Heart versus Head

STUDIES IN LEGAL HISTORY

Published by the University of North Carolina Press
in association with
the American Society for Legal History

Thomas A. Green and Hendrik Hartog, editors

Heart versus Head: Judge-Made Law in Nineteenth-Century America

Peter Karsten

The University of North Carolina Press

Chapel Hill and London

Design and composition: Wilsted & Taylor Publishing Services

The paper in this book meets the guidelines for permanence and
durability of the Committee on Production Guidelines for Book
Longevity of the Council on Library Resources.

LIBRARY OF CONGRESS CATALOGING-IN-PUBLICATION DATA

Karsten, Peter
    Heart versus head: judge-made law in
nineteenth-century America / Peter Karsten.
      p. cm.—(Studies in legal history)
    Includes bibliographical references and index.
    ISBN 0-8078-2340-6 (cloth: alk. paper)
     1. Judge-made law—United States—History—19th century.
I. Title.   II. Series.
    KF4575.K37 1997
    347.73—dc20
    [347.307]   96-43690
                              CIP

01 00 99 98 97   5 4 3 2 1

An earlier version of Chapter 5 appeared in the *American Journal
of Legal History* 34 (1990): 213–61; an earlier version of Chapter 7
appeared in *Law and History Review* 10 (1992): 46–92.

The publication of this volume was aided by generous support
from the Richard D. and Mary Jane Edwards Publication Fund
in the Faculty of Arts and Sciences, University of Pittsburgh.

To Peter & Sam, Janelle, Bill & Stanley

(It sounds like a law firm)

Good Colleagues so dandy.

You encouraged my look at the Law of the Past;

I tender this book in payment, at last.

One of the most fundamental social interests is that law shall be uniform and impartial. . . . Therefore in the main there shall be adherence to precedent. There shall be symmetrical development, consistently with history or custom when history or custom has been the motive force, or the chief one, in giving shape to existing rules, and with logic or philosophy when the motive power has been theirs. But symmetrical development may be bought at too high a price. Uniformity ceases to be a good when it becomes uniformity of oppression. The social interest served by symmetry or certainty must then be balanced against the social interest served by equity and fairness or other elements of social welfare. These may enjoin upon the judge the duty of drawing the line at another angle, of staking the path along new courses. . . .

Justice Benjamin Cardozo, *The Nature of the Judicial Process*, 1921

No man can be great in . . . the law, without *a soul of benevolence and truth*. . . . The affections of the heart have . . . much to do in sustaining right. . . .

Justice Hugh Henry Brackenridge, *Law and Miscellanies*, 1814

Our [legal] *science* (which embraces morals) expands the understanding and furnishes the heart with the purest principles of action. . . .

David Hoffman, *A Course of Legal Study*, 1836

[The law] calls into activity, before the public all the qualities and faculties of mind and heart. . . .

Judge Thomas Mellon, Fl. Pittsburgh, 1859–69

His written language was a transcript of his mind. It gave the world the very form and pressure of his thoughts. It was accurate, because he knew the exact boundaries of the principles he discussed. . . . An opinion of his was an unbroken chain of logic from beginning to end. . . . Next after his wonderful intellectual endowments, the benevolence of his heart was the most marked feature of his character.

Pennsylvania's Justice Jeremiah Black, eulogizing Chief Justice John Bannister Gibson (7 Harris 10), May 7, 1853

Wisdom is as much the offspring of the heart as of the head.

Chancellor James Kent to Columbia University Students, 1824

Contents

xv   Acknowledgments

1   An Introduction to This Tale of Two Voices

Part One. Old Channels and Moorings: A Jurisprudence of the Head

25   *Chapter One.* The Anchors of Precedent, Principle, and Symmetry: Understanding the Jurisprudence of the Head

47   *Chapter Two.* Plus ça Change: Contract's Westminster Anchors in Nineteenth-Century America

79   *Chapter Three.* On Historical Developments and Barriers to Injured Plaintiffs: Continuity in Tort Law

129   *Entr'acte.* Eddies: A Jurisprudence of the Hand

Part Two. Strong Currents: A Jurisprudence of the Heart

147   *Chapter Four.* Abandoning an Unneighborly Rule: Putting Out the Ancient-Lights Doctrine

157   *Chapter Five.* Bottomed on Justice: Allowing What Her Labor Was Worth to the Worker Who Quit

191   *Chapter Six.* Enabling the Poor to Have Their Day in Court: The Sanctioning of Contingency-Fee Contracts

201 *Chapter Seven.* "Larmoyant" Law: Explaining the Fight over the Attractive-Nuisance Doctrine

235 *Chapter Eight.* Children at Play and Heroic Risks: Big Holes Punched in the Contributory-Negligence Defense

255 *Chapter Nine.* Pain, Suffering, and the Sensitive Pocket Nerve: Discovering the Deep Pockets of Reckless Railroads

293 *Conclusion.* What We Found, and Some Explanations of the Jurisprudence of the Heart

325 Notes

475 Index of Characters

481 Index of Cases Discussed

485 General Index

Illustrations

125 Railroad construction "navvies" in late-nineteenth-century New Zealand

155 "Dead walls" at the back of Charles Crocker's mansion on Nob Hill, late 1870s

202 Late-nineteenth-century "Armstrong" turntable belonging to the Illinois Central Railroad

237 Young newsboy jumping aboard streetcar in turn-of-the-century Boston

238 Children playing in the street in New York City; train moving out of the Pennsylvania Railroad station, Pittsburgh, 1870s

239 Poster warning of dangers to children, Philadelphia, 1839

Tables and Maps

TABLES

177 1. Different Rules Adopted by States in Quitting Cases

274 2. Median Damage Awards for Other-than-Fatal Personal Injury
     Suits, Affirmed by American Courts, 1823–1896

307 3. Doctrinal/Innovative Rank Ordering of Supreme Courts by
     Aggregate Count on Twenty-nine Issues

MAPS

 75 1. State Supreme Court Gatekeeper Rule Regarding Suits of
     Third-Party Beneficiaries to a Contract, 1800–1899

205 2. States Adopting or Rejecting the Attractive-Nuisance Rule,
     1873–1924

309 3. Doctrinal/Innovative State Supreme Courts

Acknowledgments

Convincing myself that I could both "retool" as a legal historian and tackle this project was made possible in large part by the encouragement of my colleagues at Pitt, Janelle Greenberg and Bill LaPiana. They also were good enough to critique parts of chapters 4 and 7. Sam Hays and Stanley Katz encouraged my effort as well. That encouragement mattered. I am grateful to the critique of most of this manuscript provided by the New York area legal history seminar that Professor William Nelson convenes at NYU Law School. I especially appreciate the careful reading that Professor Nelson, Charles Heckman, Robert Kaczorowski, Allen Boyer, Peter Hoffer, and other participants whose names I failed to record gave to an earlier version of this book. Others who have listened to me describe or have read elements of this include Robert Hayden, Marc Galanter, Bernie Hibbitts, Richard Seeburger, John Komlos, Van Beck Hall, Richard Oestricher, Haggai Hurvitz, G. Edward White, Donald Rogers, Rande Kostal, Randy Bergstrom, Chris Tomlins, Bill Novak, and Christine Rosen. I have benefited from their advice, even if I have not taken all of it. Several of my students have been good critics of parts of this, and some have contributed ideas or evidence on their own right. I particularly want to mention Jack Burkman and Kurt Pirman in this regard. Two reference librarians at the University of Pittsburgh Law Library, Spencer Clough and Mark Silverman, were constantly "there" for me. I am grateful as well to Joel Fishman, Director of the Allegheny County Law Library and Jeffrey Kintop, Manager of the Nevada State Archives, Carson City. The ASLH series editors, Dirk Hartog and Tom Green, teased and provoked me through a substantial revision of this book; you, Gentle Reader, are the clear third-party beneficiary of their advice, consideration, and contractual terms, and if I have failed to fulfill these, you have standing to sue me, unless you live in one of those jurisdictions slavishly following Westminster's every twist and turn (see map 1).

Heart versus Head

An Introduction
to This Tale
of Two Voices

The law speaks in many voices. Some may sound ethereal, others "efficient," still others benevolent. So it is; so it was.

I am not referring here to the law as pronounced by legislatures—to statutory (or "positive") law or to such rights, duties, and limitations as were
expressed in federal and state constitutions. I will have something to say
about those kinds of law, but only with regard to how various state and federal supreme court justices of the nineteenth century ("jurists") reacted to
them, because this book is about those jurists and the rules that they administered, determined, and sometimes created regarding private suits in the
realms of contract, property, and tort. In short, I ask how American jurists
of the nineteenth century dealt with the common law and equity rules of
"private" law.

I am concerned here with that law's voice in nineteenth-century America.
I will frequently (and necessarily) refer to the voices of English jurists of the
nineteenth and of previous centuries as well, and will occasionally allude to
the colonial era and the twentieth century, but the American judiciary of the
nineteenth century will be the focus of our attention. I offer two reasons for
this focus. First, if one wants to know about jurists and what they may have
done to the rules of law, it is difficult to speak with much authority about the
eighteenth century. We know *some* things about supreme court justices and
how they functioned in that century in *some* of the colonies, but the available materials simply do not allow us to discuss with much confidence their
positions and views. The matter is altogether different for the entire nineteenth century, for, beginning in the 1790s, a steadily growing stream of
published appellate court reports, supplemented by homegrown treatises,
supply us with abundant means of hearing what American jurists were saying about, and sometimes doing to, the English judge-made rules of law that

their more obscure predecessors may well have also known and addressed. (For more on this explosion and its significance see chapter 1.)

Second, and more significant, a large body of scholarship produced in the fields of law and history treats jurists of the first sixty years of the nineteenth century as major players in the development of law, the polity, and the economy. The antebellum jurists who sat on the benches of Massachusetts, New York, Pennsylvania, and the U.S. Supreme Court, in particular, have been represented as men of genius, shaping new rules best adapted to their countrymen's needs and wants, particularly those of the burgeoning economy. Called by some "the Creative Period," by others "the Golden Age of American Law," the years before the Civil War were ones in which jurists wrote in a "Grand Style."[1] This is a much celebrated judiciary, but the fact is that there would be giants like Doe, Holmes, Appleton, Harlan, Field, Dillon, Cooley, and Ryan in the *postwar* years as well. Moreover, men relatively unknown to us, sitting on the benches of Illinois, Iowa, Kansas, Kentucky, Missouri, New Hampshire, Tennessee, Wisconsin and even little Rhode Island, had important and interesting things to say too, things that were sometimes not in accord with their respected northeastern compeers. Numerous rules adopted in Massachusetts, New York, and Pennsylvania were rejected in many other jurisdictions. And this was particularly so of rules that seemed to favor corporate defendants. Yet this has not been appreciated. Chief Justice Lemuel Shaw of the Massachusetts Supreme Judicial Court is well known; his counterparts in Illinois, Iowa, Kansas, Kentucky, Missouri, and Tennessee are not, though it was often *their* rule, *their* law, that prevailed in most of the states by the 1890s.

One tendency, then, of those who have written of this Golden Age of American Law has been to focus on a relatively small number of well-known jurists and jurisdictions. Another tendency has been to focus on the economy as the motive behind legal innovations or as the beneficiary of them. We have been told, variously, that jurists embraced the ideology of "market liberalism's umpired contest of selfish interests," that they "redefined" rules, "recast" doctrines, of the law of contract, property, and tort in order to "release new economic energies," to "aid entrepreneurs" at the expense of "the weak," to force "subsidies to growth" from "the victims of the process," or to ensure that scarce economic resources were utilized efficiently.[2] These are slightly different ways of expressing what happened. The authors of these phrases disagree with one another in significant ways to be sure, but that need not concern us here, for more important than their disagreements is what they agreed upon, which is this: In various ways the developing American economy, its agents, and its ideological spokesmen led antebellum jurists to replace a common law that embodied "earlier protective and paternalistic doctrines" with a colder, impersonal set of rules ultimately serving "the juggernaut of economic growth" at the expense of those crushed in its path.[3]

These interpretations can be thought of as a single paradigm, one I will refer to as an "economic-oriented" one, or simply as "the reigning paradigm." Every leading text and sourcebook,[4] and most major monographs produced by the current generation of American legal historians, reflect one or another of these perspectives. There *is something* to what they claim. The amazing thing is how little that something amounts to. In my view, these economic-oriented interpretations have got it almost entirely backward: To begin with, jurists of early- and mid-nineteenth-century America did not do a great deal of tinkering with the common law. They "received" common-law precedents, rules, and principles from English court reports and treatises, and they then applied these to cases at hand, with little alteration or variation. They believed that they required considerable justification for contravening the wisdom of generations of sage jurists whose legal logic and "principles" they could appreciate and whose judgments they respected. This was the Jurisprudence of the Head.

In some instances, however, some American high courts chose to differ with their English (and usually with their Westminster-facing New England) counterparts with regard to specific rules they found to be illogical, inappropriate, or unjust. We will explore these particulars largely in the second part of this book, but suffice it to say now, these innovative moments almost never produced rules friendlier to corporate entrepreneurs than the former English ones; they produced just the opposite—that is, the new rules favored relatively poor litigants. They were almost uniformly "pro-plaintiff" and *anti*–corporate entrepreneur (the Jurisprudence of the Heart). In fact, the propensity of nineteenth-century American jurists to alter common-law rules in order to *aid* the weak and the poor is so clear that I marvel that someone else has not written this book before me.[5]

Furthermore, the years of judicial innovation began later, in the 1830s, and persisted longer, well into the late nineteenth century, than has been thought. The conventional wisdom divides the history of American common-law making in the nineteenth century into an innovative antebellum era of "instrumentalism" (the use of rules by jurists as an instrument to achieve some pragmatic end) and a postbellum era of "formalism" (when jurists applied precedent and acted as if all legal rules were immutable).[6] I hereby declare that division null and void. Jurists initiated changes infrequently in the first quarter of the century. (I count only four that originated then.) They initiated far more in the second and third quarters of the century. (I counted ten and eleven, respectively, that were introduced in those years.) While I identified only three that had their origins in the century's final quarter, many of the innovations created in one or another state court in the third quarter of the century spread to others in the final quarter. I suspect that, were I to have extended the range of my inquiry to the first quarter of the twentieth century, I might have found that several innovations usually associated with those years had roots in decisions of one or another state court's decision in the late nineteenth century. But this is mere speculation. What I do feel confident in saying is that the lion's share of noteworthy judicial innovations appeared between the 1830s and the early 1880s. And this is not the conventional wisdom.

THE JURISPRUDENCES OF HEAD AND HEART

Most nineteenth-century American jurists were fundamentally conservative in that they generally deferred to English precedent and yielded to the "logic" and "principle" of the "doctrines" or "rules" to be found either there or in the opinions of their respected northeastern compatriot colleagues. Theirs was a "doctrinal" method—that is, they did *not* conceive of their role as the weighing of "the practical consequences of deciding a particular case in one way or another," but instead searched for the "essential nature" of the issue before them "to be found in certain premises dictated by the nature of law and legal relationships."[7] These premises, often shaped into doctrines or rules, they sought in the words of the great English jurists of the past (and a number of homegrown American legal geniuses as well) in their appellate reports and treatises. They practiced a Jurisprudence of the Head. And this is as true of those of the allegedly "creative" antebellum years as it is of the allegedly "formalist" late nineteenth century. But many of these jurists were, on occasion, driven by conscience and principle to alter certain common-law rules in order to produce "justice." Generally, on these occasions their motives were of Judeo-Christian origin and served the needs of relatively poor plaintiffs, not corporate defendants. At these moments, they practiced the Jurisprudence of the Heart.

Some jurists occasionally signaled in mere dicta their *wish* that they could aid this or that litigant for some reason were it not for the existence of a rule or precedent. On other occasions they actually did so, by interpreting a rule in a novel way, by creating a principled exception to it, or by rejecting it outright. In a very few of these instances, the new rule benefited entrepreneurs, and I indicate this and report such instances wherever I found it to be so; but the fact is, these instances were extremely uncommon (I found only

4

two). The far more frequent use by jurists of law as an innovative instrument of policy, the far more common instances of judge-made change, essentially benefited the weak and the poor, the *victims* of "soulless" corporations or insensitive employers. We can clearly detect evidence of numerous instances of their finding ways around an obnoxious rule or, indeed, of their *changing* it in order for those victims to emerge victorious. Specifically, these instances included: acting "*in favorem libertatis*" in slave manumission cases; helping fugitives, sojourners, and their abolitionist friends; permitting workers "what their labor was worth" when they quit special contracts they had not entirely fulfilled; allowing poor litigants to enter into contingency-fee agreements with attorneys to gain their "day in court"; providing "superior servant," "different department," "safe tool," and "safe place" exceptions to the fellow-servant rule; devising "competent servant," subcontractor, complaint-of-the-hazard and no-warning-of-the-hazard exceptions to the assumption-of-risk rule; creating an "attractive nuisance" fiction to make trespassing children injured by dangerous objects into "invitees"; refusing to view those injured while attempting heroically to rescue or protect others from danger as being contributorily negligent; ceasing to impute the contributory negligence of a parent to a child injured by a negligent driver in the street; affirming damage awards to victims of railway, streetcar, and steamboat accidents three times as large as those levied against other such tortfeasors; sanctioning damage awards for "loss of enjoyment" and "nervous shock"; refusing to allow defendant railroad physicians to examine injured plaintiffs without their permission; refusing to deduct insurance payments to the beneficiary of one wrongfully killed from damage awards; allowing third-party gift beneficiaries to a contract to sue on the contract; sanctioning charitable bequests and spendthrift trusts; finding their way around the nonliability rule for road and bridge authorities whose negligence had led to injuries; abandoning as "unneighborly" the "ancient-lights" easement; and allowing agricultural tenants the value of their improvements. There *were* "instrumentalists" on nineteenth-century American high courts, but their instrumentalism, their use of law as a purposive instrument to achieve a goal, was far "kinder and gentler" to those suing corporations, or being sued by creditors, than the reigning paradigm has maintained.[8]

With a tiny handful of exceptions, nineteenth-century jurists did not create any new rules favoring Capitalists. Moreover, they were not cut off from the egalitarian reform impulses, the child-centered culture, or the "christian civilization" around them. On the contrary, most were very much a product of their age, and their opinions reflect this fact with a frequency that makes it astounding that their basic humanitarianism has been so little noted. Jurists on several state courts created notable innovations in legal rules, and I want to direct our attention to these changes in the law, nearly all of which can fairly be described as efforts to apply democratic/republican values and Judeo-Christian ethics to legal problems addressed inadequately by existing rules.[9]

I suppose many readers are not primarily interested in the purely legal facets of this book. They should be aware that the story of Heart versus Head is very much a part of the greater story of nineteenth-century America. The interaction of power and culture sometimes produces offspring. Among the seats of power are those of supreme court benches, and those who occupied them in the nineteenth century were the creatures of their culture, a culture that became increasingly egalitarian and humanitarian. The rules these jurists created, therefore, had one or more of these characteristics: they were child-centered, reflected a concern with "community" and "neighborliness," and were responsive to the needs of the poor and weak and to human suffering in general. In these regards they reflected the larger culture, and we can learn more of that culture in the story of the creation of these new rules.

The opinions that announced these innovations were often buttressed by "good public policy" dicta, often referring to "neighborly" or "Christian" behavior and sometimes offering biblical references or locating the offensive, older rule's origin in a "feudal past." Such archaic rules would be set aside for others "bottomed on justice"[10] and promising more "humane" public policy. The public policy rationales for these pathbreaking opinions sometimes emphasized the inequity of the case or the social conditions of the plaintiff: The archaic rule (champerty, in this case) had "shut . . . the door of justice . . . to the poor, who may be oppressed," whereas the new rule (regarding spendthrift trusts, in this case) placed trust funds left to "the poor and helpless" beyond "the reach of unprincipled schemers and sharpers," so as to "keep the gaunt wolf of grinding poverty from the home door of those near and dear."[11] On other occasions the rationales more generally referred to the "barbarous" archaic rule, in contrast to "the humanity of the law" as properly stated by the court.[12] On still other occasions these two rationales were joined, as when Pennsylvania's Justice Daniel Agnew condemned "the doctrine which imputes the negligence of the parent to the child" as one "repulsive to our natural instincts and repugnant to the condition of that class of persons who have to maintain life by daily toil."[13]

There were "humane" innovations, then. But not every jurisdiction adopted them. A powerful conservative impulse held many jurists, especially those in the original thirteen states, to the doctrines of the past. Drawn to the "principles" to be found in English precedent, and to the "symmetry" that their application and reapplication produced, they resisted many of the innovations. Law, according to this view, should flow from the Head, not the Heart.

That was the dichotomy that Perry Miller settled on in his famous study of "The Legal Mentality" of the years from the American Revolution to the Civil War. The "great issue of the nineteenth century," he wrote, was "the never-ending case of Heart versus Head," and the "legal mentality's" "real controversy with their society was that they stood for the Head against the Heart." Miller's jurists were conservative and pessimistic, distrustful of "enthusiasm," revivals, and reform. He offered U.S. Supreme Court justice William Johnson as authority: "It is the unenvied province of the Court to be directed by the head, and not the heart."[14] Jurists who emphasized the need to draw upon "benevolent affections" in judging cases and "finding" the law were treated by Miller as if they were engaging in a vast subterfuge designed to mislead the public. Thus, while he noted the words of Chancellor James Kent ("Wisdom is as much the offspring of the heart as of the head") and Jesse Bledsoe ("An able and upright judge does, among men, perform the office of God's vicegerent"), he dismissed them as "strategies" intended to "confound their opponents." Jurists were "employing a masterful subtlety" when they reversed the order of the Head versus Heart dichotomy in defending their profession.[15]

Miller's "legal mentality," however, was unidimensional. Drawing too heavily upon eastern voices for authority, his story missed the diversity and complexity captured by a Heart versus Head dichotomy. It missed, for example, the voice of the Tennessee Valley, offered by Justice John Haywood, that associated "every heart" of that state's high court bench with the "humanity" of the law, as well as the voice of the Iowa Cornbelt, offered by Justice S. M. Weaver, in an opinion adopting the humane "attractive nuisance" rule: This new rule, Justice Weaver and his colleagues believed, reflected "the instincts of the heart."[16] The tension between Heart and Head is the central story of the common law in nineteenth-century America, and Heart won out over Head in such contests as it entered as often as it lost. The story of this tension, of these contests, can be seen in the following chapters. It was in some ways a struggle between a Westminster-facing, tradition-bound northeastern judiciary and their western colleagues on the benches of the newer states, but it was also a personal, inner struggle for many ambivalent individual jurists.

Part I, "Old Channels and Moorings," introduces the reader to "the

taught legal tradition," to the Jurisprudence of the Head. After describing
and attempting to explain the strength of this approach to judicial decision
making in chapter 1, I offer two examples of it from the domain of property
law. In chapters 2 and 3 I offer more elaborate sets of illustrations of this jurisprudence's persistence in the use of the familiar channels and markings of
the English common law in the fields of sales, agreements for the benefit of
a third party, and negligence suits. A brief "Entr'acte" offers the two examples of the Jurisprudence of the Hand (be it visible or invisible) that I detected, the prudent-investor rule and the "balancing of the equities" in pollution nuisance suits, mere "eddies" in the stream of nineteenth-century
private law in the United States. Part II, "Strong Currents," consists of six
chapters documenting the opening of six new gates for relatively poor and
previously helpless plaintiffs in the fields of negligence and contracts for personal service, as well as the closing of another gate that had led to the construction of rather unneighborly walls. These are my illustrations of the Jurisprudence of the Heart.

REPLACING THE ECONOMIC DETERMINIST
PARADIGM WITH A HEART VERSUS HEAD MODEL

My pathway toward the writing of this book ought to be made known in order that you may judge better my objectivity and better understand my perspective. While a graduate student in American history at the University of
Wisconsin in the mid-1960s I drew deeply from the same economic interpretations of our past that lie behind the work of economic-oriented legal historians. I found myself more comfortable with the views of Charles Beard
and William Appleman Williams (two who emphasized the importance of
economic issues in public policy), for example, than with those of their critics, and my first book reflects that.[17] I minored in law and took both of
Willard Hurst's courses while at Wisconsin. In the late 1960s and early 1970s
I read all of the books and articles representing the reigning paradigm,
particularly those of Lawrence Friedman, Morton Horwitz, and Richard
Posner. Hence, when I began to offer a course on American legal history at
the University of Pittsburgh in the late 1970s, I found myself assigning
Friedman's text, Hurst's *Law and the Conditions of Freedom*, articles by
Posner and Horwitz, and copies of many of the cases that one or another of
these scholars had identified as significant or illustrative of the pro-
entrepreneurial instrumentalism of the antebellum years.

But no sooner had I begun to offer the course than I began to have doubts
about these interpretations of judicial behavior. In the University of Pittsburgh's history department I had been learning of the new ethnocultural

interpretation of nineteenth-century American politics and society. A number of careful grass-roots analyses of mid-nineteenth-century American sociopolitical life written in the late 1960s and 1970s describe a tension in the North and West throughout the second half of the nineteenth century between the "Party of Public Morality" (Republicans), populated by Pietists, and the "Party of Personal Liberty" (Democrats), populated by members of liturgical faiths. Each of these careful studies had thoroughly rejected earlier visions of nineteenth-century American politics as being class-oriented, with "propertied elites" of the Whig Party, and later of a "tariff-oriented" Republican Party "dominated" by manufacturers, merchants, and railroad men, pitted against stolid workers and farmers of Jacksonian democracy.[18] Rather, the new ethnocultural histories saw members of all classes and occupations—farmers, miners, merchants, laborers—equally represented in the two-party system throughout the North and West, with the political arena serving as a cultural battleground between "Puritans" (as many Democrats called Republicans) struggling to drive "sin" (drink, immorality, slavery) from public life and those in the ranks of the Democratic Party, who separated public and private affairs and thus tolerated slaveholding in southern states as well as plays, dance halls, and "beer gardens" open for business on Sunday afternoons.[19]

Whichever their vision of the role the state should play in enforcing behavior, the voters of each party in the North and West agreed on one thing: Questions of moral behavior and limits to personal freedom defined the political debates far more than any workers-employer rivalries, entrepreneurial opportunities, or rich-poor distinctions. *Values* mattered more to people than class or money. Independently substantiating these findings, for me, was Michael Barton's content-analysis of Civil War diaries and letters, for Barton found reference to the values of "morality," "religion," and "humanitarianism" in (on average) 76.3 percent of them, 28 percent more often than appeared any reference to the values of "progress," "achievement," "materialism," "activity," or "efficiency."[20]

At the time, I was not entirely convinced by these findings that class struggle or entrepreneurial activity were essentially secondary aspects of nineteenth-century American life (and I remain satisfied that the legislators chosen by these political cultures often concerned themselves with measures designed to produce economic activity). Nonetheless, the "new" political history clearly raised doubts as to their importance and explanatory power with regard to the values that informed the everyday behavior and deep-seated ideologies of Americans in the age of Jackson and Story, Lincoln and Dillon. Moreover, these new insights into nineteenth-century

American life seemed to me to be consistent with an older literature that described antebellum American reform impulses and revival evangelicalism, and with a newer cultural history of "benevolence" and the "child-centered" American/Victorian family.[21] The second quarter of the nineteenth century, in the words of Daniel Walker Howe, "was a time of social innovation, and religion was at the cutting edge of this innovation."[22]

Howe was speaking of the temperance movement, the women's rights movement, and the movements to abolish slavery, corporal punishment, and the death penalty, but his words apply as well to the Jurisprudence of the Heart: These were the years that jurists began to sanction contingency-fee contracts, quantum meruit payments to workers who quit "entire" labor contracts, and charitable bequests in "Mortmain" states, years when they first bent rules to help children injured by negligent drivers, used legal fictions to permit those injured on defective roads and bridges to recover damages in the absence of state statutes specifically sanctioning such suits, years when they first sanctioned truly enormous jury awards to accident victims, as well as years when they ignored statutes and the legal principle of comity to aid manumitted, fugitive, and sojourner slaves. Both the republican spirit of the age and the evangelical faith in the perfectability of man inspired the jurists of the nineteenth century; there was at least a little of each spirit in the heart and mind of each and every American jurist, from James Kent to John Forrest Dillon.

Many of these opinions were taken from the Bible, "the book of all others for lawyers as well as divines," as Daniel Webster styled it.[23] Thus one jurist, rejecting the imputing of parental contributory negligence to the child, compared it to "the old doctrine," rejected by God in Jeremiah 31:29 and Ezekiel 18:2, "of the father eating grapes, and the child's teeth being set on edge." Another indicated that such a rule visited "the sins of the fathers upon the child to an extent not contemplated in the decalogue."[24] A third, voiding as insufficiently charitable a bequest to create a Quaker boarding school without a "means" test, offered the words of Jesus ("I was hungry and ye gave me meat") in support of his definition of what constituted a charitable bequest.[25] Others relied on "the common feeling of mankind, guided by the second branch of the great law of love" (that is, "love thy neighbor as thyself") in adopting the newly created attractive nuisance rule, rejecting the "other doctrine" because it "would illy accord with Christian civilization."[26] These jurists were responding to a "fundamental" law that spoke to their hearts, and were rejecting precedents that spoke to their heads.

10 How was one to reconcile these views with the economic-oriented vi-

sion?[27] These jurists did not appear to have been insulated from these non-economic currents of nineteenth-century American culture. Nor had they been corrupted or co-opted by such corporate clients some may have served as attorneys en route to their seats on the high courts. One prominent legal historian, James Willard Hurst, the architect of the "release of economic energies" interpretation of antebellum American law, has argued that "lawmakers" *were* essentially insulated from these cultural currents. Humanitarians and abolitionists might have concerned themselves "with slavery and drink and the rights of women," but these were but occasional distractions from the nineteenth century's primary concern, for the century "put all the energy and attention it could into economic interests." True, "from time to time" a zealous minority concerned with human suffering, ethically sound business practices, or "the public good" might "whip up a general, emotional reaction," but "in most affairs one senses that men turned to noneconomic issues grudgingly or as a form of diversion and excitement or in spurts of bad conscience over neglected problems."[28]

I came to doubt this perspective. *Could* jurists have been indifferent to the "policy of christian civilization"[29] being debated all around them? I suspected that, like most of their contemporaries, they were *not* indifferent, that many of them were profoundly affected by the cultural currents of their day. The question appeared to me both intriguing and challenging: Could one "test" the claims of the reigning paradigm by exploring selectively and systematically the nature of judicial thought and decision making in nineteenth-century America?

In short order I realized that I was formulating an alternative paradigm. I could simply announce that I am hereby "rejecting" the economic-oriented paradigm out of hand and then proceed to offer my own as elegantly as possible, but that sort of storytelling is not a method I am very comfortable with. I will not subject you here to a narrow bibliographical dialogue with those I am criticizing in the text, but I will carry on some of that dialogue in my endnotes. You may or may not find these of interest, and you can certainly avoid this dialogue if you wish, but I feel a professional obligation to include it. If one is challenging the viability of the majority views of a field of study, one owes it to the holders of those views as well as to the greater audience to explain in sufficient detail why those views ought to be discounted by virtue of what one's story tells. And given the nature of this subject, such a process makes excellent sense, because many of the very "texts" that the legal historians I disagree with have used to establish their stories are ones I will be using to establish a contrary one. These "texts" (most of them appellate cases) have, in the past generation, been given great weight in the teaching of American legal history.[30] To the extent that they have been misinterpreted or are unrepresentative, it behooves one seeking as I do to improve on these "stories" to occasionally guide the reader through a re-analysis—an explication de texte. In short, I propose to engage at times in what the late E. P. Thompson called a "discourse of the proof" in order to "bring to trial" the reigning paradigm,[31] but it will be a discourse virtually confined to the notes.

Let me offer two modest examples of how one can learn something of how jurists decided cases and how their values can be detected in their written opinions. The first case concerned the sale of a horse that had been loaned to the seller "to go a journey into the northern part" of Vermont. The owner reclaimed it from the buyer, who sued for recovery in 1802, citing "several cases from the English books" to establish that he qualified as a protected bona fide purchaser. Chief Judge Jonathan Robinson of Vermont's supreme court, however, pointed out the lack in Vermont of the customary law and statutory markets that these English precedents relied on and explained that the relevant rule was "*caveat emptor*, look to it, buyer, that he from whom you purchase has a right to sell." But he did not stop there, as he might have. Were the purchaser to defeat the owner's title, the result would

> abridge that friendly intercourse among men which ameliorates
> society, for if the law is, that a man must consider, that every time he
> loans his horse to a poor neighbor to go to the mill, or to call aid to
> his wife in the hour of nature's difficulty, that he risks the sale of the
> property by the borrower, . . . this will tend to restrain those acts of
> neighborly kindness, which, when exercised by the opulent towards
> the poor, assume a portion of that charity which is the ornament of
> christian and social life.[32]

Theoretically, Chief Justice Robinson might have observed that those who had purchased in good faith deserved the law's protection lest traders in the general marketplace become leery of all offers and the costs of transactions would accordingly rise. He might have referred the owner for redress to the dishonest fellow to whom he had been foolish enough to lend the horse. That sort of rule would, at least, have been defensible in terms of its economic efficiency. He did neither of these things. Instead, he spoke of a law that protected "that friendly intercourse . . . which ameliorates society," of "neighborly kindness," of "charity," and of "christian and social life."

Example two: As I have indicated, jurists sometimes merely expressed their sympathy in dicta with the party that seemed "oppressed" by an unduly "harsh" rule that they nevertheless felt compelled to enforce. Sometimes they also took advantage of this opportunity to welcome the day that the legislature might alter the law, a not uncommon way that the judiciary sent a signal to the legislature. I have noted these dicta with interest, but I readily acknowledge that such dicta cost their author little and generally had no long-term useful consequences. It is the more forthright challenges to the "harsh" rule that will primarily concern us in the ensuing chapters. Nonetheless, for my second example I want to offer such regretful dicta as a general illustration of how one must be sensitive to tone or choice of adjectives, to "discourse," in order to comprehend as much as one can from "the text" as to what the values of antebellum American jurists might have been.

The case was this: One Pike leased property in New York in the 1840s from an owner who covenanted to pay him for such improvement as he might build in the way of a brick dwelling place. Pike, like his more famous New York predecessor, Duncan Fyfe, was a cabinetmaker, and he sought, and thought he had obtained, a variance via an oral agreement with the landlord for a brick cabinetmaker's shop to suffice as the brick dwelling place "improvement." But the landlord was shrewd; he realized that an oral agreement was inferior in law to a written lease and that Pike would not succeed in efforts to compel him to pay for the building when he terminated the lease. To the landlord's surprise, Pike won the first appellate review; but the New York high court (after 1848, the court of appeals) reversed the lower court's ruling with the observation that neither law nor equity (now joined in New York) could "afford relief without substituting the undefined and therefore dangerous discretion of a court, for the fixed principles upon which the law in relation to contracts should be administered."

Pike lost. And a rock-ribbed economic determinist scholar might well cite this as evidence that mid-nineteenth-century American high court jurists were class-conscious (or unconscious) supporters of propertied elites. The problem with such a reading of the case would be that it would have failed to account for the rest of the opinion's language. Justice Addison Gardiner, you see, also spoke critically of "the settled determination of a selfish man to claim the full benefit of the agreement." This behavior had not *quite* constituted fraud; yet it was "harsh and repulsive." Defendant's "enforcement of a legal right" had operated "oppressively" in this "particular case."[33] Gardiner was clearly distressed at the law's inability to help Pike. His views are not those of a court that believed it could reshape the law to serve the needs of this entrepreneur. But his language reflects the same humanity and distress with unfairness that would drive other jurists at times to alter some rules at the *expense* of employers, entrepreneurs, and corporations.

Our "texts," like those of Robinson's and Gardiner's, were written with care, were read from the bench, and were often printed in newspapers. And then many or most of them (depending on the jurisdiction) were printed in formal "state reports." Sometimes dicta such as Gardiner's were read back to them at a later date by counsel for another appellant litigant. Gardiner's court had not altered the rule, but voices like his could in this way be heard again on "oppression." It is these opinions, generally containing elaborate summaries of the facts of the case, the disposition of the case at trial, and the arguments placed before the high court jurists by counsel for the litigants,[34] further supplemented by the views of treatise writers and law journal essayists, that form my central evidence base.

What happened was this: I was led to various rules or legal principles by comments in nineteenth-century legal journals, by asides offered in late-nineteenth- or early-twentieth-century treatises, or by recent claims made about their having been altered to spur economic growth or to aid entrepreneurs. I then proceeded, in most instances, to read everything I could about each of these issues—every first, second, and often third and fourth impression case that appeared in every appellate legal jurisdiction of the nineteenth century, as well as every mention of the issue in every treatise and law journal article of the age that I could identify.[35] I have not limited myself to the opinions and treatises of jurists from Massachusetts and New York, or for that matter from any particular state or region, but have attempted to grasp the entire picture.

I searched my texts to see which legal rules had been altered by jurists, looking particularly for evidence of innovations that really "mattered." Some legal rules, if altered, cause some risks to shift, cause some obligations and duties to change. But prospective litigants take those changes into consideration; they engage in slight readjustments and calculations to nullify any possible long-term consequences. One thinks in this regard of seller warranties or buyer caveats in contract law, or of some easement doctrines in property law. The typical potential litigant is a buyer in one transaction, a seller in the next, a creditor for one purpose, a debtor for another, a farmer claiming a right-of-way one moment from one neighbor and denying it to another in the next. Or, to put the issue in the words of Pennsylvania's Chief Justice John Bannister Gibson, "The capitalists are the . . . great purchasers, the great traders, the great manufacturers, the great borrowers, and consequently the great debtors."[36] Courts might alter legal rules in these and other instances without having much impact on society or economy.

But other rules have more import. "Gatekeeper" rules matter.[37] Whether or not the plaintiff has "standing," whether she has a legal right to sue for redress, or whether one is automatically barred or subject to nonsuit by virtue of one's action or one's failure to act in a prescribed way matters. Rules imposing obligations on corporations, or the lack of them, matter where they prevent plaintiffs from suing. When I detected that some jurists were opening new gates, or closing old ones, I wanted to know more. Moreover, I was struck by the disparity of power in many of these issues between the litigants. To be sure, many cases pitted one individual against another, one corporation against another. But in a great many other cases jurists were being asked to decide between an individual and a corporation (as in accident, pollution, or "takings" disputes) or between an unpropertied employee and a propertied employer.

Part I of this book concerns, in part, the propensity of "gatekeeper" jurists to keep certain rules and doctrines as they were. Part II deals with the willingness of these and other jurists to change other gatekeeper rules. The Jurisprudence of the Head won the struggles I describe in Part I; that of the Heart won those described in Part II; but within each story of doctrinal warfare, one can hear both Heart and Head, parrying and thrusting at one another.

AN EXAMPLE OF HEART VERSUS HEAD:
SLAVES, SOJOURNERS, AND FUGITIVES

I believe I can illustrate both the Heart-Head tension on nineteenth-century benches and the propensity of innovation to take place where legal "gatekeeping" was at issue with a review of judicial decisions concerning that "peculiar institution," slavery. A number of the scholars who have analyzed decision making in this field, Robert Cover, A. E. Keir Nash, William Nelson, Mark Tushnet, and Paul Finkelman, have alluded to what they variously call "fairness and formalism," a "moral-formal dilemma," or a "law/ sentiment dichotomy."[38] These tensions are what I call Heart versus Head.

In the antebellum South a "specially troubled"[39] number of state supreme court jurists struggled to provide a "justice of the heart"[40] in cases involving crimes by or against slaves and in suits by slaves claiming their freedom on the basis of their master's will (manumission) or as a consequence of their sojourn in a free state or federal territory. Especially in Jeffersonian-era Virginia, pre-Jacksonian-era North Carolina and Mississippi, and Louisiana and Tennessee throughout the antebellum years, some jurists referred to "the influence of the mild precepts of Christianity," to "feelings of humanity," the "march of benignant policy and provident humanity," the "moral sense and humanity of the present age," or, more simply, to "humanity"[41] in providing common-law defenses to slaves charged with violations of criminal statutes,[42] in using equity discretion to interpret wills and manumission statutes, "*in favorem libertatis*," and in deciding on slave claims to freedom based on their sojourn in a free region and the principle of comity.[43] In the process, they referred to "Christianity" and "the four gospels upon the clerk's table" as being "part of the law of the land." They urged their less daring colleagues to "step into the moral world and contemplate the unbiased principles of our nature" to "discover for the exercise of our discretion a wide range between humanity and cruelty." They spoke at times of "law, reason, Christianity and common humanity" being united in protecting slaves from treatment not strictly permitted by statute.[44]

Southern legislatures steadily limited this discretion, especially in the 1830s, 1840s, and 1850s, and, by the 1850s virtually all southern jurists were beholden in one way (their own election) or another (appointment by a popularly elected governor) to an electorate that expected them to treat blacks, whether enslaved or free, with less respect than whites. Thus, in the 1850s elected jurists in Georgia and Mississippi criticized the "fervid zeal in behalf of humanity to the slave" that I have cited from some of these earlier opinions, opinions these newly elected jurists characterized as having been "founded mainly" upon such "unmeaning twaddle" as "the influence of the 'natural law,' 'civilization and Christian enlightenment,' in amending, *proprio vigore* the rigor of the common law." They cited an English decision, *The Slave Grace* (1827), as being "the true rule" to follow and spoke of being "compelled to return to the English doctrine."[45] This Jurisprudence of the Heartless, or of the Fist, thus put on the *mask* of "doctrinal" law (the Jurisprudence of the Head) in the service of slavery but was at its base quite political and should not be confused, in my judgment, with the more genuine deference displayed by other practitioners of "the taught legal tradition" to precedent and "ancient legal doctrines" throughout the nineteenth century. But it is important to note that these elected "fire-eaters" felt the need to rely on "the rigor of the common law" or "English doctrine," rather than simple social expediency, to justify their rejection of unpopular rules.

When southern state courts of the 1850s became less tolerant of examples of an earlier Jurisprudence of the Heart, a few jurists on those benches who sought to continue such "humane" law found themselves offering "doctrinal" rationales as well—that is, they defended the earlier decisions "*in fa-*

vorem libertatis" as rules that were "now too firmly fixed by a uniform series of decisions to be disturbed."[46] The forerunner to the *Dred Scott* decision is a case in point. In *Scott* v. *Emerson* (1852) a majority of the Missouri Supreme Court abandoned the practice of its predecessors regarding comity and sojourners. In the past, Missouri's jurists had applied the comity principle to honor northern statutes and court rulings that freed slaves taken into those states voluntarily by their masters and kept there beyond prescribed time limits or conditions. Justice William Scott, a recently elected proslavery figure, spoke for that majority. The "dark and fell spirit" of abolitionism was alive in the North. Conditions were "not as they were when the former decisions on this subject were made." Many northern courts had ceased to observe the comity principle; Missouri could no longer afford to continue to honor it. Chief Justice Hamilton Gamble, a Whig with "moderate" views on slavery who was also recently elected (outpolling his fire-eating colleague, Scott), dissented from this Jurisprudence of the Fist:[47]

> The judicial mind, calm and self balanced, should adhere to
> principles established when there was no feeling to disturb the view of
> the legal questions upon which the rights of parties depend. . . .
> Times may have changed, public feeling may have changed, but
> principles have not and do not change; and . . . there can be no safe
> basis for judicial decisions, but in those principles, which are
> immutable.

Here was an eloquent statement of Head jurisprudence, echoing the voices of a generation of Missouri jurists and echoing as well the voices of many, perhaps most, *northern* state and federal jurists.[48] Robert Cover and Paul Finkelman have identified numerous instances in which northern jurists expressed themselves unable and unwilling to ignore the positive law of the Congress (the Fugitive Slave Acts), the fundamental law of the U.S. Constitution (which they understood to call on the North to respect the rights of southern slave owners), and the principle of comity.[49] Thus New Hampshire's Jacksonian member of the U.S. Supreme Court, Justice Levi Woodbury, spoke of the law's "path" with regard to the Fugitive Slave Act of 1793 as being "a straight and narrow one." He could follow it only where "the laws lead" and would not travel "without or beyond them." Similarly, his scholarly predecessor from Massachusetts, Justice Joseph Story, wrote privately that, while he had "been opposed to slavery" all his life, "I take my standard of duty *as a Judge* from the Constitution." And Justice John McLean, Woodbury's Conscience Whig colleague from Ohio, would urge a federal jury in Indiana to follow "the law, and not conscience," in deciding

whether slave owners who sought damages against those who had interfered with the recovery of their fugitive slaves should recover damages.[50]

But juxtaposed to this "black letter" northern voice of the Jurisprudence
of the Head, on virtually[51] every state supreme court from the 1830s to the
Civil War, could be heard the "humane" voice of the Jurisprudence of the
Heart, rejecting the comity principle, defying or circumventing the Fugitive
Slave Acts, and defending the northern states' "personal liberty" laws. For
example, in Pennsylvania, Chief Justice William Tilghman's Head voice
was answered by Justice John Bannister Gibson's Heart; New York's Justice
Thomas Clerke's by that of Justice William Wright; Connecticut's Justice
Clark Bissell's by that of Chief Justice Thomas Williams; Ohio's successive
Chief Justices Thomas Bartley's and Joseph Swan's by those of Justices
Ozias Bowen and Jacob Brinkerhoff; Wisconsin's Justice Samuel Crawford
by that of Justice Abram Smith.[52]

The dialogue on the Wisconsin high court in 1854 over the fate of one
Sherman Booth may serve as an illustration of this tension between Heart
and Head over fugitive slaves. Booth, an abolitionist editor, was charged in
federal court with a violation of the Fugitive Slave Act of 1850 for the assistance he had provided a fugitive. He secured a writ of habeas corpus from
Justice Smith, and the federal authorities appealed this decision to the state
supreme court, where Justice Smith and Chief Justice Edward Whiton affirmed Smith's order. In the process, they argued that the Fugitive Slave Act
was unconstitutional. Smith's opinion placed "fundamental law" above the
"might and authority of judicial determinations" that had held northern
"personal liberty" laws supportive of fugitives and their friends to be void
with the passage of the federal Fugitive Slave Act of 1850. "Authors of such
determinations" were "subordinate to a superior law," a law that Justice
Smith had "found." Well aware that his was a chartless course, Smith relied
on his sense that slavery was an unmitigated evil. He explained that he had
been guided by "my conscience" and hoped that "I may stand approved of
[by] my God." His colleague, Justice Samuel Crawford, disagreed. "The
duty of a judicial officer is to expound the law, not to make it." He was
"bound to yield obedience" to the decisions of the U.S. Supreme Court on
federal questions and could "feel the control of former adjudications" by
other courts "composed of men of the most eminent endowments."[53]

Wisconsin's high court thus voted two to one to hold the "might and authority" of statutes, precedent, constitutional language, and comity to be
"subordinate to a superior law," whereas Ohio's bench turned that view
away by a three to two vote.[54] Similarly, the Connecticut Supreme Court divided three to two over a related issue, the status of a slave brought to live in

the state by an owner. Nancy Jackson had been taken from Georgia to Connecticut by her owner in 1835 to be his family's servant. After two years, the owner returned temporarily to the South and Nancy Jackson sought her freedom in Connecticut's courts. The state's supreme court narrowly held that the 1784 statute abolishing slavery for all those "born in this state," when read in conjunction with another statute barring the importation and abandoning of slaves, allowed the court to rule that slaves born elsewhere who were brought into the state and "left" there were free. Slavery was "contrary to the principles of natural right and to the great law of love" (that is, "love thy neighbor as thyself"), as Chief Justice Thomas Williams put it warmly in his opinion for the majority.

Justice Clark Bissell, writing for the two dissenters, was appalled at this "experiment" in law making. His job was "to administer the law," not to respond to "moral and political writers summoned to the bar" as they had been in this case to tell of the evils of slavery. "As a man," Bissell might well "admit the injustice and immorality of slavery," but "as a jurist," he was to view only "that standard of morality which the law prescribes." He and his colleagues should limit their inquiries and concern "with the laws as they are."[55]

The Supreme Court of Ohio and its counterpart in New York (the Court of Appeals) also divided over the question of whether sojourner slaves were entitled to emancipation. When Henry Poindexter, a slave in Kentucky, was sent by his master on errands into Ohio, he initiated an action in that state, claiming that his having sojourned in the free state of Ohio entitled him to freedom. Three of Justice Jacob Brinkerhoff's colleagues concurred with his opinion that comity was inappropriate: A "principle of righteousness which is the soul of all law worthy of the name" led him to "*nullify*" slavery in such cases "*because it is wrong*, rather than to lend it an indirect sanction through a morbid exaggeration of the spirit of courtesy." Chief Justice Thomas Bartley was appalled at such a setting aside of the time-honored rule of respect for the law of a neighboring state, the comity principle: "We do not sit here to administer the divine law . . . [but] to declare the law as it is, not to change it." New York's Court of Appeals divided five to three in a similar sojourner case on the eve of the Civil War, with the majority deciding for freedom, with references to "principle," and the dissenters emphasizing "purely legal questions."[56]

Jurists elsewhere joined this dialogue, but we need not delve further into the details of this discourse; the point is, simply, that there *was* a discourse, an impassioned one, over the plight of fugitives and sojourners in the North, and that it nicely illustrates the tension between the Jurisprudences of Heart and Head. The tensions described elsewhere in this book were of this basic character as well. They involved different actors, in different states, in different decades, dealing with entirely different doctrines. Often virtually everything was different except the nature of the judicial dialogue—Heart versus Head.

DEFENSORIBUS DOCTRINAE

One final observation: Some of what follows could be condensed out as "doctrinal" legal history—that is, in many sections I am necessarily concerned with the rules and doctrines that jurists referred to and occasionally altered or created, since these are the major windows available into my primary subject matter: American jurists of the nineteenth century and their thought and values. When doctrinal disagreements arose, I wanted to know why they arose as well as why these disagreements were resolved in different ways in certain courts. Since others have styled this sort of analysis "doctrinal," I will accept the term, but I prefer to think of this as intellectual history, and *comparative* intellectual history at that, since I invariably compare judicial thought and behavior in England with that in over thirty different American jurisdictions.

Some legal historians have recently reacted to the writing of the history of legal rule making with what ranges from polite disinterest to outright disapproval. The rules pronounced by high court jurists, they explain, exist in a rarified domain of their own—iceberg tips that do not tell us much of the great mass of trial court litigation (let alone the out-of-court settlements of disputes) lying beneath them. This rarified domain is not where the *real* action is, where "the rubber meets the road."[57]

I agree completely that doctrinal history is not the *only* place where the rubber meets the road, and that there is much merit in the work of those who focus on lower court behavior, as well as those of the "law and anthropology" genre who explore the even greater domain of *non*judicial dispute resolution, that of popular norms of behavior. That is why I refer to widely held cultural beliefs, to deeply felt values from time to time in explaining one or another of the "kinder, gentler" innovations of common-law rules wrought by nineteenth-century American jurists. It is why I have devoted a large part of chapter 9 to the behavior of nineteenth-century trial court juries in personal injury negligence cases. It is why my next book compares formal ("high") and informal ("low") legal cultures in the United States, Britain, Canada, Australia, and New Zealand in the eighteenth and nineteenth centuries. And it is why I codirect the Pittsburgh Center for Social History.[58] But I insist that until those who hold to this critique describe with greater accuracy and more evenhanded emphasis the various twists and turns of nineteenth-century American high court doctrine, this book *is* necessary: If scholars have inaccurately reported the creation of probusiness or "efficient" doctrines in America's appellate courts of the nineteenth century, as I maintain they have, such analysis of doctrine as mine is can hardly be faulted as antiquarian and inappropriate.

As to the claim that high court doctrine does not explain or determine lower court behavior, I allow that there is certainly some truth to this, warranting the continued exploration of trial court behavior. Edward Purcell's study of the role of federal "diversity" jurisdiction in the late nineteenth and early twentieth centuries makes it clear, for example, that corporations defending against personal injury suits found "removal" to a distant federal court to be a powerful procedural weapon.[59] Procedural questions of jurisdiction and "standing" clearly matter, and we must note how the high courts ruled on these as well as those involving the substantive law, and whether the lower courts followed these rules. But I ask first: How can one tell whether the trial court judge is ignoring or seeking to vitiate the rules and doctrines of his high court superiors unless one first has a firm grasp of what those rules actually were? Second: Is it really true that trial court judges were not generally scrupulous in following the rules set forth by the high court jurists? Once the state's supreme court had spoken on the subject of lawyer-client contingency-fee contracts or on the question of whether parental contributory negligence could continue to be imputed to a child injured by a negligent driver (to cite but two examples of doctrinal questions addressed in this study), where is the evidence that trial court judges were willing to ignore the rule, or that the counsel for one or the other of the parties were so blissfully unaware of his duties as to fail to know the rule and to ask for the proper ruling or instruction to the jury? In my own sorties into about four hundred cases of tort and contract in the trial court records of Nevada and Colorado county courts and those of Allegheny County (Pittsburgh) Pennsylvania, I detected evidence that both attorneys and trial judges knew the high court rules. And both Gordon Bakken's study of California attorneys in the nineteenth century and Randolph Bergstrom's study of tort actions in New York City trial courts in the late nineteenth and early twentieth centuries make this clear as well.[60]

Surely there were instances where a trial judge was either unaware of, or oblivious to, some particular high court doctrine. That, after all, was the reason that the decisions in such cases were reversed by supreme courts—that is to say, the attorney whose client's interests had been adversely affected by the error was well aware of it. I allow that trial court errors were sometimes not appealed from, because of attorney ignorance or client parsimony, or because a threatened appeal had led to a settlement. Knowing how often this might have been the case with regard to the fellow servant rule, or with the rule denying quantum meruit recovery to a laborer-plaintiff who had breached an "entire" labor contract by quitting before the specified date would be worthwhile, and a research effort directed at discovering the frequency that such supreme court rules were not observed at the trial level would, indeed, be valuable. But until the evidence is in, the rebuttable presumption ought to be that supreme court rules were generally observed and followed by trial courts, that they were generally understood by their attorneys when litigation loomed likely, and that they were known and applied by a significant number of citizens in planning their behavior.[61] Once a high court had decided (for example) to allow poor litigants to enter into contingency-fee contracts with attorneys, isn't it plausible to suppose that lower courts became aware of this and sanctioned such contracts?

To the extent, then, that these presuppositions are correct, this book becomes more than an exercise in the disembodied history of ideas. It is an inquiry into the reasons that jurists decided either to transmit or alter certain "received" rules of common law and equity that were of real consequence to many Americans in the nineteenth century.

Part One

Old Channels and Moorings: A Jurisprudence of the Head

The Anchors of Precedent, Principle, and Symmetry: Understanding the Jurisprudence of the Head

Common law is the perfection of reason, arising from the nature of God, of man, and of things, and from the relations, dependencies, and connections: It is universal and extends to all men, in every possible situation; and embraces all cases and questions that can possibly arise; it is in itself perfect, clear, and certain; it is immutable, and cannot be changed or altered, without altering the nature and relation of things; it is superior to all other laws and regulations, by it they are corrected and controlled; all positive laws are to be construed by it, and wherein they are opposed to it, they are void.

Jesse Root, introduction to *Connecticut Reports, 1789–1793*, 1798

His first inquiry in every case was of the oracles of the law for their response; and when he obtained it, notwithstanding his clear perception of the justice of the cause, and his intense desire to reach it, if it were not the justice of the law, he dare not to administer it.

from Horace Binney's eulogy for Pennsylvania's Chief Justice William Tilghman before the Law Association of Philadelphia, 1827, in *Addresses . . . to Celebrate the Centennial of the Law Association of Philadelphia, 1802–1902*, 1902

He clung to the common law as a child to its nurse, and how much he drew from it may be seen in his opinions. . . . He seldom changed his opinion.

Chief Justice J. B. Gibson, eulogizing Pennsylvania's Justice John Kennedy, 4 Barr (Pa.) 6 (1846)

Has it ever been supposed that [a judge] . . . was at liberty to disregard all precedents, however solemnly repeated and observed, and by giving effect to his own abstract and individual opinions, to disturb the established course of practise in the business of the community?

James Madison to Charles Jared Ingersoll, June 25, 1831

The foregoing opinion [*Mann* v *Oriental Print Works*, 11 R. I. 152 (1875)] . . . will not fail to commend itself to all lovers of justice. But from that large class of the profession who, from habit or education, look *first* to symmetry and then to justice, it may possibly encounter some distrust. . . .

Isaac Redfield, 14 *American Law Register* (N. S.) 728 (1875)

We have continued, as you, to cite the decisions of Mansfield and Eldon and their successors. The divergencies have been so slight, compared with the whole body, that like the mountains of the moon, they are lost to the distant eye.

David Dudley Field, "Address to Dalhouise Univ. Law School Convocation, Halifax, Nova Scotia, 1885," *American Law Review* 19 (1885): 617

Let me begin with what is an utterly heretical claim in my corner of the historical profession: American jurists did not change many of the rules of common law and equity in the nineteenth century. Continuity, not change, characterized their work. I cannot say exactly how many rules changed and how many remained the same from 1800 to 1900 in all American jurisdictions; there were, literally, hundreds of rules of common law and equity by 1800. But some were more central to the field, more important, than others. I have explored over seventy rules, many of which could fairly be said to constitute the core of tort, contract, and property disputes in these years. Only about one-third (twenty-nine) appear to have been altered in one way or another, either by the creation of a "principled" exception to it or by its outright abandonment. That may seem like a large percentage, until one considers that over half of the rules of contract, tort, and property I analyzed were the very ones that other legal historians claimed had been altered by jurists determined to spur economic growth or to create "economically efficient" rules. (This is why the notes to this book often refer to the work of these scholars.)

From this perspective, then, if I had found that fully two-thirds of the rules that were said to have been altered for economic motives had in fact been transformed, I would have still felt comfortable saying that there was considerably more continuity to the legal order followed by jurists in the nineteenth century than has been allowed. Since I found, in fact, that far fewer rules that were said to have been altered for economic ends actually were altered, I feel justified in saying that nineteenth-century judge-made law in America was characterized at least as much by continuity as by change. In this and the next part of this book I will point out that virtually all of these rule changes were pro-plaintiff in nature, driven by a moral sense, generally derived from the jurists' ideological or spiritual mores—that they were of the Heart, not of the "visible" or "invisible" Hand. But the main point here is that, whatever may have inspired the specific changes jurists wrought in the rules of common law and equity, the majority of rules remained essentially unaltered.

Most American jurists were extremely uneasy about upending rules that had come down to them from generations of respected English (and some American) jurists. Sometimes, if they felt that the rule was, indeed, unfair—that it had outlived its original purpose—they called upon the legislature to abrogate it and simultaneously bemoaned the "fact" that they were not empowered, under their self-imposed set of professional standards, to alter the offending rule themselves.[1] On other occasions they broke with tradition, either by creating a "principled exception" to the rule or by rejecting it outright as "bad law." But they had been "taught" a "legal tradition," as Roscoe Pound once put it, as the centerpiece of their professional training, and they were not easily persuaded, by counsel, social circle, or public opinion, to set this perspective aside.

Most of my evidence for this judicial devotion to legal tradition appears in the final section of this chapter and in the next two chapters. The central question that the first half of this chapter asks is how I might be "right" on this and so many of my predecessors "wrong." What was it that led them to perceive change in the opinions of nineteenth-century American jurists where I see continuity? Here, as elsewhere in this book, the answer has much to do with a radically different reading of certain "texts."

THE ANCHORS OF PRECEDENT, PRINCIPLE, AND SYMMETRY

According to the author of a leading textbook on American legal history, the better antebellum jurists, such as Lemuel Shaw, the chief justice of the Massachusetts Supreme Court of Judicature (1830–60) and John Bannister Gibson, chief justice of the Pennsylvania Supreme Court (1827–53), "could write for pages without citing a shred of 'authority.'" Moreover, "they did not choose to base their decisions on precedent alone; law had to be chiseled out of basic principle."[2] Far from being checked by hide-bound English precedents, jurists of the Golden Age of American Law were willing and able to create new rules from time to time consistent with the needs of a new and burgeoning America. This is the view of Professor Laurence Friedman in his widely used *History of American Law*, and it is shared by others. I think it is essentially off the mark.

To be sure, there is something to it. First, it must be allowed that many associate and chief justices of the eighteenth century, and some as late as the first decades of the nineteenth century, were virtually untrained in the law. Of thirty Massachusetts justices who sat between 1701 and 1776, for example, only four had been lawyers. Chief Justice Thomas Hutchinson, the lieutenant governor of Massachusetts, knew no precedents because he knew no law. John Adams reported that when Hutchinson heard a case cited as authority he "wriggled to evade it." His counterpart in the 1790s in New Hampshire, Chief Justice Samuel Livermore, "having no law learning himself, did not like to be pestered with it" by an attorney familiar with English authorities. These authorities, Livermore told one such attorney in 1791, were "musty old worm-eaten books," and the precedent cited from them was dismissed with the remark that "every tub must stand on its own bottom." One of Livermore's associate justices, John Dudley, a farmer and trader, dismissed Coke and Blackstone, "books that I never read and never will." Another farmer served as the chief justice of Rhode Island's supreme court from 1819 to 1826.[3]

Furthermore, jurists in the early Republic possessed only limited means to acquire precedents to cite. As late as 1783 only about 1 in every 5 of the nearly 150 volumes of published reports of the opinions of English courts were, in fact, available in America. The Charleston South Carolina Library Society Catalogue listed only 2, those of Salkeld and Yelverton. A full generation later, by about 1810, as the high courts of the new Republic's states addressed the appeals from lower court decisions in law and equity, there were available as published guideposts to such jurists as were able to procure them a handful of English treatises (such as Sir William Jones's essay on bailment), a smaller handful of alphabetically organized topical digests (most notably Charles Viner's *Abridgement*), William Blackstone's Oxford lectures, *Commentaries on the Laws of England* (4 vols., 1765–69), Sir Edward Coke's formidable *First Part of the Institutes of the Laws of England; or a Commentarie upon Littleton* (1628), and a little over 100 volumes of reports of sixteenth-, seventeenth-, and eighteenth-century decisions of the English Courts of Common Pleas, King's Bench, Exchequer, Chancery, and the House of Lords.

When the law library of Theophilus Parsons Sr., the late chief justice of the Massachusetts Supreme Judicial Court and one of the most erudite and best-informed jurists in America, was sold in 1814 it was found to consist of some 282 (chiefly English) law books, about half of which were legislative journals and statutes.[4] Some of these available English court reports, those of Godbolt, Latch, Keble, Barnardiston, Sayer, Noy, and several of the "Modern" series, were of dubious quality,[5] and digests such as Viner's offered its users little in the way of guidance, being at times no more than a listing of the bare facts and outcomes of cases involving comparable issues. (Witness the bewildering array of cases concerning the rights of a third-party beneficiary to a contract to sue, some seeming to allow the action, others to deny it, to be found, willy-nilly, in Viner's pages.) And while Bostonians such as Parsons might possess English reports and treatises, jurists functioning farther inland were sometimes less fortunate. Hugh Henry Brackenridge's legal practice had been in frontier Pittsburgh in the late eighteenth century before he was named to the Pennsylvania Supreme Court. In 1814 he defended the use by that court of post-Independence-era English reports, both because there was "much excellent sense to be found in them" and because the "old books, . . . the year books, and Dyer and many others are little seen. Many of them are out of print, and not to be got at with us at all."[6] As for the reporting of the decisions of the state high courts in the new Republic, according to Nathaniel Haven, the "best library of American reports that could be summoned by money or magic, within the circumference of the Union in 1800, might have been borne on [the horse of one riding the judicial] circuits in a portfolio."[7] English reports were becoming available, but not widely available as late as the 1820s, and there were simply very few American reports. Antebellum jurists certainly did believe that law was chiseled from principle, and some (especially Gibson) were indeed capable of writing paragraphs in a "grand style" without "a shred of 'authority.'" But in this regard they were doing nothing inconsistent with the grandest of "styles" offered by any of the great English common-law jurists whose reported judgments often appeared without the citation of a single case.

Nonetheless, as early as the 1770s, jurists in New Hampshire, New York, and the middle and southern colonies often followed English precedent, citing from those English reports, treaties, and digests that had made their way to these shores, while those in Massachusetts, Connecticut, and Rhode Island were treating such citations as persuasive, if not binding, authority.[8] And since increasing numbers of American jurists of the late eighteenth and early nineteenth centuries *were* trained in English law, they and the trained attorneys who argued cases before them carried a wealth of common-law precedents in their memory banks. Thus "the law" was constantly being "rediscovered" by jurists who remembered (or were reminded of) how a similar case had been decided ten years earlier by themselves or their predecessors. This had been the case with English courts before the seventeenth century, and it was not an impossible situation, to be sure. Morton Horwitz thus misrepresents the dilemma that Justice Ambrose Spencer described in *Sands* v. *Taylor* (1810). A brewer bought "southern wheat" after first sampling it. He accepted delivery of some, found it unsuitable for malting, and rejected the rest; whereupon the seller sold the balance at auction and sued for the difference between the price at auction and the price the brewer had agreed to. Horwitz quotes Spencer as saying that there were "no adjudications in the books, which either establish or deny the rule adopted in this case,"[9] and he concludes that the court thereupon "created" a new rule, permitting the action the seller had taken.[10] But this is not the way I understand what the three members of the New York Supreme Court who decided the case did. In *their* opinions, Spencer's colleagues, James Kent and William Van Ness, both cited English precedents and treatises as authority for the expectation damages.[11] And while it is true that Justice Spencer, less versed in English "black letter" law than his colleagues,[12] found "no adjudications in the books," he did agree with plaintiff's counsel that "the case of *Heermance and Radcliff* v. *Yeomans*, decided in this court many years since, of which no report is extant," adopted the same principle empowering "the vendor of goods, to resell them and call on the vendee for the difference of price." "I recollect the case," Spencer said. "The principle now adopted was recognized in that case."[13] Memory and the oral tradition *could* serve as the means of transmission of common-law rules.

The printing press provided a more reliable means. "The uncertainty and contraction of oral reports of cases," Zephaniah Swift observed in his *System of Laws of the State of Connecticut* in 1795, "has been the subject of much complaint." A Boston bar member noted the "great inattention" with regards to "the presentation of the decisions of our courts of law" in the *Columbian Centinel* in 1801. The consequence of this inattention was that jurists, offered "the loose and interested recollections of counsel," had to "depend wholly on British decisions." Thus New York's first major court reporter, William Johnson, in concert with that state's chief justice of the Supreme Court of Judicature, James Kent, began to publish that court's opinions, asking rhetorically in the preface to his first volume in 1804, "Must [these opinions] float in the memories of those by whom they are pronounced, and the law, instead of being a fixed and uniform rule of action, be thus subject to perpetual friction and change?"[14]

By 1824, as men like Johnson and Kent struggled to establish printed records of that state's common law for the benefit of practitioners, colleagues, and the next generation, there had appeared some 30 volumes of reports of New York's supreme court and 7 of its chancery. J. Elihu Bay's 2 volumes of reports of the South Carolina's supreme court from 1783 to 1804 (published in 1812) "aided in bringing justice to abide by rule arising from precedents," according to that court's future chief justice John B. O'Neall, who added that before the publication of Bay's reports "all was chaos in our legal world." Indeed, by the 1840s the very efforts of men such as Kent, Bay, Swift, Shaw, Gibson, Joseph Story, and their colleagues throughout the Union to spell out the principles and rules of common law and equity in published reports, treatises, and the occasional summary statement[15] had produced over 650 volumes of reports, several useful native-grown treatises, numerous "American editions" of English treatises, several American editions of Blackstone's *Commentaries*, and a set of English common-law and Court of Chancery reports, published by Gregg and Elliott of Philadelphia.[16]

Shaw, Gibson, Kent, and Story wrote in a "grand style" because they knew that each case of "first impression" in their jurisdiction enabled them to provide guidance (as well as to demonstrate their erudition and genius) to an admiring profession, not because they were seeking to set English precedent aside in order to make "new law" for American enterprise. The cases other American jurists would now cite as precedent might not differ in their statements of "the true rule" from available English reports, but they now bore American authorship, they were *American* authorities.

Eventually these efforts began to overwhelm their audience. "Every question of doubt must be [or, at least, *was* being] argued *de novo* in each State, as the exigency occurs, and the vast mass of English and American authorities" must be "passed on," S. F. Dixon wrote in the *American Jurist and Law Magazine* in 1835. The whole business was getting very complicated as the corpus of American "law" grew up in each state. Hence one member of the American bar had praise in 1843 for "abridgers" of a law "now oppressed by the multitude of precedents." Without their "mechanical assistance" (he was reviewing Francis Wharton's *Digest of Cases in the Supreme Court of Pennsylvania*) a busy profession would fail to appreciate "the light" shed by "the experience of even our contemporaries."[17] Some went so far as to call for the law's codification in order "to have a starting point—something irrevocably fixed as settled principle." As Joseph Story put it bluntly, a "positive text" could give practitioners "the true rule, instead of leaving it open to conjecture and inference by feeble minds."[18]

Of course, those "feeble minds" lacking that "positive text" could and did fall back on what was, by the 1820s, the most reliable means of knowing "the true rule"—namely, the precedents to be found in published reports, identified for practitioners in treatises and digests. Thus in 1858 New Hampshire's Chief Justice Ira Perley deferred to the prior judgments of "judges who must certainly be reckoned among the most eminent jurists that New England has produced." He named "Parsons and Shaw in Massachusetts," "Mellen and Shepley in Maine," and "our own learned and excellent [former] Chief Justice Richardson in this State; names which carry with them an irresistible weight of authority on all legal questions . . . in New England."[19]

This trust in precedent was bound up with a rule of its own, that of stare decisis, whereby courts were, by the 1820s if not earlier, bound to follow prior decisions on any given issue so long as the ratio decidendi (or the judicial rationale that such decisions were grounded in) appeared to be "sound." In that event, the matter was proclaimed to be "well settled," and attorneys and their clients alike could thereafter rely on the court to treat like problems in the future in the same fashion. Predictability was simply good public policy. Thus Pennsylvania's Chief Justice John Bannister Gibson held in 1843 that the use of rules drawn from European civil law in a debtor-creditor dispute "would require some intolerable mischief . . . to justify us in overturning the decisions of more than two centuries," while his colleague, Justice Jeremiah Black, argued in 1856 that courts were not "at liberty to overthrow the doctrines of their predecessors," inasmuch as that would render "our system of jurisprudence . . . fickle, uncertain and vicious." The rules of property, "which ought to be as steadfast as the hills," would become "as unstable as the waves." In the words of New York's James Kent,

> If a decision has been made upon solemn argument and mature
> deliberation, the presumption is in favor of its correctness, and the
> community have a right to regard it as a just . . . exposition of the law,
> and to regulate their actions and contracts by it. It would, therefore,

be extremely inconvenient to the public if precedents were not duly regarded and pretty implicitly followed. It is by the notoriety and stability of such rules that professional men can give safe advice to those who consult them, and people in general can venture with confidence to deal with each other.[20]

Antebellum chief justices of state supreme courts sometimes spoke of their desire to "unravel a complicated case . . . in a manner consistent with the plain dictates of natural justice."[21] They sometimes protested against "blind veneration for ancient rules, maxims, and precedents"[22] and noted that prior decisions "founded on mistaken principles" of "inconvenient" rules might be ignored by "a subsequent court" that would thereby decide, not that their prior decisions were "bad law but that they are not law."[23] Some have interpreted such expressions as evidence that "law is what the courts say it is."[24] They quote at length[25] from New York's famed James Kent's recollection of his experiences upon being named chancellor to the relatively new equity system in that state in 1814:[26]

> I took the court as if it has been a new institution, never before known to the U. S. I had nothing to guide me, was left at liberty to assume all such English chancery powers and jurisdiction as I thought applicable under our constitution. This gave me great scope. . . . I might once & a while be embarrassed by a technical rule, but I most always found principles suited to my views of the case.[27]

It certainly sounds as if Kent and Chipman, Swift, and Shaw (the other three chief justices just quoted) might have been signaling their "instrumentalist" propensities in these passages, that they may have understood the common law to be a mere instrument in the hands of a jurist to achieve whatever end he and his colleagues sought at a given place and time. As one authority puts it, early-nineteenth-century American jurists escaped from "strict eighteenth century conceptions of precedent." "By 1820 . . . law was no longer conceived of as an eternal set of principles expressed in custom and derived from natural law. Nor was it regarded primarily as a body of rules designed to achieve justice only in the individual case. Instead, judges came to think of the common law . . . as an instrument of policy."[28]

It is certainly *plausible* to read these passages in that way, but there is another way to read them, a more accurate way, I contend, more faithful to their authors' true intents; and this alternative reading does not find them to be revealing any instrumentalist propensities. Instead, it finds these passages to be no more than a familiar restatement (à la Coke, Holt, and Blackstone) of the "declaratory" theory of the common law: Legal principles had, over the centuries, been "discovered" and could be learned; once learned they could be applied to a given fact situation to produce justice; and any prior decision that had failed in this regard could be ignored or rejected because it simply did not constitute "the law."[29] To Chief Justice Lemuel Shaw the common law consisted of "a few broad and comprehensive principles, founded on reason, natural justice and enlightened public policy." These were modified and adapted to the circumstances of all the particular cases that came before the jurists. When "new practices spring up" or "new combinations of facts arise," and when "cases are presented for which there is no precedent in judicial decisions, they must be governed by the general principles."[30] It was perfectly true that the common law was "progressive and expansive, adapting itself to the new relations and interests which are constantly springing up in the progress of society," as Rhode Island's Chief Justice Richard Greene put it in 1850, "but this progress must be by analogy to what is already settled."[31]

James Kent's passage offers us a slightly different problem, for Kent, it must be kept in mind, was assuming the office of chancellor, head of the equity system. Kent has *served* as chief justice of the (common-law) New York Supreme Court, where he contented himself "with administering the common law, as he f[ound] it, without the rashness to presume himself wiser than the law, or the vanity of distinguishing himself by innovation."[32] But in 1814 he was taking over a different legal system, one of relatively recent origin, without published reports. He had, as he put it, "nothing to guide me." Hence he assumed "such English Chancery powers and jurisdiction as I thought applicable," which gave him "grand scope." But now note the following: "My practice was, first, to make myself perfectly and accurately . . . master of the facts. . . . I saw where justice lay, and the moral sense decided the court half the time; and I then sat down to search the authorities until I had examined by books."[33] What is there in this passage of Kent's that is so remarkable? Does it not describe precisely the proper behavior of an equity judge in early America? The English Court of Chancery, to be sure, had rules and some published reports, but it had not yet established the rigidity that Kent's English contemporary, Lord Eldon, was building into it, and, in any event, its premises differ from those of common-law courts. Equity judges are *supposed* to gather the facts and utilize a "moral sense." That was why they were created in England once the common-law writs had been frozen and the common law's remedies and growth had slowed in the late Middle Ages.[34]

Nevertheless, those who would see in Kent's words the arbitrary will of a judge whose "moral sense" might well be on the side of the upper class or the merchant class or the entrepreneurial class would do well to consider other evidence of his judicial behavior. Kent referred to "the moral sense" elsewhere, at a lecture to students at Columbia in 1824, when he bonded "a lively sense of justice" to the cherishing of "the benevolent affections" that "sharpen the perceptions of the moral sense." "Wisdom," he added, "is as much the offspring of the heart as the head."[35] At the age of twenty-three he wrote Simeon Baldwin that the common law "can only be discerned and known by searching into the Decisions of the English Courts, which are . . . regarded with us as authentic Evidence of the Common Law & therefore are cited as *Precedents binding* with us." And later, as chancellor he wrote (in *Manning* v. *Manning* [1815]):

> I consider myself bound [by decisions of the English Chancery court] . . . . I shall certainly not presume to strike into any new path, with visionary schemes of innovation and improvement. *Via antiqua via est tuta.* It would, no doubt, at times be very convenient to disregard all English decisions as of no authority and to set up as a standard my own notions of right and wrong. But I can do no such thing.[36]

This is why Joseph Story's review of Kent's equity opinions praised the chancellor for being "exact, and methodical; always reverencing authorities, and bound by decisions; true to the spirit, yet more true to the letter of the law."[37] Jurists such as Kent sought to serve what they conceived to be the ends of justice and the "Public Good," but they did so within the scope of the existing body and principles of the law.

English cases, then, were the primary authority for legal questions in American courts, despite the fact that America had by 1815 fought two wars to free itself from British regulations and interference. When the proxies of two states sued one another before the U.S. Supreme Court, in *Robinson* v. *Campbell* (1818), that bench explained that "the remedies in the courts of the United States are to be . . . according to the principles of common law and equity, as distinguished and defined in that country from which we derive our knowledge of those principles." Indeed, in 1814 Pennsylvania's Justice Brackenridge believed he and his colleagues "have been in the habit of paying more deference to English decisions than the most technical of the English judges themselves." By 1836 David Hoffman could confidently advise prospective students of the law that "our numerous volumes of reports daily illustrate that, with trivial exceptions, what is the law of real property at Westminster Hall is equally so in the various tribunals throughout our extensive country."[38]

The jurists of one jurisdiction might, of course, differ at times from those of another as to exactly which English precedents to follow in certain particulars; some found one rule in a given matter to be the "sound" one, others found a contrary rule to be the one "well-settled."[39] Some jurists were capable of writing opinions that either rejected a bit too casually or simply ignored precedents opposed to the positions they had staked out. Although this may sometimes have been their silent way of securing a result other than the one that precedent appeared to dictate, I am convinced that, in most instances, the authors of these opinions felt justified in this behavior because they were convinced that the precedent they had either rejected or ignored was "bad law." Sometimes they felt it necessary to say as much; other times they felt that their colleagues would simply understand a lack of necessity for such a statement. On other occasions they were either fooling themselves or deliberately seeking to deceive the readers of their opinions. But I believe that they rarely wrote deliberately to deceive. Instead, they believed they were judging, professionally, which precedents were "good law" and which were bad. William P. LaPiana has recently illustrated a case of genuine disagreement (over the question of negotiable instruments and antecedent debt) between the high courts of the United States and the state of New York in the 1840s, with the jurists of other state courts offering still other versions of the "true" law. His point is that, although differences of opinion existed, none of the jurists involved saw themselves as instrumentalists, as "making" law. They simply disagreed, intellectually, over how properly to apply "scientifically" certain common-law principles to complex commercial transactions in order to know which rule was the "principled" one.[40] We will consider another clear example of that phenomenon in chapter 2, in the debate over whether a third-party beneficiary to a contract should be allowed to sue on the contract.

Jurists of "the creative era" did not think of themselves as innovators; it would take *much* self-convincing on the part of those who *were* to bend certain rules for them to do so. The notion that "settled" doctrines might be set aside by jurists "to suit their own views of convenience or policy" was to Justice Joseph Story of the U.S. Supreme Court "a most alarming dogma, subversive of some of the best rights of a free people." To Story a jurist was not to "consider what in theory ought to be the true doctrines of the law," but rather to administer the common law as he found it, "in the path of authority." Indeed, when he wrote in another decision that he was "content to stand *super antiquas vias*; and to go where they lead," he was actually quoting (without attribution) the views of Lord Kenyon on the judicial obligation to follow precedent. Story's contemporary, Chief Justice Stephen Titus

Hosmer of the Connecticut Supreme Court of Errors was more forthright in that regard when in 1823 he rejected the notion that "this court can promulgate as law any provision which will meet a particular mischief." That would amount to "an assumption of legislative power." Hosmer would have none of that; rather, he took "pleasure in declaring" the words of "a very eminent judge [Lord Kenyon]: 'It is my wish and my comfort to stand *super antiquas vias*: I cannot legislate; but by my industry, I can discover what our predecessors have done, and I will servilely tread in their footstep.'" Hosmer continued: "I deprecate a departure from the old highway of the common law, by the indulgence of a disposition to decide on principles of equity and convenience, which often are notional and imaginary."[41] So profound was the power of precedent to New York jurists in the 1850s that Jeff Hoyt aptly writes of Justice James Roosevelt's innovative but unsuccessful attempts to enjoin the city council from sanctioning graft-ridden street improvements with pathbreaking opinions that ignored existing rules: "Flickering defiantly against the smothering weight of precedent, these decisions merely singed the foundations of municipal law."[42]

Note that these jurists spoke of applying principles "scientifically."[43] Law was inductive science to its seventeenth-, eighteenth-, and early-nineteenth-century practitioners, long before Christopher Columbus Langdell spoke of law as a "science" at Harvard Law School in the 1870s. Good jurists could identify general principles of law from the particulars of a case. In fact, Craig Klafter has recently argued that American jurists of the early nineteenth century were more concerned with logic and principles than they were with mere precedent. They may well have been. Thus Virginia's governor, John Tyler, in criticizing the use by Virginia's bench of the less noteworthy English nisi prius reports, called on his colleagues in the judiciary to rely instead on the "principles and maxims" that had been distilled from the work of generations of jurists: "We should prove the proposition by the axiom—so would old Euclid have done."[44] And Pennsylvania's fabled early leader of the Bar, Peter DuPonceau, noted that while English jurists followed precedent slavishly, American courts respected an "appeal to the power of logic, or the supremacy of principles." Pennsylvania's equally fabled chief justice, John Bannister Gibson, told the profession in *Hoopes* v. *Dundas* (1848): "We are not going to overturn our decision here because it has pleased the [English] Chancellor to overturn the old decisions there."[45] English practice and procedures were followed in our "creative era" far more than some have allowed,[46] but some American state supreme courts had been sufficiently freed by provincial or antebellum legislatures from the formalities of special pleading or the writ system to deal with the substance of disputes coming to them on appeal. The more skillful jurists engaged in the assessment of precedents that appeared to conflict with, or be qualified by, other precedents. They looked to the author of the opinion, judging some to be better authority than others; and in the absence of a clear guidelight from this inquiry, they looked to the relative merits of the opinions' logic, of the "principles" to be found therein. Thus James Gould claimed in a treatise on "Pleading in Civil Actions" (1832) that law in America was a science of "consistent and rational principles."[47]

One recurrent term symbolized this celebration of the precision and order of a "principled," "scientific" system of rules and doctrines—the "symmetry" of the law. In the "private wrongs" section of his *System of the Laws of the State of Connecticut* (1795), Zephaniah Swift spoke of "the beautiful order and symmetry" of jurisprudence. Connecticut's Justice Tapping Reeve worried about innovations which might "mar the symmetry of the law, and the presence of symmetry in our system." Vermont's Chief Justice Isaac Redfield correctly associated the search for symmetry on the part of a "large class of the profession" to "habit or education."[48] Justice Story put it this way: "We have regular systems, built up with symmetry of parts; and the necessary investigations in new and difficult cases are conducted with more safety, because they are founded on inductions from rules better established and more exactly limited."[49]

TWO EXAMPLES OF THE JURISPRUDENCE OF THE HEAD

Economic-oriented accounts of American courts of the nineteenth century have offered two tales of alleged innovation in the law of property for the benefit of entrepreneurs and economic growth that I want to retell here. I do so because I am convinced that, instead of illustrating a kind of Jurisprudence of Growth, as had been claimed, these stories actually characterize the anchors of precedent, principle, and symmetry that held many common-law rules fast in the currents of nineteenth-century American history.

The English Rule Regarding the Lateral Support of
Buildings Stands, Unshaken, in the New World

We have been told of a "radical break" in antebellum America "with common law tradition" regarding the lateral support of buildings owed landowners by adjacent landowners. Courts in the early nineteenth century "turned their attack" on these "monopolistic and exclusionary predilections of property law," preferring rules with "a strong tendency to encourage competitive improvement of land."[50] That is not the way I understand the evidence regarding this problem. As I read what they were saying, American jurists addressing this question remained largely doctrinal in their approach throughout, searching for the case's "essentials" and applying the rules to be found in English precedents from the moment in 1815 when the issue of the duty that an adjoint landowner owed to the lateral support of a neighbor's building was first discussed in the appellate record here until at least 1877.[51]

The claims advanced regarding this problem property owners faced all too often rest on an understanding of a decision of Chief Justice Isaac Parker of the Massachusetts Supreme Judicial Court in the case of *Thurston v. Hancock* (1815), a "widely influential case."[52] William Thurston acquired land on Beacon Hill, Boston, in 1802 and built a house in 1804 within two feet of his lower boundary line. Some ten years later the owner of the land below him on the hill began excavation for a house of his own, keeping at all times from five to six feet from the boundary line. Despite this, land from the foundation of the first house began to fall away, leaving the building highly vulnerable. Thurston felt compelled to remove his family from it and to have it taken down and reconstructed at a safer distance from the boundary line. He then sued the lower lot owner for damages. Chief Justice Parker is said to have "dramatically shifted the idea of dominion of land" in ruling that the loss incurred to the building was not actionable, albeit nominal damages might be recovered for the displacement of any of the soil up to the side of the foundation itself. This distinction between damage to mere soil and damage to the more valuable building itself was (according to this historian) "circular and contradictory" but had the "effect of freeing economic development from the legal restrictions that a rule of priority imposed on competitive land use." The result was the "first [decision] in the nineteenth century to hold that in certain kinds of economic activity there existed no correlative rights and obligation's between adjoining landowners." Thus "American courts first established the general principle that a landowner owed no duty at all to support buildings on adjoining land."[53]

This is not the way I read *Thurston*. It did not constitute a "radical break with common law tradition" but was wholly consistent with it; and Parker's opinion did not hold that "there existed no correlative rights and obligation's between adjoining landowners"; on the contrary, it asserted and explained them.

The English common-law decisions, dating from as far back as 1639 on this subject were clear: If A built too close to B's property line "within the memory of man," were B to chose to do the same, no action would lie for damage to A's house because of B's excavation, "because it was A's own fault that he built his house so near the land of B, for he by his act cannot hinder B from making the best use of his own land that he can."[54] It might be otherwise were the original building truly "ancient," where the "circumstances of antiquity" might warrant a prescriptive claim to an easement, a kind of property right adhering to the building.[55]

In *Thurston* Chief Justice Parker noted that, in the past, English courts had only recognized prescriptive rights of this sort where the building had "the marks of antiquity about it" and one "may well suppose that all its privileges of right appertain to the house," or when it could be proved to have existed for some sixty years (though he allowed that nisi prius dicta of Lord Ellenborough raised the question of whether twenty years enjoyment of the lateral support—still a *long* passage of time—would suffice to create the easement). Neither condition, however, would help this plaintiff, inasmuch as he had built only ten years before. Moreover, he insisted, the principle to be found in "the cases anciently settled" in England was a reasonable one: The plaintiff should be held responsible for the risk he took in building so close to his neighbor's line. Such a rule was "the dictate of common sense and sound reason," and the court had "not been able to discover that the doctrine has ever been overruled nor to ascertain any good reason why it should be." It was clear that the plaintiff, in building so close to his downhill-side neighbor's land, had assumed the risk. One who builds too close to a neighbor's property line "ought to foresee the probable use" his neighbor might put his land to. Thurston "built at his peril." The sensible and neighborly thing to do, Parker explained, was to "secure himself against future interruption and inconvenience" by "a different arrangement of the house" on his land or "by convention with the neighbour."[56]

Other American opinions on this subject over the next sixty years applied the English rules in equally doctrinal fashion. Thus in 1877 Chief Justice Horace Gray of the same Massachusetts Supreme Judicial Court reviewed the same English authorities that his predecessor had, as well as a host of more recent ones, and then, referring to *Thurston*, observed that in a comparable case, "it would be unjustifiable and mischievous for the court to change a rule of law which has been established and acted upon here for sixty years."[57] One finds little innovative or "radical" in the common-law rules used by American jurists of the nineteenth century when it came to lateral support of buildings. What one does find is a devotion to English precedent and legal principles.

There are two exceptions to this generalization. In 1873 Georgia's high court abandoned altogether the English (and American) prescriptive right, the easement, that a landowner might acquire to lateral support of a building near his neighbor's property line after a passage of twenty or more years. Justice R. P. Trippe pointed out that a similar rule had led to the unneighborly building of blank walls to prevent the neighbor from acquiring an "ancient-lights" easement (see chapter 4), and it was capable of leading to the same "churlish" behavior involving the lateral support of buildings— that is, a neighbor might remove the soil from the vicinity of another's building that had been raised too closely to the property line in order to prevent a future prescriptive claim, even though this might undermine their neighbor's new foundation. Virginia's Supreme Court was taken by this reasoning and also abandoned the prescriptive right, Justice Lewis worrying in dicta about similar "unneighborly acts."[58] Thus two courts abandoned the rule, but because of its potentially antisocial quality, not for any economic reason.

America's Streams Follow Old England's Legal Channels

Another story told of common-law innovation in the service of entrepreneurs concerns riparian rights. An ancient rule protecting the "quiet enjoyment" of the "absolute dominion" of one's river frontage, it is said, allowed no alteration in the "natural flow" of water. Property in flowing water "was not essentially an instrumental good or a productive asset" in late-eighteenth-century America, "but rather a private estate to be enjoyed for its own sake." In 1795 the New Jersey Supreme Court "regarded the legitimate uses of water as those that serve domestic purposes and husbandry, requiring insignificant appropriations of the water's flow." Exploitation of water resources for dams "was thus limited" and conflicts were "invariably resolved in favor of economic inactivity." These "fundamentally antidevelopmental premises of the common law" slowly yielded to "the utilitarian world of economic efficiency" in the nineteenth century. A prescriptive "prior occupancy" doctrine, borrowed from recent English opinions, emerged that, though it might also be used to *block* development, was now "put forth" on the "offensive . . . to promote economic development," and this, in turn, yielded to a "reasonable use" doctrine when a second, more powerful milldam was built that adversely affected the first mill.[59]

Chief Justice Lemuel Shaw's opinion in *Cary* v. *Daniels* (1844) is offered in this tale as the culminating victory for large textile mills. Jurists like Shaw were "so captivated by the spirit of improvement that they were willing to manipulate the concept of property to conform to their own notions of the needs of industrialization." Shaw "took account of the 'usages and wants of the community' and 'the progress of improvement in hydraulic works'" to rule that a prior user of water power might be lawfully guaranteed a "monopoly" right to such use where later dams might adversely affect his power.[60]

How plausible is this alleged transformation of the law of riparian rights? The traditional "natural use" rule in *Merritt v. Parker*, the New Jersey opinion of 1795, actually appeared in the trial judge's charge to the jury as the first in a sequence of legal rules that he offered. The others he read them were the ones that were supposed to have "evolved" in the early nineteenth century. This judge clearly conceived of them in 1795 as being in full bloom and of one piece. Yes, all riparians had a right to the "natural use" of the water. But prior milldam owners had claims affecting more recent ones, who had the right to use water so long as they did not diminish significantly the flow to the prior millowner. All of Horwitz's "stages" of legal development were already there in this charge to the New Jersey jury: natural use, prior occupancy, and reasonable use. And this case was no preindustrial, agrarian standard-bearer. Both litigants were millowners!

Parker, the defendant, had acquired statutory authority for a sawmill constructed in 1780. Merritt, his upstream neighbor, had built another, without such authority, in 1793 by cutting a trench from Parker's millpond through his land to drive his waterwheel, and then sending the water through Parker's own land and back into the stream *below* Parker's mill. Parker had retaliated by raising his dam, thus backing water onto Merritt's waterwheel. Merritt then sued. The trial judge, after summarizing the various strands of the law of riparian rights, told the jury that he thought the law and evidence indicated that the plaintiff had not been justified in cutting the trench, draining waterpower from Parker's lawfully acquired millpond, and channeling that water onto Parker's land. The jury agreed.[61] We are told of two other early-nineteenth-century Pennsylvania cases to establish the preindustrial role of the natural use rule. But both of these *also* involve suits of one millowner against another, and both conclude as did *Merritt v. Parker* that one cannot unreasonably cause damage to an existing mill.[62]

Furthermore, the allegedly innovative decision of Lemuel Shaw in 1844, *Cary v. Daniels*, was not a victory for large cotton textile mills, as alleged, and Shaw's reasoning was foursquare in alignment with *Merritt v. Parker* and the two Pennsylvania cases nearly half a century earlier. Two men had worked two milldams a quarter of a mile apart on the Charles River at Medway as tenants in common for several years. The upper, larger dam, a sawmill, had enjoyed the right to release backed-up water when the lower dam created such a backup by sending a worker downstream to open the lower dam's waste gate. The two sold their common property to another, who then resold the upper milldam to its former tenant, Cary, and the lower one to a new miller, Daniels. Daniels abandoned the existing dam and built another some 750 feet further downstream but at a somewhat higher level. The upper millowner sued for damages because water from the new dam often backed onto his wheel. A jury awarded him three hundred dollars in damages for this, and another one hundred dollars for the fact that the new downstream dam had no waste gate, a relief measure he claimed to belong to him under the terms of the earlier common tenancy.

Chief Justice Shaw began his opinion with the same first-stage, natural use statement of the law of riparian rights that the leading voice of judicial transformation of law to serve entrepreneurs cites from *Merritt* v. *Parker*. "It is agreed on all hands," Shaw wrote, "that the owner of a parcel of land, through which a stream of water flows, has a right to use and enjoyment of the benefits to be derived therefrom, as it passes through his own land." Then Shaw went on to explain that "each proprietor is entitled to such use of the stream, so far as it is reasonable, conformable to the usages and wants of the community, and having regard to the progress of improvements in hydraulic works, and not inconsistent with a like reasonable use by other proprietors . . . , above and below." He did *not* then go on to allow, as has been claimed, that "a mill owner who did not 'wholly' obstruct a stream might claim that 'the needs and wants of the community' justified his using more than a proportionate share of the water."[63]

It is true that he observed that when "the descent [of the water] may be so gradual as only to admit of mills at considerable distances," then "prior occupancy gives a prior title to such use." But Shaw *also* hypothesized the other situation, where the fall of water per mile was great enough for several mills easily to be established without one injuring another's operation in close proximity. The opinion has several such hypotheticals, involving low waterwheels, high waterwheels, land held in joint or common tenancy, separately owned adjacent riparian land, and the like. Yes, the first dam builder could maintain his right to whatever water levels he had already created against new owners whose works threw water back on his. But this did not grant him a "monopoly." It is clear that Shaw did *not* view as damnum absque injuria the act of one raising a dam after others had already established milldams whenever the works of those dams would be thereby impeded. And any claims the dam raiser might offer as to the "needs and wants of the community" was and would be of no avail.

Shaw concluded that the upper millowner was entitled to the three-hundred-dollar award, but not the one-hundred-dollar one, because his past right to the waste gate had been enjoyed when he was a joint tenant, sharing costs and profits of the two mills. Since he and his partner might have chosen to "favor one [mill] at the expense of the other, as the exigencies of their business might require," he had acquired no easement because his use of the waste gate "was not adverse." Shaw's decision was straightforward common-law reasoning, with no innovative or pro-entrepreneurial twists.[64]

We can further verify that there was no transformation from common-law rules protecting "inactivity" to those rewarding entrepreneurs in the aquatic domain of riparian rights by examining a number of decisions of the Massachusetts Supreme Judicial Court in the years that Horwitz identifies as the era of transformation—the three decades prior to *Cary* v. *Daniels* (and the several decades ensuing). We begin with the suit of Mercy Hatch. She purchased a disused mill at Northhampton on (of all places) the Mill River in 1817, and was soon confronted with the fact that neighbors five rods downstream had built a new gristmill that backed water up onto her ruin, rending it "useless" as a future millsite. She sued for damages, but the counsel for the new mill pointed out to the court that the location of her disused mill was "not so convenient a site as that where the new one had been built." This appeal to economic efficiency did not impress the high court in 1821; it affirmed a lower court award of annual damages amounting to the interest on her investment.[65]

The same bench decided another appeal involving two millowners seven years later, in 1828. The new upstream dam had been "lawfully" constructed, drawing no power away from its downstream predecessor. But when that entrepreneur then decided to raise the level of *his* dam, he caused water to back onto the wheels of the new mill, "to its damage." Chief Justice Isaac Parker, in reading the court's opinion upholding the claim of the smaller (if newer) upstream plaintiff, noted that "the plaintiff had a right to calculate upon the state of things as they existed when he erected his mill."[66] Simultaneously, the court affirmed the right of access of a smaller sawmill to water unneeded by a "cotton factory," and ordered the larger mill to lower its flume boards.[67] Four years later, the court heard *Bemis* v. *Upham*. Two milldams were built too close to one another, with the first dam, a smaller, more traditional one, being completed only a month before the other, "a cotton manufactory" with "very expensive factories." When the smaller one sued the larger for the loss of riparian rights, the question was sent to the high court, and the new chief justice, Lemuel Shaw, answered it to the advantage of the smaller mill owner; he was free to seek an injunction, and Shaw particularly recommended that he ask for an abatement in the level of the lower factory dam.[68]

Continuity characterizes the law of riparian rights in these years. We find the same ancient common-law rules determining each of these decisions of the New Jersey, Pennsylvania, and Massachusetts courts from 1795 to 1844. They are in the instructions read to that New Jersey court in 1795 and Chief Justice Shaw's opinion in 1844. And we can track these rules in Massachusetts at least as far back as the 1760s, and at least as far forward as the 1880s.[69] William Nelson, who has examined county as well as supreme court decisions in Massachusetts from 1760 to 1830, cites over a dozen such cases (including some that I have just described). He tells us that the rule in the 1760s was that one who was first on a stream with a milldam acquired the continued right to water necessary to operate his mill and the power to "bring suit against anyone who interfered with that use." And as late as 1830, Nelson says, the Massachusetts courts "continued to protect" these same riparian rights.[70] I agree, but would add that this practice continued well beyond 1844 in Massachusetts, and that this was the case in Maine, Connecticut, Ohio, West Virginia, Iowa, Pennsylvania, Michigan, and Louisiana as well.[71]

The differences that some have drawn between the relative weights that the federal, Pennsylvania, Massachusetts, and New York courts gave in the second quarter of the nineteenth century to "prior occupancy" versus "reasonable use" have been greatly overstated. The rule applied in those jurisdictions throughout these years was the same as that used in the eighteenth century, and if a few of these decisions concluded that the older dam was not entitled to damages by virtue of the creation of a more recent milldam, this was not because of a change in the common law. Either a jury had decided that the damages claimed were inconsequential, and thus the use of the water by the new dam owner "reasonable," or the plaintiff had failed to create the necessary prescriptive right to his millpond by overflowing the lands of those above him.[72] Differences did exist between the law of riparian rights in the water-rich East, where water served in-stream power purposes, and the law in the water-scarce West, where its primary purposes were consumptive, for mining, or for irrigation.[73] But where the needs of miners collided with those of farmers, the contests tended to be won by the latter in California's high court. Doctrinal application of the rules of riparian rights were defended there with reference to "public rights" rather than being set aside with a more instrumentalist "public policy" rationale.[74]

In short, most nineteenth-century American jurists appear to have dealt doctrinally with questions of riparian rights, just as they had with regard to those involving lateral support for buildings, working their way through the facts and the rules to a "just" resolution of each conflict.

My lengthier tales of the power of precedent and "principled" continuity, of the Jurisprudence of the Head, of the defense of law's "symmetry," begin in chapter 2, with matters of contract law that are said to have been transformed in nineteenth-century America. I argue that they were not—that continuity, not change, characterized the "creative era." In chapter 3 I make the same case for a set of tort doctrines central to negligence suits.

Chapter Two

Plus ça Change: Contract's Westminster Anchors in Nineteenth-Century America

The rules of contract law remained largely unaltered throughout American's legal jurisdictions in the nineteenth century. Jurists followed longstanding English doctrines with regard to the law of sales and most questions of the law of contracts for services; they differed as to *which* English doctrine to follow when it came to contracts made for the benefit of a third person (third-party beneficiary contracts). In this chapter continuity in the law of sales is the central story, but we will also explore the strange career of the doctrine pertaining to third-party beneficiaries to a contract. These stories are evidence of the strengths of Westminster's anchors in nineteenth-century American common law, stories of the Jurisprudence of the Head. Later, in chapters 5 and 6, we will see two rules of the law of contracts for personal services that yielded to the Jurisprudence of the Heart.

One might well ask (my students sometimes do) why it is necessary to tell stories of continuity. If nothing is changing, why not simply say so and move on? Why guide the reader through centuries of English law and dozens of pages of case analyses? The answer is that the claims I am making, of continuity, are controversial ones. The reigning school of thought on these issues describes the law of sales in antebellum America as a field of flux. So I will introduce each issue by acquainting the reader with the point of view that I do not share before explaining my own position.

THE LONG LIFE OF CONTRACT'S RULES REGARDING SALES

Several doctrines central to the core of contract law, it has been said, were significantly altered in America in the early and mid-nineteenth centuries. A "sound price doctrine" of the seventeenth and eighteenth centuries was "sudden[ly]" "overthrown" in the early nineteenth century by the doctrine of caveat emptor. In the place of this "fairness doctrine," jurists "asserted for the first time" that the source of the obligation of contract was the "convergence of the wills of the contracting parties." Jurists no longer tolerated equitable inquiries into the adequacy of consideration as an element determining contractual liability. "The first recognition of expectation damages" is also said to have occurred in these years, as executory sales contracts assumed a "central place in the economic system" in "futures" agreements. In order to "accommodate the market function of such agreements," jurists reordered the rules to "grant the contracted parties their expected return." This development correlated with the "development of extensive internal commodities markets around 1815" and reflected "a pervasive shift in the sympathies of the courts" from one expressing "the legal and ethical culture of the small town, of the farmer, and of the small trader" to one "whereby courts came to reflect commercial interests."[1] Jurists are also said to have blurred ancient distinctions between various types of secured transactions due to "pressures to buy and sell" on the "highway to progress and wealth." And they are said to have "defied the prevailing rules" and to have "invented" a "new doctrine," the third-party beneficiary contract, in order to allow creditor beneficiaries of contracts drawn up by two other parties to enforce those sorts of agreements.[2]

This story of innovation has had its share of detractors,[3] but it has survived them and forms the central thesis regarding contract law of every recently published text and reader on American legal history.[4] I will refer to it from time to time in this chapter, but it is fair to say that it is not the story I will tell here. My reading of the "texts" on this subject from the sixteenth to the nineteenth century convinces me that continuity best describes the world of contracts, and that American jurists of the nineteenth century practiced the Jurisprudence of the Head with regard to the issues addressed in the previous paragraph—that is, they followed existing English rules.

FAIRNESS, ADEQUACY OF CONSIDERATION, AND THE WILL OF THE PARTIES

"A substantive doctrine of consideration" is said to have existed in eighteenth-century English and provincial American law that was "essentially antagonistic to the interests of commercial classes." This survivor of the medieval "sound price" rule allowed courts to inquire into the adequacy of consideration, the "fairness" of a contract, and to turn aside the suits of grasping plaintiffs too shrewd for their "distressed," unskilled, or ill-informed defendants. But with the emergence of a market economy in the early nineteenth century, American jurists are said to have replaced this "fairness doctrine" with a "will theory" of contract: So long as the evidence revealed the "will of the parties," so long as it established that there had

48

been a "meeting of minds," both would be held strictly to all the contractual terms. This will theory was hotly contested in the 1820s in some cases and treatises, but finally emerged victorious in the treatises of Joseph Story (*Equity Jurisprudence* [1836]) and his son, William W. Story (*Treatise of the Law of Contracts* [1844]). Its success there and in the courts was "part of a more general process whereby courts came to reflect commercial interests."[5]

What evidence *is* there of a fairness doctrine in the eighteenth century or before? How *did* courts deal with claims that contracts should be set aside or corrected due to the inadequacy of the consideration paid? When *did* the will theory emerge?

We find little evidence from the eighteenth-century record of a fairness doctrine in English or American jurisprudence affecting contracts.[6] Consider the very passage from Joseph Story's *Equity Jurisprudence* that has been offered to establish that "American law finally yielded up the ancient notion that the substantive value of an exchange could provide an appropriate measure of the justice of a transaction":

> Inadequacy of consideration is not, then, of itself, a distinct principle of relief in Equity. The Common Law knows no such principle. . . . The value of a thing . . . must be in its nature fluctuating, and will depend upon ten thousand different circumstances. . . . If Courts of Equity were to unravel all these transactions, they would throw everything into confusion, and set afloat the contracts of mankind.[7]

If these precepts were, indeed, new to Story, and his generation, we would have clear support for the claims of "transformation." But they were not. They appeared almost verbatim in Lord Chief Baron Eyre's opinion in *Griffith* v. *Spratley* (1787). A sailor, "in distress" and needing money, conveyed his reversionary interests in properties on Grub Street for an annuity of thirty-four pounds per year. Then, acting on advice, he sued to recover the conveyance from the buyer, charging that the consideration paid was grossly inadequate. Sailors in distress, easily defrauded, were protected by statute, like infants and the insane, as "wards of the court."[8] But although agreeing that the consideration here was much less than what the interests' value might be said to have been, the Court of Exchequer refused to set this contract aside as unfair. Eyre knew

> of no such principle; the common law knows of no such. . . .
> Common sense knows no such principle. The value of a thing is what
> it will produce, and admits of no precise standard. It must be in its

nature fluctuating, and will depend upon ten thousand different circumstances. . . . Now if Courts of Equity are to unravel all these transaction, they would throw everything into confusion and set afloat all the contracts of mankind. Therefore I never can agree that inadequacy of consideration is in itself a principle upon which a party may be relieved from a contract which he wittingly and willingly entered into.[9]

Story does not cite Eyre, nor did other nineteenth-century American jurists cite Lord Kenyon when they borrowed "we do not sit here to make, but to enforce contracts" from *Cook* v. *Jennings* (1797).[10] Perhaps they assumed that the words would be familiar to other jurists; in any event, there was no "plagiarism" stigmata in a profession that followed precedent and revered past English judicial luminaries. The point here is that Story did not invent; he merely used the "wisdom of the past."

A number of other examples can be offered of eighteenth-century chancellors rejecting bills to set contracts aside as unfair due to inadequacy of price.[11] But English chancellors *did* set aside a *few* sales between 1686 and 1787 where the inadequacy was "*so strong, gross, and manifest, that it must be impossible to state it* to a man of common sense without producing an exclamation at the inequality of it."[12]

Uniformly, the handful of cases that fit this description were those involving the sale by young, "distressed" expectant heirs of future estates worth many thousands of pounds.[13] And although this indicates that English chancellors set some outer limits to contractual behavior, short of fraud, when the price paid was "grossly inadequate," it is also clear that, throughout the nineteenth century, both American chancellors and common-law jurists set precisely the same outer limits, setting aside the notes, land transfers, and sales contracts of "distressed" parties to agreements of "unconscionable inequality between the value of the property . . . bought and the consideration . . . paid for it."[14] This was also the case when one party was found to have failed to bargain in good faith[15] when one party used undue mental, physical, or economic duress to secure the acceptance of the other,[16] or when the parties were deemed to have lacked equal bargaining power (as with railroads and most of their customers).[17] If these *exceptions* to the general rule in eighteenth-century England that inadequacy of consideration was no grounds for avoiding the terms of a contract somehow constituted a "fairness doctrine," then it is clear that the "doctrine" was still present as late as the time of the American Civil War.

50 If we don't find a fairness doctrine in the eighteenth century, perhaps it is

because those who believe it to be there have their timing of the alleged in-strumentalist changes wrought by the bench off by about a half-century or two. Winifred Rothenberg has demonstrated that a market economy emerged in New England half a century before it was previously believed, and Bruce Mann has shown that within this market economy merchants were holding debtors firmly to their debts by making them sign promissory notes. Moreover, eighteenth-century England was not a likely shelter for a fairness doctrine. After all, as Brian Simpson says, "England, even in the first half of the eighteenth century, was the greatest trading nation in the world," its trade "supported by a sophisticated mercantile community."[18] Perhaps English jurists had simply been responding to the commercial revo-lution of the eighteenth century; perhaps the fairness doctrine is to be found in the opinions of English chancellors of the precommercial era of the six-teenth and seventeenth centuries.

But a search for the doctrine in these years yields even less evidence of it than we found in the eighteenth century. Every one of the decisions (be-tween 1552 and 1683) that addressed the claim of inadequacy of considera-tion or price turned those claims away.[19] Virtually any price offered, virtu-ally any quid pro quo, was deemed sufficient, "be it ever so small." So long as something of detriment to one party, benefit to another, had passed, the contract was good. "The smallness of a consideration is not material, if there be any."[20] This was an age when hiring contracts and sales agreements were sealed with the passing of "God's penny," when men were recruited for the Queen's Service with the passing of a shilling or a half-crown. It was the age of the sea raiders, not yet the era of the great overseas traders. Appar-ently jurists did not need a commercial or industrial revolution to know that "one who is necessitous must sell cheaper than those who are not" (as Charles II's lord keeper of the great seal, Sir Francis North, put it in a case involving an expectant heir).[21]

Will it profit us to search for long *before* the sixteenth century for a fair-ness doctrine? I doubt it. As early as the fourteenth century there was no such doctrine in English law; rather, the rule was that promises ought to be kept.[22] Although medieval Continental courts did void contracts when the price was more than 50 percent above or below "true" value, the fact is that this "true" value was not fixed or "objective"; it was derived by the courts from the "common estimate," the *market price*.[23] And, in any event, for all the sharing of ideas between the medieval civil and common law, they devel-oped along different trajectories. English common law never adopted such a "50 percent" rule.

If there was no fairness doctrine in precapitalist England, where does that leave the reigning paradigm's claim that a "will of the parties" theory of contract, reflecting "commercial interests," replaced it in the second quarter of the nineteenth century? When did the rule that courts would not interfere with a contract evidencing a "meeting of minds" originate? We see clear signs of it in the eighteenth-century record.[24] Professor Adam Smith of Glasgow University referred to the "will of the parties" in a lecture on contract law in 1762.[25] The same chancellors who were reluctant to inquire into the "fairness" of the price were also "not very anxious" to impeach a bargain "upon such loose expressions as hard and unconscionable." One who agreed to terms "with his eyes perfectly open" had no grounds for relief either at law or equity.[26]

Yes, there were two sales contracts that the Court of King's Bench rejected as "impossible" and "not to be taken advantage of"; one in 1665, the other in 1705. But these hardly constitute evidence of a fairness doctrine or of the absence of a will theory. Let us first appreciate that they were the infamous "catching bargains," wherein shrewd, algebraically inclined defendants had "caught" quantitative-illiterate plaintiffs in the sale of a horse, in the first instance for so many units of barley per nail in the horse's shoe, "and doubling it every nail," and for the transfer of five pounds, in the second, in exchange for two grains of rye the first day, and then four, eight, sixteen, and so on, "every Monday" for a year (amounting to millions of bushels). These were hardly characteristic of bargains made by the typical merchant or farmer in either the pre- or postcapitalist marketplace. Rather, they are merely the odd effervescence of several centuries of assumpsit appeals. Let us also take note that both Holt, J., and Powell, J., indicated that the "foolish" party "ought to pay something for his folly." Hence, though specific performance of the fantastic agreement was not to be ordered, "yet he shall answer in damages," for the contract "would hold in law."[27]

The will theory, moreover, was not an invention of the eighteenth century, for we also see clear signs of it in seventeenth- and sixteenth-century reports. A decision of the Court of Common Pleas in 1615 referred to a rule that contracts "containing the will and intent of the parties" were to be construed according to "that intent."[28] Counsel arguing on both sides of the appeal of Reniger against Fogossa before the Court of Exchequer in 1551 defined a contract four times as "a mutual assent of the minds" and once as a "union, collection, copulation, and conjunction of two or more minds in anything done or to be done," while Sergeant Richard Catline referred to the "intent of the parties" no less than seven times *in arguendo* before King's Bench in 1553. He also argued that "in contracts it is not material which of the parties speak the words, if the other agrees to them, for the agreement of the minds of the parties is the only thing the law respects in contracts."[29]

We see, then, that the courts of young King Edward VII and of "Bloody Mary" held to a will theory of contracts in the age of sea raiders, nearly three centuries before the Age of Trade and early nineteenth century "market" was supposed to have given rise to it. Apparently this legal concept did not depend on capitalism for its sustenance, unless it required the protocapitalist mentality of Tudor England to bring it to life. That is possible, but my sense is that there is no good reason to see capitalism as a necessary condition for a "will of the parties" rule in actions of assumpsit. Contracts were privately made agreements between free persons. To be sure, there were differences between the sixteenth-century jurist's preoccupation with breach of promise and the nineteenth-century jurist's focus on offer and acceptance; to be sure, the earlier jurists spoke of the necessity of an "instant of mutual assent" in bilateral agreements, while those of a later age would accept the legal fiction of an offer-by-mail that remained constant in time until received by the other party; to be sure, there were some new rules regarding mistakes and damages, but these were at the periphery, not the core, of contract law, and these modest innovations were not inspired by judicial concern for "the economy" but by their application of "logic" and contractual "principles" to new (but not *radically* new) fact situations.[30]

CAVEAT EMPTOR

The caveat emptor rule (or doctrine) has it that the seller must specifically "warrant" that what she is selling is "sound and good" (which implies: or your money back) in order for the buyer to recover the price if he discovers upon delivery that the thing sold does not meet those standards. The "warranty" is necessary in the absence of evidence of fraud—that is, in the absence of proof that the seller knew the goods to be other than as described and used artifice to disguise that fact. In short, where there was no express or implied general warranty in sales; the rule is, let the buyer beware.

The story told in legal histories today is that "both the sound price doctrine" and its "underlying conception of objective value" were "suddenly and completely overthrown" in the early nineteenth century by this "clearly proseller" counterpart, caveat emptor. Jurists took this step because the law of sales "reached maturity in a period when economic relations between economically sophisticated 'seller-insiders' and relatively unsophisticated 'buyer-outsiders' were becoming dominant."[31]

Several questions form themselves: *Did* caveat emptor "suddenly overthrow" a "sound price" doctrine in the first decade of the nineteenth century? *Was* it created to aid "seller-insiders" against "buyer-outsiders"? Indeed, did it *ever* serve that function? Let us take these questions one by one.

Caveat emptor enjoys an "ancient lineage" in English law. Coke refers to it as the "old rule," and we find Prisot, J., telling a buyer about caveat emptor in 1458. Fitzherbert may especially have breathed English life into it in his *Natura Brevium* in 1534, when he described it: "If a man do sell unto another a horse and warrant him to be sound and good and the horse be lame or diseased . . . , he shall have an action. . . . But . . . if he sell the horse without such warranty, it is at the other's peril and his eyes ought to be his judges in that case."[32]

The rule appears as well in even stronger form in the successful argument of an unnamed sergeant before King's Bench in 1615: One who buys a horse from another who warrants it to have both eyes when it has but one "is without remedy, for it is a thing which lies in his own con[nai]sance, and such warranty or affirmation is not material, . . . but otherwise it is in the case where the matter is secret, and lies properly in the con[nai]sance of him who warrants it, and cannot be known to him who buys or makes the contract."[33] The rule crops up as well in the Court of Chancery in *Sergeant Maynard's Case* (1676), where Lord Chancellor Nottingham, disposing as well of the fairness doctrine, explained that "the Chancery mends no man's bargain." Instead, he offered the "advice . . . *caveat emptor*."[34]

When Chief Justice James Kent of the New York Supreme Court applied the rule in *Seixas* v. *Woods* (1804), he showed remarkably little indication that he wanted to "overthrow" a sound-price doctrine to help "seller-insiders."[35] Instead, he observed that "if the question were *res integra* in our law, I confess, I should be overcome by the reason of the [Civil Law]"—that is, he would have *preferred* a sound-price doctrine. But, the chief justice sighed, such was not to be, because the common-law rule was caveat emptor, and he cited several of the authorities that I have just offered in support of this opinion.[36]

Caveat emptor's lineage, then, was "ancient" after all. But today's legal histories can still be half right—that is, if it was not a new rule in 1800, it might still have served to aid "sophisticated 'seller-insiders'" against "relatively unsophisticated 'buyer-outsiders.'" As one account puts it, caveat emptor was a "harsh" rule in nineteenth-century America, for "it was one thing to examine a horse in advance of buying it, quite another to assess goods made and packaged by machines." Another account holds that caveat emptor provided "an indirect subsidy" to "an expanding economy." It "allowed an end to the transaction rather than permitting endless suits to decide who knew what when."[37] Modern buyers were at a distinct disadvantage under the caveat emptor regimen.

Or were they? Kim Lane Scheppele has studied some eighty-two contract cases involving caveat emptor defenses for defective or imperfectly described products before New York's high courts in the nineteenth century[38] and has found that they consistently "assigned the loss to the party who *in the pair* in *court* was in the best position to know about the defect." In the antebellum years, this tended to be the buyer-manufacturer (as in *Seixas* v. *Woods*), who knew more of the raw or partially processed material he was buying from the New York harbor seller-merchant than did that middleman; later in the century, however, the courts tended to assign the loss to seller-manufacturers whose increasingly sophisticated products were better known to them than to their buyers. This *sounds* like a "shift" from caveat emptor to caveat venditor (or from an express warranty rule to an implied warranty one). But such labeling masks the fact that the court had applied the same rule, consistently, throughout the century.

As Scheppele points out, this insistence that the party with better information should suffer the loss was not economically "efficient," by Law and Economics lights. The court's rigid adherence to the privity rule prevented buyers from suing the original producer, a most inefficient rule in itself, but one that might still have *allowed* for "efficiency" if buyers had been granted their claims for an implied warranty rule or a sound-price doctrine. Why? Because this would have forced sellers to exercise greater care and led losing, middleman-sellers to sue in turn the real villain from whom they had acquired the misdescribed goods. Instead the courts were behaving like "contractarians" (here she is using John Rawls's term)—that is, confronted with individual appellants and appellees, they were trying "to do justice" to these litigants "and not some other." They displayed "concern for what happen[ed] to individuals as the social good is sought."[39]

New York's jurists may have been exceptional in their contractarian consistency. South Carolina's simply rejected caveat emptor altogether from the very start,[40] while other high courts may just as stubbornly have applied it without any of New York's sensible "best-position-to-know" measure of assigning the loss.[41] But the Massachusetts and Pennsylvania courts, and those of England as well, show signs of having reached the same sort of formula as that used by their brethren in New York.[42] And in Pennsylvania Chief Justice John Bannister Gibson defended caveat emptor with an economic rationale exactly the *opposite* of that proposed by Law and Economics theorists. Were the buyer permitted to claim an implied warranty of soundness in sales, it "would put a stop to commerce by driving everyone out of it by the terror of endless litigation." Gibson intended this rationale to be a justification of the existing rule.

The case was *McFarland* v. *Newman* (1839), involving the sale of a colt. Gibson knew he was not striking out in a new unprecedented direction, and he clearly did not intend to do so, for he criticized the buyer's call for an implied warranty rule. The buyer had asked the seller to warrant the "soundness" of the colt, and Gibson pointed out that the seller had answered: "I never warrant." Here was a four-square example of caveat emptor, and Gibson rejected the buyer's attempts to introduce a rule of implied warranty imported from "the civil law" because of what he called "this violence" done "to the ancient principles of the law." Precedent and "principle" mattered greatly to Gibson's court. But so did "responsible individualism." Like a number of his peers throughout the early Republic, Gibson found ideologically appealing the republican notion that freedom was, in large measure, *defined* by one's ability to enter into whatever contracts one wished. Adult Americans were free of all feudal, status-based duties that limited their social, political, or economic beings; but with this freedom came responsibilities. One might contract with anyone else to buy or sell goods, services, or credit, but once that contract was made, its terms were final and courts would enforce them. Gibson may have been offering his major premise when he observed in *McFarland* that "he who is so simple as to contract without a specification of the terms, is not a fit subject of judicial guardianship."[43]

In any event, this much seems safe to say: First, caveat emptor helped unsophisticated seller-middlemen far more than it did "sophisticated 'seller-insiders.'" Second, for every entrepreneur-winner, there was an entrepreneur-loser. And, third, the rule was severely eroded by implied warranties of merchantability in sales by sample and in the sale of land.[44] Thus there was probably more "fairness" in the common law of sales by 1890 than there had been in 1590, quite independent of any statutory changes. And in any event, there was nothing new about the caveat emptor rule in nineteenth-century America; jurists there followed English precedent on the subject.

CONDITIONAL SALES, CHATTEL
MORTGAGES, AND BAILMENT LEASES

"In one of the great triumphs of form over substance," jurists in the nineteenth century are said to have begun to treat chattel mortgages as if they were the same as the newer, less-encumbered, conditional-sales agreement, thereby freeing the economic relationship between buyers and sellers of expensive forms of personal property from the older equity-based redemption right. Sellers were now free to make "exploitative use" of the conditional sale qua chattel mortgage. Buyers who had previously enjoyed a right to an equity of redemption proceeding for several months after being unable to meet payments were now stripped of the property in a swift common-law debt proceeding that favored the seller. The bailment lease, the third of these three security devices, "became almost indistinguishable" from the other two in the nineteenth century as judges responded to the public pressures to buy and sell on credit on the national "highway to progress and wealth." The three devices "all came out the same in the end" because "the resistance of the lawmakers" to those who sought to retain their legal distinctiveness was "absent or transient or weak." Or so we are told.[45]

Did courts sanction conditional-sales contracts in order to eliminate the equity of redemption rights of buyers of goods under chattel mortgages? What were the problems that led those using one or the other of these two forms of personal property transaction to seek the court's assistance? Did jurists come to treat these three security devices as indistinguishable in order to facilitate the sale on credit of expensive durables?

The first point we ought to get clear is that neither the conditional sale nor the chattel mortgage nor the bailment lease were invented in the nineteenth century. The chattel mortgage was created (by statute) in England and the colonies to protect sellers who extended credit to the buyer and transferred the property to the buyer for use while retaining a security interest in it. This protected them against an unscrupulous buyer who sought to resell the property or to pledge it to another for credit. A chattel mortgage registered in a place of public record put such third parties on notice.[46] A "conditional" sale did not. A bailment lease did not transfer any title to the leased property, but a prospective creditor of the lessor might be unaware of this; bailment leases need not be recorded in public places. Conditional sales (or "conditional liens"), bailment leases, and chattel mortgages were in widespread use in eighteenth-century England.[47] (Given the property-related nature of the early law of contracts, that would hardly be surprising.) Thus early-nineteenth-century American courts that approved of conditional sales were simply applying English precedent.[48] Not a creature of "the factory years" designed for the sale of such expensive durables as reapers, rolling stock, or sewing machines,[49] the conditional sale, like the chattel mortgage, served distinctly preindustrial uses, involving such commodities as jewelry, hemp, sheep, cattle, candles, furniture, and raw wool. The first cases of conditional sales involving manufactured goods in appellate reports appear in the 1840s and 1850s, and do not differ in outcome from their preindustrial counterparts.[50]

Jurists applied the law with no sense that they were serving the interests of manufacturers of expensive durable goods, or, more generally, "progress and wealth."[51] As New York's Chief Justice Samuel Nelson put it in the case of a conditionally sold canal boat that had been seized in a sheriff's sale, "Upon general principles, and in a practical point of view, as a question of public policy, it is of very little importance which set of creditors are allowed to seize the property."[52]

But if Chief Justice Nelson and his colleagues felt there was no important "developmental" public policy question at stake, they still had to decide which party had the superior claim to the canal boat. The problem that arose was essentially the same since the Middle Ages: A buyer of an object under a conditional sale, chattel mortgage, or bailment lease might represent himself as its "free and clear" owner and either "pledge" it for credit or sell it to another who then claimed to be its bona fide purchaser. Most courts, in these instances, drew a distinction: If the property had only been *leased* ("rented" or "hired") to one who then fraudulently represented himself as its owner to a third party, then its owner retained a claim to title and repossession superior to that of the third-party creditor or bona fide purchaser. But if the property had been *sold* under a conditional sale, the third party who acquired it in "good faith" from the buyer was seen as having the superior claim to title; he was not privy to the contract of sale. The seller's only remedy was to sue the buyer with whom he had privity. That was the only way to protect creditors and bona fide purchasers from "secret liens."[53] And the losers under this view of the law were none other than the greatest theoretical gainers under the "new" conditional-sale rule, the conditional sellers of expensive new reapers, threshers, railroad cars, engines, and boilers. In the federal (and numerous state) courts, attempts by manufacturers (or their dealers) to protect their stake in such specific hardware as "one oscillation thresher, size 6, 30 inch cylinder" or "one 10 hp engine and boiler, James Leffel make" by chattel mortgages were shunted aside as being "too indefinite and uncertain" a description of the property, thus permitting creditors of the bankrupt users of the machinery to retain them.[54]

Manufacturers also sought to protect conditional-sale arrangements from their buyers' creditors by "leasing" the object for sale (a fictive bailment lease). Would courts tolerate this arrangement as a means of facilitating the sale of expensive durables? A case in point: One manufacturer of railroad cars, seeking to protect its security in a conditional sale of its cars from creditors of a potentially bankrupt corporate buyer, arranged for the sale of its cars to have the appearance of a mere rental (a bailment lease). The United States Supreme Court saw through the ruse. The transaction was a chattel mortgage, it concluded, not a lease, and the buyer had not recorded the lien as Missouri law required. Hence, the cars were properly subject to creditor seizure.[55]

Some courts did not draw such distinctions,[56] to be sure, but at *least* those of Illinois, Pennsylvania, Kentucky, New York, and the United States did,[57] to the disadvantage of manufacturers of expensive machinery and equipment. Four of these were rather important jurisdictions, and the effect of the distinctions drawn in those jurisdictions ran against the interests of manufacturers like McCormick and Singer Sewing Machine. The other courts were simply endorsing as familiar and legitimate one or another security device that had for centuries been part of the common law, and focussing their solicitude on "small merchants, especially beginners in business," who had "no other means of securing their creditors for the stock they purchase" than by agreeing to a recorded chattel mortgage for their regularly replenished store inventory.[58] Consequently, it seems incorrect to speak of either of these sets of rules as "exploitative" or to dismiss nineteenth-century judicial sensitivity to nuances as "absent or transient or weak" when several important courts did draw distinctions between bailment leases and the other two security devices in order to protect bona fide purchasers from "secret liens." At most, one might argue that the courts of certain less-industrialized states such as Iowa, Alabama, Mississippi, Nebraska, Vermont, California (but also Michigan, New Jersey, and Ohio) were allowing the inventories of "small merchants, especially beginners in business," the protection of a chattel mortgage, while the federal courts, as well as those of more industrialized states such as Illinois, Pennsylvania, and New York (but also Kentucky), insisted on retaining the ancient distinctions between the three security devices in order to protect the creditors of the industrial buyers of expensive durables. Were jurists in the former jurisdictions displaying something of a Jurisprudence of the Heart in this regard, those in the latter, a Jurisprudence of the Head? Perhaps. In any event, they differed only in how they interpreted the conditions that would meet their state's statutory requirements for a chattel mortgage.

EXPECTATION DAMAGES AND "FUTURES" TRANSACTIONS

One who sold goods or securities in 1700 or 1800 might contract to sell either for immediate transfer and delivery or for delivery at a future date. But what happened if the price of the object sold fell sharply between the dates of transaction and delivery and the buyer now refused to accept delivery? A seller, paid only with "hand money," would find herself holding tons of perishable butter or grain, or hundreds of shares of a stock the value of which was plunging. The dilemma was reversed in a market of rapidly rising prices for a particular bond, stock, or commodity. There the buyer might find himself unable to hold the seller to the agreed-upon delivery and price, and that buyer might be a cotton manufacturer, a baker, or a financier whose plans had been built on that "futures" reliance.

According to the economic determinist paradigm, it was not until the nineteenth century that courts in England and America allowed such distressed parties to "cover" in the open market and sue for their reliance or "expectation" damages at common law. "Expectation damages were not recognized by eighteenth century courts." They "first arose in connection with stock speculation" in the early nineteenth century. Their application to commodities contracts "correlates with the development of extensive internal commodities markets around 1815" in America, though not until 1825 in England.[59]

Associating the development of expectation damages with early-nineteenth-century American commodities markets is a mistake, however. The rule granting expectation damages, based on the difference between the contract price and the market price at time set for delivery, was a centuries-old rule of the law merchant, to be found in English courts as early as 1532.[60] Both this sixteenth-century case and another in 1712 involved brewers who were "left without malt" because of nondeliveries of barley and were "compelled to buy malt at a far greater price."[61] The rule is evident as well in four cases from the early eighteenth century involving futures transactions for stock in the South Sea Company, the East India Company, a copper mine, and a construction firm. In one of these, *Thompson* v. *Harcourt* (1722), the stock had fallen in value and the House of Lords ordered the buyer to accept delivery of the stock at the price agreed on. In another, *Gardiner* v. *Pullen & Phillips* (1700), the stock had risen just as sharply, and the seller was ordered by Chancery to transfer the stock as agreed. Where the plaintiffs had turned to King's Bench for relief, in *Dutch* v. *Warren* (1720), that court awarded such expectation damages as gave him the "benefit" of the bargain. And in the final case involving the sale of stock, undelivered in a rising market, *Cuddee* v. *Rutter* (1720), the lord chancellor chose to deny the master of the roll's award of specific performance, preferring to direct the plaintiff-buyer "to his Remedy at Law for Breach of the Agreement to recover Damage" as one would who contracted to deliver grain "upon a Day certain at . . . such a Price" and found that the buyer refused to accept it. There, the lord chancellor explained, the buyer was obliged to pay "the Difference between the Price agreed on by the Parties, and the Price of Corn upon the Market Day" in damages.[62] But whether the recovery of the relied-upon expectation was by bill in equity for specific performance or action at law for damages, the aggrieved parties were well served by English courts long before any of the leaders of the American Revolution (or of the industrial or commercial revolutions, for that matter) were born.

A. W. B. Simpson and Kevin Teeven have made this clear.[63] I have culled only a few additional references, all supporting their views, a propos the law merchant, English, and provincial American experiences.[64] But one of these *is* worthy of a little elaboration. Simpson explains that "the law as it was pronounced by the King's Chancellor and the King's courts in London" did not reflect a "relatively simple and primitive economy," either with regard to expectation damages, fairness, sound price, or pleas of inadequacy of consideration, but he does allow that the law might have been otherwise "as it was spoken in small borough courts and village tribunals."[65] The qualification is a reasonable one, but I think he would not be taken by surprise by the way the rule of expectation damages was understood either by Georgian Age justices of the peace or, more significantly, by farmers and grocers of the Georgian Age. Consider the note that dairy farmer Elizabeth Purefoy of Shalstone sent to the regular buyer of her butter, Anne Warr of Buckingham, in 1737. Warr had written that she was refusing acceptance of 149 pounds of butter at six pence a pound, the previously agreed-upon price, and that, furthermore, she was canceling her contract to purchase any more at that price. Elizabeth Purefoy was irate:

> I recd your letter & admire you should chose me of all your
> customers to make a fool on. I do assure you if you don't pay . . . £31
> 4s. 6 d. I will order you to be sued forthwith, and if you refuse to take
> the fourteen pounds of butter I send this day at 6 d a pound, I have
> ordered by servant to sell it in the market, & if it fails to fetch 6 d a
> pound you must up the deficiency to
>
> E. P.[66]

Elizabeth Purefoy's rural contract for the regular sale of her butter in 1737 was not as substantial a matter as the futures transactions of American cotton planters and textile manufacturers in 1837, but she invoked the same rule for damages in its breach as they would. The rule might have had a capitalist progenitor; it certainly served the needs of both sellers and buyers in futures transactions. But it was centuries old when it reached America.

THIRD-PARTY CONTRACT BENEFICIARIES:
A DOCTRINAL GATEKEEPER DEBATE

Among the nineteenth-century judicial innovations in the field of contract law is said to be a "new doctrine," "invented" in *Lawrence* v. *Fox* (New York, 1859), which allowed a person not actually a party to a contract to enforce it in court since the contract was intended to benefit him or her. Prior to *Lawrence* v. *Fox*, the common law had resisted the transfer of abstract rights to another, but this resistance was said to have been "inconsistent with the world view of nineteenth-century contract. Contract had faith in the market; now almost any interests and values could be effectively transferred and sold."[67] Hence the birth of the third-party beneficiary contract.

To the contrary, if we probe into the history of this "gatekeeper" rule we find much more continuity than change. *Lawrence* v. *Fox* did not "begin the career"[68] of the third-party beneficiary rule. There was precious little "invention" of "new doctrine" in that case. The rule allowing third-party beneficiaries to sue on a contract existed as early as the sixteenth century and was reiterated in England, Massachusetts, New York, and several other state courts literally dozens of times before the decision in *Lawrence* v. *Fox*. Moreover, while *Lawrence* v. *Fox* would be styled the "leading American case" for the rule by the early twentieth century,[69] it was not treated in such a fashion by any state high court for some time after its appearance, and it would be more accurate to say that *Lawrence* v. *Fox* really represented an eloquent plea for the *retention* of a rule that was increasingly being abandoned as bad law in the most important of common-law judicial jurisdictions.[70]

How did jurists rule with regard to the acceptability or unacceptability of third-party beneficiary suits? Can their rationales be identified as "doctrinal," "utilitarian," "instrumental"? We can readily imagine an opinion sensitive to the importance of credit relationships in the currency-scarce world of antebellum America. Imagine the common circumstance: a debtor secures from another the promise to pay a third party monies owed that party by the debtor; the debtor then leaves the state, and the third-party creditor-beneficiary finds it necessary to sue the promisor for the funds. There could well have been an interest among instrumentalist jurists in a legal device designed to facilitate the flow of secure and conveniently arranged credit and the payment of debts by using an intermediary figure who received some valuable consideration from a debtor in exchange for a parol promise to pay the debtor's creditor (the third-party creditor-beneficiary). One can well imagine a utilitarian or instrumentalist judge saying something like the following:

> Where the debtor has left the state or for some other reason cannot realistically be expected to return to sue on his creditor's behalf, the creditor must be allowed to sue despite his lack of privity and despite the fact that no consideration moved from him to the defendant. Otherwise creditors would be remediless, many debts would go unpaid, the cost of credit would rise, its availability would decline, and both justice and the greater community would be the losers. The defendant's English precedents notwithstanding, this plaintiff must be let in. We weight precedents; we do not simply count them. The lack of privity and consideration may trouble those whose vision of the law is limited to technical niceties, but they are not of sufficient weight to those whose concern for the public consequences of such technical niceties is grave, and whose duty, in any event, is to provide justice according to the intentions of the original contract.

That would be a plausible thing to expect, were economic considerations to have made a significant difference to English and American jurists. Yet in the 357 opinions[71] dealing with the issue from the late sixteenth to the late nineteenth century, that sort of rationale appeared only *once*, in 1899.[72] The opinions reeked of doctrinal thought and reasoning and gave no hint of utilitarianism or instrumentalism.

The Findings: Gift-Beneficiaries Fare Better

The first thing we learn from analysis of the appellate court record is tentative confirmation of what I have claimed about *Lawrence* v. *Fox*—namely, that it did not "begin the career" of the third-party beneficiary rule. In 72 percent of the cases prior to that case American courts allowed third-party beneficiaries to sue on the contract, while in only 55 percent of the cases decided after *Lawrence* v. *Fox*, but before 1900, did courts permit such suits. We will want to take a close look at the opinions in *Lawrence* v. *Fox* to see if there is any language which breaks new ground and warrants the case's distinction, but that will not be our central concern, for whether *Lawrence* v. *Fox* is an "instrumentalist" decision or no, our hypotheses will stand or fall on what we find in a comparably close reading of the other 304 nineteenth-century American appellate cases.

The next thing that we learn from a simple analysis of case outcomes is that gift-beneficiaries (persons whom the promisee sought to benefit gratis, such as a bastard child or a spinster daughter) rather consistently fared better than creditor-beneficiaries, both in England (until 1861, when both types were barred common law remedies) and in America (until 1899, forty years after *Lawrence* v. *Fox* and the outer limit of our analysis). Gift-beneficiaries were allowed to sue in 82.3 percent of the English cases and 76.2 percent of the American ones, while creditor-beneficiaries were allowed to sue in only 70.6 percent of the English and 60.3 percent of the American cases. This pattern does not seem consistent with a vision of an instrumentalist judiciary that transformed the common law in antebellum America essentially to facilitate and simplify economic activity, though it *would* be consistent with a vision of an instrumentalist judiciary that sometimes bent the law slightly to help a class of poor and helpless litigants.

But percentages tell only a small part of our story. We must still see how the judges *explained* their decisions, still see whether these opinions were doctrinal, instrumentalist, or utilitarian. We begin with the pre-nineteenth-century English record.

Two impulses drew third-party beneficiary plaintiffs by the early seventeenth century to the action of trespass on the case on assumpsit (undertaking). First, assumpsit was a child of that "fertile mother of actions,"[73] trespass, and trespass and her progeny were born after the emergence of juries; consequently, no "wager of law"[74] was available to a defendant (as with the actions of debt and account) with such a writ. Second, by the early seventeenth century assumpsit had been extended in both Kings Bench and Common Pleas to encompass mere executory contracts—that is, to promises, for consideration, where no monies or land had actually been received as yet by the promisor, and where nonfeasance (a damaging nonperformance) was at issue.[75] The result was that in the seventeenth century, "action on the case in assumpsit" became the action of choice for third parties (both donee and creditor) who sought to hold promisors to beneficial agreements.

Assumpsit was, in the seventeenth century, viewed essentially as a breach of promise action. It had not yet developed into its more modern shape, contract; in particular, courts did not require that the plaintiff be "in privity" with the defendant, and there was very little attention to or requirement of "consideration" passing from plaintiff to defendant, except the occasional suggestion that such consideration might be implied by the facts.[76] Thus when a father gave a son goods on the promise that the son would pay a third party the sum of twenty pounds, and the son took the goods but did not pay the money, the Court of Kings Bench in 1651 upheld an action of case in assumpsit.[77] The defendant-son's counsel argued that the third-party beneficiary-plaintiff had offered no consideration for the money, but Rolle, C. J., responded:

> There is a plain contract, because the goods were given for the benefit of the plaintiff, though the contract be not between him and the defendant, and he may well have an action upon the case, for here is a promise in law made to the plaintiff, though there be not a promise in fact, and there is a debt here and the assumpsit is good.

Similarly, when a father offered to forgo the cutting of timber on land he was leaving his son if the son would pay his sister a thousand pounds by a certain date, and the son agreed but did not make the payment, the daughter was allowed to sue as a third-party beneficiary (in *Dutton v. Poole* [KB 1677]) on the grounds that the natural affection of the father for his child constituted a "moral consideration."[78] Lord Mansfield cheerfully accepted the *Dutton* precedent in 1776 with the observation that "it is a matter of surprise" that any "doubt could have arisen" as to the outcome of that case.[79]

Thus the third-party beneficiary of a contractual promise *seemed* to be secure in his right to a day in court as late as the eighteenth century, and in 1703 the *Trade-Man's Lawyer* was to advise his readers that an action would lie for a promise "made to another for my use," albeit he added "upon a good consideration."[80] Nevertheless, if the right of a third-party beneficiary to sue on the contract was the *standard* in the English sixteenth and seventeenth centuries, and if it survived into the eighteenth century, a contrary current was underway in creditor-beneficiary cases, founded on the principle of consideration. A third-party beneficiary, by definition, had offered the defendant-promisor no consideration; he/she had not been a participant in the contract process. As the "principles" of contract law were iterated by the courts, abridgers, and reporters, some jurists began to insist that third-party creditor-beneficiaries lacked "privity" and must find their remedies via actions of their debtors, the contract's promisee. In 1669 Parrie, in debt to Bourne, sought from Mason a promise, for consideration, to pay Bourne. Mason broke his promise and Bourne sued in indebitatus assumpsit. But the Court of King's Bench gave him "*nil capiat per billam*" because Bourne had done "nothing of trouble to himself, or benefit to the defendant, but is a mere stranger to the consideration." Fifty-eight years later the same court acted in the same fashion in a similar creditor-beneficiary case, *Crow v. Rogers*.[81] The 1791 edition of Charles Viner's *General Abridgement of Law and Equity* summarized (under "action: who shall have an action of assumpsit") over twenty of the third-party beneficiary cases we have examined. The majority of these cases, as we have seen, allowed the third party beneficiary relief, but the two obvious inconsistencies, *Bourne* and *Crow*, clearly left the issue unsettled, and Viner's *Abridgement* offered no guidance or resolution for the reader.[82]

In 1823 King's Bench permitted a third-party creditor-beneficiary suit, as did Common Pleas in 1835,[83] but all other third-party beneficiary plaintiffs between 1790 and 1861 in common law (as well as one in equity) were turned away on the grounds that no consideration had moved from the plaintiff and that he (or she) was not privy to the contract.[84] Thus the 1842 edition of *Chitty on Contracts* noted that while cases of third-party beneficiaries to a contract "seem to have been contradictory" in the past, it was "now a rule of law" that "the consideration for a promise must move from the plaintiff."[85]

Vernon Palmer has recently offered three explanations for the adoption of the privity-consideration standard, barring third-party creditor-beneficiaries from relief in assumpsit suits at common law. He notes first that the Statute of Frauds (1677) required that all promises to pay the debt of a third person, all assignments of any trust, all contracts in consideration of marriage, and all executors' promises to answer damages out of their own estates now had to be made in writing. As these were "important kinds of beneficiary contracts," the statute had "the effect of drying up" these sources of third-party litigation by forcing some contracts under seal, and thus into the domain of covenant, while forcing other litigants to turn to the Court of Chancery. Second, the increased negotiability of bills of exchange and the increased acceptability of promissory notes provided some merchants and traders with clear and secure alternatives to the third-party beneficiary suit. And, finally, the emergence of the modern trust, and Chancery's exclusive claim to its enforcement by 1700, deprived the common-law courts of their jurisdiction over defendants to whom property had been transferred for the "use" of a third-party beneficiary.

As Palmer puts it, late-seventeenth-century "contemporaries may not have appreciated" the extent to which the victory of Chancery over common law in trust actions, the terms of the Statute of Frauds, and the emergence of negotiable instruments weakened the third-party beneficiary's claims in actions of assumpsit.[86] Contract's concrete form was slow in setting. The third-party beneficiary to a contract continued to press his claims at common law, but his access to the court waned, limited finally to gift-beneficiary cases. In 1861 it was cut off in those cases as well.

If *Lawrence* v. *Fox* has been seen as the leading case on the question in the

United States, *Tweddle* v. *Atkinson* (1861) is viewed as the leading case in England. It serves as an excellent example of the "doctrinal" mind at work, the approach that increasingly characterized our English cases. Two fathers orally agreed to provide gifts of one hundred and two hundred pounds respectively to the son of one and the daughter of the other on the eve of their marriage. After the marriage they reduced this agreement to writing, giving the young couple a right to sue for the monies if either party to the covenant failed to pay. One did, and the husband sued. The law courts, as we have seen, had become increasingly unwilling to allow creditor-beneficiaries from whom no consideration had moved to sue; in *Tweddle*, for the first time, an English court turned away a donee-beneficiary on those same grounds, decisively overruling *Dutton* v. *Poole*. Crompton, J., observed that "the modern and well-established doctrine of the action of assumpsit" did not permit a stranger to the consideration to sue. He offered a solidly doctrinal explanation for the change:

> At the time when the cases which have been cited were decided the action of assumpsit was treated as an action of trespass upon the case, and therefore in the nature of a tort; and the law was not settled, as it now is, that natural love and affection is not a sufficient consideration for a promise upon which an action may be maintained; nor was it settled that the promisee cannot bring an action unless the consideration moved from him. The modern cases have, in effect, overruled the old decisions; they shew that the consideration must move from the party entitled to sue upon the contract. It would be a monstrous proposition to say that a person was a party to the contract for the purposes of suing upon it for his own advantage, and not a party to it for the purpose of being sued. . . . By reason of the principles which now govern the action of assumpsit, the present action is not maintainable.[87]

Crawford Hening maintained that the English jurists of the fifteenth and sixteenth centuries had allowed third-party beneficiaries to sue in account because "the judicial instinct recognized" that such persons "ought to recover";[88] but if such behavior characterized English jurists in the era of the Tudors, the same certainly could not be said of their Victorian age descendants. English jurists almost never offered dicta concerning the economic or social appropriateness of their decisions, whether it be for or against the third-party beneficiary-plaintiff. What they *did* offer was considerable attention to precedent, logic, and "the principles" of contract. As such, they constitute examples of the power of "taught legal tradition."

But no one will be terribly surprised that nineteenth-century *English* jurists behaved doctrinally; few have argued that Jeremy Bentham's utilitarian critique of the procedure-bound common law had a truly significant impact then on England's judicial community.[89] And in any event, it has not been they, but rather antebellum *American* courts that have been styled "instrumentalist," that have been seen as willing, in the "grand style," to innovate, that have been called practical, seeking to "release economic energies" in early- and mid-nineteenth-century America.[90]

John Bly testified in 1692 at the trial of Bridget Bishop of Salem Village, one of those accused of witchcraft, that "he bought a sow of Edward Bishop . . . and was to pay the price agreed unto another person." In this and other such records of the transactions of colonial Americans we know that the practice of creating third-party beneficiaries to contracts existed here.[91] I could not locate any clear court tests of the rights of third-party beneficiaries before 1796, but it seems quite likely that judicial decisions in pre-1800 America regarding third-party beneficiaries would not have differed from those of the early nineteenth century, since the courts of the first quarter of nineteenth-century America uniformly allowed third-party beneficiaries to sue on the contract, citing English precedent in the process. Chief Justice Lemuel Shaw of the Massachusetts Supreme Court felt that these English "authorities no doubt had their influence in settling the law here, before the period at which the Massachusetts Reports commence,"[92] and this sounds quite likely. With the exceptions of *Bourne* and *Crow*, English courts before 1800 had persistently upheld the right of a third-party beneficiary to sue on the contract, and it is quite possible that *Bourne* and *Crow* were not known to many early American jurists.[93]

In any event, between 1801 and 1820 the high courts of the first four American jurisdictions to address the problem spoke as one in applying "the decisions of the English courts," that "when a promise is made to one, for the benefit of another, he for whose benefit it is made may bring an action for the breach." This "repeatedly sanctioned" principle "was settled as early as Roll's time" and "it being cited by Lord C. B. Comyns, in his Digest [as "Action on the Case upon Assumpsit"] without any question of its authority, it is to be received as a sound principle."[94]

Thereafter the English application of privity and consideration standards to the question began to impress some American courts, who thereupon denied the third-party beneficiary the right to sue on the contract.[95] The process was a slow one, and it did not arrest the adoption of the older rule by fourteen new jurisdictions;[96] hence, by 1859, when *Lawrence* v. *Fox* was decided, some seventeen jurisdictions allowed third-party beneficiaries to sue, whereas seven others either did not or severely limited such suits. Moreover, a number of those courts that either chose or retained the older, more liberal rule were forced to address the newer English one. Hence opportunities existed for treatise writers, counsel, and jurists to offer rationales for the rule they defended. Was the language used by jurists in these years, in deciding for or against the third-party beneficiary's plea, "utilitarian" or "instrumentalist," or was it essentially "doctrinal" or "formalist?"[97]

Counsel and jurists made frequent use of available treatises, but although such works appear to have influenced the way some justices reached a decision on the third-party beneficiary's right to an action, the more commonly offered approach stressed the authority and language of prior decisions themselves. Until American jurisdictions had created sufficient case books of their own, these precedents were entirely English, and even after a number of American precedents were available, many of the English cases still served as important authority in both first impression and ensuing cases.[98]

By the 1840s the oft-cited Massachusetts and New York high courts were acknowledging the "somewhat contradictory"[99] character of the English cases. At first, both courts were unmoved by the English inconsistencies. Thus in *Carnegie* v. *Morrison* (1841) Massachusetts's Chief Justice Lemuel Shaw held that the court would follow a "leading and decisive" decision of the Massachusetts high court in 1822, a decision that had drawn upon "respectable [English] authorities." These "authorities" had exercised great "influence in settling the law here." Differences now existed between English and Massachusetts law on this subject, due to "a considerable course of practice, on both sides of the water," which had "insensibly led the judicial tribunals, respectively to different results." So be it; the chief justice and his colleagues chose to observe stare decisis locally rather than be redirected by the new English privity rule.[100] Illinois's high court agreed with Shaw's decision and the English precedent he cited, as did the courts of Iowa, Mississippi, Kansas, Colorado, Texas, Nebraska, Florida, and California.[101]

Twelve years later the New York Court of Appeals also clung to the older rule, in *Lawrence* v. *Fox* (1859).[102] But this high court was divided. Three justices joined with Justice Hiram Gray to uphold the third-party beneficiary's right to sue. Gray cited New York and Massachusetts precedent and argued that it was "as if [Fox] had been made a trustee of property to be converted into cash with which to pay." With the creation of a new state constitution in 1846 and the adoption of the New York procedural Code for 1848 (the "Field Code"), the separate Court of Chancery was eliminated, and the new Court of Appeals was told that "the distinction between actions at law and suits at equity, and the forms of all such actions and suits heretofore existing, are abolished."[103] Thus Gray and his three allies were blending the actions and reliefs of law and equity, but they were doing so at the direction of the legislature.

Nonetheless, Justices Grover and Comstock offered a vigorous dissent from Gray's view. A third-party beneficiary might be allowed to sue when he or she was truly a cestui que trust—that is, when a true trust relationship had been created, "but further than this we cannot go without violating plain rules of law." The two dissenters cited recent English case law to establish that the rule in *Dutton* v. *Poole* was flawed and had been abandoned.[104] Thus in 1859 the New York court was following the path of earlier English courts in granting third-party beneficiaries their day in court, but it had also felt the first strong undercurrents of modern doctrine tugging at the old rule's support pilings.

But if some courts had considered and rejected the new trend in English doctrine regarding third-party beneficiaries, others, including those in Georgia, Michigan, and Massachusetts itself, were moving in doctrinal fashion to adopt the new English reasoning. New Hampshire's high court was the first to react. It turned a third-party creditor-beneficiary away in *Butterfield* v. *Hartshorn* (1834). No consideration had moved from him, and his lack of privity barred his action on this contract despite his being named as the beneficiary of it. This new rule had been "received as settled law in England." It was "the better opinion," being "established on sound legal principles."[105]

Later the New Hampshire court was pleased to see that its neighbor, Massachusetts, had abandoned its "anomalous [third-party beneficiary] doctrine," one so "at war with established principles."[106] In 1854 Justice Theron Metcalf, who had written approvingly of the rule fifteen years before in *American Jurist*, was persuaded in *Mellen* v. *Whipple* to abandon the old and adopt the new English rule.[107] Plaintiff's counsel cited English and Massachusetts cases to establish her right to sue. Joel Bishop, for the defendant, responded with an aggressive summary of the new English rule. Metcalf accepted Bishop's argument, that the new mortgagee was not in privity with the new owner of the property, no consideration having moved from her. He also took note of the doctrinal objections to such suits offered by the courts of Virginia and Pennsylvania. Metcalf explained that "by the recent decisions of the English courts," the right of a third-party beneficiary to a contract to sue was now "restricted within narrower limits than formerly; and the general rule, to which it is an exception, is now more strictly enforced."[108] And thereafter the Massachusetts court showed little inclination to find third-party beneficiary-plaintiffs to fall within the "exceptions" rather than "the general rule."

North Carolina's high court took the same path. In its third-party beneficiary "first impression" case, *Carroway* v. *Cox* (1852), the court found an "implied" privity between plaintiff and defendant "in equity and good conscience," but in 1860 it followed New Hampshire and Massachusetts in adopting the English "general rule."[109]

Missouri's high court wrestled with the problem for a decade, offering conflicting judgments in four decisions in the 1840s. The state's legislature adopted the Field Code in 1849, abolishing the formal distinction in pleading between actions at law and suits at equity. This step *should* have facilitated the adoption of Justice Metcalf's first "exception" to the rigid English rule, but for some time it did not. Missouri's jurists, like those of every other common-law jurisdiction, had been trained to regard the older distinctions, forms, and pleas as important, possessing an inner logic, understandable to one who grasped the scientific principles of the common law and equity. Hence, despite the code, Missouri's high court adopted the new, rigid English rule in 1858; the court had read Pennsylvania and English precedent and was now convinced that a plaintiff not in privity with the defendant could not sue on a contract made for his benefit. Justice Ephraim Ewing reiterated that view in 1862, citing Massachusetts and Pennsylvania precedent.[110] But Missouri was not to remain for long in the rigid English camp.[111]

The Supreme Courts of Maryland and Indiana moved in the fashion of Missouri's—first allowing third-party beneficiary suits, then adopting the English privity rule against them and finally returning to their original position.[112] The Indiana legislature adopted the Field Code, in 1852, abolishing distinctions between common law and equity in all actions, but the high court showed some initial reluctance (in 1855) to reject a "doctrine uniformly held by this Court" by allowing a third-party beneficiary to sue on a contract without privity. The doctrine had been "drawn up with great care and ability" and should be followed, "through it may seem a great hardship in this particular case."[113] By the outbreak of the Civil War, Indiana's high court was signaling the end to the defense of privity of contract or lack of consideration moving from a third-party beneficiary claimant by noting that "under the system of procedure now in force, there being no distinct court of equity," a third-party beneficiary's suit could lead to all of the interested parties being brought into court "in the nature of an old bill in chancery."[114] One is led to conclude that Indiana's court eventually abandoned its English doctrinal rule because of the legislature's reform of procedure, and not for any utilitarian or instrumentalist motive; in any event, there was no language of a utilitarian or instrumentalist nature in any of these Indiana high court opinions, any more than there was in those of the Maryland, Missouri, North Carolina, Massachusetts, or New York Supreme Courts or those of any of the other high courts in the land.

In six jurisdictions the doctrinal debate was augmented by one that *could* be styled utilitarian, but jurists on each side of the debate advanced procedural utilitarian critiques of the others' position. Pennsylvania first fell in line with the older view of things, allowing the third-party creditor-beneficiary to sue,[115] but it then backed off of that mark. In *Blymire* v. *Boistle* (1837) Justice Thomas Sergeant turned a creditor-beneficiary away; he found "reasons of substantial justice" that prevented any but the original debtor-promisee from suing, for if such third-party beneficiary-plaintiffs were allowed to maintain their suits, then defendant-promisors "would be subject to two separate actions at the same time, for the same debt, which would be inconvenient, and might lead to injustice." The problem was a particularly urgent one in Pennsylvania, because until 1859 her courts were granted only very limited equity powers by the legislature, and what was needed in this case was an equity court's ability to join the real parties at issue.[116]

The supreme courts of Vermont, Virginia, and Connecticut offered the same objection to the third-party suit. Thus in 1838 Vermont's Justice Isaac Redfield offered a critique similar to Pennsylvania's in a creditor-beneficiary case. "No case can be found in the books," Redfield wrote, where the consideration moves from one person, "and the contract is made with such person," and another person interested as a third-party beneficiary "can sue in his own name": "This would involve the absurdity, that either of two distinct parties, at the same time, could sustain an action upon the same contract, and recover for the same identical thing."[117] But if the high courts of Pennsylvania, Vermont, Virginia, and Connecticut found the right of the third-party beneficiary to sue in assumpsit to be "inconvenient" and potentially unjust, those of Nevada and Colorado were to defend it as "more convenient" than the English rule in that it "avoids multiplicity of actions"; they could "see no possible evil to result from it."[118] Nevada and Colorado had both adopted the Field Code by the time these opinions were written, whereas the legislatures of Pennsylvania, Vermont, Virginia, and Connecticut resisted such reform,[119] and this surely goes a long way toward explaining the different attitudes taken by these high courts. Since the real parties to the controversy in Nevada and Colorado could with facility be brought into court on a single action, the litigants there faced none of the procedural problems that had upset Justice Sergeant and his compeers.

Missouri's supreme court, it will be recalled, had adopted the "new" English rule in 1858. But the adoption of the Field Code, complied with the circulation of Parsons's influential treatise on contracts, finally led Missouri's jurists back to the "ancient" rule (with a reference to language in "our practice act" regarding third-party beneficiary suits).[120] No utilitarian or instrumentalist language can be found in this transformation process.

While Missouri's courts were switching from the new to the "ancient" English rule, the federal courts were moving decisively in the opposite direction. As late as 1876 Justice David Davis of the U.S. Supreme Court would write of "the right of a party to maintain assumpsit on a promise not under seal, made to another for his benefit" as being "now the prevailing rule in this country," albeit it was "much controverted." But in 1878 the court united behind Justice William Strong to limit such creditor-beneficiary suits to those in equity. Strong, who came to the court from the Pennsylvania Supreme Court, borrowed Justice Sergeant's mix of legal logic and procedural utilitarianism in *Blymire* v. *Boistle* (albeit he made no reference to that case). The federal courts thereafter held to this rule consistently throughout the late nineteenth century.[121]

By the 1870s it was clear that the judicial successors on the New York Court of Appeals of those who decided *Lawrence* v. *Fox* were unhappy with the broad and sweeping scope of the language of Justice Hiram Gray's opinion in that "leading case." Time and again the court spoke of its "doubts" regarding "the principle" upon which the doctrine in that case was founded, of the difficulties in ascertaining its elements "when the number and variety of its alleged foundations are considered,"[122] and of its disinclination "to extend the doctrine of *Lawrence* v. *Fox*" to cases not clearly "within the precise limits of its original application."[123] It was not the cases of gift-beneficiaries that concerned them. They cited *Dutton* v. *Poole*, Lord Mansfield, and Chancellor Kent, in addition to *Lawrence* v. *Fox*, to establish the soundness of the concept in *Dutton* that a third-party gift-beneficiary could be brought into privity with the defendant-promisor by the moral consideration that moved from the parent-promisee to the third-party wife or child.[124] Doctrine and humanity were not seen as being at odds for gift beneficiaries; thus in one instance the court praised one of their predecessors who, "in an opinion that does honor to his heart as well as to his intellect, quotes with approval *Dutton* v. *Poole*"[125] to sanction the suit of an illegitimate child to secure his father's gift to him on the promise of another. And on another occasion the court scolded a defendant for his "designed evasion of obligation."[126]

What bothered New York's high court jurists after the Civil War were the suits of creditor-beneficiaries. Of the fourteen such cases that I identified, the court denied the third-party creditor-beneficiary's right to sue in all but two,[127] despite the "leading case" of *Lawrence v. Fox*, which was itself a creditor-beneficiary case. The weak (widows and children, be they legitimate or illegitimate) could still utilize the doctrine of *Lawrence v. Fox*; but, increasingly, the strong (mortgagees and creditors of corporations and partnerships) found that, for doctrinal reasons, they could not. As Francis Wharton observed in 1883, the courts of New York were "apparently swaying to and fro under the pressure of sympathy with hardship at one time, or at another of loyalty to the principle that to a contract two consenting minds are essential."[128]

Several of those state high courts that had by 1860 decided that third-party beneficiaries could sue now followed New York's new path. Indiana's experience may serve as an example. That court had allowed third-party beneficiary suits since the 1850s, and it continued to do so in many creditors and all gift-beneficiary cases after 1860.[129] But in 1874 it began to apply New York's creditor-beneficiary exceptions to the doctrine in *Lawrence v. Fox*, citing the New York court on the necessity of a prior debt of the promisee to a third-party mortgagee-beneficiary.[130] In fact, by 1875 some eight jurisdictions allowed gift-beneficiaries to sue, but denied that right to all or most creditor-beneficiaries in doctrinal language[131] (see map 1). Among those first addressing the issue after the Civil War, only Rhode Island's high court permitted third-party creditor-beneficiaries to sue while denying the same right, on doctrinal grounds (citing the harsh English decision of *Tweddle v. Atkinson*), to third-party gift-beneficiaries.[132]

The mode of judicial decision making in cases where third-party beneficiaries to parol contracts sought to sue in nineteenth-century America, then, was overwhelmingly doctrinal in character. Whatever the outcome, the rationale offered was rarely utilitarian, and almost never instrumentalist, in nature. Moreover, the high court jurists of antebellum America were just as doctrinal as those of the allegedly formalistic post–Civil War years. Guided by treatise writers[133] and the rule of stare decisis, antebellum as *well* as post–Civil War American appellate judges appear to me far more doctrinal than they have to members of the economic-oriented school. It sometimes troubled them to turn an apparently deserving gift- or creditor-beneficiary away,[134] but although they "should have been better pleased to have come to a different result" to alleviate "a great hardship in this particu-

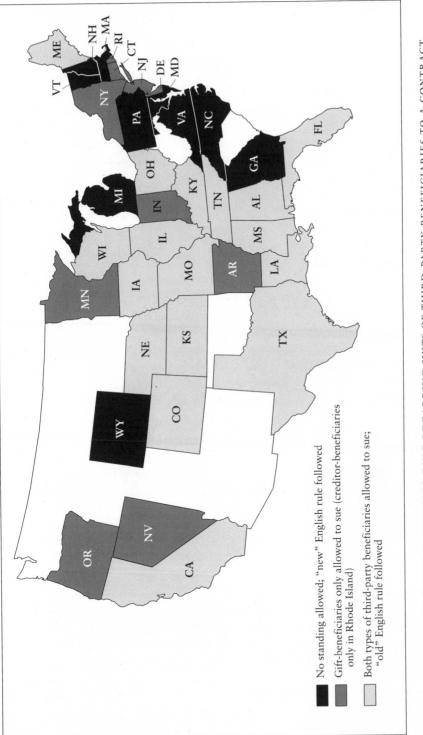

MAP 1. STATE SUPREME COURT GATEKEEPER RULE REGARDING SUITS OF THIRD-PARTY BENEFICIARIES TO A CONTRACT, 1800–1899

Legend:

- No standing allowed; "new" English rule followed
- Gift-beneficiaries only allowed to sue (creditor-beneficiaries only in Rhode Island)
- Both types of third-party beneficiaries allowed to sue; "old" English rule followed

lar case,"[135] their devotion to doctrine almost always prevented them from doing so. America's nineteenth-century appellate courts, both after *and* before the Civil War, approached the claims of third-party beneficiaries to actions of assumpsit with a respect for doctrine, precedent, and legal principles. American jurists in the nineteenth century might disagree as to whether the earlier or the more recent English rule should be followed, whether this exception or that one should be allowed; but they did not believe that a rule based on sound legal logic and principle should be bent or broken in order to satisfy the "economic" needs of a class of creditors, however compelling those needs might appear, however important the security of credit might be, generally, to nineteenth-century Americans. If the creditor of an absconded debtor, a reorganizing partnership, a manufacturing firm, or a railroad wanted access to a common-law court, he would have to find the right legal key. If a widow or illegitimate daughter sought in assumpsit to compel another to turn over the gift that he had promised a loving husband or parent to hold for her, she would have to convince the court that the rule in *Dutton* v. *Poole* was still good contract law.

Nonetheless, as I have already pointed out, widows and bastards—giftbeneficiaries—fared somewhat better than creditor-beneficiaries. The court might turn away some gift-beneficiaries with the remark that "she is in the wrong forum," but it often spelled out for the plaintiff's counsel a way the technical problem might be avoided by suing again in equity, or in the name of the administrator of her husband's estate.[136] A few courts may have favored the suit of a third-party gift-beneficiary because, as the opinion noted, she was "without means and in need of support,"[137] but such "situation-sense," where the language used in either the summary of the facts of the case or the legal exposition suggested an extralegal, humane concern with one or another of the parties, was uncommon. It may well be that the ancient English rule of *Dutton* v. *Poole* was sufficiently humane in principle and effect to satiate the typical jurist's thirst for justice. Creditorbeneficiaries, a doctrinal jurist might have reasoned, always remained entitled to sue their debtors directly, as well as to call upon their debtors to sue the defaulting party to the contract on their behalf, whereas the giftbeneficiary whose donor has died (or changed his mind and tried to alter the donation) would be without recourse to the courts if her deceased donor's estate administrator was not willing to sue on her behalf (to say nothing of the case of a living but no longer generous "donor"). Moreover, the donor, having suffered no pecuniary loss himself due to his promisor's nonperformance, might lose on the merits if he *was* willing to sue. This favoring of gift-beneficiaries flowed, in my judgment, from a purposive judicial concern with the effects of the decision, with a concern with what the rule ought to be in order to produce justice, and nine state benches did meld the old English rule for gift-beneficiaries with the newer, less-hospitable one for creditor-beneficiaries in this fashion (see map 1). These jurists were "discovering" rules purposively, though one of these rules was of a sixteenth-century, and the other of a late-seventeenth-century, English vintage.

Why did some state high courts fully adopt the newer English rule barring all third-party beneficiaries from suing while others ignored it completely and held fast to the older one? Scanning the map gives a powerful clue to one answer: seven of the ten jurisdictions that followed the new English rule were of the original thirteen states, and an eighth was the fourteenth state, Vermont. Only four of the nine jurisdictions that barred creditor-beneficiaries from the courtroom but allowed gift-beneficiaries were "original" states, and the one jurisdiction that barred gift-beneficiaries but allowed creditors, Rhode Island, was one of the Westminster-inclined "originals." All twelve of the jurisdictions that ignored the new English rule completely were created in the nineteenth century, in the South, Midwest, and West. Led by New England's doctrinal jurists, a number of disproportionately older state courts followed English courts in the mid-nineteenth century in revising their "gatekeeper" rule regarding third-party beneficiaries, whereas more recently created state courts in the South, Midwest, and West tended to ignore the Mother of All Common Law on this question.

Here and there, legislatures responded to specific requests for relief from common-law rules that denied a third-party beneficiary a right to sue on a contract made for his or her benefit. Some legislatures, in states whose courts were not yet willing to sanction certain kinds of third-party beneficiary suits under their understanding of the common law, began to respond after the Civil War to the advice of such interested parties as insurance companies and state insurance commissions, realty, contractor, and materialmen trade associations. Some passed statutes enabling mortgagees to sue a grantee of the equity of redemption who had promised to assume the mortgage.[138] Others gave materialmen the right to sue as third-party creditor-beneficiaries of a contractor's indemnity bond[139] (though many such statutes were limited to publicly financed works[140]). Some legislation gave creditors the right to sue where the debts of a firm had been assumed by a promisor.[141] Other legislatures gave third-party beneficiaries the right to sue on covenants.[142] Still other legislatures, in states whose courts denied to the beneficiary of a life insurance policy the right to sue in his or her own name, provided that right by statute.[143]

Legislatures, then, played a substantial role in "bending" the common law in states where jurists had decided to apply the rigid English rules of contract to third-party beneficiary suits. The typical jurist, be he of the antebellum years as well as the "age of formalism," be he of giant stature or of the most humdrum sort, believed that law was an unchanging domain, discoverable with inductive scientific method, and that justice could be served by the rigorous application of those ageless principles.[144] Sometimes the well-reasoned opinion of a highly regarded jurist from a court of "eminent respectability," or the eloquence and authoritative language of a popular treatise writer, might serve to influence a court "discovering" the law in a "first impression" case. But once a rule had been discovered, it was uncommon for that court to reverse itself. Hence legislative intervention, "positive law," proved to be a more potent vehicle of legal change than "creative" jurists.[145]

Chapter Three

On Historical Developments and Barriers to Injured Plaintiffs: Continuity in Tort Law

The common-law rules of tort law with regard to negligence in nineteenth-century America were, like those of contract and property, essentially unaltered from those of seventeenth- and eighteenth-century England. Once again, continuity, not change, largely characterized the law and its doctrines: the Jurisprudence of the Head generally prevailed. There are several clear and strong exceptions to this pattern: Some, with regard to the assumption of risk and fellow-servant rules, are noted in this chapter; others, dealing with the contributory-negligence rule and the processing of damage awards, belong, in my view, altogether to the Jurisprudence of the Heart and are described in chapters 7, 8, and 9. But it is fair to say that my characterization of the rules regarding negligence as being part of a "taught legal tradition" is controversial.[1] Most accounts of these rules in America describe them undergoing substantial change at the hands of common-law jurists. That is why we began with a summary of their views.

According to the reigning economic-oriented paradigm, jurists "in the first part of the nineteenth century . . . generated rules that put serious obstacles in the way of actions for personal injury." One prominent text writer is "certain" that these new "rules favored defendants over plaintiffs, businesses over individuals," that they "showed a definite preference for enterprise, for business defendants." Another tells us that the rise of what he calls "the private law negligence principle" must "be seen as a phenomenon of industrialization." It "became a leading means by which the dynamic and growing forces in American society were able to challenge and eventually overwhelm the weak and relatively powerless segments of the American economy." Still another has it that the resulting legal system was "unresponsive" to injury victims, establishing and maintaining "roadblocks and hurdles" that "only lucky and persistent litigants could surmount."[2]

This general thesis has several particulars: Jurists replaced a "strict liabil-

ity" tort standard with one requiring the injured plaintiff to prove the defendant negligent; defendants who responded that their action was only the remote rather than the "proximate" cause of the accident were protected
from liability; and plaintiffs whose contributory negligence had been a necessary cause of the accident, as well as worker-plaintiffs who had "assumed
the risk" that led to the accident or who had been injured by the negligent
act of a fellow worker, were now nonsuited by the judge as a matter of law.

That is not the story I will be telling in this chapter. Injured plaintiffs did
not have an easy time of it in collecting damages in the nineteenth century,
as Thomas Russell, Randy Bergstrom, and Edward Purcell have separately
shown.[3] But they faced no *new* "roadblocks and hurdles." Neither the fault
principle, nor the proximate cause, nor contributory negligence, nor assumption of risk, nor fellow-servant defenses were new, but can be seen
clearly in the English precedents cited by American jurists who applied
them.

This is a story of continuity, then, part of our saga of the Jurisprudence
of the Head. But it also contains elements of innovation: exceptions to the
contributory negligence, assumption of risk, and fellow-servant defenses,
and thus offers clear evidence of a Jurisprudence of the Heart. Moreover,
when you examine the proximate-cause and contributory-negligence rules
with care, to assess their effects on the outcome of suits, you can see that
these were pretty ineffective "roadblocks and hurdles."

Perhaps jurists of the nineteenth century can be faulted for relying on a
Jurisprudence of the Head in adopting existing English negligence rules.
Perhaps more of them should have offered opposition to the adoption of the
fellow-servant rule, should have been more vigorous and thorough in hedg-
ing that rule and its companion, assumption of risk, with strong exceptions.
Perhaps they should have insisted on the European Civil Law's "comparative" (rather than the contributory) negligence rule. But their failures to do
so have been explained by remarks that they either sympathized with nascent industry and corporate entrepreneurs or (to the same effect) that they
simply espoused the same market ideology as these corporate defendants.[4]
All but one of these assessments incorrectly assumed that these jurists had
invented the fellow-servant and assumption-of-risk rules.[5] When one appreciates that they did not, it becomes easier to understand why they found it
difficult to abandon them. Westminster's anchor chains were very long. A
Jurisprudence of the Head pervaded the eastern states and held many western and southern jurists, however imperfectly, to most English rules of tort
as well. Consequently, attorneys representing injured workers preferred to

invoke a "principled" exception to one or the other rule, or to attack the defendants' "facts" and witnesses, rather than to engage in what might prove a hopeless effort to persuade the bench to ignore "the law."

FROM STRICT LIABILITY TO NEGLIGENCE?

According to the reigning paradigm, one injured in the premodern era had only to prove that the defendant's act had caused the injury to establish the defendant's liability; an action of trespass vi et armas would thereby lie. And this was so even if the defendant's role was indirect, as when one's employee had caused the accident, or when one's own act had indirectly caused it, here an action of trespass on the case would lie. By the mid-nineteenth century, however, it is said, a plaintiff injured by a train, carriage, or other object had the new obligation of establishing the defendant's negligence or fault—the defendant's failure to live up to a duty of reasonable care.[6] Several scholars, however, have expressed doubts that such a shift from strict liability to negligence ever took place.[7]

Stephen Gilles has recently offered a sophisticated analysis of the issue. His reexamination of the evidence of English trespass and case law in the five centuries before 1800 establishes that the plaintiff did indeed have to prove the defendant negligent. What Gilles has added to the century-long debate is convincing evidence that, until the 1760s, the test of culpability was not whether the defendant had behaved as a "reasonable" or "prudent" person ought to have behaved, but whether he had taken all "realistically possible" measures to avoid the accident. The difference is real, but it is also subtle. The late medieval rule was that the defendant had to "have taken all practically possible care from at least the point at which the danger of a harmful event became apparent." But this is also the mid-nineteenth-century rule in *Davies v. Mann* (10 M. & W. 546 [1842]), that the defendant was liable, despite any contributory negligence of the plaintiff, if he had been the party with the "last clear chance" of avoiding the accident and had failed to act accordingly. In any event, as I understand Gilles, juries and jurors of the seventeenth century held defendants to essentially the same level of liability as they would in the nineteenth century. The central difference between the burdens of proof in actions of trespass and case by the seventeenth century, according to S. F. C. Milsom, was that in trespass the defendant had to prove that he had *not* been negligent, whereas in case the plaintiff had to prove that he *had* been.[8]

One of the problems with any analysis of medieval and early modern English common law is that the role of the jury in civil actions is sometimes mysterious; as J. H. Baker has pointed out, we see little discussion of negligence in early reports of appeals from suits where the action had been trespass, because the proper defense to such an action was "not guilty." Since the evidence of "guilt" was one of fact for the trial court *jury* to decide, and since the appellate court never got the jury's "fact" question of sufficiency of proof as a "law" question, we cannot tell from the appellate reports alone whether *lack* of negligence was being proved as a defense.[9]

Actually, the question of what the jury was deciding is not entirely without clues in the reports. We can sometimes see what the jury's role was from the appellate record, or what the appellate jurists *said* was the jury's mission. Exhibit 1: In 1290 the Court of King's Bench heard the case (*Brainton* v. *Pinn*) of a father and son sued by an innkeeper for their "ill sense and carelessness and failure to look after a lighted candle" that had led to a fire with much ensuing property damage. The trial court jury had found that the son had indeed gone to bed with the candle left burning and had consequently assessed damages at one hundred pounds. Exhibit 2: In *Gibbons* v. *Pepper* (K. B. 1696), the plaintiff had been struck by a frightened horse ridden by the defendant. The plaintiff's action was trespass for assault and battery (vi et armas) and the defendant's counsel pleaded "it was no neglect in him" in that "the negligence of the defendant did not cause it." This plea was questioned, and on appeal defendant's counsel explained that if the horse ran away "against his will, he would have been found *not guilty.*" But since the formal plea had not been "the general issue" (or "not guilty"), the Court of King's Bench appears to have allowed the lower court nonsuit for faulty pleading to stand. We thus learn what a defendant was expected to prove in a "non guilty" plea (even if this defendant had failed to plead it), and it clearly amounted to a lack of negligence. Exhibit 3: In *Ogle* v. *Barnes* (K. B. 1799), a ship collision suit, the plaintiffs charged in a trespass on the case that the defendants had "negligently" managed their vessel. Grose, J., noted that "if, on the trial it had been proved" that the collision was "occasioned by [the defendants'] willful act," rather than their mere negligence, the plaintiffs would have been nonsuited because then the action should have been trespass vi et armas instead of case, "but the jury having found a verdict for the plaintiffs, we must consider that the complaint set forth in the declaration was proved." This clearly meant that the jury was expected to decide whether the defendants had behaved "negligently." Exhibit 4: In *Wordworth* v. *Willan & Others* (N. P. 1805), Rook, J., "left it to the jury to say whether the accident had been occasioned by the defendants' coachman having driven so near to the plaintiff's horse that the action arose from that cause." This, again, reads like a test of the coachman's use of due care.[10] To be sure, these clues are not enough to lay the question to rest. But there is more evidence in a number of cases and treatises, ranging from the thirteenth to the early nineteenth centuries, that may.[11]

The earliest evidence I report is Bracton's remark on homicide-by-chance: "If he used such care as he could . . . it is not to be laid to his account." Cavendish, C. J., of King's Bench offered an analogous view regarding a contractual undertaking by a smith "to cure my horse" in 1374: If the horse "is harmed by his negligence . . . , it is just that he should be liable. But if he does all he can and applies himself with due diligence to the cure, it is not right that he should be guilty." Addressing the Court of Exchequer in 1551, Atkins, Appr., maintained that "in our law . . . there are some things that happen which may not be prevented by foresight . . . and when such a thing happens . . . the law will not punish him for it; . . . for if the law should punish a man for an accident, . . . it would be utterly against reason."[12]

Throughout the seventeenth and eighteenth centuries, both in England and the colonies, plaintiffs sued in trespass, charging "negligence,"[13] and defendants answered that it had been "an inevitable accident" and that they were "utterly without fault" and had "committed no negligence."[14] Thus when John Beach of New Haven Colony felled a tree in 1643 that killed a passing cow, the owner sued Beach. A witness was reported as having told the court that Beach had seen the cows coming and had not "done what in reason he might and ought to have done" to avoid injury to the cattle. "If he had been so careful as he might, no hurt need have been done." Beach was ordered to pay five pounds in damages. This may not be the "reasonable man" standard, which was not supposed to have appeared in America until the 1850s, or the "foreseeability" principle, which was not supposed to have emerged until the late nineteenth century, but *Smyth* v. *Beach* certainly sounds as if it could have been tried in the 1890s under the same rules and jury instructions.[15]

Morton Horwitz points to *Clark* v. *Foot*, a New York Supreme Court opinion in 1811 involving the spread of a fire from one farmer's stubble to another's woods and buildings, as a "dramatic departure from the common law of strict liability for fire" and "the first generally recognized American case in which a court denied recovery in the absence of negligence." But *Clark* is anchored by Blackstone's *Commentaries* (cited by the court). Moreover, the court in *Clark* merely affirmed a finding by a jury of this farmer's peers that the plaintiff had failed to prove the defendant negligent. Furthermore, one can find the same rule being applied in Plymouth as early as October of 1645. Roger Cooke and William Lathame sued John and Ann Barker in trespass on the case for "the burning of their house accidentally, but the jury could not give in a verdict, and the matter was ended, and the said John was content to give the plaintiffs 20 shillings towards their losses" (or one-twelfth of what they had sought). Richard Morris, who styled the law of tort in colonial America as the "Doctrine of No Liability Without Fault," maintained that there was "no evidence that any . . . general rule imposing absolute liability was ever encouraged or even recognized" in the American colonies,[16] and this still sounds right. In short, the defense of "no negligence" was at least as old as the late Middle Ages.

Nonetheless, as John Baker points out, until the seventeenth century, English common-law courts may have been reluctant to impose a duty of care on one who could not be viewed as having undertaken some such obligation to the plaintiff (as in the case of an innkeeper, common carrier, blacksmith, or by custom, a neighbor who kept a fire in his stubble or hearth). A tort, after all, is a breach of a duty that society *expects*, and duties toward strangers were not common coinage in the Elizabethan Age. Thus Walmsley, J., in *Bradshaw v. Nicholson* (1601) observed that "here there is nothing alleged except negligence, and I have never known an action to lie for negligence save where one is retained to do something and does it negligently; and the reason why it lies in that case is because he had undertaken to do it."[17]

But even in Walmsley's lifetime, a major source of accidents involving strangers was emerging. Throughout the seventeenth and eighteenth centuries all forms of transportation flourished, keeping pace with the flowering of commerce. More and more ships, barges, skiffs, and ferries crowded England's rivers and harbors. More and more horsemen and horsewomen, carts, buggies, carriages, and stagecoaches moved along its streets and highways. By 1775 there were some four hundred stagecoaches operating in the country, and nearly seventeen thousand other four-wheeled carriages.[18] Inevitably, collision, running-down, and overtaking accidents, and those caused by runaway horses, "daily increasing," led more "stranger" plaintiffs to charge "stranger" defendants with neglecting a lawful duty owed to them. The broad and general rule, reiterated by Holt, C.J., in *Tenant v. Goldwin* (1705), had been that of the Latin maxim *Sic utere tuo, ut alienum non laedas*, or in Holt's English, "Every man must use his own so as not to damage another." That would suffice for a case involving the collapse of a common retaining wall (as in *Tenant*), but a more elaborate standard was needed for a collision or running-down suit. "The rules of the road," for both water-borne and terrestrial traffic, emerged as the "customary" standards, and Lord Bathurst put the general rule in the 1740s this way: "Wherever a man receives hurt through the default of another, . . . if it be occasioned by negligence or folly the law gives him an action to recover damages for the injury so sustained [so long as he] prove that the injury was such as would probably follow from the act done."[19]

The owner of a cart might inexplicably swerve from the left side of the road into the center, grazing the wheel of an oncoming cart and plunging its occupants headlong into a ditch. A coachman might "heedlessly" look behind him to talk to a colleague, "without attending to the road where persons [were] passing" and "thereby" run over a child. A young and spirited horse, without a curb chain, might be startled by a noisy butcher's cart, and if its owner pulled the wrong gig rein, the bolting animal might force the gig's shaft against a wagoner's horse, killing it. Courts faced with these fact situations instructed the juries to ask themselves (whether the suit be in case *or* trespass)[20] if the defendant's act, or that of his servant, had been "careless," "negligent," "heedless," or "entirely without default."[21] There had been no *shrinking* of liability, from an "absolute" standard to one requiring proof of fault; rather a *new* standard of care, one due *strangers*, had been added to both the existing *sic utere* rule regarding property owners and the misfeasance rule for those blacksmiths or surgeons "undertaking" a duty, and both of these rules *already* required a failure to use due care.

In articulating this duty due strangers from strangers, Sir William Jones in 1781 anticipated the "reasonable man" standard of care of Lemuel Shaw and Oliver Wendell Holmes Jr., by two generations in proposing the "generality of rational men," as a "fixed mode or standard of diligence." Some English and American courts were certainly using this standard long before either Shaw or Holmes addressed the question. Thus Tindal, C. J., maintained in *Vaughan* v. *Menlove* (1837), that with regard to liability the "care taken by a prudent man has always been the rule laid down."[22]

In any event, there was no shift *from* "strict liability" to negligence. Indeed, a very real proxy *for* "strict" product liability was alive in the late eighteenth century and would continue to flourish in the nineteenth century as well.

PRODUCT LIABILITY BEFORE *MACPHERSON* AND *ESCOLA*

Strict product liability has been one of the more important innovations in tort law during the twentieth century. Conceived in Justice Benjamin Cardozo's opinion in *MacPherson* v. *Buick Motor Co.* (N.Y. 1916), nurtured by Dean William Prosser's treatise on torts, and drawing strength from Chief Justice Roger Traynor's concurring views in *Escola* v. *Coca-Cola Bottling Co.* (Cal. 1944), liability attached for the first time to a manufacturer for foreseeable harm caused by ordinary use of a product, despite the fact that no formal contractual "privity" existed between manufacturer and user.[23] This reversal of the English "privity" rule in *Winterbottom* v. *Wright* (Ex. 1842) made product liability "a *Wunderkind* of 20th-century tort law," or so we are told.[24]

Yes and no. There would be very few who were to recover *directly* from the manufacturer of a faulty product that had injured them before *Mac-Pherson*. Nonetheless, most of those injured by such defects had still been able to obtain redress (damage awards) in English and American courts throughout all of the nineteenth century, and these awards were about as substantial as the typical product liability award of the present day![25]

First, let us remember that plaintiffs in the nineteenth century had rarely *purchased* the defective objects (either directly from a manufacturer or a middleman retailer) that had caused them injury. One did not *buy* a stage-coach, steamboat, or railroad carriage; instead, one "let" a place on one from a company that had (usually) not built the object itself but had purchased it from a manufacturer. And since one's ticket for the "common carrier" stage, steamboat, or railroad was contractual, an implied duty of care was read by jurists into the contract, rendering the common carrier liable unless it could prove itself to be free of responsibility. That turned out to be very difficult, as I will now try to demonstrate.

When judges explained (to juries) or interpreted (to appellants) the liability of the owners of common carriers to passengers, they made clear that the rule was unlike the "strict liability" rule with regard to baggage. Baggage was inert and insensate; it could not protect itself, nor could it behave in a contributorily negligent manner. Humans were different, and the ticket of passage was not an insurance contract.[26] But what jurists thereby allowed, they thereupon quickly qualified so thoroughly as to produce, in *practice*, a virtual absolute liability of common carriers toward passengers.

Exploding Boilers

One leading text on the history of American law maintains that "the spirit of the age" in the nineteenth century "was a spirit of limits on recovery. People lived with calamity." It then provides a journalistic, fictionalized account of a steamboat disaster to demonstrate the failure of the law to hold steamboat owners liable for careless or reckless behavior:[27]

> In the novel by Mark Twain and Charles Dudley Warren [*sic*],
> *The Gilded Age*, written in the 1870s, there is a description of a
> terrible steamboat disaster. Twenty-two people died; scores more

were injured. But after an investigation, the "verdict" was the "familiar" one, heard "all the days of our lives—'NOBODY TO BLAME.'"[28]

The judicial record, however, does not support this verdict. Steamboat and steamship owners *were* held liable for injuries both to passengers *and* crew when their boilers exploded.[29] Judges told juries of their "solemn duty" to use "the strong arm of the law" to "put an end if possible to these terrible disasters."[30] Rather than suggesting that negligent steamboat entrepreneurs were to be shown some sort of consideration for their contribution to the economy, judges told grand juries to display "no mawkish sensibility, no false hopes of clemency," to "screen" any such men who might be guilty of manslaughter. Justice John McLean reminded a federal court jury that "every passenger sleeps and treads upon a fiery volcano," and that the SS *Virginia*'s engineer, on trial for manslaughter, might, indeed, be found guilty of the loss of lives when the boiler exploded, for "the culpable instruments of such unmeasurable calamity should not go unpunished." Another federal judge told a similar jury of "the spirit of rivalry and the spirit of gain" that "stimulate [steamboat] owners and officers to attain the highest speed of velocity known to be attainable," obviously forcing the boiler beyond its safe limits. Chief Justice John Sedgwick of the New York Superior Court criticized the berth design of the steamer *Algeria* in 1880, "intentionally planned by the defendants to increase their profits by holding a large number of sleeping people," and held that negligence should thereby be presumed when these berths collapsed, leading to a passenger's injury.[31] In short, jurists had no patience with steamboat men who hazarded the lives of their passengers and crew. And well they might. After all, "riding circuit," something all of these jurists did, often involved the use of a steamboat; they knew the peril. Indeed, one of their number, Justice Isaac Preston of the Louisiana Supreme Court, was killed on the SS *St. James* in 1851 when its boiler exploded.

The closest case in the appellate reports to the steamboat accident described by Clemens and Warner occurred on the Mississippi, on November 3, 1864, when two boats, the *John Ramsey* and the *Albany*, were racing in route to St. Paul, Minnesota. The boiler of the *John Ramsey* exploded because weights had been placed on its safety valve and the captain had ordered the water level in the boiler to be lowered, which is to say he ordered an increase in steam pressure (as had been the case in Mark Twain's story). A number of deckhands injured on both vessels by the explosion sued. The owners maintained that the engineer and officers were fellow-servants of the plaintiffs, as was the case in British law,[32] and that, in any event, the deckhands had assumed the risk. But neither the trial judge, jury, nor appellate jurists were impressed with their arguments. The Minnesota high court declared the engineer and captain to be agents of the owners, the unlicensed engineer to be an incompetent servant, and the machinery unsafe (three exceptions to the fellow-servant rule). They rejected the assumption-of-risk reasoning as well, and reminded the owners that a bursting boiler was prima facie proof of negligence and liability.[33] Here was a case where Clemens's and Warner's headline might have read, "Everybody in Charge to Blame and All Those Injured Recover Compensation."

Exploding steamboat boilers were not the only ones that injured persons and property in nineteenth-century America. For example, in 1872 one Losee sued a boiler manufacturer, a paper company, and two of the paper company's trustees in trespass for property damage when an exploding boiler smashed through the wall of his building, creating chaos. Justice Robert Earl spoke for the New York Court of Appeals in its decision on the case: The rules of undisturbed use of property were "much modified by the exigencies of the social state": "We must have factories, machinery, dams, canals and railroads. They are demanded by the manifold wants of mankind, and lay at the basis of all our civilization."[34]

Morton Horwitz, quoting Earl's dicta, observes that it "reflected a fundamental transformation" in the law of negligence over the previous seventy years, the "primary effect" of which had been "to force those injured by economic activities to bear the cost of these improvements."[35] Horwitz's "transformation" never occurred. Earl's dicta ought to be placed in proper context. Losee's suit against the manufacturer had been dismissed on the grounds that the manufacturer was unable to monitor the boiler's use and maintenance by the paper company and because of the lack of privity between plaintiff and manufacturer.[36] His suit against the paper company, however, had resulted in an award of $2,703.36, but that against the two trustees had been dismissed, and it was from these verdicts that Losee appealed. His attorney argued that "proof of negligence was not necessary to establish defendants' liability, and proof that there was no negligence is inadmissible." He relied on the recent English "bursting reservoir" case, *Rylands* v. *Fletcher*.[37] It was this reasoning, and this alone, that Justice Earl and his colleagues rejected. They insisted that negligence was still the standard of liability in cases in which no explicit duty was owed the plaintiff (as with a passenger and common carrier), but the court accepted the jury's finding of negligent maintenance and operation of the boiler as the cause of this damage and *affirmed* the judgment against the paper company.[38] Makers of defective or poorly maintained dangerous machinery were not liable to any but their immediate buyers, and then only for a reasonable period of time, but the owners and users of this machinery were held to a high degree of liability.[39]

Defective Stagecoaches

This high degree of liability with regard to manufactured products had for long clearly been the case as well with regard to stagecoaches. Proprietors of stagecoaches were held to be "bound" to carry passengers "safely and properly." And if the plaintiff could prove that an axletree, dickey, or harness had broken in transit, causing the accident, the courts held that a prima facie case of negligence had been established, since they "would expect a clear landworthiness in the carriage itself," as Best, C. J., put it: "Every coach proprietor warrants to the public that his stage coach is equal to the journey it undertakes, and that it is his duty to examine it previous to the commencement of every journey." The suit at issue, in assumpsit, had been brought in 1824 by a passenger on the "Kentish-town stage" after the dickey he and his son had been riding on had come loose, throwing them to the ground. The manufacturer of the coach had been called by the defendant proprietor to testify that the defective part could not have been discovered by external examination, but, on cross-examination, he had allowed that its breaking could have been the result of previous instances of overloading of the dickey. That was enough for the judge and jury; the injured plaintiff received fifty-one pounds in damages.[40] Best offered another version of the high standard of liability courts set for stagecoach proprietors the next year:

> The coachman must have competent skill. . . . He must be well
> acquainted with the road he undertakes to drive; he must be provided
> with steady horses, *a coach and harness of sufficient strength and
> properly made*, and also with lights at night. If there be *the least
> failure in any one of these things*, the duty of the coach proprietors is
> not fulfilled, and they are *answerable for any injury for damage that
> happens.*[41]

Yes, a plaintiff had to make out a case for the cause of the accident; the standard was not "strict liability." But it was close enough: For example, a woman was thrown from a coach and her leg broken when baggage shifted on a coach with no iron railing to keep it from striking her as she sat on a rear exterior seat. The jury found "improper construction of the coach" to have been the cause of the accident. The coach proprietor's counsel allowed as

89

much, but argued on appeal that, as such, the manufacturer, and not the owner-operator, should be sued. But Lord Tenderden and King's Bench disagreed, holding that as the proprietor had accepted and used the defective coach, it was liable to the passenger for its "malconstruction."[42] In 1833 Alderson, J., of the Court of Common Pleas, offered a rationale for this rule holding coach proprietors responsible for defects in their vehicles in language that the Law and Economics school could be comfortable with: Courts held such a proprietor liable for "all defects in his vehicle which can be seen at the time of the construction, as well as for such as may exist afterward, and be discovered on investigation," because otherwise "he might buy ill-constructed or unsafe vehicles, and his passengers be without remedy."[43]

American courts held consistently to the same standards as their English counterparts with regard to stagecoach accidents. Thus in 1823 the Massachusetts high court turned away the argument of counsel for a hackney-coach owner who had unsuccessfully argued (à la Clemens and Warner) that the damage the coach had done to a chaise was "occasioned by a mere accident, for which no one is to be blamed." Similarly, in 1856 the Illinois Supreme Court held coach proprietors liable for injuries due to an axle that had broken, probably, due to extremely cold weather, with the words: "They are held to strict care and vigilance." And in 1854 the Virginia high court also rejected the argument of counsel for a stagecoach proprietor charged with liability for a passenger's injuries in an accident. Counsel had maintained that "sound policy" forbade the adoption of "the very harsh rule" that "seemed to look upon carriers of passengers as criminals to be punished" rather than as "useful citizens to be encouraged and protected." Justice William Daniel, for the court, brushed that entrepreneurial *defensoribus* aside. He first restated the law: A carrier must warrant that there will be no mishap "arising from defectiveness of material or workmanship or faultiness of [coach construction] for which there is a known remedy." Then he offered this public policy rationale: There was developing a lust for "rapid traveling" that was "daily betraying the managers and conductors of every species of conveyance into a fatal disregard" of all precautions. With an apt metaphor, Daniel observed that the Virginia Court did not believe that the law "should slacken the reins" that held these common carriers "in check." For reasons, therefore, of "policy, humanity, and reason," the jury's award of nine thousand dollars to the plaintiff was affirmed.[44]

Did American courts hold stagecoach operators *strictly* liable for injuries to passengers? No. Not any more than had English courts. Thus in 1845 the Massachusetts high court remanded the case of a passenger injured when the iron axletree of a stagecoach broke due to a hidden defect. The plaintiff had sued in assumpsit, claiming an implied warranty of safety, but the court decided that, where the defect in the manufactured axle was entirely hidden, and the coach operators had inspected the axle externally in a proper manner, they should not be held liable. Nonetheless, this was the same court that nine years earlier had held a turnpike company liable for injury to a traveler due to a latent defect in the road. As Chief Justice Lemuel Shaw had put it, the toll paid was "an adequate compensation for the risk assumed," and "by throwing the risk upon those who have the best means of taking precautions against it, the public will have the greatest security against actual damage and loss."[45] This certainly *sounds* like Traynor's language in *Escola*.[46]

Fare-paying passengers were not the only plaintiffs capable of holding common carriers to these (virtually) strict-liability standards. Those carried free of charge were entitled to them, as were pedestrians run down when a proprietor's reins failed. In either case the defendant "was bound to have proper tackle."[47] Employees ("servants") could recover as well,[48] unless the fellow-servant or assumption-of-risk rules barred them; the latter rule prompted the "leading case" in preproduct liability law, *Winterbottom* v. *Wright* (1842). The plaintiff, a mail-coach driver for the government, was injured because of a "latent defect" in the coach. Citing *Priestley* v. *Fowler*, (1837), his counsel appeared to acknowledge the problem his client might have in suing. Moreover, as the driver, he had been responsible for inspecting the coach to detect any developing deterioration or weaknesses. But a "latent" defect, one undetectable by inspection, his counsel argued, might be laid at the doors of the manufacturer. The Court of Exchequer thought otherwise. The driver clearly had no contractual privity with the manufacturer, whose duty it had been to construct sound coaches for the postal service that had employed him. Unless the postal service had failed in some manner in its duties to its driver (and the court gave no indication that it suspected as much), this accident was damnum absque injuria. *Winterbottom* clearly placed drivers injured by "latent defects" beyond all hope of recovery[49] until judicial adoption of a strict product liability doctrine (or statutory abrogation of the assumption of risk doctrine). But what has not been appreciated is how small a population of injured parties the privity rule in *Winterbottom* reached.

Defective Railroad Equipment

My claim that a virtually strict product liability rule existed throughout nineteenth century America may be tested with regard to accidents caused by defective railroad equipment. Courts held the owners of these heavier, faster, more lethal common carriers to a still higher standard of care than that fixed on stagecoach operators.[50] (And keep in mind that until 1812 the English common law did not even *permit* tort actions against corporations. These were first sanctioned at the very point in time that courts are alleged to have been bending rules to protect corporate entrepreneurs!)[51] Where axles, rails, switches, or other apparatus failed,[52] injured passengers almost invariably prevailed against railroad corporations;[53] they were at no disadvantage in being unable to sue the manufacturer of the defective object. As Chief Justice Lemuel Shaw put it in 1849 (in a damage suit involving a derailment caused by a defective switch), it was the railroad company's duty to employ "the most exact care and diligence" in the "structure and care of the track, and in all the subsidiary arrangements" necessary for safety, as well as "to see that the switch was rightly constructed, attended and managed." New York jurists of the early 1850s held railroad entrepreneurs in their state liable "of course" for "even the slightest neglect" and obliged them to prove "that the accident occurred without [their] fault." In 1850 a Western Railroad car axle gave way because it lacked a "safety beam" that had been introduced in the country ten years before the accident (but still not used "by the New England roads"), designed to hold the axle and wheels in place in the event of axle failure. The railroad's counsel introduced evidence that the axle had been "made of the best quality of iron," that it was "well made," and that it had been "examined from time to time, and that no external defect could be discovered." But the appellate court approved as "correct" the trial judge's instructions to the jury that "it was no apology" that the safety beam was not in use in New England and that the company was "responsible for this defect to the same extent as if the axle had been manufactured by themselves." The railroad should have made the manufacturer test the axle's torque strength. Passenger cars lacking window bars were defective if passengers leaned an arm out of the window and suffered injury from a passing train or mail hook. Chief Justice John Bannister Gibson of Pennsylvania instructed a jury that the carrier was bound to provide a railroad carriage "perfect in all its parts." The equipment, bridges, engines, and machinery, Chief Justice Robert McKinney of Tennessee believed, were to be *"perfect*, and constructed according to the present improvements in the art," and the company was consequently responsible for injuries to a young engine hand when its bridge had not been so constructed.[54]

Perhaps the most extreme statement of this all-but-strict liability to which railroad corporations were held in nineteenth-century America was *Alden* v. *New York Central RR* (1862). A passenger sued for damages after a car axle became brittle and broke on an extremely cold night. The breaking of such axles had been reported by railway chief engineers as early as 1834 to be a leading cause of accidents. In this case, however, the break seemed to have been unpredictable and unavoidable. A small crack, "impossible" for the company to "discover without taking the wheel off" (an act requiring "a power equal to 25 or 30 tons") was deemed the cause. Nonetheless, the company was held liable. Justice George Gould, for the New York Court of Appeals, allowed that the rule was a "hard" one, but he insisted that it was

> plain and of easy application, and when once established, is distinct notice to all parties of their duties and liabilities, and, practically, it will be likely to work no more burdensome results to carriers of passengers than to have them, with an uncertain criterion of responsibility, to the trouble and expense of strongly litigated contests before juries.[55]

Lord Denman and Queen's Bench had held the London and Brighton Railway to a similarly high standard of care in another derailment case (due to defective rails), and American Courts soon cited his opinion,[56] but in 1860 Denman's successor on Queen's Bench, Cockburn, C. J., treated Denman's standard as unreasonably strict in a nisi prius trial. A defectively welded wheel had caused a derailment, and the injured plaintiff charged the Eastern Counties Railway with liability. That company's witnesses testified that the defect had been undetectable. Cockburn charged the jury that it would be unreasonable to hold the company to a standard more fit for the "microscopic eye of science" to "pick out flaws" than for "the practical working of railroad business. . . . The business of railways and of life could not go on if this were required." This time the jury found for the railway; two years later similar instructions in a virtually identical case resulted in the opposite verdict when the jury found that excessive speed and poor brake power had exacerbated the wheel's failure. But in 1869 Queen's Bench affirmed Cockburn's limitation: A railway company should not be held liable for an accident due to the failure of a defective wheel weld that was invisible to the eye when the company had engaged in a reasonable schedule of inspection and maintenance of its equipment. The court specifically rejected the strict standard set by Justice Gould in *Alden* v. *N. Y. Central*.[57]

Almost immediately, the high courts of Pennsylvania, Tennessee, and New York stepped a bit back from the *Alden* "absolute" approach and echoed the new English view. Nevertheless, there remained much support for the older standard imposing a virtual strict liability on railroads for the safety of their equipment. A commentator in the *Southern Law Review* defended Lord Ellenborough's earlier language ("as far as human care and foresight can go") and condemned "the modern English judges, with their pockets full of railroad shares," for having "diminished" the carrier's liability "to that ordinary care," "even where he drives his carriage by steam at six times the speed of the old stagecoach." Similarly, Irving Browne, editor of both the *Albany Law Journal* and the *American Reports*, sagely observed of the "minority" of American courts who had adopted the English view: "The passenger cannot look to the manufacturer; the carrier can; therefore the passenger can look to the carrier. Any other rule leaves the passenger remediless."[58] The railroad corporation remained liable for any detectable defects in its equipment, even if recently acquired from a reputable manufacturer, and remained bound to see that all such equipment was regularly inspected, tested, and maintained.[59] This was not a product liability targeted on the manufacturer; it was one targeted on the lessor of the equipment, but it protected passengers and often workers as well long before *Macpherson* and *Escola*.

Other Defective Products

And this liability was not restricted to common carriers. We have already observed that it extended to users of steam boilers on land.[60] It extended as well to cities offering steam-powered drying machines to the public for injuries "caused by the negligent construction" of the dryer "set up by the defendants"; to apartment and office building partnerships for "having contracted" for them poorly designed roofs that held and then dropped snow and ice several stories on passersby; to city fire departments for defects in firehouse doors; to warehouse owners for poorly designed warehouses; to racecourse and exhibition entrepreneurs for defectively built grandstands and staircases; to manufacturing companies for their imperfectly built or imperfectly repaired equipment that injured their employees; to the owners of elevators for almost any failure of that apparatus; and to telegraph, telephone, and electrical power companies for shocks due to poor insulation, poor installation, or inadequate maintenance of their lines.[61]

In the case of electricity, the Kentucky Supreme Court was not impressed by expert testimony that "there is absolutely no perfect insulation except at great cost, which prevents it being used extensively." Justice B. L. D. Guffy found that fact "no excuse" for the failure of the Louisville Electric Light Company to "have had perfect protection on its wires." And where the defendant was not the manufacturer of the defective deodand, as with elevators, California's high court held, as with coaches and boilers, that those injured properly sued the owner-operator of the device rather than the manufacturer, because "the manufacturer was their agent or servant in the construction of the elevator, and they are responsible for any want of care of the maker or builder."[62]

Occasionally jurists revealed a sympathy for a litigant class or group in these defective products suits. These instances, however, do not provide support for the theories of those who argue that innovative instrumentalist courts favored entrepreneurs in negligence law. I offer two cases in point. When a developer had a warehouse built to his specifications and leased it to others, the Pennsylvania Supreme Court held him liable for damages when it collapsed, and Justice George Woodward's majority opinion contained this assessment: "Such is the eagerness of capitalists for large rewards, that when they undertake to build for the profits of rents, the temptation is strong to cheapen and slight the work. . . . [S]afety . . . is lost sight of in the dazzling prospect. . . . The defects [are] all the more pernicious and unpardonable, because concealed." Similarly, when a hydraulic elevator failed in a California department store, injuring those in it, Justice James Thornton affirmed judgment for one plaintiff with the observation that "the aged, the helpless, and the infirm are daily using these elevators" to the "profit" of their owners. Hence any "careless use of such contrivances" would "fall on the weakest of the community," a "cruelty" that the supreme court condemned as being contrary to the public good.[63]

Justice Thornton was not Roger Traynor; *Escola* was still over a half century in the future. Nonetheless, those injured by defective products in eighteenth- and nineteenth-century England and America had generally been able to obtain redress under the law, and this has not yet been reflected in our "stories," texts, or casebooks.

CONTRIBUTORY NEGLIGENCE: HOW MUCH A BARRIER TO TORT PLAINTIFFS?

One of the major defenses to a suit claiming damages due to negligence has for long been that the damage would not have occurred without the contributory act of negligence of the plaintiff herself. In the nineteenth century, according to Lawrence Friedman, this defense proved to be a "barrier" to the suits of such plaintiffs. If an injured party was negligent herself, "however slightly, she could not sue on the basis of defendant's negligence." By the 1850s, Friedman tells us, the trial judge was expected to take the case from the jury by nonsuiting the plaintiff who had not established that she was guilty of no contributory negligence. The doctrine was "harsh," but "extraordinarily useful": "It became a favorite method through which judges kept tort claims from the deliberations of the jury. . . . If plaintiff was clearly negligent himself, there could be no recovery. . . . A judge could take the case from the jury and dismiss it."[64]

Friedman's (and everyone else's) authority for this description of the rule is Wex Malone's seminal essay on "the formative era of contributory negligence."[65] Malone based his view of the rule on cases from the state of New York:

> The stage on which the story unfolds is, of course, nationwide, but little can be gained from a random sampling of cases from diverse jurisdictions. . . . The *general* outline is about the same everywhere. A more comprehensible picture can be gained from a compact study of a single jurisdiction. . . . The decisions of the appellate courts of New York seem to afford us a fairly representative cross section of judicial experience for our purposes.[66]

Both Malone and Friedman cite from *Haring* v. *New York & Erie RR* (1852) as "typical of these cases." John Haring was killed by a train while crossing the tracks in a sleigh driven by a friend. The trial court judge nonsuited the plaintiff, Haring's wife, imputing the contributory negligence of the sleigh's driver to Haring. The intermediate appellate court, citing a prerailroad-era New York precedent for judicial nonsuit, in a tort action, affirmed the trial judge's action. Friedman quotes dicta from Justice Seward Barculo's opinion:

> We cannot shut our eyes that in certain controversies between the weak and the strong—between a humble individual and a gigantic corporation, the sympathies of the human mind naturally, honestly and generously, run to the assistance and support of the feeble. . . . Compassion will sometimes exercise over the . . . jury an influence which, however honorable to them as philanthropists, is wholly inconsistent with the principles of law and the ends of justice.[67]

There is some truth, to be sure, in what Malone and Friedman have claimed; careful analysis of the development and denouement of a given rule in a single jurisdiction over a century or more can yield valuable insights, as Kim Scheppele's study of caveat emptor cases in nineteenth-century New York appellate courts demonstrates, and as Wex Malone's fine study did as well. Malone pointed out that New York jurists, confronted with a growing stream of appeals involving contributory-negligence claims, developed a "physical facts approach" that led them to nonsuit plaintiffs when the evidence clearly indicated that they had crossed the tracks of an oncoming train without care, despite the presence of smoke or noise, that they had not looked or listened for the train and had a clear view of its approach. He indicated that courts used this reasoning when they were "determined that recovery is not to be allowed," and he opined that "courts everywhere" subscribe to "the bare proposition that careless plaintiffs cannot recover for the sole reason that they are unworthy of legal protection."

But, paradoxically, Malone also demonstrated that many New York appellate decisions involving contributory-negligence defenses resulted in plaintiff *victories*, despite the practice of nonsuiting utterly unworthy complainants. Even though judges were now controlling access to the jury, some sort of objective "justice" still may have prevailed. Trial judges nonsuited only one in every six tort plaintiffs suing corporations in New York City in 1870, 1890, and 1910.[68] Negligent railroads could not escape liability via a judicial nonsuit where the evidence of the plaintiff's contributory negligence had been contested; the issue was then for the jury to decide unless the evidence was "uncontrovertible." Such "uncontrovertible" instances, however, were "rare." In *Haring* Justice Seward Barculo of the New York Supreme Court (*not* the state's highest court) might criticize juries in his dicta in 1852, but the views of jurists on the highest court in the state were more likely to criticize the railroad defendants' "struggle" to "induce the courts to resort to artificial refinements for the protection of wrongdoers." "Human life" was more important than "the objects of commercial and corporate enterprise," wrote Justice John Porter of the Court of Appeals in his *long* opinion in *Ernst* v. *Hudson River Railroad* (1866), and no stop-look-and-listen dictum would be read to empower a judge to bar the plaintiff's access to a jury finding.[69] Moreover, in "most" of the cases where the plaintiff's nonsuit had prevailed (or been ordered), the reason appeared to be that evidence of the railroad defendants' negligence "was meager," whereas the plaintiff's had been significant: "Usually the victim's conduct had produced a situation with which the defendant could not reasonably be expected to cope."[70]

Contributory negligence, then, had served to defeat many tort plaintiffs in nineteenth-century New York State, and the same defense would continue to defeat many of them throughout most of the twentieth century. But Malone's insightful, if paradoxical account is flawed in two significant ways. First, he claimed that when children were hit at railroad crossings or in street accidents, courts "had no difficulty" in "retaining the practical benefits of the contributory negligence doctrine as a jury control device" by means of the "amazingly simple trick of *imputing* the parents' negligence" to the child.[71] (I will consider and dispute Malone's claim in this regard in

97

chapter 8.) Second, Malone was incorrect in claiming that "the decisions of the appellate courts of New York" constituted "a fairly representative cross section of judicial experience" on this subject,[72] because with regard to the most important aspect of the subject, the right of judges to nonsuit plaintiffs who had not established a prima facie case that they were free of contributory negligence, New York jurists were part of a distinct *minority* of American jurisdictions.

Contributory negligence was a defense to tort actions as long ago as the fourteenth century. It is clearly present in *Goodson* v. *Walkin* (1376). A dismounted rider's horse bolted through a town center, injuring a woman who had responded to the rider's calls for assistance by trying to catch hold of the reins. When the injured woman sued, the defendant's plea was that the plaintiff's injuries were "due to [her] foolishness and fault" in her "attempt to stop the horse." One can hear judicial nonsuits based on it as early as *Bayly* v. *Merrel* (1606), where it was said of the plaintiff that "being his own negligence, he is without remedy." Defendants' barrister in *Newby* v. *Wiltshire* (1785) told King's Bench that a farmer was not "liable to pay for an accident arising from the neglect of his servant, who was wrongfully riding on the shafts" of a wagon when the horse "took fright" and the servant fell and was run over. He believed the plaintiff should have been nonsuited for his contributory negligence.[73] Some English opinions dating from the late eighteenth century and first decade of the nineteenth century, however, appear to have left the question of the significance of the plaintiff's negligence up to the jury,[74] and at least one of these cases seem to place the burden of proof in this regard on the defendant.[75] Some of these cases involved vehicles colliding, the sorts of cases Malone and Friedman identify as the impetus for the contributory-negligence rule; but several of them involve more traditional, static problems of the years before the transportation revolution.[76] What would be the rules that the various American jurisdictions would adopt as the transportation revolution produced increasing numbers of accidents in the nineteenth century?

Some state high courts did as New York's did: they held that, in addition to showing "some negligence and misconduct on the part of the defendant," a tort plaintiff was expected to show "ordinary care and diligence on his own part."[77] The plaintiff who failed to establish that he had been free of contributory negligence might well find himself nonsuited by the judge, though this would be likely to happen only in "extraordinary" circumstances.[78] By the 1880s this was the law in New York, Massachusetts, and five other jurisdictions. But by 1900 over twenty other jurisdictions (including the federal system in diversity cases) required defendants, not plaintiffs, to prove the plaintiff guilty of contributory negligence, and since these claims were invariably contested by the plaintiffs, the high courts of these jurisdictions directed that the question of the plaintiffs' contributory negligence should be left to the jury.[79]

This pronounced propensity of most American benches, contrary to what Wex Malone had claimed, to leave to the jury the question of whether the plaintiff should lose on the grounds of her contributory negligence clearly mattered. How do we know? We now have studies of trial court jury verdicts in 776 tort actions against corporations between 1835 and 1910 from two counties and one federal court in California, two counties in Illinois, one county in Wisconsin, the courts of St. Louis, Missouri, a county in southern West Virginia, and the courts of New York City and Boston. Plaintiffs won 551 (71 percent) of these.[80] Some of these were brought by employees, others by passengers. In the former of these instances the contributory-negligence defense was less valuable to defendants than the assumption-of-risk and fellow-servant defenses; in the latter, contributory negligence was often an ineffective corporate weapon against paying passengers.

Its most common and crucial use by corporate defendants was in railroad crossing, streetcar, and road and sidewalk suits. Randolph Bergstrom provides a breakdown of personal injury jury verdicts in New York City for the years 1870, 1890, and 1910 in which the defendant was the government. These primarily involved road and sidewalk injuries. Plaintiffs won 76 percent of these (37 of 49). He also tells us that plaintiffs won at 72 of 126 trials in which the plaintiff had been injured by a streetcar, but he does not disaggregate these further into those lost by nonsuit or dismissal and those lost by jury verdict. I have extrapolated from his separate table that *does* disaggregate trial outcomes in that fashion from his column of data where the defendant was a corporation, as streetcar companies were. When one takes midtrial settlements, judicial nonsuits and dismissals into account, it seems likely that in cases in which plaintiffs were injured by streetcars and the case went to the jury, the verdicts were for the plaintiff about 80 percent of the time.[81] When we recall that a tort plaintiff in New York had to prove both that the defendant had been negligent and that she had *not* been contributorily negligent, we can see that, for the jury to have found for the plaintiff, it had to have been satisfied by the plaintiff's evidence on both accounts. If we assume that each of the degrees of difficulty of these burdens of proof was about equal, then we can calculate the approximate frequency with which juries found for defendants because of plaintiff contributory negligence (rate of jury verdicts for defendants attributable to plaintiff contributory negligence = overall rate of jury verdicts for defendants divided by rate of jury verdicts for defendants on grounds of defendants' lack of negligence, where both subrates are about equal). This rate is about one in every eight instances, and it is a rate that finds confirmation in the remark of counsel to one defendant corporation in California in 1891 who asked the Supreme Court not to let his client be "handed over to the tender mercies of another anti-corporation jury."[82] It finds further confirmation in the responses of some 31 trial judges from around the country surveyed by Wex Malone on this subject in the early 1940s. Thirteen of these judges said that juries "never" found plaintiffs guilty of contributory negligence and eight others said that they "generally" didn't; only seven said that juries *were* willing to find for defendants on these grounds.[83]

What is the significance of all these calculations? If judges nonsuited plaintiffs for contributory negligence in only one of every six trials in which the question arose, if three times as many jurisdictions did not *permit* judges to nonsuit these plaintiffs but left the question as one of fact for the jury, and if plaintiffs lost jury verdicts because of their contributory negligence in only one of every eight instances, then the contributory-negligence defense was a rather modest "barrier" to tort plaintiffs. "Mr. Dooley" once remarked that a rule that seemed to be an impenetrable wall to others could appear as "a Triumphal Arch" to an attorney. "Ambulance chasing" attorneys in the second half of the nineteenth century did not view the contributory-negligence defense as a Triumphal Arch, but neither need they have viewed it as a really dangerous bar to the progress of their client's case.

Plaintiffs' counsel were not, however, forced to rely solely on the "tender mercies" of (generally) anticorporate juries in tort actions. In the second half of the nineteenth century they teased from sympathetic benches some still more effective rules against tort defendants. Among these were: the rule that a defendant was held to have received "constructive notice" of a dangerous condition (such as ice on a sidewalk) if it had existed for enough time that it *should* have been detected by ordinary prudence;[84] the rule that a plaintiff injured or killed while going to the aid of another was not to be regarded as having so acted in a contributorily negligent manner;[85] the rule that a plaintiff injured or killed in circumstances in which the defendant's negligence "spoke for itself" had no burden of proof of that negligence to overcome;[86] and the rule that the party (often the defendant) with the "last clear chance" of avoiding the accident would be regarded as being liable for the injury despite evidence of plaintiff contributory negligence.[87] The tendency of many jurists to mitigate the harsh effects of the contributory-negligence rule is captured nicely in this passage from the appellate opinion of President Judge Clark Hare of the Philadelphia District Court in a case involving the running down of a youth by a tram car in 1868:

> The thoroughfares of a great city . . . are often filled with an incessant stream of carriages of various kinds, and hours may elapse before the way is clear. [One] pressed by the claims of business or duty, may be unable to wait, and compelled to venture into the throng; under these circumstances, the surrounding vehicles should obviously be driven with the utmost care, and stopped, if necessary, to allow him to cross in safety. If any presumptions are indulged, they should not be against the weaker party, who may be presumed to have endeavored to avoid a collision by which he must necessarily be the sufferer.[88]

PROXIMATE CAUSE, LOCOMOTIVE SPARKS, AND *RYAN V. N.Y. CENTRAL RR*

Related to the issue of contributory negligence is the doctrine of proximate cause. According to several accounts, American railroad attorneys in the 1860s, 1870s, and 1880s, in concert with the legal essayist Francis Wharton and jurists in New York and Pennsylvania, developed a "brilliant" way to defeat a pesky class of negligence claims with the proximate-cause defense. Under the umbrella of proximate cause, a defendant was not held liable for damage flowing from an act of his negligence unless the damage complained of was caused in a "direct and natural," interconnected, or "proximate" fashion by the negligent act. Any intervening force or actor that altered the flow of events eliminated the liability of the negligent defendant, as his causality then became "remote" from the harm. The principle was traced to Lord Chancellor Bacon's first maxim, *In jure non remota causa, sed proxima spectatur* (The law looks for proximate, not remote causes in assessing liability or guilt). The maxim itself was ancient; its use in the mid-nineteenth century on behalf of railroads however, was innovative, or so we are told. The most noteworthy case of this is said to have occurred in 1866, *Ryan v. New York Central RR*. The New York Court of Appeals "let down the veil" and used in *Ryan* the proximate-remote distinction that other courts had "manipulated . . . in other cases to limit entrepreneurial liability."[89] A fire had spread from a railroad shed to fields and houses and ultimately to a house 130 feet from the shed. When the owner of that house sued and the case reached the New York high court, Justice Ward Hunt opined that the spread of fire in this fashion was "not a necessary or a usual result" and that, in any event, holding the railroad liable as the actor having created

101

the proximate cause of the damage "would subject it to a liability against which no prudence could guard, and to meet which no private fortune would be adequate."[90] The court had utilized the proximate cause rule to protect an important railroad corporation from the "deep pockets" reach of a potentially proplaintiff jury.[91]

One account focusses on *Ryan* in explaining the "strong and supple" doctrine of proximate cause; other accounts are more interested in proximate cause's jurisprudential critic, Nicholas St. John Green, and its defender, Francis Wharton.[92] In 1870, Green's essay on the subject appeared in the *American Law Review*. Rejecting the medieval Scholasticism of the "natural sequence" test used by judges and jurists, he offered John Stuart Mill's concept of multiple causation in its place. Instead of mindlessly tracing causality as if things, and not persons, were at fault, jurists should be asking who was responsible for what "might reasonably have been foreseen." In 1874 Wharton responded. He railed against those critical of the "proximate cause" test, those who preferred to speak of "multiple causation" and "foreseeability." Such attention to foreseeability would mean that "non-Capitalists" would avoid their liability as plaintiffs and juries went after "the rich corporation": "Here is a capitalist among these antecedents; he shall be forced to pay."[93]

Wharton, a deeply religious attorney who became a "low church" Episcopal theologian in the 1860s, actually spent far more of his critique metaphysically arguing with John Stuart Mill and with American pragmatism about free will and "the materialistic view" of causality; his concern for the "deep pockets" and future of capitalists, stockholders, and employees occupied very little of his attention. But economic-oriented accounts do not misrepresent Wharton. He, and Justice Hunt, the author of *Ryan*, clearly do serve up arguments for a narrow and conservative understanding of corporate liability under the proximate cause doctrine. But one may still ask how fairly economic-oriented legal history has represented the judiciary's use of proximate cause to railroad advantage in the nineteenth century by drawing our attention almost exclusively to *Ryan* or Wharton.[94] Was the proximate-cause defense as much a creature of the age of railroads as has been said? How new was it? And exactly how useful was it to railroad counsels? Was it distinguished from, and in jurisprudential conflict with, a "foreseeability" principle, allegedly enunciated first in the writings of Charles Peirce and Nicholas St. John Green in 1870 and the lectures of Oliver Wendell Holmes Jr. in 1881? Was this "foreseeability" principle not given any practical weight by practicing jurists until Justice Benjamin Cardozo's famed *Macpherson* v. *Buick Motors* opinion in 1916?

Railroad attorneys certainly did argue that the damages plaintiffs had suffered were remotely, rather than proximately caused by the alleged negligence of company agents. But they were making use of a defense that was in widespread use in tortious actions by the time that locomotive sparks began to ignite fires that damaged property, locomotives began to plough into hogs and cattle, or conductors began to eject drunks from passenger cars. We are told that Thomas Shearman and Amasa Redfield "cited the only four American cases they could find on proximate cause" in the 1869 edition of their treatise on negligence, and that the "defense of proximate cause was almost unknown in antebellum America." How many times *did* courts address the proximate-cause issue before Shearman and Redfield's treatise appeared?

I can identify a (very incomplete) list of some twenty-five such cases (not counting at least four English cases on the subject in these years). Let us turn first to the cases in which no railroad was involved. Plaintiffs and defendants had been arguing about what was proximate, what remote, in cases involving lighted squibs flung into crowds, threats that allegedly led to economic loss, the spread of infectious disease in herds and flocks, the illegal or inappropriate sale of liquor, goods damaged on canalboats, and a donkey fettered in a highway at night. By the late 1840s American jurists had available to them the language and citations in Simon Greenleaf's and Theodore Sedgwick's treatises on the laws of evidence and damages on the subject: For the plaintiff to prevail against this particular defendant, the wrong suffered had "always [to] be the natural and proximate consequence of the act complained of."[95] Defendants won only one in eleven of these arguments (one in three of those in England).[96] Did *railroad* defendants fare any better?

I identified some twenty-six suits charging railroads with negligence between 1847 and 1880 (fourteen of them before 1870) where either counsel or the court discussed a proximate/remote cause defense; needless to say, *Ryan v. New York Central* (1866) was one of these. The "remote cause" defense was successful, as had been the case with nonrailroad defendants, in only two[97] of these twenty-six cases.[98] Consistent with their policies regarding damage to freight, injury to passengers or strangers at crossings, eminent domain "takings," and child trespassers,[99] courts held railroad corporations to a higher standard of care in these cases than they did other negligence defendants who had raised the "remote, not proximate" defense. Railroads, they repeated, were dangerous, they were profit-making, and they were "common carriers."

On balance, then, the proximate-remote distinction appears to have been a very weak reed for a defendant to lean upon, even if the defendant's name ended in "RR." But how did jurists deal with Justice Hunt's reasoning in *Ryan*? How did they answer Francis Wharton's various metaphysical and practical objections? Several met these head on. Generally, they offered two responses: one from the Head, the other from the Heart. The first was a matter of logic and science. For Hunt to call the spread of fire from one building over a field to another building, and thence to a third, "not a necessary or [a] usual result" struck several jurists as outrageous, illogical, and unscientific. Justice Reuben Chapman of the Massachusetts Supreme Court of Judicature addressed *Ryan* two years after its appearance. Sparks from an Eastern Railroad locomotive had created a fire that spread steadily to a thirty-five-acre woodland some half a mile from the tracks. The railroad's counsel, citing *Ryan*, argued on appeal that the damage was "remote and not proximately caused." Chapman offered a different view of what was meant by "proximate cause" with regard to such fires, a view widely shared both in England and nearly all American jurisdictions. The railroad was as liable as if it had "caused a bullet" to be "fired from the train":

> If, when the cinder escapes through the air, the effect which it produces upon the first combustible substance against which it strikes is proximate, the effect must continue to be proximate, as to everything the fire consumes in its direct course. This is so, whether we regard the fire as a combination of the burning substance with the oxygen in the air, or look merely at its visible action and effect.[100]

Similarly, a sawmill operating in East Saginaw, Michigan, without a spark arrester precipitated wood embers from a chimney some three hundred feet to one building, which then communicated the fire to a hotel. In 1874 the sawmill's counsel sought to overturn a verdict for the hotel owner by arguing that the jury should have been told that the sawmill owner was only liable for the loss of property in "actual contact" with the first object to burn. Its liability should cease, as in *Ryan*, "where there is an intervening space between" the subject of the "proximate" fire and the "remote" one, inasmuch as property owners were expected to be on their guard against such "remote" dangers. But the Michigan Supreme Court treated this argument as "ludicrously absurd." It was "an axiom in natural philosophy that no two particles of matter actually touch each other," but that did not lead one to conclude that one who fired one particle should not be responsible when the adjacent particle burst into flames as well. Juries were free to use their common sense in deciding whether a defendant, whose negligently caused fire to spread from property A to properties B_1 to B_{1+n} under weather conditions C, should be regarded as being the cause of damage to property

B_{1+n}, and since this jury had found the defendant liable, under proper instructions, the judgement was affirmed.[101]

The second response to *Ryan* and Wharton reflected the nineteenth-century judicial concern for morality and fairness. A farmer whose unfenced hogs strayed onto the Cleveland, Columbus, and Cincinnati Railroad's right-of-way and were killed won an appeal to the Ohio Supreme Court in 1854. He successfully charged the engineer's negligence with being the proximate cause of the accident, and Chief Justice Thomas Bartley, citing *Davies* v. *Mann*, agreed. Bartley concluded the opinion with a ringing reaffirmation of the maxim *Sic utere tuo, ut alienum non laedas* (Use your property, but not to the injury of others). It stood, as in this case, for the "protection of which the *weakest* are entitled, and from the observance of which, the most *powerful* are not exempt."[102]

Similarly, when a railroad-generated fire spread from one house to another and the latter sued, Illinois chief justice Charles Lawrence, in a frequently cited opinion, rejected the railroad counsel's argument that the *Ryan* rule had to be adopted or "these companies would be in constant danger of bankruptcy." Inasmuch as Lawrence wrote this in the fall of 1871, he may have had rather immediate knowledge of what one great urban fire, "proximately" caused by Mrs. O'Leary's cow on October 8, 1871, had done. If so, he was, indeed, conscious of the risk of bankruptcy for fire liability. Lawrence allowed that this danger might exist and he also allowed that "the railroads" were "useful . . . to the regions they traverse," but he reminded counsel that "they are not operated by their owners for benevolent purposes, or to promote the general welfare. Their object is pecuniary profit." If, by placing the loss where it belongs, "on the head of the guilty," the consequence was to be "the bankruptcy of a railway company, we may regret it, but we should not . . . hesitate in the application of a rule of such palpable justice." *Ryan*, he observed,

> proceeds upon the assumption that if a great loss is to be suffered, it had better be distributed among a hundred innocent victims than wholly visited upon the wrongdoer. As a question of law or ethics this proposition does not commend itself to our reason. We must still cling to the ancient doctrine, that the wanton wrongdoer must take the consequences of his own act, whether measured by a thousand dollars or a hundred thousand.

Wisconsin's Chief Justice Luther Dixon took a similarly unsympathetic view of the argument of counsel to the Chicago and Northwest Railroad. A fire created by sparks from one of the company's locomotives had spread from the overgrown and untended railroad right-of-way to adjacent property, jumped a brook three feet wide, and eventually burned the plaintiff's haystacks, shed, and stable some one-half mile from the tracks. Counsel had pressed the logic and precedent of *Ryan* upon the high court, but Dixon and the majority did not feel that the plaintiff and other landowners were obliged to plough precautionary fire breaks at the outer perimeters of their property because the railroad had not properly cleared its right-of-way. The plaintiff was "not his [railroad] neighbor's guardian or keeper, and not to answer for his neglect." To expect such measures would be to impose "a great tax upon his time and patience." Such a doctrine of avoidance might require that whole houses and buildings would have to be removed, and valuable timber cut down and destroyed, whereas it was "vastly easier, by a few slight measures and a little precaution," for the railroad simply to maintain a right-of-way free of combustible matter.[103]

Law and economics devotees may not be entirely satisfied with the American judiciary's lack of appreciation of the economic inefficiency, the consequent unfairness, of this rule, but one member of that school has readily acknowledged that this *was* the view of a distinct majority of American jurists in the second half of the nineteenth century.[104] *Ryan* was "bad law" or "no law at all."[105]

Quite independent of the question of proximate cause in these cases of railroad fires was the more fundamental one, of the negligence of the railroad with regard to the release of the coals, sparks, embers, or cinders. On this subject, two jurists did not lean as far in the direction of the farmers' point of view as did most, but offered Learned Hand's cost-benefit reasoning. In England, Williams, J., instructed a jury in 1860, regarding the London and Northwestern Railway's liability with regard to its failure to use the superior "American spark catcher," that "if the damage to be avoided were insignificant, or very unlikely to occur, and the remedy suggested were very costly or troublesome," they should find the railroad innocent of negligence.[106] Similarly, U.S. Supreme Court Justice Samuel Miller, riding circuit, offered these instructions to a jury in a case where a steamboat's sparks had been the proximate cause of fire damage to a plaintiff: "If steamboats must adopt various apparatus thereby increasing their expenses, they must charge them upon the products of the country transported by them. On the other hand, if they can dispense with such things without too great danger, it is to the interest of the people for them to do it."[107]

Learned Hand and Richard Posner of the Law and Economics school would have found these instructions quite "efficient" within the framework of their formula (negligence attaches if the cost of avoidance of the damage is less than the probable damage). But they would have to acknowledge that the much more common position taken on the subject was that of Iowa's Justice Joseph Beck on behalf of a rule imposing virtually absolute liability on railroads in that state for fires caused by sparks and cinders from locomotive stacks. The rule was just, Beck maintained, because it "will stimulate discoveries of contrivances and the making of experiments, with a view to ascertain means that will most nearly remove all [company] liability [for] fires communicated by railway locomotives."[108] In the meantime, railroads would pay for fires they caused, despite any "remote" causal neglect of the farmers whose homes, barns, wheat stacks, hay ricks, and woodlands were consumed by the flames. As Missouri's Justice Philemon Bliss put it, the plaintiff-farmer's negligence was "remote": "The wrongful act of kindling the fire is the proximate cause of the injury, and not the neglect of cleaning up the fence corners, of which, unfortunately, most of our farmers are guilty."[109] Consequently, most railroad companies ordered their firemen "to feed the engine cautiously, aiming at 'smokeless firing'" in order to prevent "engine sparks, which," as James Ducker says in his study of the Atchinson, Topeka and Santa Fe, "caused the Santa Fe great financial difficulty when they set fire to farmers' crops."[110]

This brings us to our final question regarding fires and other property damage along rights-of-way caused by railroad negligence: Is it true that the intellectual origins of "foreseeability" is to be found first in the writings of those theorists in the 1870s, a full generation before the principle's courtroom appearance as an element of the law of negligence in Cardozo's *Macpherson* decision?[111] I think not. Jurists in England and America were using the foreseeability test in negligence cases at least sixty-five years before any of these three legal philosophers wrote a word on the subject.[112] In ten of twenty-three appellate cases involving proximate-cause defenses to charges of negligence that appear in the appellate reports *before* 1870, the courts clearly applied a foreseeability test. The authors of these opinions defined the "reasonable care" expected of defendants as the "probable consequences" that could be "anticipated," or as care that should be appropriately "proportioned to the probable dangers of injury." Defendants were responsible only for what might "be foreseen by ordinary forecast," for things that were "a necessary or a usual result."[113] Thus if "the damage was not too remote of accordance to the usual expectation of mankind," Justice Dwight Foster of Massachusetts explained in 1867, "the result was to be expected," and in the case before him, he thought the evidence indicated that the results had been "likely to ensue from the act," that the chain of accidents could be said to have been a "foreseen result" of the defendant's negligence.[114] In the process, Foster criticized Lord Chancellor Bacon's proxima maxim as being "not particularly useful." He was not alone among jurists in these years in this regard.[115] Others recognized its shortcomings. Thus when Vermont's famed former chief justice, Isaac Redfield, commented on Nicholas St. John Green's essay critiquing the maxim as having "no application to the exposition of the law," it was to say that he "had come to the same conclusion long before [h]e received Mr. Green's article; but of course, upon less investigation and study."[116]

ASSUMPTION OF RISK: MAKING WORKERS SUBJECT TO EMPLOYERS' POWER?

When Nicholas Farwell, an engineer for the Boston and Worcester Railroad, was injured by a switchman's error in 1837, he sued the company. The case found its way to the Massachusetts Supreme Court in 1842, and Chief Justice Lemuel Shaw's opinion for the court became one of the most cited in legal history. Shaw grounded the court's rejection of Farwell's claims on a "rule" and a "doctrine": the fellow-servant doctrine (which we will consider in the next unit of this chapter) and the assumption-of-risk rule. The latter had it that in accepting work as a railroad engineer for "a higher rate than the plaintiff had before received as a machinist," Farwell had, by implication, contracted to assume in exchange certain risks associated with the job. As such, he was unable to claim damages from his employer for injuries incurred in the ordinary course of his employment.[117]

Shaw's ruling has had its share of critics. "Shaw freed some capital for further business investment" by this ruling, "and, thereby, provided through the law an indirect subsidy for early industrial expansion."[118] The assumption-of-risk rule in *Farwell* meant that "*free-willed* actors" could both "take on 'ordinary risks and perils' and be made to 'follow the directions of their employer.'" The worker thus became "subject to the employer's power."[119]

How warranted are these verdicts? *Was* the *Farwell* decision an innovative boon for Capitalists? How remarkable is it that workers could be seen both as "free-willed" and as subject to "the directions of their employer"? *Did* the rule reduce the employee to a powerless being unable to sue when injured after having been ordered to engage in hazardous work? *Should* courts have held that a kind of disability insurance was implied in the labor contract?

The assumption-of-risk rule was "harsh," but it was not new, nor was it an unreasonable instance of a new "contract ideology" that "emasculated all prior conceptions of substantive justice."[120] The principles in Farwell

108

(and its English predecessor, *Priestley* v. *Fowler* [1837])[121] were not molded for entrepreneurial use in the emerging industrial age, but were of more ancient lineage. Shakespeare understood them. His Henry V, in disguise on the eve of Agincourt, tells one of his soldiers that "the Master" is "not bound to answer the particular endings" of his servant, any more than the king is "of his soldiers," because master and monarch alike "purpose not" their servants' death "when they purpose their services."[122] Servants and soldiers assumed risks in Georgian England, just as they had in Elizabeth's time. Thus counsel for the defendant in an appeal to King's Bench in 1785 argued, successfully, that there was "no implied contract" to compensate one injured in the service of his master.[123] Fifty-one years later, on the *eve* of *Priestley*, the Virginia Supreme Court was told that miners were paid "a premium, in truth," of 25 to 30 percent "greater . . . than for ordinary service" for "the risque incurred."[124] The liability of employers for workers injured on the work site was clearly limited by the assumption-of-risk concept before *Priestley.* That was why a reader of Saunders's *Law of Pleading and Evidence* (1837 ed.) who turned to "Master and Servant" learned that questions of contract were at the heart of master liability to a servant, and was referred not to "Tort" but to "Agents" for additional information.

Moreover, workers, no less than employers, judges, and jurymen understood the risks when they accepted hazardous work, just as they understand them now. Some may have had few obvious options available to them; young men coming of age in mining communities come to mind here. But others clearly did have options. No one in eighteenth- or nineteenth-century America was *obliged* to accept the recruiting sergeant's shilling, and those who did realized that they might be killed in military service. One who worked on a farm understood that he or she had assumed certain risks (sinkholes, charging bulls) that could not lawfully be charged to the landowner.[125] One who took service on a whaler or merchantman said farewell to his loved ones with a clear sense of the perils of the sea. Work as a pony express rider, an overland stage driver, a miner, a circus roustabout, or, yes, a railroad engineer was just as dangerous, and seen as such, in 1850 as deep-sea fishing, high-rise construction, and most professional sports in the 1990s.[126]

Charles (probably "Charlie") Clifford sued the Overland Mail Company in 1862 for wrongful discharge. His complaint allowed that his compensation included the risks he had agreed to take. The route he was to drive (Arkansas to Los Angeles) was "full of danger," a risk that he had himself "set out as inducement to the contract for wages." He had been "grievously wounded by the hostile Indians infesting said rout," and he "would not have engaged to drive and work" with "the dangers of said road" unless the company had agreed to pay him seventy-five dollars per month (which they had for six months) and to allow him "to work for the company as long as the plaintiff saw fit."[127] Similarly, John Cook and his wife signed a contract with the Western and Atlantic Railroad for wages that were "more than he can get elsewhere" in consideration for his taking "upon himself all risk connected with . . . his position on the road." And the Cook's contract was not unique. The *implied* assumption of risk in Nicholas Farwell's case was, by the next decade, being made quite explicit in some railroad employment contracts.[128]

In reaction, railroad workers took steps to insure themselves against the risks of their trade. Private insurance firms in midcentury charged "enormously heavy rates," styling their work "extra hazardous."[129] Consequently, in 1867 the Locomotive Engineers' Union formed the Locomotive Engineers Mutual Life Insurance Association. Other such associations of firemen, conductors, and trainmen followed. By 1870 some 129 life insurance companies in the United States were distributing some $26 million per year to beneficiaries, some $39 million by 1880.

Many companies offered their own insurance funds. In 1869 the Central Pacific Railroad asked its employees for $6 per year (about 1 to 1.5 percent of the typical worker's annual salary) for full medical and hospital care, and in 1880 the Baltimore and Ohio Railroad organized the B&O Employee's Relief Association. The company assumed the costs of administration and donated a substantial initial endowment. Membership was compulsory. Employees paid one-thirtieth of their monthly wages and received up to fifty-two weeks of sickness or death benefits. Some 4,167 claims were processed in the first year of the association's existence, and the association became a model for other railroad companies. By 1907 some 49 percent of all workers involved in accidents in New York state carried accident insurance. A number of railroad, textile, and mining companies without such funds paid injured workers or their spouses as much as $5,000 in gifts or settlements, among them a donation of $720 to Nicholas Farwell *after* he had lost the appeal of his case before the Massachusetts Supreme Court; but many other employee victims got little or nothing.[130]

I am not implying that the summary effect of mutual associations, company hospitals, company sickness and death funds, and company largesse amounted to just and adequate compensation for those maimed or killed in the service of enterprise. Nor do I believe that the statutory creation of workman's compensation and the abrogation of the assumption of risk rule were unwise or unnecessary. Quite the contrary. I simply mean to point out that nineteenth-century workers understood that they had assumed the risks of injury on the job, that they accepted, however reluctantly, that it was their responsibility to insure themselves against the risks of injury or death from hazardous work, and that they did so, either privately, through trade unions, or company associations.

In English courts workers suing their employers for injuries faced the very real prospect of being nonsuited by the trial judge on the ground that they had assumed the risks. "It may be inhuman," Bramwell, B., opined, for an employer to use equipment "more or less dangerous to his workmen," but the practice didn't "create a right of action" for the worker who knew that this was so. Hence, as Pollock, C. B., put it in the same case, "there was nothing for the jury [properly to have been left to decide]."[131] Crompton, J., was even more explicit in his instructions to a jury in 1865, which he "left" to "decide" whether the defendant railroad had failed in its duty to employ competent co-workers for one injured, or whether the injured plaintiff had assumed the risk in his employment contract. After reviewing the evidence, he had concluded that "if you should find a verdict . . . for the plaintiff, I should hardly think it satisfactory. . . . You ought to find for the company." The Court of Exchequer decided, as well, that the case of a sheet roller injured in a Sheffield steel works had also been properly taken from the jury: "He was aware of [the dangers], and took his wages on that footing, and it has been held that he has, under those circumstances, no more claim than the soldier who takes the Queen's shilling, for danger in the service. . . . Cases of this kind ought not to be left to the jury on a mere spark of evidence."[132]

However, what may have been "held" in England was sometimes released in America. The benches here generally allowed *juries* to decide, as a question of fact (or as "mixed fact and law"), whether the plaintiff had, as alleged by the defendant, indeed assumed the risk of the injury she suffered as one of the terms of her contract. Treatises on the law of negligence, or that of master-servant relations, published in the 1870s and 1880s, as well as the notes to the cases cited in the various assumption-of-risk subcategories to the massive "Master and Servant" entry in the Century Edition of the *American Digest* (1897), clearly demonstrate that in the vast majority of appeals involving the assumption-of-risk defense, American jurists left the question as one of fact to the jury.[133]

Moreover, many courts interpreted the rule far more "liberally" than did their English counterparts. The American worker assumed "ordinary" risks, Indiana's Justice Andrew Davison noted in 1856, "but this can only be intended to mean such 'dangers and perils' as necessarily attend the business when conducted with ordinary care and prudence. He can not be presumed to have contracted with reference to injuries inflicted on him by negligence [!]"[134]

Specifically, the assumption-of-risk defense could not protect one who had negligently injured a slave (before 1866) or a chain-gang convict (after 1866), neither of whom had been parties to any employment contract when their masters leased their labor.[135] The defense also failed, and employers were held to be liable if they had not provided a safe place and safe equipment for their employees,[136] had not provided competent fellow servants,[137] had failed to make known to them any extraordinary risks that the employees might not easily discover themselves,[138] or ordered them to perform unfamiliar dangerous duties for which they lacked training and skills. Thus when a laborer was crushed to death coupling cars under orders from a superintending foreman, and his survivor was nonsuited at trial in 1868, her appeal to the Illinois Supreme Court succeeded in overruling that nonsuit, which allowed the question of whether her husband could fairly be said to have assumed that risk to be put to a jury. Chief Justice Sidney Breese pointed out that this laborer's status had been "so subordinate as to compel him to yield implicit obedience" to the foreman's command. "The law would be lamentably deficient did it furnish no remedy in such a case." Isaac Redfield, the former chief justice of Vermont's Supreme Court and author of the leading treatise on railroad law, agreed. The rule holding an employer liable for injuries to an employee ordered to do unfamiliar work "commends itself to all lovers of justice," even though it "may encounter some distrust from that large class of the profession who, from habit or education, look *first* to symmetry and then to justice."[139]

Similarly, when employees complained of defects and hazards, and were told to continue working, American courts generally held employers liable despite their appeal to the assumption-of-risk rule. Iowa's Chief Justice James Day quoted approvingly Thomas Shearman and Amasa Redfield on the subject in 1871: It was "unjust" to nonsuit such a plaintiff, for "the dependent position of servants generally makes it reasonable to hold any notice on their part sufficient, however timid and hesitating, so long as it plainly conveys to the master the idea that a defect exists, and that they desire its removal."[140] Employees "act in subordination" to employers, Missouri's Justice David Wagner observed a propos the issue, and they rely "wholly on the judgement" of those above them in the company. To nonsuit employees injured after they had warned employers of dangers and then continued working was "a cruel and inhuman doctrine" (to Virginia's Justice Robert Richardson) because employees "may be virtually compelled to remain by the stern necessity of earning the daily bread essential to keep away starvation itself."[141]

No one put the case against the assumption-of-risk rule more forcefully than former St. Louis Court of Appeals judge Seymour Thompson. In 1897 this self-taught midwestern Solon, treatise writer, and counsel to corporate giants exploded in anger at those among his colleagues in Missouri who regarded the rule as sufficient defense against the claims of the survivors of brakemen killed atop cars when struck by low bridges. His opening attack has a Law and Economics flavor, but he quickly moved from his Head to his Heart:

> I do not want my professional brethren to think for one moment that I balance the life of a railway brakeman against the slight expense to a railway company of blocking its frogs and switches. I should be sorry to have them think that I ever was willing to balance the life of railway brakeman against the slight expense to a railway company of building the upper works of its bridges sufficiently high for a brakeman to stand upon the top of his car without coming in contact with them. These are murder-machines; and the rule of judge-made law which holds the servant at all times and under all circumstances, bound to avoid them at his peril, is a draconic rule. It is destitute of any semblance of justice or humanity. It is cruel and wicked. It illustrates the subserviency of the American judiciary to the great corporations. . . . It puts the wealthy capitalist, corporate or unincorporate, upon the same equality in this respect, as that of the starving laborer, who must carry his meager dinner pail to his employment, no matter how dangerous it may be, in order to get a little food, clothing and shelter for his suffering family. . . . Those who can reconcile their consciences to the cold brutality of the general rule with reference to the servant accepting the risk, are at liberty to do so; I envy neither their heads nor their hearts.[142]

In short, jurists *appreciated* that workers were "subject to the employer's power" and relaxed the rigors of the assumption-of-risk rule accordingly. And it did not help for the employer to produce a written contract signed by the plaintiff-employee indicating that she had assumed all the risks. Such contracts were void for want of consideration, wrote New York's Justice Rufus Peckham (some fourteen years before his more famous opinion upholding the right of bakers in New York to contract to work longer than ten hours a day), and this infamous defender of "freedom of contract" went on to opine that these assume-all-risks contracts were probably void as being against good public policy as well.[143]

THE FELLOW-SERVANT RULE: IN THE SERVICE OF ENTREPRENEURS?

There was a time, in preindustrial England and America, when masters and servants lived together in the master's home in harmony and community, or so we have been told. If the servant was injured by a fellow servant, the master felt legally, or morally, responsible to care for the injured servant and to compensate him or her for medical expenses, lost wages, and suffering, either out of a sense of legal duty or "out of benevolence or charity." But industrialization began a "gradual decay" of this "paternalistic and hierarchical relationship among employers and workers." "Only after this breakdown . . . do we find laborers turning to courts to seek compensation for injuries arising from their employment." In any event, that is what we are told.[144]

According to these accounts, the Court of Exchequer took the first step in 1837 in the vitiating of this doctrine of master responsibility (respondeat superior) in *Priestley* v. *Fowler*, but the major blow was dealt by Chief Justice Lemuel Shaw in Massachusetts five years later, in *Farwell* v. *Boston & Worchester RR*. Insisting that the employment contract, and not "the normatively superior customary law," determined the issue, Shaw created both the assumption-of-risk rule and the fellow-servant doctrine. The latter had it that the master was only liable for his own negligence or that of his duly appointed agents; hence an injury caused by a mere fellow servant was not to be imputed to the master. Shaw offered a public policy rationale for this doctrine: If workers were unable to sue fault-free employers whenever injured by negligent fellow workers, they would be more watchful of their fellow workers, to the benefit of all who used the railway's services.[145] Other American high courts "eagerly swallowed the doctrine," which "thereby socialized (or ignored)" the "economic impact of railroad accidents" on workers, "relieving the roads of one possible heavy cost; or so an enterprise-minded judge might have thought." In the process, the injured worker "was thus thrown back on his own resources, or, if he had none, left to the tender mercies of the poor laws." He might sue the fellow servant whose negligence had caused his injury, but this was "pointless," because the fellow servant "was equally poor," "almost certain not to have much money."[146] Moreover, Shaw's "watchful-workers" public policy rationale had little value, for there was "no particular reason to think that an employee would be more

114

concerned about his personal safety from a workplace accident than about physical threats of retaliation if he were to turn in a fellow worker."[147]

This is the way the reigning paradigm interprets the fellow servant rule. I find this tale to contain a respectable measure of truth, but in several ways it is well off the mark. The rule was a cruel one, to be sure (which is why it was not applied by Kentucky's high court until 1886, was abrogated by legislative fiat in Georgia, Iowa, Montana Territory, Kansas, Massachusetts, and Wisconsin between 1855 and 1875, and eventually replaced by workman's compensation legislation).[148] But the rule's harshness is not at issue. What are the shortcomings of this tale, told by those who tend to interpret legal history with economic lenses? First, the fact is that some negligent fellow servants clearly *were* sued by injured workers, and many of these defendants *did* have assets capable of compensating those whom they had injured. Second, the "watchful-worker" rationale may well have had *some value*; careless workers *were* fired, saving lives and limbs. Third, the rule was not the outrageous instrumentalist innovation that it is said to be, but the application of longstanding English legal principles to an essentially new multiemployee work environment,[149] and its adoption throughout the common-law world had less to do with "enterprise-minded judges" than with the power of precedent and "the taught legal tradition"—that is, with the Jurisprudence of the Head. Finally, the real story of "judicial innovation" with regard to the fellow servant rule is one of the creating of heartfelt exceptions to it, limiting its scope and bite.

Suing the Negligent Fellow Servant

Language in opinions of the English Court of Exchequer and the Supreme Court of Massachusetts in 1855 and 1856 suggested that an injured employee unable to sue his employer was also unable to sue his superintending superior, and the leading authority on this subject gives us the impression that these cases barred suits against fellow-servants.[150] But these dicta were almost immediately rejected, in England, in Massachusetts, and elsewhere in America. Courts throughout the second half of the nineteenth century clearly entertained suits brought by injured workers against negligent supervisors who had not qualified as agents of the employer.[151] The superintendent of a wire factory in Massachusetts might have been, in law, only a "fellow servant" of a carpenter injured by a falling tackle block, but if the company was free of liability, the negligent superintendent was not. The fellow servants had "made no contract with," and had "received no compensation from, each other." Hence the carpenter had not assumed the risk of injury from the negligent act of his "fellow" worker, the factory superintendent.[152] As Indiana's Justice Samuel Perkins put it, while the company's liability might be limited by the fellow-servant rule, that protection did not extend "in the little community of employees of the same employer" to a negligent general superintendent. To hold otherwise, as had Sir Fredrich Pollock Jr., C. B., would be to say that "the common duties of man to man, in society generally, should cease to exist."[153]

But we are told that such suits against fellow servants were "pointless" because such defendants were "equally poor." Certainly this would be true of accidents caused by a railroad switchman or most foremen. But how true could it have been of the typical railroad conductor or engineer, let alone a yard, plant, mine, or factory general superintendent? Since these "fellow" servants were charged with negligence in the lion's share of industrial accident cases in the nineteenth century, suits against them clearly were *not* "pointless." Superintendents were obviously men of some means and property. But what about conductors and engineers? Walter Licht provides us with figures of the value of taxable property for railroad conductors and engineers in Philadelphia for the years 1860 and 1870. The average for conductors was $15,216; for engineers, $3,367. Even "foremen" employed by the New York Central Railroad in 1855 were paid wages ranging from $720 to $1,200 per year, when the median head of household earned less than $400.[154] These superior "fellow" servants were labor's "aristocracy." Most were *not* judgment-proof paupers.

The Watchful-Worker Rationale at Work

This still leaves a great many judgment-proof fellow servants at large—fellow common laborers, miners, and factory operatives, railroad switchmen and flagmen, and by the common-law rules of some state courts, many foremen. Chief Justice Shaw's "watchful-workmen" rationale had it that the fellow servant rule would prompt workers to report and thereby screen out careless comrades. Was this public policy rationale mere window dressing for a subsidization of nascent industry? *Were* workers reluctant to complain about careless co-workers? Discharge records of the Erie Railroad for 1873 and the Chicago, Burlington and Quincy for 1877 and 1878 (n=968) suggest otherwise. If we exclude the 13 percent fired for "illegal" strikes ("breaches" of contract), we find that 63 percent of the rest were fired for behavior that could have held them to be "negligent" in a court of law— such as "excessive drinking," "neglect of duty," "disobeying orders," "carelessness," "lying," "negligence," "sleeping," and "incompetence" (a category characterized by such entries as "unreliable," "unsteady," "not attending to duty," "left switch open," "forgot train orders," "bad company," "[went on a] spree," "not answering dispatcher," "not a sound operator," "tampering with watch," "unfaithful," "treacherous," and "inaccuracy").[155]

Are we to attribute the decisions to fire these trainmen, switchmen, and laborers to the shrewd observations of superintendents and foremen alone? Were not some of these decisions due to complaints made by fellow workers alarmed by the "careless," "unreliable," or "unsteady" behavior of those in whose hands their lives lay? Industrial accidents were often caused, to be sure, not by worker carelessness, but by corporate cost-cutting that left too few brakemen or repairmen at work for safety, or by a "speed-up" that over-taxed both workers and the machinery they operated.[156] Nonetheless, to a *certain* extent, Shaw's "watchful-workmen" rationale must have done *some* good. Some confirmation of this may be found in the remarkable fact that mine accident fatalities in the twenty-three leading mining states *rose* by 23 percent after the statutory abrogation of the fellow-servant rule and its replacement by workmen's compensation.[157]

Instrumentalist Invention or Jurisprudence of the Head?

How innovative *was* the fellow-servant rule? Was it really the case that "if one worker injured a second worker, the second worker could sue their common employer?"[158] Or would it be more accurate to say that English masters before 1837 were never held liable for personal injury damages their servants experienced, whether incurred at the hands of a fellow servant or a third party?

My reading of the English reports, treatises, and cultural ephemera suggests that the Latin maxim respondeat superior was not understood to mean anything more than "the master is liable for the sanctioned acts of his servant." Was he responsible for the servant's *negligent* acts? At least in the early fifteenth century, this question was still moot. As Hull, J., put it, in a case of a man charged with having "negligently" caused a fire, it "would be against all reason to put blame or fault upon a man where there was none in him; for the negligence of his servants cannot be said to be his own."[159] Rolle had it that "if my servant without my notice put my [cattle] into another's land," he would be "the trespasser and not I." "No master," wrote Holt, C. J., in 1699, was "chargeable with the acts of his servant" except when he acted "in the execution of the authority given him."[160]

Yet English courts generally did hold masters liable for damages caused to third parties by the negligent acts of their servants when those servants were acting within the scope of their employment. But before 1837 the reports and treatises are silent on the master's liability to a *servant* injured by a fellow servant.[161] *Priestley* v. *Fowler* (1837) is, simply, the very first case to raise that question. Prior to *Priestley* the only clues we can get as to the liability of masters to disabled servants are to be found in the handful of cases in which these servants had been injured, not by fellow servants, but by third parties or mere chance, or where the servants had simply become ill and had incurred medical expenses. The case of *Newby* v. *Wiltshire*, decided by Lord Mansfield's Court of King's Bench in 1784, offers the clearest evidence of the limits to the master's liability in this regard. A young hired hand, sent with a farmer's wagon to market, was injured when the "horse took fright and started aside," whereupon the boy fell off the shafts of the wagon "and had his leg and thigh fractured by a wheel of the waggon going over him." The accident having occurred some distance from the master's farm, a surgeon was called. After amputating the boy's leg, he presented a bill for thirty-two pounds to the master, who refused to pay. Lord Mansfield spoke critically at first of the master's lack of "humanity," but he then asked "but what is the law?" The master's counsel had pointed out that "the legislature has wisely thrown charges of this kind upon the parish at large," that is, upon the overseers of the Elizabethan poor law "as they have in cases of actions against the hundred, not upon a principle of negligence, but that the burden may be divided." Were the court to require the master to pay, "it will great[ly] discourage yearly hirings." Mansfield and his colleagues agreed; the master had no duty to pay.[162]

A similar story unfolded in 1802. A servant suffered a broken arm while driving his employer's team of horses. As the accident occurred in the immediate proximity of his home, the servant's mother sent for the employer's physician, who then presented the employer with his bill. But the Court of Common Pleas held that the employer was not liable for medical services rendered the servant. Lord Alvanley, C. J., maintained that there was "no authority in the law of England to be found" warranting such liability. The proper authorities to provide such medical care were the parish poor-law officers. They could call upon the entire community's resources. Chambre, J., went so far as to say that for this very reason any other rule "would be very disadvantageous to the servants themselves if it were adopted." Heath, J., agreed, as did Rooke, J. Holding a master liable for expenses flowing from an injury to one of his servants had never been the law, and it was well that this was so: "Many persons who are obliged for the purposes of their trade, to keep a number of servants, would be unable to fulfill the duty imposed upon them by the law. It must be left to the humanity of every master to decide whether he will assist his servant according to capacity or not."[163]

This describes the way sick and injured servants, as well as other, less theoretically eligible day laborers, were cared for in early modern England, colonial America, and early-nineteenth-century Massachusetts: While some of these servants may well have been cared for by "humane" masters, they were not legally entitled to medical services, and consequently in 1803 and 1829 Massachusetts courts held that these costs could be charged against their wages.[164] The injured servant or laborer was "thus thrown back on his own resources, or, if he had none, left to the tender mercies of the poor laws" long before the arrival of the fellow servant rule.[165]

The jurists who decided *Priestley*, *Farwell*, and the other early fellow-servant/assumption-of-risk cases were in the mainstream of what Roscoe Pound called "the taught legal tradition." Hence it is hardly surprising that they, uniformly, pointed out that these rules governing injuries to workers were *not* innovations, but were based on "general principles"[166] and were "thoroughly understood" to be the law "before attention was called" to them, "for if it had not been so," said Pollock, C. B., "we could hardly have lived into the present century without having actions brought over and over again."[167]

Thus counsel for the South Carolina Railroad told that state's high court in a fellow-servant decision that predated *Farwell* by a year: "These accidents . . . have for ages been of daily occurrence. The blacksmith, the carpenter, the ship owner, in fact, in every occupation where a joint effort is required to perform any piece of business."[168]

Just so, the railroad's counsel in *Farwell* spoke hypothetically of the absurdity of the rule in accidents involving blacksmiths, play actors, and farmers pitching hay. Chief Justice Lemuel Shaw made the same point in his *Farwell* opinion: Had the liability of masters for a servant's injury at the negligent hands of a fellow servant been the law, "it would be a rule of frequent and familiar occurrence, and its existence and application, with all its qualifications and restrictions, would be settled by judicial precedents."[169]

This was precisely why Lord Abinger in *Priestley* offered three fellow-servant examples in his litany of "alarming" hypothetical consequences of any new rule that would impose liability on the master for a servant's injuries not caused by the master's fault: "The master, for example, would be liable to the servant for the negligence of the chambermaid, for putting him up in a damp bed . . . ; for the negligence of the cook, in not properly cleaning the copper vessels used in the kitchen. . . . The footman may have an action . . . for drunkenness, neglect, or want of skill in the coachman."[170] Abinger would not have spoken in such fashion had these in fact been the legal obligations in the memory of anyone living who might read his opinion.

Moreover, note that none of his examples were drawn from the modern industrial setting of a railroad yard or factory; the hypothetical negligent parties were chambermaids, upholsterers, cooks, butchers, house builders, and coach makers. So were those that Judge George Taylor offered in instructions to jurors in rural Huntingdon County, Pennsylvania, in 1852: They might appreciate the rationale behind the fellow-servant rule for railroads were they to remember that, if it were not for such a rule, "if you should employ two men to dig you a well, or fell your timber, or work your thrashing machine, it would be at the risk of having one of them, through the fault or negligence of the other, and without any fault of yours, a pension upon you to the end of his days."

Similarly, New Hampshire's Justice Charles Doe described the fellow servant rule in 1860 in terms of the responsibilities of one "who hires two laborers in harvest, and two carpenters to erect a staging and shingle his house."[171] Consider as well examples offered by Lord Ardmillan in a case decided in Scotland in 1856. Even though the plaintiff was a worker for a railway, the Lord Ordinary's hypothetical illustrations of who was and who was not a fellow servant in the same "department" as the servant injured included a painter at a "country house" who might be injured by the gardener, a dairymaid who might be run over by the coachman, a clerk in a shipping company who might fall through a ship's hatchway, two colliers, two sawyers felling a tree, and finally, a ploughman employed by a railroad who might be hit by a company train while ploughing a patch of company-owned land![172] The master-servant model in the minds of jurists who first described the fellow-servant rule was a preindustrial one, the principles utilized were of preindustrial origin, and the fellow-servant rule itself reflected a distinctly preindustrial manner of imagining employer liability.

Exceptions to the Rule: Enter the Jurisprudence of the Heart

The fellow-servant rule was soon adopted by the vast majority of American courts, but it was not "eagerly swallowed" by them, as one leading legal historian maintains. Indeed, the very example he offers,[173] Wisconsin's adoption of the rule in *Moseley* v. *Chamberlain* (1861), demonstrates that the contrary was so. Wisconsin's court had first *rejected* the *Farwell* rule in 1860. When the question was raised again the next year, Chief Justice Luther Dixon indicated that he remained of the view that the fellow-servant rule was bad law, but, inasmuch as the Ohio Supreme Court had now reversed itself and fallen in line with the majority, Wisconsin's opposition stood virtually alone. Hence he and his colleagues would "yield to this unbroken current," but only because of "that deference and respect" due to the "well considered opinions of others."[174]

Jerrilyn Marston has told this story for the antebellum years especially well. The jurisdictions that accepted the rule in *Priestley* and *Farwell* did so "not because they were instrumentalists attuned to economic developments within their jurisdictions" (they had no more railroad trackage than those jurisdictions that initially *rejected* the rule), "but rather because their training and intellectual bias required them to adhere to certain common law myths" that law was "discoverable," that rules could be deduced from basic principles, and that a fellow-servant rule deduced by such distinguished courts as those of Exchequer and Massachusetts, and expounded as convincingly as Shaw had done in *Farwell*, should be presumed correct.[175] Here was pure Jurisprudence of the Head.

Some of those who adopted the rule, however, did so very reluctantly. Yes they deferred to Shaw's "able" and "powerful" reasoning, but, like Missouri's Justice David Wagner, they simultaneously laid on the record the observation that "were the question *res nova*, I should hesitate long before I would give to the rule unqualified approbation. In many cases it produces the grossest injustice, and grants an immunity or exemption which shocks the moral feelings."[176] Jurists who could describe the rule in this fashion were certain to adopt the exceptions to it that quickly appeared, as we shall see. But let us first visit with a court that both Chris Tomlins's and Jerrilyn Marston's acute antebellum foci failed to detect, a court that for over twenty years managed to swim against the tide.

Kentucky's high court rejected the rule altogether in 1865, several years after the courts of Ohio and Wisconsin, earlier dissidents, had reluctantly fallen in step with the majority point of view. The author of this flung gauntlet was none other than Chief Justice George Robertson, the author of *Lexington and Ohio RR* v. *Applegate* (1839), an oft-discussed, allegedly prorailroad case.[177] Robertson does not sound very prorailroad in *Louisville & Nashville RR* v. *Collins* (1865). He dismissed the rule in *Priestley* and *Farwell* as "anomalous," even when qualified by exceptions. Instead, the law should hold the employer strictly liable for a reason of public policy unlike the one that his counterparts in Massachusetts had used to defend the assumption-of-risk rule. The "assurance of protection" by employers to workers that they would be compensated for job-related injuries "would enable the corporation to obtain and keep better employees, and at cheaper rates" (since no premium for any "assumption of risk" need be offered) by "inspiring more confidence" that employers were concerned with employee safety. "This doctrine," Robertson insisted, was "the only safe clue to lead the bewildered explorer to the light which shows the sure way of right and proves the true doctrine of American law." He claimed for his rule nothing less than the title of "enlightened" law in "this clearer day" of Jurisprudence's "ripening maturity."[178] Here was a clear example of the Jurisprudence of the Heart.

Kentucky's high court held to the rule in *Collins* for some twenty-one years,[179] but, standing alone, almost half a century before this reasoning would finally impress itself upon the nation, it attracted few adherents. Isaac Redfield had glowing words for it in his treatise on railroad law; it was cited approvingly in supreme courts of Indiana and the United States; but inasmuch as Robertson had been unable to cite "a single authority" in 1865 that had not been overruled, the Texas Supreme Court rejected its value as precedent in that state's "first impression" case addressing the fellow-servant rule,[180] and that was characteristic of how *Collins* was generally treated.

Nonetheless, the fellow-servant rule was not applied as heartlessly and coldly in most American jurisdictions as it was in England and New England. Just as the creation of the "safe tools," "safe worksite," "competent servant," "constructive knowledge," and "extraordinary risks" exceptions soon tempered the ruthlessness of the assumption-of-risk rule, so the development of the "vice principal" (or "superior servant"), the "different department," and the "subcontractor" exceptions soon weakened the bite in America of the fellow-servant rule. Were there similar exceptions made in England? In 1862 Byles, J., of the English Court of Common Pleas, allowed that a defendant's employee who was "superior" in rank to and injured plaintiff could fairly be regarded to be the agent of the employer or corporation, and was not to be regarded merely as the plaintiff's fellow servant. But this view did not prevail in the British Isles. After all, Exchequer had already declared that one's foreman was also one's fellow servant. Rejected in England (1864) and in Scotland (1868), Byles's "vice principal" (or "superior servant") exception was a dead letter in Britain thereafter. Negligent general managers, superintendents, chief engineers, and ships's masters were all mere "fellow servants" (in law) with regard to those employees whose injuries they had caused.[181]

This was the rule in Massachusetts by 1850 as well,[182] but in 1854 the Ohio Supreme Court soundly rejected it. The conductor of a train was the supervisor and superior of all trainmen, and was acting as the corporation's agent when his negligence injured one of his subordinates. Hence his negligence was not that of a fellow servant but was imputable to the company.[183] This Ohio "superior servant" rule, it is said, was uncommon, largely unaccepted by others.[184] I don't agree, at least for the 1860s, 1870s and 1880s. In my scan of the terrain over this next generation, I detected ten high courts that applied the exception to such controversial categories as foremen and conductors, and I strongly suspect that there were others. Tennessee's Justice Robert McKinney (whom we will meet again)[185] applied it in 1859, mindful that if it were not the law, a corporation might "evade liability in all cases by entrenching itself behind its officers and agents." His successor, Justice James Shackelford, wrote an opinion seven years later affirming McKinney's "superior servant" exception with a similar public policy rationale: "The increasing numbers of corporations, with the concentrated wealth they draw to them, is a strong and forcible reason why they should be held to a strict rule for the acts of their officers."[186]

Louisiana adopted the exception in 1860, as did Minnesota in 1866, New Jersey in 1870, and Missouri in 1871.[187] An employee injured when the train's engineer left the locomotive in the hands of his fireman was successful in an appeal before the Missouri Supreme Court for the same reason that workers had prevailed in Tennessee. As Justice David Wagner put it, to turn this plaintiff away, "would be to . . . allow corporations to escape all responsibility for accidents occurring by the negligence of their executive agents, and thus make it profitable for such institutions to manage all their affairs in that way, . . . a principle contrary to law and sound morality." A worker who "acts in subordination" to a superior was not to be regarded as the "fellow" of his superior.[188]

In the next twelve years Illinois, New York, Rhode Island, the federal courts, Wisconsin, Colorado, Texas, and West Virginia adopted the superior-servant exception for foremen and section bosses.[189] Federal Circuit Judge John Forrest Dillon treated foremen as "superintending" agents rather than fellow servants, and his judgment was affirmed by the U.S. Supreme Court in 1873. Nicholas St. John Green's edition of Story on Agency in 1874 supported the Ohio superior-servant exception, and in 1877 Horace G. Wood's *Treatise on the Law of Master and Servant* described it as well as being "more consistent with principle and strict justice" than its harsher English and New England counterpart. Charles Beach's treatise on the subject called it "certainly the rule of humanity." In 1884 the Northwest's fabled federal district judge, Matthew Deady, commented on the "hardship and injustice" that "has been seen and felt" in certain unyielding applications of the fellow-servant rule. "Accordingly, the tendency of the more modern authorities" had been to "modify and limit" the rule to protect "lives and limbs." So he told a jury that a section boss whose negligence caused injury to a laborer was not to be viewed as the laborer's fellow servant. But in 1893 the United States Supreme Court declined to call an engineer the superior servant of a fireman, and it held a narrow view again (by a

123

vote of five to four) in 1904. The Congress finally stepped in and abrogated the fellow-servant rule altogether for interstate railroad workers in 1908.[190]

The worker in a "different department" of a company from that of a fellow worker whose negligence caused his injury persistently claimed as well that the fellow-servant rule was inapplicable: He had been unable to observe the behavior of his careless comrade, and since the "safety through watchfulness" rationale for the rule had been thus rendered impossible, the rule should not apply. That was what Nicolas Farwell's counsel, Charles Loring, had argued, unsuccessfully, in 1842. Chief Justice Shaw had not found the argument to apply to a switchman and an engineer. But, as Jerrilyn Marston has shown, Joseph Story found the "different department" logic worthy of favorable comment in his treatise on agency in 1844. By 1860 the courts of Indiana, Georgia, and Scotland had adopted and applied the exception; several other American high courts followed suit.[191]

A question similar to that of one injured by the negligence of another from a "different department" was addressed in mid-nineteenth-century England as well: Was a worker's employer liable for injuries he incurred at the negligent hands of a worker employed by his employer's subcontractor? Similarly, was a railroad company liable to an employee injured by the employee of another railroad company sharing the first company's track? These were not mere hypotheticals. Many injuries at work involved persons employed by different firms: The carpenter's apprentice who injured the plumber's apprentice; the stevedore's laborer injured by the ship's mate; the yard section hand injured by the fireman. English courts originally treated these as simply falling under the fellow-servant rule.[192] But in 1860 the Court of Exchequer decided that, unlike the fellow servants of a single employer, in these instances the doctrine of respondeat superior did, indeed, apply. The injured worker had only contracted to assume a risk of injury at the hands of his employer's workers, not those of another.[193]

American courts did not wait for Exchequer to come to this conclusion. As early at 1851 the New York Supreme Court had taken this view, and by 1872 at least eight other high courts had held as well that one injured by the employee of a subcontractor or different employer was not barred by the fellow-servant rule from suing that employer.[194] Only the Massachusetts bench proved to be especially resistant to the idea.[195]

The fellow servant rule, then, was grounded in preindustrial common-law rules, and was adopted by American jurisdictions, after its English formulation in 1837, due to the power of precedent and the taught legal tradition. Its harshness was soon made smoother in some places by the creation of certain exceptions. But workers still won only 32 percent of personal in-

These railroad construction "navvies" in late-nineteenth-century New Zealand clearly "assumed" considerable risks in cutting track passages through terrain that could collapse around them if their timber shoring proved inadequate. The question of whether the foreman who directed their work was their fellow servant or the railroad's agent was, in each common-law jurisdiction, one for the courts to decide. (New Zealand Archives, Wellington, N.Z.)

jury lawsuits against employers at the trial level in New York City in 1890 and 1910, and they won only 40 percent of such cases that were appealed to supreme courts in Wisconsin, California, New Hampshire, and Pennsylvania in the second half of the nineteenth century.[196] Conceivably the fellow-servant rule's watchful-worker rationale did produce a somewhat safer work environment, but it also gave employers less incentive to spend on safety than its alternative, employer liability, as Chief Justice George Robertson had pointed out in *Collins*.[197]

Christopher Tomlins has faulted mid-nineteenth-century jurists in England and America for failing to adopt the Civil Law rule of respondeat superior, as in France, for workers as well as strangers and passengers.[198] He has a point. It is certainly true that the American adoption of the fellow-servant rule was not foreordained. After all, for the first fifty years of the nineteenth century Scottish jurists held employers responsible for injuries due to negligence suffered by their employees, and some American jurists were aware of this and responsive to it. Moreover, the first full-fledged American test of the English *Priestley* rule (*Murray* v. *South Carolina RR* [1841]) contained a strong three-member dissent that argued that "the more liability imposed on the railroad company, the more care and prudence would be thereby elicited." And as Tomlins points out himself, several midwestern courts doubted the rule in *Farwell* or created exceptions to it in the 1850s. But to say that a rule need not have persisted has a ring of judgmental hindsight to it, and in any event does not come to grips with exactly why the rule persisted. Attorneys then (as now) regarded as professionally irresponsible the notion of directly challenging authoritative precedent, given the likelihood of success. They preferred either to attempt to persuade the court to "distinguish" the facts in their client's case from the precedent-encrusted rule that barred their path, or to lobby for a principled exception to it. Tomlins appreciates this; he simply gives less weight than Jerrilynn Marston or I do to the pull of the "taught legal tradition," to what Marston calls the "myth" of "harmony and judicial 'discovery.'"[199]

American jurists overcame English rules that had lost their "symmetry" in these years in other corners of the common law; we will see several examples of this in a moment. But they found it impossible to do so in this instance, largely, I suspect, because the contract worker *did* seem to them to constitute a principled exception to the respondeat superior rule: American and English jurists seemed to be drawn to the fact that passengers had paid, while workers had *been* paid; their "Heads" therefore held them fast to the reasoning in *Priestley* and *Farwell*. But although that explains, it does not excuse their lack of Justice Robertson's vision, and in that sense Tomlins is right. As Lawrence Friedman puts it in one of his many deft turns of phrase, the fellow-servant rule "did not have the courage of its cruelty, nor the strength to be human."[200] Mercifully, with regard to jurists and the common law in general in nineteenth-century America, this outcome with regard to work accidents was more the exception than the rule.

Eddies:
A Jurisprudence
of the Hand

In this part of *Heart versus Head* we look exclusively at questions of property law. Although common-law rules regarding the "private" law of contracts and torts remained largely the domain of the jurists, largely untouched by legislatures until the late nineteenth century, the same cannot be said of property law. The rules governing the use and transfer of real and personal property have always had substantial "public" qualities and character to them.

In the first century after their declaring independence of king and Parliament, the new American state legislatures lost little time in establishing or proscribing a wide range of property rules. They abolished primogeniture and entail; they established married women's property laws; they created mechanic's lien laws and "homesteader" mortgage exemptions; they authorized milldam manufacturers to back waters onto the fields of upstream landowners subject only to the payment of annual damages; they empowered chartered corporations to take land for public uses, while compensating the owners, under the principle of "eminent domain," in order to stimulate the construction of turnpikes, canals, bridges, railways, waterworks, gasworks, and other enterprises "vested with public interest"; they taxed property (especially these new corporations) to operate public schools and build roads; and they ultimately voided ownership in billions of dollars worth of property by adopting the Thirteenth Amendment, abolishing slavery. Legislatures and publicly sanctioned state constitutions played an active role in directing these and other alterations in the ways that Americans used their property in the first century of independence.

Courts played a much more modest role in this process. They sometimes expressed doubts about the propriety of the laws, and they occasionally declared taxation or "taking" statutes void due to their conflict with constitutional or "fundamental" principles. But they generally confined themselves

129

to interpreting and applying these statutes, within the broader context of the common law of property.[1] There were some rules of property law, however, left largely unaltered by statute. These rules of "private law" were also left, for the most part, unaltered by jurists as well. But they did alter a few rules: I detected five innovations, four of which I describe in this chapter, the other in chapter four.

Jurists generally decided on rules intended to advance "the public good." "Transcending mere considerations of policy," they held that, imbedded in all legal principles, there were "obligations that government owed the public," as Harry Scheiber puts it.[2] Jurists respected the "rule of law," and this respect sometimes led them to block the path of dynamic new entrepreneurial forces that were ignoring certain rules. They did not always stand in the way of entrepreneurial initiatives to be sure, but in resolving such "tensions" of rights they weighed the claims of the parties against the common-law principles involved, each of which invariably contained a "public good" rationale at its core.[3]

William Novak argues that jurists of the early Republic, far from being free-wheeling allies of an emerging entrepreneurial class, were quite traditionally concerned with the regulation of rights and property for the public good. To this general end they held that the common law was to be "received and modified" according to what U.S. Supreme Court Justice James Wilson called its "accommodating spirit." This is not evidence of a new propensity to treat the common law as an instrument to achieve social or economic ends deemed appropriate to a new age by jurists ("instrumentalism"), but rather that of a widespread judicial view that the common law and equity could constantly be restated and refined by jurists of genius as "circumstances, and exigencies, and conveniences change." The object of this search for "higher degrees of perfection" was not new rules that might spur economic growth, but rather the refining of old rules "to protect and to improve social life." The law managed to do this, according to U.S. Supreme Court Justice Henry Baldwin, by "sending its equitable energies through all classes and ranks of men," defending "the poor from the rich, the weak from the powerful, the industrious from the rapacious, the peaceable from the violent, the tenants from the lords, and all from their superiors." Thus the laws of shipping (for example), "founded as they were upon the experience, the necessities, and usages of the merchants generally" in the distant past, were (according to Theophilus Parsons Jr.) "characterized by a profound rationality and exact justice" and were "seldom, if ever, materially affected by the rights or prejudices of caste or class." Was this so much empty rhetoric? Novak does not think so, and neither do I. Nineteenth-century American jurists did release some new "energies" into American society, as we will see in Part II of this book, but virtually all of these energies were "equitable," not economic, ones.[4]

One judge-made change in a property rule appeared to have had the public good in mind, but its immediate effect on the litigants was to benefit tenants at the expense of landlords. The English rule that, at the termination of a lease, the landlord had the right to any agricultural buildings (barns, sheds, gins, corncribs and the like) that his tenant had erected was rejected in America. As Justice Story put it, the public "had every motive to encourage the tenant to devote himself to agriculture, and to favour any erections which should aid this result." Were the tenant, in "the comparative poverty" of a newly settled region "to lose his interest therein by the very act of erection," little "of much expense or value" would be built. Chancellor Kent praised the new rule as one promoting a good "public policy" that encouraged "improvement" and economic growth, as, indeed, it may well have, but take note that it was an innovation that accomplished this by specifically "favouring" tenants. Thus New York's Chief Justice Spencer "confess[ed]," in a case in 1822 holding that a tenant's cider press and mill belonged to him, that he "never could perceive the reason, justice, [or] equity of the old cases which gave to the landlord such kind of erections. . . . The rules anciently were very rigid."[5]

I do allow that, on *rare* occasions, jurists did set aside a few ancient rules regarding private rights to create new rules that had the potential of releasing new economic energies and aiding entrepreneurs. But I could identify only two such rules created by jurists in the nineteenth century that could be said to have these developmental qualities. Two doctrines out of some twenty-nine new ones identified in this book is pretty modest evidence of any "trend" or judicial predisposition. At best this evidence of a "Jurisprudence of the Visible Hand" constitutes no more than a few eddies or backwaters in the stream of American legal history in the nineteenth century. But they are part of our story; so here they are.

TWO INNOVATIONS IN THE LAW OF TRUSTS

The prudent-investor rule, created by the Massachusetts high court in 1830, was "quite permissive" to the "mercantile dynasties" that some Boston Brahmins were creating for their families.[6] Ignoring older, English trust requirements that assets be held in government securities or land, the court sanctioned more flexible investment practices, including the purchase and trading of corporate stocks and bonds. Justice Samuel Putnam justified this policy because of the court's confidence in the "substantial and prudent directors" of private corporations, whom they compared favorably to those who managed "the engagements of the public." Moreover, one could, as a stockholder, sue to "compel" corporate directors "to do justice," whereas "the government can only be supplicated." So long as the trustee behaved prudently, he was secure from suit by the beneficiaries.[7]

Here was a rule that energetic new entrepreneurs would appreciate, one that released dynastic millions for investment purposes in new enterprises. And it was adopted by most of Massachusetts's admiring New England neighbors. But every other high court in nineteenth-century America *rejected* it. Some specifically condemned the risks in bank stocks;[8] others in railroad stocks;[9] still others in both.[10] Pennsylvania's bench explained that when benefactors from "our agricultural districts" called in their wills for "money at interest" to be paid to their cestui que trust, they had in mind mortgage money. "Our farmers, unengaged in speculation, trade or manufactures," did not intend for trustees to purchase stock in the Bank of the United States, and neither did the Jacksonian Democrats who occupied seats on the local orphan's court or the state's supreme court.[11]

The historian who has offered the best account of the emergence of this rule suspects that the dynastic trusts of the great mercantile families were "relatively rare, a fact which perhaps kept the Massachusetts doctrine from spreading."[12] But Boston was not unique in 1850. Philadelphia had long been a commercial giant; New York had become one. Yet the courts in neither state permitted trustees to purchase securities of any private corporation. There would be millionaires in other states whose trust assets would be kept out of reach of the new banking, railroad, and manufacturing enterprises, some of which had been the very sources of their wealth. The prudent-investor rule had a decidedly pro-entrepreneurial side to it, but its scope and popularity remained *notably* limited.

Did the judicial sanctioning of "spendthrift" trusts in the Gilded Age constitute further evidence of judicial sympathy for "those of their social class" who displayed "the dynastic urge" in their creation of trust funds for their irresponsible heirs?[13] Or were they evidence, instead, of a Jurisprudence of the Heart, of jurists genuinely concerned with the plight of poor and helpless survivor-heirs? Assets held under the terms of a spendthrift trust were to be doled out to the beneficiary in a systematic monthly fashion, but never to be turned over en masse; the beneficiary was not free to sell his or her interest in the life estate; and the assets were to be placed beyond the reach of a bankrupt beneficiary's creditors. This was a way of providing for the family of a bankrupt or near-bankrupt heir. Moreover, when one reads the first and second impression cases that gave authority to the spendthrift trust in the Gilded Age, it becomes clear that these trust funds were much more modest in scope than those of any "dynastic rich"—that is, the trust's creators had not been wealthy, and the courts balked at protecting any spendthrift arrangements that were "extravagant or unreasonable."[14] Furthermore, the losers in almost every one of these cases were creditors— that is, enterprising businesses.

Jurists in North Carolina, Alabama, and Rhode Island rejected the creation of such a trust, citing English precedent. The Rhode Island court added that spendthrift trusts were unfair. Businessmen might extend credit to the beneficiary of such a trust on the assumption that they might turn to the trustee for payment if the beneficiary declined or if he declared bankruptcy.[15] But the courts of Pennsylvania, New York, Connecticut, Kentucky, Illinois, Vermont, Virginia, West Virginia, Massachusetts, and the United States, drawing on comparable "caretaker" trusts created in the early nineteenth century for precedent, had no difficulty approving these trusts and turning such creditors away.[16] Rejecting the English chancery rule barring such trusts, Justice Samuel Miller of the U.S. Supreme Court drew analogies to state "homestead" laws and noted that one contemplating the extension of credit to such a beneficiary was perfectly capable of consulting the copy of the will in the local public records office. Just how *practical* a matter that might be for the typical businessman did not concern him.[17] Businessmen could look out for their interests; some of these beneficiaries apparently could not, which was why their benefactors had created the caretaker or spendthrift trust in the first place. Listen to the ways that jurists described these benefactors and beneficiaries. The mother who had left assets in trust for her daughter and grandchildren in Virginia was protecting "poor and helpless relatives."[18] The child being provided for in Illinois was "effectively placed beyond the reach of unprincipled schemers and sharpers."[19] The real estate left an aged husband from the separate estate of his dying wife in West Virginia was also to be free from his creditors in order that her failing spouse be kept "from trudging his weary way over the hill to the poor house" and (the court must have assumed that more metaphors would help) "so as to keep the gaunt wolf of grinding poverty from the home door of those near and dear." "Ours is a humane rule," Pennsylvania's Justice John Read wrote of the spendthrift trust, "whilst the English one is hard and unnecessarily severe."[20] Some of this language we might dismiss as stilted rhetoric, but the frequency of its appearance weighs against such a view.

Harvard Law's Royall professor, John Chipman Gray, would react to the spendthrift trust by excoriating it and warning that it went hand in glove with calls for "the socialistic Utopia." Jurists had been "influenced, unconsciously it may well be, by those ideas . . . of the last few years . . . fermenting in the minds of the community . . . of paternalism, which is the fundamental essence alike of spendthrift trusts and of socialism."[21] But he was ignored. The weak, poor, and helpless would be protected from "the reach of unprincipled schemers and sharpers," albeit from ordinary businessmen and other respectable creditors as well. As such, this alteration in the rules of trust law does not appear to be a product of the Jurisprudence of the Visible Hand; it seems a better candidate for that of the Heart.

THE NUISANCE OF POLLUTION: TO BALANCE OR NOT TO BALANCE?

The reigning economic-oriented paradigm holds that most American jurists abandoned an older, "absolute dominion" view of the law of nuisance in the nineteenth century. This older, English view held that one whose use of property caused material damage to another could be enjoined from such use. Since most jurists were partial "toward economic development," judges began to establish a variety of "ingenious variations" on this general rule. In the first place, they turned private nuisance actions away with the observation that since the damage alleged had affected others as well, only the public prosecutor might press the complaint. In the second place, once satisfied that the right plaintiff was before them, they refused to enjoin polluting manufacturers or railroads if, upon "balancing the equities," or interests, of the parties, they decided that the plaintiff's damages were significantly less than the public benefits flowing from the defendant's continued operations. Thus polluters were allowed to continue "if the benefit from continuing to pollute exceeded the cost to the victims of pollution of either tolerating or eliminating it, which ever was cheaper."[22] The nineteenth-century American law of nuisance was an example of law "uncannily follow[ing] economics."[23]

Yes; but a highly qualified yes. More so than in any other legal domain, nineteenth-century American jurists appeared willing to bend the law of nuisance to the advantage of railroads and manufacturers. Given the relative interests of some of the litigants, it is hard to imagine that it could have been otherwise. For a homeowner in the seventeenth century to convince a court to enjoin an offensive pigsty or blacksmith's shop was one thing. Such businesses were to be located in secluded settings, and if they were not, the costs in relocating them were not impossible to manage, and were, in any event, of little consequence to any but their owners. But a Gilded Age factory, employing hundreds of tax-paying citizens and converting raw materials into valuable, useful, and taxable products, was quite another matter. Could one, in all justice, read preindustrial precedent in such a way as to shut such a factory down simply because it had done fifty or sixty dollars in annual damage to a neighboring farmer's orchards or crops? Here, certainly, was proper material for judicial cost-benefit analysis.

The innovative decisions of courts willing to abandon the strict English rule and to "balance the equities" usually offered both legal logic and "public policy" rationales, and yet the power of precedent, the "taught legal tradition," the past's firm grip continued to hold many other courts to preindustrial anchorages. I will not offer a complete jurisdictional breakdown of those courts holding to older, preindustrial views as opposed to those opting for one more sympathetic to railroads and manufacturing. Other scholars have been engaged in this analysis of several different jurisdictions,[24] and although the sum of their current output does not yet constitute a *complete* depiction of the landscape, enough of it is visible to say that it has a decidedly piebald appearance. The courts of Ohio, Tennessee, and Delaware appear often to have "balanced the equities" of the parties in nuisance cases, while New York's and Pennsylvania's vacillated, "balancing" in some years, but rejecting the practice in others. New Hampshire's jurists preferred an alternative, "reasonable use" test, but those of New Jersey, Massachusetts, Maine, Maryland, California, and Connecticut appear only rarely to have approved of either "reasonable use" or cost-benefit analysis in determining the relative merits of the litigants. They held to the older "absolute dominion" view.[25]

This "absolute dominion" position was never as "strict" or "absolute" as some historians would have us think.[26] It was not the case that "any interference" with a neighbor's property rights were either enjoinable or actionable at law for damages under the older English law of nuisance. The injury had to be more than mere aesthetic damage; it had to be material, something that affected the effective and necessary use of one's property.[27] The rule was *de minimus non curat lex* (law doesn't deal with trifling matters), and it was not a rule that "appeared" only in the late nineteenth century.[28] This was why the nine consecutive nuisance damage lawsuits filed by two Ohio farmers in the 1830s and 1840s against a millowner who had overflowed "a few acres of low, swampy, wet prairie of little or no value" were of no avail. Seven juries gave them nothing. One gave them 1 cent; another, $2.50. When the case finally reached the Ohio Supreme Court in 1843, that court, not surprisingly, turned them away for having failed to establish material injury to their property.[29] *Their suits* had been the nuisance!

The Public/Private Distinction

It has been said that jurists in nineteenth-century America "reshaped" the distinction between private and public nuisances, thus creating "a major barrier against individual interferences with the process of internal improvements."[30] But Michael McBride has analyzed nuisance cases in the state reports prior to 1866 and has found little truth to this claim. English jurists of the seventeenth and eighteenth centuries were as reluctant as their mid-nineteenth-century American counterparts to entertain either private suits at law charging defendants with having damaged plaintiffs by maintaining a nuisance, or bills in equity to enjoin such defendants from engaging in the allegedly damaging activity. But so long as they were satisfied that the plaintiff suffered a particular and material loss to his or her property, it was immaterial how many others in his neighborhood may also have suffered; the action was good.[31] McBride gives the term "aggregation" to these sorts of private nuisance actions, after the term used by Chief Justice George Bigelow in *Wesson* v. *Washburn Iron Co* (Mass. 1866).[32] And he shows that all American courts were willing to entertain private nuisance suits of this character.

The matter was different if the plaintiff claimed to have suffered the loss of a *right* common to others, as to the use of a stream, canal, highway, or wharf. Jurists in Delaware, Massachusetts, and Connecticut required those claiming the loss by defendant's nuisance of a "public right" to apply for relief to the attorney general's office, as they had been required in England, but McBride has demonstrated that this was not the case in Wisconsin, Georgia, New York, Maine, Vermont, Rhode Island, or Louisiana. There such plaintiffs were successful where they could establish an "injury in fact," such as being prevented from continued use of a navigable river or highway.[33] Paul Kurtz takes a position similar to McBride's on this subject for the years from 1870 to 1916: "Clearly, plaintiffs more easily satisfied the special damage requirement during this period."[34]

My own reading of the evidence sustains these views: Private nuisance suits, be they of the "aggregation" or even of "public rights" sort, were generally successful in the mid- and late nineteenth century.[35] The one state supreme court that I looked to with particular attention on the subject was that of Massachusetts. Here was one of the most industrial states in the nation. Its high court is widely regarded as having been friendly to industry. And on it for the better part of the last two decades of the century sat the Great Utilitarian himself, Oliver Wendell Holmes Jr. Surely if any court was likely to render decisions friendly to companies charged with creating nuisances, it would be that of Massachusetts.

Between 1828[36] and 1899 the court heard some forty-one appeals involving private and public nuisances polluting water, air, and land, affecting property values and "enjoyment of life." Some involved small-scale, traditional polluters, whose cesspools, pigstyes, privies, or slaughterhouses had damaged others. Some involved more substantial undertakings: petroleum and kerosene refining smells, iron furnace noises and smoke, paper mills, coal company dust, chemical company gases, steam engine and stonecrushing machine noise and vibration, and municipal corporate sewage. Thirty of these suits were brought by private citizens. Overall, plaintiffs won all but five of the forty-one (twenty-seven of the thirty private) nuisance-suit appeals. The Massachusetts bench was tough on polluters. Chief Justice Lemuel Shaw, to give one example, spoke for the court in one such private nuisance case against the New England Worsted Company: "It is sufficient that the effluvia are offensive to the senses, and render habitations uncomfortable. . . . The mill act affords no warrant or excuse for erecting or continuing a nuisance."[37]

Three of the five appeals that were won by defendants involved older, small-scale nuisances (slaughterhouses, wool-pulling); two, newer and larger ones (a paper mill, a steam engine). (A trial jury had found for the defendant paper mill; a statute protected the defendant with the offensive steam engine.)[38] Holmes wrote two doctrinal opinions; no utilitarian dissents.[39] The Massachusetts court, as one might have predicted after reading this much of our story, did not strike out in an instrumentalist, procorporate fashion; it followed English precedent and principles in upholding, generally, the rights of those whose polluting neighbors were corporate entities.

The Industrialization Defense

Next issue: Did courts develop "a new substantive defense for the industrial entrepreneur," an "industrialization defense"? A defendant otherwise guilty of a nuisance was "shielded from liability if he could show that the general geographical area in which the defendant was situated had been given over to industrial or nuisance-producing pursuits." But the proponent of this theory offers only two examples of this for the entire nineteenth century, and in one of these the plaintiff was referred to his action at law for damages.[40] I can offer one more example of it, a decision of the Pennsylvania Supreme Court in 1868.[41] But I must also note nine examples of the rejection of this defense. The burning of coal at a factory in Pittsburgh too near to dwellings was enjoined in 1867. A factory in Connecticut was held to be a nuisance in 1887, even though it was located in the poorer section of a city. A carpet-cleaning establishment emitting smells and fumes near a "thickly settled neighborhood" was enjoined in Pennsylvania in 1891. Seven home-owners on Burnet Street in New Brunswick, New Jersey, complained of dense, cinder-filled smoke coming for twelve straight hours twice a month from a nearby pottery. Chancellor Abraham Zabriskie turned aside the company's "industrialization defense" in 1868 with the observation that it was not true that only "the wealthy" had the law's protection. The New Jersey court would not "fail to secure to the artisan and their families the fewer and more restricted comforts which they enjoy." He enjoined the pottery. Twenty-four years later the same court quoted Zabriskie's views in enjoining a dyeworks from doing further damage to the property of a home-owner.[42] And in 1904 the Pennsylvania Supreme Court turned away J&L Steel's "industrialization defense" of its use of a particularly dirty coal in coking operations in Pittsburgh.[43] The "industrialization defense" appears to have been a chimera.

Coming to the Nuisance

Another shortcoming to the "favoring the company" claims regarding nuisance law was the reaction of jurists when the plaintiff had "come to the nuisance." A decision of the Court of King's Bench in 1600 found a defendant to have acquired prescriptive rights after twenty years to a use of his property, thus barring a newly arrived neighbor's later action of nuisance. This view was echoed by Blackstone and others in later years: A noxious activity practiced in a rural setting for twenty years was free from a bill to enjoin it by a homeowner who "came to the nuisance."[44] Surely industries locating expensive factories apart from settled communities could expect this rule to be observed by sympathetic courts.

But it was not. With what appears to be uniformity, mid-nineteenth-century American jurists *rejected* this rule. Industrial polluters could gain no such prescriptive rights. In 1856 the Massachusetts Supreme Court supported a public-nuisance injunction sought by the Commonwealth on behalf of homeowners who had moved into the vicinity of a twenty-year-old slaughterhouse. Chief Justice Shaw rejected the most recent English authority for the rule as "mere *obiter dicta*" of Abbott, C.J., at nisi prius. He preferred the authority of his colleagues in New York in 1845, who had allowed homeowners in Brooklyn to move in and enjoin a nuisance created by a brewery.[45] These views were echoed in the supreme courts of New Jersey,

Iowa, Maryland, Georgia, Kentucky, Pennsylvania, the United States, Indiana, Connecticut, Michigan, and Illinois.[46]

Courts, then, did not break radically with English tradition in defining nuisances; they did not turn private nuisance plaintiffs away unduly; they did not even turn away plaintiffs who had "come to the nuisance." But several did sometimes engage in "balancing the equities," in cost-benefit analysis, to determine whether or not a polluter should be restrained from operation. And this *was* new. The English Court of Chancery did not "balance the equities."[47]

Balancing the Equities

Nevertheless, the mere fact that a supreme court engaged in such cost-benefit analysis was no evidence that its decisions would be pro-entrepreneurial. Something similar to what courts would do on both sides of the attractive nuisance fight (chapter 7) was happening with regard to pollution nuisance cases as well. Thus the Michigan Supreme Court enjoined the operation of a forging mill, complete with four steam hammers, in 1875, concluding that the damage to the plaintiff's property was "very large, and in comparison with it the value of the defendant's establishment proper is a mere trifle."[48] Christine Rosen has shown us that when Pennsylvania's court *did* engage in cost-benefit analysis (in the fin de siècle), it generally loaded the equation in favor of the defending manufacturer, counting his "value" broadly, while counting those of the plaintiff quite narrowly, as if no one else in the community had suffered any losses. Conversely, the New York high court (and occasionally that of New Jersey) sometimes loaded the equation in the opposite fashion, and consequently shut down the operations of a number of manufacturers. This she attributes to the political balance between the Democratic and Republican Parties in those two states, which forced jurists to be attentive to public opinion, whereas she proposes that the Republican Party's dominance in Pennsylvania and its close financial and ideological ties to industrial enterprise produced for many years a bench unlikely to enjoin polluting corporations.[49] This interpretation sounds right and seems consistent (for Pennsylvania) with a "subsidization of industry" thesis. It finds confirmation in economist Richard Ely's observation in 1886 that "the Supreme Court of Pennsylvania, once renowned for intelligence and integrity, is now a byword and a reproach, and an author of a legal work finds it necessary to warn his students not to attach weight to its decisions, as it is a tool of corporations."[50]

This indictment of the Pennsylvania court in the 1880s and 1890s may, as

I have said, sound right, but certain things should be said in mitigation. As late as 1880 Pennsylvania jurists refused to answer the rhetorical question put to it by counsel for the Pennsylvania Lead Company as the company's counsel intended. "Shall one-fifth the entire lead product of the United States," he asked, "cease to enter the market because Mr. McIntyre's 40 acres have fallen in value?" "Hundreds of thousands" of dollars would be lost "to the people of Pittsburgh" were the lower court injunction against this company to be upheld. The lead company's attorney asked the high court for a judgment "balancing the scales of advantage and disadvantage." This Justice Isaac Gordon and his colleagues would not give him, preferring to let the injunction restraining production to stand. Citing English authority and Horace Gay Wood's *Treatise on the Law of Nuisance* (1875), Gordon found: "Where justice is properly administered, rights are never tolerated because it may be to the advantage of the powerful to impose upon the weak. Whether it be the great corporation with its lead works, or the mechanic with his tin shop, the rule is the same. 'So use your own as not to injure another.'"[51]

In the next several years this court turned away two appeals by the Pennsylvania Coal Company from damage judgments (not injunctions) for pollution of substantial farmer's water supply. It was not until the company had been heard on its third appeal (of a $2,873 award) that a sharply divided court finally agreed (four to three) to "balance the interests" and overturn the lower court judgment.[52]

Pennsylvania Coal Co. v. *Sanderson*, III, may be the baldest example of what Morton Horwitz describes in all of the nineteenth century, but the very fact that it took the company three expensive appeals and a considerable lobbying effort to obtain that four-to-three judgment, establishes just how difficult it was to secure a bench dominated by a pro-entrepreneurial instrumentalist majority. And, in any event, the Pennsylvania jurists had not become transformed into the lockstep Allies of Industry in 1886 with *Sanderson*, III. Rejecting a balancing test, they enjoined the Chemical Fertilizer Company from creating dust and smells in a rural area.[53] Moreover, recall that while Christine Rosen finds Pennsylvania's bench to have behaved at times as Ely's "tool of corporations" when engaging in cost-benefit "balancing of the equities," she finds those of New York, a state just as industrialized as Pennsylvania but less dominated by a single, pro-entrepreneurial political party, to have used the "balancing" rule as often to the disadvantage of corporate polluters as to their advantage. To be sure, when New York's high bench "balanced," they had thereby strayed from an earlier view of one's right to undisturbed enjoyment of property. But the end result still favored plaintiffs in half the cases.

One case has been singled out as a premier, early example of the use of cost-benefit analysis. In *Lexington and Ohio Railroad* v. *Applegate* (1839) Kentucky's chancellor had issued an injunction against the railroad for the nuisance that it constituted on the streets of Louisville. The Kentucky Court of Appeals dismissed this injunction, and these dicta from Chief Justice George Robertson's opinion have been quoted widely: "Private injury and personal damage . . . must be expected from . . . agents of transportation in a populous and prospering city. . . . The onward spirit of the age must, to a reasonable extent, have its way. The law is made for the times, and will be made or modified by them . . . and, therefore, railroads and locomotive steamcars . . . should not, in themselves, be considered as nuisances."

The "candid utility" of this opinion, we are told, was clearly designed "to adopt the law of nuisance to the demands of economic development."[54] Yes and no. Robertson's dicta may be read as being developmental in tone. But we have not been told all of the facts of this case, facts which both help us to understand why the private suit of Mr. Applegate and his associates was dismissed. First, the people of Louisville were particularly enthusiastic in their support of this railroad. Hence the mayor of Louisville, the council, and several of its citizens opposed Applegate's suit. Their affidavits and testimony disputed Applegate's claims that property values would decline and that the railroad would be such a hazard to traffic as to constitute a nuisance. Second, Robertson's opinion did not "balance" these conflicting views; it assessed their credibility. The Chief Justice concluded that Applegate's property value might just as well rise as fall due to the proximity of his business to the railroad's stop, and he agreed with the Mayor that the slow-moving, mechanically controlled train might well prove *less* dangerous to traffic than the steadily rising number of less-controllable carts, hacks, and coaches.[55] (Robertson was probably correct. A study conducted by the French government in the late 1870s is of interest in this regard. It compared accident rates of stagecoaches and railroads from the 1830s to the 1870s and found railroads to have been sixty times safer per passenger-kilometer than stagecoaches. Pedestrians are not passengers, but the ability to control a vehicle run by an inanimate force on a fixed track, as opposed to one driven by an animal capable of bolting in almost any direction, surely mattered to pedestrians, too.)[56]

Moreover, the legislature had chartered the railroad and had authorized it to use the main street of Louisville. This mattered to the court, as such evidence later would to other courts. Legislatures in Connecticut, Massachusetts, Illinois, and elsewhere sometimes defined a steam engine or particular trade as being a nuisance *per se*; they also pronounced specific uses of certain machinery or other property *not* to be nuisances.[57] And to these guidelines courts almost invariably deferred,[58] as they always had.[59] But when a railway went beyond the terms of its charter in extending its tracks into a populated part of a city, it *was* enjoined as a public nuisance in 1838, only a year before *Applegate*, with the observation that "important" as railroads were as "highways of incalculable value to commerce," they must function within the law "else they might become the tyrants of the day." Later in the century, a citizen of Covington, Kentucky, sought to enjoin a railroad that was operating, not under state statutory authority but under a municipal ordinance, from operating trains on city streets. The Kentucky Court of Appeals distinguished the case from *Applegate* and upheld the chancellor's injunction. The trains ground to a halt.[60]

Damages at Common Law versus Injunctions

Whether by balancing the equities, or by deciding the nuisance to be too slight, or by some other measure, some nineteenth-century American jurists, sitting as chancellors in equity proceedings, refused to enjoin many alleged nuisances. This Paul Kurtz has made clear. He allows that these jurists might refer some plaintiffs to their common-law remedy of damages, but he dismisses this as inconsequential. A common-law suit for damages "could be annoying," but "the entrepreneur could spread the cost of litigation, as well as the judgments themselves, among investors or consumers."[61]

I am not as sure of that. Nor was the Pennsylvania Coal Company in the Gilded Age when it pursued those three appeals from damage awards to Mrs. Sanderson.[62] The company finally faced a $2,873 judgment, but it knew that it faced more than that, because this was not its only mine and not the only water supply it was likely to be accused of polluting. Realizing that many others were capable of claiming the same sorts of damages as the plaintiff they faced now, many textile mills, iron foundries, slaughterhouses, municipalities, railroads, and refineries, as well as coal operators, treated such damage suits quite seriously. It is true, as Kurtz notes, that a "perpetual" injunction represented "permanent interruption of business operations," whereas damages amounted only to a forced "taking" with compensation. But, as he points out himself, there was very little English precedential authority for actually enjoining polluters.[63] Moreover, in a number of states in the antebellum era equity jurisdiction was still quite limited. It was defined and sanctioned, as deemed appropriate, by the legislature. For example, it was not until 1827 that Massachusetts courts were allowed to hear nuisance suits in equity, and then only when the plaintiff's remedy at law was deemed to be in doubt or inadequate.[64] Nonetheless, industrial polluters sometimes escaped injunctions because courts worried about their economic consequences, and that is sufficient cause to say that something like a Jurisprudence of the Hand may have been moving on those benches then.

John McLaren has said of England's judiciary that its efforts to curb industrial nuisances in the nineteenth century "failed not because of doctrinal weakness, but because it was no match for the social problems spawned by industrialization." Its "basically reactive quality" ultimately had to be aided by the more anticipatory law of statutory regulation.[65] Something of the same sort of judgment might be passed on America's nineteenth-century judiciary: It generally stuck to its guns, but some of them were "Quaker" guns and others were smoothbore in a rifled world.

Part Two

Strong Currents:
A Jurisprudence of the Heart

Chapter Four

Abandoning an Unneighborly Rule: Putting Out the Ancient-Lights Doctrine

In Part I we caught glimpses of a Jurisprudence of the Heart in the American judiciary's partiality toward gift-beneficiaries and its propensity to create "principled" exceptions to the assumption-of-risk and fellow-servant rules. In the next six chapters we see this jurisprudence in other action, creating new rules and abandoning old ones in one sector of the private law of property and several sectors close to the core of contract and tort law.

THE JURISPRUDENCE OF THE HEART: OPENING
GATES FOR PREVIOUSLY POWERLESS PLAINTIFFS

In the relatively static field of property law, jurists abandoned a rule in the domain of easements that had produced unneighborly behavior (chapter 4). As we saw in chapter 2, jurists remained faithful to centuries-old precedents and principles in the fields of sales contracts, but they proved to be more willing to aid the propertyless and powerless when it came to the law of service contracts (chapters 5 and 6). In chapter 3 we saw that in tort suits for damages due to personal injury, jurists continued (the operant word) to require that the accident had been foreseeable, that the defendant be proven to have been at fault, and that the plaintiff not have been at fault herself (the venerable contributory-negligence, assumption-of-risk, and fellow-servant defenses). In chapters 7 and 8 we will see that they relaxed some of the elements that plaintiffs had to prove and abandoned some of the defenses available to corporations charged with having caused their injuries when the plaintiffs were children or Good Samaritans. They also abandoned the sovereign-immunity defense that municipal and county authorities had enjoyed to block suits by adults as well as children who had been injured on defective roads and bridges (chapter 9). And they sanctioned the unprecedented picking of corporate "deep pockets" by nineteenth-century juries (chapter 9).

In each of the next six chapters I try to explain the particular innovation at issue, relying, in large measure, on the rationales offered by jurists themselves but also looking beyond them to socioeconomic and cultural contexts. In a concluding chapter I offer three more general explanations for this propensity to make proplaintiff changes in the rules of law, for this Jurisprudence of the Heart.

ANCIENT LIGHTS, IMPLIED GRANTS, AND GOOD NEIGHBORS

Several legal historians have reported the "overthrow" in antebellum America of longstanding English legal authority regarding the "ancient-lights" easement. In the past, one could acquire a prescriptive right by "adverse possession" after the uninterrupted passage of twenty years or more to the light entering one's windows through the air above a neighbor's property.[1] This easement was antidevelopmental in character and was thus "out of place—or so the courts thought—in a country bent on economic growth, trying to promote, not curb, the intensive use of land." Hence jurists extinguished the ancient-lights doctrine here in proper developmentalist fashion.[2]

Or did they? The occasional appearance of progrowth dicta in a few American cases involving claims of ancient lights turns out to be utterly misleading. American jurists addressing this question remained largely doctrinal in their approach throughout, from the moment in 1815 when this doctrine was first discussed in the appellate record here until at least 1880. And when they did indicate that they felt the doctrine of ancient lights was not applicable in America, they often gave quite *un*developmental reasons for rejecting it. Ultimately, the rule was abandoned because of its antisocial ramifications—that is, because it led to un-Christian behavior.

The doctrine of ancient lights *was* virtually extinguished in America, but not in the manner that the reigning paradigm would have it. Before we can appreciate what it was that eventually did this doctrine in, it might be appropriate to ask what the doctrine actually consisted of in 1815, when the first American high court was asked to rule on it.

Both sunlight and moonlight were important sources of illumination until well into the late nineteenth century. Whale oil, kerosene lamps, and, by midcentury, gas lighting were improvements in illumination over the more modest (and expensive) candlepower of the more distant past, but it was not until the turn of the century that electric power became available to the typical urban home or shop. And England was high in latitude, with short winter days. Those who could afford to built living and dining rooms with high ceilings and many windows rising nearly to the ceilings in order to capture as much of the morning and evening light as possible. Hence the struggle over legal access to sun and moon rays was not insignificant. But so was the struggle for space in the increasingly crowded communities of eighteenth- and nineteenth-century Britain. Both the population and the tendency of commercial activities to be centralized were on the rise. London was becoming a megalopolis.[3]

In the sixteenth and seventeenth centuries the English common law had it that one whose windows had enjoyed the light shining through them from over the land of a neighbor for over forty years had thereby acquired a prescriptive right (easement) to that light, barring the neighbor from building anything on his or her property that would block those "ancient lights."[4] However, in 1761 Justice Wilmot, instructing a jury at nisi prius, reasoned that, since other easements required only *twenty* years of adverse possession, it was "absurd" to hold that the easement of ancient lights should take any longer.[5] His view of the law was not reviewed by a court en banc, but it was reported by the fabled Sergeant Williams and thus reached American shores by the early nineteenth century.[6]

With continued urban growth in the late eighteenth and early nineteenth centuries, English jurists made it clear that before one could secure either an injunction against, or damages for, the obstruction of his or her ancient lights by a neighbor's new building or wall, one had to establish that there had been a "real injury" to one's effective use of a home or business.[7] And even then, despite Wilmot's instructions, one might recover only nominal damages. Parliament deemed it necessary in 1832 to assert positively that one might acquire the perpetual right to light through one's windows by the uninterrupted enjoyment of it for only twenty years. In pursuit of a public policy that the future Charles III might applaud, they also abrogated the legally recognized "custom" in London of permitting property owners to raise buildings "to whatever height [they] might think fit."[8] At least one English jurist found this statute distressing, sensitive to what he called "the growing necessity for lofty buildings." Lord Cranworth also offered this developmental guideline for judges instructing juries: "The steady spread of buildings in and round large towns gradually, but surely, obstructs some of the light and air which the houses of the interior of the place formerly enjoyed, and in estimating the damage . . . we must not omit the consideration that the place in which he complains of obstruction to light and air is a large and populous city."[9] And when one property owner "put up a screen" on the edge of his line as the twenty-year limit approached, Lord Wensleydale complained (in 1859) that "it is going too far to say that a man is bound" to shut out the light from his neighbor's window "to prevent a right being acquired against him" by that neighbor.[10]

Nonetheless, for all their growing impatience with the doctrine of ancient lights, English jurists of the nineteenth century remained true to an associated, equally old, and perhaps ultimately more significant rule regarding the right to light for one's windows from the space above a neighbor's property. Where a contractor owning two or more lots sold or leased a windowed building that had been erected close to the next lot's line, that contractor was barred from building anything on that adjacent, now "servient" lot that might block the lights of the first building. Nor would his selling or leasing that servient lot to another with such an object in mind create such a right. And no significant passage of prescriptive time was necessary to vest the owner of the first building with an easement claim to the light. Rather, the grant of light was regarded by the courts as having been implied immediately in the contract of sale.[11] Some home construction took the form of a row or crescent of houses with common walls. But others were intended to stand alone, with contractors building sequences of houses, one house being completed and sold before the contractor's financial means to break ground for others might be in place. Hence this rule of an implied grant of light led builders to leave enough space on at least two sides of each lot for light to be accessible to all. Some of this space, in western London, might become garden; some to the east might be mere alleys. But space for light and air there would be in any event.[12]

What, exactly, did American courts do with these two legal legacies? Between 1785 and 1880 some sixteen jurisdictions adopted one or both of them. Several courts applied the doctrine of "ancient lights" in the early nineteenth century. However, as in England, judicial resistance to the ancient-lights doctrine appeared in 1838 and led four such jurisdictions by 1877 to overrule earlier opinions adopting that rule.[13] To these four may be added eight other state high courts that rejected the doctrine from the start,[14] leaving only five clinging to it by 1880, albeit a sixth, New York, rediscovered it in the era of the elevated railway and the skyscraper.[15] As for the "implied grant" rule, as late as 1880 all supreme courts, excepting Ohio's and Pennsylvania's,[16] continued to espouse the rule that grants of light from adjacent undeveloped lots were implied in a sale by one who owned both lots.[17]

While a few opinions limiting or rejecting the ancient-lights doctrine do contain instrumentalist dicta (in the nature of public policy rationales) that have a prodevelopmental ring to them,[18] several other opinions rejecting it are doctrinal in nature, reflecting, and citing, the qualms English courts were having with its "want of sound principle."[19] Some noted that the rule conflicted with the generally understood rule that a property owner's fee ran from the center of the earth perpendicularly to the heavens ("the owner of the soil owns the sky, and the lowest depths"); the ancient-lights doctrine would be "a perpetual restraint, upon his dominion over his own."[20] It was, New York's Justice Greene Bronson maintained, with numerous citations, "clearly a departure from the old [English common] law," arising from "the custom of London."[21] As such, Illinois's high court concluded, it had not been the part of the common law of England at the time the American colonies were settled.[22] In any event, as both Bronson and Maine's Justice Ether Shepley explained, the doctrine "misapplied" the "principle by which . . . easements are acquired," in that with "ancient" windows there was little of the overtly adverse use made of another's property that might put the other on notice of impending loss, as with other easements.[23] This, after all, had been the reason that the original, pre-Wilmot, English rule had required some *forty* years of adverse use, whereas all other prescriptive use rules required only twenty. The doctrine, especially in its twenty-year-limit form, violated good common-law principles and was unreasonable.

Other opinions rejecting the doctrine may appear at first glance to offer a prodevelopment rationale for that course, but on closer reading, their reasoning seems quite *anti*developmental. Ask yourself, as Henry George did in Chicago in the 1870s, which policy is more developmental: one whereby vacant lots remain undeveloped for as long as their speculator-owners chose, with no adverse legal consequences (the state of affairs prevailing *after* the rejection of the ancient-lights doctrine), or one whereby such speculators lose the right to build as they might wish if they fail to do so within twenty years of their neighbor's constructing a building? In a very real sense, the ancient-lights doctrine had *developmental* consequences, whereas abandoning it served to reward those who preferred merely to wait for the activities of their neighbors to increase the value of their own lots,[24] or those who were too capital-poor to be able to develop the land. Listen to Justice Molton Rogers of the Pennsylvania Supreme Court on the doctrine: "[It] should be introduced with caution. Many vacant lots in our cities and towns are owned by persons who reside at a distance, and who are either *unable* or unwilling to improve them. It would be inconvenient to compel them to do so, on the penalty of forfeiting a valuable right by neglect."

To these jurists, then, those who were seen to benefit from the abandoning of the ancient-lights doctrine were either unproductive speculators or people of modest means. In neither event could these objects of judicial so-

151

licitude be confused with energetic Capitalist developers. On the contrary, they worried about constraints the rule would place on a neighbor seeking to enlarge his house "according to the demands of a growing or improving family."[25]

To add complexity, I offer a case where both reason and the Bible were invoked. Indiana's supreme court rejected ancient lights in 1877. Justice Horace Biddle found the rule to be unreasonable: "To give a right of property in light . . . is to make the incident greater than the principal, and allow the shadow to control the substance." But while he cited the authority of New York (*Parker* v. *Foote*) and those state high courts that followed New York's lead, Justice Biddle also cited a higher authority: " 'And upon whom doth his light arise?' Job 25, 3 . . . 'The wind bloweth where it listeth, and thou hearest the sound thereof, but canst not tell whence it cometh, and wither it goeth.' St. John 3, 8."[26]

There is, ultimately, a more important problem with the current interpretation of the extinguishing of the ancient-lights doctrine. Those interpretations draw our attention to the alleged developmental concerns of New York's Justice Greene Bronson in the leading American case for the rejection of the rule, *Parker* v. *Foote*: "The doctrine cannot be applied in the growing cities and villages of this country, without working the most mischievous consequences." What are we to understand Justice Bronson to have meant by "mischievous consequences"? Morton Horwitz clearly intends for us to understand that Bronson had antidevelopmental consequences in mind,[27] but when we see the remark in context, we realize that he was placing a completely different problem before the reader.

The ancient-lights doctrine, Bronson explained, often led one who wanted to avoid the loss of his right to build, to erect a temporary dead wall "20 to 50 feet high" along his property line, blocking his neighbors windows, simply to overcome the rule whereby the enjoyment of that light might ripen into a bar on his future right to build. Bronson knew that; he had read English cases in which those were the facts at issue, and he knew that "indeed, an attempt had been made to sustain an action for erecting such a wall" only three years before in his own court. This was *Mahan* v. *Brown* (1835), in which the doctrine of ancient lights had been applied by the former chief justice of the New York Supreme Court, John Savage, to a case involving such a wall, with little ado. The ancient-lights rule was applicable, and it was "too well settled to require discussion or authority to support it" (though he cited some).[28] To Bronson's colleague in *Parker* v. *Foote*, Justice Esek Cowen, Savage's reading of the common law had been correct. Cowen dissented from crucial elements of Bronson's decision. But Bronson carried the new chief justice, Samuel Nelson, with him and together they overruled *Mahan v. Brown*. Why? Because the building of such a wall was an extreme and unneighborly act that ought to be discouraged by the law. "A wanton act of this kind . . . is calculated to render a man odious," Bronson observed, and who would have disagreed with him? This antisocial behavior flowed logically from the ancient-lights doctrine, in Bronson's judgment, and it was this propensity that constituted its "mischievous consequences."[29]

New York's neighbor, Vermont, elaborated on Bronson's "good neighbor" policy in *Hubbard v. Town* (1860). The establishing of the ancient-lights doctrine in Vermont, Justice John Pierpont opined, would be bad public policy: "It would require a man to erect a building or wall that he did not need . . . for the sole purpose of excluding the light from his neighbor's windows[. It] would lead to continual strife and bitterness of feeling between neighbors and result in much mischief."[30]

Morton Horwitz in particular relies on *Parker v. Foote* in his economic-oriented analysis. But he also notes a lecture delivered by attorney William Curtis Noyes to the Law Association of New York City (and published the next year in *American Jurist*) as further evidence of the prodevelopmental character of that decision.[31] That does little justice to Noyes's lecture. Noyes, who had represented the successful defendant in *Parker v. Foote*, began by noting the distress expressed in the city over "the erection of a wall apparently useless except to shut out the light" to "the upper story of a new banking house, recently put up by the Bank of the United States" at an appropriately named address, Wall Street. Noyes noted that "malice or wantonness" was often associated with such stopping of lights. He then reviewed English and New York case law to establish, as would Maine's Ether Shepley in 1847,[32] that Justice Wilmot's nisi prius instructions in 1761 had "misled" later courts to allow an easement for light after the passage of a mere twenty years. Wilmot's reasoning was "founded altogether in false analogy" since there was "no manual or pedal occupation" of land to put the other owner on notice of adverse possession as there was when one secured a right-of-way, depastured a common, or took fish from another's waters. With lights, the possession was "merely ocular." And, after all, Wilmot's instructions to the jury had not been reviewed "by the judges in bank" but had merely been reported by Sergeant Williams in his edition of Sir Edmund Saunders's reports. Some of what the English reporters offered could safely be dismissed: "Let your minds be well stored with legal principles," Noyes told his colleagues, "and there is little danger of being lost or being led astray among the mass of cases."[33]

Noyes had no doubt that truly old buildings *were* entitled to ancient lights, and he cited both *Bury* v. *Pope* and *Mahan* v. *Brown* approvingly in this regard. The rule that an enjoyment of light for over forty years constituted an easement was "rational." He also regarded as proper the rule implying a grant of light when a builder sold a house with windows close to the property line of an adjacent lot that the builder had not yet developed.[34] Noyes's message was that there was no *need* for unneighborly walls. Forty years of uninterrupted enjoyment of light was a *lot* of enjoyment, longer than any Wall Street developer was likely to allow a neighbor. Noyes assured his colleagues that Wilmot's flawed dicta could safely be ignored. Vacant lots could be left vacant for reasonable periods of time. No one need slap up any window-darkening walls.

Noyes spoke to the New York legal profession about the window-darkening wall on Wall Street in 1839. Herman Melville, Lemuel Shaw's son-in-law, wrote of another in 1853. His story of "Bartleby, the Scrivener, A Story of Wall Street" is narrated by his employer, a "Master in Chancery" with an office on Wall Street.[35] Could the "lofty brick wall, black by age and everlasting shade," that stood but ten feet from Bartleby's sole window and steadily drew him into "dead-wall reveries" have been such a preemptive wall? Was the lack of sunlight that so plunged Bartleby into depression and unsocial behavior due to the antisocial consequences of the easement provision in the doctrine of ancient lights? Perhaps; but, alas, we cannot (or, in any event, we *will* not) further deconstruct Bartleby's premodernist wall.

But we can offer a real "dead-wall," built in San Francisco in 1877, to shed some light on the question. The California railroad baron Charles Crocker found that his less affluent neighbor on Nob Hill, one Nicholas Yung, would not agree to Crocker's offer to purchase Yung's little lot and house. Crocker reacted by building a thirty-foot-high wall around three sides of his neighbor's property (see illustration 2). If Yung sued Crocker, the pleas of the parties were consumed along with all others from this era in the fire that followed the earthquake of 1907. But we can at least hold it likely that Crocker's attorney would have defended him against the claim that this was a "spite" fence by calling it a preemptive wall necessary to protect Crocker's rights under the ancient-lights doctrine, which had not as yet formally been abrogated in California. In any event, if there was ever a "wanton act . . . calculated to render a man odious," one that "would lead to continual strife and bitterness of feeling between neighbors and result in much mischief," it was Crocker's wall. In addition to the anger that Yung felt, it inspired two rallies of Dennis Kearney's Workingmen's Party, complete with threats by Kearney to tear the wall down and beat Crocker "with sticks."[36]

*Charles Crocker, head of the Southern Pacific Railroad, raised these "dead walls"
at the back of his mansion on Nob Hill, San Francisco, around three sides of the
property of Nicholas Yung in the late 1870s. (Department of Special Collections,
Stanford University Library)*

What light has been shed by our story of the window of opportunity that
opened when the doctrine of ancient lights was extinguished in nineteenth-
century America? We have found two doctrines, only one of which, ancient
lights, was rejected, but not until midcentury, and then not everywhere. It
appears to have survived, at least as high court doctrine, in New Jersey, Mississippi, Delaware, North Carolina, and Louisiana, was rediscovered in
New York, and was only extinguished in Massachusetts by legislative fiat,
in 1852.[37] The other, less ancient, implied-grants doctrine survived everywhere but in Ohio and Pennsylvania. Yes, some jurists incorrectly used pro-

developmental language in discussing ancient lights; but more jurists chose doctrinal reasons in rejecting its twenty-year prescriptive version. Other jurists, including the author of the "leading case," offered good-neighbor public-policy rationales; and still others offered *anti*developmental reasoning that would have troubled Henry George (and Richard Posner). On balance, the reigning paradigm has greatly overstated the developmental bias of nineteenth-century American jurists and has misunderstood the reluctance of some jurists to approve a rule that, although developmental in character, was nevertheless unacceptable because it was decidedly unneighborly.[38] If "good fences make good neighbors," no walls made better ones, and nineteenth-century jurists were interested in finding common-law rules that would help make good neighbors.

Chapter Five

Bottomed on Justice: Allowing What Her Labor Was Worth to the Worker Who Quit

The Jurisprudence of the Heart skirmished with the Jurisprudence of the Head over issues involving personal breaches of labor contracts in the nineteenth century, winning over half of these skirmishes after its first victory in 1834. At stake were the social relations of employers and employees in the "moral economy" that many jurists hoped would prevail in the new Republic. In any event, that is the way I read the "texts." The reigning paradigm reads them quite differently. So we begin with its statement of the case.

Some legal historians have argued that America's jurists displayed a "class bias" in shaping the rules regarding labor contracts during the antebellum "Golden Age" of American law. According to one, the law of labor contracts constitutes the "most important class of cases" in which the "painfully obvious . . . alliance" of judges and commercial-industrial interests overpowered the social compact that farmers, villages, and small traders had enjoyed. The "discriminatory application" by those judges of "the recently discovered chasm between express and implied contracts" with regard to labor meant that labor contracts were now being treated as "entire," indivisible legal entities, "a change in contract law" necessary "to meet the needs of the newly emergent market economies in England and America." In the early nineteenth century workers, for the first time, were being held strictly to the terms of their employment contracts. A worker who quit after eleven months of a twelve-month contract for services would find that appellate courts would not permit him or her to recover any wages that might have been held back pending completion of the contract, or so this view maintains.[1]

Since most such contracts held back substantial fractions of pay until "completion," courts that treated such contracts as "entire," and required completion of its terms as the "condition precedent" to payment are seen as having systematically placed worker-plaintiffs at a disadvantage, useful to employers who sought to instill work discipline. Courts resolved "all ambiguity" in such contracts "in favor of the employer's contention that they were 'entire.' " Consequently, employers were increasingly tempted to treat workers badly "to create conditions near the end of the term that would encourage the laborer to quit," and some employers unfairly fired their employees and refused to pay them the monies held back.[2]

We are told that there were two exceptions to this pattern. First, New Hampshire's court allowed workers who quit to collect the value of their labor for the months and days their employer had benefited from their work (on a quantum meruit count "off the contract"). But this case, *Britton* v. *Turner*,[3] was "the solitary challenge" to the "new . . . doctrine against *quantum meruit* recovery in labor cases." New Hampshire stood alone, and the decision's value to workers was weakened by its providing offset damages to employer-defendants for losses to property.[4] Second, appellate courts distinguished labor contracts for personal service (farm laborers, operatives, servants, and artisans) from those of road engineers and house builders. These latter sorts of "contractors" were permitted to recover sums "off the contract," even if they did not complete the work or meet the standards set out in the contract, through pleas of quantum meruit (for the value of the labor) and quantum valebant (for the value of materials) if the other party did not clearly refuse their product as "unworkmanlike" or if the other party had any benefit of the product. This was so because road engineers and house builders were themselves small entrepreneurs, and, as such, received "special solicitude" by courts because of their "class bias." "The result was that in Massachusetts and in most other states two separate lines of cases were developed, one dealing with service contracts, for which recovery in quantum meruit was barred, and another applying to building contracts, for which recovery 'off the contract' of the reasonable value of the performance was permitted."[5]

How accurate are these descriptions of the development of the law of labor contracts in the nineteenth century? Was the plight of service workers worsening in the manner they relate? Were workers more vulnerable to unscrupulous employers, as argued, near the end of the contract's term because of the "all-or-nothing" rule? How uncommon was the allowance of quantum meruit recovery in the fashion of *Britton* v. *Turner*? And was it the case that road and house builders were favored over farm laborers and operatives in quantum meruit recovery?

I will argue that these views on breaches of labor contracts are quite misleading: that the plight of service workers under the law was *not* worsening, but that, to the contrary, such developments as occurred in the law of labor contracts in nineteenth-century America operated to the *benefit* of service workers, and that builders were *not* favored by courts over service workers as has been claimed. As such, I conclude that some jurists acted doctrinally, applying the law as they received it, while others attempted to soften the harsher edges of that law, to the disadvantage of their own socioeconomic class.

THE ENGLISH AND SCOTTISH BACKGROUND, 1600–1800

One searches in vain for an idyllic past in the history of British labor law. The Parliament and royal courts of medieval and early modern England were no source of strength for the unpropertied laborer. Medieval year-books contain many damage suits (in trespass) by employers against tilers, sowers, mowers, shepherds, smiths, roofers, millwrights, ditchdiggers, joiners, and carpenters who had "failed to carry out" their contractual agreement and were thereby to forfeit a penal bond they had posted. The Ordinance of Labourers (1349) and Statute of Labourers (1350–51) impressed workers during the Black Plague in the mid-fourteenth century, and remained available to local sheriffs and justices thereafter to require work of all and to prohibit one from leaving such work until the end of its term. By 1355 actions "for departure," founded on the statute, can be found in the yearbooks, preventing the quitting of tillers, reapers, mowers, and most artisans. Carpenters who covenanted to serve "when required," however, were not perceived as retained servants and could not be compelled to work, but by 1500 a carpenter could be sued for nonfeasance damages if he did not complete on time a house that he had agreed to build by a certain date "just as well as if he had made it badly" (in the words of Justice Spilman in *Pickering v. Thoroughgood* [1533]).[6] The Master and Servant Act of 1747 gave justices of the peace the authority to punish those laborers who left their employers before the harvest was home with wage abatement, imprisonment, and whipping. An amendment to the act in 1765 observed that workers "who contract with persons for certain terms" too often "leave their respective services before the terms of their contracts are fulfilled; to the great disappointment and loss of the persons with whom they so contract." Consequently, the amended act made such breaches of the contract a criminal offense. In 1823 Parliament added a new crime: If, upon entering into a written labor contract, one changed one's mind and failed to *commence* the work, one could be criminally prosecuted.[7] As late as 1875 about two thousand agricultural laborers were still being convicted and imprisoned each year for leaving or threatening to leave their employers or for "surly behavior" at work.[8]

Most farm laborers and colliers in England and Scotland were hired for "the one year binding" in the sixteenth, seventeenth, and early eighteenth centuries, and operatives in the first English factories (such as those of Richard Arkwright) signed labor contracts of three or six months, or one, three, or five year's duration. The "yearly hire," common to agriculture, "was very early extended too far beyond agricultural work to conditions which it did not fit at all,"[9] but many industrial managers soon replaced "the long hire" with piece-rate contracts or shorter contracts with clauses holding back two weeks' or one months' pay as a period of "notice," and many colliers and other unionized workers eventually secured extremely short-term contracts, enabling them to strike on short notice without loss of pay.[10]

Not so with agricultural laborers. Hiring fairs at Petty Sessions in the spring brought farmers and laborers together for "the binding" of the long-term agricultural labor contract, which typically included "victuals" and some small sum of "earnest" money (called "God's penny" or "the fastening penny") in down payment (the "consideration" in contract law) and the promise of small sums in the early months, slightly larger sums during the heat of the summer and harvest period, a larger harvest payment ("Michaelmas money"), and a substantial sum held back until the completion of the year.

The "early" payments tended to be larger in southern England, where yearly hired men (formally called "farm servants") competed with day laborers from the villages who were hired for the harvest season, and where specialized grain farming led to a more compressed (six-month) season. In Scotland and northeastern England, where mixed farming required attention for a longer season, the "long hire," with most of the salary held back until the end of the term, was deemed "well suited" as a means of disciplining the sparser labor market.[11]

For our purposes, it is worth nothing that the courts tended to assume a yearly hire, in the absence of evidence to the contrary, whenever an employee had worked for several months. As William Blackstone put it in 1765: "If the hiring be general without any particular time limited, the law construes it to be a hiring for a year, upon a principle of natural equity, that the servant shall serve, and the master maintain him throughout all the revolutions of the respective seasons; as well when there is work to be done as when there is not."[12]

Blackstone's language, his reference to "natural equity," to the obligations of masters as well as servants, suggests a "moral economy" of fair play,
enforced by law. The legal record of eighteenth- and early-nineteenth-century England reveals a harsher, more one-sided reality in the legal relations
of employers ("masters") and employees ("servants"). In the first place, the
labor contract was not deemed to imply free medical care. Thus workers
who broke arms or legs while in the service of others might be obliged to pay
for their own physicians or surgeons or have their wages abated.[13]

In the second place, English workers and servants were subject to rather
arbitrary and legally enforced cuffings, threats, and fines, imposed by their
master, for signs of insubordination, inattention, immorality, or sloth, and
they were subject to dismissal and forfeiture of all payment for brief unex-
cused absences.[14] Thus when a young female domestic, denied permission
by her mistress to visit her dying mother, went anyway for one evening and
was fired without pay, the Court of Exchequer unanimously denied her appeal of wrongful dismissal.[15] And when a farm servant with only a few
months remaining on an annual contract, who had just completed several
hours of work and was sitting down to dinner, refused his master's order to
walk a mile immediately to fetch a horse, he was fired and denied all of his
annual salary. He sued in assumpsit and, at nisi prius, was told by Lord Ellenborough that his master was completely within his rights and that he had
no claim to a farthing of wages.[16] The justice of the peace in Kelso, in the
lowlands of Scotland, was quoted on the same subject in 1807: "It was a mistake in [farm] servants, hired by the year or half year, to suppose that, after
their ordinary work hours, they are at liberty to dispose of or absent themselves as they please without their master's leave; that, on the contrary, all
such servants are bound to be at their master's call, at all times during their
service, by day or by night, when occasion requires."[17]

In the third place, workers who left voluntarily (that is, quit) before the
completion date (or other condition) of the "entire" contract were not allowed to recover any apportioning of the contract in the nature of a quantum meruit for the value of their rendered services. The end-of-contract
lump-sum payment "stood as a bond for good and faithful service," as two
English legal historians recently put it. That was the rule as early as the fifteenth century, when an English court of Westminster found that "if a priest
be retained for a year to serve by chanting, etc. and he depart within the term
he has no remedy for his salary because the contract is entire." It was the rule
in 1622 when Michael Dalton wrote in *Country Justice*: "If a servant of his
own accord shall depart from his master before his time expired, he shall

161

lose all his wages." It was the rule in 1687 when a rent collector on an annual, "entire agreement" died with three months left in his contract; his estate received nothing. It was the rule as Charles Viner described it in a note written in 1747 and published in a later edition of his *Abridgement of the Laws of England*, and it was the rule set down by John Williams, serjeant-at-law and editor of Sir Edmund Saunders's *The Reports of Cases in the Court of King's Bench in the Time of the Reign of Charles II*. Thus wives of seamen who had died before the final port in the shipping articles had been reached, seamen whose ship had been lost in a storm, seamen dismissed by the master before the end of the voyage, painters, weavers, farm servants, and factory winders who had quit before the end of the term were all denied any apportioning of the labor contract by the courts. Such a rule "had prevailed," Lord Kenyon noted in one such frequently cited case, *Cutter* v. *Powell*, "so long as to be reduced to an axiom in the law"—to wit, no recovery on a quantum meruit in the breaching of an express, "entire" contract.[18]

THE STATE OF LABOR LAW IN COLONIAL AMERICA

Neither England nor Scotland in the seventeenth, eighteenth, and early nineteenth centuries offered solace in their courts to laborers who had worked for months and who sought to prevent wrongful dismissal, or abusive treatment, or who sought recovery on a quantum meruit count "off the contract." Colonial America does not appear to have offered much solace either. To begin with, the institution of slavery was created and imposed on blacks imported from Africa and the West Indies. That was as ugly an innovation in labor law as one might imagine, but there was more. Many white laborers enjoyed less permanent, but virtually as grim a form of long-term bondage if they entered into an indenture of service in exchange for free passage to the colonies. Indentured servants "could not marry without their master's consent, vote or engage in trade," and court records "are full of complaints" by them "about beatings, bad food, nakedness, cold and general misery."[19] Indentured servants who broke their contractual terms were often sentenced to serve as many as ten days for every one they had missed, and to whippings and periods of imprisonment.[20]

Slavery and indentured servitude aside, what of those who remained free to bargain for their labor services? How did they fare in the colonial courts compared to their English and Scottish counterparts? Wages could be higher in the colonies (although there were serious and often successful efforts in the first century by towns, county councils, and colonial legislatures to set maximum limits to service contracts).[21] Colonial coopers, sawyers, smiths, glaziers, tanners, shoemakers, hatters, sailmakers, and those in the clothing trades were generally paid piece-rate. Seamen were paid by the voyage, forge and furnace workers by the day, week, or month. Farm laborers generally contracted for "the yearly hire."[22]

But whatever their terms, these contracts were treated as being "entire" in the courts. Hired hands, bookkeepers, coopers, and servants in seventeenth-century Maryland often entered into signed and sealed agreements ("covenants") to work for so many pounds of tobacco "per Annum" for "the space and time of one whole year" (or some other term), to be paid only when the term was "fully to be compleat and ended," the cooper to forfeit so many pounds of tobacco if his hogsheads were undelivered by a certain date. They and their employer would then "binde themselves each to other in the sume of" so many pounds of tobacco (the "penal bond").[23]

What happened to the hired hand or sharecropper who quit before the term of the contract was "compleat" and sought partial payment? He lost. In 1662 Samuel Price sued his employer, John Wheeler, for the value of two and a half months' work on a one-year sharecropping contract ("for a share of corne and tobacco"). His employer noted that Price's board (the "diat that hee had") "was more worth then his worke." Price had worked in Charles County, Maryland, from March to mid-May, but he then "went away and broake his Covenant," working "in other places," and his employer felt that he "thearfor desarved nothing." The county court agreed, and nonsuited Price, ordering him to pay costs. Seamen who left their ship before the completion of the agreed-upon voyage were unable to recover anything (other than what might already have been freely advanced them) in the common pleas or vice-admiralty courts of the provinces of Massachusetts, Connecticut, Maryland, Virginia, and South Carolina and forfeited some or all of their wages for absence-without-leave or disobedience.[24] In 1651 New Haven's town court sought to order one seaman to "goe the voyage and doe his service" and ended in imprisoning him for his "stubborne" behavior and for giving "uncomely answers." In 1697 Maryland's council, reacting to an employer's petition, ordered Richard Lewis, a carpenter, to the "Dungeon, there to Remain" until he pledged to "better behave himself and make due complyance in following his work."[25] Manuals for justices of the peace published in the eighteenth century in Virginia and North Carolina explained how overseers absent from work were to have their wages and in-kind shares forfeited, and damages to crops caused by their absence or mismanagement levied against them.[26] Those on personal service contracts in seventeenth-century Springfield, Massachusetts, found that John Pyncheon, the justice of the peace (and a major property owner), treated their contracts as "entire"; they could but rarely recover anything "off the contract" and might find that the bonds they had entered into to ensure their performance as a ploughman or a joiner were now forfeit.[27] A young female domestic servant who fled to her parent's home for two days after having been struck by her mistress was ordered by Pyncheon to "the house of correction" and her father was given a suspended fine for abetting her breach of the contract.[28] In some colonies domestic servants and those employed at inns were made to surrender all tips they received to their masters. In short, most traditional elements of the law of labor contracts were often enforced in the colonies as they were in England, to the discomfort of some who were engaged in the sale of personal services for a living. But inasmuch as this was what they had known in the British Isles, workers in colonial America probably accepted these rules without ado. Thus when James Hopkins quit after serving for a short period of time as the Rev. Ebenezer Parkman's hired hand on his farm in Massachusetts in 1780, his employer noted in his journal that Hopkins asked for no payment and offered to "pay the Damage of Disappointment."[29]

Nonetheless, there are indications that some colonial courts may have been more evenhanded with laborers than were their English and Scottish counterparts. "Free" artisans and hired hands could at least quit "entire" contracts by the eighteenth century without fear of being arrested, imprisoned, or compelled to return to work. Some courts offered no relief to servants who complained of being abused or fired while seriously ill,[30] but others ordered masters to pay the doctor's fees of ill or injured servants.[31] And a few cases can be found, in the Dutch civil law courts of New Amsterdam, the Rhode Island Vice-Admiralty Court, and courts of seventeenth-century West Jersey, Plymouth Plantation, Maryland, North Carolina, and eighteenth-century New York City, which allowed appropriate recovery to laborers and artisans who had sued for wages or claimed they had been unfairly fired.[32]

Consequently, it may be that, on balance, colonial laborers were slightly better off than their British counterparts in litigating labor agreements, by virtue of the fact that punitive master-servant statutes were often not applied, and breaches of contracts by *employers* were not tolerated in many colonial courts. Did the courts impose a new rigor in the days of the early Republic (1780–1860)?

PERSONAL SERVICE CONTRACT
LITIGATION IN THE EARLY REPUBLIC

I believe I have now established that there was no historical retrogression
with regard to the law of labor contracts—that is, there was no erosion of
"fairness" or decline of a seventeenth- and eighteenth-century "moral economy" that yielded to strict interpretations of "entire" labor contracts in
nineteenth-century courts. Courts on both sides of the Atlantic in the years
between 1600 and 1800 appear to have been especially hard on laborers who
breached contracts.

Nonetheless, nineteenth-century courts may still have favored employers
over employees and contractors over personal service workers if judges were
interpreting the law in ways helpful to entrepreneurs. Before consulting the
record of judicial behavior with regard to labor contract disputes in
nineteenth-century America, let us first take note of the state of the labor
market—of the practices of farmers and farm laborers, factory owners and
mill operatives, in the forming of labor agreements in these years—in order
to understand and appreciate the reasoning used by the judges as well as the
effect that judicial decisions had on the parties.

Farmers, Farm Laborers, and the Labor Contract

The first thing to note about the farm labor contract in these years is that
farm labor was scarcer, and thus more expensive, than it was or had ever
been in England. The annual pay of a farm laborer in the northern United
States in the early or mid-nineteenth century was such that he had more buying power than his English counterpart in the land market. A case in point:
The annual wages of an English farm servant in 1850 would buy one-tenth
of an acre of good English farm land, while the wages paid to a hired hand
in Michigan or Illinois (about $160 plus board) would buy from fifteen to
eighty acres of unimproved but largely tillable government-owned land in
those states.[33] Such labor scarcity had produced slavery in the colonial
South, indentured servitude throughout the colonies, and debt peonage in
the Spanish West, but most labor in the northeastern and mid-Atlantic
states was free by 1800, and as such the bargains farm laborers could make
with their employers were, by English and Scottish standards, quite respectable ones.[34]

Their treatment at the hands of their "masters" was also better than that
meted out to their English and Scottish counterparts. Mature farm laborers
were not subject to cuffings or blows.[35] Labor scarcity, coupled with republican values, had led to civility and egalitarianism on the American farm. One

farm laborer from the south of England who migrated to North America in the early nineteenth century wrote home: "I have plenty of employment for this winter season. . . . It is the custom of the country to be boarded and lodged, let you work at what you will. . . . There is no distinction between the workman and his master, they would as soon shake hands with a workman as they would with a gentleman." Another wrote that "it is not here as in England if you dont liket you may leaveet et is here pray do stop i will raise your wages." Another told his brother: "We have no overseers to tred us under foot." Patrick Shirreff, a Scottish farmer, toured the United States in 1833 and noted that the pay of hired hands was "ample" and "their treatment is good, living on the same kind of fare and often associating with their employers."[36]

Many farmers needed additional hands on occasion, as at harvest time, just as farmers did in Britain, but the labor scarcity in the United States meant that these additional hands, be they day, weekly, or piece-rate workers, had to be offered sums substantially larger than the rates that hired hands on annual or semiannual contracts were earning. Consequently, the temptation was constantly there for hired hands to slip away for a period to earn the high premiums being offered in an nearby farm or adjacent county, or, if that proved too risky, at least to avoid the hardest labor during the periods of intense work when day and piece-rate workers were being used. About 20 percent of the farm labor contracts of the Ward family of Shrewsbury, Massachusetts, between 1787 and 1860 ended by the worker quitting before the term had ended, and in the 1820s hired hands engaged in tough bargaining with the Wards, as if from positions of strength. The Massachusetts commissioner for labor wrote in 1872 of farm laborers in that state, "hired for the season," who "secretly murmur or openly rebel, at the apparent inequality between their condition and that of others hired by the day, in respect to wages paid them, and the hours of labor required. They naturally desire, and, if possible, contrive in some way to balance this inequality, however much they may injure their employer thereby."[37] Needless to say, such a sense of "apparent inequality" might prompt behavior that would ultimately lead the farmer and his hired hand to court.

Textile Workers and the Labor Contract, 1785–1875

Once again, by comparison with Britain, a labor shortage of sorts existed for factory owners in the first several decades of the nineteenth century. Skilled workers and operatives alike were sometimes able to bargain with millowners or their agents for wages or contract durations, and they fully understood what it was they were doing. Unskilled workers would begin at wages substantially lower than those who had already been trained, but either their wages were raised as their skills improved (as was the case in many mills)[38] or they might seek and find work elsewhere. A Mr. Richards played one mill off against another in bargaining for a 20 percent increase in wages in Southbridge, Massachusetts in the 1820s. As the mill superintendent there told the owner: "He gave me till the next day to decide—as I understood it—and the next day I agreed to pay him his price." In 1845 another woolen mill operative, Thomas Midgley, wrote to Samuel Slater's company: "I shall be willing to change if I can make a Bargain with you to suite us boath." Still another textile worker, an Englishman skilled as a coverer of carding rollers, sought of a mill superintendent in Massachusetts "the terms that I should like" in 1854 and asked the superintendent to make him an offer.

Of course, the mere fact that some workers were able to bargain for higher wages does not mean that millowners were at the mercy of employees in the making of labor contracts in antebellum America, but there are other indications that labor scarcity, occasional worker solidarity, and, in some cases, the millowner's sense of fair play could produce contract terms favorable to operatives and skilled factory hands.[39] For the first several decades of textile manufacturing owners tried to discipline the work force with April-to-April "entire" contracts, holding much of the worker's pay back until the end of the year. But, according to Jonathan Prude, these efforts were "easily circumscribed," and the owners were forced to "retreat" to monthly or "even bimonthly" payments.[40] By the 1830s the standard in the mills of New England and Pennsylvania was for from one to four week's notice to be required of both parties before terminating the employment contract, with these wages to be held back "in trust."[41] One Pennsylvania millowner, Samuel Riddle, testified that "we have always paid back wages when persons left us without giving two week's notice, after holding it a little while." But he allowed that "a great many" other millowners "in such cases retain it."[42] In any event, the practice continued. One mill worker in Massachusetts in 1869 complained of "the trustee process," which "swallow half of a man's month's wages," and another spoke of "the great grievance to the workingmen, in the law between the employer and the employed, in regard to recovering wages. Many men are put to great inconvenience and expense before they will apply to the courts to get their wages."[43]

This was almost certainly the case with many aggrieved workers; court suits have always been inconvenient. Despite the fact that mid-nineteenth-century lawyers took the cases of many poorer clients on a contingency-fee basis (at no cost to the client, win or lose), despite the fact that there were a number of attorneys associated with political cliques who offered their services as the "friends of labor," and despite the existence of labor unions, cases to recover fifteen days of wages must still have been too expensive or perplexing for many workingmen. Nevertheless, there were a number of cases of this kind that worked their way up to the appellate courts of several industrial states in the early and mid-nineteenth century.

Quitting: The Right of Recovery

Nineteenth-century American jurists, like their English compeers, had no complaints when trial court judges instructed juries to use the quantum meruit standard to calculate damages due employee-plaintiffs who had quit contracts that had no specified wage or rate schedule or completion date. "Jurors are acquainted with the ordinary transactions and business of society, and perhaps no one thing is so well known as the values and prices of labor," Justice Joseph Underwood said in 1829 of a case in which a Kentucky jury had been left to decide the value of a plaintiff's labor in making bale rope on an unspecified oral contract.[44] But the matter was very different for the far more common specified, "special," or "entire" contract. The harsh English standard of "entire" contracts was maintained in a substantial number of states throughout the first century of American independence, but a growing number of jurisdictions abandoned this standard for one "bottomed on justice." Beginning in 1834, increasing numbers of state courts allowed workers who quit before the end of their contractual term of service to recover the value of their services, and a few of those state high courts that had originally stood by the stricter English standard later jumped ship for the American rule, until, by 1900, about half of the jurisdictions held to the Jurisprudence of the Head and half clasped the Jurisprudence of the Heart.

The first published treatises and cases of early-nineteenth-century America, of course, offered the strict English standard. Zephaniah Swift, Litchfield Law School lecturer and former chief justice of the Connecticut Supreme Court, explained in his *Digest* of Connecticut law that no quantum meruit was allowed on special, "entire" contracts and cited *Cutter* v. *Powell* and a New York case, *Jennings* v. *Camp*.[45] The third American edition of John Simcoe Sanders's *Law of Pleading and Evidence in Civil Actions*, published in 1837, explained that "a servant in husbandry cannot sue [for the value of his services] unless he completes the year's service"; like Swift, Sanders cited *Cutter* v. *Powell*.[46] New York's appellate courts were quite comfortable with that view; the state's admiralty court appears to have taken such a position in 1786, nine years before *Cutter* v. *Powell*, in *Nasworthy* v.

The Glaudina and *Bush* v. *McRath*, both of which, like *Cutter*, also involved the right of seamen to collect wages if they completed only a portion of the agreed-upon voyage.[47] Some twenty-nine years later, in 1815, the New York Supreme Court clarified the matter in *McMillan & McMillan* v. *Vanderlip*.[48] Mr. Vanderlip had entered into an agreement with Messers J. and A. McMillan to spin yarn for ten and a half months at 3 cents per run. After three months and 845 runs, he quit, and sought to recover the value of the work he had rendered the McMillans. At the trial court level the jury awarded Vanderlip $22.35 (inasmuch as he had already been paid or advanced $3.00 by the McMillans). The McMillans appealed; their attorney cited *Cutter* v. *Powell* and other English cases and treatises establishing the rule of "entire" contracts. Justice Ambrose Spencer, for the court, agreed. Vanderlip, he noted, was a "novitiate in spinning." Other, more skilled workers had testified at the trial that they were to be paid 5 cents per run and were provided with free board as well. It was clear to Spencer that, as a novice, Vanderlip "would have been more profitable to his employers in the later part of the term," and he drew a direct analogy to "the binding" of farm servants: In offering an annual or semiannual contract "at so much per month, the farmer . . . takes his chances of the good, with the bad months. It is well known that the labor of a man, during the summer months is worth double the labor of the same man in winter."

To permit a worker to take such advantage of his employer was unconscionable. It was the reason for the all-or-nothing rule. Spencer cited *Cutter* v. *Powell* and other, similar English cases and reversed the lower court award.[49] The next year the New York Supreme Court ruled on the matter again in *Jennings* v. *Camp*.[50] Mr. Camp had agreed to clear and fence ten acres of Mr. Jenning's land for sowing at a rate of $8.00 per acre. He completed only part of the clearing and provided no fence. Justice Spencer cited *Cutter* v. *Powell* again and quoted Lord Kenyon's view that "entire," express contracts barred any recovery in assumpsit on a quantum meruit count, a rule that "has prevailed so long as to be reduced to an axiom in the law." And it remained an axiom in the law of New York throughout that state's first century.[51]

The federal circuit court for the District of Columbia was the next to speak on the question. In *Lewis* v. *Esther* a mechanic on a contract to work a year for $125 abandoned work before the year had ended and sued to apportion the contract under a count of quantum meruit. His attorney was unable to sway the court with reference to the plight of a "poor mechanic." The contract was "entire." No apportioning of it was permitted.[52]

A year later, in 1824, the Massachusetts high court heard a comparable   **169** case. John Stark agreed to work as a hired hand on Thomas Parker's farm for $120 for one year. He received some payment from Parker in the course of the term and quit after working for a little over two months. A jury, instructed by the trial judge that it might award "a sum in proportion to the time [Stark] had served," awarded him $27.33 pro rata. Parker appealed,[53] and Justice Levi Lincoln, for the court, reversed the award. A pro rata apportioning of such an express contract as this one would be "utterly repugnant to the general understanding of the nature of such engagements":

> It cannot but seem strange to those who are in any degree familiar with the fundamental principles of law, that doubts should ever have been entertained upon a question of this nature. The usages of the country, and common opinion upon subjects of this description are especially to be regarded, and we are bound to take judicial notice of that of which no one is in fact ignorant.
>
> . . . In no case, has a contract in the terms of the one under consideration, been construed by practical men to give a right to demand the agreed compensation, before the performance of the labor, and . . . the employer and employee alike universally so understand it. The rule of law is in entire accordance with this sentiment, and it would be a flagrant violation of the first principles of justice to hold it otherwise.

If "sometimes" a "different rule of construction" may have prevailed in lower Massachusetts courts, as Stark's counsel had claimed, such a rule would have been "a great departure from ancient and well-established principles," and "no law."[54] Justice Lincoln cited *McMillan* v. *Vanderlip, Jennings* v. *Camp*, several English cases, and "the elementary writers" in support of his argument.[55]

Several years later, in *Olmstead* v. *Beale*,[56] the Massachusetts court upheld a jury verdict in favor of a farmer (the employer) sued by a hired hand who had left after completing only five months of a six-month contract. Justice Marcus Morton explained that "laborers . . . may excite sympathy, but in a government of equal laws, they must be subject to the same rules and principles as the rest of the community." Since the rule precluding quantum meruit recovery on "entire" contracts "prevails in all civilized countries, and is supported by an unbroken chain of decisions in England, our sister states, and our own," there was no escaping the court's affirmation of the jury's denial of all wages.[57]

In 1825 Indiana's high court adopted the same standard. A hired hand sued for recovery on a ten-month "entire" contract despite evidence that he was working elsewhere from July to September. Justice Jesse Holman observed that "it is well known that the labor of a man is more valuable in the spring and summer than in the winter months" and affirmed the jury's judgment in the farmer-defendant's favor.[58] Two years later Alabama's high court took the same position in a case involving a man who left his employer before the completion of his term and reiterated it in two similar decisions fifteen years later, one involving a man who agreed to manage a grocery store, the other an overseer. The court cited *Cutter* v. *Powell* in the latter case.[59] Missouri's high court became the sixth American jurisdiction to follow the harsh English standard in 1833.[60]

But a different perspective was afoot. In 1834 Justice Joel Parker and his fellow justices on the New Hampshire Supreme Court broke new ground with regard to those who quit labor contracts for personal services in the case of *Britton* v. *Turner*. The plaintiff had agreed to serve as a hired hand from March 1831 to March 1832 for $120 and board. He left in December of 1831 and sued for recovery of $100. A jury awarded him $95. His employer's attorney appealed and cited *Cutter* v. *Powell*. He allowed that "in modern times" American courts "have, to a certain extent, relaxed from the strict rules formerly adopted, and have sustained a count in quantum meruit in cases where the plaintiff had not fully performed his contract." He was referring to *Hayward* v. *Leonard*,[61] a Massachusetts case involving a house contractor who had been allowed to recover on quantum meruit and quantum valebant counts because the defendant had not signaled nonacceptance of the house. But he proposed to distinguish the facts in *Britton* v. *Turner* from the "immoral tendency" embodied in *Hayward* and urged the court to cling to "the old law."[62] Justice Parker, speaking for the court, refused to do so. Parker had grown up on a farm in Jaffrey, New Hampshire, and knew both the importance of community in rural New England and the economic value of farm labor. He was later to praise Jaffrey and its neighbors, "these 'little Democracies,' as Tocqueville has called them," for their "brotherhood, . . . social intercourse, [and the] kindly feeling toward [one an]-other" that one found there. Here, indeed, was the "moral economy" of the propertied farmer and the unpropertied hired hand. In his opinion Parker insisted that the farmer who contracted for personal services "for a certain period" did so "with full knowledge that he must, from the nature of the case, be accepting part performance from day to day." As such, he was realizing benefit from his employee and was bound to pay the value of the services rendered, despite any breaches of the express contract. Parker maintained that such a principle, "by binding the employer to pay the value of the service he actually receives, and the laborer to answer in damages where he

171

does not complete the entire contract," would leave "no temptation" to the employer to drive the laborer from his service near the close of his term, by ill treatment, in order to escape from payment, and would, by permitting damage offsets, sufficiently safeguard the employer.[63] This was the proper legal rule for the "moral economy."

Britton v. *Turner* was to have a significant impact on the law with regard to employee breaches of labor contracts in America. Several treatise writers, among them James Kent, George W. Field, Floyd Mechem, J. C. Perkins (the American editor of *Chitty on Contracts*), and Theophilus Parsons (a colleague of Joel Parker's at Harvard Law School in the late 1840s), were to cite it favorably.[64] Irving Browne, the American editor of Campbell's *English Ruling Cases*, did so as well in noting that the rule in *Cutter* v. *Powell* had been countered in America by quantum meruit recovery, a "wide departure" from the *Cutter* v. *Powell* standard.[65] Several high courts that had not yet spoken on the subject did so in the next generation, and, while some of these adhered to "the old rule," six adopted the *Britton* v. *Turner* standard in their cases of first impression, and a few of those that had already spoken turned from the *Cutter* standard to *Britton* over time. Parker had struck a sympathetic chord, but jurists were slow in turning from their heads to their hearts.

Vermont's high court tried to straddle the fence. It heard its first "quitting" cases in the same year that Parker was shaping the *Britton* standard, but before it had been published. Consequently, in *Philbrook* v. *Belknap* the court refused to sanction a penny of wages for an edge-tool artisan employed by a master mechanic on a three-year "entire" contract who left after five and a half months. The artisan, William Belknap, had tried to renegotiate the contract (from $96 to $120 per year) without success. Justice Samuel Phelps, however, regarded him "amply compensated" by the training he had acquired "and the enhanced wages which he may obtain elsewhere in consequence," and he rejected the argument that Alfred Philbrook, the master mechanic, had benefited unfairly from Belknap's labor: Philbrook gained "nothing," as he lost "the services of the plaintiff when they became more valuable."[66] In similar cases involving a ship-joiner, a steamboat captain, two farm hired hands, and a journeyman tailor the Vermont court reaffirmed the *Philbrook* ruling, frequently citing *Cutter* v. *Powell*.[67] Justice Isaac Redfield was certain that when men, "hired for the farming season," quit in midseason, they were not entitled to any quantum meruit recovery, for "the loss of a single month's labor might cost the loss of the products of the entire season."[68] But Redfield allowed that the contracts of men working "by piece" *could* be apportioned, either pro rata or quantum meruit, as appropriate. In one such case, *Dyer* v. *Jones*, decided two years after *Britton* v. *Turner*, Redfield allowed a woodcutter paid to clear "as much [land] as he pleases at $2.75 per acre," to recover on a quantum meruit count despite the landowner's claim that the work was "done in such a manner" that the cleared land was "of no value to him."[69] In another, *Booth* v. *Tyson*, Redfield, like Parker, rejected that older view of the value of personal service as one of "some harshness and severity, if not injustice."[70] The landowner "will and must" have derived "some benefit" from the work, and "the laborer is entitled to his own labor, or its product, where it is in such a shape that he cannot carry it away," as was the case with this woodcutter.[71]

Despite the views of Parker and Redfield, the rule in *Cutter* v. *Powell* still had plenty of life. Louisiana adopted it in 1837, Illinois in 1845, Maine and California in 1852, Tennessee and Georgia in 1853, New Jersey in 1854, and Ohio in 1860.[72]

Britton v. *Turner* had its enthusiasts in these courts, but it had its critics as well. Nelson Rowe, a hired hand in Illinois on an eight-month "entire contract" for ninety dollars that began in late February 1843, told colleagues that he wanted "to go to the South" in late June and "did not know" whether his employer "would let him off." When his employer refused, he quit anyway. He was awarded thirty dollars by a local justice and a county court jury, but his employer, Barnabas Eldridge, appealed to the supreme court. One "A. Lincoln" appeared on behalf of Rowe, the hired hand, and "relied upon the case of *Britton* v. *Turner*." The court rejected that response, preferring the appellant-employer's appeal to the "rule of law," though Justice Gustavus Koerner dissented.[73]

Eli Heald, another hired hand in Illinois, quit after three months of a six-month contract to go to Pennsylvania "whether [I] got one cent from [my employer] or not." After quitting, he accepted $8.00 as a token compensation from his employer, shook hands with him, and "did not claim any more." A witness reported that both parties "seemed satisfied" at that parting, but Heald had a change of heart. He sued and succeeded in securing a quantum meruit award at the trial court level (Justice Koerner presiding), but his employer appealed, citing *Cutter* v. *Powell* and *McMillan* v. *Vanderlip*, and the supreme court reversed the award.[74] Swan Erickson, another Illinois hired hand, had no more success. Justice Sidney Breese reversed the jury's award to him of $67.50 with these dicta: "He left his employer in the midst of the harvest, probably under the promise, from some meddlesome person, to give him higher wages. This is contrary to justice and good morals, and cannot be tolerated."[75]

Ohio's high court was divided about the indivisibility of "entire" labor contracts. Justices Peter Hitchcock and William Peck spoke critically of *Britton* v. *Turner* and quantum meruit apportioning. The principle it espoused "is admitted to be of modern invention," something anathema to judges attentive to "the rule of law" and the doctrine of stare decisis. It was "mischievous." "We are not as yet prepared to adopt it." It "tends to encourage" the violation of contracts. "Perhaps, in most cases," the *Britton* rule "would do complete equity," but "so radical a change . . . should originate with the legislature, and not with the judiciary."[76] Justice Nathaniel Read dissented from the views of his colleagues. The "main current of modern decisions," he believed, sanctioned the apportioning, with damage offsets allowed, of incomplete contracts, and that current was one that Read was willing to join.[77]

Britton v. *Turner* was hotly debated in Maine's case of first impression on the subject. The plaintiff worked "in the woods" for a lumber company on a "lumbering season" contract for some three and a half months before quitting. The trial court allowed him the value of his labor, less costs, and the company appealed. His attorney cited *Britton* v. *Turner* and noted that it had been "cited with approbation" as being "sensible and just" in several recent American cases and in the American edition of Chitty on contracts.[78] The lumber company's attorney responded by allowing that *Britton* v. *Turner* was "obviously against us." But he argued (predictably) that that decision, "far from being founded on the law, was but an evasion of the law and in conflict with the whole current of authorities." The company, he argued, had "never consented to receive and pay" for work for any duration "less than the lumbering season." Justice Samuel Wells, for the court, agreed with that view, citing *Cutter* v. *Powell* and *Stark* v. *Parker*: "If it were permitted to the laborer to determine the contract at his pleasure, no well founded reliance could be placed, at any time, upon a due observance of it."[79]

The high court of Tennessee held to the same position. N. E. Cannon, hired to prize tobacco in Tennessee, left after serving three months of an eight-month contract; he "could get better wages elsewhere." His employer was unable to replace him for three months. Cannon sued for a portion of the sum that had been promised on the contract. His employer appealed the trial court judgment, and Justice Robert Caruthers voided the award, offering both the English rule and the parable of the laborers in the vineyard (Matthew 20:13) as authority. To apportion the contract or to order the farmer to pay Cannon for the value of his labor "would encourage bad faith and destroy the sanctity of contracts." The employer who "arranges his business and pitches his crop" owes nothing to one who "works in seed time, but fails to bear the 'heat and burden of the day' at harvest."[80]

Common-law tides are slow to turn; this one began to turn in the age of Jackson and continued to come in with the advent of the Republican Party. In the same year that Tennessee announced for the "old" English standard, Indiana reversed its position. Three years later, so did Missouri.[81] First impression cases in Michigan and Iowa appeared in 1858 and 1859 adopting the *Britton* v. *Turner* standard in personal services cases of workers who quit and sought payment for services rendered.[82] A farm "hired hand" who quit without giving notice or cause in Connecticut found support from a high court critical of the "earliest" decisions regarding "entire" contracts. The "rigid and unreasonable rule" regarding such agreements "has recently been relaxed, and it is now generally, if not universally held," that wages may generally be apportioned, a view "more in accordance with the true character of such a contract, the presumed intention of the parties, and the demands of justice."[83] A lumberjack in Michigan was "remediless" under "the strict common law rule." "But the doctrine has now grown up," wrote Justice James Campbell, "based upon equitable principles, that where anything has been done from which the other party has received substantial benefit, and which has been appropriated, a recovery may be had upon a *quantum meruit*."[84] A hired hand in Iowa who quit after four months of a six-month contract benefited from the new standard.[85] Justice John Dillon of that state's high court defended *Britton* v. *Turner*: "Its principles have been gradually winning their way into professional and judicial favor. It is bottomed on justice, and right upon principle [notwithstanding the fact that it was a variance with] the technical and more illiberal rules of the common law as found in the old cases."[86]

Before the Civil war had ended, five states (only one of them a slave state) had adopted the *Britton* v. *Turner* standard; ten (four of them slave states) held firmly to the older rule.[87] The concentration of slave states in the column of those falling in the mold of the alleged pro-entrepreneurial model is curious, for these, although certainly operating within a capitalist arena, are imperfect examples of a "newly emergent market economy."[88] Instead, they reflect an older world of "status." In four of five of these slave states the "workers" who quit and sued in these leading cases were overseers. Since there were relatively few other free laborers in the labor market of the slave states, these suits by overseers are not surprising, but they are still noteworthy, for what they represent. Overseers were, by comparison with mill operatives and hired hands, members of a "labor aristocracy"—in fact, plantation foremen were the vital henchmen of a slave labor system. The obiter dicta of Justice Henry Careton of Louisiana's high court in one such overseer case puts the relationship between the slave economy and the older legal standard well: "The agricultural interests of the [Southern] country are mainly under the control of [overseers], and if they could abandon their employers in times of greatest need . . . , it is plain that great and remediless mischief would ensue."[89] Thus the harsher *Cutter* v. *Powell* standard in cases of employee breaches of personal service contracts was maintained in the older, status-determined political economy and increasingly abandoned in the domain of free contract economy north of the Mason-Dixon line.

After the Civil War, the "more equitable" standard of *Britton* v. *Turner* inched forward again. In 1872 the Montana Territory's high court announced itself on the side of the older, "all-or-nothing" standard (in a hard case of a five year contract where the "servant"-plaintiff quit and sought apportionment after the first full year),[90] but in 1871 Kentucky declared for *Britton* v. *Turner*, as did Kansas in 1879 and Nebraska in 1880 (see table 1). Justice Amasa Cobb of Nebraska's supreme court allowed a hired hand to recover the value of five months' labor on a one-year "entire" contract with the remark that *Britton* v. *Turner* was founded on "principles approved by the profession and the people" and was now law "considered to be pretty generally settled throughout the western states."[91] Minnesota, Wisconsin, and Mississippi declared for the older, all-or-nothing rule in the late nineteenth century, but North and South Dakota and Texas declared for the *Britton* v. *Turner* rule in employee breaches of employment contracts in the fin de siècle, and North Carolina, Virginia, New York, and Illinois moved to join Vermont, California, and Oregon in allowing pro rata (apportioned) recovery where monthly payments were being made.[92]

The existence of a "liberal" trend in the law regarding employee breaches of labor contracts does not, of course, mean that nineteenth-century America was a worker's paradise. It does, however, mean that workers in America who quit before the end of their contracts were treated more generously by nineteenth-century America's high courts than they ever were in previous centuries.

To be sure, a few jurists can be found who appear to be responding directly to the appeals of industrial entrepreneurs (speaking through their attorneys), but they are uncommon. Maine's Chief Justice Ether Shepley may be one. He seemed particularly responsive to the counsel for the Salmon Falls Manufacturing Company in 1853. A worker, Almeda Harmon, had quit and had insisted that she had not understood the contract of employ-

TABLE I. DIFFERENT RULES ADOPTED BY STATES IN QUITTING CASES

Harsher English Rule of Cutter *v.* Powell *(N=12)*	*Redfield's Middle-Ground Rule of* Dyer *v.* Jones *and* Booth *v.* Tyson *(N=9)*	*Joel Parker's More Generous New Hampshire Rule of* Britton *v.* Turner *(N=11)*
Pennsylvania, 1806[a]		
(New York, 1815)[b]		
(Massachusetts, 1824)		
(Indiana, 1825)		
Alabama, 1827		
(Missouri, 1833)		
(Vermont, 1834)	Vermont, 1836[a]	New Hampshire, 1834[a]
Louisiana, 1837	Massachusetts, 1837	
(Illinois, 1845)		
(California, 1852)		Indiana, 1853
Maine, 1852	Connecticut, 1854	Missouri, 1856
Tennessee, 1853		Michigan, 1858
Georgia, 1853	California, 1859	Iowa, 1859
New Jersey, 1854		Kentucky, 1871
Ohio, 1860	Oregon, 1879	Kansas, 1879
Montana, 1872	Virginia, 1885	Nebraska, 1880
Minnesota, 1882	North Carolina, 1886	South Dakota, 1893
Wisconsin, 1883	Illinois, 1891	Texas, 1895
Mississippi, 1894	New York, 1913	North Dakota, 1915

Note: The middle-ground rule allowed pro rata apportionment in quitting cases wherever feasible but did not allow the more liberal quantum meruit recovery of *Britton.*
[a]Dates are those of the first impression case.
[b]States in parentheses are those that later altered the standard to Parker's or Redfield's.

ment to permit the company to hold back as forfeit two weeks' wages for her failure to give notice. A notice to that effect had been shown to Harmon, but she had not signed anything indicating that the sixteen-day rule had been explained to her. J. N. Goodwin, for the company, had argued that the company had done all that was necessary and sufficient, and that the court should support the company's view as one "indispensably necessary for protection against 'strikes.'" Shepley agreed:

177

The only valuable protection, which the manufacturer can provide
against . . . what are in these days denominated "strikes," is to
make an agreement with his laborers, that if they willfully leave
their machines and his employment without previous notice,
all, or a certain amount of wages that may be due to them shall
be forfeited. . . . The rule of law . . . is too important for the
prosperity of business, for the security of honest dealings, and for the
maintenance of good order in the community, to be lightly regarded.[93]

This is clearly an opinion benefiting entrepreneurs. But note that two
years later, the New Hampshire Supreme Court, hearing a virtually identical case involving a worker who quit without notice his job with the same
Salmon Falls Manufacturing Company (doing business in both states), *rejected* an identical argument offered by the company's counsel, who cited
the Maine court's opinion in the process. Chief Justice Andrew Woods
maintained that the question of whether the sixteen-day severance rule had
been properly explained and could reasonably be expected to have been
understood had been properly left to the jury by the trial court, and he upheld the jury award of wages to the worker. And note that Chief Justice Isaac
Parker of the Massachusetts Supreme Court wrote a similar opinion in a
similar case.[94] Courts did not mistreat workers.

Why did some jurists adopt the "liberal" quitting standard of *Britton* v.
Turner? One answer may be that a number of them believed this new standard to be a fairer interpretation of the principles of contract than those
they had "received" from England. Courts, they believed, ought to recognize the inequity in denying any and all pay to employees who had quit after
working for several months, for labor that had clearly benefited their employers. Allowing unpropertied laborers who had breached "entire" contracts to collect on a quantum meruit count was a principle "bottomed on
justice," as Justice John Dillon of Iowa's high court put it. "A farmhand is
not a capitalist," as Justice John Kellogg of New York put it in another case
of a hired hand who had breached an "entire" contract by quitting. He
should receive the value of his labor, for the "modern" rule "seems to be
just."[95] Juries (or auditor-arbitrators) ought to be free to decide what a
man's labor had been worth to an employer whom he was disappointing.
They ought also be free to decide whether the employer had suffered damages due to that breach of contract; and the record shows that when juries
and auditors were allowed to make such decisions, they generally awarded
the worker all or most of what he or she sought.

178   Wythe Holt argues that those courts that did not accept the rule in *Brit-*

ton v. *Turner* were defining "matters of valuation" only "from the stand-point of the employer." He is critical of jurists like Sidney Breese and Ambrose Spencer who faulted apprentices for claiming to be worth as much in their first months as they would be once trained, and who scolded hired hands for quitting "during the summer months" when their labor was worth "double the labor of the same man in winter."[96] Holt is in distinguished company on this point: Oliver Wendell Holmes Jr., in his essays on the common law, raised essentially the same question when he observed that

> the most important element of decision is not any technical, or even any general principle of contracts, but a consideration of the nature of the particular transaction as a practical matter. Suppose A promises B to do a day's work for two dollars, and B promises A to pay two dollars for a day's work. There the two promises cannot be performed at the same time. The work will take all day, the payment half a minute. How are you to decide which is to be done first, that is to say, which promise is dependent upon performance on the other side? It is only by reference to the habits of the community and to convenience. It is not enough to say that on the principle of equivalency a man is not presumed to intend to pay for a thing until he has it. The work is payment for the money, as much as the money for the work, and one must be paid for in advance. The question is, why, if one man is not presumed to intend to pay money until he has money's worth, the other is presumed to intend to give money's worth before he has money. An answer cannot be obtained from any general theory. The fact that employers, as a class, can be trusted for wages more safely than the employed for their labor, that the employers have had the power and have been the law-makers, or other considerations, it matters not what, have determined that the work is to be done first. But the grounds of decision are purely practical, and can never be elicited from grammar or from logic.[97]

What *were* the "grounds of decision" in antebellum America? The records show that smaller payments to apprentices and "novitiates" in industrial jobs during the initial learning period was a standard practice, as was the practice of holding back the bulk of the pay of the "hired hand" until after the harvest was in.[98] Moreover these practices were centuries old, were understood by farmhands and apprentices, and, by the lights of modern Law and Economics theorists,[99] were efficient ways to allocate scarce capital resources. For farm employers to have paid their hired hands pro rata (to say nothing of *pre*paying them advances) would have meant holding back

179

some capital for that purpose in the planting season, capital that could otherwise have been dedicated to the costs of land, clearing, seed, and tools.

Moreover, a farmer or planter with a crop to cultivate and harvest could well have been injured if left in the lurch by a worker lured by high seasonal day wages on another's farm. Since many hired hands hoped to be (and many of these *were* to be) farm "entrepreneurs" themselves in time, many could and did appreciate why farm laborer contracts of six months or more were treated as being "entire" in many courts. Hence they entered into such contracts with their eyes open, accepting their terms. Thus when Nelson Rowe quit, he knew that his employer, Barnabas Eldridge, had housed and fed him from February to June and consequently doubted whether Eldridge "would let him off." And when Eli Heald quit "in the midst of the harvest," "whether he got one cent from [his employer] or not," and was offered eight dollars as a gesture by his employer, he "did not claim any more," shook hands and (originally) "seemed satisfied."[100] Room and board, after all, was worth at least ten dollars per month[101] in the antebellum Midwest, and the means to pay for them without a "hired hand" contract in off-season winter months were not easily acquired in the antebellum grain belt, where both Rowe and Heald lived.[102] Hence, Rowe and Heald must have appreciated that they had already received substantial in-kind payment for their labor.

But we need not restrict ourselves to remarks about the capitalistic countryside of nineteenth-century America. Workers and managers on twentieth-century cooperative or collective farms in socialist states could also have appreciated that quitting "in the midst of the harvest" would hurt the very social order that Holt prefers to the individualistic, capitalist world.[103] It is not "capitalism" that is responsible for nearly all workers, whether in early modern England, nineteenth-century Illinois, or the former Soviet Union, to be paid *after* a period of work. The resources that must be garnered and pooled, either by "capitalist" farmers and industrialists or socialist "planners," are scarce. No society has yet concluded that it would be either "fair" or sensible to prepay workers with funds drawn from these scarce resources. Hence, if some nineteenth-century American courts were (in Holt's words) defining "matters of valuation . . . from the standpoint of the employer" when they ruled that workers who quit "entire" contracts should not be allowed quantum meruit recovery, we should not be as surprised as he is.

This is not to say that the standard in *Cutter* v. *Powell* was as "just" as the one in *Britton* v. *Turner.* In my judgement *Britton* is "better law" because of its equitable emphasis. But my opinion matters not one whit. Once we come to know and appreciate the antebellum preindustrial economy, we become less inclined to fault the Breeses and Spencers and more understanding of why a genuine difference of opinion existed by the mid-nineteenth century among honest jurists regarding what was just, fair, and "good policy" in cases of workers who quit "in midstream." Many outside of the judiciary believed that those who breached special contracts ought to suffer some consequences, and that sometimes parties to such agreements ought to be enjoined from breaking them. After all, the North's refusal to let "Confederate" states secede from the constitutional compact they had entered into in 1788, and the southern insistence on their right to breach the compact, was the central reason Secession was met with force.

One question, however, remains: Just why *did* state high court jurists come to such differing conclusions? One powerful reason must have been that the facts in the "first impression" employee breach of contract cases that came to them differed from state to state. If one compares the numbers of months worked on the contract in the "first impression" cases heard in the states that held to the older, harsh standard, to those worked on the contract in the first impression cases of *Britton* v. *Turner* and its progeny, one finds that the workers quit in the former after, on average, only about 45 percent of the time in the contract had passed, while they quit in the *Britton* v. *Turner* cases after, on average, about 60 percent of the agreed-to number of months. The two chief contrasting "leading cases," *Stark* v. *Parker* and *Britton* v. *Turner*, form even starker contrasts. In the former, the hired hand left after only a little over five of twelve months, and after having been paid in full for the first three; in the latter, the hired hand quit after working nine and a half of twelve months without pay, deserting his employer only for the winter months, those when the least farm labor was done. This difference is what Karl Llewylln called "situation-sense." Fair-minded jurists in Massachusetts could turn away the claims of John Stark, as they did, with reference to "the rule of law," "the usages of the country," and "common opinion." Other fair-minded jurists, sitting in the adjacent state of New Hampshire only ten years later, found it more difficult to ignore the plea of Britton. Quantum meruit seemed appropriate where the employer had had the benefit of the worker's labor throughout "the 'heat and burden of the day' at harvest."[104]

One other possible explanation for the increasing acceptability of *Britton* v. *Turner* in the 1850s and 1860s occurs to me. There is some evidence that by the mid-nineteenth century farm labor contracts were becoming shorter in duration, both in the United States and England, and a *new* "custom of the country" was unfolding, a custom which (in the words of a Michigan agriculturalist writing in 1850) "has almost destroyed the obligation of contracts between the employed and the employer. The first thinks he has a right to leave when he pleases, and the last expects he will go when he likes." To the extent this was so, a simultaneous change in judicial treatment of quitting cases would be understandable.[105]

Employer Breaches: The Law and Unjust Firings, 1800–1880

Thus far we have restricted our attention to cases in which employees simply quit. Morton Horwitz has argued that the strict enforcement by courts of "entire" labor contracts meant that employers "had every inducement to create conditions to create conditions near the end of the term that would encourage the laborer to quit."[106] What evidence is there that employees took such action? What was the fate of the worker who quit under those circumstances, charged the employer with a breach of contract, and sought to recover wages?

There are very few cases in the appellate records of federal courts and those of the thirty-six states that existed by 1880 of employees charging employers with conduct that merited their abandoning the personal-service contract. In all, I found nine such cases. That is not to say that employers were careful observers of the terms of personal-service contracts. Any student of nineteenth-century American labor knows that this is far from the case. Some employers laid workers off with considerable regularity. Of course, many of these took the precaution to write one-, two-, three-, or four-week "notice" clauses into the contract. But others did not, and I found sixty-seven cases in the appellate records of twenty-one states and the federal courts in which employers either fired the worker "without cause," in bold violation of the contract (forty-one cases), or fired the worker and then claimed as defendants in court that the *worker* had breached the contract (twenty-six cases). In short, it appears that employers rarely tried to get workers to quit in order to use the terms of the *contract* to deny wages; they simply fired them and made them sue to recover. Let us see how workers fared in each type of action.

The handful of cases in which employees charged employers with "ill usage" as an excuse for the worker breach of the contract are not consistent with the "inducement to quit" thesis. A seaman whose master threw scalding water into his face exchanged blows with the master and mate, quit, and was denied his wages. In 1806 a U.S. district court ordered that his wages be paid.[107] Another seaman was first struck with a club by the mate for not tarring a rope while strapping a block and then offered to a British warship's press gang. He escaped, returned to New York, and sued. The New York Supreme Court affirmed the judgment of a lower court in 1812 that he receive full wages for the voyage.[108] A hired hand in Indiana on a one-year contract who quit after three months, claiming ill treatment, was denied recovery when the court was not convinced of the sufficiency of his evidence.[109] A domestic servant in Vermont, offended by advances from the father of her employer, was unable to convince the jury that she should have her wages, but in 1851 the Vermont Supreme Court applauded her concern for her chastity, reversed that judgment, and ordered that the wages by paid.[110] A milliner who quit after taking offense at insulting criticisms made by her employer was denied recovery by the Colorado Territorial Court in 1871.[111] A hired hand in Vermont quit after having been criticized twice by the farm owner for poorly managing a hoeing crew. His grounds for abandoning the contract were not deemed sufficient by the jury, and he was denied recovery in 1855.[112] A slave, leased for a year in Tennessee, was whipped by the lessee. He slipped away and returned to his owner, who refused to allow the lessee to reclaim him. The Tennessee court reversed a lower court decision that granted the owner a quantum meruit recovery.[113] Hannu, a Hawaiian laborer on an entire contract bagging guano on the Phoenix Islands in 1860, quit when provided an inadequate water supply. Chief Justice Elisha Allen concluded that his employer had breached his agreement. "Labor in dust and dirt and under a hot sun is very exhausting," he wrote. "The system must be supplied with food and water as nature demands." Allen directed the company to pay Hannu the value of his labor ($38.15).[114]

Significantly, in only one of these cases (the one involving the leased slave) had the worker completed so much as the first half of the term or voyage contracted for—that is, in only one of these cases was there in play any end-of-term incentive for the employer to tempt the worker into a recision of the contract. And, in that case, the employer clearly did not *want* the worker to do so, because he sought him out at his master's home and tried to persuade the master to return the slave to complete his contract term!

What was the outcome in the forty-one cases in which employees claimed that they had been fired without cause? Courts upheld awards to workers in *every single case*.[115] This was so for plasterers in Maine and Kentucky; drivers and factory superintendents in Pennsylvania; ministers in Connecticut; mail carriers and agents in Illinois; ship stewards in California; hired hands in Vermont, Missouri, Minnesota, and North Carolina; seamen and railroad superintendents in New York; painters in Minnesota; lumberjacks and woodcutters in Ohio, Pennsylvania, and Maine; overseers in Arkansas, Georgia, and South Carolina; engineers in Missouri; salesmen in Maryland; riverboat pilots in Indiana; and sharecroppers in Kentucky, Vermont, Pennsylvania, and Massachusetts.[116] Some of these workers' attorneys cited

Cutter v. *Powell* on their behalf. In each of those states that had held to that "all or nothing" standard when *workers* breached "entire" contracts by quitting "without good cause," and for which I found cases in which the *employer* had breached the contract by firing the worker "without good cause," the awards were for the *full value* of the contract, not merely for the value of those services rendered.[117] In other words, those courts that had been tough on workers when *they* had violated their contracts were just as tough on employers who violated theirs.[118]

Consistent with its standard in *Britton* v. *Turner*, New Hampshire's high court chose not to apply an all-or-nothing rule to the case of a hired hand fired without cause in 1870; instead it enthusiastically approved a jury award considerably greater than a pro rata one. The man "had worked through the very best of the season" and was fired in late October, six months into a one-year contract. Since he could have earned more as a day laborer during the summer and harvest, his employer must pay more than the mere pro rata monthly rate if they were to terminate his contract in October—that is, they must pay him quantum meruit, what his labor was worth.[119]

The employer often responded to the worker's suit for wages in an unjust firing with a claim that the worker had violated the terms of the contract herself and had justifiably been discharged. Under those circumstances the workers won in twenty-two of twenty-six contests. Let us examine these, looking first at claims that the employee became ill, next at claims that the employee was "insolent" or "abusive," and finally at claims that the employee violated the "rules of the shop."

Workers who, employers claimed, had abandoned the contract due to illness were able to recover wages in eleven of twelve cases. Hired hands, glassblowers, mill operatives, and well drillers who were unable to continue due to illness or injury were allowed the "reasonable value of their labor," with no damage setoff allowed their employer for time and value lost in replacing them, because such disabling was an "Act of God," releasing them from the terms of their special contracts.[120] Only in Alabama (an all-or-nothing state) was the estate of an overseer who died before the end of the contract's term unable to recover any wages.[121]

"Insolence" or "abusive conduct" was another employer response to worker's suits for wages. It rarely sufficed. A female domestic servant in New Jersey, fired for insolence in the twenty-fifth day of her (monthly) contract, took her employer to court and convinced the jury that her employer was exaggerating. The jury awarded her a month's wages, and she won the high court appeal as well.[122] Several overseers on annual contracts in Virginia, South Carolina, and Mississippi, "turned off" for abusive language toward their employer's family or abuse of the slaves under their control, won recovery of the full value of their labor.[123] In the leading case, *Byrd* v. *Boyd*, South Carolina's Justice David Johnson pointedly rejected English precedent, which would have denied any such recovery on an "entire" contract, and held for quantum meruit recovery, more consistent with "my notions of natural justice."[124] It took the brutal killing of a slave under an overseer's control for a Missouri high court to agree that the planter had a right to fire the overseer, one Bird Posey, on grounds of "mercy and humanity."[125]

Still another employer response was that the worker had violated "the rules of the shop" (or of "the ship"). In four of seven such cases, the worker was successful; in another, the issue was unresolved (that is, the case was returned to the trial level for a jury ruling).[126] Two of these decisions are worth particular attention.[127] In *Sloan* v. *Hayden* the plaintiff was told that 25 percent of his wages, held in bond by his employer, a Massachusetts factory owner, had been forfeited because of alleged violations of "the rules of the shop." He sued. The trial jury found that his dismissal has been without sufficient cause, and when his employer appealed, the high court affirmed the award. For the court, Justice Marcus Morton held that "the provision that the [wage] fund is to be held by the defendants until the contract is fulfilled to their entire satisfaction, must be construed to mean their reasonable satisfaction."[128]

In a comparable case, a weaver employed by the U.S. Flax Manufacturing Company in Rhode Island, reported off "sick" one day in 1879 but actually went on "a pleasure excursion." Fired, he sued, claiming wrongful discharge. His contract had stipulated that he give two weeks notice of a desire to quit or forfeit two week's (withheld) pay. He sought to recover the two week's forfeiture. The trial judge refused to accept and read to the jury the instructions prepared by the company's attorney, to the effect that the single day's absence might be deemed sufficient grounds for the dismissal. On appeal, Chief Justice Thomas Durfee ruled for the worker, observing that "a man does not quit the service of another when he merely takes a holiday without the others consent." Responding to the company's argument, he added: "It is . . . urged that scarcely less mischief would result from such an intermission of service than from its total abandonment without the notice. That may be so, but in order to remedy the evil we cannot give the contract a strained and unnatural construction."[129]

Justice Samuel Hubbard of the Massachusetts Supreme Court offered similar obiter dicta in *Hunt* v. *The Otis Co.* Elvira Hunt's contract required that she give four week's notice but did not indicate that wage forfeiture **185** would ensue if she did not do so. The company's attorney sought to treat the contract as an "entire" one and stressed the importance of the outcome to the company's management of its work force. Hubbard was listening, but he did not respond as the company hoped. The court, he said, "looked at the circumstances of this case with care, as it is said that this regulation of [the Otis Company] is important to them in the due management of their business, not merely in regard to this case, but as to others." But the court could find no grounds for the wage forfeiture that the company sought to impose in this badly written contract. Hence it upheld the jury award of back wages to Hunt. Floyd Mechem, a treatise writer of the era, wrote of this decision, "The Law abhors forfeitures and will not lightly imply them."[130]

The lesson to be derived from this look at the appellate record[131] with regard to alleged breaches of personal service contracts is that the claim that judges had read the law in ways that helped entrepreneurs at the expense of workers appears to be disproved. American courts appear to have been more evenhanded with workers than earlier English courts had been. George Comstock, the editor of the eleventh edition of Kent's *Commentaries*, was on the mark when he wrote in 1867 of the English standard, vesting the employer with wide-ranging power with regard to firings: "No case in this country, it is believed, goes so far in upholding the authority of the master."[132]

Road and Building Contractors: Special Consideration?

Unpropertied laborers locked in contract litigation with their employers were clearly better off in antebellum America courts than they were in those of colonial America or seventeenth- and eighteenth-century England and Scotland. Nevertheless, the suits of road and house builders could have received better treatment in the courts than those on personal service contracts, as has been claimed.[133] But they did not. I identified some sixty-eight "contractor" cases in American courts (and a smaller number of English cases) and found very little difference between the ways that courts treated "contractors" and other workers. Contractors fared no better, no worse, than laborers in suits to recover in quantum meruit (and quantum valebant).[134] These contractor cases can be described using the same categories we had used for our "employees": In twenty-four instances contractors abandoned the work before completion ("quit"); in six cases they were simply prevented from continuing work by the other party (that is, they were "fired without cause"); and in thirty-eight cases the contractors were unpaid because of a dispute over the quality or timeliness of the work (comparable to employees "fired for sufficient cause"). Let us briefly examine each category.

Recall that when workers quit, they were eventually able to recover for the value of their work, less any legitimate damages their employer incurred, in about half of the American states whose high courts spoke on the subject. Contractors who quit before completing the job were less fortunate. By the 1870s the courts of only seven states sanctioned quantum meruit or quantum valebant recovery in such cases, and only where the other party clearly received some benefit (generally through use) from the partially completed work,[135] while those of thirteen states and the U.S. circuit court for Massachusetts refused any such recovery, even where the other party received benefit.[136] Chief Justice Thomas W. Bartley of Ohio's high court noted in 1856 that there was no "well-founded distinction in the principles of the law" between "contracts for specific jobs of work, such as the erection of buildings, etc., and those arising on ordinary contracts for service."[137]

What of those cases in which the contractor had been prevented from completing the work by the other party to the contract ("firing without cause")? The English rule was that an act of prevention constituted a breach of contract on the employer's part and warranted recovery of the full value of the contract price, independent of the amount of work actually done.[138] That rule was applied strictly by the high courts of New York and Texas (and the latter also allowed the house builder "to be compensated the damages he has sustained" if he was "thrown out of employment and lost time by the failure of the defendant to furnish the materials according to his understanding");[139] it was applied less strictly in Alabama and Kentucky, where the contractor's recovery was limited to the value of the work and materials actually expended.[140] Where employers failed to pay contractors sums as the work progressed in accordance with the terms of the contract, and the contractor consequently halted work, courts allowed the contractor pro rata recovery for the work and time completed.[141] In every regard, however, contractors "fired without adequate cause" received the same protection of the courts as had laborers.[142]

Finally, what of those cases where the work of contractors was rejected by the employer on the grounds that it was completed too late to be of use or was too imperfect to be of value? The English rule was that "unworkmanlike" or "untimely" efforts did not entitle a contractor to any payments[143] unless the employer "acquiesces" by using the building, or unless he "sees" the work progressing "and never objects."[144] These were essentially the

standards used in American courts. Builders who had been late in completing a seawall or a broom factory were held liable for damages when an alternative wharf had to be rented or a crop of broomcorn was ruined, just as
they had in medieval England.[145]

Judges and juries in America *may*, over time, have become somewhat less
strict than the English in deciding when an employer had received benefit
from the contractor's work,[146] but contractors still did not win in these sorts
of "firing for cause" cases as often as did hired hands, domestic servants,
and mill operatives. In twenty-six cases where "unworkmanlike" or "untimely" claims were made (70 percent of the total), the trial court found that
the employer had clearly received benefit or use from the contractor's work
or had acquiesced in it as it progressed and the appellate court upheld the
verdict for the contractor.[147] In twelve cases appellate courts voided these
awards (or upheld the nonsuiting of the contractor-plaintiff), noting that
the evidence established that the road engineer or builder had failed to fulfill
his terms of the contract.[148] (Laborers, it will be recalled, had won in
twenty-two of twenty-six, or 87 percent of such cases.) In short, the courts
had no favorites. As Justice William F. Allen of the New York Supreme
Court put it in *Sinclair* v. *Tallmadge* in 1861: "The law imposes no liability
on, and exacts no . . . penalties of, the mechanic. It will see that justice is
done to the employer, but at the same time it will do no injustice to the
laborer."[149]

CONCLUSION

A close look at the law of quitting and firing reveals a picture quite unlike
the one drawn by those who have previously addressed this issue. The law
was changing, but in a direction opposite to the one they had described, and
road and house builders did *not* receive "special solicitude" from
nineteenth-century American courts in comparison with the justice meted
out to hired hands, domestic servants, and mill operatives. Most judges did
not speak of the policy implications of their decisions in obiter dicta, but
some (in perhaps one in four of these cases) did; so law as instrument, instrumentalism, can be found in these cases, but it points in two directions at
once. Those who defended the older, English rule of entire contracts, men
such as Ambrose Spencer (New York), Levi Lincoln (Massachusetts), Jesse
Holman (Indiana), Robert L. Caruthers (Tennessee), and Sidney Breese (Illinois), argued that *Cutter* v. *Powell* was both good law *and* good policy. Industrial workers on annual contracts should not leave employers immediately upon acquiring the "mysteries" of their trade; hired hands should not
leave "in the midst of harvest" and expect wages. The old rule with respect

to entire contracts had both "the rule of law" *and* a powerful policy logic behind it, one that many judges, all of whom were familiar with the cycle of the farm seasons, could fully appreciate. Those who preferred the "more equitable" rule in *Britton* v. *Turner*, men such as Joel Parker (New Hampshire), James Campbell (Michigan), John Dillon (Iowa), and Amasa Cobb (Nebraska), argued, to the contrary, that *Cutter* v. *Powell* was *bad* law, both because it was unfair and because it was bad policy: The employer who had received the daily benefit of a worker's labor should be obliged to pay for that labor (less any damages he could prove to have suffered due to the employee's untimely departure). Otherwise the employer might take advantage of the worker's vulnerability as the contract's termination date approached. Such behavior would be disruptive of "brotherhood" in the workplace.

The newer rule of *Britton* v. *Turner* could only have been enunciated under the substantially altered conditions of the American labor market. Labor was more expensive here, and many workers were themselves aspiring property owners. Courts made fewer class distinctions in America than in England because there *were* fewer class distinctions. Only in such an atmosphere of "brotherhood" and republicanism[150] could the law of labor contracts take a new turn, but it still took an extraordinarily bold jurist like Joel Parker to turn it and a kind of bravery on the part of other jurists to follow in his path. Some followed Parker; others, the "taught legal tradition."

When judges in industrializing states were explicitly invited by attorneys representing manufacturing firms to rule in ways beneficial to the "rules of the shop" that those firms sought to use to enforce worker discipline, they nearly always declined to do so, preferring to enforce the law of contracts with equanimity.[151] Judges wanted to believe that the law represented good policy, but, with the exception of the very few pathbreakers such as Joel Parker and perhaps Isaac Redfield, most antebellum jurists were primarily concerned with precedent and "the rule of law." Nonetheless, once the new gate had been opened and the current was flowing, other courts, chiefly in the Midwest and Great Plains, were willing to follow Parker and to cite *Britton* as good law.

Chapter Six

Enabling the Poor to Have Their Day in Court: The Sanctioning of Contingency-Fee Contracts

> **The inhabitants of [England] are lost in the law, such and so many are the references, orders and appeals, that it were better for us to sit down by the loss than to seek for relief. . . . The price of right is too high for a poor man.**
>
> John Warr, *The Corruption and Deficiency of the Laws of England Soberly Discovered,* 1649

An intriguing development in nineteenth-century American law consisted of the increased availability to wronged Americans of the legal services of skilled attorneys at affordable prices. Nineteenth-century America saw the creation and sanctioning of the contingency-fee contract, an agreement between plaintiff and lawyer wherein the latter offered to represent the former free of charge until a settlement or judgment had been obtained, at which time the lawyer was to receive a percentage of the award (ranging from 5 to 50 percent), depending on the type of action, the likelihood of recovery, and the anticipated preparation costs and labor. This distinctly "proplaintiff" innovation has not received the attention it deserves. Others have *noted* the emergence of these contracts (albeit they have identified them incorrectly as emerging in the *late* nineteenth century),[1] but to date no one has systematically described or interpreted their approval by the bench. Why had contingency-fee contracts not been tolerated before the nineteenth century? Why were they tolerated in America by the midnineteenth century?

THE ENGLISH RULE

Since the Middle Ages in England, those who offered to assist or assume the pleading of the legal claim of a stranger for reward were barred from doing so by both penal statutes and the common-law doctrine of champerty: Rich and powerful men had sought to acquire additional wealth and power by aiding those with claims on the property of others, "stirring up suits" and "oppressing the possessors," in exchange for a portion of that property.[2] Both private men and public officials were the targets of such statutes, which eventually included penalties of three years' imprisonment and fines for "pleaders and attorneys."[3] In 1617 Sir Henry Hobart, chief justice of the Court of Common Pleas, styled one attorney who had offered a contingency-fee contract to the plaintiff in a slander suit "a champertor": "If an attorney follow a cause to be paid in gross," Hobart said, "when it is recovered, that is champerty."[4]

Eighteenth- and nineteenth-century English high courts held to the same standard, barring all "champertous" contingency-fee contracts. In 1843 one of England's leading jurists seemed impatient with a rule that prevented attorneys from assisting those without the means to advance them their costs and fees in order to seek justice. Lord Abinger, the author of the assumption-of-risk and fellow-servant rules in 1837,[5] offered these dicta in 1843: "If a man were to see a poor person in the street oppressed and abused, and without the means of obtaining redress, and furnished him with money or employed an attorney to obtain redress for his wrongs, it would require a very strong argument to convince me that that man could be said to be stirring up litigation or strife."[6]

Abinger was hypothesizing a Good Samaritan, not a solicitous solicitor who advanced resources for affidavits and court fees to promising clients. Nonetheless, I think his dicta indicates that he understood that there existed a humane rationale for the contingency fee, however inadequate that rationale ultimately might have been to him and his colleagues.

Ten years later a British inspector of coal mines named Mackworth described a dilemma that could, theoretically, have served as the grounds for the sanctioning of the contingency-fee contract in Britain. The survivors of those killed in mine accidents, he noted, "have no one to plead their cause. However gross may have been the neglect which caused the husband's death, all interests are arrayed against the survivors. The colliers, the [propertied] jury, the means of legal redress, . . . the difficulty of obtaining a solicitor who will undertake the odium [sic] and the risk, unite in forming an insuperable bar to the widow and the fatherless."

In England, the *losing* party was generally obliged by the court to pay the attorney's fees of the *winning* party, and since these could be quite substantial (often amounting to a sum greater than what was being recovered in damages in the suit itself), the prospect of paying costs of court *and* the fees of both party's attorneys was daunting.[7] Example: The coal mine inspectors managed to convince the secretary of state the next year, in 1854, to pay for the costs of one widow's suit and unsuccessful appeal in the test case of *Parkinson* v. *Caldwell*. The government's costs ran to £187 13s. 11d., and one inspector lamented that the statute enabling the widows of workers killed in industrial accidents to sue for their wrongful death ("Lord Campbell's Act") was "comparatively inoperative, as regards collieries, owing to the poverty of the suitor."[8]

THE AMERICAN "RECEPTION" AND REJECTION OF THE RULE

Contingency-fee arrangements between clients and attorneys may have been common in late colonial America, if Pennsylvania's experience was at all typical, and if that state's Justice Hugh Henry Brackenridge is to be believed. In 1813 he claimed that "parties not monied" sometimes chose "to stipulate for something out of what was recoverable," with attorneys "taking what are called contingent fees." Brackenridge suspected that the practice may have arisen from "the scarcity of circulating medium" in cash-scarce colonial Pennsylvania. In any event, "at an early period, it was tolerated, and has become common." But Brackenridge believed the "most eminent" members of the bar still viewed the contingency-fee contract as "unlawful," and he himself felt the arrangement was the cause of suits with little merit.[9]

Most of the earliest reported antebellum American decisions on the subject held contingency-fee arrangements to be champertous and void.[10] South Carolina's high court, anticipating Lord Abinger, was not averse to a Good Samaritan who was to "lay out money in . . . a suit to recover a [tract of land] of which his poor neighbor had been deprived, and without which he must lose it," since "right, humanity and justice would approve it." But an attorney who was to "do it upon a stipulation that he shall receive one half of the field, if it be recovered, he is . . . a champertor." New York's chancellor, James Kent, was equally adamant in adhering to the English rule. An attorney, aware of the issues in a suit for recovery of the value of promissory notes for pipes of wine, had purchased from the plaintiffs their right to sue (their "chose in action") for $359. After he had secured a judgment in New York for $5,987, the original suitors sought justice in that state's equity system. Chancellor Kent easily identified this attorney's behavior as having all the elements of champerty: "The object of the rule is to remove the temptation to imposition and abuse, for clients must apply to attorneys for assistance." This man had come to the plaintiffs "as an attorney"; he had hidden from them his grounds for belief that he might succeed where they had failed. He had secured the right to litigate in exchange not for 10, 20, or even 50 percent of the judgment, but for what turned out to be 94 percent (6 percent of its value). *And* he had paid for this "right" outright. This, Kent wrote, was champerty in its most "obnoxious" form, and champerty was as wrongful in New York in 1821 as it had been in England in 1621.[11]

Other reported cases of champertous contracts between lawyers and clients in the 1820s were less obviously offensive contingency fees, for 10 percent, a quarter, a third, or a half of the debt or property being claimed. Well-connected and accomplished litigators like Henry Clay, Amos Kendall, Linus Child, and Daniel Webster provided their services on contingency-fee bases to such diverse clients as the Western Cherokee, Mississippi slaveowners, the heirs of Philadelphia millionaire Steven Girard, merchants suing foreign governments, and diplomats suing the United States.[12] Conflicting and overlapping land claims in several of the newly settled states of Kentucky, Tennessee, Maine, and Ohio poured into the courts in the early nineteenth century. Holders in due course of colonial land grants vied with Revolutionary War land scrip holders and squatters bearing occupancy titles, some with registered land warrants, others without. Settlers who had purchased "titles" from mere squatter-enclosers and had built homes, cleared farms, and paid taxes for years, now found themselves ejected, their improvements treated as mere offsets for "rent" they had not paid to the "true" land grantees.[13] Disseized settlers, desperate, entered into contingency-fee arrangements with attorneys to defend their rights at trial or on appeal.[14]

Charles Hammond appeared before the Ohio Supreme Court in 1823 on behalf of such a contract. Hammond noted that "from the commencement of our jurisprudence, the legal profession" in Ohio had been "in the habit of stipulating for conditional and contingent fees, very frequently, . . . to be paid out of the sum recovered, and in proportion to the amount." A poor individual, "placed in the power of unfeeling and rapacious men," had been "illegally and oppressively stripped of his property, and turned, with his family, destitute, desolate, and hopeless upon the world." "The feelings of humanity" demanded that Ohio's judiciary reject a common-law rule created by tyrannical descendants of "the Norman conqueror" who had "subjugated the country and despoiled" the Saxons of their land. Inasmuch as "the right of making contracts" was "a high personal privilege of the citizen," Hammond (who also served as the supreme court reporter for Ohio in these years) asked that the court order the upholding of an arbitrator's award of 25 percent of the value of recovered property to his attorney-client. Hammond's client and his partner, however, had included in their contract with their disseized client the provision that he not settle the case out of court without informing them and securing their assent. They, after all, were proposing to spend time, labor, and monies to build their client's case; they felt it only fair that they be a party to any settlement. The Ohio Supreme Court felt otherwise, particularly offended by this stipulation, which might have the effect of mitigating the "injunction of sacred writ . . . which invites us to agree with our adversary." This contract would result in maintaining a dispute that litigants would have been willing to resolve, and this was contrary to good public policy and therefore void.[15]

Justice Jacob Burnet also denied Hammond's claim that contingency fees were commonplace, but Burnet may have been engaging in wishful thinking; the appearance of these suits in more than just a few jurisdictions in antebellum America suggests that Charles Hammond's description of contingency fees in early Ohio was neither fanciful nor unique. Benjamin Hardin, Esq., defending his own 1817-vintage contingency-fee arrangement before the Kentucky Supreme Court in 1823, maintained that the "old, forgotten and obsolete doctrine" of champerty should remain "buried under the rubbish of two hundred years." In Kentucky it was "frequently" the practice for the plaintiff to promise "contingently" part of what was "in contest" to his attorney, and he offered this public policy rationale: "[The client] may not have anything else to give, and without the aid of the matter in contest, he can never sue for his right, not having otherwise the means to employ counsel, the precise case here."

His client, one Rust, offered clear substantiation of Hardin's point during the trial when he told the equity judge that he was "so poor" when he had entered into this agreement that he had, really, been without any option. He "had to" agree to "a contingent fee" for "the purpose of obtaining counsel," as "one hundred dollars was charged by other counsel" to whom he had spoken. The chancellor treated this champertous contract as void, but allowed Hardin, off the contract, "a liberal compensation for his services" on a quantum meruit, as would the high courts of Massachusetts and Alabama. And note that *everywhere* in the United States courts did not oblige the losers of suits to pay the legal costs of the winners, as they did in England. Those of modest means need not fear the crushing weight of a railroad corporation's legal fee.[16]

Justice George Woodward of the Pennsylvania Supreme Court also attested to the antebellum popularity of contingency-fee arrangements when he called them "common," though criticizing them as being "more frequent . . . than they ought to be." They had "attracted the animadversion of this court, more than once," he continued.[17] But whereas his colleagues in Massachusetts, Rhode Island, South Carolina, Ohio, Alabama, Indiana, and Michigan would continue for some time to declare these contracts void, sometimes in very doctrinal fashion,[18] in 1852 Woodward and the Pennsylvania Supreme Court joined New York (1824), Louisiana (1834), Kentucky (1836), Tennessee (1836), and Delaware (1840) in sanctioning such contracts.[19] In the next two decades the high courts of Iowa, the United States, California, Illinois, Virginia, Arkansas, Georgia, Texas, New Hampshire, and Wisconsin held contingency fees to be enforceable, and in the years following the Civil War, Connecticut, Missouri, New Jersey, Michigan, and Utah followed suit. (New Jersey's chancellor went so far as to reject the English rule barring any payment to a barrister assigned to aid a pauper [*in forma pauperis*]. An attorney who had been assigned by the court to represent a poor woman seeking to recover on an insurance policy had asked for 50 percent of what he recovered for her, and that state's chief equity official held this to be a valid agreement.)[20] Indeed, by the 1850s state auditors and county commissioners were employing attorneys on contingency fees to recover escheated lands and taxes.

How is it that a practice that courts had for centuries regarded as a "temptation to imposition and abuse," a tendency "to promote useless and unjust litigation" and to "greatly multiply" the number of lawsuits[21]—in short a contract contrary to good public policy—could by the 1850s increasingly come to be deemed acceptable? Chief Justice Isaac Parker of the Massachusetts high court allowed that the contingency fee was "useful and convenient, where one has a just demand which he is unable from poverty to enforce," but he and his colleagues regarded themselves (as ever), to be bound by the old English champerty statutes and by common-law precedent and principles until the state legislature were to act to change the law.[22] In 1839 the legislature of Virginia passed such a statute, narrowing the scope of champerty and maintenance substantially and indicating that attorneys were "free to contract" such fee arrangements with their clients as the parties chose. Theodore Sedgwick argued in 1840 that American attorneys were free from the English tradition and practice that limited barristers to "honoraria" payments from clients or solicitors, who then recovered this from his client or the losing opposite party as part of the court-ordered bill of costs, and consequently American attorneys ought to be free to contract with clients as they wished, like other professionals, artisans, and tradesmen. David Dudley Field's report to New York's legislature on procedural reform called for freedom of contract for attorneys, and the resulting Code of Procedure in 1848 banned all rules "regulating the costs or fees of attorneys." A few of the other states adopting versions of the Field Code also sanctioned contingency-fee contracts by a statutory route.[23]

196   The contingency-fee arrangement, so useful to poor plaintiffs, entered

through the positive law door, then, in four or five states. But in many other, noncode states it entered through the portals of the state's supreme court. Champerty's "venerable" lineage might hold doctrinal courts like that of Massachusetts in tow, but others were more impressed by utilitarian-instrumentalist arguments than by mere precedent. One such rationale was advanced in the mid-1850s by both Justice Lucas Thompson of the Virginia Special Court of Appeals and Justice Onias Skinner of the Illinois Supreme Court. They reasoned that contingency-fee contracts constituted "a better guaranty" of the "fidelity, energy and proper zeal" of one's attorney "than a fee certain." An attorney who was to receive payment only if he was successful would work harder to achieve that goal. And he would not waste the time and resources of the state's judicial system, his client, or his opponent with a case that was without merit. Judge Edwin Countryman of New York took the same view, describing the contingency-fee arrangement between attorney and client as an "advantageous bargain" for both parties, "as they are equally dependent on each other for service and support generally."[24]

The other, more commonly expressed rationale, however, more exclusively concerned the welfare of the plaintiff. The plea that Benjamin Hardin, Esq., had offered before the Kentucky Supreme Court in 1823, to bury champerty "under the rubbish of two hundred years" in order to help a poor man to "sue for his right," finally found a sympathetic audience in the 1830s, 1840s, and 1850s. Thus in 1836 Tennessee's Justice William Reece sanctioned a clearly champertous agreement between a "very poor" woman and her attorney regarding her inheritance rights with the observation that it was "no quixotism" to "redress the wrongs of the indigent and the injured," but was rather "a grave and highly honorable duty of the profession."[25] When a champertous attorney's attorney asked the Delaware high court in 1840, "How is the poor man to assert his rights?" he was pleased to hear Justice Samuel Harrington answer: "The poor suitor may not have the present means of payment, and this *policy* [of voiding contingent fee contracts] may deprive him of counsel. . . . His rights are nothing unless he can have the means of enforcing them."[26]

Justice Christopher Scott offered the same rationale for sanctioning contingency fees in Arkansas in 1857. Citing Lord Abinger's dicta on the subject, he added his own ("the door of justice is not shut to the poor, who may be oppressed") and those of Justice Harrington's ("rights are nothing . . . [without] . . . the means of enforcing them").[27] Virginia's Justice Lucas Thompson reasoned in 1855 that such contracts "are in fact based on [the client's] ability to pay. Abrogate the right to so contract, and . . . you virtually close the doors of justice upon the party aggrieved in many cases. . . .

The genius of this practical and utilitarian age" renders old rules "as inapposite and inappropriate, in reference to the affairs of mankind in this age, as would be the code of chivalry promulgated by the Knight of LaMancha to the common every-day concerns of life." New Hampshire's Chief Justice Samuel Bell noted similarly in 1862 that "it is not uncommon that attorneys commence actions for poor people, and make advances of money necessary to the prosecution of the suit upon the credit of the cause. Thus a man in indigent circumstances is enabled to obtain justice in cases where, without such aid, he would be unable to enforce a just claim." Similar sentiments were expressed by appellate jurists in Texas, Iowa, Missouri, New Jersey, and Utah.[28]

The arrangement was never sanctioned for purposes deemed to be contrary to "good public policy," of course. That meant, in practice, that it would not be available to one seeking alimony or a divorce, to criminal defendants, or to clients seeking an attorney-lobbyist to secure some purely private statute or order from a legislature or cabinet officer.[29] But this left a vast field of law open to its use, including actions for debts, inheritance, land title, and, increasingly, personal injuries. Poor litigants could now "afford" skilled legal services and were not as intimidated by the prospect of their "costs of court" (fees for jurors, witnesses, and documents, as well as the court's own fee). We know something of the socioeconomic backgrounds of tort plaintiffs in nineteenth-century American courts: about 12 percent were professionals, proprietors, or their spouses; approximately another 25 percent were low white-collar workers or farmers or their spouses; about 15 percent were skilled manual workers; about 20 percent were semiskilled; and about 10 percent were unskilled workers or domestics.[30] Hence, while some tort plaintiffs were capable of paying for legal representation, others clearly would not have been able to do so were it not for the judicial sanctioning of contingency-fee contracts. This innovation opened the "doors of justice" in most jurisdictions to indigent and working-class plaintiffs in the same mid-nineteenth-century years that civil juries were beginning to award large damages to accident victims of corporations (as we will see in chapter 9).

While sanctioned in increasing numbers of jurisdictions, contingency-fee contracts continued to be criticized in the mid- and late nineteenth century by railroad attorneys, physicians facing malpractice claims, and some treatise writers, law review editors, and jurists. Some arrangements that had grown up around the contingency-fee lawyer specializing in personal injury suits, such as the employment of "lead men," "touters," and "chasers" to solicit business, were prohibited.[31] But the contingency-fee contract itself survived. As Alexander Robbins, editor of the *Central Law Journal*, put it in 1904, the "final argument" on its behalf was that "the public" favored it: "Where claims are uncertain, or where the parties plaintiff are in poor circumstances, the request is nearly always made by the client that the advocate undertake the case on a contingency fee."[32] Arguments persist as to the propriety of some of the rates charged today for relatively easy tasks, and proposals continue to be advanced regarding these and other aspects of the arrangement, but its utility to the poor and the cash-scarce plaintiff remains its chief raison d'être.[33]

Chapter Seven

"Larmoyant" Law: Explaining the Fight over the Attractive-Nuisance Doctrine

> On Monday I fired off a decision cutting the turn table cases (children hurt when playing on them) down to somewhat more precise limits. My brother Clarke uttered a larmoyant dissent that seemed to me more sentiment and rhetoric than reasoning, but the Chief Justice and Day agreed with him.
>
> Oliver Wendell Holmes Jr. to Sir Fredrick Pollock Jr., regarding *United Zinc & Chemical* v. *Britt*, 258 U.S. 268 (1922)

One sunny summer Sunday, August 17, 1873, an Irish-born day laborer named Fitzsimmons, "of very limited circumstances,"[1] living in a shack in Fort Leavenworth, Kansas, sent his twelve-year-old son, Jerry, to fetch the family's cow. The animal had been left on an "open common" grazing area near the local sheds and yards of the Kansas Central Railroad. Fitzsimmons had warned his son to stay away from the railroad company's trains, but he had never mentioned, and may never have known of, a curious device that stood near the commons. For the past three years a large iron turntable had served to reverse the direction of the company's locomotives (see ill. 3). The Fitzsimmons family cow had wandered to a spot close to this turntable, and Jerry Fitzsimmons climbed onto this device as two or three older children began to turn it around. The Fitzsimmons boy sat on the end of the table with his legs hanging over its rails. Before he realized what was happening, the rails of the turntable came into alignment with those of the adjacent track, and his left leg was caught between the two rails and badly mangled, requiring its amputation. His father sued the company for negligence and a jury awarded him three thousand dollars and court costs. The company appealed the decision, and the Kansas Supreme Court ordered a new trial, but in 1879 it upheld that second jury's award and finding of the company's liability. The high court cited decisions of the U.S. Supreme Court and of the Minnesota Supreme Court in its opinion.[2]

This late-nineteenth-century "Armstrong" turntable, belonging to the Illinois Central and located at Woodville, Mississippi, was the type involved in several of the early turntable cases. Manually operated, the Armstrong was described in Daniels v. N.Y. & N. E. RR, *154 Mass. 349 (1891) as having "large, upright standards or guys, 12 to 15 feet in height, which could be seen from a considerable distance." (Illinois Central Railroad)*

Almost five years later, on May 27, 1878, a circus advertised a performance in Jefferson, Missouri, a city of some five thousand souls. The circus managers pitched their tents on "open ground" near the state capitol, a flour mill, several houses, and the local roundhouse of the Missouri Pacific Railroad, on a field that had served as "the principal playground for the boys" of the area. Two of the Nagel children, Alice (age eleven) and Albert (age six), asked their mother if they could go to the circus grounds to see a lady tightrope-walker whose performance had been announced. Mrs. Nagel agreed, placing young Albert in his sister's care. The tightrope-walker's performance was delayed, and Alice became bored and returned home, leaving her brother, who wanted to stay and see the performance, at a lemonade stand. Albert finally tired of waiting as well and joined a group of boys exploring the circus grounds. They soon left the circus and entered the railroad company's property, where the roundhouse and its curious turntable stood, "in the shadow and within a stone's throw of the Capitol." This machine was "not unlike the circus' merry-go-round," and it was free, unlocked, and unattended. Neither the boy nor his sister or mother had ever seen the turntable, and young Albert was unaware of any risks he was taking when he climbed onto the device as the older boys began to turn it. When his legs were caught and mangled, young Albert did not survive his injuries.

Mrs. Nagel sued the company, and her attorney introduced evidence establishing that other children had previously been injured by the turntable and that the company's agents had been warned of the danger in leaving the device unlocked and unattended. A jury awarded her $1,050. The company appealed the award, but in 1882 the Missouri Supreme Court upheld the lower court action, citing as precedent decisions of the U.S. Supreme Court and those of Minnesota and Kansas.[3]

A turntable claimed the life of another young lad in the town of Cambridge, Idaho, on May 13, 1900. George York, a farmer, took his family and hired hand to town in his wagon to see a baseball game. He responded cheerfully when asked to play himself. Shortly thereafter, he later recalled, he heard the laughter of children coming from an adjacent property and saw a large group of boys playing on a curious mechanical roundabout, a device unknown to him and his family. Somewhat uneasy, he started toward the device and then broke into a dash when he heard his wife scream. He met one of his older sons carrying his four-year-old boy, Joseph, his right leg dangling and covered in blood. The boy had been another victim of a revolving turntable, this time turned by his own older brothers. The lad died three hours later, and York sued the turntable's owner, the Pacific and Idaho Northern Railroad Company, for negligence in leaving this dangerous machinery unlocked and unattended in the vicinity of a public recreational area. A jury awarded York $2,000. The company appealed the verdict, unsuccessfully, to the Idaho Supreme Court whose justices, like their Kansas and Missouri compeers, cited precedent to uphold the lower court findings.[4]

One final turntable case, with a very different outcome, serves to complete my setting of the stage for this chapter's inquiry. In 1904, "just before the 4th of July" ceremonies in the village of Kent, Ohio, a five-year-old boy joined a pair of older boys (ages ten and thirteen) in play on a turntable of the Wheeling and Lake Erie Railroad. Sitting on the revolving turntable "with his left leg hanging down over one end," the boy's leg was "caught between the end of the table and the head block." He lost the leg. His father sued the company and established in court that the company's station agent had known that boys played on the turntable and that the turntable was unlocked and unattended at the time of the accident. A jury awarded him $6000, but when the company appealed the award, the Ohio Supreme Court, reversing its earlier decision that had held a railroad company liable for injuries to a ten-year-old boy playing with signal torpedoes on the company's property,[5] agreed that the company was not liable. It cited the views of Justice Frank Hooker of the Michigan Supreme Court: "A man's home has always been considered his castle. . . . In our anxiety to prevent personal injuries, we should not go so far as to overthrow private rights."[6]

Ohio thereby joined a tiny but growing number of high courts that were choosing to reject a doctrine regarding the liability of property owners of dangerous machinery which was attractive to trespassing children, a doctrine that had prevailed in almost every state whose high court had announced a "first impression" ruling on the subject in the course of their history. What was happening?

I have offered some glimpses at a series of cases, known by the late 1880s as "the Turntable Cases," out of which emerged by 1900 the doctrine of the "attractive nuisance."[7] By the mid-1890s no fewer than twenty American jurisdictions, including the federal courts themselves, were consistently holding railroad companies and other owners of dangerous man-made objects seen as alluring and attractive to children liable for injuries to those trespassing children. But beginning in New Hampshire (in 1883) a number of eastern state high courts, several in industrialized states, broke with this pattern. By the turn of the century the states of New Hampshire, Massachusetts (1891), and New York (1895) had decided that the rights of the property owners precluded any claims that the trespassing children might have for damages caused by their dangerous machinery. By 1907 the high courts of eight more eastern states had joined this property-oriented chorus, among them Pennsylvania and Ohio, whose high courts had overturned their own earlier decisions. By 1925 the ratio of states holding to the older rule to those following the more recent decisions of New Hampshire, Massachusetts, Michigan, Pennsylvania, New Jersey, Connecticut, and New York, was about two to one. A clear majority of high courts still favored the more "generous" rule, but a trend away from it, led by eastern industrial states, seemed well underway (see map 2).

Were we to judge what had happened in the high courts of fin de siècle America on the basis of these glimpses alone, we would likely conclude that the pro-entrepreneurial instrumentalism that has been ascribed to antebellum American jurists was still serving industrial entrepreneurs in the so-called Age of Formalism.[8] The high courts of highly industrialized eastern states were apparently breaking new ground, clearly favorable to the corporate world, in rejecting a rule of law that protected trespassing children against injury from unguarded and attractive machinery, the dangers of which they were unaware.

Were that to have been our conclusion, we would have misunderstood almost entirely what had transpired. In the first place, the trend visible in the

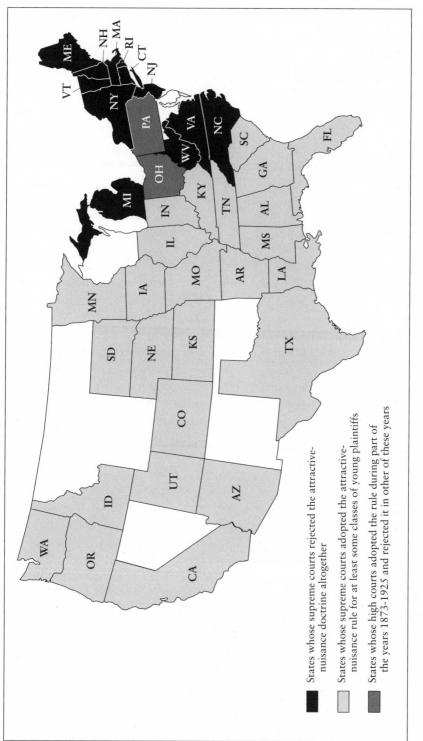

MAP 2. STATES ADOPTING OR REJECTING THE ATTRACTIVE-NUISANCE RULE, 1873–1924

early twentieth century against the attractive-nuisance doctrine did not prevail. The Supreme Courts of Ohio and Pennsylvania reversed themselves again on the doctrine, within a decade, and the American Law Institute's *Second Restatement of Torts* in 1934 contained a section (339) entitled "Artificial Conditions Highly Dangerous to Trespassing Children" which clearly accepted, but went *beyond*, the doctrine.[9] The doctrine grew (as did tort liability rules in general) not only in most of the states in which it had already established a home, but in several of those that had, for a time, like Ohio and Pennsylvania, rejected it as well.[10]

In the second place, the "trend" we *thought* we had discerned had been a totally deceptive one. The eastern, industrial state high courts had *not* broken new, instrumentalist ground in protecting railroad, utility, and manufacturing defendants in these suits; rather, they had been reiterating in formalistic tones older rules in *rejecting* a doctrine that was itself an instrumentalist invention, a doctrine that was itself a pure "legal fiction" designed explicitly to avoid a rule which had for *centuries* precluded any recovery for trespassers whose injuries had occurred unintentionally on another's property.[11] The attractive-nuisance doctrine was not an ancient accident rule that had been bent out of shape by late-nineteenth-century eastern industrial state courts friendly to entrepreneurs; it was in fact a nineteenth-century invention of non-eastern jurists who were friendly to children and unsympathetic to negligent industrial entrepreneurs. Moreover, many of the children in these suits were of a "lowly station in life," "poor," "of small means," from "the congested districts" in their community.[12] The creation of this attractive-nuisance doctrine, to borrow the phrase of a recent American president, amounted to a "kinder, gentler" instrumentalism in the Age of Formalism than legal historians have thought possible. And it was an instrumentalist invention that mattered—one that has saved thousands of lives and limbs and has required millions in damages to be paid to the persons or estates of those not saved. As such, its story is further evidence of the bankruptcy of the claims that nineteenth-century American jurists were pro-entrepreneurial instrumentalists who, by the late nineteenth century, became formalists, applying law according to its rules and internal logic and exhibiting no willingness to bend the law to serve social or economic needs.[13] It is also a story of a struggle between Head and Heart.

How did this attractive-nuisance doctrine emerge from English rules preventing damage suits by trespassers? How did its creators define its perimeters? And why was the doctrine embraced in twenty-five jurisdictions but rejected in thirteen others by 1925? Why did jurists claiming the same common-law traditions come to such starkly different conclusions about attractive nuisances? Why, in particular, did *eastern* jurists alone reject the rule? And what light does this inquiry shed on the larger question of the nature of judicial decision making in late-nineteenth-century America, the Age of Formalism?

THE ORIGINAL ENGLISH DOCTRINE

English and American jurists of the seventeenth, eighteenth, and early nineteenth centuries understood a property owner's duty to those injured on that property to vary according to the status of the injured party: One had a very high degree of duty toward a paying guest (a duty akin to an innkeeper's common-carrier liability for loss or damage to that guest's property). One had a less absolute (but still substantial) duty, one of "active vigilance," toward a guest (an "invitee") whom one had invited to visit, either personally or by implication (by such a gesture as placing a "welcome" sign before one's door). One had a less substantial, but still lawful duty, of "reasonable care," toward one whom one merely tolerated on one's land, from whose presence one derived neither economic nor societal benefit (a "licensee"), a duty to refrain from injurious behavior. But one had no duty (except to avoid deliberate and unwarranted maliciousness) toward one who came on the property without permission or invitation (a "trespasser").[14]

Thus if one deliberately set a baited and scented trap on one's property in order to draw dogs and other predators of one's livestock to their death, a neighbor's dog, drawn by an "instinct which he cannot resist," would be viewed only nominally as a trespasser. Property owners *did* owe a duty to their neighbors not to entice such creatures deliberately and maliciously to such traps and snares. And one who set spring-guns to punish trespassers was liable for injury to one who, unaware of the risk, pursued an escaping fowl onto that property, tripping a wire and causing one of these guns to discharge buckshot into his legs. That unneighborly behavior was viewed in 1828 by Best, C. J., as both "unchristian" and unlawful. But where a mare, "straying" into a neighbor's field in early-seventeenth-century England, stumbled into a ditch and was killed, the Court of King's Bench would not allow his owner a suit of action on the case to recover damages. The landowner's ditch, "in his own soil, was no wrong to the other"; the mare had been lost without grounds for recovery ("*damnum absque injuria*"). Tindal, C. J., illustrated the rule in an English opinion in 1830: "If a man puts a dog in a garden, walled all round, and a wrong-doer [trespasser] goes into that garden, and is bitten, he cannot complain in a Court of Justice of that which was brought upon him by his own act."[15]

Neither could one recover damages who fell into a quarry on unfenced

207

wasteland belonging to another, or who was injured by the unguarded machinery of a mortar mill on another's property, or whose trespassing sheep were run over by a negligently driven train. One injured while playing with an oil-cake crushing machine that had been left unattended, for sale, in a public market was viewed by the Court of Exchequer as a trespasser, and thus unentitled to an action for damages, and it did not matter that the injured party was a four-year-old child unmindful of the risk he had taken.[16]

The sole exception to this unyielding standard for trespassers seeking damages for their injuries was the case of *Lynch* v. *Nurdin* (Q. B., 1841). An egg merchant's servant left his cart unattended for fifteen minutes in New Compton Street, Soho, a place where children often played. One such child climbed into the cart; another, six years old, climbed onto one of the cart's wheels. When the first child took the bridle and drove the horse forward, the other was thrown from the wheel, which then ran over and broke his leg. His father sued and won a jury award for damages. On appeal, the merchant's counsel argued that the boy's act flowed from his "unlawful . . . trespass," a statement that the Court of Queen's Bench accepted but did not regard as sufficient grounds to rule a nonsuit. In the words of Lord Denman, C. J., this boy's act, while amounting to an "unlawful" trespass, flowed from "the natural instinct of a child, in amusing himself with the empty cart and deserted horse," and the jury had properly been allowed to compare the culpability of the child with that of the egg merchant's servant whose "most blameable carelessness" had "tempted" the youngster.[17]

Other English jurists, however, were soon to express doubts regarding Lord Denman's dismissal of the significance of the boy's trespass, and as late as 1870 the law in England did not permit trespassers, be they adults or children, to recover damages for injuries unintentionally incurred on another's property.[18]

THE EMERGENCE OF THE AMERICAN RULE

Several American high courts in the 1830s and 1870s adopted and applied the English rule; trespassers could expect no damage awards if unintentionally injured on another's property.[19] Intentional injuries to trespassers, as in England, were a different matter. The suit of a sixteen-year-old boy injured by the hound of a property owner who had deliberately set the animal upon the trespassing hunter was allowed to go to the jury by the New York high court in 1837 because, in Justice Esek Cowen's words, "the defendant . . . transgressed the plainest outlines of his duty. He put his neighbors in danger without the semblance of benefit to himself." A less malicious property owner would have no cause to worry about suits by injured trespassers, Cowen noted, with a republican's nod to the public, because "so long as one keeps upon the side of humanity, there is little danger that a jury of his neighbors will not place a correct construction upon his acts." Justice Roger M. Sherman of the Connecticut Supreme Court was similarly unsympathetic to a property owner who maliciously poisoned trespassing fowls with arsenic despite that man's evidence that he had warned the neighboring owner of the offending animals. Any other rule, Sherman felt, "would tend to impair the moral sense."[20] But these opinions were no more, no less, than applications of the English common-law rules, amply supported by appropriate citations of English precedent. Two opinions handed down in Tennessee and Connecticut in 1858 had a somewhat different character.

In Connecticut a three-year-old girl, walking too close to a train track on the railroad company's property, was injured by a train coming around a walled-in curve at a speed that was not deemed "careful and prudent" by either the trial or the appellate court. In affirming the jury's damage award, Justice W. W. Ellsworth noted that "if" the child was a trespasser, she was "only technically so," for she had been moved by "childish instincts" to venture into the "place of danger" and was consequently not chargeable with contributory negligence. Ellsworth did not speak of the train track as having "attracted" her to it, which would syllogistically have excused her trespass. He simply sidestepped the trespass problem altogether.[21]

Chief Justice Robert J. McKinney of Tennessee's high court in that same year was less evasive. A three-year-old boy who lived near a paper mill had lost several fingers to two uncovered, unattended, turning cogwheels fifteen inches from ground level, located some twenty feet from a public street, while the papermill's workers were on a lunch break. Eighteen years later, upon attaining the age of twenty-one, he sued. A jury found him to have been a trespasser and exonerated the millowner of liability. When the young man appealed that verdict, the state's high court agreed and set aside the jury verdict. The chief justice observed that the plaintiff, when injured "in playing about the cogwheels," had been "but indulging the natural instinct of a child" in "yielding to the temptation" to play with that strange object, a temptation "into which he was led by the negligence of the defendants." In this regard he noted that the evidence "shows that the wheels might have been boxed at a very trifling expense."[22]

In one sense, the high courts of Tennessee and Connecticut did not claim to be making any new law in 1858, for both opinions cited *Lynch* v. *Nurdin*, and, even if they were aware that this case had been "doubted" by Queen's Bench in 1854, they could fairly have laid claim to it, for it had not been explicitly repudiated. But, in another sense, the Tennessee court, in particular, **209** did venture onto the new ground that Lord Denman's opinion had created in *Lynch* v. *Nurdin*, for both explained away the youngsters' trespasses with the same words: the careless defendants' "temptation" of those who were merely yielding to "the natural instinct of a child."[23] Nonetheless, neither jurist went so far as to say that this "temptation" by the negligent property owner amounted to a full-fledged "invitation" to the child, a step that would have shifted him from the category of "trespasser" to that of "invitee" and would have given him clear rights to sue for injuries; it would be several years before that step would be taken.

The case of *Railroad* v. *Stout* (U.S., 1873) is widely regarded as the source of the doctrine of attractive nuisance.[24] It certainly represents an important piece of the puzzle. In 1869 Henry Stout, a boy of six, lived in Blair, Nebraska, a hamlet of 150 persons, three-quarters of a mile from a turntable belonging to the Sioux City and Pacific Railroad. One day he went with two older boys (nine and ten) to the company's yard. The older boys began to turn the unfastened, unguarded turntable and young Henry's foot was crushed as he stood on the machine's baserail, trying to climb onto the rotating track. His father sued in federal court (in diversity), and, after a first trial ended in a hung jury, the case was retried in 1872 before Judge John Forrest Dillon of the federal circuit court for the Nebraska District. The court heard testimony about the machine and the circumstances of the accident, and it heard one railroad employee testify that he had seen children playing on the turntable before the accident and had chased them away. Dillon, describing the case to the jury as a "novel and important case," instructed them that the company could be held liable if they were persuaded by the evidence that the machine was a "dangerous" one "which, if unguarded or unlocked, would be likely to cause injury to children" and if the company had "reason to anticipate that children would be likely to resort to it." He also instructed them to regard the testimony of a railroad witness that other companies left their turntables unlocked and unguarded at times too as "important" but "not conclusive."[25] The jury awarded Stout seventy-five hundred dollars and the company appealed. The next year the U.S. Supreme Court affirmed the award and approved Dillon's instructions, citing "the well known case of *Lynch* v. *Nurdin*" as well as the cases from the Connecticut Supreme Court in the process.[26]

Judge Dillon's instructions had staked out the *grounds* for ignoring an injured child's trespasser status, in the fashion of *Whirley* and *Lynch*, but they did not include the explicit language that would lift the child from the "trespasser" status to the role of an "invitee"—that is, they had not observed that the placing of an attractive machine where children would see it was an act that "invited" them onto the owner's property. As such, that problem remained, at least for those jurists who would insist on observing the invitee/trespasser distinction.

The solution was provided only two years after *Stout* by Justice George Brooke Young, a young Harvard-trained jurist who had recently migrated to Minneapolis. In the same year that Dillon allowed the question of the turntable owner's negligence to go to a jury, another trial court judge in Minnesota nonsuited a plaintiff with an identical complaint, a seven-year-old trespassing boy whose right leg had been caught between a turntable's rail and one on an adjacent wall, requiring the leg's amputation. Judge William Sprigg Hall told that jury that such accidents were deplorable, but that no legal grounds existed for the plaintiff to sue since he had been a trespasser. "It is apt to strike the mind," he allowed, "that from accidents of this nature, the community does stand in need of some protection," but "established principles of law" required a finding for the company. For relief from such a harsh rule of the common law "resort must be had to . . . the legislature by virtue of its general police powers to establish such regulations as may furnish such protection."[27]

When the boy's guardian appealed Judge Hall's decision to the Minnesota Supreme Court, however, the issue left unaddressed by Lord Denman, Chief Justice McKinney, and Judge Dillon was met head-on by the young, thirty-three-year-old associate justice assigned to write the opinion. For the court, Justice George Brooke Young found the railroad liable for the youth's injury, citing *Lynch*, *Birge*, *Whirley*, and *Stout* in the process, and particularly praising Judge Dillon's instructions to the *Stout* jury. But the young Harvard Law graduate[28] went beyond these opinions. Justice Young allowed that the railroad had not left its turntable unfastened "for the purpose of injuring young children." It had not deliberately attracted or invited them to use this admittedly dangerous machine. Nonetheless, the company *had* "presented to the natural instincts of young children a strong temptation," a "very attractive" object. They had "allured into a danger" those whose childish judgments could not appreciate that hazard. They had "induced" children to come toward what was the legal equivalent of "a trap." The company had reason to know that the unfastened turntable "was likely to attract and injure children." As such, they had extended to these children an invitation, at least by implication, for "what an express invitation would be to an adult, the temptation of an attractive plaything is to a child of tender years."[29] Here was born a legal fiction, an instrumentalist invention in the service of unwary children: Railroads had "invited" children to use their turntables and were consequently to be held to the "reasonable care" standard property owners owed to "invitees."

The Doctrine According to Dillon and Young spread with the publishing tide of law journals, court reports, and treatises. *Stout* was cited by Judge Reynolds of the Brooklyn (New York) City Court as early as January 1874, in his reversal of a trial court's nonsuit involving a trespassing four-year-old child who had been "drawn by the curiosity of a child" to the sight of a "whirring engine" a few feet from a sidewalk on Baltic Street and there crushed by a descending, unattended coal yard elevator car.[30] Both *Stout* and *Keffe* were cited favorably (along with *Lynch* v. *Nurdin*) in an Alabama opinion favoring an injured trespassing child in 1875, a Kansas opinion of 1879 (involving a trespassing boy injured on a turntable), and a Missouri opinion of 1882 (involving a trespassing boy killed on a turntable), while Pennsylvania's Chief Justice Daniel Agnew relied on a broad interpretation of the Latin maxim *Sic utere tuo, ut alienum non laedas* (Use your property, but not to the harm of others) in 1877 to affirm a jury award to the estate of a boy killed by a poorly secured heavy platform in an alley accessible to children.[31]

An additional, important voice was added in 1880 when Seymour Thompson, Judge Dillon's master in chancery and the associate editor of his *Central Law Journal*, published his first treatise, *The Law of Negligence*. Thompson praised Dillon's charge to the *Stout* jury; it was an "able re-sume" of the elements of attractive-nuisance liability. He also cited *Whirley* (the Tennessee case of 1858), *Birge* (one of the Connecticut cases), and *Mullaney* (the Brooklyn City Court case of 1874), and called Justice Young's opinion in *Keffe* an "able judgement." He rejected the Exchequer's *Mangan* decision (the oil-cake crushing machine case) as one "plainly contrary to reason and to the dictates of humanity," and, in his 1886 edition, he claimed (excessively) that the English Court of Queen's Bench had recently "de-nied" the "correctness" of the rule in *Mangan* (in *Clark* v. *Chambers*).[32] But it was Thompson's own vigorous language in describing the reason for the attractive-nuisance fiction, language that would be cited or quoted by ju-rists in first impression attractive-nuisance opinions over the next two de-cades,[33] that deserves attention here: "It would be a barbarous rule of law that would . . . exempt [the property owner] from liability for the conse-quence of leaving exposed and unguarded on his land a dangerous machine, so that his neighbor's child, attracted to it and tempted to intermeddle with it by [strong] instincts . . . might thereby be killed, or maimed for life. Such is not the law."[34]

In the 1880s the trickle of jurisdictions adopting the attractive-nuisance fiction became a torrent; to the high courts of the United States, Minnesota, Alabama, Kansas, and Pennsylvania were added those of Nebraska (1881), Texas (1882), Missouri (1882), Kentucky (1884), Georgia (1885), South Carolina (1885), Indiana (1886), Ohio (1887), and Mississippi (1887).[35] In the 1890s the supreme courts of Washington (1890), Louisiana (1891), California (1891), Illinois (1895), and Arkansas (1895) entered the stream. Nine more American jurisdictions joined the now more sedate flow in the next quarter-century, in the same years that the highest court of the British isles, the House of Lords, accepted the doctrine as well, its members unconventionally citing American precedent (*Stout* and *Keffe*) in a case involving a four-year-old Irish lad injured by an unlocked turntable.[36]

A number of the many clarifying, "second impression" cases in each jurisdiction applying the attractive-nuisance doctrine to the benefit of the injured child involved accidents on a railroad company's turntable;[37] indeed, "the Turntable Cases," as the first generation of attractive-nuisance cases were sometimes called, read like a *Who's Who* of America's railways west of the Hudson River. But the doctrine was soon extended in several states to accidents involving trespassing children injured by things other than that great merry-go-round of amputation and death. Some courts extended the rule to other "attractive" machinery, but not to all machinery;[38] some extended it to explosives left lying about, but not to those kept in an enclosure;[39] to electrical wires in easy reach of trespassing children, but not to those requiring considerable effort to touch;[40] to unguarded vehicles at rest, but not in every jurisdiction, and never to vehicles already in motion;[41] to vats and pits of scalding grease or water in some jurisdictions, but not others;[42] to carelessly piled railroad ties, I beams, or heavy cement pipes;[43] to smoldering, untended fires, but not stump fires;[44] to barrels of oil left unsealed, but not to kerosene lanterns left near an excavation;[45] to excavations leaving dangerously fragile slopes or overhanging precipices, to rusty barbed-wire fencing in settled communities, but not to revolving doors;[46] to artificially created watercourses in some jurisdictions, but not all jurisdictions;[47] to artificially created bodies of dangerously deep standing water, but not to naturally forming bodies of standing water.[48] In short, the *Stout* rule had been clarified by the early twentieth century in most jurisdictions to hold property owners liable for injury to trespassing children if the artificial object causing the injury was attractive to children,[49] if the company should have known it to be dangerous to them,[50] if it was visible or known to them off the property,[51] and if the child did not know of its dangers.[52]

These defining qualifications limited a company's liability, to be sure, but   213 they also created liability for a wide range of accidents involving trespassing children that had not been permitted prior to the last quarter of the nineteenth century. The average jury award in the forty-two of these cases for which I was able to detect figures was $3,158 (median of $3,000, low of $250, high of $10,000). Lawrence Friedman believes that "from the modern standpoint," damage awards in the late nineteenth century (which he found to be slightly higher than these) "fell short of full compensations."[53] I am not sure what he means by "the modern standpoint," unless it is anachronistic hindsight. One must judge the "fullness" of compensation from the perspective of the jury that was doing the compensating. I believe that, by the rules and wage-earning expectations of their time, these juries were offering compensation that was as full as their ethos and their economy could be expected to provide. Keep in mind that these figures include damage awards to those with no more serious an injury than a burned hand or a broken limb as well as to those seriously maimed. One must also keep in mind that many jurisdictions had statutory maximum wrongful-death limits of $5,000, and rules that minimized recovery by heirs or administrators in the death of a child.[54] Moreover, one must keep in mind that the annual income of the typical American wage earner in the late nineteenth century was only about $410, and that jury awards in 1979 in San Francisco and Chicago averaged $105,000 when the median American household earned $16,841.[55] In that light, these awards appear at *least* as generous as those of today.

A "Legal Fiction"

The clearly fictive character of the attractive-nuisance doctrine (the defendant's "invitation" to the youthful plaintiff) is evident in several of the first-generation cases. Property owners were said to be "enticing" children, they were said to be creating things "calculated to attract children," their "exposed" machines were said to be "an invitation to ['allured' children] by implication," they were "regarded as holding out implied invitations to such children," the "enticements" on their property were said to have been "tantamount to an invitation to visit," their "allurement or inducement" was said to have constituted an invitation to go upon the premises, "implied" by virtue of "the attraction [their dangerous objects] offered."[56]

This instrumentalist reliance upon legal fiction to move plaintiffs into a category requiring "prudent" or "reasonable" care on the part of the property-owning defendants offended some legal minds of the Age of Formalism. Treatise writers such as Thomas Cooley, Christopher Patterson, Amasa Redfield, and Thomas Shearman, unlike their western counterpart, Seymour Thompson, almost immediately rejected the law in *Stout* and

Keffe as "miscarriages of justice," holding rather to the older English distinctions as spelled out by Exchequer in the *Mangan* case. The "allurement" rule "tends to place responsibility for the safety of small children everywhere except where it belongs—with their parents." This "resort to a fiction" in order to allow trespassing children to sue offended formalists upset by such patently instrumentalist jurisprudence.[57]

New Hampshire's high court agreed. In 1883 Justice William Allen turned away the claims of a four-year-old boy's estate administrator who claimed that a disused city reservoir had lured more than one boy in Manchester, New Hampshire, to their deaths. Allen denied both the allegation that the artificially created reservoir constituted a "trap" and that the city had "allured" or in any way invited boys to swim there. Even "machinery . . . attractive and dangerous to children" would not be seen as having lured trespassing boys, he added in dicta. The rule that the "owner of land may manage it in his own way for his own benefit" was "too well established" to be abandoned. His colleague, Justice Lewis Clark, made the point even more explicitly four years later in a case of a seven-year-old lad injured on an unlocked turntable sixty feet from a public street (but in a fenced area). "We are not prepared to adopt the doctrine of *RR Co.* v. *Stout* and cases following it," Clark wrote. "The owner is not an insurer of infant trespassers."[58]

Turntable cases decided by the supreme courts of Massachusetts (1891) and New York (1895) made it clear that the jurists of those two influential jurisdictions had reached the same conclusion as Cooley, Patterson, Shearman, and the New Hampshire Supreme Court.[59] In a case with facts reminiscent of the Exchequer's *Mangan* decision, Justice Oliver Wendell Holmes Jr. of the prestigious Massachusetts high court characteristically penned the most citation-worthy, hide-bound rationale offered up by the eastern establishment in rejecting their frontier-colleagues' innovative legal fiction. A seven-year-old girl had lost three fingers after thrusting them into an unattended coffee-grinder in a grocery store. Upholding the trial judge's directed verdict for the defendant, Holmes wrote: "Temptation is not always invitation. As the common law is understood by the most competent authorities, it does not excuse a trespass because there is a temptation to commit it, or hold property owners bound to contemplate the infraction of property rights because the temptation to untrained minds to infringe them might have been foreseen."[60]

The most forceful critique of the attractive-nuisance doctrine, however, came from the pen of another Brahmin, Jeremiah Smith, in a *Harvard Law Review* article in 1898. For Smith the attractive-nuisance rule flew in the face of true doctrine, sound logic, and good public policy. The rule as ex-

215

pressed by Dillon and his western progeny was against "the weight of reason," "utterly untenable," with "misleading" rhetoric, "an entire perversion of language and a total confusion of legal distinctions," and it had *not* been adopted by English courts. (Smith was kinder to his fellow Harvard Law alum Justice George Young of the *Keffe* decision, suggesting that his words had been misunderstood by later jurists.) In particular, Smith fumed at the invention of a fictitious "invitation." This would "annihilate the distinction between negligence and intention" in the common law, and it was also morally wrong. It was "unfair" to enhance the alleged moral obliquity of the defendant's conduct "by imputing to him an intent which exists only by construction or fiction." After all, "no sane man believes that people who are making beneficial use of their own land do in fact entertain the intention of thereby alluring children to their destruction." Moreover, if the question of the defendant's negligence were allowed to reach the jury, that popular institution would invariably find for the injured, "invited" child, despite the fact that the parents of that child, at "moral fault" for allowing the child to trespass into danger, would be the ones who would, "practically," reap financial benefit as the recipients of that portion of the child's estate created by the wrongful death judgment.[61] Smith's brief against the attractive-nuisance rule was thorough and, for some, it was persuasive.[62]

The courts of New Hampshire, Massachusetts, and New York, the treatises of Patterson, Shearman, Redfield, and Thomas Cooley, and the pen of Harvard Law's tort expert Jeremiah Smith—with such authoritative voices as these, it is not surprising that others in the early twentieth century would join in the formalist rejection of the attractive-nuisance rule. First impression cases in West Virginia's and New Jersey's high courts attacked the rule and its implied "invitation" as "novel and startling," lacking "a solid foundation": "What a constant menace to ownership of real estate! What an infringement upon domain over private property!" When courts stuck to the "bedrock principles" that a man had the right to use his property as he chose for lawful purposes, and owed no duty to "use it in any particular way for the safety of trespassers, we have a certain, fixed guide."[63]

The supreme courts of Michigan, Rhode Island, Virginia, and Connecticut joined the formalist ranks between 1901 and 1906; Ohio and Pennsylvania overruled their prior acceptances of the rule in 1907; and those of North Carolina, Vermont, and Maine climbed aboard with their own first impression cases between 1908 and 1915.[64] The western authors of the attractive-nuisance rule had "left the solid ground of the rule that trespassers cannot recover for injuries . . . due merely to the negligence of the person trespassed upon." It could not honestly be said that a property owner "invites or allures children because no such intention in fact exists." The implication of consent had been "obviously fictitious," and the true motive behind it had been "to escape the imputation of making law, rather than declaring it."[65] A virtually solid block of eastern states, then, bounded by North Carolina to the south, West Virginia, Ohio, and Michigan to the west, and the Atlantic Coast to the east, chose by 1915 to reject the attractive-nuisance rule. Why? Why did this area remain doctrinal,[66] true to the older common-law rule, on this issue? Why did the rest of the state courts bolt from that rule? Let us consider the possibilities.

EXPLAINING THE DIFFERENCES: ALTERNATIVE HYPOTHESES

Jurists can hold to positions, at least in theory, for a number of reasons— among them, what they ate for breakfast, their class or political predisposition, the type of cases that came before them, differences over what constitutes good public policy, honest confusion regarding "the law" in cases on the borderline of existing and conflicting doctrines, personal values, and the process under which they received their legal training and were "programmed" to think about their professional duties. Each of these observations constitutes a potential explanation of the fin de siècle rift over the attractive-nuisance rule, but only two truly do the job.

The "Nature of Children" Explanation

Conceivably, the jurisdictions that chose to reject the rule were populated by jurists who simply didn't like children. It is certainly the case that those courts adopting the rule spoke very endearingly of "little children, who, like the bees and butterflies, wander everywhere," whose "little hearts tell them they are welcome everywhere," who "must be protected from dangers they know not of."[67] Most of these accidents involved young boys,[68] and some jurists had a more gender-specific warmth for the victims, reflecting, perhaps, their own childhood memories. An oak tree through which a poorly insulated electrical line passed was "just such a tree as the small boys of any community would be attracted to, and use, in their play," and this jurist wondered whether the power company officials "had forgotten that they were once small boys themselves." Another jurist found the appeal to small boys of a railroad turntable understandable:

> Everybody knows that by nature and by instinct boys love to ride,
> and love to move by other means than their own locomotion. They
> will cling to the hind ends of moving wagons, ride upon swings and
> swinging gates, slide upon cellar doors and the rails of stair-cases,

pull sleds up hills in order to ride them on the snow, and even pay to ride upon imitation horses and imitation chariots, swung around in a circle by means of steam or horse-power. This last is very much like riding around in a circle upon a turn-table.

The editor of the *Central Law Journal*, took issue with Kentucky's Justice J. P. Hobson in the same way: Justice Hobson must have had "a peculiar sort of childhood" for him to have found that certain electrical guy wires of the Mayfield Water and Light Company were uninviting to a child. They clearly offered to such a child "a glorious slide to the ground," something that "a bright boy" would recognize as "fun as soon as he saw it and would about fight for his turn to climb and slide." Similarly, Irving Browne, editor of the *American Law Review*, observed wryly of the attractive-nuisance rule in 1897 that "the leaning of judges in this matter is probably much influenced by their observation of their own small sons, if they have any." Browne had "regarded" the doctrine "askance" in the past, "but since I have been blessed and bothered with a grandson, I have become quite reconciled to it."[69]

Those who wrote opinions adopting the attractive-nuisance rule, then, described children tenderly and lovingly, while those rejecting the rule or its extension beyond narrow limits were often less generous. Trespassing children were "willful," "annoying," "venturesome," and "intermeddling," they were "adventurous truants," a "lawless class," who sometimes added "peculation" to the trespasses and on other occasions engaged in "youthful recklessness." Some there were, "in nearly every community," who were "abnormally mischievous and disobedient, who not only defy parental authority but public authority as well." This sort were mere "hoodlums, disregarding property rights from mere love of mischief, and taking risk out of mere bravado, or in conscious defiance of moral and legal restraint."[70] Did a law review commentator reveal a vision of Original Sin and a need for young men to wash away that heritage from their souls in these remarks?

> Looking back on my boyhood, containing an average of youthful transgressions, this writer can find little sympathy with the view that even a child of tender years is necessarily an unconscious and instinctive transgressor and therefore an allured and "innocently baited victim." Some of those who have discussed this topic either must be a trifle forgetful or else must have passed through a most sweet, innocent, and sheltered childhood.[71]

Now it is *conceivable* that one could explain the differences between the adopting and rejecting jurisdictions as one of a "good" versus "evil" view of human nature in children, but that would require that we believe that all those concurring in these opinions were governed by the same compelling vision of children. It would also require that we believe that eastern jurists had a far more negative view of children than westerners, when, in fact, most of both the "good" *and* the "evil" views just offered came, not from eastern, but from southern and midwestern jurists.[72] And, more significantly, it would require that we ignore the fact situations in the cases from which these passages are drawn—ignore the fact that several of the cases in which boys were described as "annoying," "reckless," or "lawless" were ones wherein a trespassing youngster had been injured as a consequence of such acts as swinging on the ladder of a moving freight train or stealing dynamite caps from a road construction team's box.[73] It seems more reasonable to conclude that the facts in some cases explained the harsh language, while in others the author of the opinion simply chose to flavor his dicta with adjectives that were consistent with a decision that had been reached on other grounds. Nonetheless, the warmth and empathy toward children expressed in several opinions upholding the attractive-nuisance rule is culturally revealing; we will have occasion to return to it later in this chapter.

The "Judicial Aid to Industrialization" Explanation

In the second edition of his *Law of Negligence* (1886) Seymour Thompson noted suggestively that opposition to the rule in *Stout* and *Keffe* was to be found "chiefly in those portions of our country which are dominated by railroads and other corporate interests." In other words, the eastern opposition to the attractive-nuisance rule might have been due to the propensity of jurists in the more industrialized states to oppose a rule unfavorable to industrial property owners. The couching of these rules in doctrinal language might simply have been convenient rhetoric, masking industry-sympathetic judicial reasoning. Lawrence Friedman puts it this way: Formalistic rulings were "the ones that fit the dominant boosterite mentality of the period. . . . Businesses as a whole were smaller and more precarious than today. . . . The deep pocket was not so deep."[74]

Turntable and other railroad-related accidents constitute a clear majority of first impression attractive-nuisance cases and are the single largest category of such cases overall in the years 1873 to 1925. Hence, it is worth noting that, as of 1890, the states *adopting* the rule had, on average, 74 percent more miles of track (4,521 versus 2,593) than had the states that would *reject* it.[75] In 1900 the rejecting states were four and a half times as densely settled as the adopting ones, and people in 1900 in those states rejecting the rule were about five times as likely to be located in cities of twenty-five thousand inhabitants or more, rather than in towns of one thousand or less, than in those states whose high courts adopted the rule.[76] The West and South in 1900 tended to be characterized by small towns; the East by larger cities. Deaths per one hundred thousand due to railroad-related accidents were slightly higher in cities than in rural communities in 1900. And the adopting states in 1900 had 17 percent more children under the age of fifteen per capita than the rejecting states.[77] Turntables, then, located as they were in depots serving the railroad, tended to be accessible to a larger fraction of the younger population in the western and southern adopting states than in the eastern rejecting ones. Would this not have meant that more turntable tragedies had actually occurred in those adopting states, prompting their protective high court reaction? The proposition is plausible, and in this regard it is worth noting that Seymour Thompson's impassioned defense of the rule referred to the owner of the attractive machinery as having tempted to his fate "his neighbor's child."

It may be that turntables presented the attractive-nuisance question somewhat more immediately to western and southern adopting states. The problem of how one explains judicial behavior, however, remains largely unsolved, for the eastern, rejecting states also had substantial numbers of turntable accidents, and, more to the point, they also had many nonturntable accidents in which trespassing children were injured or killed by attractive machinery or other industrial objects (electrical wires, pulleys, cables, elevators, cogwheels, etc.). The risks to trespassing children were sufficiently substantial in the rejecting states to doubt that this turntable-availability explanation is sufficient to provide an answer to the geographical split over the doctrine. Moreover, it is important to recall that the courts of the eastern, more industrialized states were not the judicial innovators, bending law to suit industry's needs; rather, they were *holding to the older rule* regarding trespassers. It was the western and southern courts that were doing the bending. Moreover, if those eastern anti-*Stout* states were *slightly* more industrial than those adopting the new rule (by about 10 percent, as to the percentage of assessed value of land and buildings investing in manufacturing), the fact remains that the overwhelming majority (88 percent) of wage-earners, and (thus) of voters, were *not* engaged in any manufacturing activity.[78]

More relevant to our inquiry is this observation: The members of those eastern high courts by the 1890s had been born before the Civil War and had been raised in a predominately agrarian, rural world. Morrison Waite, chief justice of the U.S. Supreme Court in the late nineteenth century, may serve as an example of this: The son of an attorney, he was born in Connecticut in

1816. Though he later moved to Ohio, he was raised in Connecticut on his father's "small farm." Moreover, for two summers, while in his teens, he lived first on one grandfather's farm and then on the other's, where (he later recalled) he "worked in farm work as boys did."

Consequently, when these jurists chose examples of the types of property that the adoption of the attractive-nuisance rule might logically extend to—that is, the types of objects from which property owners might be expected to protect trespassing children—it is not surprising that they invariably chose rural, not industrial, examples: "blue-berry pastures," "the high barn," "the pretty horse," "the dam that contains water to turn the mill wheel," "the canal with its towpath and frogs," the "pond necessary for [a farmer's] cattle," "the high cherry tree," "the bright red mowing machine," the "farm tool."[79] In short, a hypothesis that eastern, anti-*Stout* jurists were motivated by the desire to aid industry does not sound very persuasive.

The "Cost-Benefit Analysis" Explanation

Another potential explanation of why some states adopted the attractive-nuisance rule while others rejected it would be that some courts saw the rule as an appropriate measure in an overall cost-benefit formula fit for all negligence cases. That formula might have been worded in different ways by different public policy–oriented jurists, but, in general, it could be stated thus: Defendant property owners should be held liable if the cost to them of avoiding the accident to the trespassing child was slight, relative to the economic viability of the enterprise, the costs to the parents of the child of preventing the child from committing the trespass, and the likelihood of the accident. Perhaps one side of the debate saw the attractive-nuisance rule as an efficient allocator of scarce economic resources, and those jurists sensitive to such public policy issues in the shaping of common-law rules thereupon came down on the side of "good economic policy." Richard Posner champions such an interpretation of nineteenth- and twentieth-century judicial decision making in this corner of tort law. Posner's recent work on this subject indicates that the minds of jurists who crafted the "ingenious solution" to the problem of unlocked turntables and unboxed machinery were alive to this cost-benefit analysis.[80]

Which faction in the attractive-nuisance debate would one have predicted to favor the rule if its reasoning had relied heavily on cost-benefit analysis? A case can be made that *eastern* jurists, located as they were in more industrial and more densely populated states, should have been the more likely proponents of the rule if late-nineteenth-century American courts gave great weight to economic cost-benefit analysis. The demographic facts placed more children per turntable or uninsulated electrical wire per square mile at risk in the East than in the South or West; thus the jurist attentive to cost-benefit reasoning in the East should have been somewhat *more* willing to impose liability than his western counterpart. Yet we already know that this was not the case. What *did* the jurists have to say about cost-benefit analysis?

It is certainly the case that there are a respectable number of Posnerian statements in the cases under consideration (in about one in every ten cases) and in the law review essays and treatise commentary on the rule (about one in every four). But the fact is that both the defenders *and* the critics of the rule used Posnerian reasoning with about equal frequency; thus it is not possible to claim that evidence of a cost-benefit analysis by courts searching for an efficient allocation of scarce economic resources sufficiently explains either its emergence or the opposition to it.

Defenders of the rule sometimes pointed out that a very modest expenditure on the part of the owner of the attractive object could have prevented a costly, grim, and likely injury. A dangerous, disused open well, covered with loose boards, was located near a saloon in Lincoln, Nebraska, close by a site where people frequently hitched their teams and boys played ball. Its owners had been warned in 1900 of the danger by city health officials. Finding the owners liable for the death of a trespassing youth, Supreme Court commissioner S. H. Sedgwick noted that the wall "could easily have been put in such condition as to have prevented this accident." He generalized: "If I can obviate the danger with very little trouble to myself, and I know that children are attracted to the area in play, I am liable to those injured by my negligence." An unfastened turntable near a park in Indiana that was a picnicking area in the summer and a skating spot in the winter could have been made safe "without great expense or inconvenience." The protruding chain and sprocket wheelcogs of a box factory in Arkansas that killed a seven-year-old boy "could have been made safe by being enclosed, or boxed in, at an expenditure of from $2.50 to $20." A bolt protruding five inches from the outer rim of the coupling of a shaft rotating at 125 rpm, that caught the clothes of a boy fishing from the timbers enclosing the shaft, fatally whirling him around the shaft and against the timbers, was also "not boxed or covered." An unfastened turntable in Pennsylvania, could have been "guarded . . . with a small expenditure of money. . . . Under the evidence in this case, a few dollars would have restored the fence surrounding the turntable, and the children of that populous neighborhood would have been protected." It would have been better for "such protection" to have been provided "by the owner of the premises with a small expenditure of money" than "that the thousands of people" in the area "be required" to employ babysitters ["nurses"] when most of these families were unable "to bear the expense, to protect their children."[81]

Couched in these public policy terms, the rule sounds as if it had been invented by a jurist versed in the views of Jeremy Bentham and anticipating those of Richard Posner. But so do the public policy rationales of those who *rejected* the rule in toto or in extenso. "Expediency, in the Benthamic sense of 'the greatest good to the greatest number'" constituted the very public policy "grounds" that Jeremiah Smith voiced in declaring his opposition to the rule in 1898. The "danger of occasional harm," to Smith, could not "outweigh the benefit to the community of leaving owners unfettered in making a beneficial use of their land in methods which cause no damage to persons outside their boundary." The "general impolicy" of imposing on landowners with so-called attractive objects a set of legal "troublesome and expensive restrictions" was "totally irreconcilable with the progress of civilization."[82] The application of the rule to a boy trying to leap aboard a moving train in Georgia seemed to that state's supreme court to "impose upon the railroads a burden which it is not reasonable that they should bear." Its application to the pulleys and cables of a coal company's machinery in West Virginia "would incur vast additional expenditure in enclosing and guarding their machinery—an expenditure wholly unnecessary, except to prepare in advance for the presence of children." Its application in Michigan to a bankrupt factory whose disused waterwheel had been turned by an eight-year-old-girl's brothers, injuring her, was "unreasonable" if it required a "company with an empty treasury and overwhelmed with debt to be [put] to the expense" of providing elaborate fencing in order to prevent "children from going across its lots to school." Its application to a railroad company's unfenced (*and* unlocked) turntable was also unreasonable in New Jersey because "no matter how carefully" the company might endeavor to protect itself with fences, "discharging the duty" the attractive-nuisance rule would require of it, "the probability of [its] failure is great." Its application in cases where a young boy and a young girl were drowned in artificially created waterways in Vermont and Arizona were unacceptable because, were it to be applied to such accidents, there would be "no practical stopping place this side of practical insurance of children."[83] It was "not necessary to make premises 'child-proof.'"[84]

We cannot explain the emergence of the attractive-nuisance rule, then, as an application, by one side of the controversy, of cost-benefit analysis. But that does not prevent us from appreciating that *some* justices, on both sides of the controversy, found such analysis valuable in offering public policy rationales of their positions. Friends of the rule might read low cost and high probability into such an equation; foes might read high cost and low probability into the equation. The former might describe the liability of landowners in the language of small change; the latter in terms sounding like long-term, high-cost "insurance" that companies would be obliged to render their property "child-proof." My point is not that one side had the equation right and the other wrong. Rather, my point is that only a relatively small fraction of jurists *engaged* in such cost-benefit analysis, and those who did were equally divided between friends of the rule and foes. There *were* Posnerian jurists in fin de siècle America, but cost-benefit analysis alone will not explain the fact that some favored the rule, weighting the equation accordingly, and others did not. Cost-benefit analysis was used, it appears, as a kind of public policy support for a position already arrived at on other grounds.

Reason versus Humanity: Formalism Contends with Instrumentalism

We seem to have been able to explain very little of the difference between pro- and anti-attractive-nuisance jurists with the two prime models of economic determinism. What judicial language remains that *will* explain it? If we listen to what these jurists said in defense of their positions, we can hear them arguing earnestly over basic principles of law and justice. The critics of *Stout* and *Keffe* are familiar to us as "formalists," men whose training and values caused them to blanch at this legal "fiction"[85] as a departure from "well established" doctrine and "settled principles of law," sustained by "reason."[86] They abhorred "sentimental" jurists who "have yielded to their sympathies" for maimed trespassers in adopting "a rule unknown to the common law."[87] Theirs was a Jurisprudence of the Head. Those who favored the attractive-nuisance rule were "larmoyant";[88] those who opposed it spoke for "a clear and scientific explanation" of the common law.[89] If the *legislature* wanted to change the law regarding youthful trespassers, then these Solons would obey, but "a wise public policy should forbid such a sweeping innovation by judicial main strength."[90]

The defenders of *Stout* and *Keffe* spoke another language altogether. To be sure, a few of them would claim that it was they, and not the eastern Solons, who were following the "well-settled principles" found in *Whirley, Stout, Keffe,* and their progeny.[91] As Jerrilyn Marston has demonstrated with regard to another tort rule created in the nineteenth century, once an important court had addressed a problem thrown up by new industrial circumstances and has articulated a "principled" rule to deal with that problem, other courts felt compelled to follow the leader.[92] Once *Stout* and *Keffe* were published, built as they were on *Lynch* and *Whirley*, they would be cited by the more acquiescent jurisdictions as "precedent," as "the true rule"[93] for courts to follow, in a process that developed a momentum of its own.

A few defenders of the rule maintained that they were, in fact, following a doctrine of even greater lineage, "the doctrine based upon humanity, the wholesome maxim *Sic utere tuo, ut alienum non laedas*," a maxim "which for centuries has protected the weak against the strong."[94] But most defenders of the attractive-nuisance rule were more explicitly instrumentalist than either of these two neodoctrinal subgroups. Most of the rule's defenders believed in "the humanity of the law," and, in that context, referred to "the instincts of the heart," to "the common feeling of mankind, guided by the second branch of the great law of love" ["love thy neighbor as thy self"], and to "the best monitor, . . . the conscience." The law to them was "alive with the spirit of justice," attentive to those "humane considerations" as would "require such a rule."[95] "Any other doctrine would so illy accord with christian civilization" as to be untenable. *Stout* was "good law and good ethics. To hold otherwise would be to exalt mere money and property and put down humanity—would be to offend against little ones; and there is high authority [Matthew 18:6] for the proposition that it were better that a millstone were hung about the neck for drowning purposes than that such offense be given."[96] A court would "violate its social duty" if it were to "magnify" property rights at the expense of "personal right—the right to life, limb, health, and safety." Precedent might exist for the nonsuiting of trespassing children injured by attractive machinery, "but an equal number of cases may be found in the books sustaining witchcraft, slavery, and other inhumanities and infamies, in the light of present-day civilization and jurisprudence."[97] Rather than follow such "unjust" precedent, the defenders of the attractive-nuisance fiction would follow their own law, "the law as written by this court,"[98] the Jurisprudence of the Heart.

The creators and defenders of the attractive-nuisance rule were instrumentalists, but not the sort that economic determinists write about; they were willing to change the common law, not to the *advantage* of entrepreneurs, but to their *disadvantage*. Eastern, Harvard-trained formalists such as Jeremiah Smith saw the common law as a defensible set of inherited, reasonable rules; western, self-taught jurists such as John Forrest Dillon, Seymour Thompson, and Frank Doster saw many of these qualities in the common law as well, but they were not quite as wedded to them, not quite as bound by them, as were their eastern counterparts. Most had not been students or colleagues of Christopher Columbus Langdell; most were not as familiar with and attentive to English precedent as were their eastern counterparts; most were not as devoted to the internal logic of the common law. Eastern formalists, by contrast, appear on our map to have been attracted to English precedent as if by a magnet, for if one draws an arc through the United States, five thousand nautical miles from the courts of Westminster, all the states rejecting the rule lie within, all those adopting it lie without, "beyond the pale."

SEVEN SKETCHES

To clarify further this tension between Heart and Head over the attractive-nuisance doctrine, let us briefly consider seven of our story's leading actors: Lord Denman, the author of *Lynch* v. *Nurdin*; John Forrest Dillon, the author of the rule in *Stout* v. *RR*; Seymour Thompson, the impassioned defender of the rule in his *Law of Negligence*; Frank Doster, the boldest extender of the fictional "invitation" reasoning;[99] Jeremiah Smith, the most eloquent and vigorous critic of the rule; Oliver Wendell Holmes, whose pithy language in *Holbrook* v. *Aldrich* was often cited by the rule's critics; and John Clarke, the author of the dissent to *Britt* that Holmes styled "larmoyant."

Thomas, Lord Denman is described by his biographer as a man who had "never" been "a great lawyer" and as one who made "a weak judge." Of "ultra-liberal opinions," he served the Whigs in Parliament for a decade as Lord Brougham's associate in the struggle for utilitarian law reform, defended the Luddite "Captain" Jerry Brandreth, supported the radical Richard Carlile's petitions, and held abolitionist and antislave trade positions in Parliament. He proposed the act (2, 3 Vic. c. 54) that allowed mothers who were legally separated from their husbands to have access to their children, as well as the act that bears his name (6, 7 Vic. c. 85), which allowed an "interested party," barred by the common law from testifying in a case, to be sworn and give testimony. He is said to have called the judicial wig "the silliest thing in England" and to have sought in vain to end its use. As such, he seems appropriately to have been the first English jurist to ignore precedent to help trespassing children injured by negligent acts.[100]

John Forrest Dillon had been raised as a boy in an Iowa frontier community. He was self-taught in law. Elected as an antislavery man and Republican to the Iowa Supreme Court in 1862, he wrote for that court an eloquent defense of the controversial and recent innovation by Justice Joel Parker of the New Hampshire high court (*Britton* v. *Turner* [1834]) permitting farm laborers to breach an "entire" labor contract and recover in quantum meruit, off the contract. He was an advocate in 1869 of the codification movement (popular simplification of the common law by the legislature). Dillon was later described as one who "saw law always as a practical implement," as one who espoused "common sense opinions" and as one possessed of an "intensely pragmatic attitude, smelling always of the plowed fields of Iowa." After leaving the federal bench in 1879, he served as president of the American Bar Association and as counsel for several railroad companies, at one time defending one (unsuccessfully) in a case before the U.S. Supreme Court against a plaintiff's attractive-nuisance claim![101]

In 1895 Dillon addressed the New York State Bar Association on the subject of "Property—Its Rights and Duties in our Legal and Social Systems." He had "no criticism" of nonviolent Socialists, who had already done "much good in securing the recognition of the unrestricted right of labor combination, shortening the hours of labor, the prohibition of Sunday labor, and of the employment of young children," as well as "securing the sanitary inspection of factories and workshops." He was critical of "ostentatious" displays of wealth and of "extreme individualists" who feared the state. He favored regulation of trusts, and recommended the creation of charitable trusts and the French progressive inheritance tax to curb vast wealth from creating dynasties. The only "doctrines" he mentioned were those of "the Heavenly Dreamer of the Galilean Hills, . . . the Blessed Savior," regarding the obligation of the rich to relieve social suffering.[102] Others have characterized Dillon as a "traditional conservative" and linked him with "robber barons."[103] He seems to me to have been closer to the social Gospel than to social Darwinism or laissez-faire.

Seymour Thompson (like George Brooke Young, the author of *Keffe*) was a (Presbyterian) clergyman's son. Born in Illinois in 1842, his family moved to Iowa in 1855, where he attended Clark Seminary. When his father and brother were burned to death in a prairie fire in 1858, he moved back to Illinois, where he worked as a farm laborer and peddler. He enlisted in May 1861, and was mustered out in 1866 as a captain. He settled in Tennessee for five years, where he worked as a policeman, a balloonist, and a clerk of court while teaching himself law. In 1872 he moved to St. Louis, attracted the attention of Judge Dillon, who offered him the position of master in chancery. In 1874 the two men founded the *Central Law Journal*. His *Law of Negligence* appeared in 1880, full of praise of the attractive-nuisance rule, equally critical of contributory negligence as being "cruel and wicked." Thompson was elected judge of the St. Louis Court of Appeals in 1880. By 1892 he was the principal editor of the *American Law Review*. In the early 1890s Judge Thompson criticized the "freedom of contract" principle as "the veriest sham" employed by "unfit" jurists, called for the direct election of senators and for laws responsive to laboring people, and attacked the U.S. Supreme Court's opinions on railroad rates and trusts. Like Dillon, he moved to New York in the 1890s but returned to Missouri, where he attacked the assumption-of-risk rule, in 1897.[104]

Frank Doster volunteered for service in an Indiana cavalry unit early in the Civil War at the age of fourteen. After two years of service he returned to Indiana for more education and then went on to Illinois College, where he studied law. He migrated with his wife to Marion County in western Kansas, where he was elected as a Republican to the state legislature in the early 1870s. A temperance man, devoted to his family, he and his wife raised five children in a modest home in a small town. He believed that a lawyer owed a duty to "the social state" and rejected Lord Brougham's dictum that an attorney's primary duty should be to his client's interests. He campaigned in the early 1890s on the theme that "the rights of a user [of property] are paramount to those of the owner." In 1893 he told an audience that "the wail of the orphan is heard louder in the courts of heaven than the chuckling glee of the money changers. I know that humanity is above property." After his election on the Populist ("People's") Party ticket to the chief justiceship in 1896, he told a reporter that his understanding of the law was "what the profession generally has learned," but he went on to say that recent common-law decisions had been "extorted from the courts by the capitalistic institutions of the country. . . . We need a return to the old ways and the common-law precedents. They will be found more consonant with theories of popular right." (He was, therefore, prepared to see the eastern, industrial state rejection of the attractive-nuisance doctrine in the least flattering light.) He would sometimes refer to himself as a Socialist in the early twentieth century and would lecture on law as a "science."[105]

Jeremiah Smith was the son of a Federalist chief justice of the New Hampshire Supreme Court. He attended Harvard Law School, married the daughter of Daniel Webster, and became a justice of the New Hampshire Supreme Court. He resigned from that court in 1874, suffering from tuberculosis, and spent some time "taking the cure" in Minnesota.[106] Returning to New England, he was appointed the Story professor at Harvard Law in 1890, where he taught torts, corporations, and legal ethics. He would later (in 1913) publish another important formalist critique of legal innovation, this one complaining of the abrogation of the fellow-servant rule and the creation of workman's compensation laws.[107]

Oliver Wendell Holmes Jr., the author of the "hard" *Holbrook* and *Britt* decisions, was the nephew of a Boston attorney and the grandson of Charles Jackson of the Massachusetts Supreme Court.[108] After over three and a half years at Harvard, Holmes served as a junior officer in the Twentieth Massachusetts Infantry Regiment during the Civil War, was wounded in action three times, lost much of his enthusiasm, and resigned in 1864. He obtained a law degree from Harvard in 1866, practiced admiralty law with the firm of Shattuck and Munroe, became a partner, edited the *American Law Review* from 1870 to 1873, and was the twelfth editor of Chancellor James Kent's *Commentaries on American Law.* In 1881 he delivered a series of lectures on law at the Lowell Institute in Boston. He accepted the Weld professorship at Harvard Law in January of 1882, but surrendered it eleven months later when named to the prestigious Massachusetts Supreme Judicial Court. He was advanced in 1899 to chief justice of that court, and to the U.S. Supreme Court in 1902. He underwent major surgery in 1922, the year of the *Britt* decision, at the age of eighty-one, retired from the court in 1933, and died in 1935.[109]

A Unitarian, Holmes was philosophically a skeptic. Drawn to scientific analysis, fully aware of Darwin's findings, he was a pessimist, with little patience for the "squashy sentimentalism" of "a big minority" of the public. He did not love mankind, as he confessed to Lewis Einstein: "Most of the great work done in the world" came from the self-centered. He recommended to entering law students in 1897 that the way to understand common-law rules was to imagine oneself "as a bad man who cares only for the material consequences which such knowledge enables him to predict." The Golden Rule was a "futile" guide. In his "years of full maturity he had but few friends." He married in his twenties a lively and charming woman, but had no children.[110]

Holmes was not a formalist. He had read the utilitarian views of the English legal philosophers Jeremy Bentham, John Austin, and John Stuart Mill and was as critical as were they of "legal theologians" who ignored the medieval, archaic origins of most elements of nineteenth-century common law.[111] He denied that there existed any natural, moral rights discoverable within the law's internal logic and principles; rather, the law reflected external values and experience, "the felt necessities of the time."[112]

Nonetheless, this utilitarian legal philosophy did not mean that, in practice, Holmes would behave as an innovative, instrumentalist judge. He sought to explain his tort decisions in language consistent with his external liability standard, but this resulted only in his being in essential symmetry with his colleagues on the bench with regard to the outcome of assumption-of-risk, contributory-negligence, res ipsa loquitur, and last-clear-chance arguments.[113] Other of Holmes's opinions, although based on different reasoning, were also almost invariably consistent in outcome with those of his formalist colleagues. Bankruptcy creditors of an insurance firm were turned away in 1888 because "the law knows nothing of moral rights unless they are also legal rights" (which prompted an "outraged dissent" from Justice Walbridge Field, "who had learned law in a law office, not in a school," and who believed "firmly that the creditor's claims were founded on natural justice"). A master-servant rule that Holmes *admitted* to be of questionable public policy was enforced in 1891 because "we are not at liberty to refuse to carry out to its consequences any principle which we believe to have been part of the common law, simply because the grounds of policy on which it might be justified seems to us to be hard to find, and probably to have belonged to a different state of society." A company's demand that an injured plaintiff submit to an examination by a specific physician in 1900 led to Holmes's observation that the jurist's "general duty is not to change but to work out the principles already sanctioned by the practice of the past. No one supposes that a judge is at liberty to decide with sole reference even to his strongest convictions of policy and right."[114] It is Justice Holmes, the pessimistic conservative, not Scholar Holmes, the mentor of legal realists, who declined to set aside the ancient rule against liability to trespassers in *Holbrook* and *Britt*.[115] He drew neither dissents nor distinguishing concurrences from his *formalist* colleagues.

Justice John Clarke's dissent in *Britt* was, according to Holmes, that of a "larmoyant" (tearful) sentimentalist. Clarke was "deeply religious," with an "optimistic faith in the reasonableness and perfectibility of man, . . . and an insistence upon the social welfare." He was willing to ignore ancient common-law rules and called big businessmen "selfish and narrow." Something of a philanthropist, he favored municipal ownership of street railways and "clashed with the interests of the clients he represented." Clarke was a progressive Democrat, active in Ohio politics. A friend of labor, he favored the vote for women in Ohio. Justice Holmes once complained to Chief Justice Taft that Clarke "sometimes decided cases in advance based on his own political convictions." He resigned from the Supreme Court shortly after his *Britt* dissent to lobby for U.S. entry into the League of Nations. In the 1930s he supported President Roosevelt's "court-packing" proposal before Congress. His biographer called him a "humanitarian idealist, deeply interested in the welfare of his neighbors." As such, his Britt *dissent* (unnoted by his biographer) was perfectly consistent with his philosophical precepts.[116]

From what we have seen in the dicta of our attractive-nuisance cases (the tension between humanity and precedent), and from what we see in these brief sketches of our seven leading actors, could we not have predicted from their biographies on which side they would have come down on the issue?

Their philosophies of life and legal training informed their courtroom behavior. The rule's creators gave much more weight to "humanity" than did its critics. And that made all the difference.

CONCLUSION

We have seen how a number of humane jurists created the legal fiction of the attractive nuisance in late-nineteenth-century America (and England), and we have seen how other, more formalistic, eastern jurists resisted the creation of that fiction. Some, on both sides of the question, sought to justify their positions with public policy rationales exhibiting efforts in cost-benefit analysis, but, inasmuch as these efforts did not adopt the same objective weightings to be applied to various elements in the cost-benefit equation, these efforts cannot be said to have been of much use to a jurist who had not made up his mind or a company president who sought to minimize his company's liability.[117]

Some of the creators of the attractive-nuisance rule were more clearly instrumentalists than others. Some swept English rules and precedent aside with reference to "higher authority," "Christianity," or morality. In the process, they behaved in exactly the opposite fashion of the pro-entrepreneurial nineteenth-century American jurist posited by the reigning paradigm. They were using law instrumentally, but this kinder, gentler instrumentalism was *anti*corporate, driven by humanitarian impulses.

Other creators of the rule were uneasy with the charge that they were upending existing rules of law. They preferred to offer the rule as one reasonably derived from an analysis of the facts of the case: an artificial object placed within sight of children by a property owner and known to be dangerous to those children had attracted those children to it. As such, the children could reasonably be said to be invitees, and the property owner owed them the duty corresponding to that status. Some of these tradition-seeking creators of the rule also repeated the Latin maxim *Sic utere tuo* as if its lineage and general charge to property owners might cancel out the seventeenth-century *Blyth* precedent. In these regard, our tradition-seeking creators and defenders of the rule all remind one of Tocqueville's observation about the English or American jurist (*legiste*) who

> denies his own reasoning powers in order to return to those of his
> fathers, maintaining his thought in a kind of servitude . . . [and]
> values laws not because they are good but because they are old; and if
> he is reduced to modifying them in some respect, to adopt them to the
> changes which time brings to any society, he has recourse to the most

incredible subtleties in order to persuade himself that in adding something to the work of his fathers he has only developed their thought and completed their work. Do not hope to make him recognize that he is an innovator; he will be prepared to go to absurd lengths rather than to admit himself guilty of so great a crime.[118]

Of whatever jurisprudential persuasion, the creators and defenders of the attractive-nuisance rule hoped to accomplish two things: to afford children an avenue of redress against those whose careless use of their property had led to their being maimed and to deter such careless use of property in the future. Railroad turntables, other exposed machinery, and electrical power lines were new hazards on the late-nineteenth-century landscape, claiming the lives and limbs of thousands of children each year.[119] But the mid- and late nineteenth century was also the era of the child in American culture—an era that redefined children as innocent, loving, heaven-sent creatures. Parents and children as recently as 1814 had been told that "too much play" created "evil habits," that children's recreation should be "lawful, brief, and seldom." By the mid-nineteenth century, they were being told of "children's rights," of the natural character and importance, indeed, the "necessity," of child's play. One was never to "find fault with children for their incapacity to keep still." It was no "transgression of the moral law" for a boy to be restless and lively, for a child "to give free vent to its animal spirits and overcome them by exhaustion."[120] Is it any surprise that jurists inspired by such advice would write of children who "wander everywhere," whose "little hearts tell them they are welcome everywhere," and who consequently "must be protected" by the courts "from dangers they know not of?"[121]

The defenders of the attractive-nuisance rule exercised their "power so as to secure, at the hands of . . . public utilities corporations, handling and controlling these extraordinarily dangerous [electrical] agencies, the very highest degree of skill and care," and their judgments in the turntable cases "probably" produced "much good" (in the words of one commentator) "in the way of forcing the guarding of exposed machinery dangerous to children."[122] I close with a concrete example of that process, uncovered by Gordon Bakken. John D. Bicknell was an attorney who frequently represented the Southern Pacific Railroad Company in tort defenses. When the company lost the "first impression" turntable case in California,[123] Bicknell wrote to the company's general counsel, Creed Hammond:

> In view of the tendency of the courts in the various states in this class of cases, I feel disposed to call your attention again, as I did some months ago, to the necessity of some means of locking or fastening

the turntables in the country towns, such as Santa Ana, where children pass near them upon the public highway and the table is not guarded by the presence of any of our employees.

Hammond responded: "I concur with you in the suggestion which you make as to fastening turntables in towns like Santa Ana."[124]

Dillon's *other* "rule" was being observed.[125]

Chapter Eight

Children at Play and Heroic Risks: Big Holes Punched in the Contributory-Negligence Defense

And the streets of the city shall be full of boys and girls, playing in the streets thereof.

> Zechariah 8:5

It is not . . . a transgression of the moral law [or] unnatural for children to run.

> *Sunday-School Journal,* November 18, 1857, 169, cited in Anne Boylan, *Sunday School* (N. H., 1988)

The children in the streets [of the Lower East Side of New York] are so numerous that it is impossible to avoid riding them down. I have run down three children [on my bicycle] while riding through these streets, but the accident was absolutely unavoidable.

> Edwin Christmae, April 29, 1896, letter to *New York Times,* cited in Cary Goodman, *Choosing Sides: Playground and Street Life on the Lower East Side* (New York, 1979)

I learned to cut across the tracks in front of an oncoming [street]car, and it was great fun to see the motorman's angry face turn scared, when he thought I was going to be shaved this times sure.

> Mary Antin, *The Promised Land* (Boston, 1911), describing life as a child in Boston in the 1890s

Kids, especially, like to pretend they don't hear [the train's whistle], and then when you are almost on them, they leap aside and laugh as if it were a good joke. . . . I've seen them get onto the track and dare each other to stay there as long as possible.

> Rex Stuart, "People Act as if They Wanted to be Killed," *American Magazine* 92 (September 1921): 38 at 125–26 (a railroad engineer's recollections of approaches to Philadelphia's main station, c. 1900)

Children in nineteenth-century America played outdoors a lot. They were not as constrained in this regard as had been their colonial American counterparts by rural isolation and long religious services or by a Puritanical culture that looked upon play as something frivolous. By the 1860s both mainstream and recently arrived immigrant cultures sanctioned active outdoor play for toddlers and teenagers alike. Nineteenth-century America's town and city streets were playgrounds for the creative child, filled as they were with fountains, pushcarts, light poles, delivery wagons, stoops, fences, horsecars (and later trolleys), train crossings, construction sites, and fire hydrants. "Tom Sawyer," Thomas Bailey Aldrich, Mary Antin, and Michael Gold in this regard belonged to the same world, a world of streets and carts.[1]

Most urban, and much small town and rural, play took place on the sidewalks and in the streets. By one estimate, for 95 percent of the children in turn-of-the-century New York City the streets were their "true homes."[2] But this playground could be dangerous. "Teasing the iceman's horse" could result in a bitten arm or leg; climbing over his car, a broken thigh, if the cart moved.[3] Stealing a ride on a moving horsecar could be deadly if a boy miscalculated and fell beneath the heavy wheel.[4] Jumping aboard moving freight trains or the fenders of a streetcar were equally hazardous. And yet many children delighted in "congregat[ing] in swarms about the [trolley] car tracks [to] torment the motormen and conductors as recreation."[5]

HOW JURISTS FOUND A LEGAL WAY TO COMPENSATE THE "WASHERWOMAN'S WAIF"

Jurists such as Georgia's Joseph Lumpkin had little patience for such "wild and wayward" children as were injured when they dashed into the path of a cart or dray. "The conduct" of such children "must be controlled," he scolded from the bench in 1859. "The failure to do this is the curse and ruin of this country."[6] Of course these reckless antics were generally the work of those nine years old or older; their six- and seven-year-old brothers and sisters sometimes ambled along, observing and imitating. They lacked the agility of their more daring elder brothers and sisters and might consequently fall beneath the wheels of a horsecart. And their still younger three- and four-year-old sisters, whom they might all have been charged by their mothers to watch out for, might toddle away, oblivious to the daring-do of the older boys and girls, into the path of a trolley or horse and buggy whose driver was himself moving at a reckless pace or whose "attention was occu-

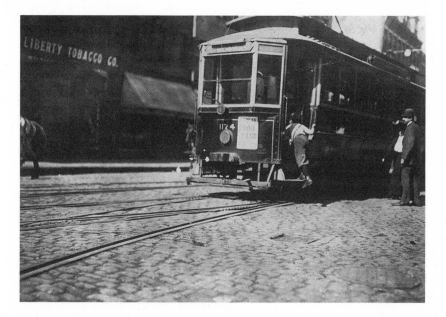

The young newsboy jumping aboard this streetcar in Boston at the turn of the century was at risk, but was much more capable of protecting himself than his younger sister might have been. (Lewis Hine Collection, National Child Labor Committee Papers, Library of Congress)

pied by a young lady standing in the door of a house on the opposite side of the street."[7]

How did jurists respond to those suing on behalf of young children injured by negligent drivers? Was the contributory-negligence rule applied to aid entrepreneurs using the highways and byways? The most famous study of that rule argues that it was, but that study is flawed and misleading and its initial premise is incorrect.

In his analysis of the emergence of the contributory-negligence rule in New York, whose courts constituted a "fairly representative cross-section of judicial experience" of the nation, Wex Malone pointed out that the contributory-negligence rule was sometimes hard on children injured by negligent defendants generally driving a vehicle of some sort. First, the child's counsel had to establish to the trial judge's satisfaction that his client's conduct had not been a substantial factor in the accident (as with adults). Were he to fail, he had (at least theoretically) an escape theory: He could claim that the child was non sui juris, not capable, by virtue of his age, of being legally negligent. Were he to succeed in this regard, however, he had also to prove that the child's parents had not been negligent in allowing the

Children playing in the street in New York City (top) could be hit by carts, buggies, or, in some streets, by streetcars or even trains, such as the one shown above moving out of the Pennsylvania Railroad station in Pittsburgh in the 1870s, hauling goods to warehouses downtown. (Lewis Hine Collection, Library of Congress; Archives of the Industrial Society, University of Pittsburgh Libraries)

Philadelphians were warned of the dangers to children of railways in this antirailroad poster in 1839. (Historical Pictures, Chicago)

child to escape from their care—that is, that their conduct as well as his own had been without fault. The problem with that was that in 1839 the New York high court had established the rule that the trial judge was free to non-suit the "negligent" child-plaintiff in such a case if the evidence satisfied him that the parent's own negligence had been established or could fairly be presumed.[8]

The first accident appeal in New York involving a small child had been decided by the state supreme court in 1826. A horse and gig being driven "very fast" had injured a two-year-old girl crawling after "some pigs" in "one of the public streets of New York City." The defendant told the child's mother that he had not slowed, because "he took her for a pig, and if he had killed it he would have paid for it." A trial court jury awarded the plaintiff seven hundred dollars. The defendant appealed, but his appeal was limited to the appropriateness of the pleading (in case rather than trespass). The Supreme Court affirmed the lower court verdict, satisfied that case would suffice, and offered no dicta regarding the possible contributory negligence of either child or parent. As such, the rule nonsuiting such a plaintiff was not announced by that high court for another thirteen years, when the next such case reached it. A two-year-old boy playing in a wintry rural road had been run over by a sleigh whose driver had failed to slacken his pace on the assumption that the object in his path was a small animal that would scamper out of the way. A trial court awarded the boy's father, pro ami, five hundred dollars. On appeal, the high court agreed that the parent's contributory negligence in permitting the child to toddle into harm's way should have been imputed by the trial judge to the child. Justice Esek Cowen held that if this were not the case, "the roads would thus become of very little use in the line for which they were principally intended."[9]

Cowen's opinion and its instrumentalist rationale places *Hartfield* v. *Roper* well within the domain of the economic determinist thesis. One such analysis of *Hartfield* offered a "guess . . . that the country was not ready for a different point of view. . . . Americans were still leaving [such victims] where they fell."[10] But the fact is that this *Hartfield* rule, which held small children to the "degree of care which a person of ordinary prudence would exercise" and that imputed parental negligence to them to boot in order to protect the "use" for which roads were intended, would not survive for long.[11] Indeed, the next decision handed down by an American supreme court on the subject, completely rejected both elements of the *Hartfield* rule. Thereafter, every American jurisdiction, including New York, ultimately joined in rejecting the first nonsuit rule (holding an injured child to the same test of contributory negligence as an adult); some severely limited the second (allowing the trial judge to nonsuit the plaintiff if its parent's negligence had clearly contributed to its injury), and a majority (nineteen of thirty-one) rejected the defense's right to impute the contributory negligence of the parents to the child altogether. Once again, mid-nineteenth-century American jurists displayed a humane concern for tort plaintiffs. Let us listen in on the dialogue between high court jurists on these subjects.

1849–1869: NEW ENGLAND, NEW YORK,
AND MARYLAND WRESTLE WITH THE PROBLEM

The next time, after *Hartfield*, that an American appellate court was to address the question of a child's degree of contributory negligence and its consequences, it was to have available to it two English cases offering the views of the chief justice of the Court of Queen's Bench, Thomas, Lord Denman, both of which limited the bite of the contributory-negligence rule in *Butterfield v. Forester*.[12] In the first case, a "taxed cart" drawn by a runaway horse hit a crippled man. Lord Denman, instructing the jury in 1832 at nisi prius, advised that "all persons, paralytic as well as others, had a right to walk in the road."[13] The second case we are already familiar with from the previous chapter, *Lynch v. Nurdin* (1841). There a six-year-old boy had been injured while playing on the wheel of a horse-drawn cart negligently left unattended in a public street. Lord Denman and his colleagues were satisfied that the jury had been properly permitted to compare the limited culpability of the child with that of the "most blameable carelessness" of the cart's driver.[14] Lord Denman's views were to be "doubted" by subsequent English courts; the contributory negligence of children would be calculated by the same standard as that use for adults. Bramwell, B., Pollock, C. B., and Alderson, B., of the Court of Exchequer and their colleagues on the Court of Common Pleas were consistently of the view that "the fact of the plaintiff being of tender years makes no difference" regarding his or her degree of contributory negligence, *and* that the contributory negligence of a parent or guardian in permitting a child to come into harm's way was to be imputed by the court to the child.[15] But *Lynch v. Nurdin* had been launched, and American courts would give her safe harbour.

The Connecticut Supreme Court was the first to embrace Lord Denman's views, in 1849. When a six-year-old boy's leg was broken by the fall of a carelessly fastened gate, Chief Justice Samuel Church cited *Lynch* in holding that a boy of that age must be seen as being "without judgement or discretion," governed largely by "childish instinct," and thus entitled to a higher threshold of contributory negligence. Nine years later that court repeated the point: A three-year-old girl struck by a train passing too rapidly around a blind curve in one of the "inhabited parts" of Norwich was not to be held to the same degree of care as an adult since "she had no discretion, or knowledge or capacity."[16]

Vermont's high court was the next to attack the New York court's rule. In *Robinson v. Cone* a four-year-old boy on his way to kindergarten in the village of Pawlet, Vermont, in February 1845, was sledding down a hill and onto an icy road when he was hit by a sleigh. Its driver first supposed the sled to be a dog, but "when he saw it was a boy he thought it would have wit enough to get of the way." The driver allowed that the hillside "was always swarming with children, and he never went into the village without finding the hill alive with them." The trial judge instructed the jury that it was to judge that child's contributory negligence by a standard of care that such a youngster was capable of, and that the child's parents were not negligent in letting the child go to school by itself. Defendant's counsel demurred, citing *Butterfield* v. *Forrester* and *Hartfield* v. *Roper*, but Chief Justice Isaac Redfield took exception to both of these precedents. "Perplexing doubts will spring up" in "the almost endless variety of incidents attending accidents" for which the "general formula" in *Butterfield* was "wholly insufficient. . . . Hence this case has been somewhat questioned, perhaps it may be said, criticized certainly." Citing Lord Denman's views, Redfield held that "what would be but ordinary neglect, in regard to one whom the defendant supposed a person of full age and capacity, would be gross neglect as to a child, or one known to be incapable of escaping danger." *Hartfield* was "less sound in its principles" than *Lynch* and was "infinitely less satisfactory to the instinctive sense of reason and justice."[17]

The Massachusetts high court was (typically) not as willing as Vermont's to ignore precedent on the question of parental negligence. It settled on a rule that often allowed judges to nonsuit *very* young plaintiffs on evidence of parental contributory negligence while leaving to the jury as a fact-finding matter the question of contributory negligence in all cases involving somewhat older (eight or nine years old) children, who might reasonably have been expected by their parents to understand dangers and respond to warnings. Massachusetts, while never going so far as to deny the defendant the right to seek to impute parental negligence to the child, generally left that question as a fact-finding task to the jury.[18]

Maine's high court, in two "hard" cases in 1856 and 1870, turned aside actions in one case on behalf of a young girl injured while returning from school when the railing to a sidewalk gave way, causing her to plunge eleven feet, in another on behalf of a nine-year-old boy injured jumping onto a moving railway drawbridge. In the latter case, the boy's counsel cited both *Lynch* v. *Nurdin* and *Birge* v. *Gardiner*. Justice John Appleton concurred in holding the girl contributorily negligent, and later, as chief justice, he wrote the opinion nonsuiting the boy for his "rash" behavior, while adding that the law in Maine would impute parental negligence to children.[19]

New York held to its *Hartfield* rule for twenty-five years. Thus in 1850 Justice Lewis Woodruff of New York's appellate Court of Common Pleas reversed an award of $55 to the parents of a seventeen-month-old girl whose thigh was broken when she was run over by a cart at Twenty-eighth Street and Eleventh Avenue. Woodruff cited *Hartfield*, but he also quoted from the New York legislature's Code of Procedure, section 168, which barred recovery to an injured child permitted "without any suitable attendant or guardian" to venture into "a street in which horse and carts and other vehicles usually and lawfully pass." Woodruff's reference to this virtual codification of *Hartfield*, however, was unique. Other jurists relied exclusively on the common law. A case in point is the New York Court of Appeal's opinion in 1864 regarding the objection of the Second Avenue Railway to a jury award of $869.50 to one Daniel Honegsberger. The plaintiff's six-year-old son, Solomon, had been run over near his school while chasing his schoolmates as they headed home "tapping each other with their books." His arm had to be amputated. Honegsberger's counsel pointed out that New York required that parents send their children to school, and that its legislature in 1853 had passed a statute requiring streetcars to use diligence in the vicinity of public schools. Hence neither the boy nor his parents should be held to be contributorily at fault: "To hold that children may not go to and from school unattended, would be to render the [school] law inoperative, as it is not within the power of the great majority of the people to furnish such attendance or guardians."

Justice Henry Hogeboom disagreed. Citing *Hartfield*, he opined that the parent's negligence could be imputed to the boy, that "the law as it is held with us" made "no distinction on account of age." Hence he held young Solomon to an adult's standard of care, to be as wise, as it were, with regard to traffic as his namesake had been with regard to jurisprudence. "An infant of tender years," he added, "is not to be permitted to occupy the highway." A rule treating a child differently would be unfair to drivers, "not practical" in enforcement, and would not "protect" the interests of "the community."[20]

Hogeboom's rationale in *Honegsberger*, like Cowen's in *Hartfield*, could fairly be said to have had the good of the economy at its cold heart. But if this was so, then New York's appellate courts eventually experienced, quite literally, a change of heart, for they soon adopted a rule consistent with *Lynch* v. *Nurdin* and the views of the Connecticut and Vermont Supreme Courts. A seven-year-old boy run over on his way to school was not to "be driven from the street, or butchered in it," wrote President Judge Joseph Mullin of the New York Supreme Court, and were the law to be understood to mean that they were to be held to an adult's standard of care, "there will be heard in every town and hamlet a cry like that which was heard in Egypt, when in every house there was one dead."[21]

If such a cry had been raised, the New York Court of Appeals had heard it. A four-year-old boy whose older sister, tending him, was busy hanging out clothes, slipped out of their home through a window and strayed into the path of a horse-drawn streetcar. The driver had caught a pigeon, which he was inspecting. He had wound the reins around the brake, and "was paying no attention to his team or to what might be on the track." At the defendant's request, the trial judge nonsuited the plaintiff on the grounds that both he and his parents had been contributorily negligent, but the New York Supreme Court ordered a new trial, resulting in a judgment for the plaintiff. In 1868 the streetcar company took this judgment to the Court of Appeals, without success. A small child was non sui juris, wrote Judge Charles Mason. Despite *Hartfield*, children were no longer to be held to an adult standard of care.[22] But with regard to such tots, defendants *were* to be held to a higher degree of care:

An infant, of even this tender age, is not an outlaw in the street. . . . Common humanity is alive to their protection, and the law, both in reason and justice, and out of compassion to their weakness and inability to protect themselves, should throw a broader shield of protection around them, against injuries from the careless conduct of the strong, than it affords to an adult, who is capable of self-defense.

Moreover, the question of whether or not the evidence warranted the imputation of parental negligence to the child was deemed to be one of fact to be left to the jury. Since that question *had* been left to the jury in the retrial of this case, Justice Mason affirmed the jury's award.[23]

Maryland's judiciary adopted the harsh *Hartfield* standard in 1865. The rules of care that persons owed to one another "must be uniform," explained Chief Justice Richard Bowie in a particularly doctrinal passage. One could not have one rule for adults and another for children "without producing an uncertainty in the law destructive of all principle." *Hartfield* was "to be preferred to *Lynch* v. *Nurdin*." But Bowie and his colleagues said this in a case of a seven-year-old boy who had been injured while climbing aboard a moving train in response to a playmate's imperative: "Boys, let's take a ride!"[24] The factual evidence in cases involving injuries to less reckless children over the next decade may have inspired them to take a second look at the principles in *Lynch* v. *Nurdin*, *Daley*, and *Robinson*. In any event, by the early 1870s, Maryland's jurists agreed with Justice Mason of New York that drivers of streetcars should display that higher degree of care ("constant watchfulness") in "large, populous" communities such as Baltimore, where both "the aged and infirm" and "children who are young and wanting in prudence and discretion" were using the roads. The "cause of humanity" demanded that "the simplicity of childishness" not be equated with an adult's standard of care. Parents were only expected to use "ordinary care" in protecting their youngsters, and the decision as to whether to impute more substantial parental negligence to the injured child as a bar to recovery was to be left to the jury.[25] The high courts of Indiana, California, Arkansas, Missouri, Kentucky, Wisconsin, Iowa, Mississippi, Louisiana, Minnesota, and Delaware adopted these rules as well.[26]

If this were all that we had to report on the development of the American rule regarding the degree of contributory negligence of a child or its parent, we would be entitled to say that American courts had produced somewhat more generous rules to deal with this problem than had English ones. But there is much more American innovation on this question to report, much of it with a decidedly humanitarian character to it. In the first place, by the 1880s, eight jurisdictions (only one of which was one of the original thirteen states) offered a new, means-tested rationale for denying the defense the right to charge the parents with negligence. In the second place, also by the 1880s, most American high courts had decided that the whole idea of imputing a parent's negligence to an injured child was illogical and unjust.[27]

1857–1889: THE WASHERWOMAN'S WAIF

The first court to apply a "means test" to the question of parental negligence appears to have been the Illinois Supreme Court. A four-year-old boy in Chicago had drowned in a city water tank, one side of which was only two feet off the level of the ground. Evidence adduced at the trial established that the boy's father was "a poor man and kept no servant." Both he and his wife "worked for a living." In 1857 Justice John Caton rejected the city's effort to nonsuit the boy's parents for their contributory negligence. Working people could not afford nursemaids to protect their children against "reckless or careless drivers" or "traps and pitfalls" left by negligent municipal authorities. To permit a nonsuit based on the parent's contributory negligence in permitting the boy to play out of doors would be both unconscionable and poor public policy: "Such a rule of law ought to depopulate a city of all its laboring inhabitants." The role that parental negligence played in such a case was to be left to the jury to decide, and since it had been, he and his colleagues approved the jury's award of eight hundred dollars to the boy's father.[28]

Missouri's high court adopted the same socioeconomic view of the question of parental negligence in 1869. A working mother dressed her two-and-a-half-year-old daughter and sent her in the company of her eight-year-old sister "to a lot across Carr street in St. Louis to play and get fresh air." While crossing the road the younger girl was hit and killed by a streetcar, the driver of which was inattentive. The streetcar company's counsel questioned the mother's measure of care, but Justice David Wagner and his colleagues, attentive to the evidence adduced at trial, would not hear of it: "To say that it is negligence to permit a child to go out to play unless it is accompanied by a grown attendant, would be to hold that free air and exercise should only be enjoyed by the wealthy who are able to employ . . . attendants, and would amount to a denial of these blessings to the poor."[29]

Attorney M. A. Low of Gallatin, Missouri, was even more specifically class-conscious in his note for the *Central Law Journal* on the rule imputing parental negligence to a child. By expecting poor parents to watch their tots as carefully as more affluent parents could, the rule "would not only debar the children of the poor from the privilege of schools, but from the exercise in the open air as well. In large cities it would doom them to close confinement in dark tenement houses and filthy alleys."[30]

The Keystone State's jurists came, in stages, to the same conclusion. They first decided that children "of tender years" whose arms or legs were crushed beneath the wheels of streetcars or trains would not be held to the same standard of care of adults. One six year old, on an errand for his father, a carpenter, in July 1855, lost both feet crawling under a lumber train left standing in the main street of Hollidaysburg. The conductor was "having breakfast" and the crew moved the train without a warning signal. The railroad's attorney cited *Hartfield* and argued for its rule, but Justice George Woodward and his colleagues preferred *Lynch* and *Robinson*: The boy "acted like a child, and is not to be judged as a man." He took a risk, but this was what one expected of a young lad. "The degree of danger would be as likely to attract as to repel him." Of a nine-year-old boy injured in like fashion, crawling under a train to get some tobacco for his father (who worked for the railroad), Justice Woodward offered the same "boys-will-be-boys" exculpatory dicta: "To many active and enterprising children risks not absolutely appalling are attractive; especially if others are at hand to witness the daring achievement."[31]

This much the New York and Massachusetts courts had said. But Pennsylvania's had more to say. The Pennsylvania Railroad's attorneys sought to impute the negligence of the mother of a two-year-old girl whose arms were crushed by a negligently managed sawmill train in Williamsport, but Justice Daniel Agnew made the court's position clear on that subject in an eloquent response that was to be quoted by other courts. Lizzie Kay's parents were "poor"; they lived in a "small shanty"; her mother was "employed that morning in washing for herself and others." But she was not to lose her suit because of that:

> The doctrine which imputes the negligence of the parent to the child in such a case as this, is repulsive to our natural instincts, and repugnant to the condition of that class of persons who have to maintain life by daily toil. . . . Here a mother toiling for daily bread, and having done the best she could, in the midst of her necessary employment, loses sight of her child for an instant, and it strays upon the track. With no means to provide a servant for her child, why should the necessities of her position in life attach to the child and cover it with blame?[32]

Justice Agnew reiterated this means-test of the imputed-negligence rule four years later. A mother near Philadelphia had fed her two-year-old child in the kitchen and had latched the kitchen door to "scrub the oil-cloth on the floor" in the next room. Five minutes later the child was brought into the house by neighbors, dying of injuries inflicted by a train "going pretty fast" down a nearby street. Agnew rejected the notion that the railroad's right-of-way would require that urban inhabitants "be imprisoned in their houses, or their children caged like birds." Was it negligence, he asked rhetorically, "for the poor [to] congregate these crowded streets?" Must they, "even in the summer heat," live "shut up in the noisome vapors of their closed tenements, without a breath of fresh air?" And "what sort of justice" was it "which tells the mother agonizing over her dying child: '*Your* negligence caused this?'" After all, her love for her child was no lesser than that of "the more favored of her sex, having servants at their beck."[33]

The judiciary of California, Michigan, Iowa, Oregon, and, ultimately, Massachusetts offered similar defenses of "poor" parents "depending upon their labor for support" or "confined to her room by sickness." Those in "such moderate condition in life" were not required to "give their personal attention and oversight to their infant child, in order to avoid the imputation of negligence."[34] Justice James Day of the Iowa Supreme Court, in offering such views as these, defended them with this comment: "Law, as a rule of human conduct, should be adapted to human necessities and conditions. In so far as it fails of such adaptation it becomes unjust and unreasonable."[35]

Such opinions were highly offensive to some railroad directors and their counsel. A case in point: Christopher Patterson was a director of the Pennsylvania Railroad, a member of the Philadelphia bar, and the author of *Railway Accident Law* (1886). He rejected as bad law the decisions that permitted the "condition in life" of the child's parents to be introduced a propos their contributory negligence. The "sentimental" views of those who had sanctioned this sort of evidence had "failed to give due weight" to the fact that the parents, not the railroad, had chosen to "bring these children into the world." The railroad was not responsible for their "condition of more or less want."[36] But Patterson and those of his persuasion were to face an even more formidable obstacle in their efforts to defend careless corporations.

1858–1891: THE SINS OF THE FATHERS

Until 1880 Pennsylvania's jurists seem to have allowed the "modest condition in life" of the parents to be introduced in evidence as a bar in law to defense efforts to impute parental negligence to the child. But the rest of the high courts that sanctioned this sort of evidence simply saw it as additional information that a jury ought to have available to it in its fact-finding role— that is, they acted to weaken substantially the defendant's case for parental negligence but still held that such a question was to be left to the jury.[37] However, beginning in 1858, jurists began to breathe life into a more complete bar "in law" to defendant efforts to impute contributory negligence to parents.

In 1858 Tennessee's judiciary heard the case of a young man who had lost several fingers to the unboxed cogwheel of a paper mill near his home when he was a small child. Upon reaching the age of twenty-one, he was now suing in his own name. The defendant's counsel argued that his parents had been contributorily negligent (citing *Hartfield* v. *Roper*). Justice Robert McKinney and his colleagues disagreed. McKinney rejected the authority of *Hartfield*, a precedent "opposed . . . to every principle of reason and justice." The idea of imputing parental negligence to a wronged child was "literally, to visit the transgression of the parent upon the child." Citing *Lynch*, *Robinson*, and the maxim *Sic utere tuo, ut alienum non laedas*, he returned the case for retrial in accordance with this rule.[38]

Henry Hogeboom of the New York Supreme Court, author of the doctrinal *Honegsberger* decision, must have come to regret his rigid application of the *Hartfield* rule; perhaps a reading of McKinney's opinion, or the Bible, had moved him; in any event his heartfelt dicta in *Lannen* v. *Albany Gas Light Co.* (1865) used the same biblical allusion. A seven-year-old girl was injured in an explosion in the basement of her home when her father reported a leak to the gas company, and the repairman the company dispatched had the notion that he might shed some light on the problem by striking a match. The gas company's attorney argued that the jury should decide whether her father's negligence, in permitting her to witness the repairman's dazzling performance, was not of a nature to bar her recovery. Hogeboom disapproved the trial judge's instructions to the jury in this particular fact situation. Imputing parental negligence here "would be, I think, visiting the sins of the fathers upon the child to an extent not contemplated in the decalogue, or in the more imperfect digest of human law."[39]

This dicta is not simply evidence of humanitarianism, nor was it merely a legal fiction in aid of children, an effort to skirt a problem of precedent or legal principle. On the contrary, with his biblical allusion, Justice Hogeboom had sensed a doctrinally unprincipled quality to the rule that allowed a wrongdoer, guilty of having harmed a child innocent of any wrongdoing herself, to seek escape from compensatory responsibility by identifying another party, the child's parents, as being wrongdoers as well. Justice John Welch of the Ohio Supreme Court offered the same sort of traditional, ethically clad metaphor in 1868 as had Hogeboom, when he compared the *Hartfield* rule to "the old doctrine of the father eating grapes, and the child's teeth being set on edge," a "parable" God rejects (in Jeremiah 31:29 and Ezekiel 18:2), but he went on to attack more directly the logic-bound core of the rule's ratio decidendi: "Can it be true, and is such the law, that if only one party offends against an infant he has his action, but that if two offend against him, their faults neutralize each other, and he is without remedy? His right is to have an action against both." Justice Welch drew support for this position from the nisi prius views of Pennsylvania's Justice George Sharswood in *North Pennsylvania Railroad* v. *Mahoney* (1867): "A child . . . is not precluded from recovery against one tort-feasor by showing that others [parents or guardians] have borne a share in it."[40]

Chief Justice Robert Brickell of the Alabama Supreme Court came at the problem from a different direction but with the same result. "There would seem to be greater reason for extending to the child a higher degree of civil protection" when the parent failed in its duty than when it had not. After all, wouldn't the child have been entitled to public protection if it had been "abandoned by its parents, thrown out a mere waif in society"?[41] Seven more high courts promptly adopted this exculpatory rule.[42] Hence by 1888, some thirteen jurisdictions had rejected the imputation of parental contributory negligence to the child by way of legal *reasoning*.

By the 1870s and 1880s the issue had been joined in the treatises. Francis Wharton quoted Welch, Agnew, and Sharswood approvingly; not surprisingly, he also considered the question in terms of the remote and proximate **249** causes of a child's injuries. Satisfied as he was that any parental negligence was remote compared to the "proximate cause," the negligence of the cart, streetcar, or railroad, Wharton rejected what he called "the English, Massachusetts, Maine, and New York rule" accompanied by a comparison of English decisions regarding the protection afforded injured children and damaged oyster beds. "The child, were he an oyster," Wharton wrote, "would be protected." The imputing of parental negligence to children was, in his view, inhumane. "The protection of the helpless from spoliation is one of the cardinal duties of Christian civilization."[43]

Christopher Patterson's *Railway Accident Law* and Thomas M. Cooley's *Treatise on the Law Torts* held to the older rule. Patterson's contempt for washerwomen and their waifs we have already heard.[44] Cooley's defense of the rule imputing the negligence of parent to child, while Posnerian in structure, offered an even more cynical verdict on parenthood and humanity. The rule was

> more likely to guard the interests of children and imbeciles than is the opposite. If a heartless parent or guardian may suffer a child to take his first lessons in walking in the crowded streets of a city, and then, when he is injured or killed, as in all probability he would be, may recover for such injury or killing, on the grounds that the child himself is too young to be chargeable with negligence, there will not, perhaps, be wanting depraved custodians of children, unrestrained by any considerations of humanity, willing enough to count upon probably gains from such reckless conduct.[45]

Cooley's views were echoed by Justice Edward Paxson of the Pennsylvania Supreme Court in 1880. A seven-year-old boy trespassing on railroad property was run over by a flatcar he was playing on. "Holding as we do [railroad] corporations to a strict responsibility for negligence," he wrote, "it is our duty to give them a clear track," a rule "necessary for the preservation of life." The boy, as a trespasser, had no case, but Paxson addressed his parents' negligence as well and justified the rule that imputed their negligence to their child in the pessimistic language of an Old Light Calvinist: "There are many unfeeling parents who not only neglect but maltreat their children. It would be cruel to such children to lay down a rule which would make it an object for unprincipled parents to expose them to injury and death upon a railroad track."[46]

In 1889, however, there appeared in Chicago Joel Bishop's *Commentaries on . . . Every-day Rights and Torts*, which offered the view of the "better authorities" that the child was not "the father's chattel" and, as such, was entitled to recovery for personal injuries despite any negligence of his parent. Bishop analogized:

> The law never took away a child's property because his father was poor or shiftless or a scoundrel, or because anybody who could be made to respond to a suit for damages was a negligent custodian of it. . . . But by the doctrine, after a child has suffered damages, which confessedly are as much his own as an estate conferred upon him by gift, and which he is entitled to obtain out of any of the several defendants who may have contributed to them, he cannot have them if his father, grandmother, or mother's maid happens to be the one making the contribution.[47]

This was precisely the point made by Ohio's judiciary in 1868 and approved by Alabama's and eight other judiciaries in the next two decades. Bishop's treatise helped to bring the important Illinois Supreme Court into this fold in 1891. Until then, that court had left to the jury the question of whether the evidence showed the negligence of the parent to be significant enough to impute it to the child to defeat any recovery of damages.[48] In 1891 it reheard the appeal of the Chicago City Railroad from an award of fifteen thousand dollars to a six-year-old boy who had lost his leg due to the negligence of the defendant's driver. The supreme court quoted from Bishop's treatise in deciding that a parent or guardian's negligence would no longer be imputed by law to a small child in Illinois.[49] Seven other high courts and three treatise writers also rejected "the conversion of the infant . . . into a wrong doer by imputation" as "a logical contrivance uncongenial with the spirit of jurisprudence" as well in the next five years,[50] and in 1934 the *American Law Institute's Restatement of Torts* opined that the law did not bar a child "from recovery by the contributory negligence of its parents."[51]

Wex Malone's claim that New York's courts were "fairly representative" of American judicial views on the rights of children injured by negligent drivers was incorrect. Most state courts went well beyond New York's in protecting those rights, despite the views of those who felt that the rights of such children must yield to others who were using "the roads" for purposes "for which they were principally intended."[52] Once again we find that a majority of American courts had rejected an English rule that inhumanely barred recovery. And, once again, we find that American courts of the Age of Formalism were willing to change the formal rules and to rely, at least in part, on "the Decalogue" for their authority. Whereas in the case of the attractive-nuisance doctrine, humanity seemed to be the prime mover in the process, here humanity had combined with legal reasoning to reject "bad law."

HEROIC RISKS: ALTERING THE
CONTRIBUTORY-NEGLIGENCE STANDARD

With children playing in busy streets and increasing risks at railway platforms and crossings and within many industrial workplaces, it is not surprising that jurists were eventually confronted with a new problem. Beginning in the 1860s they heard appeals from nonsuits brought on behalf of individuals or their survivors who had protected or saved the lives of others and had themselves been injured or killed in the act. In about half of these appeals the injured appellant-protector had rescued a child in the path of a streetcar or train; in about a third of them it had been a worker's fellow workers, or an engineer's passengers, who had been the recipients of his or her valor. Half of the rescued persons were known to their protector, or were the protector's own child or parent; in the other instances, they were utter strangers. About a third of the appellant-protectors were female; most of these were the mothers of the rescued child. How did our jurists deal with these appeals?

The English rule in such cases, the cause of the nonsuits, was that a person who placed himself in harm's way to save another was a "mere volunteer" and was behaving negligently, despite any noble intentions as might have inspired the reckless act. Hence any injury they suffered in saving another was due to their contributory negligence, offsetting any negligence on the part of the defendant. This was so even in the case where the injured rescuer was a child's own grandmother.[53] The English rule may have been the product of the Jurisprudence of the Head, but this was a hard-headed jurisprudence indeed.

This rule was followed in the first case of this sort that I could detect in an American court, *Evansville & Crawfordsville Railroad* v. *Hiatt* (1859).[54] A young man lost a leg to an onrushing train, while pushing his old and deaf father off the tracks. He was deemed contributorily negligent by the Indiana Supreme Court. But just as *Hartfield* v. *Roper* was rejected by Heart jurists in cases involving children hit in streets, neither the English rule nor *Hiatt* were ever followed by any American court.[55] It was cited approvingly, however, by two jurists in what was to be the leading case in this field, *Eckert* v. *Long Island Railway*, decided by the New York Court of Appeals in 1871. The case was this: On his way home from work on November 26, 1867,

Henry Eckert noticed a three-year-old child in the path of a train coming to East New York from Jamaica. He also noticed that the engine had no cow catcher and was sounding neither a bell nor a whistle. Eckert ran to the track and threw the child aside but was struck and killed. His wife, Anna, sued, and the railway appealed a jury verdict for her on the grounds that Eckert had contributed to the accident by his daring but reckless act. Justices William Allen and Charles Folger agreed. "The company is not the insurer of . . . those who of their own choice" placed themselves in the paths of their trains. They cited English precedents as well as *Hiatt* and *Hartfield*. But they wrote in dissent. Justice Martin Grover's majority opinion had the heartfelt support of Rufus Peckham, Charles Rapallo, and Chief Justice Sandford Church. "The law," he wrote, "has so high a regard for human life that it will not impute negligence to an effort to preserve it." Justice Grover cited no case law at all in support of this judgment, for there was none to cite.[56]

Three of Pennsylvania's jurists rejected *Eckert* as "nothing beyond an emotional basis of admiration for heroism, very creditable in human nature, but having no proper place in the administration of justice." But their four colleagues disagreed and adopted the *Eckert* rule in the case of a lad who had gone to the aid of a friend overcome by gas in a deep trench left unattended by those working on the gas mains and had been overcome by the gas himself.[57]

Eckert was also followed in Massachusetts (1879), where a man had been gored by a bull after he had tried to help another who was being gored, in Missouri (1884) and Alabama (1899), where mothers had sought to save their children from the paths of trains, in Louisiana (1889), where a visitor to a fair who pushed a drunken friend from the path of a train had "suffered great pain," and in Illinois (1900), where another mother's toddler had run into the path of the Halsted Street cable car. The rule was praised in the Louisiana case as "tending to foster a proper spirit of generous impulses" and as "resting on sound principles of humanity."[58] Perhaps no clearer example might be offered of the Jurisprudence of the Heart than a rule justified, not by analogy to any existing principle to be found in any citable English precedent, but by the "sound principles of humanity."

It was also good law in Ohio in the case of a man killed saving a stranger's child from an onrushing freight train at an unguarded crossing in a heavily populated section of East Toledo late one afternoon in 1885. Justice Joseph Bradbury regarded the man as having responded to the "strongest dictates of humanity" and refused to treat such an act as negligence that might excuse the Pennsylvania Company from its own culpability in the incident.[59]

Bradbury's sentiments were shared widely in cases of these kinds. Thus President Judge Charles Thompson of the Colorado Court of Appeals praised a father and mother who had been badly shocked trying to pull their child from a live wire he had grasped. To find the mother contributorily negligent, Thompson said, "would be to shock a sentiment which is as universal as mankind." The law was "not the creature of cold-blooded, merciless logic." Its "inherent justice and humanity" would "never for a moment permit the act of a mother in saving her offspring, no matter how desperate it may have been, to be imputed to her as negligence."[60]

Engineers might find themselves switched onto the wrong track facing a certain collision and their own death. When they stayed at their posts to help slow their train and lessen the force of the blow for their passengers, instead of jumping to safety as some of their firemen had done, their surviving spouses were not nonsuited, and their courage was commended. "Who shall sit in judgement upon this brave engineer?" asked Wisconsin's Justice Harlow Orton, sitting in judgment on his spouse's suit in 1879. The man had died "after great agony and suffering." His "heroic bravery," the product of his "true manhood," was "most praiseworthy and commendable, and an occurance worthy of lasting record in the book of heroic deeds." As such, it was not negligence. Neither was the act of another engineer killed in similar circumstances near Valpariso, Indiana, on March 1, 1879. "The law has for him no censure," wrote Indiana's Justice Byron Elliot, "but has, on the contrary, high commendation and respect." When another engineer was killed at his throttle in Georgia trying to lessen the force of a collision, his act was hailed as a "martyrdom to public policy" rather than treated as culpable want of self-preservation by that state's chief justice, James Jackson, a martyrdom entitling the man to "a kinship to Christ." American jurists thus wrote a final stanza to "The Ballad of Casey Jones," enabling his widow to recover damages.[61] Listen as well to the voice of this Jurisprudence of the Heart in Maryland's Justice James Pierce. An experienced tapper in Maryland Steel's foundry was killed when he discovered that molten steel, negligently tended by a man the assistant superintendent had failed to train, was about to spill onto men working below. "Though moving in a humble sphere, he has given an example of genuine and heroic manhood and has demonstrated that in his estimation, 'the duties of life are more than life.'"[62]

Chapter Nine

Pain, Suffering, and the Sensitive Pocket Nerve: Discovering the Deep Pockets of Reckless Railroads

> **The establishment of the fact that surgical operations**
> **may be performed without pain has been properly**
> **described as "Good News for Travelers by Railways!"**
> *Punch*, January 30, 1847

We have seen in the last two chapters, as well as in sections of chapter 3, that many American high courts in the nineteenth century began to diverge significantly from English negligence rules, to the advantage of injured plaintiffs. In the process of analyzing these developments, I noticed that the damage awards noted in these cases were often quite substantial for their times and there was much attention to the victim's "pain and suffering." Could it be that our humanely innovative nineteenth-century American jurists had also pioneered in another proplaintiff tort domain—damage awards allowed for pain and suffering? These awards, I will maintain, had been, proportionately, at *least* as large in the mid and late nineteenth century as the tort awards of the modern "liability crisis" era of the 1970s and 1980s.[1] This came to me as a complete surprise and led me to ask when juries were first permitted to award large sums for pain and suffering negligently inflicted.

BRITISH BEGINNINGS

The first awards of damages for pain and suffering negligently inflicted in the common law predated my "American Age of Humanity." English courts of the late-eighteenth-century Enlightenment appear to have pioneered in upholding damage awards of that nature. In any event, late-eighteenth- and early-nineteenth-century English treatises (Chitty and Wentworth on Pleadings) offered sample pleas in actions for personal injury where the plaintiff alleged that she had "suffered and underwent great pain" or "tortures both of body and mind."[2] Thus in 1822 counsel for a man who sued a surgeon for negligent treatment of his wife would speak of the "right to sue for damages for personal grievance" and of "the suffering endured by the wife."[3] I argue in chapters 3, 7, and 8 that the early-nineteenth-century common law of torts was not moving from proplaintiff standards of strict liability, as has been claimed, to more restrictive rules requiring that the plaintiff prove fault on the part of the defendant, but that, to the contrary, it was becoming easier for plaintiffs to establish defendant liability in a number of particular tort actions. Here, we see that this may have been the case with regard to damage awards as well—that is, recovery for pain and suffering was becoming available to plaintiff-victims of negligence.

Nonetheless, although English courts sanctioned such damage awards, they saw to it that the sums awarded were "reasonable," by which they appear to have meant "token" or "modest." The woman "thrown to the ground with great force" in 1673 by a coachman negligently breaking in fresh horses in Little Lincoln's Inn Fields was "seriously crushed and broken in her body and limbs," made "lame," and "mutilated." She and her husband sought £200 in damages; a jury awarded only £12 6s.[4] The unfortunate youth who lost both his eyes to the lighted squib thrown as a prank into a marketplace (the celebrated case of *Scott v. Sheperd*[5] [1773]) asked for £40 in medical expenses and £500 in damages; the jury awarded him a total of £100, affirmed on appeal. A passenger whose arm was broken when the Chester mailcoach overturned in 1794 was awarded £60. Another, injured in similar fashion in 1798, received £12 12s. One who was injured in 1811 when she tumbled down an uncovered cellar entryway one night was awarded £20. Another injured in a stagecoach accident in 1820 had to see the case through an appeal in the Court of Exchequer to collect £50. Others, victims of poor roads, were awarded variously £50 and £51 in 1824. An eleven-year-old boy whose leg was broken when a tradesman's iron cellar door fell on him received £25 later in that decade. A female servant struck by a cabriolet on High Street, Aldgate, in 1838 was awarded £30. An elderly woman who was knocked down, "much bruised," and had "some of her teeth knocked out" by a negligent carriage driver was awarded £25 in 1839, while another woman struck by a cart in the same year received £15. A man hit by a negligently driven coach suffered much pain from a broken thigh. The jury found the defendant to be liable, but awarded but a farthing in damages. On appeal to Queen's Bench in 1843, the plaintiff sought a retrial for only £10, 5s. 6d., the surgeon's bill.[6]

Passengers on early English railroads soon came to be injured in derailments and collisions, and on December 29, 1845, the *Times* called for tougher legislation designed to generate greater safety; but it also observed that suits against company directors to achieve these ends would "be quite idle. . . . It is notorious that no respectable lawyer, except in very peculiar circumstance, would advise such an action." This view did not prevail. Transport companies of all sorts were increasingly held liable for the wrongful behavior of their employees, and Willes, J., was frank in explaining that one public policy rationale for this was that "there ought to be a remedy against some person capable of paying damages to those injured by improper driving."[7]

Nevertheless, when some of those injured did sue, they found resistance to the notion that they might be compensated for more than their medical bills and loss of income. In *Armsworth* v. *South Eastern Railway Company* (1847) Parke, B., warned the jury against giving "the utmost amount" which it "think an equivalent for the mischief done. Scarcely and sum could compensate a labouring man for the loss of a limb, and yet you don't in such a case give him enough to maintain him for life." Similarly, counsel to a bookseller injured in a railway accident in 1853 was told by Sir Fredrick Pollock, C. B., during oral argument:

A jury most certainly have a right to give compensation for bodily suffering unintentionally inflicted, and I never fail to tell them so. But when I was at the bar [the 1830s and 1840s] I never made a claim in respect of it, for I look on it not so much as a means of compensating the injured person as of damaging the opposite party. In my personal judgement it is an unmanly thing to make such a claim. Such injuries are part of the ills of life, of which every man ought to take his share.[8]

The bookkeeper's jury award of thirty-five pounds for medical expenses and one hundred pounds for loss of profit was reduced by the Court of Exchequer to thirty-five pounds. Pollock's memory might be questioned, but not when it can be confirmed by that of Sir Fredrick Thesiger, counsel to the Midland Railway, who told the Court of Queen's Bench in 1852 that some eight years earlier, Sir Fredrick Pollock "avowedly withdrew from consideration as a subject of damages the bodily suffering which the plaintiff (a passenger in a speeding train that had become derailed) had undergone." Moreover, Sir Fredrick added, the plaintiff "himself concur[ed] in the adoption of this view."[9] The evidence indicates that damage awards for wrongful death in the third quarter of the nineteenth century in England tended to be set by juries at a figure equaling only about three to four times the annual wage of the victim. Parliament was made aware of this trait and chose to set a cap in such damage actions of three times the deceased's last year's wage in the Employer's Liability Act of 1880.[10] Mid-nineteenth-century Britain, then, appears to have all the qualities of what Leon Green and Lawrence

Friedman have styled a "culture of non-compensation."[11] Jurors were men "of sufficient Freeholds" to look askance at the mulcting of propertied defendants; jurists were appointed, not elected, and belonged to the upper or upper middle class. Seeking damages for pain "unintentionally inflicted" on oneself was "unmanly." Victorian gentlemen would "keep a stiff upper lip."[12]

EXPLAINING THE RISING PRICE OF PAIN
IN MID-NINETEENTH-CENTURY AMERICA

Eighteenth- and nineteenth-century English judges and juries were not nearly so generous as modern American juries,[13] but this will come as no surprise; after all, the award for unintentionally but negligently[14] inflicted pain seems to have been created only in the late eighteenth century, and there were few "deep pockets," at least until the emergence of railway corporations in the mid-nineteenth century. However, this is precisely what makes the nineteenth-century *American* experience with pain and suffering awards so remarkable. No, American jurists did not *create* the new award; that honor appears to belong to those of late Georgian Britain. But mid-nineteenth-century American trial court judges and juries, as well as appellate court jurists, quickly established their independence from British practice in one crucial regard: American negligence awards for injuries with pain and suffering were *much* more generous than English ones. The median English jury award for personal injury between 1773 and 1875 was £100 (n= 38), whereas the median American award upheld at the appellate level (n= 149) for personal injuries negligently inflicted that were accompanied by pain and suffering between the years 1826 and 1896 (median case year: 1871) was $5,000,[15] a sum some seven or eight times as large as those in England, and substantially larger than the median personal injury award granted by allegedly "increasingly generous juries" in the United States in the late 1980s. To be sure, the cases from which my median award was derived had all been appealed to state (or federal) high courts,[16] and I am not claiming that this group of cases represents precisely the typical *trial* court award; my figure, being derived from appellate cases, is clearly higher than the median for trial court awards. Randolph Bergstrom's study of personal injury suits before the New York Supreme Court (sitting as a trial court) in 1870 reports an average award of $3,637 (n=12), and Lawrence Friedman has reported that the average trial court personal injury awards in his late-nineteenth-century California courts was $3,725.00 (n=50).[17] These are about 74 percent as large as my typical "pain and suffering" personal injury negligence award affirmed at the appellate level. But other characteristics of my *appel-*

late award cases, and of Friedman's Alameda County and Robert Silverman's Boston *trial* court cases, are comparable. Essentially the same percentage of plaintiffs were suing on behalf of children (ranging from 11 to 14 percent), were female (ranging from 30 to 40 percent), and were suing municipal corporations, typically for defective roads, bridges, or sidewalks (ranging from 13 to 24 percent), or transportation companies (trains, stagecoaches, ships, and streetcars) (ranging from 65 to 73 percent).

Most significantly, even *Friedman's* average damage award figure compares favorably to the typical Alameda County award a century later, in the "liability crisis" era (something Friedman seems unwilling to allow). The median income in the United States in 1988 was $16,618. In 1989 the national median state court jury award for automobile torts or other personal injuries was slightly over $31,000, or almost exactly twice the median income. The median Alameda County jury award in vehicular accidents or street hazard cases in the early 1980s was only $27,045.[18] Since the typical American wage earner of the early 1870s (median award year: 1871) earned only about one-fortieth as much as the typical American worker of the early 1980s (due to inflation and economic growth), it may be that the typical award was substantially *larger* in 1871 than in 1981, and, according to a recent Rand Corporation study, only about one in every ten accident victims today even considers a lawsuit. Perhaps the mid-nineteenth century constituted the *real* liability crisis in American courts. The Massachusetts legislature that enacted (ch. 270, sec. 3) a law fixing a maximum of $4,000 that juries might award employees suing for personal injury damages in 1887 must have thought it was capping *something*. During the Civil War a commutation fee payable to the Union to avoid being drafted cost $300 (in 1863), and when that fee was eliminated in 1864, the cost of a draft substitute on the market to avoid the considerable risks of combat ranged from $400 to $1,000 throughout the North. The typical worker in the United States in 1870 earned a little over $400.[19] When one, therefore, compares the value of $5,000 in 1871 (or $3,700, the average *trial* court figure) to the value of these modern awards, in 1988 dollars, one can only marvel at the generosity of *nineteenth*-century juries and the liberality of the high court jurists who affirmed the awards.

Lawrence Friedman and Thomas Russell, among other legal historians, have not found nineteenth-century juries and jurists to have been as generous as I have. Reporting on personal injury awards by trial courts in the Alameda County (Oakland) California Superior Court and the federal district court for northern California for the years 1880–1900, they style that era "an age of restraint," in contrast with the current "explosion" of damage award figures, and describe "the legal culture" of the late nineteenth century as "a culture of noncompensation."[20] They claim that "the behavior" of nineteenth-century juries reflected this "culture of low expectations with regard to tort compensation." Juries "did not fully subscribe to the deep pocket theory" of mulcting negligent defendants. Plaintiffs "received precious little for their pains."[21] The "general expectation of compensation" was to be a twentieth-century phenomenon. "In the nineteenth century, personal injury recoveries were small," they write, though Friedman allows that he knows of "no reliable information about average awards" for the mid-nineteenth century. Friedman maintains that pain and suffering awards by juries in the mid-nineteenth century were "mostly backward-looking: What has plaintiff suffered so far? Courts and juries were less comfortable with the future, with 'damages' to be caused by future suffering or from an impaired and injured life." But it was "not hard to understand" why this would be so: "Who, after all, would pay for inflated damages? Businesses as a whole were smaller and more precarious than today. The deep pocket was not so deep. . . . There was no general theory of compensation, no notion of total justice. . . . [P]ast juries did not . . . try [to] compensate for a lifetime of suffering, . . . a broken body, . . . ruined expectations."[22]

Leon Green, and more recently, Randolph Bergstrom, regard nineteenth-century victims of railroad and stagecoach accidents as lacking an urge to sue. In Green's words, "They were inured to hardship. They could have a leg sawed off or an eye removed without the aid of an anesthetic. They accepted their misfortune as their lot."[23]

Friedman and Green are off the mark with regard to their timing of the changes in the propensity of Americans to sue and of juries and jurists to grant large damage awards. Drawing on the insights of Robert Rabin, Friedman describes "three stages" in the development of "modern tort law": "First, a stage in which accidents were seen as a product of chance or fate; second, a stage that stressed individual failings (both of these created cultures of low liability); and third, a stage in which theories of causality became more complex, and responses tended to be social and preventive."[24] He is quick to point out that these three stages "overlapped and coexisted in the past" and "do so still." I agree. But where Friedman, Green, and others see the third stage falling almost entirely in the twentieth century, I see a *substantial* portion of it falling in the nineteenth.

At the very least, I want us to see that American juries and jurists of the *mid*-nineteenth century did *not* look upon accidents as did their British contemporary, Sir Fredrick Pollock, as "part of the ills of life, of which every man ought to take his share."[25] Nor did they "stress individual failings" in contributory-negligence or trespassing-child cases, as I hope I have demonstrated.[26] Legislators eventually acted to require safety devices, speed limits, bell and whistle signals, crossing gates and school crossing guards, streetcar operator licenses, and intersection regulations,[27] but, in the meantime, the essentially conservative, precedent-led mid-nineteenth-century American courts, with clear "theories of causality" in their minds and on their lips, were bending and sometimes breaking principles of tort law for "social and preventive" reasons. Juries offered, and jurists sanctioned, remarkably generous personal injury awards throughout nineteenth-century America—an example of congruence between popular and "high" legal cultures, both responding to their own sorts of Jurisprudence of the Heart.

Why might mid-nineteenth-century juries and jurists have been more solicitous to suffering than their seventeenth- or eighteenth-century predecessors? The fact that, by the 1850s, most of the pain was caused by a new monster, the negligent corporate railway, is at the heart of the answer, as we shall see, but the *pattern* was already set in the 1830s and 1840s with the affirming of pain and suffering damage awards against townships for accident-causing road and bridge defects, and against horse "omnibus" or small stagecoach operators for defective equipment or careless drivers.[28]

In any event, the question ought to be put in a more comprehensive form. Let us begin with what appears to be a sea-change in popular attitudes toward suffering. Plaintiffs, juries, and jurists were part of a culture in which people "no longer" felt "that we are called upon to face physical pain with equanimity," as William James would put it in 1901, describing "a strange moral transformation" that had "within the past century swept over our Western world."[29] In the second quarter of the nineteenth century, drugs that had been only toyed with before (like nitrous oxide and morphine) became more frequently used in American surgery and dentistry, along with newer "painkillers," ether and chloroform. One medical historian has argued that humans did not *feel* pain as severely prior to the modern age, but Daniel de Moulin has recently demonstrated that there exists no evidence to support such a hypothesis and plenty of evidence to refute it. Humans may have sought to *deal* with bodily pain in the nineteenth century, but not because it was new. What, then, *had* changed? Precisely what William James had claimed—humanity's *tolerance* for pain. Mid-nineteenth-century American surgeons and physicians had available to them a number of painkillers. One may have resigned oneself to pain before such "painkillers" were available. One need no longer do so by the 1840s. Some surgeons and dentists praised anesthesia as "humane"; others condemned it as danger-

261

ous or nontherapeutic. (Pain was "necessary" for both its diagnostic and purgative properties.) But whatever debate might have raged among *professionals*, *patients* voted with their pocketbooks for less pain. Voluntary major surgeries rose sharply in hospitals offering anesthesia in the 1850s; dentists found that their practice fell off sharply if they refused to offer ether or nitrous oxide.[30] The war with pain had been joined and was being won. Why, then, in this popular "revolution of rising expectations," should not those whose careless acts had led to pain and suffering be made to compensate their victims?

The "moral transformation" of popular attitudes toward pain appears to have its roots in the late eighteenth century and to have been coincidental with changes in English, American, and some European attitudes toward criminal punishments, torture, the treatment of the wounded in the field of battle, military flogging, slavery, and cruelty to animals.[31] This sense of "sensibility" in the Enlightenment was also coincidental with, and *may* have been a consequence of, the rise of capitalism and economic growth in the age of the first industrial revolution. Thomas Haskell has argued that as human relationships in the West became less dependent upon status, family, and community, and more dependent upon contractual agreements with strangers, there developed a conscience regarding that outer social arena.[32]

Haskell's theory is intriguing, but he offers little evidence on its behalf, and as I have found none in its support, it seems to me that it is inadequate. It is true that *some* English and American jurists of the nineteenth century developed a simultaneous admiration for the views of Adam Smith and Jeremy Bentham, on the one hand, and a jurisprudence of "moral responsibility," holding litigants firmly to their contractual or quasi-contractual obligations, on the other.[33] But *these* were not our Heart jurists, the defenders of *Britton v. Turner*, the advocates of the attractive-nuisance rule, the creators of the "best interests of the child" doctrine, the generous affirmers of hefty personal injury damage awards in negligence cases. These Benthamite jurists tended to be *less* "sympathetic" to injured trespassing children, for example, than were others.[34] To account for "humanitarian" jurists we must look to other, contemporary movements for causal linkage—namely, the rise of constitutional democracy and mass movement politics, the Second Great Awakening of the 1820s and 1830s, and the humanitarian reform impulse.

A society that views law as the edict of the sovereign, a people who do not enjoy jury trials, who perceive no constitutional way of altering the law through their legislatures, cannot easily create effective public pressure groups to abolish slavery, flogging, cruelty to animals, or capital punishment. But societies that viewed "the common law" as rules emanating from both the natural order and "general customs,"[35] who believed that they possessed the capacity to give positive shape and form to the law in their jury deliberations and legislatures, in fact *did* create such lobbies, *did* award substantial damages in personal injury negligence cases, and *did* bring forth (here one might also, in America, read "*elect*") jurists who softened the harsh edges of the common law.

Contrasting Assault and Negligence Awards

We can gain perspective on the extent to which the discovery of deep pockets in the mid-nineteenth century led to princely solatia by making one simple comparison. Plaintiffs who were injured *intentionally* in an assault and battery were, in England and most states, entitled to exemplary damages ("smart money") "not only to compensate the plaintiff, but to punish the defendant."[36] Yet when we compare the damages granted *these* plaintiffs by nineteenth-century American juries (1823–96) and affirmed by appellate courts (n=43)[37] to those granted plaintiffs injured by *negligent* acts, generally by corporations, in these same years (n=141), we find the median award to the *former* to be only one thousand dollars[38] (highest: eight thousand dollars; lowest: fifty-one dollars; median year: 1867), whereas the figure for the *latter* was five thousand dollars. What was going on?

Very simply, twenty-six of these forty-three "smart money" assailant-defendants were *individuals*, not agents of corporations, and it was most uncommon for any of them to be possessed of enough wealth to enable the juries to award what they might have liked to. And were they to award a sum, assessing several defendant-assailants jointly, without differentiating these defendants according to their means of paying, they would find themselves scolded by jurists for not identifying the "one of them" of greater "wealth, situation, or talents" and mulcting him more than "the others of . . . poorer circumstances."[39] Hence the average award in *these* twenty-six cases was only[40] $868, whereas it was $3,135 for the seventeen "smart money" cases involving assaults by the employees of carriers (two ships, fifteen railroads). The essence of this distinction, which was not confined to the New World, is captured in this exchange between Harcourt, Q. C., representing the London and Northwestern Railway, and Cockburn, C. J., in 1869. Harcourt was arguing that the jury award (for negligence) to the Reverend Campbell Fair had been excessive:

Had this been a common street accident, of which there are hundreds in the year, no such amount of damages would have been given.

Cockburn, C. J. (interrupting): They generally occur to poor persons who are satisfied with comparatively small compensation, which is readily given them. . . . In many cases of compensation against private parties, juries will look to their means of paying damages, and so will moderate them; but in a railway accident they feel that they are not so restrained, and so give full damages.[41]

Comparing Medical Malpractice and Negligent Railroad Awards

Plaintiffs whose damage awards against nineteenth-century physicians and surgeons were affirmed by American appellate courts received considerably more (median award = fifteen hundred dollars) than those *deliberately* injured by individuals.[42] Medical malpractice suits were skyrocketing in the 1840s, 1850s, and 1860s, their rise exceeding the rate of population growth for the first time in the nation's history, and exceeding it for those decades by a factor of six! Thereafter, from 1880 to 1950, medical malpractice suits continued to increase at a rate faster than population, but at a lesser (three-fold) rate.[43]

Many patients in the past had accepted their fate, had (in the words of one physician's attorney in a malpractice suit in Maine in 1823) "trusted to the healing power of nature" conscious that there were "some interior injuries" that a doctor's "art could not reach." Kenneth DeVille has recently argued that, as the medical profession improved in its ability to treat dislocations, set fractures, and anesthetize surgery patients in the 1840s, and as physicians claimed that new expertise, the public began to expect more of practitioners in this regard. (Fully two-thirds of malpractice suits in these years involved fractures and dislocations.) Moreover, the Second Great Awakening, which stressed one's personal responsibility for one's religious fate, may have encouraged people to blame others, be they physicians or corporations, rather than an amorphous destiny, for injuries and suffering that befell them.[44]

My own readings of the views of both trial judge John Bredin of the Beaver County Court (Pennsylvania) and Pennsylvania's Supreme Court Justice George Woodward in *McCandless* v. *McWha* (1853) suggests that there were jurists with attitudes identical to those that DeVille attributes to jurors. James McWha's broken leg, set by Dr. Alexander McCandless, had mended two inches shorter than his good one. He sued. In his charge to the jury President Judge Bredin remarked, in an aside that Justice Woodward charitably styled "irrelevant" and "harmless," "If suits were more frequently brought, we would perhaps have fewer practitioners of medicine and surgery not possessing the requisite professional skill and knowledge that we now have."[45]

This invitation to clear out the deadwood was tolerated by a high court that appears to have shared the view that the time was ripe for such malpractice suits. Justice Woodward, for the court, noted, in remarkable dicta, that "discoveries in the natural sciences for the last half-century" had "exerted a sensible influence" on the field of medicine, "whose circle of truths has been relatively much enlarged." Experimentation, study, and diversification had led to "a positive progress in that profession." The "standard of ordinary skill is on the advance," and "he who would not be found wanting, must apply himself with all diligence to the most accredited sources of knowledge," for "the physician or surgeon who assumes the exercise the healing art, is bound to be up to the improvements of his day." Dr. McCandless had failed in this regard, and since "the patient is entitled to the benefit of these increased lights," the state's Supreme Court affirmed the lower court jury's award of $850, reduced by Judge Bredin's remitter to $500.

In Iowa a jury verdict and award of $2,000 to a man whose doctor failed to treat his broken wrist was reversed by a majority of that state's supreme court jurists who felt that the standard of care set down in the trial judge's instructions to the jury had been too high; physicians were only expected to perform at the "average" level of care in their profession. This was not the view of Chief Justice Joseph Beck. He agreed with his compeers on the Pennsylvania bench. "For centuries," Beck wrote, "the science of medicine was stationary." But "within our days" it had made "constant and wonderful progress." And this being so, why was "average" care any longer acceptable? "Is not diseased and afflicted humanity entitled to all of the benefits of this progress?" Physicians should be held to the standard of a properly trained modern practitioner.[46] Once again, at least some juries and jurists seemed to be on the same wavelength, the J curve of rising expectations.

The medical profession reacted with outrage at the "lack of gratitude" shown by patients (some of whom had been treated for a nominal fee). It condemned the "tricky" lawyers on contingency fees who sought damage awards or "blackmail" settlements, and the "jury of laborers" whose awards were "a farce and a disgrace to our country." One doctor wrote that the ultimate "evil" lay "in the imperfection and prejudices of the twelve specimens of human nature in the jury box."[47]

Nevertheless, the medical profession was better off than the corporate world in two important regards: In the first place, the jury awards in medical malpractice suits, many of them just as shocking in the degree of suffering

265

and loss of sight or limb as those caused by negligent "iron monsters," were not nearly so large as those levied against corporate "spoliators." Juries seemed to be responsive to the argument that damage awards ought not deprive doctors of their life's savings and thereby frighten such professionals from offering their services to the community. An attorney defending a physician in a malpractice suit in Maine in 1827 offered such a rationale for jury leniency: The doctor who lost such a suit might well thereby be lost to the community if as a consequence he suspended his practice or moved. (Indeed, in this case the town leaders in Eastport, where this physician practiced, were alleged to have spoken to the three Eastport men on the panel to persuade them to exonerate him. In any event, the jury could not agree on a verdict.)[48] Similarly, a defendant/doctor, "destitute of counsel," argued before the Connecticut Supreme Court in 1832: "What men, even of skill and talents, would undertake to practice in the healing art, if some little failure or ordinary skill, or ordinary diligence, or even some trifling want of carefulness, might sweep from him the whole earnings of life of toil and drudgery?"[49] Maine's Justice Samuel Wells seemed to be responding to this doctor's hypothetical sixteen years later in *Howard* v. *Grover*:

> The practice of surgery is indispensable to the community. . . .
> Surgeons should not be deterred from the pursuit of their profession
> by intemperate and extravagant verdicts. . . . The compensation to
> surgeons in the country is small in comparison with what is paid in
> cities . . . and an error of judgement is visited with a severe penalty,
> which takes from one a large share of the surplus earnings of a long
> life.[50]

In the second place, medical malpractice trials that went to judgment were generally *won* by the physician-defendant, and half of those judgments that were thereafter appealed were also won by the defendant.[51] This pattern contrasts with evidence of trial judgments in personal injury negligence suits in several nineteenth-century communities where corporations were the defendants. There, *plaintiffs* tended to prevail, at both the trial and appellate level. This was so in rural Illinois and Chicago, 1872–1902, Alameda County, California, 1880 and 1900, Los Angeles County, 1889–95 (all jury verdicts of negligence suits against railroads); Chippewa County, Wisconsin, 1855–94, Boston, 1880 and 1900, St. Louis, 1835, 1850, 1865, and 1880, New York City, 1870, 1890, and 1910, and Southern West Virginia, 1872–1900 (where plaintiffs only broke even with defendants at the trial level). Some 776 of these judgment trials were by jury; plaintiffs won 71 percent of these (551). Another 88 trials were bench trials (both parties agree-

ing to be tried by the judge alone); plaintiffs won only 40 percent of these
(35).[52]

Yes, there was an increase in the number of medical malpractice suits in
mid-nineteenth-century America, but these plaintiffs were not as successful
as those who alleged that negligent corporations had injured them. And this
was so despite the additional fact that juries and jurists were rarely persuaded by physicians' attorneys that patients had been guilty of contributory negligence by virtue of their posttreatment behavior.[53]

Comparing the Not-So-Immune Municipal
Corporate Defendants to Entrepreneurial Ones

Robert Rabin has recently argued that the mid-nineteenth century saw
courts expand upon the doctrine of sovereign immunity to protect county
commissioners, municipal corporations, and their offspring (road districts,
fire and police departments, gas and waterwork authorities, and the like)
from tort claims.[54] There certainly were some new government services offered where the injurious negligent conduct of those providing such services
was not viewed by courts as constituting liability under common-law tort
rules. These include fireworks displays, schools, police, and, generally
speaking, fire departments; one injured by the negligence of someone providing one of these services could only sue if a statute or ordinance sanctioned such a suit.[55] Moreover, several eastern high courts, following the English rule in *Russell* v. *Men of Devon*,[56] would not permit a common-law
tortious action for certain accidents occurring on county-maintained
bridges or roads or in county courthouses or town halls, in the absence of a
statute specifically sanctioning it.[57]

These applications of sovereign immunity certainly did limit the ability
of those injured by defective roads, bridges, and the like to sue, but, in most
cases, there was nothing innovative going on; neither eighteenth-century
English nor American courts had ever imagined that *counties* were liable in
tort under the common law, and the original American colonies had created
such tort liability for municipal corporations as they wished by statute and
ordinance. These statutory provisions, however, often imposing double
damages for injuries caused by defects in roads and bridges, were significant; by the second quarter of the nineteenth century towns and cities were
clearly paying out substantial sums regularly to persons injured due to such
defects, if notice had been given of the defect to a "substantial" inhabitant
of the town.[58]

Jurists of the newer western and southern states created after the separation from Britain generally did not feel bound by the New England practice

requiring statutory authority to waive the sovereign immunity of municipal corporations and road districts. They cited a new English decision[59] to support their view that such entities, having been created by the state at the request of individuals, being empowered thereby to raise revenues and seize property, were necessarily held liable in exchange for the safe condition of the roads, sidewalks, bridges, buildings, sewers, and gas- and waterworks they constructed.[60] Indeed, no special statutes, in the fashion of those of colonial New England, were by midcentury any longer deemed necessary for the courts of Pennsylvania, New York, Maryland, or Georgia to find municipalities liable by this same reasoning.[61] And these courts ignored other English decisions that continued to exempt municipal road authorities from vicarious liability when the act of omission of a municipal road employee or the negligence of a contractor led to the injury of a traveler, decisions that rejected the plea that statutory grants to municipalities of authority to spend funds on roads created a kind of "debt" liability for negligent maintenance.[62]

Why were increasing numbers of American jurisdictions waiving the sovereign's immunity from lawsuit for injuries on roads and bridges by 1850? Were roads getting worse? Accidents increasing? The opposite seems to have been the case. Until well into the nineteenth century roads everywhere in America were so poorly designed and maintained, were "so bad" that "accidents often occur by upsetting."[63] That was why Chancellor James Kent had been reluctant in 1820 to find any language in New York statutes that specified the duties of overseers of roads and commissioners of highways that might hold counties or road districts liable in tort for accidents caused by defects they had been warned of. Their liability under the statute was limited to breach of duty suits for ten dollars.[64] However, John McAdam's technique of constructing durable roadbeds had spread from Britain to the United States in the second quarter of the nineteenth century. By 1830 over sixty turnpikes had been built in Massachusetts alone, and the number of stagecoach lines in that state had doubled between 1825 and 1832. By the 1850s his self-hardening crushed-stone surface (and an alternative urban "Nicholson" roadbed of wooden bricks and tar) facilitated the safer transit of vehicles at faster speeds with less maintenance. Thereupon, highway speeds increased from four to five miles per hour (in 1750) to ten to fourteen miles per hour (by 1830).[65] In cities, where such roadbeds were now affordable, expectations rose, as they had with regard to the setting of fractures by physicians and surgeons in the same era. Thus Chief Justice Lemuel Shaw of Massachusetts, in affirming a jury's award to a man injured on a defective street in Boston in 1848, held that cities were obliged to make streets "harder, smoother and more uniform to render the road safe and consistent," whereas the countryside, with its more limited resources, would not be held to the same standard of liability.[66]

With the ensuing building up of the nation's transportation infrastructure, county and municipal authorities were, at their request, empowered by statute to "levy all needful taxes" for such purposes. Consequently, some courts were increasingly prepared to find that the additional obligational language in these new statutes (such as "and to pay . . . all claims . . . authorized by law")[67] made these government corporations liable in tort as well as "taking" proceedings and contract disputes. Other courts simply inferred such liability, in the absence of that additional language, on the grounds that when groups voluntarily received authority from the legislature to raise taxes and seize property, they were offering in consideration a promise to maintain those roads and bridges carefully.[68] *Here* was the innovation in the common-law rules regarding sovereign immunity—and it did not *expand* that immunity, it contracted it.

I detected in dicta only three public policy rationales for this abandoning of the requirement of legislation imposing tort liability: I have already noted the views of Chief Justice Shaw of Massachusetts on the virtues of macadamized roads. A second was offered by Shaw's contemporary, Illinois's Chief Justice Walter Scates. Responsive to the reasoning of the plaintiff's attorneys (the law partnership of Lincoln and Herndon), Scates held that the question of Springfield's liability to Oliver Browning for his leg broken due to a street defect should go to the jury, despite the absence of a statute authorizing such suits against municipal corporations. A recent English case justified such a decision, Scates indicated, but besides, a rule holding municipalities liable would be "keeping pace with the progress of the improvements of the age."[69] The third public policy rationale I detected was Posnerian in tone (though it is not to be found in one of our personal injury cases, but in one involving injury to a horse). In 1851 Justice Samuel Foot of New York's Court of Appeals offered this cynical (but perhaps realistic) cost-benefit analysis of the politics of tort. Were the high court not to impose tort liability itself on New York for failing to illuminate and guard an open excavation on Broome Street,

> innumerable applications to the common council for redress,
> legislatively, . . . would bring in their train an organized body of
> soliciting parties and agents, the allowance sometimes of extravagant
> and unjust claims, the rejection, at other times, of meritorious ones,
> in a word, all the evils attending a legislative body having control over

large funds and exposed to the solicitations of a corps of artful and
unscrupulous claimants, and their hired or interested [contingent
fee?] agents. . . . Where the city now pays, in accordance with just
principles, hundreds of dollars it would probably then pay
thousands.[70]

In any event, whatever their specific rationale might have been, the tendency of mid-nineteenth-century jurists with regard to sovereign immunity
was clear: Modern municipalities with the legal means and economic capacity to pay for injuries they had caused should be obliged to compensate
their victims.

Nevertheless, if municipalities and road authorities were now liable in
tort, juries appeared to make a distinction between the measure of compensation expected from such municipal and county pockets (being of medium
depth and belonging to the public treasurer) and those of railroad and other
deeper corporate pockets. The plaintiffs of some thirty-eight suits against
municipal and county corporations affirmed between 1831 and 1895 had
suffered accidents just as serious in their nature as those eighty-seven plaintiffs whose awards were affirmed against railroad, stagecoach, steamboat,
streetcar, and manufacturing companies in the same years. The former had
tumbled into unguarded excavation holes, or had been flung from their buggies, horses, or wagons, plunging off bridges, into ditches, or down ravines.
Their legs, hips, and arms had been broken; their skulls fractured; their
kneecaps, noses, and teeth shattered. Yet the median award to the former
group was $2,250; to the latter, $6,000.[71] The deeper the pockets, the larger
the award.

This explains why the average trial court award in New York City in 1890
and 1910 was $6,315 where the defendant was a railroad corporation (n=
20), but only $1,205 where the injury was due to a sidewalk or roadway de-
fect (n=69) and the defendant was either an individual or the city. It would
also explain why the eight partners who operated a coach that injured a passenger through negligence in England in 1820 were mulct only £50 by the
jury; why a man, injured when his carriage was hit by a passing stagecoach
in 1836, recovered only $60 from its owners even though the jury has been
allowed to award exemplary damages since the driver has "betrayed a disregard for the ordinary dictates of humanity which require every man to suc-
cour his fellow man in distress" when he drove on despite the evident injury;
and why the owner of a horse omnibus that hit a woman at the juncture of
Third Avenue and Twenty-sixth Street in New York in 1847, fracturing her

leg and crippling her, paid only $500. As Martin, B., told a parliamentary committee in 1875, "There is a higher scale of damages given against railway companies than would be given against private individuals for the same injury."[72]

RAILROADS AND GENEROUS JURIES

Why were those suing railroads so successful? Charles Francis Adams Jr., chairman of the Massachusetts Board of Railroad Commissioners, felt that he knew. In 1878, close to the median year of our damage award population, he noted that juries "proverbially have little mercy for railroad corporations, and, when a [train] disaster comes, these [corporations] have practically no choice but . . . to settle." William Swift, former president of the Philadelphia, Wilmington and Baltimore Railroad, offered the same judgment in 1853 when he wrote that "we paid more than it was honest for the parties to receive" because of "the effect upon juries of ingenious advocates who are working for a contingent fee." Similarly, in 1897, Justice Oliver Wendell Holmes Jr. noted "the inclination of a very large part of the community" (that is, juries) "to make certain classes of persons insure the safety of those with whom they deal."[73] "Iron monsters" had "deep pockets."

Americans, after all, had ambiguous feelings about railroads and factories.[74] Most recognized that tremendous economic and social benefits would come to communities that attracted these new instruments of celerity and progress. And most probably realized that the railroad was a much safer means of transportation than a stagecoach. (A French government study had reported it to be *sixty times* safer per passenger kilometer in 1878). Moreover, as time passed, the public may also have sensed that railroads were steadily becoming safer still, as safety devices like the Miller Platform and Buffer, the Westinghouse Air Brake, and the interlocking signal systems were introduced. A British study in 1878 found that injuries to railroad passengers were five times less frequent in that year than they had been thirty years earlier. To the extent that this was so, the public's expectation of train safety and lack of patience with negligent train operators would have become quite high, just as it had with regard to fracture-setting and macadamized roadbeds.[75]

But many also realized that these machines had more than a price tag of construction on them; they had a price tag of *destruction* as well. This was what troubled the editor of the *Worcester (Mass.) Palladium* in 1843, who complained of the new signs that the Boston and Worcester Railroad had posted: "Look out for engine while the Bell Rings." This put things backward, the editor wrote: "The corporations must look out for the *people*—and not the *people* for the *corporations*."[76]

One rarely is able to hear directly from the jurors themselves on whether negligent corporations ought to be made to feel "the pocket nerve," but I have detected a few of the sorts of sentiments that Adams, Holmes, Swift, and a good many railroad lawyers associated with juries. In 1870 four jurors in a suit in Illinois against the Chicago and Alton Railroad for failing to give the statutorily required signals at crossings indicated in voir dire that they were inclined to "lean against" the railroad, and one said that he would do so "because the company [was] able to stand it," whereas a private individual should "have a little mite the advantage." No challenges for cause were sanctioned by the trial judge. Sixteen years later a juror from the same state in voir dire in a personal injury suit against the Chicago and Western Indiana Railroad said that his sympathy would be with "the young man that lost his limb" and that he "would have no sympathy for the railroad." When asked more directly by the judge whether he could try the case fairly, he replied that he could, and the judge then refused the railroad counsel's challenge for cause. Justice John Scott of the Illinois Supreme Court felt that this juror's remarks provided "not the slightest grounds" for such a challenge. "Certainly the possession of so kindly a spirit would not disqualify a citizen." William Dye of Populist-peopled Kansas was called as a juror in 1895 to hear the suit of a laborer who claimed to have been injured in a fall from a handcar derailed due to the negligence of the Atchison, Topeka and Santa Fe Railway. On his voir dire, Dye "admitted that he had a feeling against railroads generally, which had existed for several years." He also allowed that it would "require a continual effort" on his part "to deal with the railroad company in the same way that [he] would deal with an individual." Needless to say, the railroad's counsel challenged Dye for cause, but this challenge was overruled by the judge, and Dye had to be eliminated with one of the company's peremptory challenges. (The empaneled jurors then awarded the laborer $14,806.)[77] Some jurors clearly behaved as Charles Francis Adams had said, with "little mercy for railroad corporations." As early as 1854 Justice Ira Harris of New York's joint trial and intermediate appellate court (misnamed the Supreme Court) could write: "Everyone who has had much experience in the trial of causes has had occasion to observe the fact that in actions against railroad corporations to recover damages for personal injuries, jurors are apt to be far more liberal in awarding damages than in other cases of a kindred character."[78] Shortly after assuming the chairmanship of the Interstate Commerce Commission, Michigan's former chief justice, Thomas McIntyre Cooley, argued similarly that a farmer, sued for injury caused by the negligent act of his laborer would be much less likely to be punished in damages than would a great railway company. The farmer would be judged by his peers and without bias; but the railway company [will be looked upon by some jurors] as a creature standing apart from human nature, soulless, heartless, grasping, an arrogant representation of monopolizing wealth.[79]

Commissioner Cooley may or may not have described accurately the motives of nineteenth-century jurors, but he clearly described modern American jurors accurately. Recent juror analyses by both Robert MacCoun and Valerie Hans have demonstrated that jurors are more inclined to mulct corporations than other defendants because they see them as soulless entities whose agents behave negligently when corporate leaders "cut corners," *not* simply because of their substantial assets.[80] This seems to me to be the same reason that both jurors and jurists were prepared to seek the "sensitive pocket nerve" of corporate defendants in mid-nineteenth-century America.

Nineteenth-century jurors appear to have been of more modest socioeconomic background and (at least in Boston) of more diverse ethnic origin than the typical civil law litigant, if studies of Boston's late-nineteenth-century civil law trial courts, of Marion County (Indianapolis), Indiana, juries from 1825 to 1855, and of Philadelphia's civil jurors in the 1840s are representative of other communities. Moreover, Robert Silverman's analysis of the Boston civil court jurors indicates that the lower socioeconomic composition of the juries did not appear to affect their decisions with regard to the socioeconomic backgrounds of civil action plaintiffs, as there was less than 1 percent difference between the fate of the suits (n=326) of identified high white-collar, low white-collar, and blue-collar plaintiffs, and less than 1 percent difference as well between their judgments of the suits (n=180) of identified first-generation immigrant and Yankee plaintiffs.[81] But, as we have seen, the attitudes and behavior of jurors toward defendants of different *dimensions* clearly *were* distinguishable by degree of damage awards. The jury acted in these cases like a tiny, legitimate arm of the ebullient nineteenth-century American vox populi, sending clear signals to the railway barons.

Why did juries appear to triple the damage award to one injured by a private corporation as opposed to a municipality or individual (see table 2)? A railroad had deeper pockets, but why were they almost precisely three times deeper (a phenomenon I have detected as well in jury awards in nineteenth-century Canada, Australia, and New Zealand)? One possibility is that they

273

TABLE 2. MEDIAN DAMAGE AWARDS FOR OTHER-THAN-FATAL
PERSONAL INJURY SUITS, AFFIRMED BY AMERICAN COURTS, 1823–1896
(N=192)

Cause of Injury	Median Damage Award
Assault and Battery (intent)	$1,000 (n=43)
When defendant an individual	891 (mean) (n=26)
When defendant a corporation	3,965 (mean) (n=17)
Medical malpractice (negligence)	1,500 (n=26)
Road/sidewalk/bridge defect (negligence)	2,250 (n=38)
Railroad/steamboat/stagecoach accident (negligence)	6,000 (n=85)

were applying the biblical double-damages rule (Exodus 22:7 and 9) and
then adding another layer to cover the plaintiffs' contingency fee to his or
her attorney. The problem with this theory is that New England's colonial
statutes sanctioning suits against towns for injuries caused by defects on
roads or bridges already contained this rule ("The county or towne through
whose neglect such hurt is done shall pay to the partie so hurt, double damages"). Another possibility is that juries were drawing analogies from
colonial-era statutes warning of "treble damage" payments from "any Person falsely pretending great damages . . . to vex his adversary," or from
early-nineteenth-century statutes authorizing the creation of aqueducts and
turnpikes and allowing these corporate entities to sue for treble damages
one who injured their property or who evaded their fees ("shunpiking").[82]
In any event, triple damages they were.

Juries could not have picked the deep pockets of corporations entirely by
themselves. Their decisions and awards had ultimately to be sanctioned by
trial judges and appellate jurists. And they usually were. Jury bias against
railroad corporations was tolerated by the judiciary far more than legal historians have previously allowed.[83] Such a bias can be said to be reflected,
collectively, in the cases that form the basis for this chapter, inasmuch as the
substantial jury biases against corporate defendants were rarely checked on
appeal. But evidence of judicial tolerance for the mulcting of railroads can
be detected as well in dicta now and then, as in *Brown* v. *Swineford*,[84] decided by the Wisconsin Supreme Court in 1878. An employee of a railroad
kicked and beat the plaintiff severely on railroad grounds. The plaintiff was
awarded $750 after his attorney, summing up, inferred that the railroad
company would reimburse the defendant. As no evidence to that effect had

been introduced at the trial, Chief Justice Edward Ryan, for the court, remanded the case for a new trial. Ryan, no fast friend of railroad corporations,[85] was not willing to permit the jury to hear such an "inference" that "in assessing damages, the power, wealth and influence of the corporation" might be seen as standing behind the defendant. This defendant might well have to pay the damage award himself, and "for all that appears in [evidence in] this case, the [defendant] may be as poor as Job in his downfall." The "popular prejudice against great corporations" evident in juries was apparent; it would be "intolerable that it should be extended to their servants."[86]

A Corporate Cost-Benefit View of the Price of Pain

Defendant's attorneys in "pain and suffering" cases certainly sounded as if they felt there was a liability crisis in the mid-nineteenth century. They persistently argued that the jury should not have been allowed to add to the damage award for medical expenses and lost earnings a "*solatium*" for past, present, and future pain and suffering. There existed "no standard to compute [it] by," and clearly no "rule of measuring [mental pain] pecuniarily." Such awards were too "conjectural" for the fact-finding "province of a jury."[87]

The clear majority of these defendants (about 65 percent of all) were railroads, and their attorneys offered additional arguments against pain-and-suffering damage awards: They were too large. "At this rate, a railroad corporation may be obliged to pay, in damages for one accident, the whole amount of their capital stock."[88] Large damage awards levied against railroads meant that "the companies are really made insurers, without having [collected] any [appropriate] premiums."[89] Holding companies liable for the pain and injuries caused by negligent agents was "a more cruel and oppressive rule than the tyranny of Caligula conceived" because it would require "absolutely perfect" agents, an impossibility. And that "would wither all public enterprise, deter capitalists from investing in these necessary works of public improvement" and "encourage licentious and speculative litigation."[90] Allowing the jury to levy these arbitrary and excessive "mulcts" of defendant corporations would (somehow) have the deleterious effect of "making drivers careless."[91] If in spite of all such prudent arguments, courts were determined to sanction "a reasonable *solatium*, or satisfaction, for loss of bodily or mental powers and pain of body and mind," then this sum should be limited to a figure suitable "to the average of mankind for similar losses and injuries." Such a solatium was calculable. Juries and jurists should take note of the fact that, by statute, the *most* the state would allow an heir to be awarded in a wrongful death action was (typi-

275

cally) five thousand dollars. The court should be mindful, of "the relative amounts of fines, compared with terms of imprisonment, imposed as punishments for crimes." Were the jurors to have been so wanton as to appear to have calculated "the amount of an annuity which the damages assessed would purchase for the plaintiff," they were in no circumstance to have allowed an addendum "for the provision of an estate for her heirs."[92]

Jurists eager to aid economic growth should have found some of these arguments about pain and suffering persuasive. What is significant, then, is that these arguments were consistently, uniformly, and thoroughly rejected by nineteenth-century America's appellate jurists. Justice Thomas Johnson of New York's Supreme Court wanted to dispel "any doubt" raised by the Auburn and Syracuse Railroad's attorney in 1851. It was time that the rule regarding pain and suffering was distinctly settled and fully understood:

> If persons or corporations engaged in the business of the defendants, intrusted daily with the lives and personal safety of hundreds of individuals, and using such an untamed power [as steam], may negligently cause serious injuries to the person, and occasion intolerable bodily pain and suffering, and only be chargeable with the loss of time, at what it may be proved to be worth, and the surgeon's and nurse's bill, [then it would be necessary for] persons trusting themselves to such protection [to] provide for more ample indemnity by special contract [of insurance].[93]

That was the rule the railroad's counsel, by implication, was calling for, but Justice Johnson and his colleagues would not have it: "Such a rule would ... be a serious general evil and be productive of the most deplorable consequences."[94]

Chief Justice Lemuel Shaw and the Massachusetts Supreme Court agreed. Charles Greely Loring, the man who had represented the engineer Nicholas Farwell in the famous fellow-servant/assumption-of-risk case in 1842,[95] represented Farwell's opponent, the Boston and Worcester Railroad, some fifteen years later against a crippled namesake of the chief justice, one Sarah Shaw. She had lost her husband, one of her arms, and the use of the other in an accident at Needham on January 27, 1852, when the couple's horse had panicked as their sleigh crossed the railroad track and was hit by a speeding train. She was now destitute, "without property sufficient for [their children's] support," and was experiencing recurring physical and mental pain. A jury awarded her $22,250, a fortune in 1857.

Loring and his colleagues, Benjamin Franklin Butler, Ebenezer R. Hoar, and George Bemis, pressed home their Posnerian arguments against pain and suffering damages with all their skill and persuasiveness; Rufus Choate responded on Shaw's behalf. Her distinguished namesake and his colleagues made the Boston and Worcester pay it all. Shaw began cautiously: "As railroad disasters . . . are often . . . attended by the most deplorable consequences, . . . it seems necessary that each case should be decided upon the fullest deliberation, and decided upon such principles that it may stand as a precedent for succeeding cases, without danger of working injustice." He then signaled the court's pleasure by offering up the "ancient maxim" *Sic utere tuo, ut alienum non laedas* (Use your property, but not to the injury of others) and indicated that Massachusetts courts would continue to sanction damages for pain and suffering negligently inflicted. Mrs. Shaw's award was then affirmed.[96]

The Iowa Supreme Court turned away the argument of a *stagecoach* company's attorney regarding pain-and-suffering awards in an 1854 decision, but Justice George Green indicated the court's concern as well with the newer, iron-rail technology, and implied a public policy rationale for the rule allowing damages for pain and suffering in negligence cases:

> The reason and necessity for this rule is becoming yearly more
> apparent. The consequence of such negligence on the part of carriers
> is becoming more and more appalling. The alarming increase of
> railroad, steamboat and stage disasters, the frightful destruction of
> life, and limbs and property, calls loudly for a strict enforcement of
> the most exemplary rules in reference to common carriers.[97]

As a nisi prius trial court judge in 1852, John Bannister Gibson, chief justice of the Pennsylvania Supreme Court, offered some remarkably generous instructions to a jury deciding on the liability of a railroad company. The centerpost on a railway bridge struck and broke the arm of a passenger who had leaned it on the sill of a car window: "There is no measure or standard of damages for a broken limb; and you therefore ought to be liberal against the author of it. You ought certainly to give enough, for it is safer to err, if at all, against the party who was the cause of the injury, than against an innocent man who suffered it."[98] The jury awarded the plaintiff twenty-five hundred dollars, and the supreme court approved their chief's "liberal" instructions and affirmed the award, but it is not for these reasons alone that we might feel called on to remember *New Jersey Railroad* v. *Kennard*: In dicta Gibson went on to observe (for the record, one suspects, as much as for the jury), in cost-benefit language Richard Posner would recognize, that such accidents could be avoided in the future were railroads to install in the windows of passenger cars "a few metallic rods set in the windows perpendicular or horizontal, or a netting of wire work, or even wooden slats." Anyone who doubts the effect of nineteenth-century judicial views regarding tort liability upon corporate conduct has only to recall (or speak to one who does recall) riding in an un-air-conditioned passenger car (that is, one whose windows could be opened) in the mid-twentieth century. Perpendicular metallic rods prevented one from leaning one's arm or head out of the window.

Later in the century, an Illinois appellate court offered another cost-benefit rationale in sanctioning an award of fourteen thousand dollars to a train conductor who had emerged from a collision in "great pain" for "long duration," had experienced no less than four surgical amputation procedures and had been left "a perfect wreck." A defective handrail that he had relied on in uncoupling the engine had led to his misfortune. Given the modest cost of such repairs, the likelihood of the accident, and the damages incurred, the court held the company to blame. "The appellant's road was," as its counsel had observed, "no doubt weak and poor," but that was only evidence that it had "been run on too economical a principle for safety to its employees and to the public."[99]

Some jurists criticized juries for having failed to award *enough* compensation. One example: Judge Roger Pryor of New York City's appellate Court of Common Pleas spoke of the outrage, "shocking to reason and a sense of justice," that he and his colleagues felt in 1890 for a jury verdict from the usually generous trial Court of Common Pleas of that city. Isabelle Smith had been badly injured by a falling bale of cloth. "In the bloom of early maidenhood," she was "prostrated by a blow which shatters her body and mind; which bereaves her of all the joy and pride of life; which denies her the felicities of the marriage relation; which dooms her, till death shall happily release her, to a bed of helpless anguish; and for this the jury thought a thousand dollars an adequate indemnity!"[100] Judge Pryor and his colleagues remanded the case for retrial with instructions for the jury designed to elicit a more substantial award.

A few jurists, of course, were ready to allow that pain-and-suffering damages and the solatium for loss of a limb *were* hard for the jury to calculate. Chief Justice E. T. Merrick of the Louisiana Supreme Court could "not think that $1000 is an adequate compensation to a laboring man for the loss of so important a member as a leg," but he deferred to the jury and to his colleagues (who had just raised the jury's award from eight hundred to one thousand dollars!). Judge Seymour Thompson of the St. Louis Court of Appeals in affirming a two-thousand-dollar award to a woman who had suffered a severe ankle sprain falling into a coalhole in a sidewalk, noted that she had introduced no evidence of medical expenses or loss of earnings; the award was, thus, "principally as compensation for the very great and long-continuing pain which the plaintiff must have suffered." He agreed with the city's counsel that "we have no scales with which to estimate the value of this suffering," but was content to leave the calculation to the jury. Justice William Strong rejected the Pennsylvania Railroad counsel's argument that pain and suffering have no discernable pecuniary value, an argument, he noted, "which has often been urged, but always unsuccessfully," but he did admit "that it is easier to answer this by authorities than it is by reasoning." Nevertheless, he and his colleagues were content to cite Chitty, *Theobald*, and the several New York decisions on the subject in affirming a ten-thousand-dollar award. Justice William Biggs said of a two-thousand-dollar award for a sprained ankle in St. Louis in 1889 that it seemed "to us to be large and rather out of proportion to the injury received," but he and his colleagues affirmed the award. Justice George Nesmith complained that juries, "in actual practice," were "apt to be much influenced" by the victim's "rank in society, or relative merits and position in life" in awarding damages for both loss of income *and* "sufferings," but while he was unhappy with that reality, he accepted it and affirmed an award of three thousand dollars to a timber merchant who now took opium to mask the pain in his arm and shoulder caused by a derailment.[101]

Some cases enable us to see precisely how the juries calculated these awards in the nineteenth century: If the plaintiff lost an eye or limb, 40 to 50 percent of the award might be given for that future loss of income, pleasure, and physical facility; another 40 to 50 percent was for his or her past and future pain and suffering, while the rest went for medical expenses. Where there was no loss of sight or limb, most of the award was for pain and suffering. This pattern is not inconsistent with current practice.[102]

Negligent defendants, then, were by the 1840s and 1850s being held liable for more than tangible medical costs and lost income. They were also made to pay the less tangible price of the plaintiff's loss of limb or faculties and the intangible price of the plaintiff's past *and* future physical *and* mental suffering. Thus when the counsel for a negligent Missouri coal operator sought to separate physical suffering (as compensable) from the "less tangible" (and thus noncompensable) *mental* suffering, his effort was described by the Kansas City Court of Appeals as "the very acme of carrying the most abstruse metaphysics of the schoolman into the practical deliberations of the jury room."[103] And when former justice B. C. Whitman protested to the Nevada Supreme Court an award of fifteen thousand dollars to a "subsistence" earner (who "though working for many years" owned nothing), he was answered by plaintiff's counsel that the jury had properly annualized his four-dollars-a-day miner's salary and then chosen a sum, which, after subtracting his attorney's contingency fee, simply paid the man for his pain and loss of income. The court agreed with this latter view, and its opinion affirming the award was praised by the editor of Nevada's *Weekly Enterprise* the next day.[104]

LOSS OF ENJOYMENT, NERVOUS SHOCK, AND THE RIGHT TO EXAMINE

We also see in some of these nineteenth-century personal injury decisions the first signs of jurists recognizing what we now call "loss of enjoyment"[105] as a legitimate ground for damages. In Indiana in 1854 a trial judge spoke of the plaintiff's right to "individual happiness." In Illinois in 1870 Chief Justice Breese spoke of the plaintiff's loss of "human happiness." In New York in 1871 a trial court judge instructed a jury to compensate a train collision victim, in part, for what the railroad had done to "impair his capacity to enjoy life." (The New York Supreme Court later affirmed their award of $20,000.) In Kentucky in 1887 a jury awarded a brakeman $10,000 after hearing instructions identical to those given by the New York judge, instructions later approved by the Kentucky Supreme Court. In Wisconsin in 1890 Justice David Taylor, affirming a $18,500 award, sympathized with a seven-year-old amputee's loss of "those things which make life enjoyable and happy."[106] Nineteenth-century (white) Americans truly enjoyed a "pursuit of happiness" in a century of unprecedented economic growth and personal liberty, and it is not surprising that their optimistic expectations of "pleasure" and "happiness" might form a part of the grounds and justification for large damage awards compensating those who had lost the opportunity due to a negligent corporation.[107]

We know that until the mid-twentieth century, most courts required that pain and suffering awards be allowed only where some actual physical injury occurred, "though that bodily injury may have been very small."[108] Was "mental suffering" that flowed from or was associated with that physical injury compensable as well? The issue was fought out in the late 1840s and early 1850s, and echoed a debate between two important American treatise writers, Simon Greenleaf and Theodore Sedgwick. Greenleaf, the successor to Joseph Story as Harvard Law's Dane professor, maintained in his *Treaties on the Law of Evidence* that tort plaintiffs should be awarded nothing other than "actual damages proved," and that, in case of personal injuries, the jury might consider, in addition to lost income, "his bodily sufferings, and, *if* the injury was *wilful*, his mental agony also."[109]

280   In New York, Theodore Sedgwick, the Jeffersonian great-grandson of

William Livingston, disagreed with these "extreme views." He felt that English and American opinions warranted compensation for mental as well as physical suffering in personal injury *negligence* suits.[110] And it was clearly Sedgwick's views that carried the day, approved explicitly over Greenleaf's in Iowa, Connecticut, and Missouri,[111] and applied elsewhere, uniformly, with less ado.[112]

As late as 1893 railroad counsels would still, unsuccessfully, be attacking, in ad hoc fashion, the call for damages for "mental anguish."[113] But they were to be confronted with additional legal problems: In 1888 the Supreme Court of Victoria (Australia) sanctioned damages of £342 against a negligent railroad for the "nervous shock" a woman experienced at a railroad crossing that later caused her to become ill. On appeal, however, Privy Council reversed and remanded. Such a suit, absent any proof of actual physical injury, would create a "wide field opened for imaginary claims." They refused to alter the common-law rule.[114] That *had* been the case in America as late as 1880.[115] But between 1889 and 1896 six American courts, more independent now of the Privy Council than was Victoria's, abandoned the requirement of a physical "touching" for pain-and-suffering damages. Where near collisions and the like produced fright that led to physical consequences ("violent convulsions" or, in female plaintiffs, miscarriage), "common sense," "reason," and "analogies of the law" told jurists that tort damages for pain and suffering should now lie. Conceivably, some courts were becoming aware of the views of Doctor Herbert Page (1883), who argued that the traumatic shock to one's nerves after a near-miss by a railroad train could produce a psychosomatic reaction. After all, Minnesota's chief justice Gilfillan explained, "the mind and the body operate reciprocally on each other."[116]

Simultaneously, plaintiffs seeking pain-and-suffering damages from negligent railroads fought, with less success, another battle with railways seeking to avoid damage awards. When carelessly maintained timbers in an Iowa railroad trestle came loose and felled a worker in 1875, he sued. The company asked the trial judge to direct the plaintiff to submit to an examination by physicians to verify the man's claims, and the judge so directed. The worker refused to submit to the examination; the railroad appealed. The Iowa Supreme Court reversed and remanded. Chief Justice Joseph Beck explained that the trial court was properly searching for "exact justice." He cited no authority for this judgment, but it is plausible to assume that he was borrowing from Chancery and common-law rules regarding rules of evidence. An equity court could require a plaintiff to take the stand in a civil action; defendants were entitled to "discovery" in order to provide justice.

281

Common-law courts could require medical examinations of plaintiffs in marriage annulment suits or claims of pregnancy.[117] The end result, however, was a rule in personal injury liability suits that gave railroad counsels an opportunity to establish that plaintiffs were exaggerating their injuries.

Defendants (all but one a railroad) made use of this decision over the next decade in Kansas, Nebraska, Maine, Wisconsin, Texas, Indiana, Arkansas, Georgia, and Alabama with some success, but they found some of these courts protective of the plaintiff's privacy and quite willing to create exceptions to the Iowa rule;[118] consequently, they called upon the state legislatures for positive direction in some important jurisdictions. Statutes authorizing the dismissal of personal injury lawsuits where the plaintiff refused to submit to a court-supervised medical examination were passed in Ohio and New Jersey to force the high courts of those states into line. But where the request for an examination came after the plaintiff had rested her case in Ohio, the court regarded the right as having been waived and affirmed a three-thousand-dollar award.[119] The courts of New York were unwilling to grant railroads any such right until compelled to do so by that state's legislature in 1893. Adaline Roberts, injured in a train collision in northern New York in 1881, would not be required to an "inquisitorial" examination by three railroad-approved physicians. "Such an invasion of the sacredness of the person, as here proposed," wrote President Justice William Learned of New York's supreme court in 1883, "cannot be permitted at this day." It "might deter many, especially women, from ever commencing actions," and many of these successful plaintiffs *were* women.[120] The high courts of Illinois, Missouri, and the United States would still not require such defendant-requested medical exams as the century drew to an end.[121]

Why were American juries and jurists so attentive and generous to those injured by tortfeasors? One reason, clearly, has just been identified: The nineteenth-century common law was simply not very tolerant of common carriers who were responsible for injury and suffering to innocent persons, be they passengers, strangers, or workers. B. C. Whitman, while still a justice of the Nevada Supreme Court, was more frank on this score about judicial motives than were any of his colleagues:

> Some idea of punishment to defendants prompted the first allowance for bodily suffering in cases of mere negligence. . . . In these times, when travelling is so much a constituent part of living, it is perhaps practically well that it is so, for the pocket nerve is a very sensitive one, and prospect of heavy damages will undoubtedly do much to prevent carelessness on the part of passenger carriers.[122]

Damage awards for pain and suffering, Whitman believed, were properly intended both to "punish" and to instruct negligent corporate defendants. "The pocket nerve" of such soulless entities was "a sensitive one" that, when touched, would produce a higher standard of care. Justices Johnson, Shaw, Gibson, and Greene seem to have said as much. So did Maine's Justice Charles Walton, when he referred to the "one vulnerable point" corporations possessed, "that is the pocket of the monied power that is concealed behind them, and if that is reached they will wince" and cease to employ "careless and indifferent agents or reckless . . . servants." Mississippi's Justice William Harris made the same point when he told counsel for the New Orleans Jackson & Great Northern Railroad that "idle capital in search of splendid investment" could not expect to "rest in comfort and security in the enjoyment of the large profits" realized "from the dangerous instrumentalities . . . set in motion." He and his colleagues thereupon affirmed an award of twelve thousand dollars to a warehouseman "greatly injured" in a collision who "never walks now without great pain."[123] This is not the sort of judicial behavior that the reigning paradigm has identified with antebellum American jurists, and four of these seven *were* antebellum American jurists (Whitman wrote in 1870; Walton, in 1869; Harris, in 1866).

There was a second rationale that jurists gave for affirming pain-and-suffering and loss-of-limb or -faculty awards, one closely related to the first, but with a different emphasis: Admonishing negligent defendants was to be accomplished by compensating wrongly injured, suffering plaintiffs. And American jurists were attentive, far more attentive than their British counterparts, to the wrongs done to this class of plaintiffs. The stagecoach passenger enroute Zanesville, Ohio, in 1838, who had been "shockingly mangled" in an accident caused by a negligent driver, had endured suffering "as great as human nature could bear," in the words of U.S. Supreme Court justice John McLean, riding circuit. He deserved compensation "for the sufferings he has undergone," in addition to lost income and medical expenses.[124] The engineer whose arm was broken in September 1855 on the banks of the Etowah River in Georgia, due to the carelessness of one working in a separate department of the Western and Atlantic Railroad, was entitled to receive damages for both his physical and mental pain. His mental suffering, Justice Linton Stephens observed, "must have been great, and the dread of the approaching collision between the two engines, though brief, must have been terrible. Mental agony has been known to turn a head gray in a night, and gray hairs are often but the effervescence of some great mental anguish."[125] A passenger who found that his train had overrun his station in Mississippi was forced to disembark without assistance. He slipped on the icy roadbed and suffered a dislocated knee. The jury's award of forty-five hundred dollars was affirmed in 1871, "notwithstanding the erroneous instruction" by the trial judge sanctioning exemplary damages. Justice Jonathan Tarbell explained the court's generosity: "Few of us, we apprehend, even of those who have passed the meridian of life, would be willing to take a permanently crippled limb with twice or thrice $4500."[126] A construction gang laborer suffered internal injuries and a crushed thigh in the shifting of a load of fill negligently undermined at the orders of agents of the Chicago, Rock Island and Pacific Railroad in 1871. The jury's award of nine thousand dollars was affirmed by the Iowa Supreme Court, where Justice Joseph Beck observed: "His sufferings were protracted and most intense, having to endure for seven weeks the excruciating torture of machinery and appliances used by surgeons."[127]

Today we would characterize these sentiments in essentially the same way that they would have been characterized in the nineteenth century—as "sympathetic," "liberal," and "humane." The jurists who wrote them displayed a concern with suffering victims and a sense, essentially indistinguishable from that of the juries, that these victims deserved a substantial solatium from corporate "spoliators" for the pain and the future misery they had been made to endure. Appellate jurists could especially empathize with injured passengers and those whose buggies were hit at crossings. After all, they "rode circuit" (be it on horseback, or in a buggy, a stagecoach, or a train) regularly in the course of their official duties—probably traveling a good deal more than the typical juror, and more than just a few jurists were killed or injured in the process.[128]

INSURANCE PAYMENTS, WOUNDED FEELINGS, AND LOSS
OF COMPANIONSHIP: WRONGFUL DEATH AWARDS

So much for personal injuries. What about "wrongful deaths"? For the survivors of a spouse or child wrongfully killed, the English courts offered little solace. Indeed, until the passage of Lord Campbell's Act (9 & 10 Vic. Ch. 93 [1846]), the rule laid down by Lord Ellenborough in *Baker* v. *Bolton* (1808) was that the right an action for negligently caused personal injury died with the aggrieved individual (*actio personalis moritur cum persona*).

Such does not appear to have been the case in some of the American colonies where statutes allowed the survivors of one wrongfully killed recovered a solatium, typically of about ten pounds, in a joint civil-criminal manslaughter proceeding. After independence, some of these statutes were repealed, but a few courts still sanctioned common-law actions for wrongful death. Thus in 1794 the Connecticut high court allowed a husband's action for deprivation of "consort" against a careless surgeon deemed responsible for his wife's death. But upon becoming aware of Lord Ellenborough's rule in *Baker* v. *Bolton*, Connecticut's jurists adopted it. Similarly, in New York, a decision of the state's supreme court in 1838, offering an award of two hundred dollars to the parents of a boy killed by a carriage, was overruled in 1859, when the same court cited *Baker* v. *Bolton* and observed, apologetically, that "the law will not bend to accommodate our private views, or gratify our personal desires." Courts must "stand by" the "ancient landmarks" of the common law.[129] The Supreme Courts of Massachusetts, Kentucky, Maine, and New Hampshire also conformed to the harsh English rule, leading some state legislatures to pass "Lord Campbell's Acts" of their own, allowing administrators and heirs to sue in the place of one wrongfully killed.[130]

Other jurisdictions, however, were not so slavish in their regard for English authority and did not await the passage of positive law to declare that a widow might sue for the loss of her slain spouse. The federal district and circuit courts in Massachusetts and the courts of Missouri and Georgia had rejected the English rule by 1860,[131] and in 1874, federal circuit court judge John Forrest Dillon spoke on the subject for the inhabitants of the Nebraska Territory. Neither the Congress nor the territorial assembly had passed any "Lord Campbell's Act" for Nebraska Territory; hence Judge Dillon reviewed the "general common law principles." After noting that both French and Scottish law allowed administrators and heirs to sue in the cases of wrongful deaths, Dillon reviewed the English and American decisions. He rejected *Baker* v. *Bolton* and its Massachusetts counterpart (*Carey* v. *Berkshire RR* [1848]) while citing favorably the contrary New York decision (*Ford* v. *Monroe* [1838]). The problem with the now-abrogated English rule was that it "cannot be vindicated on considerations of reason, justice, or policy"—that is, in addition to being illogical and unjust, it was not "good public policy" to allow railroads and other negligent corporations to kill people and get away scot-free. Dillon literally invited the U.S. Supreme Court to affirm or reject his views.[132]

Nevertheless, the wrongful-death actions, be they by statute or common law innovation, generally limited the victim's legal representative to the recovery in damages of economic loss—that is, how much money the loss of the victim would be likely to cost his or her legal representative in past medical expenses (if the victim had not died instantaneously) and in the loss of the victim's contributed earning power. Recovery for the loss of a spouse's companionship had been limited in England to husbands whose wives were so disabled or disfigured as to deprive them of the companionship they had enjoyed (consortium).[133] A wife could not maintain such a suit for the loss of her husband's society, nor a child for a parent's, for, as Blackstone put it, "the inferior [wife and child] hath no kind of property in the company . . . of the superior [husband] as the superior is held to have in those of the inferior." But after the passage of Lord Campbell's Act, no damages for loss of society survived the death of either spouse.[134]

Such was not the rule in several American jurisdictions. New York's Supreme Court chose to "take a humane view" in construing that state's wrongful death statute in allowing damages to the grown children of a forty-five-year-old seamstress killed due to a railway conductor's carelessness for their loss of her "intellectual culture and moral training."[135] And in Pennsylvania a husband was allowed damages for the loss of companionship of his wrongfully killed wife, despite the language in the statute limiting damages to economic loss. Justice Daniel Agnew explained that "certainly the service of a wife is pecuniarily more valuable than that of a mere hireling." The loss of her "attention" and "tender solicitude" was to be compensated.[136] The California Supreme Court allowed damages for loss of companionship, but limited it to "the case of a wife . . . or a mother." The Connecticut Supreme Court of Errors went so far in 1865 as to read into that state's wrongful-death statute authority for a jury's award of fifteen hundred dollars above and beyond the twenty-five hundred dollars in economic losses it had calculated for the pain and suffering the deceased had experienced before dying. After all, Justice Charles McCurdy observed, the common-law rule barring such recovery was but "a strange fiction."[137] Other courts were less inventive, and it took the action of the state legislature in South Carolina and Florida before the legal representative of one wrongfully killed could be awarded damages for the loss of a spouse's society or for the mental anguish he or she suffered.[138]

All damages for economic loss were, under the American wrongful-death statutes, to be calculated so as to cease at age twenty-one if the victim had been a minor contributing to a family's living expenses. And these sorts of damages could be substantially offset if the child had been too young yet to have contributed to the family's income, on the grounds that the parents would have had to expend funds for such a youngster's upbringing for several more years before any significant monetary returns might have been expected. English courts rarely provided any compensation for the loss of children under seven years of age, whereas some New York decisions in the mid-nineteenth century affirmed awards to the parents of such wrongfully killed youngsters amounting to approximately four times the median American wage earner's annual income, but other such awards in New Jersey were disapproved on appeal as excessive. In fact, an action for the wrongful death of the child of a *middle*-class family was likely to result in only the most nominal damage award, since "the children of such parents receive far more primary aid . . . from their parents, then their parents from them."[139]

This too would pass. As the birthrate fell throughout the nineteenth century in America, children became more emotionally precious. Pediatrics emerged as a separate medical field in the 1880s. Social historians speak of a "revolution of feeling" about the death of a child, "a magnification of mourning," a "sacralization" of the child in the second half of the nineteenth century. Pressure steadily grew for courts to require tortfeasors whose careless actions had led to a child's death to pay for the family's emotional suffering in addition to their less significant economic loss. The "priceless" child had arrived.[140]

Few courts were willing to create this new category of compensation without legislative authority, and these socially responsive institutions eventually provided just such a mandate in a number of southern and western states. The first of these appears to have been Virginia's statute in 1873, which allowed the jury to take into consideration "the grief and mental anguish of [close family members], and their loss in being deprived of the care, attention and society" of the victim. West Virginia's rule followed the path of Virginia's. California's legislature allowed for the parent's loss of companionship, as did Wisconsin's, Utah's, Idaho's, Florida's, Missouri's, and Washington's. In every instance, the supreme courts of these states upheld these statutes and interpreted them broadly to allow compensation for both the loss of the child's future "care, attention and society" and a "further sum" for "solace and comfort" for "the sorrow, suffering and mental anguish" the parent had endured.[141] Once again, the northeastern states appeared less humane than their southern and western counterparts.

Jurists in nineteenth-century America tended to be more doctrinal and conservative with regard to expanding the categories of compensation in wrongful death actions than they had been in assessing the defense of imputing parental contributory negligence to a child, or in deciding whether contingency-fee contracts between prospective plaintiffs and their attorneys were honorable. But if they did not invent these innovations in compensation, they both welcomed and sheltered the legislatures' creations when they came before them.

With the rise of the insurance industry in the mid-nineteenth century, some plaintiffs whose spouse or parent had been wrongfully killed received death benefits from an insurance contract in addition to such damages as they might win at trial or be offered in settlement. Railroad attorneys sought to have courts subtract these payments from the damage awards they were ordered to pay, and in England their views prevailed in the instructions to the jury offered by Lord Campbell, presiding at a nisi prius trial in 1857, and approved by the Court of Exchequer in 1863.[142]

That practice was never adopted in the United States. Here courts uniformly regarded the benefits flowing from a life insurance contract as belonging exclusively to the beneficiary of the contract. The spouse or parent "effecting the insurance paid full value for it, and there is no equity in the claim of the defendant to the benefit" of it. To allow a railroad to reduce their liability because the person it had wrongfully killed had purchased life or accident insurance "would seem to be a perversion of justice to subrogate the wrongdoer." The English rule was inequitable and was rejected. Juries were not to be told of any insurance payments being made to plaintiffs.[143] Once again, American courts favored plaintiffs over corporate wrongdoers.

The Vox Populi

What impulses other than empathy and deeply ingrained Christian values might have drawn juries and jurists together against careless corporations? There remains one more impulse, one that we have only alluded to so far, that may explain some of the considerable judicial tolerance of high damage awards. Beginning in midcentury, an increasing percentage of the nation's state appellate justices were no longer appointed but elected to their office. James Hunt's analysis of appeals of cases in nineteenth-century North Carolina involving negligence suits for personal injuries against railroads indicates that that state's supreme court appeared to be decidedly "pro-plaintiff" during the years when Radical Republicans (1869–79) and Populists (1895–99) dominated the bench, and "pro-railroad" in the years when developmentalist Whigs (1840–62) and Bourbon Redeemer Democrats (1879–94) controlled it.[144] The vox populi might speak through the juries, but it had also acquired the capacity to be heard by those seeking a seat on a state's high court.

One does not want to overstate the strength of this impulse. Two sophisticated studies by Kermit Hall of the judicial-political process demonstrate that state high court jurists in the years 1850 to 1920 were usually renominated and reelected if they sought to continue in office, and that their performance on the bench shows little indication that they feared voter rejection or were tailoring their opinions to curry voter support. Thus it was the newly *elected* jurists in Ohio who overcame their appointed predecessors' resistance to the fellow-servant rule in the 1850s. And it was newly elected jurists in Missouri in 1876 who overruled a previous statutory interpreta-

288

tion of that court, effectively reinstating the fellow-servant rule in that state. When the Republican Party in Wisconsin would not support Justice Erasmus Cole for reelection in 1861, fearing that his opinions affirming the foreclosure of farm mortgages for worthless railroad bonds would lead to his defeat, he ran as an independent against a popular assemblyman who attacked Cole's opinions. Cole won by some five thousand votes. Chief Justice Luther Dixon found it necessary for him to take the same step in 1863; he won by three thousand votes.[145]

Nonetheless, about one in every ten of those state high court jurists who sought reelection in these years were defeated, and although most of these appear to have lost in landslide elections that swept all candidates bearing the wrong party label from office,[146] a few jurists must have been defeated "on the merits"—that is, due to voter dissatisfaction with that individual jurist's judicial philosophy.

A case in point noted by Hall is the defeat of California's Justice William Van Fleet, a Republican, by Judge Walter Van Dyke, a Democrat, in the election of 1898. Hall pointed out that Justice Van Fleet's opinion for the court in *Fox* v. *Oakland Consolidated Street Railway* (1897),[147] remanding as excessive a jury award of six thousand dollars to the parents of a four-year-old boy killed by a negligently operated streetcar, was criticized on the eve of the election by the *San Francisco Examiner*.[148] Let us briefly explore this case and its issues. Van Fleet first turned away the streetcar counsel's argument that the company had not been negligent. The evidence of such negligence was on the record. He then turned to the other questions raised by the streetcar's counsel. Counsel for the parents of Lorin Fox had introduced evidence of their low economic status to defeat the streetcar's defense that they were negligent in the safeguarding of their son. They lived only one hundred feet from the tracks. However, the boy's father was at work "at his trade," and his mother, who had just warned the boy to stay in the yard, was washing clothes on the back porch as a supplement to the family's income. The parents were not held by the trial court to the same standard as the wealthy, who could afford a constant attendant for their children, and as such no contributory negligence of theirs was imputed to the boy.[149]

Justice Van Fleet was not convinced of the wisdom of this rule. He read from Christopher Patterson's fiercely prorailroad treatise, *Railway Accident Law* (1886):

> The ["bad law"] judgements . . . seem to have been largely influenced by the sentimental reflections of the judges on the poverty of the plaintiffs, and their consequent inability to employ servants to watch

their children. . . . But those learned judges failed to give due weight to the consideration that the railway was not responsible for the acts of the parents in bringing these children into the world, nor for that degree of misfortune which retained those parents in a condition of more or less want.[150]

But Van Fleet left that issue as a quaere and remanded the case on the final issue—the excessive damages. He decided that the boy would have been "a subject of expense and outlay to his parents, without the ability to render peculiar return" for "many years" and took judicial notice of the fact that boys tended to follow the career pattern of their fathers. Consequently, he and his colleagues felt the jury award of six thousand dollars revealed prejudice on the part of the jury and sent the case back to be retried.[151] It was of this opinion that the editorial writer of Hearst's *San Francisco Examiner* observed: "Van Fleet is the judge who rendered the Loren [*sic*] Fox decision, declaring that the life of a poor man's child is not nearly as valuable as that of a rich man's darling." Kermit Hall then observed that, following the publication of that editorial, Justice Van Fleet lost his seat by nine thousand votes.[152] He provided no further details regarding this election, inasmuch as his reference to this case was illustrative, offered in passing in a highly quantitative essay that moved on to other issues. Consequently, I felt the need to ask whether this nine-thousand-vote margin was anti–Van Fleet, inspired by the *Fox* case, or merely a part of a Democratic landslide.

California voter turnout in the 1890s had ranged between 68.6 percent of eligible voters in the presidential years to 63.4 percent in the off years, as consistent in San Francisco County as elsewhere. The Democratic gubernatorial candidate was outpolled in San Francisco County in 1898 by an 8.4 percent margin (28,218 to 24,630), whereas the Democratic Supreme Court candidate running against Justice Van Fleet, Judge Van Dyke, outpolled Van Fleet in that county by a 7.4 percent margin (23,762 to 20,436). While Van Fleet's Republican colleague on the high bench, Justice T. B. McFarland, was also outpolled in San Francisco County by the Democratic-Populist ("Fusion") candidate, William Coley, and by an even *larger* margin of 11.4 percent (25,598 to 21,715), Justice McFarland's opponent may have been better known. Perhaps he was tarred by the same brush that had tarred Van Fleet in the voters' eyes. Probably the fact that his opponent had Populist as well as Democratic support added to the magnitude of that Republican jurist's defeat. In any event, the likelihood is considerable that the *San Francisco Examiner*'s condemnation of Van Fleet's *Fox* opinion had indeed struck sympathetic chords in the breasts of some voters. [153]

CONCLUSION

What have we learned in this excursion into the world of nineteenth-century personal injury damage awards? First, we have found that those who have claimed that American juries and jurists were "fault-oriented," noncompensational, and proentrepreneurial in the mid- and late nineteenth century have misdated by at least half a century a major change in Anglo-American legal culture. As early as the 1830s and 1840s, American juries were awarding injured plaintiffs large sums for their pain and suffering, by comparison to either English courts of their day or those of present-day America. Second, we have found that as soon as careless corporations appeared on the scene, they were sent signals about accountability and carefulness via their "pocket nerve." These signals were sensitive to the pocket's contents: The individual who assailed paid less than the doctor who delicted, who paid less than the careless city, which paid less than the reckless railroad.[154] The availability of entities that could compensate may have been related to the emergence of a "legal culture of compensation." Third, we have found further evidence that some American high courts were willing to break with English precedent when their sense of justice was enraged by the inequity or illogic of the English rule, further evidence of the Jurisprudence of the Heart. This was so with regard to the sovereign immunity of road and bridge authorities, the wrongful-death rule, the deducting of insurance payments from damage awards, and the *Coultas* rule with regard to "nervous shock." Finally, we have confirmed what we have found in previous chapters, that, while "highbrow" American jurists (especially, as ever, those of the Massachusetts Supreme Judicial Court) were reluctant to depart from these English "principles," "middle-brow" jurists elsewhere were more in sync with trial court judges and juries, more in sync with popular legal culture. They were, after all, elected in democratic America by these jurors; they "rode circuit" on the very vehicles being held to common carrier standards of liability; and they saw that liability damages might lead these common carriers to acquire innovations that would save American lives and limbs, pain and suffering, and future enjoyment.

Conclusion: What We Found, and Some Explanations of the Jurisprudence of the Heart

Equity enforces benevolence where the law of nature makes it our duty.

> Lord Kames, copied by Thomas Jefferson into his placebook, noted in Peter Hoffer, *The Law's Conscience* (1990), 68

Judge Lyon had reverence for precedent, but he had greater reverence for justice. Where it seemed to him that some mouldy, medieval precedent would work absolute wrong in the case before him, he was very apt to say with a twinkle in his eye, "well, I think this is a case where we will have to use a little *main strength*"; and the precedent was very apt to go by the board.

> Wisconsin's Chief Justice John Winslow, on Wisconsin justice, later chief justice, William Penn Lyon (1871–94), in *Wisconsin Magazine of History* 9 (1926): 250 at 283

The religious habits of Americans form not only the basis of their private and public morals, but have become . . . thoroughly interwoven with . . . the very essence of their government. . . . Religion presides over their councils, aids in the execution of their laws, and adds to the dignity of their judges.

> Francis Grund, *The Americans, in Their Moral, Social, and Political Relations*, 1837

Parables go strait [*sic*] to their mark and are rarely misunderstood. Conscience, seated in the inner recesses of the human bosom, is quick to perceive and understand what is meant.

> *The Evangelist*, May 3, 1883

What, in summary form, have we learned? First, we have rediscovered the power of long-standing English rules, maxims, and doctrines. Conveyed to American courtrooms by both oral tradition, treatises, and published English reports, this Jurisprudence of the Head was far more important in the early nineteenth century than has been reported. Jurists were trained to follow precedent, the "heaped-up wisdom" of the past, and the "principled" views of their predecessors. As such, the propensity of antebellum jurists to innovate, to "bend" rules for whatever reasons, has been exaggerated.

Second, such rules as had "distributive" qualities, like those governing master-servant relations, were generally not nineteenth-century innovations but medieval, based on long-standing principles and practices. Moreover, some of these "ancient" rules, and most of the newly created ones as well, had "good public policy" rationales that reflected the judiciary's (and *Zeitgeist*'s) desire to provide a "well-regulated society" for the general welfare, for the public good.

Third, such innovations as nineteenth-century jurists did produce should not be characterized as having been intended to spur economic growth or aid entrepreneurs.[1] Rather, almost all were designed to aid those who had been *hurt* by the course of that economic growth, those who lay wounded in its wake. This proplaintiff propensity is surely what has characterized the judge-made alterations in the common law in *twentieth*-century America— alterations like the imposition of strict product liability on manufacturers, the termination of charitable immunity from damage suits for hospitals, the creation of the "emotional distress" tort, the abrogation of the "accepted work" doctrine in contracts for the sale of new buildings and the related "implied warranty of habitability" in sales and leases, to name some of the best known.[2] But these twentieth-century innovations did not reverse an alleged pattern of nineteenth-century procorporate "transformations" of the law such as the reigning paradigm has claimed to identify. Rather, they extended and built upon a proplaintiff process that got underway in the antebellum years and continued to churn out new rules throughout the nineteenth century. Proplaintiff innovations, it turns out, are a longstanding American judicial tradition.

Finally, we learn other, extralegal things about nineteenth-century America from this sort of analysis of conflict in the courts: We learn that "the poor," "the weak," common laborers, and children were better off under the rules of common law and equity by the 1890s than they had been in the 1790s because of judicial innovations. We learn that railway travel was safer than earlier forms of transportation, that railway companies paid dearly for land seized under eminent domain "takings," contributed substantially in taxes for the new public schools, and were ordered to turn over much larger sums than other defendants whose negligence had also caused injuries.

GETTING SPECIFIC: ACCIDENTS

The "fault" doctrine did not overcome one of "strict liability" in the nineteenth century, as has been claimed; the negligence standard had long been a necessary element in tort actions for personal injury. But the advent of macadamized roadbeds, railways, and steam power did result in an explosion in the number of suits claiming (under the old common-carrier rationale) a *virtually* strict "product" liability for those who offered dangerous machinery or vehicles for the use of others. Steamboat, stagecoach, and railroad companies in particular found it extremely difficult to escape liability to passengers for defects in their equipment. They found as well that, despite their central role in the nineteenth-century economy, they were held liable to the public for the slightest negligent act of any of their employees that led to injury, and held strictly liable for damage to freight.

Corporations had available to them the contributory negligence of the plaintiff as a defense in actions for personal injury, but this turned out to be a much weaker reed to lean on than has been believed. The same may be said of the proximate-cause defense. Moreover, jurists created several exceptions to the contributory-negligence rule, including the rejection of the rule imputing parental contributory negligence to a child, and the rejection of the "trespasser" defense in cases in which children had been injured by a dangerous artificial object on defendant's property. Here the humanity of southern, midwestern, and prairie state jurists in the child-centered world of the Victorian era led them to create a "legal fiction": the defendant, in placing the "attractive" object before the child, had "invited" him to it. Northeastern jurists who rejected this innovation did so not because they were heartless, probusiness instrumentalists, but because they were penned in by precedent, because they were dedicated to doctrine.

The legal culture of nineteenth-century American trial court juries and judges hearing cases of personal injury was not "noncompensational" as has been said, but generous—more generous than that of its English counterparts and just as generous as today's legal culture. American juries gave victims greater awards for pain and suffering, loss of enjoyment, and loss of companionship than the stoical English. They seemed to have been inspired by a sense of rising expectations with regard to the setting of fractures by physicians, the macadamizing of roads by municipalities, and the increasing capabilities of railroads to conduct train movements safely. Hence when these expectations were not met, the tort-feasor was made to pay. And they picked the deep pockets of railroad, steamboat, and manufacturing corporations as soon as those pockets appeared, giving plaintiffs injured by these tortfeasors three times what they gave to the victims of medical malpractice or defective municipal roads and bridges, and six times what they demanded of intentional tortfeasors in assault and battery awards. When corporations appealed these awards as excessive, jurists who "rode circuit" on the same engines of destruction that had injured these plaintiff-appellees affirmed them, indicating that the railroad corporations should be sent a message regarding safety via their "sensitive pocket nerve."

Injured workers fared as well as passengers if they could get their cases to the juries, but the ancient law of master and servant raised the assumption-of-risk and fellow-servant defenses against them, and even though several exceptions to these defenses were created in many state courts, the doctrinal propensity of jurists to resist change eventually meant that these defenses had to be eliminated by the legislatures.

GETTING SPECIFIC: PROPERTY

Our exploration of judicial interpretations of several issues in the law of property also found little support for the economic-oriented perspective. Jurists occasionally engaged in cost-benefit analysis, but they often did not balance the equation in ways that entrepreneur-defendants would have liked. And when they did sometimes strike out in some new direction, abandoning as antisocial a common-law doctrine or rediscovering a forgotten rule of equity, it was, generally, to aid the less powerful members of society or to create a greater sense of social togetherness.

There are exceptions to this generalization: The "balancing the equities" innovation in nuisance actions sometimes aided polluting entrepreneurs, and the adoption in Massachusetts of the prudent-investor rule was of some help to entrepreneur-capitalists in a few northeastern states. But generally speaking, jurists were just as doctrinal, and just as humane, in deciding property appeals as they had been in deciding negligence cases. The Jurisprudence of Head and Heart won out over any Jurisprudence of Visible or Invisible Hand in this domain as well.

GETTING SPECIFIC: AGREEMENTS

The law of contract in nineteenth-century America was driven by doctrine. When those who interpreted it on high courts sought to explain the public policy purposes of its rules, as jurists sometimes did, they almost never offered developmental rationales. Once in a rare while one or another might offer the cost-benefit language of economic efficiency.[3] But usually contract's rules and doctrines were applied as they had been for centuries in England and the provinces. The third-party beneficiary contract was not invented in America in the nineteenth century, but in early-seventeenth-century England, and when those same English courts reversed themselves in the early and mid-nineteenth century, denying third-party beneficiaries a right to sue on such contracts, most American courts clung to the older English rule as the more principled one in doctrinal fashion. There was no fairness doctrine before 1800. The will theory of contract was very much in evidence, at least as early as the 1550s. There was no sound-price regimen in seventeenth- or eighteenth-century England. Caveat emptor was the rule, and when it was applied in nineteenth-century America it did not help "economically sophisticated 'seller-insiders' " but managed to do just the opposite: Uninformed middlemen-sellers won out over relatively better informed buyer-manufacturers. The law of sales was at least as "fair" in 1890 as it had been in 1590. Conditional sales, chattel mortgages, and bailment leases were of ancient origin. They were not applied in an "exploitative" fashion by nineteenth-century courts, and several important jurisdictions drew rather sharp distinctions between each, contrary to what has been claimed. Moreover, these distinctions tended to serve the interests of "weak" bona fide purchasers, *not* manufacturer-entrepreneurs. Finally, the rule allowing expectation damages when one party defaulted in a commodities "futures" transaction was in place centuries before 1815, and it appears to have been understood as early as the 1730s by relatively small-scale farm businesswomen. The "capitalist transformation"[4] of antebellum America thus had little impact on this or any other of the aspects of contract law addressed in chapter 2. Continuity, not change, characterizes most contract law over the seventeenth, eighteenth, and nineteenth centuries.

This continuity theme does not make a very exciting story. I know how entrancing the different story can be: of how industry, commerce, and economic growth generated the need for such "innovations" as the "fault-must-be-proved" rule, the fellow-servant doctrine, the "release of energy" principle in property law, innovations with regard to riparian rights and lateral support of buildings, the will theory of contract, conditional sales, expectation damages, and the harsh rule against quantum meruit recovery for workers who quit—all of which allegedly serve as evidence of a propensity of jurists to "transform" the law for economic or ideological ends. I once taught that perspective, and recognize how plausible it sounds. It is much less interesting for a class to wend its way through evidence, counterevidence, argument, and counterargument, to the conclusion that, with regard to these rules, virtually nothing changed, that courts seemed largely indifferent to econometric reasoning or to the various forces transforming the economy. Indeed, some of my classes may well have wondered why they had been led down such an ultimately uninteresting trail in the first place. Isn't history supposed to be about change? Moreover, it is very difficult for some students to *believe* that much of the law of tort, property, and contracts was not transformed in the century after the American Revolution, especially after they have read Horwitz, Hall, or Friedman. And yet it is true.

The saving grace is that one can point to several previously un- or underreported humane innovations as evidence that many jurists *were* willing to alter some rules to ensure more equitable results; in the field of contract workers could recover "what their labor had been worth" their employers "off" an "entire" contract; poor litigants could acquire "their day in court" via the contingency-fee contract. These innovations may not have constituted a raging Transformation, but the current was still a robust one. And it bore poor plaintiffs along, not corporate defendants. What appeared to others to be a legal current bearing corporate defendants to new riches turns out to be a few minor backwaters and eddies, of little assistance to most entrepreneurs.

THE ECONOMIC-ORIENTED REIGNING PARADIGM

I have sought to tell my own story, a story of tension within the ranks and individual souls of America's nineteenth-century jurists, a tension of Heart against Head. But in the course of telling this story, if largely in my notes, I have also reported my disagreements with a reigning economic-oriented paradigm. I will say no more here of my differences with most of those with whom I have disagreed in these notes, because those differences relate to certain specific claims and views these historians have offered, not to the whole of their accounts, arguments, and propositions.[5] The matter is different with both Richard Posner's Law and Economics perspective and Morton Horwitz's "subsidization of growth"/"aid to entrepreneurs" thesis in *The Transformation of American Law, 1780–1860*. My understanding of the antebellum judiciary is pretty thoroughly at odds with the Horwitz account. He is on track when it comes to describing some important aspects of the law with regard to pollution nuisances, for some jurisdictions at least. But I differ thoroughly with his accounts of innovations in other corners of private law—lateral support for buildings, riparian rights, ancient lights, sales and service contracts, negligence, and the fellow-servant and assumption-of-risk rules.[6] And, more generally, I find his claim that courts subsidized enterprise by "transforming" legal rules to be way off the mark.

I found more evidence of American jurists in the nineteenth century behaving as Richard Posner suggests they did[7] than as Horwitz claims, but the evidence is spotty and much of it constitutes a second level of justification, subordinate to the core ratio decidendi and often untrue to the basic premise of the Law and Economics perspective. Thus the cost-benefit analysis in many proximate-cause, pollution-nuisance, and attractive-nuisance cases was weighted by the opinion writers in ways that supported their major premises but only by failing to take fairly into account important variables on one or the other side of the cost-benefit equation.[8]

Posner's observations with regards to the economic efficiency of a number of other common-law rules are not borne out by my analysis. The abandonment of the ancient-lights rule in the law of easements ran counter to econometric reasoning, as did the creation of certain exceptions to the assumption-of-risk and fellow-servant rules, and other "wealth maximizing" rationales regarding futures transactions, sales contracts, the imputation of parental negligence to children, and pain-and-suffering awards were ignored or rejected outright.[9] Jurists seemed ultimately to have been more concerned with inspiring what they thought of as moral and socially responsible behavior than economic efficiency, and these two ends were often *not* the same.[10]

This is not to say that a Jurisprudence of the Invisible Hand would have been (or is today) wrong-headed. Much of the economic analysis of law sounds plausible to me. But that's neither here nor there; my task here is to help comprehend the past. And in that regard, I detected so little evidence of jurists in nineteenth-century America making use of economic analysis that I feel confident in saying that the Jurisprudence of the Invisible Hand was itself virtually invisible.

If I fault Posner and Horwitz somewhat more than I do others whom I associate with the economic-oriented paradigm, I think my story so antithetical to that paradigm that I am, in effect, declaring the whole of it to be essentially bankrupt, or null and void, to borrow some terms from the field of analysis. And how could it not have been so? I will not be the first to note that the legal rules of other industrializing, commercial nations of the nineteenth century were quite different from those allegedly pro-entrepreneurial innovations American jurists were said to have adopted. If the economic imperatives of industrialization and commercial growth in antebellum America had led jurists to change common-law rules, would not the same economic forces in France and Germany in these same years have led to the same sorts of legal innovations? If the legal process was inexorably "shaped" and "molded" by external forces in the United States, we might expect to see the same results elsewhere.[11] If the economic-oriented accounts regarding the pro-corporate character of American legal innovations are to be believed, then why did English common law rules often differ from those of many American jurisdictions, and why did the Civil Law industrializing nations of France and Germany develop rules imposing strict liability on employers for injuries to workers at the hands of negligent fellow workers while English and American courts were simultaneously releasing these same defendants from liability under the fellow-servant rule? Were European jurists indifferent to growth? Were they simply less intelligent than American jurists? Or were the differing rules of both simply irrelevant? Conversely, one can find doctrines in Roman or medieval law that are alleged to have been the products of the antebellum commercial-industrial revolution.[12] How can they be both the instrumentalist creations of pro-entrepreneurial jurists and the doctrines of a pre-commercial-industrial era? As Brian Simpson asks of one such claim: "If, for example, the rule in *Hadley* v. *Baxendale* (1854) is, as it has been argued, peculiarly appropriate to mid-nineteenth century industrial capitalism, what was it doing in Orleans in the 1760s?"[13]

Legal rules and innovations were not driven so much by external economic forces as has been claimed, but rather by a "legal culture" with roots deep in the legal traditions of each nation. Certainly those with "civil" or Roman law traditions had differed in several particulars from England's common-law rules in the preindustrial age, and it would have been surprising had the force of these traditions *not* resulted in some different approaches to problems generated by industrialization. In any event, the extent to which the courts of industrializing America actually did generate rules friendly to industry and railways has been badly overstated by the economic-oriented.

And that leaves the question: How could such a paradigm have come into being and dominated the field for so long—from the 1950s (Hurst) through the 1960s and 1970s (Friedman, Posner, and Horwitz) and the 1980s and early 1990s (Holt and Tomlins)? I think the answer is that these scholars were drawing on scholarly traditions that gave overwhelming significance to economic issues. This goes without saying for Richard Posner, whose paradigm is explicitly that of the discipline of economics (that is, the economics of Adam Smith, Jeremy Bentham, and Ronald Coase). It describes as well the handful of able Marxist historians in the field who draw upon the insights and theories of Marx, Engels, and their twentieth-century heirs. But it also pertains to those who drew on the work of "legal realists" of the early twentieth century as well as on the accounts of mainstream American historians who charted the history of the nineteenth century for us in the mid-twentieth century, for guidance, insight, and authority. The work of Karl Polanyi, Matthew Josephson, Charles and Mary Beard, W. W. Rostow, and Arthur Schlesinger Jr., to name but a few of the better known of these scholars, posited the centrality of economic growth to the story of what mattered in the nineteenth century. The research pointing to the importance of cultural and religious values that I referred to in the introduction, chapters 6 through 9, and later in this conclusion, is of comparatively recent origin, and would not have informed (or in any event, clearly did not inform) the perspectives of some of those of the reigning paradigm. Their training either did not include this literature or, were they made aware of it, it did not persuade them, as it did me, to reconsider their assumption that jurists, like legislators and the populace as a whole, were inspired to alter rules by concerns with economic growth and prosperity.

But the timing of this newer body of research does not tell the whole story, for there were plenty of foreshadowings of the significance and importance of cultural values vis-à-vis economic ones in an earlier American historical literature. One thinks of the work of Whitney Cross, Alice Felt Tyler, indeed, of Perry Miller.[14] Our economic-oriented legal historians had plenty of opportunity to learn of the power of non-economic impulses in nineteenth-century America. They simply chose to give these impulses little weight.

Historians holding to such an economic-heavy perspective could and did find judicial language that appeared to constitute evidence of concerns with the economy. But a closer look at this language and its context, as well as a reading of cases drawn from a net cast much further into the legal currents of the nineteenth century, has seemed to me to provide a very different perspective. This one finds almost no judge-made changes inspired by concerns for the economy or economic efficiency. It finds a core of concern for continuity, for the "symmetry" of doctrines of property, tort, and contract, past and present. And it also finds considerable evidence of heartfelt willingness to change such rules as were deemed to be inhumane or inconsistent with equitable "benevolence."

It is possible, of course, to argue that those jurists who held to certain past precedents and principles were not so much doctrinal traditionalists as has been implied, inasmuch as their resistance to the innovation of jurists on other state high courts sometimes amounted to a kind of innovation of its own. The application of an old rule in a new context, it can be argued, could produce a result quite different from that which the original rule was intended to accomplish. Does this describe those who "held fast" to ancient lights, champerty, or the all-or-nothing rule in labor contracts? To argue that this was so would ignore the developmentalist role that the ancient-lights doctrine's time limit played, forcing the owner of vacant land to build. It would also require that we ignore arguments still extant in much of the rest of the common-law community of nations affirming the continuing good public policy reasons for the champerty and all-or-nothing rules. This view of precedent holding *may* describe those who refused to regard injured child trespassers as "invitees." The creators of the medieval rule regarding the low level of liability property owners owed to trespassers injured on their land had sinkholes and ditches in mind, knowing nothing of turntables, electrically charged wires, whirling cogwheels, or "inviting" swimming pools. Those who in the fin de siècle rejected the principled creation of the attractive-nuisance rule as a "mere legal fiction," in effect, relieved property owners of a duty in a way that the rule's medieval creators had not specifically intended. But we must not confuse slavish following of archaic rules by unimaginative men[15] with deliberate and subtle assistance to entrepreneurs. After all, other jurists treated as imprudent all trust investments other than those in land or government securities and refused to permit any "balancing of the equities" in pollution-nuisance cases (entr'acte). Yet both of these instances of doctrinal traditionalism ran against the interests of nineteenth-century American Capitalists.

Consider as well the judicial application in America of common-law rules against regrating, engrossing, and forestalling (think of them as "futures," "options," and "cornering"), rules that had been abrogated in Britain by two acts of Parliament in 1772 and 1824 as interfering with "a free trade" in commodities and discouraging the market's "growth."[16] Richard Posner argues that rules sanctioning "futures" and "options" are economically efficient, in that they give "people a stake in forecasting prices correctly" and "increase the amount of price information in the market."[17] I do not dispute his logic, but most nineteenth-century American jurists did. Futures or options contracts of the sort in which neither party intended to possess or use the commodities being traded (which is to say most of today's transactions) were declared void, since they were "against good public policy." Why? Because they tempted men to speculate beyond their means in "Wall Street gambling,"[18] they caused a "vast amount of misery and suffering," they were "demoralizing to the community," affecting "the humblest housekeeper,"[19] they might "agitate the markets," "derange prices to the detriment of the community," and "bring down financial ruin upon the heads of the unwary,"[20] and they rewarded the "unscrupulous speculator," "sharpers and blacklegs."[21] Justice T. Lyle Dickey of the Illinois Supreme Court *defended* an options contract between businessmen in the Chicago Board of Trade in 1876. They were necessary in "a large city" in the "competition in the trade in grain" in order to "secure to the producer an active market for his products." That was the purpose of the Board of Trade—to facilitate impersonal trading among men "without the trouble and time of inquiring as to their pecuniary responsibility."[22] This was the voice of Law and Economics, but it was the lone voice of dissent in a six-to-one vote *against* the legitimacy of the contract. A small handful of jurists spoke in the language of economic efficiency, but the rest spoke the ancient morality of the common law,[23] reminding their "new look" colleague of the South Sea Bubble, the Panic of 1873, and of "black Fridays."

The Jurisprudence of the Head may, occasionally, have served Capitalists' interests, inadvertently, but it just as often served to deny them what they sought. In any event, my belief is that those who were drawn to the defense of ancient doctrines threatened by other judicial innovators simply valued tradition more than their innovative compeers.

I included in the scope of my analysis a number of issues central to the law of contract, tort, and property, claims having been advanced regarding most of them by one or more economic-oriented legal historians. To these I added several "gatekeeper" rules as well as other issues that came to my attention in the course of my inquiries. Needless to say, though, there are many rules of common law and equity in the nineteenth century that I did not investigate. For example, I have only tentatively explored two issues in contract law: One is "undue influence" (a form of duress) which Kevin Teeven believes to have been raised in nineteenth-century American courts "to protect the weakened"; the other is "detrimental reliance." Teeven identifies those held to have relied to their detriment on promises not kept in nineteenth-century America as coming "frequently . . . from protected classes, such as charities, holders of an equity of redemption, debtors subject to large forfeitures, and employees making employment decisions." Teeven is somewhat tentative about the extent to which the rules regarding these defenses differed from English ones and cites only illustrative cases.[24] I have taken the questions no further. (One sometimes simply runs out of steam.) I welcome tests of my claims and invite others to report on whether their research does or doesn't uncover evidence of a Jurisprudence of the

Heart. It is perfectly possible that were one to explore an entirely different set of issues, or to focus on judicial treatment of family law or criminal law in these years, one might tell a very different story.

But I doubt it. Michael Grossberg's fine study of family law in the nineteenth century (*Governing the Hearth* [1985]) provides plenty of evidence of the same humane, child-centered propensities that I detected in both trust and tort law. The "best interest of the child" doctrine, for example, is a creature of the same era that produced the changes documented in chapters 7 and 8. Once again, a harsh English rule (*patria potestas*), treating the child in a separation case as being the virtual property of the father, whatever his moral qualities or capacities, was condemned by the aberrant English voice of humane innovation, Lord Denman, as a rule so repulsive "as to make all the judges ashamed of it."[25] And once again one hears American jurists quote the Bible and refer to "the deepest feelings of the human heart" in rejecting the *patria potestas* rule.[26]

Similarly, Marylynn Salmon has shown that chancellors in New York, Maryland, Virginia, and South Carolina created rules allowing married women to own property separate from their husbands. "Over time, the degree of independence granted to women in these jurisdictions increased," and by 1830 the right to control property and wages free from their husband's interference "was exercised with relative ease." Craig Klafter notes similar judicial innovations in Connecticut, New York, and Virginia protecting against wife beating and providing widows with a dower right of the equity of redemption of mortgaged property. Barbara Welke has shown that jurists applied negligence and contributory-negligence rules quite differently in suits involving accidents that took place while women were alighting from a vehicle, with female plaintiffs treated more solicitously than males.[27] The paternalistic legal culture of Victorian America favored women as well as children.

Similarly, we see evidence in the work of Kenneth Winkle and Amy Dru Stanley on vagrancy laws targeted on beggars in the 1820s and 1830s and the 1870s and 1880s (and in my own sortie into the subject of vagrancy ordinances for the years in the 1840s, 1850s, and 1890s) that judges in Massachusetts, Illinois, Ohio, New York, Georgia, North Carolina, Alabama, Pennsylvania, Michigan, and California were quite willing to "break new ground" to allow poor transients to relocate and claim poor relief, by voiding vagrancy laws as unconstitutional, or by releasing the alleged vagrant because of the inadequacy of the evidence or the failure of the constable, policeman, or magistrate to follow common-law rules and procedures.[28] In Allen Steinberg's study of the shift from private to public prosecutions in Phil-

304

adelphia's lower magistrate courts, 1800–1880, we see that appellate jurists "wedded to traditional legal culture, uneasy about the transformation of criminal justice" taking place, criticized the police when they acted without probable cause, warrants, or sworn accusations. And in A. E. Kier Nash's analysis of appellate review of murder convictions in the antebellum South, we learn that southern jurists showed no sympathy or favoritism toward whites convicted of murdering blacks.[29] We might find that a thorough analysis of appellate review of criminal cases in these years would provide further evidence of a judiciary guided by common-law rules and constitutional guarantees, but benign, perhaps even "humane," in "hard" cases. But I don't pretend to know anything particular on this score. As Kermit Hall says, "One of the ironies of contemporary American life is that . . . its historians know next to nothing about the evolution of substantive criminal law."[30] Perhaps someone more willing than I am to work her way through the reports to this end will address this challenge.

EXPLAINING THE JURISPRUDENCE OF THE HEART

And now we come to the knottiest issue. In the last six chapters I described something that I have come to call a Jurisprudence of the Heart.[31] You have met jurists who altered "obsolete," "inhumane" rules in order to provide "justice" for "poor" or "helpless" litigants, and you have noticed that, in the process, they sometimes referred to a biblical parable or offered words from "Christ's teachings" as a kind of authority for abandoning the older rules. I now want to try to explain their behavior. Explaining past human behavior (motivation, causality) is a lot harder than describing it. Often we must settle for tentative, alternative answers no matter how "thick" our description might be. I find myself in that dilemma and consequently must offer three explanations. No one of these is a "sufficient" one, but I believe that the sum of them is.

Explanation One: Procedural Reform

There are a number of potentially viable explanations for the observable propensity of jurists in a number of instances and jurisdictions to alter existing common-law rules to the advantage of relatively powerless plaintiffs. My first is largely technical, nonideological, in character: Perhaps the simplification of pleading, the abolition of the writ system, the merging of law and equity in the procedure reforms of the 1840s, 1850s, and 1860s, made it seem easier to some jurists to reach for equitable remedies to problems embedded in common-law rules. This *might* explain the toleration of quantum meruit recovery by jurists in some states in cases in which laborers quit "entire" contracts. But such procedural reform did not lead to the acceptance of quantum meruit recovery in one state that adopted it (Indiana) and did not hasten the acceptance of such recovery in the state that pioneered procedural reform (New York: though the continued separation of law and equity in New York may explain why New York did not move from the harsh English rule until a half century after the procedural code reforms). Procedural reform clearly explains the acceptability of third-party beneficiary suits in the Field Code states of New York, Kentucky, Indiana, West Virginia, Minnesota, and Missouri, but it does not explain why courts in the "code" states of North Carolina, Connecticut, Georgia, and Wyoming did not permit such suits.[32] We might find that it explains other innovations that I was unaware of. But, given its limitations, I can offer the increased access to equitable remedies only as a possible explanation for some of the changes produced by the Jurisprudence of the Heart; it might serve as a "necessary," but not as a "sufficient" explanatory cause, and it could not claim to explain very much; the difference between "code" and "noncode" states in the ratios of innovative/doctrinal rules that I computed (see table 3) are very slight (.62 versus .58). After all, procedural reforms were purely technical in nature, externally imposed on courts. Their existence or lack of existence does not mean that one jurist would approach any given issue differently from another jurist. In short, the facilitating nature of certain procedural innovations provided by legislatures says nothing of why jurist A might decide to use the new procedural code to alter rule X while jurist B might disagree, insisting that the legislature's reforms had provided no such authority.

Explanation Two: Distrust of Corporations and Democracy

Democracy, distrust of corporations, and the election of jurists by the mid-nineteenth century could well account for much of our Jurisprudence of the Heart. Furthermore, these historical phenomena may also explain why the Jurisprudence of the Heart appears to be regional—much stronger on the Great Plains, for example, than in Massachusetts, where jurists were still appointed, or late-nineteenth-century Pennsylvania, where corporations were politically powerful. Some state supreme courts behaved in decidedly doctrinal ways throughout the nineteenth century; others were more willing to innovate. This propensity can be depicted, as we saw in the maps in chapters 2 and 7. I will now depict it in aggregate fashion with appropriate caveats. I gave equal weight to each of twenty-nine instances of judicial innovation of one sort or another noted in this book,[33] and counted the number of times that the various supreme courts adopted either the doctrinal or innovative position (ignoring the "missing values" when a bench took no

TABLE 3. DOCTRINAL/INNOVATIVE RANK ORDERING OF SUPREME
COURTS BY AGGREGATE COUNT ON TWENTY-NINE ISSUES

Nebraska	(5–0)	1.00
Texas	(9–1)	.90
Kansas	(6–1)	.86
U.S.	(8–2)	.80
New Hampshire	(8–2)	.80
Oregon	(4–1)	.80
California	(9–3)	.75
Tennessee	(9–3)	.75
Illinois	(11–4)	.73
Arkansas	(5–2)	.71
Missouri	(11–5)	.70
Kentucky	(9–4)	.69
Indiana	(10–5)	.67
Georgia	(10–5)	.67
New York	(15–9)	.625
New Jersey	(10–6)	.625
Vermont and Iowa	(8–5)	.61
Connecticut	(11–7)	.61
Wisconsin	(9–6)	.60
Colorado	(9–6)	.60
Pennsylvania	(10–7)	.59
Virginia	(7–5)	.58
Mississippi	(4–3)	.57
Delaware and South Carolina	(5–4)	.55
Maryland	(6–5)	.54
Minnesota	(7–6)	.53
Michigan	(8–8)	.50
North Carolina	(3–3)	.50
Rhode Island	(5–5)	.50
Ohio	(7–8)	.47
Louisiana	(5–6)	.45
Alabama	(6–8)	.43
West Virginia	(2–3)	.40
Massachusetts	(6–16)	.27
Maine	(2–9)	.18
Total	(272–182)	.60

Note: Table shows ratio of innovative to total positions taken (minimum of five).

position on an issue, and counting courts only where they took at least five positions). This produced an aggregate rank ordering of these courts on a "degree of innovativeness" scale (see table 3).

This is, admittedly, a very crude measure, inasmuch as it treats each innovation as being of equal significance, ignores missing data, and equates innovations adopted by courts early in the century with those adopted by other courts much later.[34] Hence I claim no more for it than that it is *suggestive* of the regional variation that seems to emerge (see map 3). But as it seems to confirm what we thought we "knew" about the doctrinal Northeast and innovative West, I offer it up.

There are a few surprises, or, at least I found them surprising. First, once a high court decided to reject a doctrine, some 60 percent of the other high courts eventually followed suit. This does not negate the propensity of all these courts to hold to many other English rules, something I have pointed out in chapter 1. But it does indicate that, once the floodgate was opened, the current that constituted the Jurisprudence of the Heart was strong enough to draw in the benches of a majority of the states. Second, the U.S. Supreme Court proved to be quite willing to adopt as its own a substantial number of these common-law innovations. Inasmuch as the court's composition generally reflected the nation as a whole, though, this propensity does not seem terribly surprising. Third, a few courts do not follow the Northeast-versus-the-rest axis—among them, New Hampshire, Louisiana, Alabama, and Minnesota.[35] But the basic pattern seems plausible. Moreover, while I found no more than three positions taken by any of the nine remaining state courts that existed in nineteenth-century America (Florida [3–0], South Dakota [3–0], Utah [3–0], Nevada [2–1], North Dakota [2–0], Idaho [2–0], Washington [2–0], Montana [1–1], and Wyoming [1–0]), if one adds up all of these positions, the result (19 innovative positions, 2 doctrinal ones) is clearly consistent with the pattern depicted in map 3, and would result in most of the blank portions of this map appearing just as it does now: white or lightly shaded, confirming the pattern I have described.

The East-West/Head-Heart distinction is also evident in such "impressionistic" evidence as the observations of attorney Henry Strong concerning the pre-bench career of U.S. Supreme Court justice Samuel Miller from the Field Code state of Iowa: Strong had come from Harvard Law, where he had been "taught to practice most strictly upon the *stare decisis* theory of the law, and to yield unquestionably to the weight of authority . . . , departing only far enough to admit that where the numbers were nearly equal, the judgements of Justice Shaw [of Massachusetts], and such as he, were

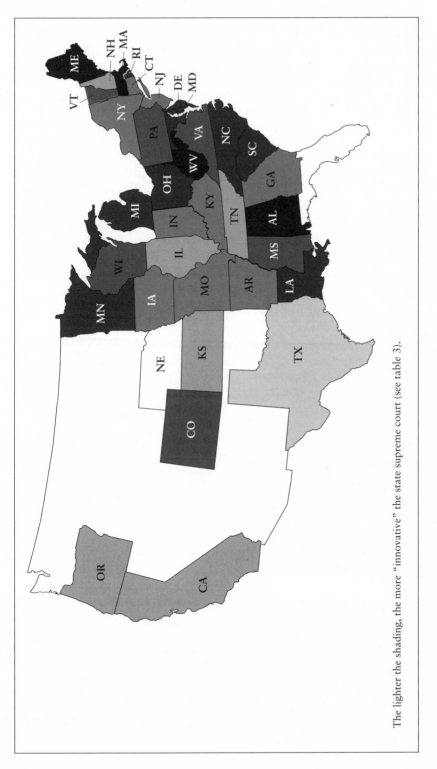

The lighter the shading, the more "innovative" the state supreme court (see table 3).

MAP 3. DOCTRINAL/INNOVATIVE STATE SUPREME COURTS

entitled to special consideration." Justice Miller's method in the 1850s in Iowa, however, "was to cite few cases, but to impress the court with the reason of the law." His "terseness in pleading particularly impressed me. A page of legal cap written in an open hand would have been for him a long declaration or answer. . . . He grasped at once the theory of the code of practice then in vogue." According to his biographer, Charles Fairman, Justice Miller's jurisprudence was just as down-to-earth. He was "more concerned with the practical result of a decision than its doctrinal basis." As such, he was "disposed to let no technicalities stand in the way of what seemed right and just." He was also inclined to think that jurists from his region were the most likely innovative leaders of the future. In 1879 he boasted in the *Albany Law Journal* that the "future Marshalls and Mansfields" to "arise and give new impulses and add new honor to the profession of the law" would be "from some western prairie town."[36] (Roscoe Pound was born in Nebraska in 1870; Leon Green in western Louisiana in 1888; Earl Warren in southern California in 1891; William O. Douglas in Minnesota in 1896; Roger Traynor in Utah in 1900.)

We see further confirmation of this pattern in data on personal injury suits against railroads in the appellate record for the first quarter of 1875. The contrast between doctrinally conservative New England, on the one hand, and the more innovative federal and western state courts, on the other, is striking. Suffering only 15.4 percent of the nation's serious railroad accidents, the West produced 30 percent of all the appellate cases of serious personal injury caused by railroads heard in the first quarter of 1875, whereas New England, with 5.8 percent of the nation's serious railroad accidents, produced only 4.5 percent of cases heard on appeal. Something was encouraging appeals in the West and discouraging them in New England. Of these appealed cases, plaintiffs had won at the trial level only 37.5 percent of the time (six of sixteen) in New England, whereas they had won in 82 percent (forty-six of fifty-six) of the western and federal trials.[37] Thus we can surmise that plaintiffs who lost in New England saw little point in going through the time, risk, and expense of an appeal; whereas it was *corporate defendants* in the western and federal courts who saw little to be gained by hazarding the appellate process. They had less fear in New England of that region's Westminster-facing jurists.

And we can also find confirmation of the regional character of this division of Heart against Head in the votes of members of the U.S. Supreme Court on the three occasions between 1884 and 1904 when they chose to speak on the question of the existence and scope of a "superior servant" exception to the fellow-servant rule in the federal courts.[38] In *Chicago & Mil-*

waukee RR v. *Ross* (1884) the court narrowly adopted the "liberal" (Ohio and Kentucky) version of this exception, finding a conductor to be the superior servant of a fireman. Justice Stephen J. Field wrote the majority opinion; the court divided five to four. Nine years later in *Baltimore and Ohio Railroad* v. *Baugh* (1893), the court backed away from *Ross*; Justice Field and Chief Justice Fuller dissented, Field with great force and passion. And in 1904 (in *Northern Pacific RR* v. *Dixon*) the court again divided narrowly, five to four, in upholding their position in *Baugh*.[39] Had we predicted the voting patterns of the individual Supreme Court membership from the figures in table 3, we would have done very well indeed. In these divisions, all those justices appointed from the basically doctrinal courts of Massachusetts (Gray and Holmes), New York (Blatchford and Peckham), Pennsylvania (Shiras), Michigan (Brown), and New Jersey (Bradley) voted for the harsher, narrow rule. All those from the more "liberal" courts of California (Field and McKenna), Iowa (Miller), Kentucky (Harlan), Illinois (Fuller), and Georgia (Woods) voted for the broader, Ohio-Kentucky superior servant exception. Those from Ohio (Waite, Day, and Matthews) divided, and those from Kansas and Louisiana (Brewer and White) voted in a fashion inconsistent with the general patterns set in their respective state courts over the century. If we assign to each vote a figure corresponding to the ratio I derived for table 3 and then compute an aggregate figure for the two groups, we find that despite the two exceptions (David Brewer and Edward White), the "liberal" justices came from states with ratios 20 percent higher, in aggregate, on the "innovative"-"doctrinal" scale, than those of the "doctrinal" justices. The U.S. Supreme Court's membership in the late nineteenth century appears, generally, to have reflected the views on the fellow servant rule of the state supreme courts from which its membership had been appointed, though this is only a tendency.

Walter Prescott Webb's "Great Plains" thesis may be of some utility here. As we saw in the fight over the attractive-nuisance rule, western and New South courts simply did not feel as constrained by English precedent as those from the original thirteen colonies. They often simply lacked *access* to both English reports and their imitative counterparts from Massachusetts and New York. Thus we find complaints by attorneys in Louisiana in the early nineteenth century and in California during the Gilded Age of the lack of both case reports and treatises. And we hear jurists in Iowa and Colorado admitting "to the profession" that their "access to [law] books is very limited." Gordon Bakken has pointed out in this regard that California's Supreme Court "gave absolutely no legal citations" in some 40 percent of the contract cases they decided between 1850 and 1890.[40] It was hard to be a formalist in the Age of Formalism if you had to render the law as you recalled it. In such surroundings, a jurist might willy-nilly invent some law, just as one of their neighbors had invented barbed wire to range in cattle.

Moreover, popular views *were* represented on the bench: the western and New South jurists were elected whereas the courts of some of the older states (Massachusetts and South Carolina, and for much of the period, Virginia as well) retained appointed judiciaries. By 1855 the legislatures of fifteen of the twenty-nine existing states had mandated short-term election of jurists, and thereafter all newly created states, as well as some of the older ones, followed suit.[41] Jurists whose opinions appeared inhumane or insensitive to children or the poor could be voted out of office, as the case of California's Justice William Van Fleet, described in the previous chapter, indicates, whereas those responsive to the child-centered culture of mid-nineteenth-century America were drawn to alter the common-law rule regarding the imputation of parental contributory negligence to tots injured by negligent drivers in the streets (chapter 8) and to evade the common-law rule of trespass via a legal fiction in order to help protect children "drawn" to dangerous objects that caused them injury (chapter 7).

Furthermore, we know that, even when jurists were appointed by governors, the perspective of candidates could be weighed in a political balance scale that sometimes tipped against corporate interests, as when Wisconsin's Granger-elected Governor William R. Taylor sought a chief justice in 1874 "who is instinctively in sympathy with the people as against aggregated capital and oppressive monopolies."[42] Jurists chosen because their values were consistent with those of the antirailroad Granger movement, or the humanitarian reform impulse were *expected* to protect "producers" against "Capitalists,"[43] fugitives against slave catchers, children against careless drivers, the "ordinary people" against the rich and powerful. We should not be surprised by the innovations wrought by men such as John Forrest Dillon, Frank Doster, Seymour Thompson, Abram Smith, Thomas Durfee, or David Wagner.

Explanation Three: Religion, Culture, and Politics

America in the nineteenth century experienced several sorts of development simultaneously. As Europeans and Canadians continued to emigrate to the newly created United States and as families grew, the population rose from four million in 1790 to forty million in 1870. With the acquisition of the Louisiana Territory, Florida, Texas, Oregon Territory, California, and the Southwest, the land mass of the nation more than doubled between 1803 and 1853. Outputs of grain, livestock, coal, iron, glassware, lumber, and clothing rose at varying rates greater than that of the population's increase. Gross farm output rose elevenfold between 1800 and 1880. Pig-iron output rose by fifteenfold between 1810 and 1860.[44] Railways, canals, and steamboats serviced the new nation. The economy was growing.

But there was another development unfolding in these years that is too often ignored, a religious development. Between 1780 and 1860 the number of religious congregations in the United States rose from some twenty-five hundred to over fifty-two thousand, a twenty-one-fold increase, nearly three times greater than the rate of population increase in the same period. Churches, especially evangelical churches, were being built by Christian communities everywhere and church attendance was rising. By the mid-1850s at least 40 percent of the total population were evangelical churchgoers.[45]

Moreover, this was no pro forma phenomenon. A generation of fresh scholarship has demonstrated that antebellum Americans, as individuals as well as congregations, were "awash in a sea of faith." They read religious tracts, they joined Bible societies, they taught Sunday school classes, and they read "the good book." For many the Bible was as important as institutionalized religion. One wrote that he had "applied" his "heart to get wisdom from God" in daily sorties into "the Scripture." Another spoke of the Bible as "a book dropped from the skies for all sort of men to use in their own way."[46] Some legal historians have drawn attention to the emphasis given by some jurists to individual responsibility: Agreements made between free persons were to be honored; injuries caused by negligence was to be compensated.[47] These sorts of republican-liberal ethics counted, to be sure. But note also that Nathan Hatch, a religious historian, speaks of "the individualization of conscience" in antebellum America.[48] Americans were increasingly concerned with the welfare of their souls, increasingly in search of "God's grace."[49]

Many, especially members of evangelical churches, were also concerned with the welfare of the souls of others. Slavery was sinful; drinking led to intemperate behavior and disrupted family life. And concern for the spirit was often joined with concern for the body. Cruelty toward children, wives, sailors, prisoners, animals, and slaves was inhumane. Christianity had a role to play, Reverend Elias Magoon argued in *Republican Christianity* (1849), as the "fortifier of the weak, the deliverer of the oppressed." It must "work for the millions rather than for aristocratic cliques."[50] Benevolent societies sprang up, organized by evangelical men and women, targeting one after the other of these customs and norms.

Many found politics and legislation the most effective means of changing the rules.[51] Evangelical Christians found early voices in the Whig, Liberty, American, and Free-Soil Parties and were the leaders of the Republican Party. Whereas less than 30 percent of eligible voters participated in the political process in the election of 1824, over 80 percent of those eligible voted in 1840, and that level of activity persisted for decades thereafter.[52] For those unable to vote, there remained the petition to legislators as the political statement in aid of temperance, children, or slaves. In this regard, note the dichotomy that Sarah Blake drew in a letter to Maria Weston Chapman in 1842 regarding her decision to sign Chapman's antislavery petition: "I was strongly tempted to sign it when you sent it, but . . . if I had done so at that time, it would have been done with my HEAD and not my heart, and now I do it with real delight."[53]

By 1890 some thirty-seven of forty-two state constitutions "acknowledged the authority of God in preambles or main articles." Most legislatures required that Protestant Bibles be used in public schools. As one Presbyterian minister put it in 1895: "Christianity in a proper sense is the established religion of this nation; established, not by statute law, it is true, but by a law equally valid, the law in the nature of things, the law of necessity."[54]

The studies I alluded to in the introduction demonstrate that American political parties from the 1820s through the 1890s were primarily reflections of the moral issues and perceptions of the day with divisions largely along religious lines, not those of class. In the words of a convert to this perspective, "Class-consciousness and economic radicalism were shallow and ephemeral characteristics of the electorate. . . . The mass of American voters . . . were prompted . . . primarily by ethno-cultural values, mostly religious and sectarian in their roots."[55] In 1856 one of Pennsylvania governor William Bigler's correspondents argued that "moral questions have much more to do with elections than formerly. . . . The development of principles draw after them the religious and moral feelings of the people." As another put it in the same year, "Our Protestant laws and constitution need Protestant officers to enforce and execute them."[56]

This political world elevated to supreme courts the jurists that this book concerns. Most state jurists were selected by governors, before the election of judges began in the 1840s and 1850s. As late as 1860 jurists in ten of thirty-four states were appointed; the rest were elected. A few western jurists, carryovers from prestate, territorial status, as well as all federal jurists, earned their appointments, politically, from the president and their districts' congressmen. But whether selected or elected, they were more or less chosen in a "political" process. Consequently, it would be very surprising if they did not reflect some of those moral and religious perspectives to be found in that political process. How much do we know about that selection process?[57]

A few political historians have identified the process of selecting antebellum federal jurists as well as candidates for supreme courts in New York, Ohio, and Pennsylvania in the 1850s and 1890s, and have given some attention to those contests. Antebellum federal appointees were often judged by the president and Senate on how they might rule in highly political, but also "moral," cases involving fugitive slaves. In 1835 Indiana's Judge Jesse Holman, a lay Baptist minister and antislavery Democrat who was accused by one of his foes of being "a fanatic on the subject of slavery . . . and religion," assured President Andrew Jackson that he had enforced, and would continue to enforce the terms of the federal Fugitive Slave Act of 1793. He was confirmed by the Senate, whereas Ohio's Benjamin Tappan, another Jackson nominee, incapable of persuading the Senate that he would do so, was not. Later, in 1858, President Buchanan's nominee for the federal district court for eastern Pennsylvania, John Cadwalader, was referred to as "one of the old school of 'black-letter lawyers' " by Horace Greeley's *New York Tribune*, which clearly feared that Cadwalader would enforce the Fugitive Slave Act of 1850. This, however, was the very virtue that recommended Cadwalader to a majority of Senators.[58]

Federal jurists were appointed; by the 1850s most state jurists were elected, and in these contests it is clear that the prior political positions taken by these candidates, and not any unspoken views they may have held on existing rules of common law or equity, led to their nomination and subsequent success or failure. But one's politics could serve as a crude voter's guide to how one could be expected, generally, to behave on the bench. As an Ohio constitutional convention delegate put it in 1850, jurists forced to stand for election or reelection would "take care that their opinions reflect justice and right, because they cannot stand upon any other bases."[59] James Campbell was chosen by the Democrats in Pennsylvania to run for a seat on the state's supreme court in 1851 because he commanded the loyalties of Philadelphia's Catholic voters. Bradford Wood was nominated for a seat on the court of appeals by the newly formed Republicans in New York in 1855 because, as a "Dry," he was "right" on new temperance legislation. Jacob Brinkerhoff appealed to most Republican leaders in Ohio in 1856 as a candidate for supreme court because he was "right" on nativist, temperance, and antislavery issues. As New York's deputy attorney general, Isaac Maynard had orchestrated measures to gain Democratic control of the state senate; this led to his nomination to run for a seat on the Court of Appeals in 1893.[60]

In any event, these elections for state high court seats largely followed

315

party lines, and these reflected religious differences, as William Gienapp's data for the Ohio and Pennsylvania races demonstrate;[61] they were not contests between jurists taking positions on the wisdom of rules of common law and equity, with voters deciding between conflicting views.[62] But that was still enough popular influence to make it likely that men of the "right" moral persuasion would make it to the nation's benches. And thus I was not surprised to come upon abolitionists indicating that they hoped "the Judges of the land" would find ways to end slavery.[63] Similarly, I was not surprised to see that when Judge Benjamin F. Wade of the Third Judicial Circuit was elected to the Senate from Ohio in 1850 his victory was attributed to the fact that he had denounced as "infamous" the Fugitive Slave Act of 1850 and had sworn not to obey it. Nor was I surprised to see that Byron Paine was elected to the Wisconsin Supreme Court in the wake of *Abelman v. Booth* in 1859 despite his youth and the greater experience of his opponent, William Lynde, because Paine had presented the brief for Booth, had been endorsed by the *Milwaukee Sentinel*, an antislavery bastion, and had (in the words of Senator Charles Sumner) campaigned "on the issue distinctly presented," the Fugitive Slave Act of 1850 and "State's Rights." Indeed, when U.S. Supreme Court justice John McLean became a serious candidate for the presidential nomination of the new Republican Party in 1856, it was said of this future *Dred Scott* dissenter that "he is a pet of the Methodists & it might help him to a good many votes."[64]

In short, given the political perspectives of nineteenth-century American voters, why should it be in the least surprising that the men their leaders nominated (and they elected) to seats on the nation's high courts would quote from the Bible from time to time in support of their rulings? These were men of the times; attuned, to one degree or another, to evangelical reform impulses and humanitarian movements. And they were not mouthing platitudes; they were speaking from their hearts.

Virtually nothing in the past is as simple as it seems though. A jurist chosen to represent one perspective sometimes finds that he had to disappoint the powers that placed him on the Bench. (One thinks of Chief Justice Salmon P. Chase's opinion in *Hepburn v. Griswold* [1870], declaring unconstitutional the very Legal Tender Act that he had sponsored as secretary of the treasury in 1862,[65] or of Chief Justice Earl Warren's remarkably unexpected opinions and leadership in the 1950s and 1960s.) Surely there were many antislavery leaders and voters in the 1840s and 1850s who found distressing the deference to both statutory and constitutional language, on the one hand, and the principle of comity (respect for southern laws) on the other, displayed by some of those whom they had placed on state and federal benches. A case in point, as Robert Cover demonstrated, was Joseph Swan, Ohio's Chief Justice in 1859. His opinion, for the majority, in *Ex Parte Bushnell, Ex Parte Langston*[66] upheld the application and enforcement of the punitive terms of the federal Fugitive Slave Act of 1850 in Ohio. Despite Swan's antislavery sentiments, which had led to his election to the court and his concurrence in *Anderson v. Poindexter* (1856), the sojourner-slave case mentioned in the introduction to this book, in the Bushnell and Langston cases he found himself unable to overcome his profession's rules: Jurists were not to ignore clear statutory mandates, constitutional terms, precedents, and general principles such as comity. Thus in *Ex Parte Bushnell* Swan appears to be a clear exception to the picture I have painted. But he is the proverbial exception that proves the rule, for his views were rejected by the Ohio Republican electorate, who did not renominate him,[67] whereas his colleagues, Jacob Brinkerhoff and J. Milton Sutliff, *dissenters* in *Ex Parte Bushnell*, won applause. And note Brinkerhoff's dicta: He refused to regard the question of fugitive slaves as having been "settled," either by the Fugitive Slave Act, the U.S. Supreme Court's opinions in *Dred Scott v. Sanford* (1857) or *Ableman v. Booth* (1859),[68] or by the Ohio court's decision in *Ex Parte Bushnell*. "When it is settled right, then it will be settled, and not till then." These were "my opinions, freely declared before I had the honor of a seat on this bench," and they remained his opinions. Moreover, the sole dissenter in the earlier Poindexter case had been Chief Justice Thomas Bartley, a Democrat who in 1860 supported John Breckenridge, the southern Democrats' candidate for president.[69]

It seems to me that those loyal to the Whig and Republican Parties proved to be the more willing to bend rules to accomplish some of these ends when the right opportunity presented itself in a doctrinal or a "situation-sense" argument. Perhaps Pietists, evangelicals, the voices of "public morality" were more comfortable with a Jurisprudence of the Heart than those of liturgical faiths, who tended to identify with the Democratic Party. The former might feel that "the facts of the case," or perhaps "bad law" embedded in an ancient rule, required that they formulate a means within the common law to provide "justice"; the latter might have been more inclined to signal in dicta that while "the law" did at times fail to reflect certain "imperatives of the moral order," that was a matter for the legislature to address: they were bound to defer to the existing rule. But Jacksonian Democratic jurists had few qualms about abandoning the ancient ban on contingency-fee contracts (champerty); they were uncomfortable with any interference with one's liberty to contract. And they were often suspicious of legal claims advanced by corporations, and consequently open to such anticorporate innovations in tort law as were described in chapters 7, 8, and 9.

In any event, it was probably no coincidence that the most doctrinal judiciary, that of Massachusetts, was also the only one that was never to subject jurists to the test of popular election in the entire century. (Yet even there we can find evidence that the popular test was intended to achieve accountability. When the question of an elected judiciary was considered in Massachusetts in 1853, support for the idea among antislavery advocates reflected their desire that the court "reflect the values of the people.")[70] Some jurists elected to the high courts of the other states may have been inspired to draw new equitable rules from their "hearts" rather than following their common law "heads" because they faced reelection and sought a popular mandate. But all had been chosen as candidates for the bench by their parties in the first place and may have been selected because, in addition to their experience and skills, they seemed predisposed to behave with imagination and compassion toward fugitive slaves, farm debtors, and temperance activists, but with rectitude and a concern for "the public good" toward factory owners and railroad barons. These selection criteria were important, but we are ultimately reduced to speaking of individual jurists and of "courts" (small groups of those individuals).

I do not want to pursue this potential Republican-Democratic distinction any further. Others may want to test the hypothesis; I am content to draw attention more generally to the religious, egalitarian, and humanitarian roots of the Jurisprudence of the Heart.

Ultimately, however, it was the views and values of individual jurists that mattered. A state high court might, *in general*, be doctrinal, but one or two of its members might regularly speak for change in dissent. And vice versa. (David Brewer's brief tenure on the Kansas Supreme Court fits this pattern, as does the career of West Virginia's Justice Marmaduke Dent.)[71] Moreover, the collective behavior of state high courts sometimes changed in the nineteenth century. The Pennsylvania bench of the 1850s and 1860s, led by such humane figures as Daniel Agnew, was very different from the court in 1886 that finally denied Mrs. Sanderson her award of damages from Pennsylvania Coal Company.

In any event, I repeat that it is the individual jurists who mattered, more than their state's economic problems or religious proclivities. After all, most jurists on the courts of the Midwest, West, and New South were born and trained elsewhere. Simply consider Louisiana's great antebellum leader, Francois Xavier Martin, born in France, with experience in North Carolina's courts, or Tennessee's respected Chief Justice Robert McKinney, a Scots-Irish immigrant. They brought values and perspectives shaped thousands of miles away to the courts of Louisiana and Tennessee.[72]

I have already singled out (in chapter 7) a number of jurists who "mattered" with regard to the struggle over the attractive-nuisance rule: Lord Denman, the leading voice of change among English jurists of the nineteenth century; John Forrest Dillon of the Iowa and federal courts; Seymour Thompson, Dillon's master in chancery, judge of the St. Louis Court of Appeals, and treatise writer; Frank Doster, the Populist chief justice of the Kansas Supreme Court; the doctrinal scholar/jurist, Jeremiah Smith; the disappointing "utilitarian," Oliver Wendell Holmes Jr.; and the "larmoyant" humane dissenter in *Britt*, John Clarke. As we have seen, Lord Denman, Dillon, Thompson, and Holmes figure in other of our stories as well, with the same results. In my account of the struggle over quantum meruit recovery in cases in which workers quit entire contracts, I drew particular attention to New Hampshire's Chief Justice Joel Parker. To the innovative and humane examples of Dillon, Doster, and Parker, I would especially add Justice Abram Smith of Wisconsin, Justice Daniel Agnew of Pennsylvania, Justice David Wagner of Missouri, Chief Justice Charles Lawrence of Illinois, Chief Justice Thomas Durfee of Rhode Island, Chief Justice George Robertson of Kentucky, Chief Justice Robert McKinney of Tennessee, and perhaps Chief Justice Isaac Redfield of Vermont, Justices W. W. Ellsworth and Roger M. Sherman of Connecticut, and treatise writers Joel Bishop and Francis Wharton as well. These men seem generally to have rejected the law's "symmetry" for what they believed to be its more irregularly (heart-)shaped "justice."

Knowing of a jurist's prebench political career, of his efforts as a Congressman or legislator to spur economic growth, merely provides *clues* as to how he was to behave once on the bench. Chief Justice Sidney Breese of Illinois is a case in point. A Democrat, Breese served in the U.S. Senate in the 1840s. There he successfully promoted a land grant for the Illinois Central Railroad, something of which he remained immensely proud. He was described in 1849 by Congressman Jacob Brinkerhoff of Ohio as "a cold-hearted, dough-faced [pro-Southern] scoundrel." Later, as an Illinois Supreme Court jurist, he wrote one of the three opinions rejecting the rule of *Britton* v. *Turner* allowing the payment of quantum meruit to a hired hand who had quit. He also authored the opinion that set aside as excessive an award of $5,750 in 1858 to a man injured at a railroad crossing: "He saw and heard the locomotive; he had time to get down and take his horses by the head, as prudent men do every day even when plowing in the fields, on the approach of a locomotive. . . . The plaintiff did not attempt to do anything, but sat in his wagon, wrapped in his buffalo-skin, whipping his horses, sawing their mouths with the reins and bits."

Yet for all the scolding tone of this passage, Breese found only that the man had been *comparatively* negligent, allowing him access to the jury in a rehearing, holding here only that the company had not been *willful* in its tortfeasance.[73] And in other opinions Breese upheld the state's regulation of the grain warehouse elevator companies, established a superior-servant exception to the fellow-servant rule for a laborer "so subordinate" to a foreman "as to compel him to yield implicit obedience," scolded negligent contractors ruthlessly, and criticized the agents of the CB&Q Railroad as "heartless" for their lackadaisical behavior while fighting a fire caused by sparks from a locomotive's stack. Railroad companies "ought to be bound to use the greatest precautions." Breese expressed revulsion at the thought that "a railroad company acting under a charter granted by this state should be so lost to all the calls of benevolence and kindness—to all the common instincts of the most ordinary humanity." In another case, the reckless management of a train by an engineer of the Illinois Central led to the death of a brakeman, and Chief Justice Breese spoke for the court in holding the company liable for retaining an incompetent servant. He added this suggestion: "Why should not railroad companies . . . institute and keep inquisitorial exams, periodically, among the . . . employees so that the unfit be condemmed and discharged, and thus afford some protection to the countless lives . . . committed daily to their care?"[74]

Breese was active in securing railway services for Illinois, but he was not willing to see those or any other corporate services managed at the expense of individual rights. His opinions reflect "the rule of law" and Judeo-Christian values; as such, those opinions will not be of much use to an economic determinist, of whatever stripe.

Of course most jurists left ambivalent trails of appellate opinion. Some have styled Thomas M. Cooley "conservative" because of his views on substantive due process and "liberty of contract." That label tells us very little. The fact that Cooley remained a Jacksonian in his respect for personal rights also means that he distrusted corporations. In his influential *Treatise on Constitutional Limitations* (1868), he spoke with alarm of the "enormous and threatening powers" of corporations. It was not an afterthought or the product of a recent conversion. As editor of the *Watchtower* in 1853, at the age of twenty-nine, he had criticized James Joy, president of the Michigan Central Railroad, and warned of the railroad's influence in the state. One of his editorials in that year, "The Age—Steam," warned of fascination with things mechanical. They could produce a "breaking up, not only of legs and heads," but of families as well: "Men and women now, like the hissing locomotive, must and will be on the *move*. . . . We must see to it that the moral sense of society is not wholly diseased as by the madness of steam!"

As a jurist, Cooley was no mere prairie Populist when applying common-law rules to railroads, but his earlier views clearly counted. They crop up in such dicta as his reference to the "moral obligations" railroads ought "in common humanity to recognize and provide for, whether required by law to do so or not."[75] Breese, Cooley, and other nonpietistic jurists with "conservative" perspectives displayed the same decidedly humane propensities that we have seen in men like Agnew, McKinney, Dillon, and Doster often enough to question whether we should not be using a more politically neutral term, or a more accurate cultural one, to describe such jurists.

That leaves us with those essentially "doctrinal" jurists, those who seemed consistently wedded to English precedent, who seem utterly "bound" by common-law "principles," utterly wedded to a Jurisprudence of the Head. Yet even the efforts of these men serve at times to illustrate the force of "humanity" as a judicial norm in nineteenth-century America. Far from being cold allies of corporate defendants, these jurists were the products of the same morally charged, child-oriented culture as their more innovative compeers. Thus Jeremiah Smith, while a professor at Harvard Law at the turn of the century, made it a habit each year, "after showing how few positive acts were demanded by law," to have his students "read the last part of the twenty-fifth chapter of Matthew ["I was hungry and ye gave me meat"] and thus to call to mind the obligations above and beyond law."[76] Hence they sometimes agonized over "hard" decisions they felt compelled to render that went against plaintiffs whose plight aroused their sympathies.

John Phillip Reid draws our attention to one such doctrinal spokesman, New Hampshire's Justice Alonzo Carpenter, whom he contrasts with Charles Doe, that court's chief justice. Doe himself was no Populist humanitarian. He condemned the "confiscating" propensity of anticorporate legal voices from "the West and South" and worried about attacks on property rights in his own state. He limited his reading, according to his landlady, to the *London Times*, a steady source of information on English legal opinion. Yet he was not as wedded to precedent as his colleague, Carpenter, a man later eulogized as one who "undertook to do no more than to interpret the law," who "believed in following established precedent absolutely no matter what the result might be."[77] As a young attorney, Alonzo Carpenter had excelled at special pleading while in practice in partnership with his father-in-law. His fellow doctrinal jurist, Jeremiah Smith, remembered him as a "worshipper of the Year Books." Justice Carpenter lived simply; he never took a vacation. Appointed to the New Hampshire Supreme Court in 1881, he was named its chief justice in 1896 after Doe's death.[78]

What caught my attention were the sentiments that Professor Reid offered from one of Carpenter's letters to Smith in 1898, shortly before Carpenter's death. Chief Justice Carpenter had just written an opinion denying recovery to a child seriously injured in a factory accident. "The case has caused me great anxiety," Carpenter wrote. "I have felt oppressed . . . by the humanitarian aspect."[79] Reid provided no further information about this subject. Curious, I read the New Hampshire reports for the term preceding this letter to try to identify the case that so distressed Carpenter. It was *Buch* v. *Amory Manufacturing Company*. Eight-year-old Carl Buch had been taken to a textile factory by his thirteen-year-old brother, who worked there in March of 1886. For a day and a half Carl helped his brother, a "back boy" in a mule-spinning room, until his hand was mangled in the gearing of the mule-spinner. Upon coming of legal age, he sued the company. Evidence that the foreman knew of the boy's presence was disputed by the company. Chief Justice Carpenter's opinion, for the court, turned the young man away. He had been a trespasser, and, as such, the company was not responsible. Carpenter explained the law: The defendants were "not liable unless they owed to the plaintiff a legal duty which they neglected to perform. With purely moral obligations the law does not deal." He offered both biblical and modern examples:

> The priest and Levite who passed by on the other side were not, it is supposed, liable at law for the continued suffering of the man who fell among thieves, which they might, and morally ought to have, prevented, or relieved. Suppose A, standing close by a railroad, sees a 2 year-old babe on the track, and a car approaching. He can easily rescue the child, with entire safety to himself, and the instincts of humanity require him to do so. If he does not, he may, perhaps, justly be styled a ruthless savage and a moral monster; but he is not liable in damages for the child's injury.[80]

Carpenter's anguish is evident. One less wedded to precedent might have found that the lad had been an "invitee," entitled to more attention from the foreman than he received, that he had assumed no risks, or that the machinery had been "attractive" to the child; Carpenter ruled that the attractive-nuisance cases "have no application here," but not because he callously favored business defendants.[81] This "worshipper of the Year Books" was simply unable to do anything more daring than to scold the company's management quite indirectly for having supervisory policies that allowed the boy to have been placed by his brother in harm's way. They might have had a moral duty to detect such child trespassers, but "the law" had not made that a legal duty, and Carpenter's lifelong concern had been with "the law."

So be it. But note the source of Carpenter's anguish: His legal culture was at war with his Judeo-Christian culture. He felt compelled to retell the biblical parable of the man who fell among thieves. A formalist such as Carpenter was moved by the same Christian moral dictates as were his less doctrinal compeers. With the possible exception of a few skeptical Unitarians such as Holmes, virtually all jurists in nineteenth-century America were believing Christians, and for many, these beliefs were sufficiently important at times to affect their judicial opinions. When this imbalance of power between the individual plaintiff and corporate defendant impressed jurists with the need to bend a rule one way or the other to correct this imbalance, sometimes the issue was more purely of an egalitarian than a moral/religious one. But on balance, I count religious convictions as accounting for somewhat more of the innovative propensity of jurists than purely secular, anticorporate ones. There is nothing necessarily dichotomous about the two; opinions that offered biblical authority in justification often offered as well a public policy critique of corporate "Capitalists." But I stand by my emphasis on religious convictions as the prime source of the Jurisprudence of the Heart. After all, long before jurists were being elected, they were finding inspiration in Judeo-Christian values. Pennsylvania's Justice Hugh Henry Brackenridge would call "the law of God" the "ground of the common law" in 1814, and in 1833 a former chief justice of the Vermont Supreme Court, Nathaniel Chipman, compared the *Sic utere tuo* rule ("So use your own right, that you injure not the rights of others") to the rule "emphantically expressed in that Command,—'Thou shalt love thy neighbor as thyself.' " It was said of Pennsylvania's Justice J. Richard Coulter, the author of the Pennsylvania Supreme Court's defense of those who aided fugitive slaves (*Kaufmann* v. *Oliver*) and a devout Presbyterian, that "his influence was on the side of religion and morality." William Strong, son of a Presbyterian minister, served as an antislavery congressman from Pennsylvania before his election to that state's supreme court, and later, after being named to the U.S. Supreme Court, he presided over the National Association of Presbyterian Churches' assembly with an agenda to help make "Christ's will as the supreme law of the land." Justice John Marshall Harlan Jr., who represented the government in the civil rights case, *U.S.* v. *Reece* in the federal circuit court in Kentucky 1873, and was later the great champion of civil rights on the U.S. Supreme Court, maintained that nothing the Bible commanded could "be safely or properly disregarded" and nothing it "condemn[ed] [could] be justified."[82]

Historians today signally fail to comprehend the legal culture of nineteenth-century America when they treat remarks of this sort casually. Just as the century's political parties reflected the deeply felt moral and religious perspectives of their constituencies, so too did the century's courts. The tension between the doctrines of the taught legal tradition and those of John Forrest Dillon's "Heavenly Dreamer of the Galilean Hills," the tension between Head and Heart, between symmetry and justice, is the key to understanding the judiciary and its alterations to the common law in nineteenth-century America. We ought to make more use of that key, to explore more of that tension, for there are more tales to tell of these two voices.

Notes

INTRODUCTION

1. Charles Haar, *The Golden Age of American Law* (New York: G. Braziller, 1965); Bernard Schwartz, "The Golden Age," in *Main Currents in American Legal Thought* (Durham, N. C.: Carolina Academic Press, 1993); Karl Llewellyn, *The Common Law Tradition: Deciding Appeals* (Boston: Little, Brown, 1960) ("Grand Style"); Mark DeWolfe Howe, "The Creative Period in the Law of Massachusetts," *Proceedings of the Massachusetts Historical Society* 69 (1947–50): 237; Daniel Boorstin, *The Americans: The National Experience* (New York: Vintage, 1965), 35 (era of greatest "creative outbursts in American legal history"); Morton Horwitz, *The Transformation of American Law, 1780–1860* (Cambridge, Mass.: Harvard University Press, 1977), 1, 16, 30.

2. One group of scholars, sometimes styled the "Wisconsin school," argues that lawmakers acted out of a sense of what rules might best "mobilize the resources of the community" to "release economic energies" by "increasing the practical range of choices" available to men of all trades and callings, as James Willard Hurst puts it in his prize-winning book, *Law and the Conditions of Freedom in the Nineteenth Century United States* (Madison: University of Wisconsin Press, 1957). The nineteenth-century United States, Hurst wrote, "put all the energy and attention it could into economic interests." Humanitarians mights have concerned themselves "with slavery and drink and the rights of women," and "from time to time" a "zealous minority interested in these matters could whip up a general, emotional reaction to them. But in most affairs one senses that men turned to noneconomic issues grudgingly or as a form of diversion and excitement or in spurts of bad conscience over neglected problems" (6, 29). (Hurst's emphasis, however, is on the innovations produced by legislatures; by comparison, he regards the courts as being less innovative [43, 54].)

More recently, this judicial propensity to recast law in ways that might advance society's economic well-being has been described in more mathematical terms by Judge Richard Posner and others of the Law and Economics school. Posner has argued that nineteenth-century jurists could "hardly fail to consider" whether the loss a plaintiff had suffered in her case in contract, tort or property "was the product of a wasteful, uneconomical resource use." In such a "culture of scarcity," this was an "urgent, an inescapable question," and common-law rules were "redefined from time to time as the relative values of different resource uses changed." Jurists, consciously or unconsciously, put existing common-law principles to the tests of cost-benefit analysis and Kaldor-Hicks efficiency theory. The nineteenth-century common law "uncannily follows economics," and the rules were thus beneficial to all. Posner, "A Theory of Negligence," *Journal of Legal Issues* 1 (1973): 29; Posner, *The Economics of Justice* (Cambridge, Mass.: Harvard University Press, 1981), 5. Cf. Richard Posner, *Economic Analysis of Law*, 3rd ed. (Boston: Little, Brown, 1986), 6, 20, 99, 234–37, 325–27.

Morton Horwitz of Harvard Law School disagrees with Judge Posner that this rulemaking was neutral. Jurists "transformed" the common law in antebellum America "functionally or purposively," as "an instrument of policy" in "alliance" with merchants and entrepreneurs "to advance their interests." They "forced subsidies to growth coerced from the victims of the process," "the weak," "the small town," "the farmer" and "the small trader." Horwitz is "skeptical" of claims by these jurists, or those made on their behalf by others (such as Hurst or Posner), that these changes were merely designed to advance the well-being of all by spurring economic growth. Such claims were mere "rhetoric," and, in any event, "what self-interested group does not" make such statements? Horwitz draws our attention to the "transformation" of the law of marine insurance, riparian rights, easements, franchises, ancient lights, eminent domain, sales and labor contracts, and the broad domain of negligence—changes framed in the neutral language of the common-law discourse, which set aside "earlier protective and paternalistic doctrines," replacing them with rules that helped those acquiring wealth and power at the expense of others, independent of the will of the people as expressed in the legislatures. Horwitz, *Transformation of American Law*, xvi, 1, 30, 99, 155, 186, 188, 220–25, 253, 255–56, 259. See also Wythe Holt, "Morton Horwitz and the Transformation of American Legal History," *William and Mary Law Review* 23 (1982): 663 at 722, maintaining that nineteenth-century American jurists hid their true intentions behind a "good for all" ideology (albeit Holt does not insist that they were self-consciously deliberate in this regard, inasmuch as they could not be expected to distinguish their own *class* interests from those that they felt to be in the best interests of all). For that matter, Horwitz himself allows at one point [34] that many jurists were "practical men" who "may never have stopped to reflect on the changes they were bringing about."

Horwitz's prize-winning *Transformation of American Law* (hereafter referred to as *Transformation 1*) "opened a whole new universe" for American historians, "the real universe of the past and present," as one of his colleagues put it in 1982. Other reviewers were sure that *Transformation 1* would "be at the epicenter" of all debates over America's legal past in the future and would "require an army of researchers to prove the author wrong." Holt, "Morton Horwitz," 663 at 688; William P. LaPiana in *New England Law Review* 13 (1977): 373; David Flaherty, *Michigan Law Review* 76 (1978): 566. Criticism of the book in several law reviews was dismissed by one of Horwitz's defenders as being a mere "volley of quibbles, distortions, misunderstandings, and even in some cases open refusals to accept the evidence." Holt, "Morton Horwitz," 666; Eugene Genovese, in *Harvard Law Review* 91 (1978): 729. Horwitz has recently extended his account in *The Transformation of American Law, 1870–1960* (New York: Oxford University Press, 1992) (hereafter cited as *Transformation 2*), portions of which we will consider as well.

Some American historians have accepted and adopted Morton Horwitz's somewhat conspiratorial, class-oriented version of "the transformation of American law." See, for example, Steven Schlossman, *Love and the American Delinquent* (Chicago: University of Chicago Press, 1977), 16, 25, 26; Theodore Ferdinand, *Boston's Lower Criminal Courts, 1814–1850* (Newark, Del.: Associated University Presses, 1992); Sanford Jacoby, "The Duration of Indefinite Employment Contracts in the U.S. and England: An Historical Analysis," *Comparative Labor Law* 5 (1982): 85 at 94; R. Kent Newmeyer, "Harvard Law School, New England Legal Culture, and the Antebellum Origins of American Jurisprudence," *Journal of American History* 74 (Dec. 1987): 820; Raymond Holger, "Labor History and Critical Labor Law," *Labor History* 30 (1989): 165; David Hoffman, "What Makes a Right Fundamental?" *Review of Politics* 49 (1987): 515 at 523; Joseph Tripp, "Law and Social Control," *Labor History* 28 (1987): 447 at 464. For over fifteen years the Social Science Citator Index has listed over twenty references per year to Horwitz's *Transformation 1*.

William E. Nelson adopted, in the conclusion of his *The Americanization of the Common Law: The Impact of Legal Change on Massachusetts Society, 1760–1830* (Cambridge, Mass.: Harvard University Press, 1975), a perspective comparable to Horwitz's: "In resolving those distributional disputes, the law came to be a tool by which those interest groups that had emerged victorious in the competition for control of law-making institutions could seize most of society's wealth for themselves and enforce their seizure upon the losers" (174). When Nelson later criticized some of the work of Critical Legal Studies scholars (in New York University Law School's *Annual Review of American Law* [1988]), he was taken to task by Robert Gordon (in an exchange published in *Law and History Review* 6 [1988]: 139). See also Richard Posner's disagreement with Horwitz that common-law rules in the nineteenth century operated to subsidize entrepreneurs and stimulate growth at the expense of others. *Economic Analysis of Law*, 233–238.

Other historians prefer a less conspiratorial version of that transformation. (See especially Robert Gordon, "Critical Legal Studies," *Stanford Law Review* 36 [1984]: 57.) Christopher Tomlins rejects Horwitz's claim that jurists were "willing agents of employers." Rather, they had embraced the ideology of "market liberalism's umpired contest of selfish interests." Tomlins's focus is on the ideology of jurists, not their reaction to economic and technological change. Yet, he finds that the "market liberalism" ideology that (he says) they espoused had distributive consequences. It amounted to "implicit or explicit endorsements of one kind of political economy rather than another, one set of social relations or vision of social order over another," legitimizing "daily interactions" in the workplace "structured by relations of dominance and subordination." Jurists were engaged in an ideological recasting of common law discourse, but the end result of this nonconspiratorial process, in Tomlins's view, was still economically oppressive. Tomlins, *Law, Labor and Ideology in the Early American Republic* (New York, Cambridge University Press, 1993), 190, xiv–xv, 217, 190, 113.

Both of the only current textbooks on the subject, respond to aspects of Horwitz's perspective, while generally offering a Wisconsin school approach. Lawrence Friedman, author of the prize-winning *A History of American Law*, believes law to be "a dependent rather than an independent variable, shaped by events and ideas from outside," "a mirror of society." He takes "nothing as . . . autonomous, everything as relative and molded by economy and society." Legal doctrines, "however quaint they may seem, must be acting as the servants of some economic or social interest." Nineteenth-century American jurists made law by deciding the rules in a given case on an "expedient economic basis." "Nothing . . . was allowed to interfere in the 19th century with what judges or the dominant public saw as the highroad to progress and wealth. Court decisions did not create economic conditions, trends, and business practices; rather, these molded decisions and laws." Friedman, "Opening the Time Capsule: A Progress Report on Studies of Courts over Time," *Law and Society Review* 24 (1990): 229 at 230; *A History of American Law*, 2nd ed. (New York: Simon and Schuster, 1985), 12, 15–16, 23, 543; *Contract Law in America: A Social and Economic Case Study* (Madison: University of Wisconsin Press, 1965), 121–22. (See Michael Grossberg's telling review of this "unrepentent" view in the second edition of Friedman's *History of American Law* (1985) in *Law and Social Inquiry* 1 (1988): 355.)

More recently, in *The Magic Mirror: Law in American History* (New York: Oxford University Press, 1989), Kermit Hall agrees with Friedman and Horwitz that "our legal past has had a persistently dark side." "Instrumentalism" (that is, the conscious use of law as an instrument by jurists) has been "the way of the law" in our past. "The courts" were "politicized instruments" of an "economic progress whose benefits spilled over to only a small portion of the population. There is no doubt that the nation's infatuation with economic progress infected many judges." The "juggernaut of economic growth" has caused pollution, personal injury and death, while lawmakers have "pulled on the masks of the law, permitting rather than alleviating injustice" (127, 335–36). (Hall seems in these latter passages to be incorporating an indictment of legislators [creators of statutory, or "positive" law] and common-law jurists. To the extent that his remarks refer to *statutory* law [which included slave codes and pro-developmental eminent domain grants to quasi-public corporations] I do not disagree.)

3. Horwitz, *Transformation 1*, xvi, 253, 259; Hall, *Magic Mirror*, 335–36.

4. Friedman, *History of American Law*; Hall, *Magic Mirror*. See Stephen Presser and Jamil Zainaldin, *Law and American History: Cases and Materials* (St. Paul: West, 1980); and Kermit Hall, William Wiecek, and Paul Finkelman, *American Legal History: Cases and Materials* (New York: Oxford University Press: 1991).

5. But I believe the research of Gary Schwartz, Robert Kaczorowski, and Jerrilynn Marston on nineteenth-century tort, Brian Simpson on contract, and Peter Hoffer and William Novak on property (referred to where relevant throughout) represent perspectives similar to mine.

6. See Horwitz, *Transformation 1*, chap. 8, "The Rise of Legal Formalism"; Grant Gilmore, *The Ages of American Law* (New Haven, Conn: Yale University Press, 1977) chap. 3; Hall, *Magic Mirror*, 221; Friedman, *History of American Law*, 383–84, 623; Llewellyn, *Common Law Tradition*, 35–39.

7. In the words of Lon L. Fuller, *Basic Contract Law* (St. Paul: West, 1947), 520.

8. Lawrence Friedman, to his credit, does acknowledge that many "judges were only human" and that certain harsh rules both of contract and tort were "disinvented" by the late nineteenth century (*History of American Law*, 277, 476, 481–82). But Friedman offers these observations only as edge-smoothing qualifications to an otherwise relatively harsh portrait of the nineteenth-century American judiciary.

9. Some jurists, admirers of Adam Smith, Jeremy Bentham, and John Stuart Mill, emphasized the element of free will inherent in the acts of free men and women in a republican society, in ruthlessly holding all litigants responsible for their individual acts of contract or negligence. See, generally, for example, the judgments of Maine's Chief Justice John Appleton, Massachusetts' Justice Oliver Wendell Holmes Jr., Pennsylvania's Chief Justice John Bannister Gibson, and Michigan's Thomas McIntyre Cooley. (Alan Jones, *The Constitutional Conservatism of Thomas McIntyre Cooley* (New York: Garland, 1987); David Gold, *The Shaping of Nineteenth Century Law: John Appleton and Responsible Individualism* (New York: Greenwood, 1990); and Tomlins, *Law, Labor and Ideology.*) I hold that these individuals, while interesting and of some importance, were not representative of their nineteenth-century contemporaries in these regards.

10. Justice John Forrest Dillon, referring to *Britton* v *Turner*, 6 N. H. 481 (1834), in *McClay* v *Hedge*, 18 Iowa 66 (1864). Dillon may have borrowed the phrase from Justice Spencer Roane in *Jones* v *Commonwealth*, 5 Va. 555 (1799).

11. Justice Christopher Scott in *Lytle* v *State*, 17 Ark. 608 at 670, 677 (1857); *Nickell* v *Handly*, 10 Gratt. (Va.) 336 at 339 (1853); *Steib* v *Whitehead*, 111 Ill. 247 at 251 (1884); Pres. J. Henry Brannon in *Guernsey* v *Lazear*, 51 W.Va. 328 at 340, 41 S. E. 405 at 410 (1902).

12. Justice Daniel Agnew in *Hydraulic Works* v *Orr*, 83 Pa.St. 332 at 336 (1877); Judge Seymour Thompson, *The Law of Negligence . . .* , 2nd ed., 2 vols. (San Francisco, 1886), 1:305.

13. *Kay* v *Pa.RR*, 65 Pa. St. 269 at 272 (1870).

14. Miller's book is without citations, but one of Pitt law library reference librarians, Spencer Clough, showed me how to run Johnson's words down with Westlaw: *The Rapid*, 12 U.S. 155 at 164 (1814).

15. Perry Miller, *The Life of the Mind in America* (New York: Harcourt, Brace and World, 1965), 100, 120, 121, 186, 189. In many ways Miller is echoing Alexis de Tocqueville's critique of sly and aristocratic lawyers in *Democracy in America*, trans. Henry Reeve, 2 vols. (New York, 1841), 1:298–306.

16. *Bob* v *State*, 10 Tenn. (2 Yerg.) 155 at 159 (1826); *Edginton* v *Burlington RR*, 116 Iowa 410, 90 NW 95 at 97 (1902).

17. Peter Karsten, *The Naval Aristocracy: The Golden Age of Annapolis and the Emergence of Modern American Navalism* (New York: Free Press, 1972).

18. Among the older visions are Arthur Schlesinger Jr., *The Age of Jackson* (New York: Book Find Club, 1946); Matthew Josephson, *The Politicos, 1865–1896* (New York: Harcourt, Brace, World, 1938); H. Wayne Morgan, ed., *The Gilded Age* (Syracuse: Syracuse University Press, 1963); Donald B. Cole, *Jacksonian Democracy in New Hampshire* (Cambridge, Mass.: Harvard University Press, 1970); and Charles Beard and Mary Beard, *The Rise of American Civilization*, 4 vols. (New York: Macmillan, 1927).

19. Especially the work of Lee Benson, *The Concept of Jacksonian Democracy: New York as a Test Case* (Princeton: Princeton University Press, 1961); Paul Kleppner, *The Cross of Culture* (New York: Free Press, 1971); Samuel McSeveney, *The Politics of Depression: Political Behavior in the Northeast, 1893–1896* (New York: Oxford University Press, 1972); Donald Jones, *The Sectional Crisis and Northern Methodism: A Study in Piety, Political Ethics, and Civil Religion* (Metuchen, N.J.:

Scarecrow, 1979); Richard Jensen, *The Winning of the Midwest: Social and Political Conflict, 1880–1896* (Chicago: University of Chicago Press, 1971); Ronald Formisano, *The Birth of Mass Political Parties: Michigan, 1827–1861* (Princeton: Princeton University Press, 1971); and William Gienapp, *Origins of the Republican Party, 1852–1856* (New York: Oxford University Press, 1987). See also Paul Kleppner, *The Third Electoral System, 1853–1892: Parties, Voters and Political Culture* (Chapel Hill: University of North Carolina Press, 1979); R. L. Moore, "The End of Religious Establishment and the Beginning of Religious Parties: Church and State in the U.S.," in *Belief in History*, ed. Thomas K. Selman (South Bend, Ind.: University of Notre Dame Press, 1991); John L. Hammond, *The Politics of Benevolence: Revival Religion and American Voting Behavior* (Norwood, N.J.: Ablex, 1979).

20. Michael Barton, *Goodmen: The Character of Civil War Soldiers* (University Park: Pennsylvania State University Press, 1981), 25.

Southern politics, after the collapse of the Whigs in the 1850s, lacked much of this pietistic-liturgical quality at times because of slavery and race, but Republicans thrived briefly in the Reconstruction decade (1868–1877), and Populist-Fusion slates of candidates for judicial office enjoyed some success in the South during the 1890s. For the only analysis I am aware of regarding the consequence of politics for judicial questions in a southern state in these years see James L. Hunt, "Private Law and Public Policy: Negligence Law and Political Change in Nineteenth Century North Carolina," *North Carolina Law Review* 66 (1988): 421.

21. As, for example, in Alice Felt Tyler, *Freedom's Ferment* (Minneapolis: University of Minnesota Press, 1944); and Bernard Wishy, *The Child and the Republic: The Dawn of Modern American Child Nurture* (Philadelphia: University of Pennsylvania Press, 1968); Schlossman, *Love and the American Delinquent*; Lois Banner, "Religious Benevolence as Social Control: A Critique of the Interpretation," *Journal of American History* 60 (1973): 34.

22. Howe in *Religion and American Politics*, ed. Mark Noll (New York: Oxford University press, 1990), 137–38.

23. Charles Lanman, *The Private Life of Daniel Webster* (New York: 1856), 104.

24. Justice John Welch in *Bellefontaine-Indiana RR* v *Snyder*, 18 Ohio State 399 at 409 (1868); Justice Henry Hogeboom in *Lammen* v *Albany Gas Light Co.*, 46 Barb. (N.Y. Supreme Ct.) 264 at 270 (1865). See chapter 8 for more on this.

25. Chief Justice Ellis Lewis in *Price* v *Maxwell*, 28 Pa. State 23 at 37 (1857).

26. Justice W. H. Holt in *Kentucky Central RR* v *Gastineau's Adm.*, 82 Ky. 119 at 125 (1885); Justice Isaac Gordon in *Biddle & Wife* v *Hestonville, M., & F. RR*, 112 Pa.St. 551, 4 atl. 485 (1886). See chapter 7. See also the views of U.S. Supreme Court justice Joseph Bradley in *The Evangelist*, May 3, 1883: "Parables go strait to their mark and are rarely misunderstood. Conscience, seated in the inner recesses of the human bosom, is quick to perceive and understand what is meant."

27. Few of the critics of the works of any of our economic determinists have noted this paradox. One who has is Stephen Diamond, "Legal Realism and Historical Method: James Willard Hurst and American Legal History," *Michigan Law Review* 77 (1979): 784 at 786 (who notes that Hurst ignores issues of religion, the family, temperance, slavery, Civil Rights, and woman's suffrage in his studies of nineteenth- and early-twentieth-century law making).

28. Hurst, *Law and the Conditions of Freedom*, 6, 29. Hurst's main emphasis

was on the work of legislatures (43, 54), but he did not explicitly exclude jurists for this generalization, and he has certainly been understood to have intended them to be included in his "release of energy" thesis. See also his interview with Hendrick Hartog, wherein he spoke of his "early enthusiasm for Charles Beard" and noted that "it's hard not to be an economic determinist. People have to find means to eat." *Law and History Review* 12 (1994): 370 at 371, 388.

29. It will be seen that this question is purely rhetorical when I cite a North Carolina Supreme Court justice, Edwin Reade, as the source of this particular expression, sympathetically offered in *Garrett* v *Chesire*, 69 N. C. 396 at 405 (1873). Reade also spoke twice in the opinion of "inhumanity" (404, 405).

30. See Presser and Zainaldin, *Law and American History*; and Kermit Hall, William Wiecek, and Paul Finkelman, *American Legal History*.

31. E. P. Thompson, *The Poverty of Theory* (London: Merlin, 1995), 41–43.

32. *Heacock* v *Walker*, 1 Tyl. (Vt.) 338 at 342 (1802) (here Robinson was offering instructions to a jury). Harold Weinberg, "Markets Overt, Voidable Titles, and Feckless Agents: Judges and Efficiency in the Antebellum Doctrine of Good Faith Purchase," *Tulane Law Review* 56 (1981): 1 at 12–13, takes note of this case, which brought it to my attention.

33. *Pike* v *Butler*, 4 N.Y. 360 at 363 (1850), reversing *Pike* v *Butler*, 4 Barb. (N.Y. Sup. Ct.) 650 (1848).

34. Sometimes the only views of counsel appearing in the published reports were those of the losing party, the court having "stopped" the winner, or the reporter having omitted or sharply condensed the winner's views for brevity's sake. Consequently, I often cannot say with authority what role counsel's argument may have played in shaping the ensuing opinions. But that level of analysis was not my focus or primary interest. The next step, which others may well chose to take before I do, is to dig in the judicial archives of the several states for such briefs and transcripts as may still exist on such cases as appear worthy of further attention. To date, I have "passed" on that task; one makes choices.

35. I do *not* claim to have dealt exhaustively with three issues; however, the number of cases in which the general question of contributory negligence, the fellow-servant rule, and the assumption-of-risk rule appear is too great to manage more than a few per jurisdiction, in search of that jurisdiction's "leading case." I read opinions both of the "courts of last resort" and of such intermediate appellate courts as existed and I could locate. These were the federal circuit reports (Fed. Cases), the New York "Supreme" Court (*after* 1848), New York City Court of Common Pleas, and the Texas, Missouri, and Illinois intermediate appellate courts of the last quarter of the nineteenth century. I also made some use of the trial court judges' instructions to the grand or petit jury, sometimes available in their own volumes (as in the federal reports and both Ohio's and Pennsylvania's district and circuit/county court reports), and sometimes in lengthy quoted passages appearing in journals, newspapers, or appellate opinions.

When others had identified a case as being innovative, I read it and the cases cited in it with particular care, and then "Shepardized" it to try to trace its impact. (I have found Shepard's pre-1884 state citators to be incomplete; one must scan later cases on a subject with care, and a close reading of some elaborate late-nineteenth-century opinions can yield opinions in the English, state, and federal reports that one might miss by relying solely on treatises and the Century Edition of the *American Digest* [1896].)

36. In *Logan* v *Mason*, 6 W & S(Pa.) 9 at 13 (1843).

37. See Richard Epstein, "The Social Consequences of Common Law Rules," *Harvard Law Review* 95 (1982): 1717, for a good discussion of these questions. See also Weinberg, "Markets Overt," 1.

38. A. E. Keir Nash, "Fairness and Formalism in the Trial of Blacks in the State Supreme Courts of the Old South," *Virginia Law Review* 56 (1870): 64; Robert Cover, *Justice Accused: Antislavery and the Judicial Process* (New Haven, Conn.: Yale University Press, 1975), 201; Mark Tushnet, *The American Law of Slavery, 1810–1860: Considerations of Humanity and Interest* (Princeton, N.J.: Princeton Univrsity Press, 1981), 37, 63, 67, 211; Paul Finkelman, *An Imperfect Union: Slavery, Federalism and Comity* (Chapel Hill: University of North Carolina Press, 1981); William Nelson, "The Impact of the Antislavery Movement upon the Styles of Judicial Reasoning in Nineteenth Century America," *Harvard Law Review* 87 (1974): 513, describes some of those jurists who took their guidance essentially from statutory and constitutional language, the principle of comity, and precedent as "instrumentalists"; I see them differently. I also differ somewhat with Robert Cover, who emphasizes the lack of courage doctrinal antislavery jurists displayed. I find this behavior understandable when viewed in the context of their professional standards (the "autonomy" of the law). See also Judith K. Schafer, *Slavery, The Civil Law and the Supreme Court of Louisiana* (Baton Rouge: Louisiana State University Press, 1994), for evidence of both formalistic rule-of-law decisions and humane Jurisprudence of the Heart decisions with regard to the treatment of slaves and slave suits for freedom where the issue was either manumission or sojourner status in a northern state or foreign country, and see Robert Kaczorowski, *The Politics of Judicial Interpretation: The Federal Courts, the Department of Justice, and Civil Rights, 1866–1876* (Dobbs Ferry, N.Y.: Oceana, 1985), 67–70, and *The Nationalization of Civil Rights: Constitutional Theory and Practice in a Racist Society, 1866–1883* (New York: Garland, 1987) 220, 260, 295–309, for evidence of a similar tension between Radical Republican and conservative jurists and Justice Department officers with regard to the freedmen during Reconstruction.

Thomas Morris and Andrew Fede properly point out that, in the antebellum South, the moral concerns of "heart" jurists amounted to a "blunted morality," inasmuch as they were either constrained by or willingly accepted, the law of slavery. T. Morris, " 'Society is Not Marked by Punctuality in the Payment of Debts': The Chattel Mortgage of Slaves," in *Ambivalent Legacy: A Legal History of the South*, ed. James Ely and David Bodenhamer (Jackson, Miss., 1984), 163; Andrew Fede, *People Without Rights: An Interpretation of the Fundamentals of the Law of Slavery in the U.S. South* (New York: Garland, 1992). This is perfectly true. My point here is a simpler one: Despite this, *some* southern jurists were willing to strain against the language of statutes and the limits of equity to provide humane treatment of slaves.

39. Cover, *Justice Accused*, 237.

40. Nash, "Fairness and Formalism," 74. See also Nash, "Negro Rights, Unionism and Greatness on the South Carolina Court of Appeals: The Extraordinary Chief Justice John B. O'Neill," *South Carolina Law Review* 21 (1969): 141; and

Nash, "A More Equitable Past: Southern Supreme Courts and the Protection of the Antebellum Negro," *North Carolina Law Review* 48 (1970): 197.

41. Justice Leonard Henderson in *State v Reed*, 9 N. C. 454 at 456 (1823); Chief Judge Mathews of New Orleans First Judicial Court in *Marie Louise v Marot*, 8 La. 475 (1835); Justice Buchanan in *Humphreys v Utz.* unreported La. S. C. case # 3910 (1856), described in Schafer, *Slavery*, 50–52; C. J. John L. Taylor in *State v Hole*, 9 N. C. 582 at 583 (1823); Judge Nathan Green in *Worley v State*, 30 Tenn. 171 at 175 (1850); Justice Spencer Roane in *Reno's Ex. v Davis*, 14 Va. 889 at 892 (1809); C. J. E. Turner in *Harry v Decker & Hopkins*, Walk. (Miss.) 36 (1818).

42. As in *Kirkwood v Miller*, 37 Tenn. 455 at 459 (1858). Similarly, in *Fields v State*, 9 Tenn. 156 (1829), the court held that a white man, acquitted of murdering a slave, a crime defined narrowly by the legislature, could still be convicted of the common-law crime of manslaughter.

43. See, for example, Justice Richard Moncure's dissent in *Bailey v Poindexter*, 14 Gratt. (Va.) 132 (1858); *Pleasants v Pleasants*, 2 Call. (Va.) 319 (1800); *Elder v Elder*, 4 Leigh (Va.) 252 (1833); *Williamson v Coalter's Ex.*, 14 Gratt. (Va.) 394 (1858); Judge F. X. Martin in *Forsyth v Nash*, 4 Mart. (O. S.) (La.) 385 (1816); and in *Lamsford v Coquillon*, 2 Mart. (N. S.) (La.) 401 (1824); Chief Judge Mathews in *Marie Louise v Marot*, 8 La. 475 (1835); C. S. Martin again in *Smith v Smith*, 13 La. 441 (1839); J. Edward Simon in *Thomas v Generis*, 16 La. 483 (1840); the dissenting opinion of Justice John Hall in *Trustees v Dickenson*, 12 N. C. 189 at 207 (1827); and, generally, A. E. Keir Nash, "Reason of Slavery: Understanding the Judicial Role in the Peculiar Institution," *Vanderbilt Law Review* 32 (1979): 7.

44. Justice Jacob Peck in *Fields v State*, 9 Tenn. 156 at 163 (1829); Justice John Hall (diss.) in *Trustees v Dickenson*, 12 N. C. 189 at 207 (1827).

45. *The Slave Grace*, 2 Hagg. Adm. R. 94, 166 ER 179 (Adm. 1827); Justice Eugenius Nisbet in *Neal v Farmer*, 9 Ga. 555 (1851); Judge William Harris in *George v State*, 37 Miss. 316 at 320 (1859). For a more temperate version of this Jurisprudence of the Southern Head, see the remarks of Louisiana's Chief Justice George Eustis in *Haynes v Hutchinson & Forno*, 8 La. Ann. 35 (1853), noted in Schafer, *Slavery*, 256–57, regarding the fate of a slave who had been freed in Cincinnati and had voluntarily returned to Louisiana: "The true rule in laid down in the case of *The Slave Grace* [an English decision], and, although more liberal views once prevailed in Louisiana, we have been compelled to return to the English doctrine," which was that her voluntary return to Louisiana was a return to slavery.

46. Justice R. L. Carruthers, writing for the court in a case upholding a manumission, *Boon v Lancaster*, 1 Sneed (Tenn.) 577 at 586 (1854). (See *Kirkwood v Miller*, 37 Tenn. 455 [1858], for evidence of Justice Carruthers' Heart jurisprudence.) For similar examples of a "humane" approach to manumission that took the form, by 1858, of a doctrinial argument see the dissents authored by Justice Richard Moncure in *Bailey v Poindexter*, 14 Gratt. (Va.) 132 (1858), and *Williamson v Coalter's Ex.*, 14 Gratt. (Va.) 394 (1858).

47. *Scott v Emerson*, 15 Mo. 576 at 586 ff (1852); Don Fehrenbacher, *The Dred Scott Case* (N.Y., 1978), 263. Gamble went on to serve Missouri as its Unionist governor from 1861 until his death in 1864.

48. The fact that most northern federal district court judges honored southern slave law and applied federal fugitive slave acts will come as no surprise to one who

has read Kermit Hall's *The Politics of Justice: Lower Federal Justicial Selection and the Second Party System, 1829–1861* (Lincoln: University of Nebraska Press, 1979). All of the presidents in the 1830s, 1840s, and 1850s making these selections belonged to and believed in "bisectional" parties, be they Democrat or Whig. All expected appointees to comply with the terms of the federal Fugitive Slave Acts (of 1793 and 1850).

49. Cover, *Justice Accused*, 120–23. See also Tushnet, *American Law of Slavery*, and Finkelman, *Imperfect Union*.

50. Woodbury in *Jones v Vanzandt*, 5 How. (46 U.S.) 215 at 231 (1847); Story to Ezekiel Bacon, November 19, 1842, reprinted in William Wetmore Story, *Life and Letters of Joseph Story*, 2 vols. (Boston, 1851), 2:431; both noted in William Wiecek, "Slavery and Abolition before the U.S. Supreme Court, 1820–1860," *Journal of American History* 65 (1978): 34 at 48–49; McLean in *Norris v Newton*, 18 Fed. Cas. 322 (C. Ct. D. Ind. 1850), noted by Paul Finkelman in "Fugitive Slaves, Midwestern Racial Tolerance, and the Value of 'Justice Delayed'," *Iowa Law Review* 78 (1992): 89. For a characteristically superb analysis of Justice Story's views, see Paul Finkelman, "Story Telling on the Supreme Court: Prigg v Pennsylvania and Justice Joseph Story's Judicial Nationalism," *Supreme Court Review* 1994, 247.

51. California's high court was dominated by prosouthern jurists throughout its brief antebellum history. See Paul Finkelman, "The Law of Slavery and Freedom in California, 1848–1860," *California Western Law Review* 17 (1981): 437.

52. See, for example, *Jackson v Bullock*, 12 Ct. 38 (1837); *In re Sherman Booth*, 3 Wis. 1 (1854); *Ex Parte Bushnell, Ex Parte Langston*, 9 Ohio St. 198 (1859); Robert Cover, *Justice Accused*, 52–53, 64–67, 80, 96, 120–23, 186. See also the more disguised voice of jurists in New York, Pennsylvania, Illinois, and Indiana, who cited Joseph Story's decision in *Prigg v Pennsylvania*, 41 U.S. 539 (1842), to hold that state statutes slave owners and their agents had relied on were null and void. See *Kauffman v Oliver*, 10 Pa. St. 514 at 517 (1849) (Justice Coulter: "We feel the genial influence of the common law on this subject"); *Graves and Others v State*, 1 Ind. 368 (1849); *Thornton's Case*, 11 Ill. 332 (1849), and *In the Matter of Geo. Kirk*, 1 Parker Cr. R (N.Y.) 67 (1846), all noted in Paul Finkelman, "Prigg v Pa. and Northern State Courts: Antislavery Uses of a Proslavery Decision," *Civil War History* 25 (1979): 5.

53. *In re Booth*, 3 Wis. 1–196 (1854).

54. In *Ex Parte Bushnell, Ex Parte Langston*, 9 Ohio St. 198 (1859).

55. *Jackson v Bulloch*, 12 Ct. 38 at 41, 57, 64, 65 (1837).

56. *Anderson v Poindexter*, 6 Ohio St. 622 at 638, 724, 727 (1856); *Lemmon v People*, 20 N.Y. 562 at 620, 633 (1860). For a good analysis of these and other such "comity" cases see Finkelman, *Imperfect Union*.

57. A term used to describe this approach by Professor Thomas Russell during the 1991 meeting of the American Society of Legal Historians in San Francisco.

58. And this is as good a moment as any to allude to our center's more recent apropos product, *Theory, Method and Practice in Social and Cultural History*, ed. Peter Karsten and John Modell (New York: New York University Press, 1992).

59. Edward Purcell Jr., *Litigation and Inequality: Federal Diversity Jurisdiction in Industrial America, 1870–1958* (New York: Oxford University Press, 1992), 36–52, 85–90. Purcell, to be sure, is also attentive to high court rules.

60. Gordon Bakken, *Practicing Law in Frontier California* (Lincoln: University

of Nebraska Press, 1991), 28–31, 149, 163; Gordon Bakken, *The Development of Law in Frontier California, 1850–1890* (Westport, Conn.: Greenwood, 1985), 7, 38, 81–82; Randolph Bergstrom, *Courting Danger: Injury and Law in New York City, 1870–1910* (Ithaca: Cornell University Press, 1992), chap. 3.

61. For examples of this, see Bakken, *Practicing Law*, 163; Bakken, *Development of Law*, 81–82; and John Phillip Reid, *Law for the Elephant: Property and Social Behavior on the Overland Trail* (San Marino, Calif.: Huntington Library, 1980).

ONE

1. See, for example, *Dobbins v R. R.*, 91 Tex. 60, 41 SW 62 (1897); and *Driscoll v Allis-Chalmers Co.*, 144 Wis 45; 129 NW 402 (1911).

2. Lawrence Friedman, *A History of American Law*, 2nd ed. (New York: Simon and Schuster, 1985), 135. He includes U.S. Supreme Court justice John Marshall in this litany; I have omitted Marshall. Marshall and his court are unique; there simply *were* no English precedents for many of the constitutional questions of interpretation of a written republican Constitution for him to turn to.

For a similar interpretation of antebellum jurists writing in a "Grand Style" guided as much by "situation-reason" as mere precedent, see Karl Llewellyn, *The Common Law Tradition: Deciding Appeals* (Boston: Little, Brown, 1960).

3. Roscoe Pound, *The Formative Era of American Law* (Boston: Little, Brown, 1938), 92; Shannon Stimson, *The American Revolution in the Law: Anglo-American Jurisprudence before John Marshall* (Princeton: Princeton University Press, 1990), 58, 173; Daniel Boorstin, *The Americans: The Colonial Experience* (New York: Random House, 1958), 199–201; Perry Miller, *The Life of the Mind in America: From the Revolution to the Civil War* (New York: Harcourt, Brace, World, 1965), 134–35.

4. Charles Warren, *History of the American Bar* (Boston: Little, Brown, 1911), 157, 338; Donald Senese, "Legal Thought in South Carolina, 1800–1860," Ph.D. diss., University of South Carolina, 1970, 46.

5. John William Wallace, *The Reporters, Arranged and Characterized*, 4th ed. (Boston, 1882), 8, 315, passim.

6. Charles Viner, *A General Abridgement of Law and Equity* (London, 1791), 1:333–37; H. H. Brackenridge, *Law Miscellanies* (Philadelphia, 1814), 53.

7. Haven, in a review of Simon Greenleaf's *Maine Reports*, *North American Review* 22 (1826): 29, cited in Charles M. Cook, *The American Codification Movement: A Study of Antebellum Legal Reform* (Westport, Conn.: Greenwood, 1981), 47.

8. Joseph H. Smith, "New Light on the Doctrine of Judicial Precedent in Early America: 1607–1776," in *Legal Thought in the United States under Contemporary Pressures*, ed. J. Hazard and W. Wagner (Brussels: Emile Bruylant, 1970), 24–34; T. Lewis, "The History of Judicial Precedent," *Law Quarterly Review* 46 (1930): 207; *Law Quarterly Review* 47 (1931): 411; and *Law Quarterly Review* 48 (1932): 230.

9. 5 Johns. (N.Y.) 395 at 406.

10. Horwitz, *Transformation 1*, 164.

11. 5 Johns. (N.Y.) 395 at 408–11.

12. Kent to Thomas Washington, October 6, 1828, in *Select Essays in Anglo-American Legal History* 1 (1907): 844.

13. *Sands* v *Taylor*, 5 Johns. (N.Y.) 395 at 406.

14. Swift, *System*, 2 vols. (Windham, Conn., 1795–96), 1:45; 1 Johns. (N.Y.) v (1804), cited in Cook, *American Codification Movement*, 9, a study to which, along with Warren's *History of the American Bar*, esp. chaps. 13 and 20), I am greatly indebted for the views in this and the following paragraph.

15. These were Kent's *Commentaries on American Law*, 4 vols. (New York, 1826–30), Nathan Dane's *General Abridgement and Digest of American Law*, 9 vols. (1823–29), Timothy Walker's *Introduction to American Law* (Boston, 1837), James Wilson's *Lectures* (1804), and Swift's *System*.

16. Senese, "Legal Thought," 391–92; Erwin Surrency, *A History of American Law Publishing* (New York: Oceana, 1990), 172; Cook, *American Codification Movement*, 132, 204. The more noteworthy of the treatises include Tapping Reeve's *Law of Baron and Femme, Parent and Child, Guardian and Ward, Master and Servant and the Powers of Courts of Chancery* (New Haven, Conn., 1816); Story's *Commentary on the Law of Bailments* (Boston, 1832), *Commentaries on Equity Jurisprudence* (Boston, 1836), and *Commentaries on the Law of Promissory Notes* (Boston, 1845); Joseph Angell's *Watercourses* (Boston, 1821); Swift's *Digest of the Law of Evidence* (1810) and *Treatise on Bills of Exchange and Promissory Notes* (1810); Simon Greenleaf's *Treatise on the Law of Evidence* (Boston, 1842); Joseph Angell's and Samuel Ames's *Treatise on the Law of Private Corporations Aggregate* (1832); Henry Wheaton's *Elements of International Law* (Philadelphia, 1836); Theodore Sedgwick's *Treatise on the Measure of Damages* (New York, 1847); Theophilus Parsons's *Treatise on the Law of Contracts* (Boston, 1853); Isaac Redfield's *Practical Treatise on the Law of Railroads*, 2nd ed. (1858); Francis Hilliard's *Law of Torts and Private Wrongs* (Boston, 1859); Thomas Shearman and Amasa Redfield's *Treatise on the Law of Negligence* (New York, 1869); Francis Wharton's *Liability of Master to Servant* (1869) and *Treatise on the Law of Negligence* (1874); Henry Mills's *Eminent Domain* (1879); Floyd Mecham's *Agency* (1889); and Seymour Thompson's *Law of Electricity* (St. Louis, 1891). Among the "American editions" were *William Jones on Bailments* (Boston, 1796); Joseph Story's edition of *Laws on Assumpsit* (Boston, 1811); *Laws on Pleading* (Postsmouth, N. H., 1808); Story's edition of *Joseph Chitty on Bills and Notes* (1809); Henry Wheaton's edition of William Selwyn's *Abridgement of the Law of Nisi Prius* (1823); and J. C. Perkins's edition of *Joseph Chitty's Practical Treatise on the Law of Contracts*, 7th ed. (Springfield, 1842). Among the American editions of Blackstone's *Commentaries* are those of Virginian jurist St. George Tucker (1803) and Pennsylvanian John Reed (1831).

17. Dixon, "Codification and Reform of the Common Law," *American Jurist and Law Magazine* 14 (1835): 284; Anon., "Wharton's Digest," *American Law Journal* 1 (1843): 231, both cited in Cook, *American Codification Movement*, 65, 206.

18. Story to Henry Wheaton in 1825, cited in Cook, *American Codification Movement*, 89.

19. *Eastman* v *Meredith*, 36 N. H. 284 at 299 (1858). See also the remarks of Rufus Choate, a prominent Boston attorney, on the law as a "mighty and continuous stream of experience and reason, accumulated, ancestral, widening and deepening and washing itself clearer as it runs on," in *The Works of Rufus Choate*, ed. Samuel G. Brown (Boston, 1862), 1:68.

20. Gibson in *Logan* v *Mason*, 6 W.&S. (Pa.) 9 at 11 (1843); Black, diss., in *Hole* v *Rittenhouse*, 2 Phila. R. 411 (1856); Kent, *Commentaries on American Law* 1:473. See also Fredrick Kempin Jr., "Precedent and *Stare Decisis*: The Critical Years, 1800 to 1850," *American Journal of Legal History* 3 (1959): 28; *Adam Smith: Lectures on Jurisprudence*, ed. R. L. Meek et al. (Oxford: Clarendon, 1978): "New courts . . . are . . . great evils. Every court is bound only by its own practice. It takes time . . . to have precedents enough to determine the practice of a court. [Until then] its proceedings will be altogether loose."

21. Chief Justice Lemuel Shaw, in a speech praising the late Chief Justice Isaac Parker, in 1830, cited in Leonard Levy, *The Law of the Commonwealth and Chief Justice Shaw* (Cambridge, Mass.: Harvard University Press, 1957), 23–24.

22. Chief Justice Nathaniel Chipman of Vermont in N. Chipman's Rep. 66, n. 1.

23. Future Chief Justice Zephaniah Swift, *A System of Laws of the State of Connecticut* (1795), 41.

24. These are Horwitz's observations on the passage of Swift just offered, *Transformation 1*, 25.

25. Horwitz, *Transformation 1*, 125; Friedman, *History of American Law*, 135–36. Friedman includes the additional passage, cited at note 27; Horwitz does not.

26. Equity courts were feared and detested by New York's colonial legislature as instruments of the royal governor. They were finally sanctioned only in the 1760s and were not extensively utilized until shortly before Kent's tenure as chancellor.

27. Kent to Thomas Washington, *Select Essays in Anglo-American Legal History* 1 (1907): 844.

28. Horwitz, *Transformation 1*, 26, 30.

29. This point is precisely made by Randall Bridwell and Ralph Whitten in their critiques of Horwitz's reading of Zephaniah Swift's statements. Bridwell and Whitten, *The Constitution and the Common Law* (Lexington, Mass., 1977), 27–28. Although I am generally impressed with and persuaded by the argument of Craig Klafter that American jurists of the early Republic emphasized reason and principle rather than mere precedent, I believe Klafter is actually describing William Blackstone's process of rejecting *bad* precedent in favor of what Blackstone called "abstracted reason." (See Klafter, *Reason over Precedents: Origins of American Legal Thought* [Westport, Conn., Greenwood, 1993], 66–67, 82.) Here are Blackstone's views on this question: "It is an established rule to abide by former precedents, where the same points come up again in litigation. . . . Yet this rule admits of exception, where the former determination is most evidently contrary to reason. . . . But even in such cases the subsequent judges do not pretend to make a new law, but to vindicate the old one from misrepresentation. For if it be found that the former decision is manifestly absurd or unjust, it is declared, not that such a sentence was *bad law*, but that it was *not* law. . . . It is wisely . . . ordered, that the principles and axioms of law, which are general propositions, flowing from abstracted reason, and not accommodated to times or to men, should be deposited in the breasts of the judges, to be occasionally applied to such facts as come properly ascertained before them. For here partiality can have little scope: the law is well known, and is the same for all ranks and degrees." *Commentaries*, 1:69–70; 3:379–80. The words of Lord Chief Justice Holt in *Lane* v *Cotton* (1 Salk. 18, 90 ER 17 (K. B. 1701) are of the same tenor (albeit he appears to have had in mind statutory language): "New things may

be governed by old laws, when they fall within the reason of those things which were the subject matter of those laws at first." Cf. *Lane* v *Cotton*, 11 Mod. 16, 90 ER 853 (K. B. 1701); and *Bole* v *Horton*, 3 Vaugh. 382, 124 ER 1124 (C. P., 1673).

30. In *Norway Plains Co.* v *B & M RR*, 1 Gray (67 Mass.) 263 (1854). Nonetheless, Shaw cited five English and three American cases as precedent in this opinion.

31. Greene in *Hodges* v *New England Screw Co. et al.*, 1 R. I. 356 (1850) (rejecting the English assumption of equity jurisdiction over corporations). See also the oft-quoted passage from Senator (C.T. of Errors) John Spencer's opinion in *Rensselaer Glass Factory* v *Reid*, 5 Cowen (N.Y.) 586 (1825): The "flexibility [of the common law] to consist, not in the change of great and essential principles, but in the application of old principles to new cases, and in the modification of the rules flowing from them to such cases as they arise, so as to preserve the reason of the rules and the spirit of the law."

32. Miller, *Life of the Mind*, "The Legal Mentality—The Hinge of Negation," 235, citing an encomium to Kent in 1838. See also Kent's opinion in *Sexias* v *Woods*, 2 Cains. 48 at 55 (N.Y. 1804), where he defers to English precedent on the rule of caveat emptor despite a preference for "the reason of the civilians" (that is, the different European rule). And see his praise of the English reporters and jurists in his *Commentaries on American Law* 1:463: "I do not know where we could resort, among all the volumes of human composition, to find more constant, more tranquil, and more sublime manifestations of the intrepidity of conscious rectitude. If we were to go back to the iron times of the Tudors, and follow judicial history down from the first page in Dyer to the last page of the last reporter, we should find the higher courts of civil judicature, generally, and with rare exceptions, presenting the image of the sanctity of a temple, where truth and justice seem to be enthroned and to be personified in their decrees."

33. Horwitz omits this passage (*Transformation 1*, 125).

34. Clyde Croft, "Lord Hardwick's use of Precedent in Equity," in *Legal Record and Historical Reality*, ed. Thomas Watkin (London: Hambledon, 1989), 121–55. See also Vaughan, C. J., in *Fry* v *Porter*, 1 Mod. 307, 86 ER 902 (Ch. 1681) "I wonder to hear of citing precedents in matters of equity; for if there be equity in a case, that equity is a universal truth, and there can be no precedent in it. So that in any precedent that can be produced, if it be the same with this case, the reason and equity is the same in itself; and if the precedent be not the same case with this, it is not to be cited, being not to the purpose."

35. Cited in Miller, *Life of the Mind*, "The Legal Mentality: Law and Morality," 189.

For good analysis of the influence of William Paley's moral philosophy on Kent and Story see Peter Charles Hoffer, "Principled Discretion: Concealment, Conscience, and Chancellors," *Yale Journal of Law and the Humanities* 3 (1991): 53.

36. Kent to Baldwin, July 18, 1786, *Law Practice of Alexander Hamilton*, ed. Julius Goebel, 5 vols. (New York: Columbia University Press, 1964–81), 1:50 n. 50; *Manning* v *Manning*, 1 Johns. Ch. 527 at 529–30 (1815); both cited in David Raack, "To Preserve the Best Fruits: The Legal Thought of Chancellor James Kent," *American Journal of Legal History* 33 (1989): 320 at 343–44.

37. In *North American Review* (July 1820); cited in Miller, *Life of the Mind*, 138.

38. Justice Thomas Todd in *Robinson* v *Campbell* 3 Wheat. 212 at 223 (1818)

(land titles and property dispute in Virginia-Tennessee border area); Brackenridge, *Law Miscellanies*, 64; D. Hoffman, *A Course of Legal Study* (Baltimore, 1836), 227; Joel Bishop, *The First Book of the Law* (Boston, 1868), 356, n. 1. See also David Nourse, "Egbert Benson-Lawyer and Justice of the New York Supreme Court," in *Egbert Benson*, ed. Wythe Holt and David Nourse (New York: Second Circuit Bicentennial Committee, 1987), on the following of English admiralty law precedent by New York jurists in the 1790s and early-nineteenth-century criticism of this practice by more political figures in New York's senate.

39. As in *Baring* v *Raeder*, 1 H.& M. (Va.) 154 (1806), where Justice Spencer Roane cited a decision of Lord Mansfield and spoke of how American jurists might "avail ourselves of the testimony of the eminent and able judiciary of England," and Justice St. George Tucker cited an English decision differing with Mansfield's views and spoke of the value of the handiwork of "able Judges upon the same law which as to this point [the testimony of a wife in a case where the husband was an interested party] prevails in this country."

40. LaPiana, "*Swift* v *Tyson* and the 'Brooding Omnipresence in the Sky': An Investigation of the Idea of Law in Antebellum America," *Suffolk University Law Review* 20 (1886): 771.

41. Bridwell and Whitten, *Constitution and the Common Law*, 6; *Leroy* v *Crownshield*, 15 Fed. Cas. 362 (Cir. Ct. D. Mass. 1820) at 369–71; *Dartmouth College* v *Woodward*, 4 Wheat. (U.S.) 518 at 713 (1819); *The George*, 10 Fed. Cas. 205 (Cir. Ct. D. Mass. 1831) at 208; *Card* v *Grisiman*, 5 Ct. 164 (1823) at 168. The passage of Lord Kenyon's is from *Bauerman et al.* v *Radenius*, 7 Term R. 664, 101 ER 1186 (K. B., 1798). See also his dedication to precedent in *King* v *Inhabs. of Brighthelmston*, 5 Term R 188, 101 ER 106 (K. B., 1793); and *Goodtitle* v *Otway*, 7 Term R. 399, 101 ER 1041 (K. B., 1797). Cf. *Butler* v *Duncomb*, 1 P. Wms. 448 at 452, 24 ER 466 (Ch. 1718). Chancellor James Kent also used the expression *Super antiquas vias* in a comment on the common law in a letter to Edward Livingston, March 13, 1826, published in *American Jurist* 16 (January 1837): 361, cited by Raack, "Preserve the Best Fruits," 362.

Lord Kenyon, of course, in turn, was probably borrowing this Latin phrase from his own venerable predecessors.

42. Jeff Hoyt, "Abuse of Public Power: New York City and the Formation of Municipal Law, 1846–1866," Ph.D. diss., University of Virginia, 1983, 195.

43. Noted in Mark F. Fernandez, "The Appellate Question: A Comparative Analysis of Supreme Courts of Appeal in Virginia and Louisiana, 1776–1840," Ph.D. diss., William and Mary, 1991, 208–11.

44. See the term's use in the 1820s and 1830s in Cook, *American Codification Movement*, 47, 125, 177, 189, and 207; see also Miller, *Life of the Mind*, passim. Chancellor Kent used the term often as well, as did the New York Law Institute's charter in 1826 (Raack, "Best Fruits," 364). See also Brackenridge, *Law Miscellanies*, iv.

45. Klafter, *Reason over Precedents*; DuPonceau, *A Dissertation on the Nature and Extent of the Jurisdiction of the Courts of the United States . . .* (Philadelphia, 1824), 174–75 (cited in Klafter, 57); *Hoopes* v *Dundas*, 10 Pa. St. 75 at 78 (1848); Stephen Siegel, "The Aristotelian Basis of English Law, 1450–1800," *American Journal of Legal History* 33 (1989): 3; Michael Hoeflich, "Legal Science from Liebnitz

to Langdell: Law and Geometry," *American Journal of Legal History* 30 (1986): 95; Barbara Shapiro, "Law and Science in Seventeenth Century England," *Stanford Law Review* 21 (1988–89): 717; Michael Lobban, *The Common Law and English Jurisprudence, 1760–1850* (Oxford: Clarendon, 1991), 10–16, 54, 83.

46. But see Friedman, *History of American Law,* 165; *Revised Law and Form Book for Business Men* (San Francisco, 1892), iii.

47. Gould, *Principles of Pleading in Civil Actions* (Boston, 1832) viii. Generally speaking, the *civil* law stressed the letter of the statutory code and general principles; the common law was, by 1800, more precedent-bound, but with the capacity to reject the "bad law" of a rule or precedent where it seemed inconsistent with a general principle.

48. Swift, *System*, 1:3; Reeve in *Bush v Bradley,* 4 Day 298 at 305 (1810); Reeve, *Law of Baron and Femme,* preface; cited in Craig Klafter, *Reason over Precedents,* 55, 70; Redfield, *American Law Register,* n.s., 14 (1875): 728. See also Justice Benjamin Tappan in *Ohio v Lafferty,* 1 Tap. R(Ohio) 81 (1817) (comparing law to the "symetry and beauty" of architecture); Thomas Roberts, *Memoirs of John B. Gibson* (Pittsburgh, 1890), 157 (common law is "symmetrical").

49. Story, cited in Miller, *Life of the Mind,* 119. Story also complained in 1821 that "a neglect of appropriate averments" deprived "our pleadings of just pretension to . . . symmetry." Story was praised by attorney Robert Waterston for the "symmetrical beauty of proportion" of his opinions (136, 150). See also Justice Joseph Bradley's juxtaposition of the two terms in *Insurance Co. v Dunham,* 78 U.S. 1 at 23 (1870).

50. Horwitz, *Transformation 1,* 102, 103; William Nelson, *The Americanization of the Common Law: The Impact of Legal Change on Massachusetts Society, 1760–1830* (Cambridge, Mass.: Harvard University Press, 1994), 10, 255.

Horwitz goes on to say that English courts "seemed to undermine the vitality" of its own rule distinguishing the right to lateral support of land from the absence of such a right with regard to buildings "when the subject first became of general economic importance in the nineteenth century" (103), but the cases he cites to support this (*Brown v Robins,* 4 H.& N. 186, 157 ER 809 (EX 1859), and *Stroyan v Knowles,* 6 H.& N. 452, 158 ER 186 (EX 1861) seem rather late in the century to constitute a moment "when the subject first became of general economic importance in the nineteenth century," and, in any event, they do not overrule any prior decisions, but concern *mining* operations that undermined adjacent property, a very different proposition.

51. For exceptions to this generalization, see note 58.

52. *Thurston v Hancock,* 12 Mass. 220 (1815); Horwitz, *Transformation 1,* 103; Nelson, *Americanization of the Common Law,* 10, 255.

53. Nelson, *Americanization of the Common Law,* 103–4. Nelson also believes that Parker ignored relevant precedent and applied others "erroneously."

54. *Wilde v Minsterley,* 2 Rol. Ab. 564 (K. B. 1639); *Palmer v Fletcher,* 1 Sid. 167, 1 Lev. 122, 83 E. R. 329 (K. B. 1664); *Peyton v Mayor of London,* 9 B. & C. 725, 109 E. R. 269 (K. B., 1829) (the rule was the same where one razed a building upon which another had been relying for support); *Wyatt v Harrison,* 3 B. & Ad. 871, 110 E. R. 320 (K. B., 1832); *Partridge v Scott,* 3 M. & W. 220, 150 ER 1124 (Ex. 1838); *Gayford v Nicolls,* 9 Ex. 708, 156 ER 301 (1854).

Nelson particularly points to Parker's rejection of one precedent cited by Thurston's counsel, *Slingsby* v *Barnard & Hall*, 1 Rol. 430, 81 ER 586 (K. B. 1617), as being imperfectly and too briefly reported. It is very brief, and its "law French" is ambiguous; moveover, Parker seemed justified in rejecting its relevance in *Thurston*, because in *Slingerby* the defendant's digging does not appear to have been confined to his own land, for the report uses the verb "undermine."

55. Cited words are in *Wyatt* v *Harrison*. See also *Palmer* v *Fletcher*.

56. *Thurston* v *Hancock*, 12 Mass. 220 at 225–29 (1815); *Stansell* v *Jollard*, 1 Selw. N. P. 444, 8th ed. (1803) (Lord Ellenborough: One who built at the extremity of the land acquired a right to lateral support after twenty years, "but it is otherwise of a house newly built"); and *Gayford* v *Nicolls*.

57. See *Lasala* v *Holbrook*, 4 Paige Ch. (N.Y.) 169 (1833); *Panton* v *Holland*, 17 Johns. (N.Y.) 92 (1819); *Shrieve* v *Stokes*, 8 8 B.Mon. (47Ky.) 453 (1848); *Charless* v *Rankin*, 22 Mo. 566 (1856); *McGuire* v *Grant*, 25 N.J.L. 356 (1856); *Moody* v *McClelland*, 39 Ala. 45 (1863); *Oneil* v *Harkins*, 71 Ky. 650 (1871); *Mamer* v *Lussem*, 65 Ill. 484 (1872); *Gilmore* v *Driscoll*, 122 Mass. 199 at 206 (1877).

The Massachusetts court decided *for* the plaintiff in *Earle* v *Hall*, 2 Met. 353 (1841), but there the defendant's workers had "dug out the earth *under* [sic] the wall of the plaintiff's house." And Horwitz also overstates the significance of *Radcliff's Ex.* v *Mayor of Brooklyn*, 4 N.Y. 195 (1850), when he claims that the New York court had gone "still further" in rejecting "even the last vestige" of English doctrine (Horwitz, *Transformation 1*, 104). He refers to Chief Justice Greene Bronson's dicta (and it was *clearly* no more than that) on the English rule that one might cause no actionable damage to recently-built *buildings* while causing nominal damage to a neighbor's *land*. (Subsequent courts described the language that Horwitz regarded as significant as having been insignificant dicta.)

58. *Mitchell* v *Mayor of Rome*, 49 Ga. 19 (1873) (the case actually involved the undermining of a house foundation by the city's repaving of a street); *Tunstall, Tr.* v *Christian, Tr.*, 80 Va. 1 at 5 (1885), reversing *Stevenson* v *Wallace*, 68 Va. 77 (1876).

59. Morton Horwitz is this story's author, in *Transformation 1*, 32–36, 42; his tale is retold in Kermit Hall's legal history textbook, *Magic Mirror*.

60. Horwitz, *Transformation 1*, 41–42.

61. *Merritt* v *Parker*, 1 Coxe L. (N.J.) 460 (1795). For evidence that the "prior occupancy" rule was centuries old in 1800, see T. E. Lauer, "The Common Law Background of the Riparian Doctrine," *Missouri Law Review* 28 (1963): 60.

62. Horwitz, *Transformation 1*, 274. *Beissell* v *Skoll*, 4 Dallas (Pa.) 211 (1800); *Livesey* v *Gorgas* (Pa. 1811) in Brackenridge, *Law Miscellanies*, 454–55.

63. Horwitz, *Transformation 1*, 41.

64. *Cary* v *Daniels*, 49 Mass. 466 at 476–77, 481, 483 (1844).

65. *Hatch* v *Dwight & Burnell*, 17 Mass. 289 (1821). Cf. *Colburn* v *Richards*, 13 Mass. 420 (1816) (where farmer upstream from established mill builds new irrigation watergate, injuring millowner, abatement allowed, citing *Brown* v *Best*, 1 Wils. 174, 95 ER 557 (K. B. 1747) (same fact situation); *Bigelow* v *Newell*, 10 Pick. (27 Mass.) 348 (1830) (where one owns an old mill or is building one, another downstream may not build a new one or raise an old one, and the Flowage Act is not relevant; one cannot wrongfully build and simply pay damages under the act.)

66. *Sumner* v *Tileston*, 7 Pick. (24 Mass.) 198 at 203 (1828). See also *Thompson*

v *Crocket*, 26 Mass. 59 (1829) (upstream mill gets damages from new, downstream mill); *Barnett* v. *Parsons*, 64 Mass. 367 at 372 (1852) (jury verdict for downstream mill damages by newer, upstream mill affirmed).

67. *Sumner* [no relation to preceding plaintiff] v *Foster*, 7 Pick. (24 Mass.) 32 (1828). The smaller millowner had "knocked away" the flue boards "several times," as the common law allowed; the court approved. See also *Hodges* v *Raymond*, 9 Mass. 315 (1812) (upper mill can enter close of lower mill and tear down wrongfully raised flume boards).

68. *Bemis* v *Clark*, 28 Mass. 452 at 454 (1831); *Bemis* v *Upham*, 30 Mass. 169 (1832). The same may be said of the Ohio Supreme Court's opinion in *Cooper* v *Hall*, 5 Ohio 321 (1832), a decision that E. P. Krauss says "typifies the . . . prodevelopmental economic policy" of Ohio's judiciary (Krauss, "The Legal Form of Liberalism: A Study of Riparian and Nuisance law in Nineteenth Century Ohio," *Akron Law Review* 18 [1984]: 223 at 231). *Cooper* v *Hall* reveals no such proclivity. The upstream milldam owner lost because the trial evidence was that, contrary to his claim, water from the downstream mill "was not caused to flow back upon the plaintiff's mill or mill-wheels" (322). In short, he lost on the merits. *Cooper* may be compared with *Boatner* v *Henderson, et al.*, 8 Martin (La.) 473 (1826), and *People's Ice Co.*, v *Steamer Excelsior*, 44 Mich. 229 (1880).

69. See Nelson, *Americanization of the Common Law*, 49, 122, 198, 234; *Thurber* v *Martin*, 68 Mass. 394 (1854); *Gould* v *Boston Duck Co.*, 79 Mass. 442 (1859); and the cases referred to in the ensuing notes. Carol Rose, "Energy and Efficiency in the Realignment of Common Law Water Rights," *Journal of Legal Studies* 19 (1990): 287, says that Chief Justice Shaw "turned with remarkable alacrity" in these cases and in *Elliott* v *Fitchburg RR*, 64 Mass. 191 (1852) (no millowners involved), to the New York Supreme Court's new "reasonable use approach." There is no new doctrine at work here, but mere applications of the same language that can be found in over a dozen of the precedents just described in this section.

70. Nelson, *Americanization of the Common Law*, 49, 122, 198, 234.

71. See *Clapp* v *Herrick*, 129 Mass. 292 (1880) (non-milldam riparian won action against milldam owner); and three "prior occupancy" verdicts affirmed in *Knapp* v *Douglas Axe Co.*, 94 Mass. 1 (1866); *Whitney* v *Wheeler Cotton Mills*, 151 Mass. 396, 24 NE 774 (1890); and *Watuppa Reservoir Co.* v *City of Fall River*, 154 Mass. 305, 28 NE 257 (1891). Cf. *People's Ice Co.* v *Steamer Excelsior*, 44 Mich. 229 (1880); *Boatner* v *Henderson*, 5 Martin (N. S.) (La.) 186 (1826); *Cooper* v *Hall*, 5 Ohio 321 (1832); *Hoy* v *Sterrett*, 2 Watts (Pa.) 327 (1834); *Wentworth* v *Poor*, 38 Me. 243 (1854); *Miller* v *Shenandoah Pulp Co.*, 38 W. Va. 558, 18 SE 740 (1893); *Moffett* v *Brewer*, 1 Greene (Iowa) 348 (1848); *Buddington* v *Bradley*, 10 CT. 213 (1834); and *Parker* v *Griswold*, 17 Ct. 287 (1845), where a farmer won a jury verdict, affirmed on appeal, against an upstream milldam that had caused a diminution in his irrigation water.

72. As in *Merritt* v *Brinkerhoff*, 17 Johns (N.Y.) 306 (1820) (new upstream mill must pay damages to older downstream mill); *Hammond* v *Fuller*, 1 Paige Ch. (N.Y.) 197 (1828) (downstream dam can be enjoined from injury to upstream dam); *Whipple* v *Cumberland Mnfg. Co.*, 29 Fed. Cas. 934 (Circ. Ct. D. Me. 1843) (lower dam must pay for damages to upstream mill); *Tyler* v *Wilkinson*, 24 Fed. Cas. 473 (Circ. Ct. D. R.I. 1827) (mill and trench owners held to arrangement regarding use

of flow in 1796 despite entrepreneurial wishes of some); *Hoy* v *Sterrett*, 2 Watts (Pa.) 327 (1834); *Cooper* v *Hall*, 5 Ohio 321 (1832); and *Hetrich* v *Deachler*, 6 Pa. St. 33 (1847).

73. See Carol Rose, "Energy and Efficiency in the Realignment of Common Law Water Rights," *Journal of Legal Studies* 19 (1990): 261; Harry Scheiber, "Public Rights and the Rule of Law in American Legal History," *California Law Review* 72 (1984): 217; Gordon Bakken, *The Development of Law on the Rocky Mountain Frontier: Civil Law and Society, 1850–1912* (Westport, Conn.: Greenwood Press, 1983). But see *Thorp* v *Freed*, 1 Montana 651 (1872), where an evenly divided court disagreed over whether a "prior use" or a "reasonable use" rule prevailed in that water-scarce Rocky Mountain territory.

74. Scheiber, "Public Rights"; *Lux* v *Haggin*, 69 Cal. 255, 10 Pac. 674 (1886). But see *Katz* v *Walkinshaw*, 141 Cal. 116 at 133, 74 Pac. 766 at 769 (1903) (Justice McKinstry worried about "monopoly" of water "in a few hands" if the English rule of percolating water were applied in California, for then those with wealth could acquire most of the water).

TWO

1. Morton Horwitz, *The Transformation of American Law, 1780–1860* (Cambridge, Mass.: Harvard University Press, 1977), 180, 160, 161, 174–75, 176, 186: "Only in the nineteenth century" did jurists come to reject "the longstanding belief that the justification of contractual obligation is derived from the inherent just or fairness of an exchange." Horwitz cites Karl Polanyi, *The Great Transformation: The Political and Economic Origins of Our Time* (Boston: 1957), 115, on the emergence of commodities markets "around 1815."

2. Horwitz, *Transformation* 1, 265–66; Lawrence Friedman, *A History of American Law*, 2nd ed. (New York: Simon and Schuster, 1985), 534–35, 542–43; Anthony Jon Waters, "The Property in the Promise: A Study of the Third Party Beneficiary Rule," *Harvard Law Review* 98 (1985): 1109, at 1111–13.

3. Morris Arnold, review, *University of Pennsylvania Law Review* 126 (1977): 246 at 247; S. Williams, review, *U. C. L. A. Law Review* 26 (1978): 1187 at 1206–1214 (pointing to research in economic history demonstrating a lack of change in the distribution of wealth from 1770 to 1915 (1210); Richard Epstein, "The Social Consequences of Common Law Rules," *Harvard Law Review* 95 (1982): 1717 at 1748–49; Kim Lane Scheppele, *Legal Secrets: Equality and Efficiency in the Common Law* (Chicago: University of Chicago Press, 1988), 269–98; A. W. B. Simpson, "The Horwitz Thesis and the History of Contracts," *University of Chicago Law Review* 46 (1979): 533.

A. W. B. Simpson's critique is the most thorough. It encompasses virtually all of Horwitz's claims regarding the law of contracts (excluding only his treatment of labor contract breaches). Despite Simpson's critique, "Horwitz on Contracts" serves as the pedagogic history-of-contract paradigm. (See Kermit Hall, *The Magic Mirror: Law in American History* (New York: Oxford University Press, 1989), 119–22.)

4. See Hall, *Magic Mirror*, 119–20, 121, 123: In the eighteenth century consideration "had to be adequate for the bargain to be made." In the nineteenth century jurists revised the law of sales "to favor the seller." The rise of caveat emptor constituted an "indirect subsidy" to "an expanding economy." See also Hall, William

Wiecek, and Paul Finkelman, eds., *American Legal History* (New York: Oxford University Press, 1991), 172 ("In [nineteenth-century America] those with the most knowledge and greatest economic power tended to dictate the terms of contracts. Thus common law generally favored sellers over buyers and employers over laborers, and served as an instrument that aided the industrial and commercial entrepreneurs of the nineteenth century."), and Jamil Zainaldin, *Law in Antebellum Society: Legal Change and Economic Expansion* (New York: 1983), 55–56. An earlier work presaging much of Horwitz's perspective on contract is William E. Nelson, *The Americanization of the Common Law: Legal Change and Massachusetts Society, 1760–1830* (Cambridge, Mass.: Harvard University Press, 1975), 143, 174.

5. Horwitz, *Transformation 1*, 167, 184–86, 200.

6. Here the "we" is more actual than editorial: I draw in this "fairness" section, in part, on the work of an honors student, Jack Burkman, who turned a few leads into a much larger number of identified cases, about half of those that I cite here, and wrote a fine honors essay, "The Impact of the Fairness Doctrine upon English Contract Law, 1500–1800," April 1988, copy on file with University of Pittsburgh Honors College Office.

7. Story, *Commentaries on Equity Jurisprudence*, 1:249–50; cited in Horwitz, *Transformation 1*, 184.

8. As in *How* v *Weldon*, 2 Ves. Sen. 516, 28 ER 330 (Ch. 1754)

9. 1 Cox. Ch. C. 383 at 389–89, 29 ER 1213 at 1215 (Ex. 1787). Eyre does allow in dicta that he would "never quarrel with a Court of Equity" which finds evidence of fraud in an inadequacy of consideration "so gross as makes it impossible that the bargain could have been fairly made," though he does not find the bargain in this case to be fraudulent. Fraud is the deliberate misleading of a party to a contract as to matters material to a true "meeting of the minds," and was just as much a grounds for the voiding of contracts in the nineteenth as in previous centuries.

10. 7 Term R. 381 at 384, 101 ER 1032 at 1033 (K. B. 1797).

11. See *Thomson* v *Harcourt*, 1 Bro. 193, 1 ER 508 (H. L. 1722); *Collier* v *Brown*, 1 Cox Ch. C. 429, 29 ER 1234 (Ch. 1788); *Floyer* v *Sherard*, Amb. 18, 27 ER 10 (Ch. 1743); *Low* v *Barchard*, 8 Ves. 133, 32 ER 303 (Ch. 1803); *Bullock* v *Saddlier*, Amb. 764, 27 ER 491 (Ch. 1776); *Stephens* v *Bateman*, 1 Bro. C. C. 22, 28 ER 962 (Ch. 1778); *Noble* v *Smith*, Quincy (Mass.) 254 (1767) (Chief Justice Hutchinson: "It would be big with mischief to oblige people to stand always prepared to contest evidence that might be offered to the sufficiency of the consideration."); *Henly* v *Axe*, 2 Bro. C. C. 18, 29 ER 9 (Ch. 1786). See also Patrick Atiyah, *The Rise and Fall of Freedom of Contract* (Oxford: Oxford University Press, 1979), 82, 149; John J. Powell, *Essay upon the Law of Contracts and Agreements* (London, 1790), 152; and John Fonblanque, *Treatise on Equity* (Philadelphia, 1807) 1:127 n. 1, 109–10, 373–74. And see *Flureau* v *Thornhill*, 2 Black., W. 1078, 96 ER 635 at 636 (K. B. 1776), where King's Bench reversed an award of twenty pounds damages for loss of a "bargain" in a real estate contract where the title was defective with the observation (by Justice William Blackstone): "The plaintiff had a chance of gaining as well as losing by the fluctuation of the price."

12. Lord Chancellor Thurlow in *Gwynne* v *Heaton*, 1 Bro. C. C. 1, 28 ER 949 at 953 (Ch. 1778). But note that Thurlow added that equity would not set aside agreements of *adults* even where the inequality of the bargain was "gross."

13. *Heathcote* v *Paignon*, 2 Bro. C. C. 175, 29 ER 96 (Ch. 1787); *Barnardiston* v *Lingood*, 2 Atk. 133, 26 ER 484 (Ch. 1740); *Nott* v *Hill*, 1 Vernon 167, 23 ER 391 (Ch. 1686) (where Lord Keeper North reversed Chancellor Nottingham's decree relieving a young heir of such a bargain, and then, in an unreported case in 1687, Chancellor Jeffreys [of the Bloody Assises] reestablished Nottingham's decree).

14. *Graves* v *Boyd*, Va. Col. Decs. (Ran. & Bar.) R47 (1730); (no specific performance of delivery of title unless a "hard Bargain"); Chief Justice Lemuel Shaw in *Parish* v *Stone*, 14 Pick. (Mass.) 210 (1833); Justice William H. Cabell in *McKinney* v *Pinckards' Ex.*, 2 Leigh (Va.) 149 at 155 (1830); *Boyd* v *Dunlap*, 1 Johns. Ch. 478 (1815); *Lester* v *Mahan*, 25 Ala. 445 (1854); *Marshall* v *Billingsley*, 7 Ind. 250 (1855); *Blackwilder* v *Loveless*, 21 Ala. 371 (1852); *Clitherall* v *Ogilvie*, 1 Des. Eq. (S. C.) 250 (1792); *Smedes* v *Wild*, 7 How. Pr. (N.Y. Sup. Ct.) 309 at 310 (1852); (contract between businessman and inexperienced woman set aside); *Sherpard & Co.* v *Rhodes*, 7 R. I. 470 (1863); *Birdsong* v *Birdsong*, 39 Tenn. 289 (1859); *Baxter* v *Wales*, 12 Mass. 365 (1815); *Esham* v *Lamar*, 49 Ky. 43 (1849); *Schnell* v *Nell*, 17 Ind. 29 (1861); *Richardson* v *Barrick*, 16 Iowa 407 (1864) (Cole, J.: Equity will "disrobe transactions of their garbs . . . adapted to . . . entrap the weak, the unlearned or oppressed." [citing English precedent]); *Deaderick* v *Watkins*, 8 Humph. (Tenn.) 520 (1847).

15. See *Reed* v *Peterson*, 91 Ill. 288 (1878) (inexperienced woman misled by lawyer); *Blackwilder* v *Loveless*, 21 Ala. 371 (1852); *Converse* v *Blenrich*, 14 Mich. 108 (1866); *Fish* v *Leser*, 69 Ill. 394 (1873) ("agent" of foreign-born lot owner in post-fire Chicago misleads owner); *Hadley* v *Hackley*, 50 Mich. 43, 14 NW 693 (1883); *U.S.* v *Hume*, 132 U.S. 406 (1889) (dealer in corn shucks misleads govt. agent re price); *Schoelhamer* v *Rometsch*, 26 Ore. 394, 38 Pac. 344 (1894) (inexperienced woman misled re value of lot); *Boyd* v *Dunlap*, 1 Johns. Ch. 478 (1815); *King* v *Cohorn*, 6 Yerg. (Tenn.) 75 (1834) (inexp. black woman misled re sale of lot by "speculating man"); *Dunn* v *Chambers*, 4 Barb. (N.Y.) 376 (1848).

16. *Bartlett* v *Wyman*, 14 Johns. (N.Y.) 260 (1817); *Nelson* v *Weeks*, 111 Mass. 223 (1873); *Cobb* v *Charter*, 32 Ct. 358 (1865); *Spaids* v *Barrett*, 57 Ill. 289 (1870); *Chandler* v *Sanger*, 114 Mass. 365 (1874); *Fitzgerald* v *Fitz. & Mallory Constr. Co.*, 44 Neb. 463, 62 NW 899 (1895); *Kellogg* v *Kellogg*, 21 Colo. 181, 40 Pac. 358 (1895); *Stewart* v *Stewart*, 30 Ky. 183 (1832); *Kuelkamp* v *Hudding*, 31 Wis. 503 (1872); *Brown* v *Peck*, 2 Wis. 261 (1853); *Kocourek* v *Marak*, 54 Tex. 201 (1881); *Oliphant* v *Markham*, 79 Tex. 543, 15 SW 569 (1891); *Parametier* v *Pater*, 13 Ore. 121 (1885); *Central Bank of Md.* v *Copeland*, 18 Md. 305 (1862); *Notz* v *Michell*, 91 Pa.St. 114 (1879); *Quinnett* v *Washington*, 7 Green. (Me.) 134 (1830); *Chamberlain* v *Reed*, 13 Me. 357 (1836); *Sasportas* v *Jennings*, 1 Bay. (So.Car.) 470 (1795); *Alston* v *Darant*, 2 Strob's L. (So.Car.) 257 (1847); *Hough* v *Hunt*, 2 Ohio 495 (1826); *Esham* v *Lamar*, 49 Ky. 43 (1849); *Burch* v *Smith*, 15 Tex. 219 (1855); *Briggs* v *Wethey*, 24 Mich. 136 (1871); *Stenton* v *Jerome*, 54 N.Y. 480 (1873); *Kelley* v *Caplice*, 23 Kans. 337 (1880); *Lingenfelder* v *Wainwright Brewing Co.*, 103 Mo. 578, 15 SW 844 (1891).

17. Railroads: *McGregor* v *Erie RR*, 35 NJL 89 (1871); *LaFayette & Ind.RR* v *Pattison*, 41 Ind. 312 (1872); *Chic & Alton RR* v *Chic. Coal Co.*, 79 Ill. 121 (1875); *Mobile & M.RR* v *Steiner*, 61 Ala. 559 (1878); *Peters, Richer & Co.* v *RR*, 42 Ohio St. 275 (1884); *Heiserman* v *Burlington RR*, 63 Iowa 732, 18 NW 903 (1884); *W.Va Trans. Co.* v *Sweetzer*, 25 W.Va. 434 (1885).

Gas & Water Cos: *N. O. Gas Light Co v Paulding*, 12 Rob. (La.) 378 (1845); *Westlake & Button v City of St. Louis*, 77 Mo. 47 (1882); *Panton v Duluth Gas & Water Co.*, 50 Minn. 175, 52 NW 527 (1892); *Leheigh Coal & Nav. Co. v Broon*, 100 Pa. St. 338 (1882). (I have benefited greatly from John Dawson, "Economic Duress: An Essay in Perspective," *Michigan Law Review* 45 [1947]: 253 with regard to the cases of bad faith and unequal bargaining and duress.)

18. Winifred Rothenberg, "A Price Index for Rural Massachusetts, 1750–1855," *Journal of Economic History* 39 (1979); and Rothenberg, "Explanation in History: In Defense of Operationalism," in *Theory, Method and Practice in Social and Cultural History*, ed. Peter Karsten and John Modell (New York: New York University Press, 1992), 134; Bruce Mann, *Neighbors and Strangers: Law and Community in Early Connecticut* (Chapel Hill: University of North Carolina Press, 1987); Simpson, "Horwitz Thesis," 539.

19. *Andrew v Boughey*, 1 Dyer 75a, 73ER 160 (K. B. 1552); *Lord Grey's Case*, H. L. Mss 2071, f. 18 v (1567); *Preston v Tooley*, Cro. Eliz. 74, 78 ER 334 (Q. B., 1587); *Sturlyn v Albany*, Cro. Eliz. 67, 78 ER 327 (1586); C. H. S. Fifoot, *History and Sources of the Common Law* (London: Stevens, 1949), 402; *Knight v Rushworth*, Cro. Eliz. 469, 78 ER 707 (K. B. 1596); *Sherwood v Woodward*, Cro. Eliz. 700, 78 ER 935 (Q. B. 1600); *Sidenham & Worthington's Case*, 2 Leon. 324, 74 ER 497 (K. B. 1585); *Barny v Beak*, 2 Chan. Cas. 136, 22 ER 883 (Ch. 1682) (bargain enforced despite inadequacy of price even though plaintiff an expectant heir); *Batty v Floyd*, 1 Vern. 141, 23 ER 374 (Ch. 1682) (same); *Hobert v Hobert*, 2 Chan. Cas. 159, 22 ER 893 (Ch. 1683).

20. *Sturlyn v Albany*; *Knight v Rushworth*.

21. *Batty v Floyd*.

22. Morris Arnold, "Fourteenth Century Promises," *Cambridge Law Journal* 35 (1975): 321; Arnold, review of Horwitz, *University of Pennsylvania Law Review* 126 (1977): 246.

23. Horwitz, *Transformation 1*, 160; Simpson, "Horwitz Thesis," 536; J. R. Gordley, "Equality in Exchange," *California Law Review* 69 (1981): 1640; Raymond De Roover, "The Concept of the Just Price: Theory and Economic Policy," *Journal of Economic History* 18 (1958): 418.

24. So did Justice Theodore Sedgewick of Massachusetts, writing in 1811: "In every contract the intent of the parties is to be carried into effect . . . all authors of respectability whom I have had the opportunity of consulting in substance agree." *Summer v Williams*, 8 Mass. 162 at 178 (1811).

25. *Adam Smith's Lectures on Jurisprudence*, ed. R. L. Meek et al. (Oxford: Clarendon, 1978), 96.

26. Lord Chancellor Loughborough in *Adams v Weare*, 1 Bro. C. C. 567, 28 ER 1301 (Ch. 1784); *Day v Newman*, 2 Cox 77, 30 ER 36 (Ch. 1788); *Chesterfield v Janssen*, 2 Ves. Sen. 146, 28 ER 94 (Ch. 1750); *Cole v Gibbons*, 3 P. Wms. 290, 24 ER 1070 (Ch. 1734); *Cory v Cory*, 1 Ves. Sen. 19, 27 ER 864 (Ch. 1747); *Thompson v Harcourt*, 1 Brown 193, 1 ER 508 (H. L. 1722); *Cann v Cann*, 1 P. Wms. 722, 24 ER 586 at 587 (Ch. 1721); *Cass v Rudele*, 2 Vern. 280, 23 ER 781 (Ch. 1692); *Mitchell v Reynolds*, 10 Mod. 27, 88 ER 610 (Q. B. 1715); *London v Richmond*, 2 Vern. 421, 23 ER 870 (Ch. 1701).

27. *James v Morgan*, 1 Lev. 111, 83 ER 323 (K. B. 1665); *Thornborrow v Whita-*

kre, 2 Ld. Raym. 1164, 92 ER 270 at 271, 6 Mod. 305, 87 ER 1044 at 1045, 3 Salk. 97, 91 ER 715 (K. B. 1705).

28. *Earl of Clanrickard v Sidney*, Hobart 273 at 275, 80 ER 418 at 420 (C. P. 1615); cited in Phillip Hamburger, "The Development of Nineteenth Century Consensus Theory of Contract," *Law and History Review* 7 (1989): 254. See also Maxim no. 46 in Charles I's Privy Counselor, William Noy's *Principal Grounds and Maximums*, 3rd ed., ed. W. W. Hennig (Burlington, Vt., 1845), 50: "An intendment of the parties shall be ordered according to law"; and the observation of Chief Justice Addison in *Armstrong v M'Ghee*, 1 Ad. (Pa. C. P.) 261 (1795) that evidence concerning the contract in question "show an agreement of mind"; and Stephen Innes, *Labor in a New Land: Economy and Society in Seventeenth Century Springfield* (Princeton: Princeton University Press, 1983), 78 (the county courts "systematically enforced contractual rights").

29. *Browning v Beston*, 1 Plow. 131, 75 ER 202 at 216–18 (K. B. 1553); *Reniger v Fogossa*, 1 Plow. 1 at 17, 75 ER 1 at 14, 20, 27 (EX. 1551). See also *Andrew v Boughey*, 1 Dyer 75a, 73 ER 160 (K. B. 1552).

30. Thus I find A. W. B. Simpson, "Innovation in Nineteenth Century [English] Contract Law," *Law Quarterly Review* 91 (1975): 247, to be consistent with my portrayal of a Jurisprudence of the Head in America regarding contract law. Such "innovations" were entirely within the domain of "doctrinal" law—that is, within the heads of jurists working out the logic of the "principles" of contract.

31. Horwitz, *Transformation 1*, 180, 164, 330. Cf. Friedman, *History of American Law*, 541, but see also Friedman's "doubt" that "majestic capitalism would have smothered in its crib without the rule of *caveat emptor*" (264). Dismissing the "supposed ancient lineage of *caveat emptor*," Morton Horwitz tells us that its modern English and American origins lie in an English decision of 1802 and a New York decision of 1804. Horwitz, *Transformation 1*, 180; *Parkinson v Lee*, East 314, 102 ER 389 (K. B. 1802); *Seixas v Woods*, 2 Cai. R (N.Y) 48 (1804).

32. Sir Edward Coke, *Institutes of the Law of England*, 4 vols. (London, 1642), 2:714; S. F. C. Milsom, "Sale of Goods in the Fifteenth Century," *Law Quarterly Review* 77 (1961): 257 at 271 (Prisot); Alan Harding, *A Social History of English Law* (London: Penguin, 1966), 102; and Kevin Teeven, *A History of the Anglo-American Common Law of Contract* (Westport, Conn.: Greenwood, 1990), 136 (Fitzherbert); Simpson, "Horwitz Thesis," 585.

33. In *Bayly v Merrel*, Cro. Jac. 386, 79 ER 331 (K. B. 1615).

34. *Maynard v* [Oswald] *Mosley*, 3 Swans. 653 at 653, 655, 36 ER 1010 at 1010, 1011; Tem. Finch 288, 23 ER 158 at 159 (Ch. 1676).

35. Horwitz, *Transformation 1*, 180, 164, 330.

36. *Seixas v Woods*, 2 Cains. 48 at 55 (1804). See also Gulian Verplanck's observation in his *Essay on the Doctrine of Contracts* (New York, 1825), 297, that *Parkinson v Lee* restated the caveat emptor rule "as it stood in the days of Fitzherbert and Croke," albeit Verplanck misjudged the extent to which the rule had been affected by the views of a successor to Blackstone's Vinerian Chair, Richard Wooddeson. Cf. Simpson, "Horwitz Thesis," 597 n. 395; and Jefferson White, "Representing Change in Early American Law: An Alternative to Horwitz's Approach," in *The Law in America*, ed. William Pencak and Wythe Holt (New York: New York Historical Society, 1989), 238–68.

37. Friedman, *History of American Law*, 541; Hall, *Magic Mirror*, 122.

38. Until 1848 New York was served by a chancery court and a supreme court, both reviewable by the state senate, sitting as a court of errors. After passage of the Code of Procedure in 1848, all of this high court superstructure was replaced by a single court of appeals. (Later in the century, for a few years, two such courts sat, as the older one cleared its docket and went out of existence.)

39. Scheppele, *Legal Secrets*, chap. 14: "Caveat Emptor, New York, 1804–1900," 288, 293, 297–98. Scheppele adds that both Hurst's "release of energy" thesis and Horwitz's aid to "sophisticated 'seller-insider'" rationale don't work here, inasmuch as the New York Bench consistently found against manufacturers, whether they were antebellum buyers or Gilded Age sellers, and it "is hard to see how this sets loose the entrepreneurial spirit." Kermit Hall's brief analysis of the caveat emptor rule is quite similar to that of Scheppele's (*Legal Secrets*, 122). So is that of Patrick Atiyah, who points out that caveat emptor "had to contend" in nineteenth-century England "with serious opposition from judges who still believed that it was part of the job of the Courts to see that contracts were fair." (*Rise and Fall*, 479). And so are the views of Friedman (*History of American Law*, 541), when he reports an Illinois Gilded Age decision where that court distinguished between "a mere dealer in produce" who "professed to be selling for other parties" and a manufacturer, who was, by 1877, held liable for unmerchantable, defective or unwholesome products. *Chicago Packing v Tilton*, 87 Ill. 547 (1877).

40. Horwitz, *Transformation 1*, 330–31; *Barnard v Yates*, 1 Nott and McCord 142 at 150 (1818) (preferring Domat, the Civil Law, and the Golden Rule to caveat emptor and the common law). See also early decisions in Louisiana such as *Dewees v Morgan*, 1 Martin (O. S.) 1 at 3, 4 (1809).

41. See, for example, *Ricks v Dillahunty*, 8 Porter (Ala.) 133 at 141 (1828).

42. *Bradford v Manly*, 13 Mass. 139 at 144 (1816), (caveat emptor defense, offered by attorney Lemuel Shaw on behalf of merchant who sold cloves by sample, rejected by Chief Justice Parker as being "so unjust and so productive of distrust . . . among traders"); *Borrekins v Bevan*, 3 Rawle 23 (Pa. 1831); but see *Jennings v Gratz* 3 Rawle 168 (Pa. 1831). Horwitz draws our attention to these developments (*Transformation 1*, 199 n. 1). See also *Jones v Bright*, 5 Bing. 533, 130 ER 1167 (C. P. 1829) (implied warrant of merchantability where copper sheathing sold for ship's hull); and *Carter v Crick*, 28 LJ (Ex.) 238 (1859) (No warranty implied in sale of barley where wholesaler-seller lacked information about quality).

43. *McFarland v Newman*, 9 Watts (Pa.) 55 at 57–58 (1839). For a different perspective on this case see Friedman, *History of American Law*, 265. For similar rejections of "judicial guardianship" see *Hawkins v Hawkins & Ballard*, 50 Cal. 558 (1875), *Bayard v McLane*, 3 Harr. (Del.) 139 at 220–21 (1840), and David M. Gold, *The Shaping of Nineteenth Century Law: John Appleton and Responsible Individualism* (Westport, Conn.: Greenwood, 1990).

44. This point is made by Simpson, "Horwitz Thesis," 585; Atiyah, *Rise and Fall*, 479; Friedman, *History of American Law*, 541; and in Horwitz, *Transformation 1*, 199, as well. And Anon. "The Doctrine of Implied Warranty on the Sale of Personal Chattels," *American Jurist* 12 (1834): 311 (cited in Simpson, "Horwitz Thesis").

45. Horwitz's treatment of this subject is cryptic; He offers no details or examples in his text, but refers to several cases and legal notes in an endnote. Lawrence Fried-

man offers a similar, if less-conspiratorial-sounding analysis. Horwitz, *Transformation 1*, 265–66, 348; Friedman, *History of American Law*, 542–43.

46. I am indebted to Charles Heckman of Quinnipiac Law School for sharing his insights into the history of chattel mortgages, but I absolve him of any errors in this account. See also Levin Goldschmidt, *Universalgeschichte des Handelsrechts [Universal History of Mercantile Law]* (Stuttgart, 1890), 1:133, 306.

47. See *Mason v Lickbarrow*, 1 H. Black. 362, 126 ER 208 at 213, 215 (Ex. 1790); *Ex parte Hunter*, 6 Ves. J. 95, 32 ER 955 (Ch. 1801); *Austen v Halsey*, 6 Ves. J. 475, 32 ER 1152 (Ch. 1801); *Bishop v Shilleto*, 2 B. & Ald. 329n, 106 ER 387n (K.B. 1809); *Shepley v Davis*, 5 Taunt. 617, 128 ER 832 (C.P. 1812); *Delauney v Baker*, 2 Stark. 539, 171 ER 792 (N.P. 1819). Cf. *Snee v Prescott*, 1 Atk. 245, 26 ER 157 (Ch. 1743); George Long, *A Treatiste on the Law of Sales of Personal Property*, 1st American ed. (Exeter, N.H., 1823), 109; William Sheppard's *Touchstone of Common Assurance*, 1st American ed. (New York, 1808), 118.

48. See *Barrett v Pritchard*, 2 Pick. (19 Mass.) 512 at 515 (1824); *Hussey v Thornton*, 4 Mass. 405 (1808); *Marston v Baldwin*, 17 Mass 606 (1822); *Ludlow v Bowne*, 1 Johns. (N.Y.) 1 (1806); *Otis v Wood*, 3 Wend. (N.Y.) 498 (1830); *Hurt v West*, 7 Cow. (N.Y.) 756 (1827); *Marsh v Lawrence*, 4 Cow. (N.Y.) 467 (1825).

49. Friedman, *History of American Law*, 542.

50. *Dresser Mnfg. Co. v Waterston*, 44 Mass. 9 (1841); *Herring v Hoppock*, 15 N.Y. 409 (1857).

51. Friedman, *History of American Law*, 543.

52. In *Strong v Taylor*, 2 Hill (N.Y.) 326 at 329 (1842).

53. *Haak v Linderman*, 64 Pa. St. 499 (1870); See also *Stadfield v Huntsman*, 92 Pa. St. 53 (1879); *Vaughn v Hopson*, 10 Bush. (Ky.) 337 (1874); *Furniss v Hone*, 8 Wend. (N.Y.) 256 (1831); *Brundage v Camp*, 21 Ill. 330 (1859). This is why several states required the recording of chattel mortgages and conditional liens. A buyer under such an encumbrance would find it more difficult to "obtain credit upon his apparent ownership" and thereby "trap innocent purchasers and encumbrancers." "Note," *American State Rep.* 1 (1887): 63.

54. *Hayes v Wilcox*, 61 Iowa 732, 17 NW 110 (1883); *Leffel v Miller*, 7 So. 324 (Miss.) (1890); *Nicholson v Karpe*, 58 Miss. 34 (1880); *Allen v Dicken*, 63 Miss. 91 (1885); *Solinsky v O'Connor*, 54 S.W. 935 (Tex. Civ. App.) (1899); *Singer Manfg. Co. v Smith*, 40 So. Car. 509, 19 SE 132 (1893); *Galveston RR v Cowdrey*, 78 US 459 (1871) (virtually reversing *Pennock v Coe*, 64 US 117 (1860)); *U.S. v New Orleans RR*, 79 U.S. 362 (1871); *McGourkey v Toledo & Ohio Central RR*, 146 US 536 (1892).

55. *Heryford v Davis*, 102 U.S. 243 (1880) (Bradley, J., dissenting). See also *McGourkey v Toledo & Ohio Central RR*, 146 US 536 (1892); and *Murch v Wright*, 46 Ill. 487 (1868) (the "lease" of a piano for fourteen months, title to pass after final payment, was a "mere subterfuge"; the transaction was a conditional sale "made with a risk on the part of the vendor of losing his lien in case the property should be levied upon by creditors of the purchaser while in possession of the latter" (citing *McCormick Harvester v Hadden*, 37 Ill. 370 (1865)). See also *Singer Mnfg. Co. v Smith*, 40 So. Car. 509, 19 SE 132 (1893).

56. See, for example, *Bailey v Harris*, 8 Iowa 331 (1859); *Sumner v Woods*, 67 Ala. 139 (1880) (overruling *Dudley v Abner*, 52 Ala. 572 (1875)); *Cole v Berry*, 42 N.J.L.

308 (1880); *Aultman, Miller & Co.* v *Mallory,* 5 Neb. 178 (1876) (conditional sale of reaper; seller's title superior to creditor's). This was the rule as well in Ohio, Vermont, California, and Mississippi.

57. In New York bona fide purchasers, but not ordinary judgment creditors, prevailed against conditional sellers-on-credit. See *Haggerty* v *Palmer,* 6 Johns. Ch. (N.Y.) 437 (1822) (dicta); *Smith* v *Lynes,* 5 N.Y. 41 (1851) (carpeting); *Steelyards* v *Isaac Singer [Sewing Machine] Co.,* 2 Hilton (N.Y. Ct. of C. P.) 96 (1858); *Western Transp. Co.* v *Marshall,* 37 Barb. (N.Y. Sup. Ct.) 509 (1862) (wheat); *Root* v *French,* 13 Wend. (N.Y.) 570 (1835). Cf. *Hoffman* v *Nobel,* 6 Met. (Mass.) 68 (1843).

58. *Gay* v *Bidwell,* 7 Mich. 519 at 525 (1859) (rejecting the New York rule); *Hughes* v *Cory,* 20 Iowa 399 (1866). But see *Robinson* v *Elliott,* 89 US 513 (1874) (rejecting this practice as a fraud on future creditors).

59. Horwitz, *Transformation* 1, 163, 176.

60. Goldschmidt, *Universalgeschichte des Handelsrechts,* 1:133.

61. *Pykeryng* v *Thurgoode,* 2 Spelman's R. 247 (Selden Soc., ed. John Baker, 1978) (K. B. 1532); and *Peeram* v *Palmer* (1712), reported in Baron Gilbert's *Law of Evidence,* 2nd ed. (Dublin, 1756), 194, cited in Simpson, "Horwitz Thesis," 552, 555. Cf. Y. B. 10 H VII 8 pl. 18 (C. P. 1505), Atiyah, *Rise and Fall,* 200, 208. Kevin Teeven points out that Chaucery was awarding expectation damages in the fifteenth century and that one could secure such damages at comon law before 1500 through an action of detinue. Teeven, *History of the Anglo-American Common Law of Contract,* 78–79, 100 n. 132.

62. *Thompson* v *Harcourt,* 1 Bro. 193, 1 ER 508 (H. L. 1722); *Gardener* v *Pullen & Phillips,* 2 Vern. 394, 23 ER 853 (Ch. 1700); *Dorison* v *Westbrook,* 2 Eq. Ca. A 161, 22 ER 137 (Ch. 1722); *Dutch* v *Warren,* 1 Strange 406, 93 ER 598 (K. B. 1720), reported also in *Moses* v *Macferlan,* 2 Burr. 1005 at 1010, 97 ER 676 at 680 (K. B. 1760); *Cuddee* v *Rutter,* 2 Eq. Ca. Abr. 161, 22 ER 137 (Ch. 1720); also reported as *Cud* v *Rutter,* 1 P. Wms. 570, 24 ER 521 (Ch. 1720); in Charles Viner's *A General Abridgement of Law and Equity* (Dublin, 1792), 5:538, pl. 21; and in Sir Robert Chambers, *A Course of Lectures on the English Law* (Oxford, 1793), 238. See also *Stephenson* v *Wardell* (1777), an unreported King's Bench case. Notes on the case were kept by Lord Mansfield. See James Oldham, *The Mansfield Manuscripts and the Growth of English Law in the Eighteenth Century,* 2 vols. (Chapel Hill: University of North Carolina Press, 1992), 1:235–36.

63. Simpson and Teeven have also examined the American cases that Horwitz cites to establish that antebellum jurists instrumentally created the rule of expectation damages to serve the new "extensive internal commodities markets." Most refer back to specific English cases or treatises for authority that "the rule or measure of damages in such cases is to give the difference between the price controlled for and the price at the time of delivery." Simpson, "Horwitz Thesis," 547–61; Teeven, *History of the Anglo-American Common Law Contract,* 165, 173 nn. 68, 69; *Lewis* v *Carradan,* described from the notes of the Pennsylvania chief justice in *Marshall* v *Campbell,* 1 Yeates 35 at 36–37 (1791), which relies on several English authorities. See other Pennsylvania cases cited by Simpson (559 nn. 138–140), making the same point. And see Justice Jacob Sutherland's reference to *Dutch* v *Warren* for the rule in *Clark* v *Pinney,* 7 Cow. (N.Y.) 681 (1827), Tapping Reeve's reference to the rule in *Cuddee* v *Rutter* in *The Law of Baron and Femme, Parent and Child, Guardian and*

Ward, Master and Servant (Albany, 1862), 384, and Nelson, *Americanization of the Common Law*, 142, 245, who reports two Massachusetts county court decisions from 1784 and 1790 awarding expectation damages.

64. These are to Goldschmidt, *Handelsrechts*; *Cuddee* v *Rutter* and Chambers, *Lectures*; Nelson's eighteenth-century Massachusetts cases; *Clark* v *Pinney*; Reeve's *Baron and Femme*; and *infra*, note 67.

65. Simpson, "Horwitz Thesis," 539.

66. *The Purefoy Letters, 1735–1753*, ed. L. G. Mitchell (New York: 1973), 72–73.

67. *Lawrence* v *Fox*, 22 N.Y. 268 (1859); Friedman, *History of American Law*, 534–35.

68. Friedman, *History of American Law*, 534. Cf. Waters, "Property in the Promise," 1109 at 1111, 1112, 1113, and 1116: *Lawrence* v *Fox* "defied the prevailing rules," constituted an "abrupt change," and made "possible the birth of the third party beneficiary rule." The rights of third parties "had long been beyond the scope of contractual obligation [in America before *Lawrence* v *Fox*]."

69. See, for example, Irving Browne, ed., *English Ruling Cases*, 13 vols. (London, 1894–99), 1:706; Samuel Williston, "Contracts for the Benefit of a Third Person," *Harvard Law Review* 15 (1901): 767, at 785; Charles Knapp, *Problems in Contract Law* (Boston: Little Brown, 1976), 1133; L. P. Simpson, "Promises without Consideration and Third Party Beneficiary Contracts in American and English Law," *International and Comparative Law Quarterly* 15 (1966): 835, at 853.

Arthur Corbin knew better; his research had identified one key New York precedent for *Lawrence* v *Fox*—*Delaware and Hudson Canal Co.* v *Westchester Bank*, 4 Denio (N.Y.) 97 (1847)—and he consequently observed that "the decision in *Lawrence* v *Fox* can hardly, therefore, be said to have created a new rule of law." Corbin, *Contracts*, IV, sec. 788, p. 303 (1951). Nevertheless, Corbin still styled *Lawrence* v *Fox* "the leading case" and had no such comment about other precedents for that case from New York, Pennsylvania, or Massachusetts courts in his massive treatise.

70. For more elaborate account and analysis of this research see Peter Karsten, "The 'Discovery' of Law by English and American Jurists of the 17th, 18th, and 19th Centuries: Third Party Beneficiary Contracts as a Test Case," *Law and History Review* 9 (1991): 327.

71. If we utilize existing digests and compilations to identify cases, and then track precedents cited in *these* cases, and we limit ourselves to English cases decided before the modern English rule clearly crystallized (the 51 cases ending with *Tweddle* v *Atkinson* in 1861), and to American cases decided until *Lawrence* v *Fox* (109 cases) and for some forty years *after* that case (another 197 cases between 1860 and 1899), then we end up with a total of 357 English and American appellate case reports that deal with our question. This has to be very close to the total universe of such appellate cases in these years. *Century Edition of the American Digest* (St. Paul: West Publishing, 1899), vol. 11, cols. 290–300, 829–72; Williston, *supra* note 69; Corbin, *Contracts*; William Moch and W. B. Hale, eds., *Corpus Juris* (New York: American Law Book, 1917), vol. 13, 602, 609, 701–12.

72. *Adams* v *Union Ry Co.*, 21 R. I. 134, 42 Atl. 515 (1899).

73. The phrase is Maitland's, in *The History of English Law*, 2 vols. (Cambridge, 1895), 2:525.

74. That is to say, the defendant could not opt to produce a passel of witnesses

who would swear that he had discharged the debt, thus nonsuiting the plaintiff without further ado. W. J. V. Windeyer, *Lectures on Legal History*, 2nd rev. ed. (Sydney, Australia, 1957), 106–9.

75. In *Slade's Case*, 4 Co. Rep. 920, 76 E. R. 1074 (K. B. & E. X., 1603). See Harding, *Social History of English Law*, 104; R. M. Jackson, *The History of Quasi-Contract in English Law* (Cambridge: Cambridge University Press, 1936), 30–36.

76. An early exception regarding "consideration" is the case of *Howlett v Osbourn*, Cro. Eliz. 380, 78 E. R. 627 (Q. B. 1595), where the third-party beneficiary's action in assumpsit appears to have failed for what would later be called lack of consideration moving from the plaintiff.

77. *Starkey v Mill*, Style 296, 82 E. R. 723 (K. B. 1651). Two justices agreed with Roll; one "doubted."

78. *Dutton v Poole*, Lev. 210, 83 E. R. 523 (K. B., 1677) affmd. on appeal to the Court of Exchecher, T. Ray. 302, 83 E. R. 156 (EX 1677). The court of King's Bench cited *Starkey v Mill* in the process. (Chancery also regarded "moral consideration" as sufficient. Windeyer, *Lectures on Legal History*, 238.)

79. *Martyn v Hinde*, 2 Cowp. 437 at 443, 98 E. R. 1174, at 1178 (K. B. 1776).

80. *Trade-Man's Lawyer* (1703), 64, cited in Palmer, "History of Privity," at 35. See also *Marchington v Vernon*, 1 (Bos. & Pull. 101n, 126 E. R. 801n (C. P. 1787), where Buller, J., supported a suit by a third-party creditor-beneficiary and cited *Dutton v Poole* and *Martyn v Hinde*; and *Israel v Douglas*, 1 H.BL. 240, 126 E. R. 139 (C. P. 1789).

81. *Bourne v Mason*, 1 Vent. 6, 86 E. R. 5; 2 Keb., 457, 84 E. R. 287 (K. B., 1669); *Crow v Rogers*, 1 Strange 592, 93 E. R. 719 (K. B., 1727). Cf. *Ward v Evans*, 2 Ld. Ray. 928, 92 E. R. 120 (K. B. 1704).

82. Viner, *General Abridgement*, 1:333–337. Cf. T. Comyns, *Comyns Digest* (London, 1762–67), at 156 (E).

83. *Carnegie v Waugh*, 2 Dowl. & R. 277 (1823); *Fruhling v Schroeder*, 2 Bing. (N. C.) 78, 132 E. R. 31 (C. P. 1835).

84. *Williams v Everrett*, 14 East 582, 104 E. R. 725 (K. B. 1811); *Price v Easton*, 4 Barn. & Ad. 433, 110 E. R. 518 (K. B. 1833); *Colyear v Countess of Mulgrave*, 2 Keen 81, 48 E. R. 559 (Rolls 1836); *Barford v Stuckey*, 2 Bro. & B. 333, 129 E. R. 995 (C. P. 1820); *Wharton v Walker*, 4 B. & C. 165, 107 E. R. (K. B. 1825); *Liversedge v Broadbent*, 4 H. & N. 604, 157 E. R. 978, at 981 (Ex. 1859); *Tweddle v Atkinson*, 1 B. & S. 396, 121 E. R. 762 (Q. B. 1861). Cf. Windeyer, *Lectures on Legal History*, 237–40.

85. Joseph Chitty Jr., *Contracts* (London, 1842), 53.

86. Vernon Palmer, "The History of Privity—The Formative Period (1500–1680)," *American Journal of Legal History* 23 (1989): 3, at 40–50, 52.

87. *Tweddle v Atkinson*, 1 B. & S. 396, at 398, 121 E. R. 762, at 763 (Q. B. 1861).

88. Crawford Hening, "History of the Beneficiary's Action in Assumpsit," in *Select Essays in Anglo-American Legal History*, 3 vols. (Boston: Little, Brown, 1907–9), 3:367.

89. But see Atiyah, *Rise and Fall*, 372–83, 481–82, 492; and Jim Evans, "Precedent in the 19th Century," in *Precedent in Law*, ed. Laurence Goldstein (Oxford: Clarendon Press, 1987), 67–68.

90. Horwitz, *Transformation* 1; Llewellyn, *Common Law Tradition*, 37; and

J. Willard Hurst, *Law and the Conditions of Freedom in the Nineteenth Century United States* (Madison: University of Wisconsin Press, 1956), 3–32.

91. John Bly's testimony is available in David Hall, ed., *Witchhunting in Seventeenth Century New England* (Boston: Northeastern University Press, 1991), 298. See also Charles Steffen, "The Rise of the Independent Merchant in the Chesapeake: Baltimore County, 1660–1769," *Journal of American History* 76 (1989): at 31 (note to Table 2); *Rayner v Sim*, 3 H.&McH. (Md.) 451 (1796).

92. *Carnegie v Morrison*, 43 Mass. (2 Met.) 381, at 405 (1841).

93. *Crow*, in particular, was first reported by Sir John Strange in his *Reports* in 1755; the next editions of Strange's *Reports*, especially the third in 1795, were more likely to have been available in America than the first. According to Daniel Boorstin, only about one-fifth of the 150 English case report volumes published by 1775 were used in the colonies. *The Americans: The Colonial Experience* (New York: Vintage, 1958), 200.

94. For these citations see Karsten, "The 'Discovery' of Law," 327 n. 64.

95. See Karsten, "The 'Discovery' of Law," 327 n. 66.

96. For these citations see Karsten, "The 'Discovery' of Law," 327 n. 67.

97. For a complete list of these and examples of their uses see Karsten, "The 'Discovery' of Law," 327 nn. 70–73.

98. See, for example, *Dunlop v Silver*, Cranch (5 U.S.) 428 (1803); *Schemerhorn v Vanderheyden*, 1 Johns. (N.Y.) 139 (1806); and *Lovely v Caldwell*, 4 Ala. 684 (1843) (where Justice John Ormond prefaced his citations of English cases on the subject with the words "it is laid down in the books . . . ."); *Cabot v Haskins*, 3 Pick. (Mass.) 83 (1825); *Crocker v Higgins, Steene v Aylesworth, Thredgill v Pintard*, and *Van Dyne v Vreeland*, 11 N.J. Eq. 370 (1857); and *Hind v Holdship*, 2 Watts (Pa.) 104 (1833).

99. Justice John Jewett in *Barker v Bucklin*, 2 Denio (N.Y.) 45 (1846).

100. *Carnegie v Morrison*, 43 Mass. (2 Metc.) 381, at 386–93, 402, 405 (1841).

101. For these citations see Karsten, "The 'Discovery' of Law," 370–71, 375–76, at notes 86, 87, and 143.

102. 22 N.Y. 268. For a detailed analysis of the case from trial court through both appellate levels see Waters, "Property in the Promise," 1109 at 1116–33.

103. Friedman, *History of American Law*, 391–92.

104. At 274 and 175. Two other jurists, Denio and Chief Justice Johnson, felt that Fox had become Lawrence's "agent." They thereby avoided the privity problem.

105. 7 N.H. 345, at 351 (1834).

106. *Warren v Batchelder*, 15 N.H. 129, at 136 (1844).

107. 67 Mass. 317 (1854); *American Jurist* (October, 1839): 17.

108. 67 Mass. 317 at 319 and 321.

109. 44 N.C. 173, at 175 (1852); *Styron v Bell*, 53 N.C. 222 (1860). See also *Draughan v Bunting*, 31 N.C. (9 Ire.) 10 (1848).

110. *Manny v Frazier's Adm.*, 27 Mo. 419 (1858); *Page v Becker*, 31 Mo. 466 (1862).

111. See text at note 120.

112. *Owings v Owings*, 1 H&D (Md.) 485 (1827) (a gift-beneficiary "trust" case); *Eichelberger v Murdock*, 10 Md. 373 (1857) (a creditor-beneficiary case); *Kalkman v McElderry*, 16 Md. 56 (1860); *McNamee v Withers*, 37 Md. 171 (1872);

Small v *Schaefer*, 24 Md. 143, at 158 (1866); *M'Gillicuddy* v *Cook*, 5 Blackf. (Ind.) 179 (1838); *Salmon* v *Brown*, 6 Blackf. (Ind.) 347 (1842); *Farlow* v *Kemp*, 7 Blackf. (Ind.) 544 (1845). See also *Britzell & Wife* v *Fryberger*, 2 Ind. 176 (1850).

113. Robert W. Millar, *Civil Procedure of the Trial Court in Historical Perspective* (New York: Law Center, New York University, 1952), 54; Justice William Stuart in *Conklin* v *Smith*, 7 Ind. 107, at 109 (1855).

114. *Beals* v *Beals*, 20 Ind. 163 (1863); *Day* v *Patterson*, 18 Ind. 114, at 115–16 (1862). Cf. *Davis* v *Calloway*, 30 Ind. 112, at 114 (1868); and *Miller* v *Billingsley*, 41 Ind. 489 (1873).

115. *Hind* v *Holdship*, 2 Watts (Pa.) 104, at 105 and 106 (1833).

116. Sydney George Fischer, "The Administration of Equity through Common Law Forms in Pennsylvania," in *Select Essays in Anglo-American Legal History*, 3 vols. (Boston: Little, Brown, 1908), 2:810–31; Frank Eastman, *Courts and Lawyers of Pennsylvania* (New York: American Historical Society, 1922), 2:411–21; *Blymire* v *Boistle*, 6 Watts (Pa.) 182, at 184 (1837).

117. *Crampton* v *Ballard*, 10 Vt. 253 (1838). See also *Town of Milton* v *Story*, 11 Vt. 101 (1839); *Hall* v *Huntoon*, 17 Vt. 244 (1845); *Corey* v *Powers*, 18 Vt. 587 (1846); and *Fugure* v *Mutual Society of St. Joseph*, 46 Vt. 362 (1874), where Justice Redfield rejected the New York rule and noted (363) that "the course of decisions in England seems in concurrence with the uniform rule in this state." (But see *Davenport, Adm.* v *Northeastern Mutual Life Assoc.*, 47 Vt. 528 (1875), and *Coleman* v *Whitney*, 62 Vt. 123, 20 Atl. 322 [1890] where third-party gift-beneficiaries were permitted to sue on contracts for their benefit.)

118. Chief Justice H. O. Beatty in *Alcalda* v *Morales*, 3 Nev. 132 at 137 (1867); Justice Ebenezer Wells in *Lehow* v *Simonton*, 3 Colo. 346, at 348 (1877). The similarity of language in these last two opinions is striking, which suggests doctrinal borrowing. They also defended it as "sustained by ample authority" (*Alcalda*, 137; *Lehow*, 348), citing Parsons on Contracts and case law.

119. Friedman, *History of American Law*, 393; Connecticut eventually did adopt a code of procedure in 1879, but it was based on the English codes of 1852 and 1854 rather than the Field Code. Millar, *Civil Procedure*, 55.

120. Justice Warren Currier, quoting Parsons, in *Meyer, et al.,* v *Lowell*, 44 Mo. 328, at 330–31 (1869); *Flanagan* v *Hutchinson*, 47 Mo. 237 (1871); Justice Wash Adams in *Rogers* v *Gosnell*, 51 Mo. 466 at 469 (1873); *Rogers* v *Gosnell*, 58 Mo. 589 (1875).

121. *Hendrick* v *Lindsay*, 93 U.S. 143, at 149 (1876); *National Bank* v *Grand Lodge*, 98 U.S. 123, at 125 (1878); *Thatch* v *Metropole Ins. Co.*, 11 Fed. 29 (1882); *Anderson* v *Fitzgerald*, 21 Fed. 294 (1884); *Woodland* v *Newhall's Adm.*, 31 Fed. 434 (1887); *Keller* v *Ashford*, 133 U.S. 620 (1889); *Jackson Iron Co.* v *Negaunee Concentrating Co.*, 64 Fed. 298, 31 U.S. App 1 (1895); *American Exch. Nat. Bank* v *Northern Pacific RR Co.*, 76 Fed. 130 (1896). Only in *Sonstiby* v *Keeley*, 7 Fed. 447 (1880), did a federal circuit court follow the local (Minnesota) rule and allow the third-party beneficiary to sue.

122. Justice Francis Finch in *Gifford* v *Corrigan*, 117 N.Y. 257, 22 NE 756, at 757 (1889). Cf. *Garnsey* v *Rogers*, 47 N.Y. 233, at 240 (1872); *Aetna National Bank* v *Fourth National Bank*, 46 N.Y. 82, at 90 (1871); *Pardee* v *Treat*, 82 N.Y. 385, at 392 (1880); and *Simpson* v *Brown*, 68 N.Y. 361, at 362 (1877).

123. Justice William Allen in *Vrooman v Turner*, 69 N.Y. 280 (1877); Justice Finch in *Wheat v Rice*, 97 N.Y. 296, at 302 (1884).

124. See especially *Todd v Weber*, 95 N.Y. 181 (1884) at 190, 193, and *Buchanan v Tilden*, 158 N.Y. 109, 52 NE 724 (1899), at 725–27.

125. Justice Edward Bartlett in *Buchanan v Tilden*, at 727, praising Justice George Danforth in *Todd v Weber*, 95 N.Y. 181 (1884).

126. *Todd v Weber* at 190.

127. *Hutchings v Miner*, 46 N.Y. 456 (1871); and *Thorp v Keokuk Coal Co. of N.Y.*, 48 N.Y. 253 (1872).

128. Wharton's note on third-party beneficiaries to a contract is in 18 Fed. Rpt. 523, at 525 (1883).

129. For these citations see Karsten, "The 'Discovery' of Law," 378, at note 175.

130. *Berkshire Life Ins. Co., v Hutchings*, 100 Ind. 496 (1884); and *Lowe v Turpie*, 147 Ind. 652, 44 NE 25, at 30 (1896). See also *Durham v Bischof*, 47 Ind. 211 (1874).

131. For these citations see Karsten, "The 'Discovery' of Law," 378, at note 174. In addition to Indiana, the courts of Oregon, Arkansas, Nevada, Minnesota, New Jersey, and Delaware all adopted the "tough" New York rule toward creditor-beneficiaries, while allowing gift beneficiaries their suits. See *Parker v Jeffrey*, 37 PAC (Ore.) 712, at 713 (1894); *Baker v Elgin*, 11 Ore. 333, 8 PAC 280 (1884); *Washburn v Interstate Investment Co.*, 26 Ore. 436, 38 PAC 620 (1894); *Thomas Mnfg. v Prather*, 65 Ark. 27, 44 SW 218 (1898); *Ferris v Carson Water Co.*, 16 Nev. 44 (1881); *Richer v Charter Oak Life Ins. Co.*, 27 Minn. 193, 6 NW 771, at 772 (1880); *Greenwood v Sheldon*, 31 Minn. 254, 17 NW 478 (1883); *Brown v Stillman*, 43 Minn. 126, 45 NW 2 (1890); *Jefferson v Asch*, 53 Minn. 446, 44 NW 604 (1893); *Union Railway Storage v McDermott*, 53 Minn. 407, 55 NW 606 (1893). But see *Sanders v Classon*, 13 Minn. 379 (1868), *Jordon v White*, 20 Minn. 91 (1873), *Starika v Greenwood*, 28 Minn. 521, 11 NW 76 (1881), and *Bell v Mendenhall*, 71 Minn. 331, 73 NW 1086 (1898), where all the proper doctrinal elements were found to be present to sanction application of the older English rule (and, once again, Parsons on Contracts served as the primary authority). *Crowell v Hospital of St Barnabas*, 27 N.J.Eq. 650 (1876), (third-party mortgagee-beneficiary turned away on grounds that the promisee owed him no debt and the contract had been rescinded before his acceptance); and *Merchant's Union Trust Co., v New Phila. Graphite Co.*, 83 ATL (Del. Ch.) 520 (1912) (third-party mortgagee-beneficiary turned away because of the promisee owed him no debt). See more generally John Norton Pomeroy, *Code Remedies*, 5th ed. (Boston: Little, Brown, 1929), sec. 77 nn. 13, 15.

132. *Urquart v Brayton*, 12 R.I. 169 (1879); *Wood v Moriarty*, 15 R.I. 518, 9 NE 427 (1887); *Adams v Union R Co.*, 21 R.I. 134, 42 ATL 515 (1899); and *Wilbur v Wilbur*, 17 R.I. 295, 21 ATL 497 (1891).

133. Western courts of the post–Civil War era tended to rely heavily on Parsons on Contracts, probably because some of those high courts lacked complete sets of all of the published English and American reports. Thus Justice Ebenezer Wells cited Parsons on Contracts in Colorado's first impression third-party beneficiary case (*Lehow v Simonton*, 3 Colo. 346 (1877) and then referred to certain cases in Massachusetts, Indiana, and California reports and "some others which are not accessible to us" but which were noted in his edition of Parsons.

134. *Buchanan v Tilden*, 5 App. Div. 354, 39 N.Y. Sup. 228, at 233 (1896); *Conklin*

v *Smith*, 7 Ind. 107 (1855); *Clapp* v *Lawton*, 31 Ct. 95, at 104 (1862); *Washburn* v *Interstate Investment Co.*, 26 Ore. 436, 38 PAC 620, at 622 (1894).

135. Justice Henry Dutton of Connecticut in *Clapp* v *Lawton*; Justice William Stuart in Indiana in *Conklin* v *Smith*.

136. *Linneman* v *Moross' Estate*, 98 Mich. 178, 57 NW 103, at 105 (1893) (where a woman sought access in a common-law court as the cestui que trust of a gift contract that, she claimed, created a trust for her, and the high court redirected her to a court of equity); *Saunders* v *Saunders*, 154 Mass. 337 (1891); and *Buchanan* v *Tilden*, 5 App. Div. 354, 39 N.Y. Sup. 228, at 233 (1896).

137. *Coleman* v *Whitney*, 62 Vt. 123, 20 ATL 322 (1890). See also *Swan* v *Shahan*, 1 Ohio Cir. CT. 216 (1885); *Todd* v *Weber*, 95 N.Y. 181 (1884); *Buchanan* v *Tilden*, 158 N.Y. 109 (1899). In contrast, see the "hard law" meted out mercilessly in *Woodland & Wife* v *Newhall's Adm.*, 31 Fed. 434 (1887).

138. Michigan appears to have been first, in 1871 (*Comp. Laws*, 1871, sec. 5150, noted in *Miller* v *Thompson*, 34 Mich. 9 [1876]). Nebraska adopted a similar statute. (See *Shamp* v *Meyer*, 20 Neb. 223, 29 NW 379 [1886]). Connecticut's legislature (*Gen. St.*, 1902, Ch. 587) abrogated the rule in *Meech* v *Ensign* 49 Ct. 191 (1881). See also *Gen. Stats*, 1918, sec. 5610. Cf. *Williston on Contracts* 1:720 (sec. 383), and Garrard Glenn, "Purchasing Subject to Mortgage," *Virginia Law Review* 27 (1941): 853 and *Virginia Law Review* 28 (1942): 445.

139. Iowa may have been the first. See *Parker* v *Jeffrey*, 37 PAC 712, at 714 (1894).

140. True of Michigan, New York, Indiana, and the United States. See *Columbia Law Review* 14 (1914): 669, and Charles Whittier, "Contract Beneficiaries," in A. A. L. S., *Selected Readings on Contracts* (1931), at 701.

141. As in Missouri in 1865. See *Meyer* v *Lowell*, 44 Mo. 328 (1869).

142. As in Missouri (*Rogers & Peak* v *Gosnell*, 51 Mo. 466 [1873]), Oregon (*Hughes* v *Navigation Co.*, 11 Ore. 437, 5 Pac. 206 [1884]), West Virginia (*Johnson* v *McClung*, 25 W.Va. 659 [1885]), Illinois, and New Jersey.

143. As in Pennsylvania (Act of 14 March 1873, Public Law 46, overcoming the problem in *DeBolte* v *Pa Ins. Co.*, 6 Whart. [Pa.] 68 [1838]). Massachusetts, California, North Dakota, and South Dakota passed similar statutes (*Williston on Contracts*, I, 690, sec. 365). Other statutes protected the interests of life insurance policy beneficiaries from revocation of their status by the policy holder (to protect a wife whose husband divorced her, or a child whose widower-father had remarried and sought to switch the policy to the new wife). *Bliss on Life Insurance* (1872), sec. 317, served the same role in some states whose legislatures had not yet passed such statutes. Bliss asserted, without citing authority for the claim, that once a policy had been issued, the insurer was not free to change the beneficiary, and were he to try, the beneficiary had standing to sue. His language was borrowed (often without attribution) by courts friendly to that point of view. (See, for example, *Washington Central Bank* v *Hume*, 128 U.S. 195 at 206 [1888]). But these sorts of statutes, treatises, and decisions simply prompted insurance companies to insert into the standard insurance policy contract a clause specifically reserving the policyowner's right to change the beneficiary. See William R. Vance, "The Beneficiary's Interest in a Life Insurance Policy," *Yale Law Journal* 31 (1922): 343.

In England, where the courts only allowed an insurance policy beneficiary her suit if she had an "interest" in the life of the insured, a parliamentary statue in 1867 was required to give her her day in court.

Louisiana's legislature required that gift contracts such as life insurance policies be notarized. *Mutual Life Ins. Co. v Houchins* 52 La. An. 1137, 27 So 657 (1899).

144. See William P. LaPiana, "*Swift v Tyson* and the Brooding Oninipresence in the Sky: An Investigation of the Ideal of Law in Antebellum America," *Suffolk University Law Review* 20 (1986): 771, for a good discussion of this view of law. See also the documents in Michael Hoeflich, ed., *The Gladsome Light of Jurisprudence* (Westport, Conn.: Greenwood, 1988).

145. Lawrence Friedman is quite sensitive of this point (*Contract Law in America: A Social and Economic Case Study* (Madison: University of Wisconsin Press, 1985), 195, and *History of American Law*, 534); Horwitz (*Transformation 1*) is not.

THREE

1. I believe, however, that the work of Robert Kaczorowski, John Baker, and Christopher Tomlins (referred to in notes 4, 7 and 9) provide support for (and often presage) elements of this chapter.

2. Lawrence Friedman, *Total Justice* (New York: Russell Sage Foundation, 1985), 53–54, and *A History of American Law*, 2nd ed. (New York: Simon and Schuster, 1985), 467, 485; Morton Horwitz, *The Transformation of American Law, 1780–1860* (Cambridge, Mass., 1977), 99; Thomas Russell, "Historical Studies of Personal Injury Litigation: A Comment on Method," *Georgia Journal of Southern Legal History* 1 (1991): 109 at 112. Friedman allows, however, that by the late nineteenth century courts had created a number of exceptions to the harsher of these rules in sympathy with injured plaintiffs. (*History of American Law*, 476, 483, 487.) Kermit Hall also seems equivocal on the subject. At one point he says that antebellum American jurists maintained a "middle ground" between "capitalists" and "victims," while on the next three pages he tells us that they replaced a "strict liability" standard that had prevailed in *both* the actions of trespass and case, with one requiring that the defendant's negligence be proved, and tells us that this new "fault standard" was "removed from jury supervision," which facilitated "economic development by insulating entrepreneurs from the costs of accidents" (*The Magic Mirror: Law in American History* [New York: Oxford University Press, 1989]), 123–26.

3. Russell, "Historical Studies"; Randolph Bergstrom, *Courting Danger: Law and Personal Injury in New York City, 1870–1910* (Ithaca: Cornell University Press, 1992); Edward Purcell, *Litigation and Inequality: Federal Diversity Jurisdiction in Industrial America 1870–1958* (New York: Oxford University Press, 1992).

4. Leonard Levy, *Law of the Commonwealth and Chief Justice Shaw* (Cambridge, Mass.: Harvard University Press, 1957), 178–79; Friedman, *History of American Law*, 300–301, 473; Hall, *Magic Mirror*, 125; Christopher Tomlins, "A Mysterious Power: Industrial Accidents and the Legal Construction of Employment Relations in Massachusetts, 1800–1850," *Law and History Review* 6 (1988): 375 at 418–21.

5. Tomlins was the first to appreciate that they were not innovating.

6. Horwitz, *Transformation 1*, 89–90; Morton Horwitz, *The Transformation of*

American Law, 1870–1960 (New York: Oxford University Press, 1992), 123; Hall, *Magic Mirror*, 124; Herbert Hovenkamp, "Pragmatic Realism and Proximate Cause in America," *Journal of Legal History* 3 (1982): 3, at 5.

7. See especially Robert Kaczorowski, "The Common Law Background of Nineteenth Century Tort Law," *Ohio State Law Journal* 51 (1990): 1127. See also Morris Arnold, "Accident, Mistake, and the Rules of Liability in the 14th Century Law of Torts," *University of Pennsylvania Law Review* 128 (1979): 361; Stephen Williams, review of Morton Horwitz's *Transformation 1, UCLA Law Review* 25 (1978): 1187; Stephen B. Young, "Reconceptualizing Accountability in the Early Nineteenth Century: How the Tort of Negligence Appeared," *Connecticut Law Review* 21 (1989): 197; Robert L. Rabin, "The Historical Development of the Fault Principle: A Reinterpretation," *Georgia Law Review* 15 (1981): 925 at 927, 960; Gary Schwartz, "Tort Law and the Economy in Nineteenth Century America: A Reinterpretation," *Yale Law Journal* 90 (1981): 1717 at 1727, 1731; Schwartz, "The Character of Early American Tort Law," *UCLA Law Review* 36 (1989): 641; Samuel Donnelly, "The Fault Principle: A Sketch of its Development in Tort Law During the Nineteenth Century," *Syracuse Law Review* 18 (1967): 728; and Percy Winfield, "The Myth of Absolute Liability," *Law Quarterly Review* 42 (1926): 37.

8. Stephen Gilles, "Inevitable Accident in Classical English Tort Law," *Emory Law Journal* 43 (1994): 575 at 634, 643–44, 645; S. F. C. Milsom, *Historical Foundations of the Common Law* (London: Butterworths, 1969), 347–48.

9. John H. Baker, *An Introduction to English Legal History*, 3rd ed. (London: Butterworths, 1990), 456. (R. H. Helmholz makes the same point regarding slander trials in seventeenth- and eighteenth-century England: The defense of a special traverse [later a general denial—"not guilty"] enabled the defendant to put the question before the jury, in mitigation, as a matter of fact. Helmholz, "Civil Trials and the Limits of Responsible Speech," in *Juries, Libel and Justice: The Role of English Juries in 17th and 18th Century Trials for Libel and Slander* (Los Angeles: W. Clark Memorial Library, UCLA, [1984], 3–36).

Morton Horwitz, in a note, allows (*Transformation 1*, 303) that "it seems obvious" that juries in early-nineteenth-century America *were* deciding whether defendants charged with trespass vi et armas had been negligent, and cites trial records to this effect, but then he decides that this evidence means, "in short," that "the negligence standard has already developed an 'underground' existence"!

10. *Brainton* v *Pinn*, (K. B. 1290), *Select Cases Court of K. B.* (London: Seldon Society, 1936), 1:181; *Gibbons* v *Pepper*, 4 Mod. 405, 87 ER 469 (K. B. 1696); also reported as *Gibbons* v *Pepper*, 1 Ld. Ray. 39, 91 ER 922 (K. B. 1696); *Ogle* v *Barnes*, 8 Term R. 188 at 191, 101 ER 1338 (K. B. 1799); *Wordworth* v *Willan & Others*, 5 Esp. 272, 170 ER 809 (N. P. 1805).

11. One could, theoretically, look to early Roman Pandects and later Roman glossators for evidence that negligence had to be proved to recover from one whose fire (for example) damaged your property (*Tortious Liability for Unintentional Harm in the Common Law and the Civil Law: Vol. 2: Materials*, ed. F. H. Lawson and B. S. Makesinis [Cambridge: Cambridge University Press, 1982], 14–15), but we will limit ourselves to the early modern common-law record.

12. Bracton, *DeLegibus*, 120b, cited in John Henry Wigmore, "Responsibility for Tortious Acts: Its History," in *Select Essays in Anglo-American Legal History* (Bos-

ton: Little, Brown, 1909), 3:487 n. 2; Alan Harding, *A Social History of English Law* (London: Penguin, 1966), 135; *Reniger v Fogossa*, 1 Plow. 1, 75 ER 1 at 14 (Ex. 1551).

13. English: *Bayly v Merrel*, Cro. Jac. 386, 79 ER 331 (K. B. 1615); *Mihael v Alestree*, 2 Lev. 173, 83 ER 504 (K. B. 1677); *Jones v Hart*, 2 Salk. 440, 91 ER 382 (K. B. 1698) (dicta of Holt, C. J.); *Turberville v Stampe*, 12 Mod. 152, 88 ER 1228 (K. B. 1698). Cf. *Coggs v Bernard*, 2 Ld. Ray. 909, 92 ER 107 (Q. B. 1703); and *Mason v Keeling*, 1 Ld. Ray. 606, 91 ER 1305 (K. B. 1700). Early American: Smyth v Beach, *New Haven Colonial Records*, I, 88 (1643); *Swift v Berry & Town of Kent*, 1 Root (Ct.) 448 (1792); *Waldron v Hopper*, 1 Coxe (N.J.) 339 (1795); *Van Cott v Negus*, 2 Caines (N.Y.) 335 (1804).

14. *Weaver v Ward*, Hobart 134, 80 ER 284 (K. B. 1616).

15. *Smyth v Beach*, *New Haven Colonial Records*, I, 88 (1643), cited in Richard Morris, "Responsibility for Tortious Acts in Early American Law," in Morris, *Studies in the History of American Law* (Philadelphia: J. M. Mitchell, 1959), 208. See also text at notes 23, 89, and 93.

16. Horwitz, *Transformation 1*, 98, 99; *Clark v Foot*, 7 Johns. (N.Y.) 421 (1810); *Records of Plymouth Colony*, ed. Nath. Shurtleff (Boston, 1857), 7:41; Morris, *Studies in the History of American Law*, 235, 201.

17. Cited in Baker, *Introduction to English Legal History*, 456.

18. Ibid., 466.

19. *Tenant v Goldwin*, 2 Ld. Ray. 1089, 92 ER 222 (K. B. 1705); Bathurst, *An Institute of the Law Relative to Trials at Nisi Prius* ["Buller's *Nisi Prius*"] (Dublin 1768), 35–36; Thomas Wood, *An Institute of the Laws of England* (London, 1724), 542 (for "daily increasing" remark about tort actions), cited in Baker, *Introduction to English Legal History*, 346. See also Kaczorowski, "Common Law Background," 1127.

20. Horwitz argues that English jurists distinguished between trespass and case as strict liability and negligence (*Transformation 1*, 90.) Horwitz cites Benjamin Oliver on this. But Benjamin Oliver says, in his *Forms of Practice* (Boston, 1828), 619: "Without any negligence or fault, . . . no action can be maintained" in either trespass or case. Thus the New York Supreme Court held, in *Blin v Campbell*, 14 Johns. 432 (1817), that "from the authorities on the subject [citing Chitty on pleading] it appears that if the injury was attributable to negligence, though it were immediate, the party injured has an election, either to treat the negligence of the defendant as the cause of action, or to declare in case, or to consider the act itself as the injury, and to declare in trespass."

21. *Brucher v Fromont*, 6 Term R. 659, 101 ER 758 (K. B. 1796); *Leame v Bray*, 3 East 593, 102 ER 724 (K. B. 1803); *Wordworth v Willan & Others*, 5 Esp. 272, 170 ER 809 (N. P. 1805); *Rogers v Imbleton*, 2 Bos. & Pul. (N. R.) 117, 127 ER 568 (C. P. 1806); *Hopper & Wife v Reeve*, 7 Taunt. 699, 129 ER 278 (C. P. 1817); *Wakeman v Robinson*, 1 Bing. 212, 130 ER 86 (C. P. 1823).

22. Sir William Jones, *Treatise on the Law of Bailments* (London, 1781), 6; Bayley, J., in *Jones v Bird*, 5 B. & Al. 837 at 845, 106 ER 1397 (K. B. 1822); *Dygert v Bradley*, 8 Wend. (N.Y.) 470 (1832) (Selden, J.: Actionable negligence "in legal phraseology," is "the want of such care or skill as the law holds every man bound to exercise."); *Vaughan v Menlove*, 3 Bing. (N. S.) 468 at 475, 132 ER 490 (C. P. 1837).

See also my text at notes 112–16 on "foreseeability" language in negligence opinions in the 1850s and 1860s.

When Lawrence Friedman tells us that Francis Hilliard's *Law of Tort* (1859) was "the first English-language treatise on the subject" (*History of American Law*, 467) he is not allowing that Sir William Jones's *Treatise on Bailments* (1781) and Joseph Story's *Law of Bailments* (Boston, 1832) were essentially treatises on torts not involving strangers.

23. *MacPherson* v *Buick Motor Co.*, 217 N.Y. 382, 111 N.E. 1050 (1916); *Escola* v *Coca-Cola Bottling*, 24 Cal 2nd 453, 150 P. 2nd 436 at 441 (1944); G. Edward White, *Tort Law in America: An Intellectual History*, 2nd ed. (New York, 1985), 120, 170, 198. Cf. George Priest, "The Invention of Enterprise Liability: A Critical History of the Intellectual Foundations of Modern Tort Law," *Journal of Legal Studies* 14 (1985): 466. Gary Schwartz, "New Products, Old Products, Evolving Law, Retroactive Law," *N.Y.U. Law Review* 58 (1983): 797; and Schwartz, "Forward: Understanding Product Liability," in *California Law Review* 67 (1979): 435, offers some early-twentieth-century examples of suits by "ultimate consumers" against manufacturers, sanctioned in California courts.

24. *Winterbottom* v *Wright*, 10 M. & W. 109, 152 ER 402 (Ex. 1842); Friedman, *Total Justice* (N.Y. 1985), 351, 355.

25. The median of such product liability awards in America in 1989 was $215,441 (B. Ostrom, D. Rottman, and R. Hanson, "What are Tort Awards Really Like?," *Law and Policy* 14 (1992): 77 at 85), or about ten times the median income; the median award for personal injury caused by defective axles on stagecoaches and trains in the nineteenth century was also about ten times the median income. See chapter 9.

26. See, for example, *Boyce* v *Anderson*, 2 Peters (27 U.S.) 149 (1829); and *Aston* v *Heaven*, 2 Esp. 533, 170 ER 445 (N. P. 1797). For a good analysis of this issue see Kaczorowski, "Common Law Background," 1127 at 1159–67. We are in Professor Kaczorowski's debt for his analysis of many of the same cases I address in this section.

27. This story's steamboat burned after its boiler exploded during a race with another. Clemens had experienced the explosion of the SS *Pennsylvania* in 1858; 150 persons had been killed.

28. Friedman, *History of American Law*, 470, 476. Several pages later (480) Friedman briefly notes for the reader the Congressional Acts of 1838 and 1852, acts which imposed criminal penalties on those using uninspected or defective steamboat boilers and equipment or misusing the same, and which stipulated that a boiler explosion was prima facie evidence of negligence.

29. They were also held liable to shippers, passengers, and crew in the event of collisions, groundings, and other accidents due to the negligence of one of their agents, contrary to the impression Friedman gives. See *Charleston & Columbia Steamboat Co.* v *Bason*, Harp. (16 S. C.) 262 at 264 (1824) (Justice John Richardson: Steamboats have "accelerated and cheapened so much the carriage of our product to market" that "I should be sorry indeed to impose any check on the enterprise of the steamboat companies." *However*, "their own financial advantage depends greatly upon the implicit confidence of the public," and, in any event, "the common

law of common carriers has been well settled, and is convenient, safe and whole-some." Hence the company was held liable for books damaged by the grounding of the vessel.); *Carlisle* v *Holton, et al.*, 3 La. Ann. 48 at 49–50 (1848) (Justice Thomas Slidell: "In the reckless race of two steamboats to catch the passengers" at the wharf at Pass Christian leading to a collision between them, the *Edna* should have "aban-doned his course to secure the safety of his vessel and passengers. . . . The practice of racing, which has become so common on our waters, is, in our opinion, highly dangerous and reprehensible; and when a collision takes place between boats thus engaged, they must not expect any relief at our hands." Hence reckless behavior of plaintiff barred any recovery by him from defendant, a verdict which should not be read as "nobody to blame."); *Simpson* v *Hand*, 6 Whart. (Pa.) 311 at 322 (1841) (Chief Justice J. B. Gibson: When a collision due to the negligence of both captains, the owner of goods shipped on one must sue that vessel; not the other.); *Camden & Phila. Steamboat Ferry Co.* v *Monaghan*, 10 Weekly Notes of Cases (Pa.) 46 (1881) (where passenger fell when ferry struck pier, no contributory negligence. "One of the great pleasures of steamboat travel is the ability of passengers to move about."); *Opsahl* v *Judd*, 30 Minn. 128, 14 N. W. 575 (1883) (steamboat towing barge party liable when passenger on barge thrown overboard and drowned when vessel hit shore); *Bequette* v *People's Transp. Co.*, 2 Ore. 200 (1867) (steamship liable for run-ning down flat boat and skiff); *The George Washington & The Gregory*, 76 U.S. 513 (1869) (a passenger injured on a ferryboat hit by a steamboat on the Hudson River can recover [ten thousand dollars] from *both* if both at fault); *Holmes* v *Oregon & Cal. Ry.*, 5 Fed. 523 (1881) (drowning at steam-ferry landing due to lack of guard); *Julien* v *Cpt. & Owners of Steamer Wade Hampton*, 27 La. Ann. 377 (1875) (pas-senger recovered for injuries when hit by barrel while freight discharged); *Miller* v *The W. G. Hewes*, 16 Fed. Cas. 363 (C. C. E.D. Tex. 1870) (eight thousand dollars, affirmed when steamer ran down skiff, the captain saying "D——the little boat!"); *The David Dows*, 16 Fed. 154 (D. C. N.D., N.Y., 1883) (collision of vessels on Lake Erie; admiralty rule, apportioning loss according to degree of negligence); *Holmes* v *Watson* [!], 29 Pa. St. 457 (1857) (steamboat liable in collision with coal barges); *Killien Hyde, et al.*, 63 Fed. 172 (D. C. S.D., N.Y., 1894) (five thousand dollars for heirs of fireman killed in collision); *Williamson, et al.* v *Barrett, et al.*, 54 U.S. 101 (1851) (award to ascending vessel struck by descending vessel on Ohio River; viola-tion of rules of road); *Duggins* v *Watson*, 15 Ark. 118 (1854) (shipper should sue car-rier, not owner of other vessel, if both vessels at fault in collision). But see *Dougan* v *Champlain Transp. Co.*, 56 N.Y. 1 (1873) (heirs nonsuited where passenger fell overboard and drowned chasing hat); *Boyce* v *The Empress*, 1 Ohio Dec. R (*Western L. J.*) 173 (1845) (plaintiff's steamboat at fault too in collision; no recovery); *Owners of S. B. Farmer* v *McCraw*, 26 Ala. 189 (1855) (flatboat run into; jury finds for defen-dant); *Broadwell* v *Swigert*, 43 Ky. 39 (1846) (plaintiff's steamboat also at fault in collision; no recovery).

30. Charge to Grand Jury by District Judge McCaleb, D. C., E. D. La., 30 Fed. Cas. 990 (1846). McCaleb referred to the Congressional Act of 1838 imposing pen-alties and fixing liability as legislation "dictated by humanity." Cf. *Poree* v *Cpt. Cannon et al.*, 14 La. Ann. 506 (1859); *McMahon* v *Davidson*, 12 Minn. 357 (1866); *Caldwell* v *N. J. Steamboat Co.*, 47 N.Y. 282 (1872); *Yeomans* v *Contra Costa Steam*

Navigation Co. 44 Cal. 71 (1872); *SS New World* v *King*, 16 How. (57 U.S.) 469 (1853) ($2,500 award to ship's waiter on free pass when vessel raced another on Sacramento River and boiler exploded).

31. *U.S.* v *Taylor*, 28 Fed. Cas. 25 at 27, 30 (C. C. Ohio, 1851); (for a number of reasons developed by his attorney, the defendant in this case was acquitted by the jury). See also *U.S.* v *Warner, et al.*, 28 Fed. Cas. 404 (C. C. Ohio 1848); *Comm.* v *Bilderback*, 2 Pars. Sel. Eq. (Pa.) 447 (1843); *The Henry Clay*, 11 Fed. Cas. 1164 (D. C. S.D., N.Y. 1852); *U.S.* v *Keller*, 19 Fed. 633 (C. C. W.Va. 1884) (drunken pilot found guilty of manslaughter in death of fifty-eight in collision on Ohio River near Mingo Is., July 4, 1882); *Smith* v *Br.& N. A. R.M. S. Packet Co.*, 46 N.Y. Super. (14 Jones & Sp.) 86 at 89–90 (1880). And see *Amer. S. S. Co.* v *Landreth*, 108 Pa. St. 264 (1885) (owners responsible for injury to passenger where handrail not available in appropriate place). But see *Yerkes* v *Keokuk N. Line Packet Co.*, 7 Mo. App. 265 (1879), where a verdict for a passenger injured when a paddlewheel broke was reversed and remanded because the trial judge's instructions (the company "must use the most perfect materials") were deemed too extreme.

32. See *Wilson* v *Merry*, L. R., S. & D. App., 1 H. L. (Scot.) 326 (1868).

33. *McMahon* v *Davidson*, 12 Minn. 357 (1867); *Connolly* v *Davidson*, 15 Minn. 519 (1870). See also *SS New World* v *King*, 16 How. (57 U.S.) 469 (1853).

Samuel L. Clemens and Charles D. Warner were referring to the results of a coroner's inquest, which would have addressed the question of whether federal manslaughter charges should be brought against the owners or officers. (*The Gilded Age* [1873], 38). Manslaughter charges clearly *were* being brought against some for boiler explosions (see note 29), but, in any event, *civil* actions in tort for damages were more frequently being brought whether or not manslaughter charges had been.

34. *Losee* v *Buchanan and Bullard*, 51 NY 476 at 484 (1873).

35. Horwitz, *Transformation 1*, 71.

36. *Losee* v *Clute* [the manufacturer of the boiler], 51 N.Y. 494 (1873). The court cited *Mayor of Albany* v *Cunliff*, 2 N.Y. 165 (1849) on this question. A city maintaining a bridge, not its architect or constructor, was liable for injury to a bridge user, because the city had commissioned and accepted the work and monitored its use.

37. *Rylands* v *Fletcher*, LR. 3 H. L. 330 (1868).

38. *Losee* v *Buchanan & Bullard*, 51 N.Y. 476 at 478–79.

39. See *Spencer* v *Campbell*, 9 W.&S. (Pa.) 32 (1845), for another example of a bursting defective boiler where its owners, operators of a grist mill, were held liable, ("They brought on the misfortune, and must therefore bear it."). And see *City of Lafayette* v *Allen*, 81 Ind. 166 (1881), for a case of city liability to an employee for a defective fire-engine boiler; and *Noyes* v *Smith & Lee*, 28 Vt. 59 (1856) (boiler exploded; engineer sued; master liable).

40. Lord Kenyon instructing the jury in *White* v *Boulton & Others*, Peake 113, 170 ER 98 at 114 (N. P. 1795) (action was "assumpsit," not "case"; jury verdict for sixty pounds, where a passenger's arm was broken due to negligence); *Aston* v *Heaven*, 2 Esp. 533, 170 ER 445 (N. P. 1797); Lord Ellenborough in *Israel* v *Clark*, 4 Esp. 259, 170 ER 711 (N. P. 1803); Best, C. J., in *Brenner* v *Williams*, 1 Car. & P. 414, 171 ER 1254 (N. P. 1824). Cf. *Jackson* v *Tollett*, 2 Stark. 37, 171 ER 564 (N. P. 1817).

41. *Crofts v Waterhouse*, 3 Bing. 319, 130 ER 536 (C. P. 1825) (italics mine).

42. *Curtis v Drinkwater*, 2 B.& A. 169 at 171, 109 ER 1106 (K. B., 1831).

43. *Sharp v Grey*, 9 Bing. 457, 131 ER 684 at 685 (C. P. 1833).

44. *Fales v Dearborn*, 18 Mass. (1 Pick.) 344 at 346 (1823); *Frink v Potter*, 17 Ill. 405 (1856); *Farrish & Co. v Reigle*, 11 Gratt. (Va.) 697 at 704, 717, 719 (1854). Cf. *Saltonstall v Stockton*, 21 Fed. Cas. 275 (C. C. Md. 1838); *Stokes v Saltonstall*, 38 U.S. 181 (1839); *McKinney v Neil*, 16 Fed. Cas. 219 (1 McLean 540) (C. C. D. Ohio, 1840); *Fuller v Talbot*, 23 Ill. 357 (1860); *Fairchild v Calif. Stage Co.*, 13 Cal. 599 (1859).

45. *Ingalls v Bills*, 50 Mass. (9 Met.) 1 at 14 (1845); *Yale v Hampden & Berk. Turnpike Co.*, 35 Mass. (18 Pick.) 359 (1836). (The defendant in *Ingalls* may have been one of the exceptions to our story because of the quality of his counsel: Simon Greenleaf and Theophilus Parsons Jr.).

46. *Escola*, 150 Pac 2nd 436 at 441: "The risk of injury can be insured by the manufacturer and distributed among the public as a cost of doing business."

47. *Nolton v Western RR*, 15 N.Y. 444 at 449 (1849); *Cotterill & Wife v Starkey*, 8 Car. & P. 691, 173 ER 676 (N. P. 1839).

48. See *Cayzer v Taylor*, 76 Mass. 274 (1857); *Ford v Fitchburg RR*, 110 Mass. 240 (1872); *Lobdell v Bullitt*, 13 La. 348 (1838); *Forsyth & Simpson v Perry*, 5 Fla. 337 (1853); *Noyes v Smith & Lee*, 28 Vt. 59 (1856); *Keegan v Western RR*, 8 N.Y. 175 (1853); *Howes v S. S. Red Chief*, 15 La. Ann. 321 (1860); *McMahon v Davidson*, 12 Minn. 357 (1866); *Yeomans v Contra Costa Steam Navigation Co.*, 44 Cal. 71 (1872); and *Lowndes v The Phoenix*, 34 Fed. Cas. 760 (D. C. S.C. 1888).

49. 10 M. & W. 109, 152 ER 402 (Ex. 1842). See also *Longmeid v Holliday*, LR 6 Ex. 761, 155 ER 752 (Ex. 1851) (manufacturer of defective lamp not liable for injury due to lack of privity with victim). As we know, however, American courts held manufacturers of "inherently dangerous" objects, such as poisons, illuminating oil, painting scaffolds, and even stepladders, to strict product liability standards as early as 1852. See *Thomas v Winchester*, 6 N.Y. 397 (1852); *Wellington v Oil Co.*, 104 Mass. 64 (1870); *Elkins v McKean*, 79 Pa. St. 493 at 502 (1875); *Coughtry v Globe Woolen Co.*, 56 N.Y. 124 (1874); *Devlin v Smith*, 89 N.Y. 470 (1882); and *Schubert v J. R. Clark Co.*, 49 Minn. 331, 51 N. W. 1103 at 1106 (1892) (manufacturers of defective stepladder liable despite lack of privity as the company was "to be deemed to have anticipated that in the ordinary course of events," the ladder "would come into the hands of a purchaser." (But see *Loop v Litchfield*, 42 N.Y. 351 (1870) (manufacturer of a balance-wheel used in sawing wood, later *repaired* by the manufacturer at the direction of the user, not liable to worker injured when defective repair failed; worker *could*, however, sue employer-user of balance wheel).

50. Several opinions made this point. See, for example, *Hegeman v Western RR*, 13 N.Y. 9 (1854).

51. The first English case to permit such a suit was *Yarborough v Bank of England*, 16 East 6, 104 ER 991 (K. B. 1812). (Actually the Massachusetts Supreme Court anticipated *Yarborough* by a year, permitting such a suit under principles of agency. See *Minot v Curtis*, 7 Mass. 444 (1811).) Herbert Hovenkamp, *Enterprise and American Law, 1836–1937* (Cambridge, Mass., 1991), 15; Schwartz, "Character of Early American Tort Law," 641 at 650; Stewart Kyd, *Treatise on the Law of Corporations* (London, 1793), 223; Horwitz, *Transformation 1*, 29–30.

52. As had been the case with steamboats, railroads were also held liable to passengers and strangers crossing tracks for negligent acts of their employees that led to collisions, derailments, and running-down accidents, but here we are concerned only with accidents that appeared to have been due to faulty equipment that might have led today to a product liability suit.

53. And see text at note 136 for exceptions in America to the assumption of risk rule for employees apropos defective employer equipment.

54. *McElroy & Wife v Nashua & Lowell RR*, 58 Mass. 400 at 402 (1849); *Holbrook & Wife v Utica & Schen. RR*, 16 Barb. (N.Y.) 113 (1852); *Hegeman v Western RR*, 16 Barb. (N.Y.) 353 at 356 (1853); *Hegeman v RR*, 13 N.Y. 9 (1854); *N.J. RR v Kennard*, 9 Harris (Pa.) 204 (1853); *Nashville & Chat. RR v Elliott*, 1 Cold. (41 Tenn.) 616 (1860). Cf. *Bradley v Boston & Me. RR*, 2 Cush. (56 Mass.) 539 (1848); *Laing v Colder*, 8 Barr. (Pa.) 479 at 483 (1848); *Phila. & Read. RR v Derby*, 55 U.S. 468 at 486–87 (1852); *Chicago, etc. RR v Swett*, 45 Ill. 197 (1867).

55. *Alden v N.Y. Central RR*, 26 N.Y. 102 at 104 (1862); Russell, "Historical Studies," 109 at 119 (on report by chief engineer on S. C. Canal & RR Co. on axle defects).

56. *Carpue v London & Brighton Ry*, 5 Q. B. 747, 114 ER 1431 (Q. B. 1844); cited, for example in *Holbrook & Wife v Utica & S. RR*, 16 Barb. (N.Y.) 113. See also *Grote v Ry*, 2 Ex. 251, 154 ER 485 (Ex. 1848); and *Burns v Cork & Bandon Ry*, 13 Ir. C. L. R. 543 at 548 (Ex. 1863) (railway, not manufacturer, liable to passengers for injuries caused by defective crank-pin in locomotive, as any other course "would be a distraction dangerous to the public.")

57. *Stokes v Eastern Counties Ry.*, 2 F&F 691, 175 ER 1243 (N. P. 1860); *Ford v London & S. W. Ry.*, 2 F&F 730, 175 ER 1260 (N. P. 1862); *Redhead v Midland Ry.*, L. R., 4 Q. B. 379 (1869). Cf. *Withers v Great Northern Ry.*, 1 F&F 165, 175 ER 674 (N. P. 1858).

58. *Meier v Pa. RR*, 64 Pa. St. 225 at 230 (1870); *Nashville & Decatur RR v Jones*, 9 Heisk. (56 Tenn.) 27 at 36 (1871); *McPadden v N.Y. Central RR*, 44 N.Y. 478 (1871); *Southern Law Review* 6, 537; *American Reports* 31 (1878): 326. See also *Grand Rapids & Ind. RR v Huntley*, 38 Mich. 363 (1878).

59. Thus as late as 1875 a locomotive's smokestack was to be "constructed . . . so perfect[ly] as to prevent the emission of sparks" by the company's "availing itself of all the discoveries which science and experience have put within its reach." *Pittsburgh, Cinc. & St. L. RR v Nelson*, 51 Ind. 150 at 153 (1875).

60. See text at notes 38 and 39.

61. *Cowley v Mayor of Sunderland*, 6 H. & N. 565 at 572, 158 ER 233 at 236 (Ex. 1861); *Shipley v 50 Associates*, 106 Mass. 194 (1870); *Kies v City of Erie*, 169 Pa. St. 598 (1895); *Godley v Hagerty*, 20 Pa. St. 387 (1853); *Carson v Godley*, 26 Pa. St. 111 (1856); *Francis v Cockrell*, L. R., 5 Q. B. 184 (1870); *Brazier v Polytechnic Inst.*, 1 F. & F. 507, 175 ER 829 (N. P. 1859); *Gregg v Page Belting Co.*, 69 N. H. 247, 46 Atl. 26 at 28 (1897); *Treadwell v Whittier*, 80 Cal. 574, 22 Pac. 266 (1889); *Goodsell v Taylor*, 41 Minn. 207, 42 N. W. 873 (1889); *Thomas v Western Union*, 100 Mass. 156 (1868); *Col. Elec. Co. v Lubbers*, 11 Col. 505, 19 Pac. 479 (1888); *Kraatz v Brush Elec. Light Co.*, 82 Mich. 457, 46 N. W. 787 (1890); *United Elec. Ry. v Skelton*, 89 Tenn. 423, 14 S. W. 863 (1890); *S. W. Tel. & Tel. Co. v Robinson*, 50 Fed. 810 (1892); *Clements v Elec. Light Co.*, 44 La. Ann. 695, 11 So. 52 (1892); *Haynes v Gas Co.*, 114

N. C. 211, 19 S. E. 346 (1894); *McKay* v *South. Bell Tel. & Teleg. Co.*, 111 Ala. 337, 19 So. 695 (1895); *Illingsworth* v *Boston Elec. Light Co.*, 161 Mass. 583, 37 N. E. 778 (1894); *McLaughlin* v *Louisville Elec. Light Co.*, 100 Ky. 173, 37 S. W. 851 (1896). Cf. *Dickey* v *Maine Teleg. Co.*, 46 Me. 483 (1859) (low lying wire upsets stagecoach); *Western Union Teleg. Co.* v *Eyser*, 2 Colo. 141 (1873) (same); *Pa. Tel. Co.* v *Varnau, et al.*, 121 Pa. ST, 302, 15 Atl. 624 (1888) (same).

62. *McLaughlin* v *Louisville Light Co.*, 37 S. W. 851 (1896) at 853, 856; *Treadwell* v *Whittier*, 22 Pac. 266 (1889) at 272.

63. *Carson* v *Godley*, 26 Pa. St. 111 at 116 (1856); *Treadwell* v *Whittier*, 80 Cal. 574, 22 Pac. 266 at 271 (1889).

64. Friedman, *History of American Law*, 302, 470.

65. Wex Malone, "The Formative Era of Contributory Negligence," *Illinois Law Review* 41 (1946): 151; cited by Friedman, *History of American Law*, 471 n. 5.

66. Malone, "Formative Era," 152.

67. Friedman, *History of American Law*, 472; *Haring* v *New York & Erie RR*, 13 Barb. (N.Y.S. C.) 9 at 15–16 (1852).

68. Randolph Bergstrom, *Courting Danger: Law and Personal Injury in New York City, 1870–1910* (Ithaca: Cornell University Press, 1992), 138.

69. *Ernst* v *Hudson R. RR*, 35 N.Y. 9 at 39 (1866).

70. Malone, "Formative Era," 168–71, 177, 179. Regrettably, this was, and still is, sometimes true. A significant fraction (about 20 percent) of work-related injuries in the late nineteenth century, for example, were attributed (by company management, coroner's inquests, and historian's analysis) to careless workers themselves. Carl Gersuny, *Work Hazards and Industrial Conflict* (Hanover, N. H., 1981), 61–66; Crystal Eastman, *Work-Accidents and the Law* (New York: Russell Sage Foundation, 1910), 86. This was especially evident in the mining industry. Thus James Whiteside observes that western miners in the 1870s and 1880s were often responsible for the accidents that befell them in their very self-directed world, due to their inadequate job of timbering, use of improper lamps, excessive use of blasting powder, and sheer haste. James Whiteside, *Regulating Danger: The Struggle for Mine Safety in the Rocky Mountain Coal Industry* (Lincoln: University of Nebraska Press, 1990), 78–82.

71. Malone, "Formative Era," 180.
Lawrence Friedman correctly refers to the "disinvention" by courts of another rule imputing the contributory negligence of a driver to an injured passenger, but his citations might inadvertently indicate to some that this rule lived in America until the mid-1880s and early 1890s. (Friedman, *History of American Law*, 476.) The English Court of Common Pleas "identified" the passenger of an omnibus involved in an accident with the contributory negligence of its driver in *Thurogood* v *Bryan*, 8 C. B. 115, 137 ER 452 (1849). This rule was immediately and thoroughly rejected by high courts in every corner of the United States as being "based on fiction and inconsistent with justice." See *Macon & W. RR* v *Winn*, 26 Ga. 250 (1858) (here the driver was the plaintiff's *slave*, not a common carrier's employee; yet Judge Joseph Lumpkin refused to impute his negligence to his owner); *Chapman* v *New Haven RR*, 19 N.Y. 341 at 344 (1859); *Danville, L. & N. Turnpike Rd.* v *Stewart*, 59 Ky. 119 (1859); *Lockhart* v *Lichtenthaler*, 36 Pa. St. 151 (1863); *Bennett* v *N.J. RR & Transp. Co.*, 36 N.J. L 225 (1873); *Brown* v *N.Y. Central RR*, 32 N.Y. 596 (1865); *Lake* v

Milliken, 62 Me. 240 at 243 (1873); *Richer* v *Freeman*, 50 N. H. 420 at 432 (1870); *Covington Transfer Co.* v *Kelly*, 36 Ohio St. 86 at 92 (1880); *Wabash, St. L. & P. RR* v *Schacklett, Adm.*, 105 Ill. 364 (1883). But see *L. S. & M. S. RR* v *Miller*, 25 Mich. 274 (1872) (accepting English rule for private carriages only).

72. Malone, "Formative Era," 152. Similarly, Crystal Eastman, a New York Employer's Liability Commission member who sagely surveyed Pittsburgh's worker injury environment for the Russell Sage Foundation, assumed, incorrectly, that Pennsylvania's common-law rules regarding worker injury (contributory negligence, assumption of risk, and the fellow-servant rule) "pretty fairly represent the common law rules of employer's liability in all the states." (Eastman, *Work-Accidents and the Law*, 171.)

73. *Goodson* v *Walkin*, in *Select Cases of Trespass from the King's Courts, 1307–1399*, ed. Morris Arnold (London: Selden Society, 1985), 1:18–19; Morris Arnold, "Accident, Mistake, and the Rules of Liability in the 14th Century Law of Torts," *University of Pennsylvania Law Review* 128 (1979): 361–364; *Bayly* v *Merrel*, Cro. Jac. 386, 79 ER 331 (K. B., 1606); Wilson, Barr., in *Newby* v *Wiltshire*, 4 Doug. 284, 99 ER 883 (K. B. 1785) (the case was decided on other grounds); William Holdsworth, *A History of English Law* (London: Methuen, 1925), 8:459. See also *Virtue* v *Birdie*, 2 Lev. 196, 83 ER 515 (K. B. 1793); and *Underhill* v *Priestly*, unpublished case, 1781, notes of Lord Mansfield reported in James Oldham, *The Mansfield Manuscripts and the Growth of English Law in the Eighteenth Century*, 2 vols. (Chapel Hill: University of North Carolina Press, 1992), 2:1137.

74. See *Cruden* v *Fentham*, 2 Esp. 685, 170 ER 496 (C. P. 1798); *Dudley* v *Smith*, 1 Camp. 167, 170 ER 915 (N. P. 1808); *Knapp* v *Salsbury*, 2 Camp. 500, 170 ER 1231 (N. P. 1810).

75. See esp. *Knapp* v *Salsbury*, 2 Camp. 500, 170 ER 1231 (N. P. 1810).

76. As in Arnold, "Accident, Mistake," 361; *Bayly* v *Merrel*, 79 ER 331; *Virtue* v *Birdie*, 83 ER 515; and an early American example, *Shepherd* v *Hees*, 12 Johns. (N.Y.) 433 (1815) (where defendant's hogs had regularly come through the plaintiff's fence and had eaten his corn, he was without relief because this was due to "his own negligence"). I am indebted to Robert Kaczorowski's analysis of these early contributory negligence cases in "Common Law Background," 1127.

77. *Lane* v *Crombie*, 29 Mass. 177 at 178 (1831). See also *Adams* v *Inhabs. of Carlisle*, 38 Mass. 146 (1838).

78. *Palmer* v *City of Portsmouth*, 43 N. H. 265 at 267 (1861), cited in Gary Schwartz, "Tort Law and the Economy in Nineteenth Century America: A Reinterpretation," *Yale Law Journal* 90 (1981): 1761. Cf. *Williams* v *Town of Clinton*, 28 Ct. 264 (1859); *Churchill* v *Rosebeck*, 15 Ct. 359 (1843); Thomas M. Cooley, *A Treatise on the Law of Torts* (Chicago, 1888), 802.

79. Depending upon which treatise writer one relies on for authority, at which moment in time, the ratio of jurisdictions allowing judges to nonsuit plaintiffs to those requiring that the issue be left to the jury varies from one to two to one to five. See *Inland & Seabord Coasting Co.* v *Tolson*, 139 U.S. 551 (1891); Malone, "Formative Era," 151 at 166 n. 37; Francis Wharton, *Treatise on Negligence*, 2nd ed. (1878); Seymour Thompson, *The Law of Negligence*, 2 vols. (San Francisco, 1886), 2:1176–84; Thompson, *The Law of Carriers of Passengers* (San Francisco, 1887), 562; Thomas Shearman and Amasa Redfield, *Treatise on the Law of Negligence*, 4th ed.

(New York, 1888), 193; Thomas Shearman and Amasa Redfield, *The Law of Negligence* (1913), sec. 123; *Century Edition of the American Digest* (St. Paul: West, 1896), vol. 38 ("Negligence"), 315–17. (In the early twentieth century the Massachusetts legislature abrogated the court's rule and placed the burden of proof on the defendant. Gen. L. C. 231 sec. 85.)

80. See chapter 9, note 53, for the citations from these studies.

81. Bergstrom, *Courting Danger*, 138, 159; Professor Bergstrom agrees with this extrapolation. Personal communication, February 10, 1993.

82. *Bellegarde v San Fr. Bridge Co.*, 90 Cal. 179 at 181, 27 Pac. 20 (1891), cited in Schwartz, "Tort Law and the Economy," 1717 at 1765 n. 357.

83. Malone, "Contributory Negligence and the Landowner Cases," *Minnesota Law Review* 29 (1945): 61 at 65–66. See also Gary Schwartz, "Tort Law in Nineteenth Century America: A Reinterpretation," *Yale Law Review* 90 (1981): 1717 at 1762 (for indications in the appellate report records that, among cases that saw light in the published supreme court reports, both juries and appellate courts in California and New Hampshire overwhelmingly found for plaintiffs where defendants had claimed the plaintiff to be contributorily negligent).

84. *Hart v Brooklyn*, 36 Barb. 226 at 229 (1862); *Todd v Troy*, 61 N.Y. 506 (1875).

85. See, for example, *Eckert v Long Is. RR*, 43 N.Y. 502 (1871).

86. See *Johnson v Hudson Ry*, 20 N.Y. 65 at 74 (1859), anticipating *Byrne v Boadle*, 2 H. & C. 722, 159 ER 299 (Ex. 1863). ("The thing speaks for itself" is of course a translation of Pollock, B.'s, Latin phrase for the phenomenon res ipsa loquitur, which he employed only during oral argument.)

87. The rule emerged with clarity in *Davies v Mann*, 10 M. & W. 546, 152 ER 588 (Ex. 1842), but it can be found as well, without the use of the specific phrase or any reference to *Davies v Mann*, in a number of mid-nineteenth-century American opinions. See *Macon & W. RR v Davis' Admin.*, 18 Ga. 679 at 687 (1855); *Littleton v Richardson*, 34 N. H. 179 (1856); *Owen v Hudson River RR*, 20 N.Y. Sup. 329 at 338 (1860); *Warner v RR*, 25 Phila. Rpts. 52 (1868); *Hankerson v S. W.RR*, 59 Ga. 593 (1877); *Morrissey v Wiggins Ferry*, 43 Mo. 380 (1869); and *O'Brien v McGlinchy*, 68 Me. 552 at 557 (1878). *Davies v Mann* is cited in *Huelsenkamp v Citizens Ry*, 37 Mo. 538 at 549–50 (1866).

88. *Warner v RR*, 6 Phila. Rpts. 537 (1868).

Judge Hare's language approaches at moments the comparative negligence standard of the next century, but it is only a flirtation; his was ultimately the all-or-nothing view of contributory negligence. Some mid-nineteenth-century high courts did adopt the civil law's comparative negligence standards, if only for a generation or less. See *Dublin v Murphy*, 3 Sandf. (N.Y. Super. Ct.) 19 (1849); *Nash. & Chat. RR v Smith's Adm.*, 53 Tenn. (6 Heisk.) 174 (1871); *Galena & Chic. RR v Jacobs*, 20 Ill. 478 (1858); *Union Pac. RR v Rollins*, 5 Kans. 167 at 191 (18); *O'Keefe v Chicago, etc. RR*, 32 Iowa 467 (1871); *Flanders v Meath*, 26 Ga. 250 (1858) and 27 Ga. 358 at 362 (1859).

89. Hovenkamp, "Pragmatic Realism," 3 at 6–7, 14–18, 26; Horwitz, *Transformation 2*, 54–58; Friedman, *History of American Law*, 469; Kermit Hall, William Wiecek, and Paul Finkelman, *American Legal History: Cases and Materials* (New York: Oxford University Press, 1991), 184–86. Horwitz, to his credit, identifies the *Ryan* decision as "an outcast," largely rejected by other courts, though he main-

tains that this was so essentially because it had "limited entrepreneurial liability" so "brazenly" that it "threatened to bring the entire intellectual system [of proximate cause] into disrepute." Both Horwitz and Hovenkamp are almost exclusively concerned with jurisprudence in their discussion of proximate cause—that is, their attention is on the dialogue between legal philosophers (J. S. Mill, C. Pierce, N. St. J. Green, F. Wharton, O. W. Holmes Jr., etc.) They tell a fascinating story, but have very little to say about what the practicing jurists were saying on the subject of proximate cause. Had they done so, I believe, they would have found that these practicing jurists were participants in this dialogue, with a lot to say (as I hope this section of the chapter demonstrates).

90. 35 N.Y. 210 at 212 (1866).

91. Friedman, *History of American Law*, 469–70.

92. Hovenkamp, "Pragmatic Realism," at 17–18; Horwitz, *Transformation 2*, 58–59.

93. Green, "Proximate and Remote Cause," *American Law Review* 4 (1870): 201; Wharton, *A Suggestion as to Causation* (Cambridge, Mass., 1874), 10; Wharton, *The Liability of Railroad Companies for Remote Fires: Proximate and Remote Cause* (St. Louis, 1879). One ought to be aware that Wharton clearly preferred the "practical" rules of Roman tort law to "the idealistic fictions of medievalism" (in his *Treatise on Negligence* [1874], preface and passim).

94. A more thorough analysis of the general subject is Mark Grady, "Common Law Control of Strategic Behavior: Railroad Sparks and the Farmer," *Journal of Legal Studies* 17 (1988): 15.

95. Greenleaf on Evidence 210 (1846), cited in *Harrison v Berkeley*, 1 Strob. (32 S. C.) 525 (1847). Cf. Sedgwick, *A Treatise on the Measure of Damages* (1847), 75.

96. *Scott v Sheperd*, 2 Wm. Bl. 892, 96 ER 525 (K. B. 1773) (defendant liable for his first act and all sequential acts of others leading to injury); *Ashley v Harrison*, 1 Esp. 48, 170 ER 276 (N. P. 1793) (jury verdict for defendant regarding threat too "remote" from damage); *Guille v Swan*, 19 Johns. (N.Y.) 381 (1822) (descending balloonist defendant liable as proximate cause of damage done inadvertently by crowd to garden of plaintiff); *Jeffrey v Bigelow*, 13 Wend. (N.Y.) 518 (1835) (infection of plaintiff's sheep the "natural consequence" of defendant's act); *Harrison v Berkley*, 1 Strob. (32 S. C.) 525 (1847) (defendant's sale of liquor the proximate cause of buyer's death); *Davies v Mann*, 10 M. & W. 545, 152 ER 588 (Ex. 1842) (wagoner who hit donkey fettered in road liable; donkey's owner's negligence remote; wagoner's proximate); *Morrison v Davis*, 20 Pa. St. 171 (1852) (defendant canalboat owner's use of lame horse on voyage where goods damaged in flood not the proximate cause of plaintiff's loss); *Littleton v Richardson*, 34 N. H. 179 (1856) (obstruction in road; defendant at fault); *Puterbaugh v Reasor*, 9 Ohio St. 484 (1859) (owner of running horses liable as proximate cause of damage to property); *Vandenburgh v Truax*, 4 Denio (N.Y.) 464 (1847) (defendant's chasing one who caused accidental damage the proximate cause of damage); *Stickney v Maidstone*, 30 Vt. 738 (1858) (bridge defect was proximate cause of damage); *McDonald v Snelling*, 96 Mass. 290 (1867) (sleigh owner liable for sleigh that he hit hitting others); *Griggs v Fleckenstein*, 14 Minn. 81 (1869) (owner of team of horses left unhitched liable for direct consequences of their running and causing others to run and do damage); *McGrew v Stone*, 53 Pa. St. 436 (1866) (owner of coal barge liable for consequential damage

to others). Cf. *Page* v *Bucksport*, 64 Me. 51 (1874) (bridge defect proximate cause of chain of events damage); *Lane* v *Atlantic Works*, 111 Mass. 136 (1872); *Hoyt* v *Jeffers*, 30 Mich. 181 (1874) (sawmill owner liable for all damage caused by fire that spread to hotel); *Smith* v *Br. & N. A. R.M. S. Packet Co.*, 46 N.Y. Super (14 J. & S.) 86 at 89 (1880) (berth collapse and steward's reaction the proximate cause of injury); *Mead* v *Stratton*, 87 N.Y. 493 (1882) (liquor sold to drunk the proximate cause of his subsequent injury).

97. These were: *Ryan*, 35 N.Y. 210 (1866); and *Pa. RR* v *Kerr*, 62 Pa. St. 353 (1869). In another three or four cases courts found what Mark Grady calls a "victim's trap"—that is, they viewed the plaintiff as being contributorily negligent for not acting to protect their property after they saw that the railroad had failed to clear its right-of-way properly or had placed them at risk in some other manner. See, for example, *Michigan Central RR* v *Anderson*, 20 Mich. 244 (1870) (not cited by Grady). (Grady, "Railroad Sparks and the Farmer," 29–35.) But other courts responded to these arguments (see text). See also *Toledo, P.&W. RR* v *Pindar*, 53 Ill. 447 (1870), where the high court remanded a verdict for the plaintiff because the judge's instructions had virtually instructed the jury to find the railroad's fire to be the proximate cause; that question was to be left to the jury.

98. Thus the defense failed in *Hart* v *Western RR*, 13 Met. (54 Mass.) 99 (1847); *Beers* v *Housatonic RR*, 19 Ct. 566 (1849); *Kerwacker* v *C. C.&C. RR*, 3 Ohio St. 172 (1854); *C. C.&C. RR* v *Elliott*, 4 Ohio St. 474 (1855); *Trow* v *Vermont Central RR*, 24 Vt. 488 at 494–95 (1852); *Vicksburg & Jackson RR* v *Patton*, 31 Miss. 156 (1856); *Hookset* v *Concord RR*, 38 N.H. 242 (1859); *Isbell* v *N.Y. & N.H. RR*, 27 Ct. 406 (1858); *Freemantle* v *London & N. W. RR*, 2 F. & F. 337, 175 ER 1086 (N. P. 1860); *Quigley* v *Stockbridge & P. RR*, 90 Mass. 438 (1864); *Cleaveland* v *Grand Trunk RR*, 42 Vt. 449 (1869); *Fitch* v *Pacific RR*, 45 Mo. 324 at 329 (1870); *Flynn* v *S. F. & S. J. RR*, 40 Cal. 14 at 17 (1870) (directed verdict for plaintiff with damages set by supreme court); *Kellogg* v *Chic. & N. W. RR*, 26 Wis. 223 (1870); *Fent* v *Toledo, P.&W. RR*, 59 Ill. 349 (1871); *Gilman* v *European & N. A. RR*, 60 Me. 235 (1872); *Henry* v *Southern Pac. RR*, 50 Cal. 176 (1875); *Pa. RR* v *Hope*, 80 Pa. St. 373 (1876); *Atch., Top. & Santa Fe RR* v *Sanford*, 12 Kans. 354 (1874); *Burlington & Mo. RR* v *Westover*, 4 Neb. 268 (1876); *Coates & Dowell* v *Mo., Kans. & Tex. RR*, 61 Mo. 38 (1871); *Longabaugh* v *Va. & Truckee RR*, Ormsby County Court Records, Nevada, Sept. 1873, affirmed in *Same* v *Same*, 9 Nev. 271 (1876); *Del., Lack. & West. RR* v *Salmon*, 10 Vro. (39 N.J.L.) 308 (1877); *Kuhn* v *Erie RR*, 32 N.J. Eq. 647 (1880).

99. See chapter 7 of this book.

100. *Perley* v *Eastern RR*, 98 Mass. 414 at 417, 419 (1868).

101. *Hoyt* v *Jeffers*, 30 Mich. 181 at 200 (1874) (Justice Thomas M. Cooley concurring). See also the lengthy response to Wharton's reasoning in the Note on Proximate Cause in *American State Reports* 36 (1894): 806 at 825–26.

102. *Kerwacker* v *C. C.&C. RR*, 3 Ohio St. 172 at 194, 199, 201 (1854). Cf. the views of Justice Sidney Breese in *Bass* v *Chic., Burl., & Q. RR*, 28 Ill. 9 at 19 (1862). But see *Walsh* v *Virginia & Truckee RR*, Storey County Ct, no. 2396, 1871, Nevada Records and Archives (suit for damages to cattle dismissed; statute required owner of cattle to fence them in).

103. *Fent* v *Toledo, Peoria & Warsaw RR*, 59 Ill. 349 at 357–62 (1871); *Kellogg* v

Chicago & N. W. RR, 26 Wis. 223 at 231–239 (1870). See also Anon., "Note," *Albany Law Journal* 5 (May and June 1872): 309 and 334; for one commentator's lengthy critique of *Ryan*, and see the views of Justice Valentine in *Atchison, T. & Santa Fe RR* v *Sanford*, 12 Kans. 354 at 378 (1874): "Even if it should bankrupt the wrongdoer, would that be any reason for not compensating the innocent sufferer?"

104. Grady, "Railroad Sparks and the Farmer," 15 at 30–36.

105. In a footnote appearing some nine pages after he tells us of Justice Hunt's instrumentalist language in *Ryan*, Friedman acknowledges that "the doctrine of the *Ryan* case was . . . not universally accepted by the courts" (478 n. 27).

106. *Freemantle* v *London & N. W. RR*, 2 F. & F. 337, 175 ER 1086 (N. P. 1860).

107. *Kellogg* v *Milw. & St. P. RR*, in 1 *Central Law Journal* 278 at 280 (1874).

108. *Jackson* v *Chicago & N. W. RR*, 31 Iowa 176 at 178 (1870).

109. *Fitch* v *Pacific RR*, 45 Mo. 324 at 327, 329 (1870).

110. James Ducker, *Men of the Steel Rails: Workers on the Atchinson, Topeka & Santa Fe, 1869–1900* (Lincoln: University of Nebraska Press, 1983), 31.

111. See the text of this chapter at note 93.

112. Here I have limited my search for evidence of such use to the twenty-one appellate cases decided before 1870 that I have identified wherein the proximate-cause defense was at issue. (See notes 96 and 98 above.) A broader search of *all* pre-1870 negligence cases would certainly reveal other evidence of the "foreseeability" principle at work. See, for example, *Cole* v *Fisher*, 11 Mass. 137 (1814) (defendant's "reasonable apprehension" of risk of horses bolting when he test-fired gun used as liability test); *Macon & W. RR* v *Winn*, 26 Ga. 250 at 254 (1858) (company lacked "anticipation"); and *Gibson* v *Pacific RR*, 46 Mo. 163 at 169 (1870). See also English examples: *Sutton* v *Clarke*, 6 Taunt. 29, 128 ER 943 (C. P. 1815); and *Coupland* v *Hardingham*, 3 Camp. 398, 170 ER 1424 (N. P. 1813).

113. *Hunt* v *Pownal*, 9 Vt. 411 (1837); *Beers* v *Housatonic RR*, 19 Ct. 566 at 577 (1849); *Morrison* v *Davis*, 20 Pa. St. 171 at 175 (1852); *Scott* v *Hunter*, 46 Pa. St. 192 at 194 (1863); *Ryan* v *New York Central RR*, 35 N.Y. 210 at 212 (1866); *McGrew* v *Stone*, 53 Pa. St. 436 at 441 (1866); *Morton* v *Inhabs. of Frankford*, 55 Me. 46 at 52 (1867); *McDonald* v *Snelling*, 96 Mass. 290 at 294, 295, 296 (1867); *Griggs* v *Fleckenstein*, 14 Minn. 81 (1869). See also the "foreseeable" language in *Kellogg* v *Chic. & N. W. RR*, 26 Wis. 223 at 246 (1870); *Smith* v *London & S. W. RR*, L. R. 6 C. P. 14 at 21 (1870); *Houfe* v *Town of Fulton*, 29 Wis. 296 at 301 (1871); *Lane* v *Atlantic Works*, 111 Mass. 136 at 141 (1872) (where the jury found that the defendant "ought to have apprehended and provided against" the accident); *Daniels* v *Ballantine*, 23 Ohio St. 532 (1872); and *Atch., T. & S. F. RR* v *Sanford*, 12 Kans. 354 at 377 (1874).

114. *McDonald* v *Snelling*, 96 Mass. 290 at 294–96 (1867).

115. See, for example, Justice William Strong in *Scott* v *Hunter*, 46 Pa. St. 192 at 195 (1863).

116. Redfield's note is in *American Law Register*, n.s., 12 (1873): 560. See Redfield's views on the subject as Vermont's chief justice in *Hunt* v *Town of Pownal*, 9 Vt. 411 (1837).

117. *Farwell* v *Boston & Worcester RR*, 45 Mass. (4 Metc.) 49 at 59 (1842).

118. Kermit Hall, *Magic Mirror*, 125.

119. Christopher Tomlins, "Law and Power in the Employment Relationship,"

in *Labor Law in America: Historical and Critical Essays*, ed. Christopher Tomlins and Andrew King (Baltimore: Johns Hopkins University Press, 1992), 73, 88; See also Friedman, *History of American Law*, 301, 473; Horwitz, *Transformation 1*, 209–10.

120. Horwitz, *Transformation 1*, 210.

121. 3 M.&W. 1, 150 ER 1030 (Ex. 1837).

122. Henry V, act 4, scene 1.

123. Especially so since he also charged that the injury was due to "the neglect" of the employee. See Wilson, B., in *Newby* v *Wilkshire*, 4 Doug. 284, 99 ER 883 (K. B. 1785).

124. *Randolph* v *Hill*, 7 Leigh (34 Va.) 383 at 387 (1836) (court upheld jury verdict that employer had failed to maintain a safe work site by a divided vote, two to two).

125. No recovery to a dairymaid hurt by a bull while bringing dairy cows to shed in *Clark* v *Armstrong*, 34 Jur. (Scot.) 640 (1862). No recovery to licensees injured on property of others in *Bolch* v *Smith*, 7 H.&N. 736, 158 ER 666 (Ex. 1862); *Indermaur* v *Davies*, L. R., 2 C. P. 311 (Ex. 1867); *Hounsell* v *Smyth*, 7 C. B. (N. S.) 731, 141 ER 1003 (C. P. 1860).

126. Stuart Dorsey finds, significantly, that a 3 percent wage increase accompanies every 1 percent increase in the probability of injury. Dorsey, "Employment Hazards and Fringe Benefits: Further Tests for Compensating Differentials," in *Safety and the Work Force*, ed. John D. Worrall (Ithaca, N.Y.: ILR Press, 1983), 94.

127. *Clifford* v *Overland Mail Co.*, no. 1524, 1862, Ormsby County Court Records, Nevada.

128. *Cook* v *Western & Atl. RR*, 72 Ga. 48 at 49 (1883); *Mitchell* v *Pennsylvania RR*, Com. Pl. Ct., Huntingdon County, Pa., *American Law Register*, o.s., 1 (1853): 717.

129. One railroad engineer ingeniously sidestepped that problem, successfully, by purchasing a death and disability policy from the Railroad *Passenger* Assurance Company, retaining proof that the company's agent knew him to be an engineer. After his death in a collision, the company was required to pay his estate the guaranteed five thousand dollars. *Brown, Admx.* v *Ry. Pass. Assur. Co.* 45 Mo. 221 (1870).

130. Lawrence Goodheart, *Abolitionist, Actuary, Atheist: Elizur Wright and the Reform Impulse* (Kent, Ohio: Kent State University Press, 1990), 144; Robert Silverman, *Law and Urban Growth: Civil Litigation in the Boston Trial Courts, 1880–1900* (Princeton: Princeton University Press, 1981), 120; Census Bureau, *Historical Statistics of the U.S. to 1957* (Wash., G. P. O., 1960), 671, 673; Walter Licht, *Working for the Railroad: The Origins of Work in the Nineteenth Century* (Princeton: Princeton University Press, 1983), 205–211; Tomlins, "Mysterious Power," 375 at 415; C. of Massachusetts, *Statistics of Labor*, I (1870), 213; James H. Ducker, *Men of the Steel Rails: Workers on Atchinson, Topeka & Santa Fe RR, 1869–1900* (Lincoln, Neb.: University of Nebraska Press, 1983), 44; *Milwaukee Sentinel*, Mar. 19, 1885; *Dillon* v *Va. & Truckee RR*, (Aug. 1869), #1204, Ormsby County Court, Nevada Div. of Archives & Records; *McIntyre* v *Va. & Truckee RR*, (1878), #3359, Storey County Court Records, Nevada; R. Posner, "A Theory of Negligence," *Journal of Legal Studies* 1 (1972): 29 at 31 n.

131. *Dynen* v *Leach*, 26 L. J., Ex. 221 at 223 (Ex. 1857). Cf. *Seymour* v *Maddox*,

16 Q. B. 326, 117 ER 904 (Q. B. 1851), and Rande Kostal, *Law and English Railway Capitalism, 1825–1875* (Oxford: Oxford University Press, 1994), 255–321.

132. *Edwards, Adm.* v *London & Brighton RR*, 4 F&F 530, 176 ER 677 (1865); *Saxton* v *Hawksworth*, 26 L. T. 851 (Ex. 1872).

133. See Horace G. Wood, *A Treatise on the Law of Master and Servant* (Albany, 1877), 727, 731–32, 734–35, 737, 751, 756–57, 761, 781; Francis Wharton, *A Treatise on the Law of Negligence*, 2nd ed. (Philadelphia, 1878); Thomas Shearman and Amasa Redfield, *A Treatise on the Law of Negligence*, 4th ed. (New York, 1888); Seymour Thompson, *The Law of Negligence . . .* , 2nd ed., 2 vols. (San Francisco, 1886); *American Digest (Century Edition)* 34 (1897): 1748–1765.

134. *Fitzpatrick* v *New Albany & Salem RR*, 7 Ind. 436 (1856). See also *Illinois Central RR* v *Welch*, 52 Ill. 183 (1869).

135. Fred Wertheim, "Slavery and the Fellow Servant Rule," *New York University Law Review* 61 (1986): 1112; Paul Finkelman, "Slaves as Fellow Servants," *American Journal of Legal History* 31 (1987): 289; *Dade Coal Co.* v *Haslett*, 83 Ga. 549, 10 SE 435 (1889); *Dalheim* v *Lemon*, 45 Fed. 225 (C. C. D. Minn. 1891); *Buckalew* v *Tenn. Coal, Iron & RR Co.*, 20 So. (Ala.) 606 (1896); *Chat. Brick Co.* v *Braswell*, 92 Ga. 631, 18 S. E. 1015 (1893).

136. See *Randolph* v *Hill*, 34 Va. 383 (1836); *Keegan* v *Western RR*, 8 N.Y. 175 (1853); *Smith* v *N.Y. & Harlem RR*, 19 N.Y. 127 (1859); *Hallower* v *Henley, et al.*, 6 Cal. 210 (1855); *Fifield* v *Northern RR*, 42 N. H. 225 (1860); *Snow* v *Housatonic RR*, 8 Allen (90 Mass.) 441 (1864); *Noyes* v *Smith*, 28 Vt. 59 (1856); *Fifield* v *Northern RR*, 42 N. H. 225 (1860); *Harrison* v *Central RR*, 32 N.J.L. 293 (1865); *Gibson* v *Pacific RR*, 46 Mo. 163 at 169 (1870) (company must use "foresight"; plaintiff-employee must have been able to "foresee" risks); *Paulmier, Adm. of Carhart* v *Erie RR*, 34 N.J.L. 151 (1870); *Baxter* v *Roberts*, 44 Cal. 187 (1872); *Plank* v *N.Y. Central & Hudson RR*, 60 N.Y. 607 (1875); *Dorsey* v *P. & C. Constr.*, 42 Wis. 583 (1877); *Hough* v *RR*, 100 U.S. 213 (1879); *Hackett* v *Middlesex Mnfg. Co.*, 101 Mass. 101 (1869); *Cooper* v *Pitts., Cinc., & St. L. RR*, 24 W.Va. 37 at 49 (1884); *Wilson* v *Denver, S. P. & P. RR*, 7 Colo. 101, 2 Pac. 1 (1883); *R. R.* v *O'Brien*, 161 U.S. 451 (1896); *Boyce* v *Schroeder*, Ind. App., 51 N. E. 376 (1898) (unsafe truck axle; owner liable to driver). Cf. *Britton* v *Great Western Cotton Co.*, L. R., 7 Ex. 130 (1872); and *Holmes* v *Clarke*, 6 Hurl. & N. 349, 158 ER 144 (Ex. 1862). But see *Hayden* v *Smithfield Mnfg. Co.*, 29 Ct. 548 (1861) (older machinery acceptable so long as risks of using it are clearly understood by worker).

137. See *Savignac* v *Roome*, 6 Term R. 125, 101 ER 470 (KB 1794); *Walker* v *Bolling*, 22 Ala 294 (1853); *Bassett* v *Norwich & W. RR*, Super. Ct. Ct, *Monthly Law Rep., n.s.*, 19 no. 9 (1857): 551; *Gilman* v *Eastern RR*, 92 Mass. (10 Allen) 233 (1865); *Louisville RR* v *Filbern's Adm'x.*, 6 Bush (Ky.) 574 (1869); *Harper* v *Ind. & St. L. RR*, 47 Mo. 567 (1871); *Laning* v *RR*, 49 N.Y. 521 (1872); *Wright* v *N.Y. Central RR*, 25 N.Y. 565 (1862); *Georgia RR & Banking Co.* v *Rhodes*, 56 Ga. 645 (1876); *Ill. Central RR* v *Jewell*, 46 Ill. 99 (1867); *Wabash RR* v *McDaniels*, 107 U.S. 454 (1882).

138. See *Perry* v *Marsh*, 25 Ala. 659 (1854); *Ryan* v *Fowler*, 24 N.Y. 410 (1862), (rejecting *Seymour* v *Maddox*, 117 ER 904); *Coombs* v *New Bedford Cordage Co.*, 102 Mass. 572 (1869); *Paulmier* v *Erie RR*, 34 N.J.L. 151 (1870); *Fort* v *Union Pac. RR*, 2 Dill. C. C. 259 (1872), affirmed in *RR* v *Fort*, 17 Wall. (U.S.) 554 (1873); *Strahlendorf* v *Rosenthal*, 30 Wis. 674 (1872); *Spelman* v *Fisher Iron Co.*, 56 Barb. (N.Y. Sup.

Ct.) 151 (1870); *Connolly v Poillon*, 41 Barb. (N.Y. Sup. Ct.) 366 (1864); *Frandsen v C.R.I.& P. RR*, 36 Iowa 372 (1873); *Mann v Oriental Print Works*, 11 R.I. 152 (1875); *Smith v Oxford Iron Co.*, 42 N.J.L. 467 (1880); *Dorsey v Phillips & Colby Const. Co.*, 42 Wis. 583 (1877) (Ryan, C.J.: "employees operating trains may perform their duties under an implied warrant that they may do so without exposing themselves to extraordinary danger"); *Lorentz v Robinson*, 61 Md. 64 (1883).

139. *Lalor v C.B.&Q. RR*, 52 Ill. 401 at 404 (1869); Redfield in *American Law Register*, n.s., 14 (1875): 728. See also *Chic. & N.W. RR v Bayfield*, 37 Mich. 205 (1877). But see *Williams v Churchill*, 137 Mass. 243 (1884) (a harsh ruling, characteristically, from the pen of Oliver Wendell Holmes Jr.); and *Wornell v Maine Central RR*, 79 Me. 397, 10 Atl. 149 (1887).

140. *Kroy v RR*, 32 Iowa 357 at 366 (1871), citing Shearman and Redfield on Negligence, sec. 96. See also *Snow v Housatonic RR*, 90 Mass. 441 (1864); *Greenleaf v RR*, 29 Iowa 14 (1870); *Ford v Fitchburg RR*, 110 Mass. 240 (1872); Francis Wharton, *A Treatise on the Law of Negligence* (Philadelphia, 1874), sec. 221. But see *Dynan v Leach*, 26 L.J. Ex. 221, 157 ER 468 (1857); *Patterson v Pitts. & C. RR*, 76 Pa. St. 389 (1874), and *Colo. Central RR v Ogden*, 3 Colo. 510 (1877), for rule that warning to company would not suffice if employee continued working without an assurance that problem would be corrected. The assumption of risk defense also failed where the employee had not notified the company of a defect, but the long-standing nature of the defect constituted "constructive notice" to the company. See *Cooper v R., C. & St. L. RR*, 24 W.Va. 37 (1884), for a good summary of the cases establishing the "constructive notice" exception.

141. *Gibson v Pacific RR*, 46 Mo. 163 at 169 (1870); *Richmond & Danville RR v Norment*, 84 Va. 167, 4 SE 211 at 214 (1887). Cf. *Holmes v Clark*, 6 Hurl. & N. 349, 158 ER 751 (Ex. 1862).

142. Thompson, "Under What Circumstances a Servant Accepts the Risk of His Employment," *American Law Review* 31 (1897): 82 at 85–86.

143. *Purdy v R. W. & O. RR*, 125 N.Y. 209 (1891). Such contracts were also held to be void, generally on grounds of being against good public policy, in *Cook v RR*, 72 Ga. 48; *Little Rock & Ft. S. Ry. v Eubanks*, 48 Ark. 460, 3 S.W. 808 (1886); *Hissong v Richmond & D. RR*, 91 Ala. 514, 8 So. 776 (1890); *Jones v Lake Shore & M. Ry.*, 49 Mich. 573, 14 N.W. 551 (1883); and *Lake Shore & M.S. Ry. v Spangler*, 44 Ohio St. 471, 8 N.E. 467 (1886). The members of Idaho's constitutional convention, however, *defeated* (twenty-two to seventeen) a proposition to make it unlawful for railroads to contract out of liability for injuries with their employees., Dennis Colson, *Idaho's Constitution* (Moscow, Idaho: Idaho University Press, 1991), 127.

144. Horwitz, *Transformation 1*, 208; Hall, *Magic Mirror*, 124; Paul Finkelman, "Slaves as Fellow Servants: Ideology, Law, and Industrialization," *American Journal of Legal History* 31 (1987): 269 at 271.

145. *Priestley v Fowler*, 3 M.&W. 1, 150 ER 1030 (Ex. 1837); *Farwell v Boston & Worchester RR*, 45 Mass. 49 (1842).

146. Horwitz, *Transformation 1*, 209–10; Carl Gersuny, *Work Hazards and Industrial Conflict* (Hanover, N.H.: University Press of New England, 1981), 48–49.

147. Rabin, "Historical Development," 925 at 942.

148. Hall, *Magic Mirror*, 202; Richard Epstein, "Social Consequences of Common Law Rules," *Harvard Law Review* 96 (1983): 1737; *Pitts., Cinc., Chic. & St. L.*

RR v *Montgomery*, 152 Ind. 1, 49 N. E. 583 (1898). Georgia's abrogation in 1855 applied to railroad workers. Iowa's and Wisconsin's legislatures first abrogated, and then reinstated the rule. The Massachusetts Supreme Judicial Court interpreted the abrogation statute quite narrowly. For the history of the Wisconsin legislation, see Donald Berthrong, "Employer's Liability Legislation in Wisconsin, 1874–1893," *Southwest Social Science Quarterly* 34 (1953): 57; and Robert Hunt, *Law and Locomotives: The Impact of the Railroads on Wisconsin Law in the Nineteenth Century* (Madison: University of Wisconsin Press, 1958), 152–53. Alabama abrogated the rule in 1884, Colorado and Indiana in 1893.

149. Christopher Tomlins has, of course, "scooped" me by several years on this. In his prize-winning essay, "A Mysterious Power," 375, he demonstrates that the doctrine existed at least fifty years before *Priestley*.

150. Pollock, C. B., dicta in *Southcote* v *Stanley*, 1 H.&L. 247 at 250, S. C. 25 LJ (N. S.) Ex. 339 (Ex. 1856); *Albro* v *Jacquith*, 4 Gray (70 Mass.) 99 (1855) (but here evidence of the superintendent's negligence was in question). Christopher Tomlins gives the impression (*Law, Labor and Ideology*, 366–67) that *Albro* was an important precedent, preventing injured servants from suing negligent "fellow-servant" superintendents.

151. *Swainson* v *N. Eastern Ry*, L. R., 3 Ex. D 341 (Ex. 1878); *Wright* v *Roxburgh*, 2 Sess. Cas. (3rd S.) 748 (Scot., 1864); *Griffiths* v *Wolfram*, 22 Minn. 185 (1875); *Hinds* v *Oneracker*, 66 Ind. 547 (1879) (award of one thousand dollars to carpenter where defendant was general superintendent of manufacturing firm, and where the carpenter had been unable to sue firm because of fellow-servant rule); *Hinds & Studebacker Bros. Mnfg. Co.* v *Harbou*, 58 Ind. 121 (1877) (superintendent liable; company exonerated); *Osborne* v *Morgan*, 130 Mass. 102 (1881) (doubting *Albro* v *Jacquith*).

152. *Osborne* v *Morgan*, 130 Mass. 102 at 105 (1881).

153. *Hinds, et al.,* v *Harbou*, 58 Ind. 121 at 126 (1877).

154. Licht, *Working for the Railroad*, 130, 304–5.

155. Ibid., 106–8. See also Eastman, *Work-Accidents and the Law*, 38, 90–93.

156. See, for example, Tomlins, *Law, Labor and Ideology*, 325–29; and Karen Orren, *Belated Feudalism: Labor, The Law, and Liberal Development in the United States* (New York: Cambridge University Press, 1991), 173–180.

157. See Price Fishback, "Liability Rules and Accident Prevention in the Workplace: Empirical Evidence from the Early Twentieth Century," *Journal of Legal Studies* 16 (1987): 305. See also Gersuny, *Work Hazards and Industrial Conflict*, 66, for evidence that worker injuries at the Lyman Textile Mills rose by over 10 percent (from an average of 35.5 per thousand per year for 1908–11 to one of 39.2 per year for 1913–16) after the abrogation of the fellow-servant rule. And see James Chelius, "The Control of Industrial Accidents," *Law and Contemporary Problems* 38 (1874): 700. Nonfatal injuries may rise because of increased reporting once workman's compensation is available, but were coal mining *fatalities* underreported for such a reason?

158. Finkelman, commenting on Nathan Dane's *General Abridgement and Digest of American Law* (Boston, 1823), 2:494, in "Slaves as Fellow Servants," 269 at 271.

159. *Beaulieu v Finglam*, 5 Year Book, Henry IV 1399–1423 at 2nd yr, fol. 18, pl. 6 (1401), as cited in John M. Wallace, *The Reporters, Arranged and Characterized* (Boston, 1882), 84–85, and in 22 NY 366n (1860).

160. *Middleton v Fowler*, 1 Salk. 282, 91 ER 247 (N. P. 1699); 2 Roll. Abr. 553; *McManus v Crickett*, 1 East 106 at 108, 102 ER 43 at 44 (K. B. 1800).

161. But see *Hull's Case*, Kelyng 40, 84 ER 1072 (K. B. 1664), where a carpenter who killed a fellow worker with a timber that his "master" had ordered him to remove from the third story of a building under construction was charged with homicide by misadventure, not the master. At least in criminal proceedings *respondeat superior* was not observed.

162. *Priestley v Fowler*, 150 ER 1030. *Newby v Wiltshire*, 2 Esp. 739, 170 ER 515 at 516 (K. B. 1784). See another report of the case in 4 Doug. 284, 99 ER 883 (K. B. 1785). See also *Watson v Turner*, reported in Buller's *Nisi Prius*, 5th ed. (London, 1788), 281; *Simmons v Wilmott*, 3 Esp. 91, 170 ER 549 (N. P. 1800) (parish liable for care for carter thrown from cart, and Lord Eldon says master "not bound to provide" medical services for this servant [93]); *Rex v Kynaston*, 1 East 117, 102 ER 47 (K. B. 1800) (parish responsible for care of injured waggon driver); *Lamb v Bunce*, 4 M. & S. 276, 105 ER 836 (K. B. 1815) (parish responsible for care to an injured "under-carter to a farmer"). The last three cases came to my attention in the endnotes to Christopher Tomlins's excellent essay on this subject, "Mysterious Power."

163. *Wennall v Adney*, 3 B.&P. 247, 127 ER 137 (C. P. 1802). Thus they rejected the nisi prius instructions of Lord Kenyon, C. J., in *Scarman v Castell*, 1 Esp. 270, 170 ER 353 (1795), that for "moral" reasons a master should be obliged to pay for medical services for a sick servant living in the household of the master.

164. *Watling v Walters*, 1 Car. & P., 132, 171 ER 1133 (1823); *Littleton v Tuttle* (1796), noted in 4 Mass. 128; Marcus Jernegan, *Laboring and Dependent Classes in Colonial America, 1607–1783* (New York: Unger, 1960), 186, 207; Christopher Tomlins, "Mysterious Power," 416, 399.

165. The passage I've just quoted is that of Lawrence Friedman, but he is attributing this dilemma to the *Farwell* decision of 1842. It was only *then*, according to Friedman, that "enterprise-minded" jurists concluded "the economic impact" of accidents should be "socialized (or ignored)." Friedman assumed, in concert with others, that *Farwell* was more innovative that it was. But as Christopher Tomlins's essay on the subject makes clear, injured workers had been left "to the tender mercies of the poor law" in preindustrial England as well. Friedman, *History of American Law*, 301–2. Tomlins, "Mysterious Power." Tomlins also points out that early-nineteenth-century "lawyers with an interest in the origins of [respondeat superior] might reasonably have been led to the conclusion that [it] specifically excused the master from liability for injuries done by one servant to another" because of a translation of Justianian's *Pandects* that appeared in the *American Law Journal* in 1808: "If the mariners occasion damage to each other, no action lies against the master." (Tomlins, *Law, Labor and Ideology*, 364 n. 94)

166. Lord Abinger, C. B., in *Priestley v Fowler*, 3 M.&W. 1, 150 ER 1030 at 1032 (Ex. 1837).

167. Pollock, C. B., in *Vose v Lancashire & Yorkshire Ry*, 27 L. J. Ex. 249, also in 2 H. & N. 728 at 734, 157 ER 300 at 303 (Ex. 1858).

168. Col. Blanding, in *Murray* v *S. C. RR*, 1 McM. 385 at 390 (1841). (See also the views of Justice Josiah Evans at 398.)

169. Tomlins, "Mysterious Power," at 434; *Farwell* v *Boston & Worcester RR*, 4 Metc. 49 at 57 (1842). The same point was made by Lord Shand, *The Liability of Employers* (Edinburgh, 1879), 8: Servants had not been "deprived of previous existing legal rights" by the fellow-servant ("comon employment") rule, and arguments to the contrary were "fallacious."

170. *Priestley* v *Fowler*, 150 ER 1030 at 1032.

171. *Mitchell* v *Pa. RR*, American Law Register, o.s., 1 (1853): 717 at 719–20; *Fifield* v *Northern RR*, 42 N. H. 225 at 238 (1860).

172. *McNaughton* v *The Caldonian RR*, 19 Ses. Cas. (2nd S.) 271 (1857).

173. Friedman, *History of American Law*, 473.

174. 18 Wis. 700 at 705.

175. Comment [Marston], "The Creation of a Common Law Rule: The Fellow Servant Rule, 1837–1860," *Univ. of Pennsylvania Law Review* 132 (1984): 579 at 597. She offers the examples of New York (*Coon* v *Syracuse & Utica RR*, 5 N.Y. 492 [1851]); Alabama (*Walker* v *Bolling*, 22 Ala. 294 [1853]); Pennsylvania (*Ryan* v *Cumberland Valley RR*, 23 Pa. St. 384 [1854]); Illinois (*Honner* v *Ill. Cent. RR*, 15 Ill. 550 [1854]); Maine (*Carle* v *Bangor & P Canal & RR*, 43 Me. 269 [1857]); Maryland (*O'Connell* v *Balt. & O. RR*, 20 Md. 212 [1863]); Virginia (*Randolph* v *Hill*, 34 Va. 383 (1836)); Vermont (*Hard* v *Vt. & Can. RR*, 32 Vt. 473 [1860]); and Iowa (*Sullivan* v *Miss. & Mo. RR*, 11 Iowa 421 [1860]). To these antebellum "first impression" cases I add only Louisiana (*Hubgh* v *N. O. & C. RR*, 6 La. Ann. 495 [1851]); and Missouri (*McDermott* v *Pac. RR*, 30 Mo. 115 [1860]).

176. *Rohback* v *Pac. RR*, 43 Mo. 187 at 193 (1869).

177. But only allegedly so. For my critique of this view of *Applegate* (offered by Horwitz and others) see text in "Entr'acte" at note 54.

178. *Louisville & Nash. RR* v *Collins*, 2 Duvall 114 at 117–20 (1865). Ten years after Chief Justice Robertson's "enlightened" opinion appeared, its precepts, regrettably, were shared outside of Kentucky only by trade unionists. As one put it in a report to the Ninth Annual (British) Trades Union Congress in 1876, "The present state of the law takes away a motive for the exercise of careful control and supervision by the employer. It even makes it his interest not to examine too minutely into the way in which his work is carried on, lest he should be held to have personally . . . become . . . liable." (Cited in Sidney Webb and Beatrice Webb, *Industrial Democracy* [London: Longmans, Green, 1920], 367.)

179. *Louisville & Nash. RR* v *Robinson*, 4 Bush (67 Ky) 507 (1868); *Same* v *Filbern's Admx.*, 6 Bush (69 Ky) 579 (1869); *Louisville, Cinc., & Tex. RR* v *Cavin's Adm.*, 9 Bush (72 Ky) 559 (1873) (John Marshall Harlan representing Cavin's Adm.); *Louisville & Nash. RR* v *Brook's Adm'x.*, (83 Ky) 136 (1886); *Same* v *Moore*, 83 Ky. 684 (1886). The Farwell rule was *finally* applied in *Casey's Adm.* v *Louisville & Nash. RR*, 84 Ky. 79 (1886). See also *Fort Hill Stone Co.* v *Orm's Adm.*, 84 Ky 183 (1886).

180. Redfield on Railways, 530; *Pitts., Ft. Wayne, etc. RR* v *Ruby*, 38 Ind. 274 (1871); *C. & M. RR* v *Ross*, 112 U.S. 377 (1884); *Price* v *Houston District Navigation Co.*, 46 Tex. 535 at 537 (1877).

181. *Wigmore v Jay*, 5 Ex. 354 (1850); *Searle v Lindsay*, 11 C. B. (N. S.) 429, 142 ER 863 (C. P. 1861); *Clarke v Holmes*, 7 H. & N. 937, 158 ER 751 (Ex. 1862); *Gallagher v Piper*, 33 L. J., C. P. 329 (1864); *Wilson v Merry & Cunningham*, L. R., S & D, App., 1 H. L. (Scot.) 326 (1868) (the "leading case").

182. *Albro v Agawam Canal Co.*, 60 Mass. (6 Cush.) 75 (1850).

183. *Cleveland RR v Keary*, 3 Ohio St. 201 (1854).

184. Tomlins, in Tomlins and King, eds., *Labor Law in America: Historical and Critical Essays* (Baltimore: Johns Hopkins University Press, 1992), 89.

185. In chapters 7 and 8.

186. *Washburn v Nashville & Chattanooga RR*, 40 Tenn. (3 Head) 639 at 642 (1859); *Haynes v East Tennessee & Georgia RR*, 43 Tenn. 222 at 227 (1866). Cf. *Nashville, etc., RR v Carroll*, 53 Tenn. (6 Heisk.) 348 (1871).

187. *Howes v S. S. Red Chief*, 15 La. Ann. 321 at 324 (1860); *McMahon v Davidson*, 12 Minn. 357 (1866); *Paulmier, Adm. of Carhart v Erie RR*, 34 N.J.L. 151 (1870) (engineer a "superior servant"); *Harper v Ind. & St. L. RR*, 47 Mo. 567 (1871).

188. *Harper v RR*, 47 Mo. 567 at 581 (1871); *Brothers v Cartter*, 52 Mo. 372 at 375 (1873) (for J. Wagner's "acts in subordination" language). In *Lewis v St. L. & Iron Mt. RR*, 59 Mo. 495 (1875); and *Hall v Mo. Pacific RR*, 74 Mo. 298 (1881), foremen were similarly adjudged not to be fellow servants.

189. *Lalor v C. B. & Q. RR*, 52 Ill. 401 (1869); *Laning v N.Y. Central RR*, 49 N.Y. 521 (1872); *Flike v Bos. & Alb. RR*, 53 N.Y. 549 (1873); *Corcoran v Holbrook*, 59 N.Y. 517 (1875); *Bradley v N.Y. Central RR*, 62 N.Y. 99 (1875); *Mann v Oriental Print Works*, 11 R. I. 152 (1875); *Union Pacific RR v Fort*, 17 Wallace (18 U.S.) 553 (1873); *Hough v RR*, 100 U.S. 213 (1879); *C. & M. RR v Ross*, 112 U.S. 377 (1884); *Gilmore v Northern Pacific RR*, 18 Fed. (C. C. D. Ore. 1884); *Brabbits v Ch. & M. RR*, 38 Wis. 289 (1875); *Thompson v Hermann*, 47 Wis. 602 (1879); *G. H. & S. A. RR v Sullivan*, 2 Unrep. Tex. Cas. 315 (1883); *Tex. & Pac. RR v McClanahan*, 2 Unrep. Tex. Cas. 270 (1883); *Riley v RR*, 27 W. Va. 145 (1885). Cf. *Richmond & D. RR v Rudd*, 88 Va. 648, 14 S. I. 361 (1892). See also *Berea Stone Co. v Kraft*, 31 Ohio St. 287 (1877).

190. *Fort v Union Pacific RR*, 2 Dill. C. C. R. 259, 9 Fed. Cas. 475 (C. C. D. Nebr. 1871); *RR v Fort*, 17 Wall. (84 N. S.) 553 (1873); Story on Agency (8th ed., Boston, 1874), sec. 564; Horace Gay Wood, *A Treatise on the Law of Master and Servant* (Albany, 1877), 856 n. 1; G. Edward White, *Tort Law in America: An Intellectual History* (New York: Oxford University Press, 1980), 53; *Gilmore v Northern Pacific RR*, 18 Fed. 866 at 870 (C. C. D. Ore. 1884); *B. & O. RR v Baugh*, 149 U.S. 368 (1893).

191. *Farwell v B. & W. RR*, 45 Mass. 49 (1842); Marston, "Comment: Creation of a Common Law Rule: The Fellow Servant Rule," *U. of Pa. Law Review* 132, 579 at 602; Story on Agency, sec. 453 (d & f); *Gillenwater v Madison & I. RR*, 5 Ind. 339 (1854); *McNaughton v The Caledonian RR*, 19 Ses. Cas. (2nd S.) 271 (1857); *Cooper v Mullins*, 30 Ga. 146 (1860); *Conlin v City of Charleston*, 15 Rich. L. (So. Car.) 201 (1868); *Nashville, etc. RR v Carroll*, 53 Tenn. (6 Heisk.) 348 (1871); *Baird v Pettit*, 70 Pa. St. 477 (1872); *Beeson v Green Mt. Gold M. Co.*, 57 Cal. 20 (1880); *Cooper v P., C., & St. L. RR*, 24 W. Va. 37 (1884); *Phillips v Chic., M., & St. P. RR*, 64 Wis. 475 (1885). But see *Foster v Minn. Central RR*, 14 Minn. 360 (1869); *Harkins v Stan-*

dard Sugar Refinery, 122 Mass. 400 (1877); *Slater v Jewitt*, 85 N.Y. 61 (1881); *Kielley v Belcher Silver Mn. Co.*, 14 Fed Cas. 461 (C. C. D. Nev. 1875); and *N.Y., L. E., & W. RR v Bell*, 122 Pa. St. 400, 4 Alt. 50 (1886); and *Northern Pacific RR v Dixon*, 194 U.S. 338 (1904).

192. *Wiggett v Fox*, 36 El. & E. 486, 11 Ex. 832, 156 ER 1069 (Ex. 1856); *Morgan v Vale of Neath RR*, L. R., 1 Q. B. 149 (1865); *Rourke v White Moss Colliery Co.*, L. R., 1 C. P. D. 556 (1876). Cf. *Reedie & Hobbit v London & NW RR*, 4 Ex. 244 at 254 (Ex. 1849); *Murry v Currie*, L. R., 6 C. P. 24 (1870).

193. *Abraham v Reynolds*, 5 H. & N. 143, 157 ER 1133 (Ex. 1860); *Johnson v Lindsay*, A. C. 371 (1891).

194. *Coon v Syracuse & Utica RR*, 5 N.Y. 490 (1851); *Sawyer v Rutland & B. RR*, 27 Vt. 370 (1855); *Smith v N.Y. & Harlem RR*, 19 N.Y. 127 at 132 (1859); *Young v N.Y. Central RR*, 30 Barb. (N.Y. Sup. Ct.) 329 (1859); *Curley v Harris*, 93 Mass. (11 Allen) 112 (1865); *Donaldson v Miss. etc. RR*, 18 Iowa 280 (1865); *Hunt v Pa. RR*, 51 Pa. St. 475 (1866); *Catawissa RR v Armstrong*, 49 Pa. St. 186 (1865); *Carroll v Minn. Valley RR*, 13 Minn. 30 (1868); *Michigan Central RR v Leahey*, 10 Mich. 193 (1862); *Burke v Norwich & W. RR*, 34 Ct. 474 (1867); *Yeomans v Contra Costa Steam Nav. Co.*, 44 Cal. 71 (1872); *Svenson v Atlantic Mail SS Co.*, 57 N.Y. 108 (1874); *Coughtry v Globe Woolen Co.*, 56 N.Y. 124 (1874).

195. See *Stewart v Harvard College*, 94 Mass. 58 (1866); *Johnson v Boston*, 118 Mass. 114 (1875); *Killea v Faxon*, 125 Mass. 485 (1878); *Hasty v Sears*, 157 Mass. 123, 31 N. E. 759 (1892). Cf. *Illinois Central RR v Cos*, 21 Ill. 20 (1858).

196. Given the standards accepted by courts, jurors, and many workers at that time (assumption of risk, contributory negligence, and the fellow-servant rule), these figures were accurate. Crystal Eastman had served as the secretary of the New York State Employer's Liability Commission before analyzing work-related accidents in Pittsburgh for the Russell Sage Foundation in 1908. She assigned responsibility, as she could best determine, to 77 percent of 410 fatal accidents there in the years 1906 and 1907. Eastman was clearly sympathetic to workers; her book for Sage, the "Pittsburgh Survey," *Work-Accidents and the Law*, was a plea for the abrogation of the fellow-servant rule and the adoption of no-fault workman's compensation statutes. Yet she concluded that fellow servants caused 27 percent of these fatalities, and that 34 percent were caused by those fatally injured themselves; the remaining 40 percent were due to employer negligence, and that was precisely the same percentage of cases won by workers or their survivors of 307 cases argued before the Wisconsin Supreme Court in the same years. Eastman, *Work-Accidents and the Law*, 86. Bergstrom, *Courting Danger*, 159; Friedman, *History of American Law*, 483; Schwartz, "Tort Law and the Economy," 1717 at 1768–69; Louise Bem, "Work Injury Suits before the Pennsylvania Supreme Court, 1850–1910," M. A. thesis, Dept. of History, University of Pittsburgh, 1985.

197. *RR v Collins*, 2 Duval (Ky.) 114 at 117–20 (1865). See also Roger Warner, "Employer's Liability as an Industrial Problem," *Green Bag* 18 (April 1906): 185 at 189.

198. Tomlins, "Mysterious Power."

199. Marston, "Creation of a Common Law Rule," 579 at 619.

200. Friedman, *History of American Law*, 484.

ENTR'ACTE

1. On this subject see my "Supervising the 'Spoiled Children of Legislation': Judicial Judgments of Quasi-Public Corporations in the Nineteenth Century," *American Journal of Legal History* 41 (forthcoming).

2. Scheiber, "Public Rights," 217 at 220. Cf. Scheiber, "Instrumentalism and Property Rights," *Wisconsin Law Review* (1975): 1.

3. Scheiber, "Public Rights," 230–32. (The case Scheiber uses to illustrate his point, is *Lux* v *Haggin*, 69 Cal. 255, 10 Pac. 674 (1886), wherein Justice McKinstry worried about a "monopoly" of water "in a few hands" (703). Cf. Justice Lucien Shaw in *Katz* v *Walkinshaw*, 114 Cal. 116, 74 Pac. 766 at 769 (1903).

4. Novak, *Intellectual Origins of the State Police Power: The Common Law Vision of a Well-Regulated Society* (Institute for Legal Studies Working Paper, Madison, Wis., 1989), 78, 80–81, 99, citing U.S. Supreme Court justice James Wilson, *The Works of James Wilson*, ed. R. G. McCloskey, 2 vols. (Cambridge, Mass., 1967), 1:183, 353–54, 88; Henry Baldwin, *A General View of the Origin and Nature of the Constitution and government of the United States* (Philadelphia, 1837), 8, 4, cited in Novak, *Intellectual Origins of State Police Power*, 83; Theophilus Parsons, *Treatise on the Law of Shipping and the Law and Practice of Admiralty* (Boston: Little, Brown, 1869), 4–5.

5. Story in *VanNess* v *Packard*, 2 Pet. 137 at 145 (1829) (a springhouse for a dairyman); Kent, *Commentaries on American Law*, 3rd ed. (New York, 1836), 2:346; Morton Horwitz, *The Transformation of American Law, 1780–1860* (Cambridge, Mass.: Harvard University Press, 1977), 55; *Holmes* v *Tremper*, 20 Johns. 29 at 30 (1822) See also *Whiting* v *Brastow*, 21 Mass. 310 (1826) (a corn-house). The offensive English precedent was *Elwes* v *Maw*, 3 East 38 at 50, 102 ER 510 (K. B. 1802) (beast house, cart house, and pump house of tenant's on farm belong to landlord).

6. Laurence Friedman, *A History of American Law*, 2nd ed. (New York: Simon and Schuster, 1985), 253.

7. In *Harvard College* v *Amory*, 9 Pick. (26 Mass.) 446 (1830).

8. *Overseers of the Poor* v *Tayloe's Adm.*, 1 Gilm. (Va.) 336 (1821); *Nyce's Estate*, 5 W. & S. (Pa.) 254 (1843); *Hempill's Appeal*, 18 Pa. St. 303 (1852).

9. *Allen* v *Gaillard*, 1 Rich., N. S., (So. Car.) 279 (1869).

10. *King* v *Talbot*, 40 N.Y. 76 (1869); *Simons* v *Oliver*, 74 Wis. 633 (1889); *White* v *Sherman*, 168 Ill. 589, 48 N. E. 128 (1897). G. W. Keeton, *Social Change in the Law of Trusts* (London: Pitman, 1958), 20.

11. *Nyce's Estate*, 5 W. & S. (Pa.) 254 at 257 (1843). This is why in his will, in 1860, Justice Peter Daniel, a Virginian on the U.S. Supreme Court, excluded the conversion by the administrator of his estate of any of his real estate into bank, railroad, or other corporate stocks or bonds "of any kind." Quoted in Tony Freyer, *Producers and Capitalists: Constitutional Conflict in Antebellum America* (Charlottesville: University of Virginia Press, 1994), 197.

12. Friedman, *History of American Law*, 423.

13. This is the view of Laurence Friedman, "The Dynastic Trust," *Yale Law Journal* 73 (1964): 547 at 585, 589; Friedman, *History of American Law*, 424.

14. Kentucky's Chief Justice Thomas Marshall in *Pope's Ex.* v *Elliott & Co.*, 8 B. Mon. (Ky.) 56 at 60 (1847).

15. *Tillinghast* v *Bradford*, 5 R. I. 205 (1858); *Ryder* v *Sisson*, 7 R. I. 34 (1862); *Smith* v *Moore*, 37 Ala. 328 (1861); *Mebane* v *Mebane*, 4 Ire. Eq. (39 N. C.) 131 (1845). See also *Heath* v *Bishop*, 4 Rich. Eq. (So. Car.) 46 at 58 (1851) (modest trust approved for a son "thriftless, of understanding not sound, and liable to imposition by artful men," but since beneficiary had vanished, payment to creditors allowed, citing English precedent).

16. See, for example, *Fisher* v *Taylor*, 2 Rawle (Pa.) 33 (1829); *Holdship* v *Patterson*, 7 Watts (Pa.) 547 (1838); *Shankland's Appeal*, 47 Pa. St. 113 (1864); *Barnett's Appeal*, 46 Pa. St. 392 (1864); *Pope's Ex.* v *Elliott*, 8 B. Mon. (Ky) 56 (1847); *Leavitt* v *Beirne*, 21 Ct. 1 (1850); *Clute* v *Bool*, 8 Paige Ch. (N.Y.) 83 (1840); *Stewart* v *McMartin*, 5 Barb. (N.Y. Sup. Ct.) 438 (1849); *Bramhall* v *Ferris*, 14 N.Y. 41 (1856); *Campbell* v *Foster*, 35 NY 361 (1866); *Exs. of White* v *White*, 30 Vt. 338 (1857); *Broadway Bank* v *Adams*, 133 Mass. 170 (1882), and the next four notes.

17. *Nichols* v *Eaton*, 91 U.S. 716 at 726 (1875).

18. *Nickell* v *Handly*, 10 Gratt. (Va.) 336 at 339 (1853).

19. *Steib* v *Whitehead*, 111 Ill. 247 at 251–52 (1884), quoted in Gregory Alexander's valuable analysis, "The Dead Hand and the Law of Trusts in the 19th Century," *Stanford Law Review* 37 (1985): 1189 at 1247.

20. *Guernsey* v *Lazear*, 51 W.Va. 328 at 340, 41 S. E. 405 at 410 (1902), cited in Alexander, "Dead Hand, 1248; *Barnett's Appeal*, 46 Pa. St. 392 at 400 (1864).

21. John Chipman Gray, *Restraints on the Alienation of Property*, 2nd ed. (Boston, 1895), viii–ix.

22. Horwitz, *Transformation 1*, 74–77; Kermit Hall, *The Magic Mirror: Law in American History* (New York: Oxford University Press, 1990), 119; Friedman, *History of American Law*, 413; Paul Kurtz, "Nineteenth Century Anti-Entrepreneurial Nuisance Injunctions: Avoiding the Chancellor," *William and Mary Law Review* 17 (1976): 621; Richard Posner, *The Economic Analysis of Law*, 3rd ed. (Boston: Little, Brown, 1986), 56.

23. Richard Posner, *The Economics of Justice* (Cambridge, Mass.: Harvard University Press, 1981), 5.

24. C. Rosen, "Differing Perceptions of the Value of Pollution Abatement Across Time and Place: Balancing Doctrine in Pollution Nuisance Law, 1840–1906," *Law and History Review* 11 (1993): 303; Robert Bone, "Normative Theory and Legal Doctrine in American Nuisance Law: 1850 to 1920," *Southern California Law Review* 59 (1986): 1101; D. M. Provine, "Balancing Pollution and Property Rights: A Comparison of the Development of English and American Nuisance Law," *Anglo-American Law Review* 7 (1978): 31; M. McBride, "Critical Legal History and Private Actions against Public Nuisance, 1800–1865," *Columbia Journal of Law and Social Problems* 22 (1989): 307; Kurtz, "Avoiding the Chancellor"; E. P. Krauss, "The Legal Form of Liberalism: A Study of Riparian and Nuisance Law in Nineteenth Century Ohio," *Akron Law Review* 18 (1984): 223; and Peter Hoffer, *The Law's Conscience: Equitable Constitutionalism in America* (Chapel Hill: University of North Carolina Press, 1990), 152–63.

25. Krauss, "Legal Form of Liberalism"; Rosen, "Balancing Doctrine"; McBride, "Private Actions against Public Nuisance"; Horwitz, *Transformation 1*;

Bone, "Normative Theory and Legal Doctrine"; Provine, "Balancing Pollution and Property Rights"; Hoffer, *The Law's Conscience*, 154–61.

26. Horwitz, *Transformation 1*, 75 ("the mere existence of an injury"); Kurtz, "Avoiding the Chancellor," 622–23 and 643 ("any interference"; "absolute liability").

27. *William Aldred's Case*, 9 Co. 576, 77 ER 816 (K. B. 1611); *Jones v Powell*, Palm. 536, 81 ER 1208 (K. B., 1628) (a brewhouse emitting "horribles vapores & insalubres" and "un smel del sea cole" a nuisance for having made life for neighbors as unbearable as the reporter's law french). See Daniel Coquillette, "Mosses from an Old Manse: Another Look at Some Historic Property Cases about the Environment," *Cornell Law Review* 64 (1979): 761, for a good discussion of the issue.

28. Kurtz, "Avoiding the Chancellor," 665–66.

29. *McCord & Hunt v Iker*, 12 Ohio 387 at 389 (1843). Krauss ("Legal Form of Liberalism," 232) and I do not agree on the interpretation of this case.

30. Horwitz, *Transformation 1*, 76. Cf. Kurtz, "Avoiding the Chancellor," 639–42. Kurtz, however, notes that private nuisance suits were increasingly tolerated by courts of the late nineteenth century (654–56).

31. See *Baines v Baker*, Amb. 158, 27 ER 105 (Ch. 1752) (private nuisance suit inappropriate; defendant's activities too public and question one of public rights); Year Book, Mich. 27 Hen. 8f. 27, pl. 10 (1535); Coke on Lit. 56a (private action good if plaintiff suffers "a particular damage" not common to others); *Crowder v Tinkler*, 19 Ves. Jn. 617, 34 ER 645 (Ch. 1816) (same); *Sampson v Smith*, 8 Sim. 271, 59 ER 108 (V. Ch. 1838) (same); *Coulson v White*, 3 Atk. 23, 26 ER 816 (Ch. 1743) (injunction will issue if nuisance continued for long time); *Att. Gen. v Cleaver*, 18 Ves. J. 212, 34 ER 297 at 299 (Ch. 1811) (injunctions rare); Robert H. Eden, *A Treatise on the Law of Injunctions* (London, 1821), 236.

32. 95 Mass. (13 Allen) 95 at 102 (1866).

33. McBride, "Private Actions against Public Nuisance," 315–22. But see *Burrows v Pixley*, 1 Root (Ct.) 362 (1792) (private suit against public nuisance okay where special injury done).

34. Kurtz, "Avoiding the Chancellor," 655–56.

35. See *Tuebner v Cal-St. RR*, 66 Cal. 171, 4 Pac. 1162 1884); *Broome v N.Y. & N.J. Tel. Co.*, 42 N.J. Eq. 141, 7 Atl. 851 (1887); *Wells v New Haven & Northhampton Co.*, 151 Mass. 46 (1890); *Waldron v Haverhill*, 143 Mass. 582 (1887); *Jackman v Arlington Mills*, 137 Mass. 277 (1884); *Manning v Lowell*, 130 Mass. 21 (1880); *Dugan v Bridge Co.*, 27 Pa. St. 303 (1856); *Heckers v N.Y. Balance Dock Co.*, 13 How. Pr. (N.Y. Sup. Ct.) 549 (1857).

When courts *did* bar private nuisance suits of a "public rights" nature, these tended to involve *public* defendants (a harbor authority, a public bridge corporation, a river-dredging authority, a waterworks; e.g., *Lansing v Smith*, 8 Cow. (N.Y.) 146 (1828); aff. 4 Wend. 9 (1829); *Vanderbilt v Adams*, 7 Cow. (N.Y.) 347 (1827) (harbormaster may order vessel at private wharf to shift berths); *Flanagan v City of Phila.*, 42 Pa. St. 219 at 233 (1862) (towboat owners cannot enjoin new city bridge that would lengthen their towlines because "their right of navigation, like all the rights of citizenship, is held subject to the common weal," and their loss was not "too great a sacrifice to make for the comfort and convenience which a bridge will furnish to the populous districts on the banks of the Schuylkill"); *Hobart v Milwau-*

kee City RR., 27 Wis. 194 (1870) (a businessman using wagons on a street where a horse-drawn streetcar was planned for "public travel" cannot enjoin such an undertaking because he does not possess the right to back his wagons up at right angles to his store, blocking half the street). See also William Novak, *"Salus Populi:* The Roots of Regulation in America, 1787–1873," Ph.D. diss., Brandis University, 1992, 310–15.

36. The pattern I detected appears to predate 1828; William Nelson, *The Americanization of the Common Law: The Impact of Legal Change on Massachusetts Society, 1760–1830* (Cambridge, Mass.: Harvard University Press, 1975), 121, 233, reports six Massachusetts county court damage judgments involving pollution nuisances between 1799 and 1828.

37. *Eames* v *New England Worsted Co.*, 52 Mass. 570 (1846). Cf. Jennifer Nedelsky, "Judicial Conservatism in an Age of Innovation: Comparative Perspective's on Canadian Nuisance Law, 1880–1930," in *Essays in the History of Canadian Law*, ed. David H. Flaherty (Toronto: University of Toronto Press, 1981), 281–322.

38. *Shepard* v *Hill*, 151 Mass. 540 (1890); *Call* v *Allen*, 83 Mass. 137 (1861).

39. *Commonwealth* v *Perry*, 139 Mass. 198 (1885); *Middlesex Co.* v *City of Lowell*, 149 Mass. 509 (1889). Cf. a nonpollution nuisance opinion of Holmes in *New Salem* v *Eagle Mill Co.*, 138 Mass. 198 (1885).

40. Kurtz, "Avoiding the Chancellor," 669. *Gilbert* v *Showerman*, 23 Mich. 447 (1871); *Huckenstine's Appeal*, 70 Pa. St. 102 (1871).

41. *Rhodes* v *Dunbar*, 57 Pa. St. 274 at 287 (1868).

42. *Fish* v *Dodge*, 4 Denio (N.Y.) 311 (1847); *Galbraith* v *Oliver*, 3 Pitts. R. 78 (1867); *Hurlbut* v *McKone*, 55 Ct. 31, 10 Atl. 164 (1887); *Rodenhausen* v *Craven*, 141 Pa. St. 546, 21 Atl. 774 (1891); *Davis* v *Sawyer*, 133 Mass. 289 (1882); *Butterfield* v *Klaber*, 52 How. Pr. 255 (N.Y.S. C. 1876); *Ross* v *Butler*, 19 N.J. Eq. 294 at 306 (1868); *Hennessey* v *Carmody*, 50 N.J. Eq. 616, 25 Atl. 374 at 380 (1892), cited in Rosen, "Balancing Doctrine." Compare the contemporary Canadian experience with the "industrialization defense" (also known as "local standards or character of the neighborhood"). Jennifer Nedelsky notes that in sixteen cases where this was at issue, plaintiffs lost only once ("Judicial Conservatism in an Age of Innovation," 291).

43. But not before Justice Samuel Gustine Thompson, dissenting, had penned this contemptuous aside about my fair city: Enjoining the use of this high-ash coal would hurt the economy of Pittsburgh, "a monument to progress and activity of the manufacturing interests." These larger socioeconomic costs ought to be counted against the value of such roofing, fabrics, carpets, shade and fruit trees of the urban plaintiffs "if such be of value amid the smoke of Pittsburgh." *Sullivan* v *J & L Steel*, 208 Pa. St. 540 at 562 (1904).

44. *Leeds* v *Shakerly*, Cro. Eliz. 751, 78 ER 783 (Q. B. 1600); Blackstone, *Commentaries on the Laws of England*, 4 vols. (London, 1765–69), 2:402; *Rex* v *Cross*, 2 Car. & P. 483, 172 ER 219 (N. P. 1826) (Abbott, C. J.).

45. *Commonwealth* v *Upton*, 72 Mass. 473 at 476 (1856), citing *People* v *Cunningham*, 1 Denio (N.Y.) 536 (1845). (See also *Ashbrook* v *Comm.*, 64 Ky. 139 (1866), and *Hackney* v *State*, 8 Ind. 494 (1856). (The New York court had creatively cited dicta in *Weld* v *Hornby*, 7 East 196 at 199, 103 ER 75 at 76 (K. B. 1806) as authority. See *Elliotson* v *Feetham*, 2 Bing. (N. C.) 137, 132 ER 53 (C. P. 1835), for an

application by common pleas of the older view (ten years' noise from an ironmonger shop no bar to one moving in to sue for damages because ironmonger only active for ten years).

46. *Ashbrook v Ky.*, 64 Ky. 139 (1866) (rejecting the English rule in *Cross's Case*, 2 C.& P. 483, 173 ER 219 (N. P. 1826); *Alexander v Kerr*, 2 Rawle (Pa.) 83 (1828); *Smith v Phillips*, 8 Phila. 10 (1871); *Wier's Appeal*, 74 Pa. St. 230 (1873); *Cleveland v Citizen's Gas Light*, 20 N.J. Eq. 201 (1869); *Brady v Weeks*, 3 Barb. (N.Y.) 157 (1848); *King v Morris & Essex RR*, 18 N.J. Eq. 397 at 399 (1867); *Susquehana Fertilizer v Malone*, 73 Md. 268, 20 Atl. 900 (1890); *Van Fossen v Clark*, 113 Iowa 86, 84 N. W. 989 (1901); *Austin v Augusta Terminal Ry.*, 108 Ga. 671, 34 S. E. 852 (1899); *Fertilizing Co. v Hyde Park*, 97 U.S. 659 (1878); *Hurlbut v McKone*, 55 Ct. 31, 10 Atl. 164 (1887); *People v Detroit White Lead Works*, 82 Mich. 471, 46 N. W. 735 (1890); *Laflin-Rand Powder Co. v Tearney*, 131 Ill. 322, 23 N. E. 389 (1890); *Ohio & M. RR v Singletary*, 34 Ill. App. 425; *Same v Elliott, Id.*, 589 (1890); *Oehler v Levy*, 139 Ill. App. 294, aff. 234 Ill. 595, 85 N. E. 271 (1908). Cf. *Campbell v Seaman*, 63 N.Y. 568 at 584 (1876). But see *Platte & D. Ditch Co. v Anderson*, 8 Colo. 131, 6 Pac. 515 (1884), for the opposite rule.

47. See John P. S. McLaren, "Nuisance Law and the Industrial Revolution— Some Lessons from Social History," *Oxford Journal of Legal Studies* 3 (1983): 155 at 220; and Nedelsky, "Judicial Conservatism in an Age of Innovation." But see James Oldham, *The Mansfield Manuscripts and the Growth of English Law in the Eighteenth Century*, 2 vols. (Chapel Hill: University of North Carolina Press, 1992), 2:887–89, for evidence of some attention to the relative interests of the parties in one public nuisance suit before King's Bench in 1757 (*Rex v White*), where Lord Mansfield noted that "this manufactory is of great utility to commerce and physick."

48. *Robinson v Baugh*, 31 Mich. 290 (1875).

49. Rosen, "Balancing Doctrine."

50. Richard Ely, "The Nature of the Railway Problem," *Harper's New Monthly Magazine* 73 (1886): 250 at 254. See also James Kehl, *Boss Rule in the Gilded Age: Matt Quay of Pennsylvania* (Pittsburgh: University of Pittsburgh Press, 1980).

51. *Appeal of the Pa. Lead Co.*, 96 Pa. St. 116 at 122, 127 (1880). Cf. *Evans v Reading Chemical & Fertilizing Co.*, 160 Pa. St. 209 (1894).

52. *Pa. Coal Co. v Sanderson*, 5 Norris (86 Pa. St.) 401 (1878) (Woodward, J., citing *St. Helen's Smelting v Tipping* and other English precedent); 94 Pa. St. 302 at 307 (1880) (Gordon, J.: mining not in public welfare but for "private gain"); 113 Pa. St. 126 (1886).

53. *Evans v Chemical Fertilizer Co.*, 160 Pa. St. 209 (1894).

54. 8 Dana (38 Ky.) 289 at 305, 309 (1839); Horwitz, *Transformation 1*, 75. See also Hall, *Magic Mirror*, 127; Kurtz, "Avoiding the Chancellor" at 646; and St. Presser and Jamil Zaimaldin, eds., *Law and American History* (St. Paul: West, 1980), 336.

55. *Lexington & Ohio RR v Applegate*, 38 Ky. 289 (1839) at 309. See Richard Epstein, "The Social Consequence of Common Law Rules," *Harvard Law Review* 95 (1982): 1717 at 1729–33, for another critique of Horwitz's reading of *Applegate*.

56. Charles F. Adams Jr., *Notes on Railroad Accidents* (New York, 1879), 231.

57. See, for example, *Nicols v Pixly*, 1 Root (Ct.) 129 (1789) (mill licensed by town not a nuisance); *Harmon v Chicago*, 110 Ill. 400 (1884) (dense smoke a nuisance per

se by statue); *North Chicago Ry v Lake View*, 105 Ill. 207 (1883) (a steam locomotive on a street a nuisance *per se*); *Call v Allen*, 83 Mass. 137 (1861) (steam engines and furnaces authorized by statute not nuisance *per se*); *Pa v Wheeling & Belmont Bridge Co.*, 59 U.S. 421 (1855) (bridge no nuisance by act of Congress); *Quinn v Lowell Electric Co.*, 140 Mass. 106 (1887) (steam engine within five hundred feet of buildings a nuisance by statute); *Hooker v New Haven & Northhampton Co.*, 14 Ct. 146 (1841) (statute explicitly barring private nuisance suits lawful); *Bristol v Housatonic Water Co.*, 42 Ct. 403 (1875) (same).

58. *Almost* invariably. Jurists did not see themselves as mere ciphers. They construed statutes "in derogation of the common law . . . strictly," wrote Justice Horace Gray in a decision enjoining a petroleum refiner operating under what he claimed was statutory authority in Winthrop, Massachusetts, in 1871. The statutes in point, Gray noted, sanctioned little more than the *storage* of petroleum. The "offensive odors" its refining generated were not authorized. (*Commonwealth v Kidder*, 107 Mass. 188 at 192 (1871)). See also Justice Pliny Merrick's similar views in the case of *Commonwealth v Rumford Chemical Works*, 82 Mass. 231 at 234 (1860); and Justice Stephen J. Field's ringing rejection of the congressional authority cited by counsel for the Baltimore and Potomac Railroad in *B. & P. RR v 5th Baptist Church*, 108 U.S. 317 at 331 (1883) (forty-five hundred dollars damages affirmed for noise and vibration by roundhouse and sixty feet from smokestacks adjacent church/Sunday school on D Street).

59. This point was made by an English jurist we will meet again (chaps. 7 and 8), Lord Denman, C. J., in *Rex v Ward*, 4 Ad. & El. 384, 111 ER 832 at 839 (K. B. 1836). Coal shippers had obstructed the Medina River at Cowes Harbour with a causeway without statutory authority. (Ships tacking into Newport harbour were "obstructed.") Denman turned away their "public benefits" defense: "No greater evil can be conceived than the encouragement of capitalists and adventurers to interfere with known public rights, from motives of personal interest, on the speculation that the changes made may be rendered lawful by being thought to supply the public with something better than they actually enjoy." But he allowed that were "a great and acknowledged public improvement" to appear, the Parliament would be perfectly able to declare the activity to be lawful (no nuisance). (Cited in McLaren, "Nuisance Law and the Industrial Revolution," *Oxford J. of Legal St* 3 (1983): 155. *Rex v Ward* was cited as authority in several American nuisance actions, notably by the New York Court of Appeals when they turned away Jacob Sharp's effort to secure a Broadway streetcar franchise from the New York City Common Council. *Davis v Mayor of N.Y.*, 14 N.Y. 506 (1856).

60. *State v Tupper*, 23 So. Car. 135 (1838), cited in G. Schwartz, "The Character of Early American Tort Law," *U. C. L.A. Law Review* 36 (1989): 641 at 652; *Ruttles v City of Covington*, 88 Ky. C. of A., 10 S. W. 644 (1889). See also *Pitts., C.&C. RR v Welch*, 12 Ind. App. 433, 40 N. E. 650 (1895), where an award for negligently caused damage to a hotel from smoke, vibration, and noxious smells was affirmed against a railroad that abused its use of the public main street.

61. Kurtz, "Avoiding the Chancellor," 644.

62. Kurtz, "Avoiding the Chancellor," 625n. And see *Att. Gen v Cleaver*, 18 Ves. J. 212, 34 ER 297 (Ch. 1811). See also John McLaren, "Nuisance Law and the Indus-

trial Revolution: Some Lessons from Social History," *Oxford Journal of Legal Studies* 3 (1983): 159.

63. Mass. St. 1827, ch. 88. (This is why Kurtz, "Avoiding the Chancellor," 624–33, finds no pollution nuisance bills in equity before 1836 from New England or Pennsylvania courts.)

64. American courts, like their English counterparts, often preferred to refer plaintiffs to their damage remedy at law when they could thereby be "adequately" compensated for their loss. See *Middleton v Franklin*, 3 Cal. 238 at 241 (1853); *Coe v Win. Lake Cotton & Wollen M. Co.*, 37 N. H. 254 at 264 (1858). See also *Bliss v Anaconda Copper Mining Co.*, 167 Fed. 342 (C.CD, Mont. 1909), which Kurtz characterizes (659) as having "denied relief" to Mr. Bliss. It is true that the federal circuit court did not grant Bliss the injunction he and his rancher/farmer associates sought, out of respect for the Congressional invitation to mining prospectors "to the exploration of the Rocky Mountains," but Kurtz does not tell us that Anaconda had offered to buy Bliss's land, that the court warned Anaconda that it would hear further testimony "to prevent the release of arsenic," and that "the courts are open to Mr. Bliss" for an action of past damages and future compensation (359–72).

65. McLaren, "Nuisance Law and the Industrial Revolution," 155. Of late, courts have, once again, acquired a central role in overseeing control of pollution. See Rosen, "Balancing Doctrine"; Samuel P. Hays, "Environmental Litigation in Historical Perspective," *University of Michigan Journal of Law Reform* 19 (1986): 969.

FOUR

1. Morton Horwitz, *The Transformation of American Law, 1780–1860* (Cambridge, Mass.: Harvard University Press, 1977), 46, 103; William Nelson, *The Americanization of the Common Law: The Impact of Legal Change on Massachusetts Society, 1760–1830* (Cambridge, Mass.: Harvard University Press, 1975), 10, 255; Laurence Friedman, *A History of American Law*, 2nd ed. (New York: Simon and Schuster, 1985), 413. Richard Posner, "The Law and Economics Movement," *American Economic Review* 77 (1987): 1 at 6, thinks the abandoning of the "ancient-lights" doctrine represented, and was based on, an efficient allocation of resources. Light here was not "a scarce commodity" since people "spread out" in America(!?).

2. Friedman, *History of American Law*, 413; Horwitz, *Transformation* 1, 44, 72, 102.

3. John Burnett, *A Social History of Housing, 1815–1970* (London: Newton Abbot, 1978), 110, 209. Cf. John E. Crowley, "Artifical Illumination in Early America and the Definition of Domestic Space and Time," in *Travail et Loisir dans Les Societés Pré Industrielles*, ed. Barbara Karsky and El. Marienstras (Nancy: 1991).

4. *Bowry v Pope's Case*, 1 Leon. 168, 74 ER 155 (Q. B. 1587); *Hughes v Keme* [or *Keymish*], 1 Bulst. 116, Yelv. 216, 80 ER 141 and 811 (K. B. 1612). Cf. *Palmer v Fletcher*, 1 Sid. 167, 82 ER 1035 (K. B. 1663). But note that English courts never supported an easement over another's land merely for "a pleasant, open view" (Friedman, *History of American Law*, 413). See *William Aldred's Case*, 9 Co. R. 576, 77

ER 816 at 821 (K. B. 1611), and George Bispham, *The Principles of Equity* (1874), sec. 441, citing English precedent.

5. In *Lewis v Price*, noted by Sgt. Williams in his comments on *Yard v Ford*, 2 Sand. 175, 85 ER 926.

6. Ibid. See, for example, the attention to it given in 1840 by William Noyes, "The Legal Rules Governing the Enjoyment of Light," *American Jurist* 23 (1840): 55.

7. *Fishmongers Co. v East India Co.*, Dick. 163, 21 ER 232 (Ch. 1752) (Lord Hardwicke: "It is not sufficient to say that it will alter the plaintiff's lights, for then no vacant piece of ground could be built on in a city"); *Attny. Gen. v Nicol*, 16 Ves. 338, 33 ER 1012 (Ch. 1809); *Back v Stacey*, 2 C. & P. 465, 172 ER 210 (N. P. 1826). Cf. *Parker v Smith*, 5 C. & P. 438, 172 ER 1043 (N. P. 1832), but here the defendant's offending building was ordered to be torn down. I am indebted to John McLaren, "Nuisance Law and the Industrial Revolution," for much of the evidence in this paragraph; he is not responsible for any errors in my interpretation of these cases.

8. Statute 2 & 3 Will. IV, c. 71 ("Prescription Act").

9. In *Yates v Jack*, 1 L. R. Ch. App. 295 (1865–66); and *Clark v Clarke*, L. R. 1 Ch. App. 16 (1865).

10. *Chasemore v Richards*, 7 H. of L. 386, 11 ER 140 (1859).

11. *Cox v Matthews*; 1 Vent. 237, 86 ER 159 (K. B. 1674) (Hale, C. J.); *Tennant v Goldwin*, 6 Mod. 311 at 314, 87 ER 1051 at 1054 (K. B. 1704) (Gould, J.: "If a man builds next to a vacant piece of ground of his own, and then sells the new house, keeping the ground in his own hands, he cannot build upon the waste ground so as to stop the lights of the house; for by sale of the house, all the lights . . . pass."); *Swansborough v Coventry*, 9 Bing. 305, 131 ER 629 (C. P. 1832); *Canham v Fisk*, 2 Tyrw. 155, 2 Cr. & J. 128, 149 ER 53 (Ex. 1831); *Roswell v Prior*, 12 Mod 635 at 639, 88 ER 1570 (K. B. 1698) (Holt, C. J.); *Palmer v Fletcher*, 1 Sid. 167, 82 ER 1035 (K. B. 1663); *Nichols v Chamberlain*, Cro. Jac. 121, 79 ER 105 (K. B. 1607); *Compton v Richards*, 1 Price 27, 145 ER 1320 (Ex. 1814).

12. Donald Olsen, *Town Planning in London: The 18th and 19th Centuries* (New Haven, Conn.: Yale University Press, 1964), 15, 19, 30–31, 90, 128, 187; M. A. Simpson and T. H. Lloyd, eds., *Middle Class Housing in Britain* (London: Newton Abbot, 1977), 10, 29, 38, 55, 63, 102, 119–20, 134–40.

13. These were: New York, in *Parker v Foote*, 19 Wend. 309 (1838); (overruling *Mahan v Brown*, 13 Wend. 261 (1835)); South Carolina, in *Napier v Bulwinkle*, 5 Rich. 311 (1852); overruling *McCready v Thompson*, 1 Dud. L. 131 (1838)); Maryland, in *Cherry v Stein*, 11 Md. 1 (1858) (rejecting dicta of Justice Walter Dorsey in *Wright v Freeman*, 5 H & J 467 at 477 (1823)); and Illinois, in *Guest v Reynolds*, 68 Ill. 478 (1873) (overruling *Gerber v Grabel*, 16 Ill. 217 (1854)).

14. Maine, in *Pierre v Fernald*, 26 Me. 438 (1847); Pennsylvania, in *Hazlett v Powell*, 6 Casey (30 Pa. St.) 293 (1858); Vermont, in *Hubbard v Town*, 33 Vt. 2 83 (1860); Alabama, in *Ward v Neal*, 37 Ala. 500 (1861); Iowa, in *Morrison v Marquardt*, 24 Iowa 35 (1867); Ohio, in *Mullen v Stricker*, 19 Ohio St. 135 (1869); Indiana, in *Stein v Hauck*, 56 Ind. 65 (1877); and West Virginia, in *Powell v Sims*, 5 W.Va. 1 (1871).

15. These were New Jersey, in *Robeson v Pittenger*, 2 N.J. Eq. (1 Greene's Ch.) 57 (1838) (dicta indicating the doctrine might not apply to "populous cities"); Mississippi, in *Gwin v Melmoth*, 1 Freem. Ch. (Miss.) 505 at 506 (1841) (dicta); Kentucky,

in *Manier v Myers*, 43 Ky (4 B. Mon.) 514 at 520–21 (1844); Louisiana, in *Durel, Adm. v Boisblanc*, 1 La. Ann. 407 (1846); and Delaware, in *Clawson v Primrose*, 4 Del. Ch. 643 (1873). Massachusetts courts applied the ancient-lights doctrine in a series of cases between 1785 and 1829 (see Nelson, *Americanization of the Common Law*, 123, 235 n. 68), but thereafter the rule was circumvented, and finally abrogated altogether, by legislative fiat. For the New York court's rediscovery of the right to light in the era of the elevated railway, see *Story v N.Y. El. RR*, 90 N.Y. 122 (1882).

16. See *Rennyson's Appeal*, 94 Pa. St. 147 (1880); and *Mullen v Stricker*, 19 Ohio St. 135 (1869). Cf. *Morrison v Marquardt*, 24 Iowa 35 (1867), where Chief Justice John Dillon came very close to a blanket rejection of the "implied grant" rule.

17. On implied grants of light see *Story v Odin*, 12 Mass. 157 (1815); *U.S. v Appleton*, 1 Charles Sumner 492, 24 Fed. Cas. 841 (Cir. Ct. D. Mass. 1833) (Story, J.); *Burr v Mills*, 21 Wend. 290 (1839); *Hazlett v Powell*, 6 Casey (30 Pa. St.) 293 at 296 (1858); *Kay v Stallman*, 2 Week. N. of Cas. (Pa.) 643 (1876); *Cherry v Stein*, 11 Md. 1 (1858); *James v Jenkins*, 34 Md. 1 at 10 (1871); *Lampman v Milks*, 21 N.Y. 505 (1860); and *Durel, Adm. v Boisblanc*, 1 La. Ann. 407 (1846).

18. See *Morrison v Marquardt*, 24 Iowa 35 at 64 (1867) ("Fettering estates and laying an embargo upon the hand of improvement which carries the trowel and the plane"); and *Mullen v Stricker*, 19 Ohio St. 135 at 144 (1869) ("unsuitable . . . where real estate is constantly and rapidly appreciating and being subjected to new and more costly forms of improvement."). But two other passages appear in opinions *upholding* the doctrine, and the other appears in one applying the implied-grant rule. Hence in these three instances the plaintiffs secured their right to the lights. In *Robeson v Pittenger*, 2 N.J. Eq. 57 (1838) at 61–62, New Jersey's Chancellor Pennington suggested that the ancient-lights doctrine "might work great inconvenience and injustice" in "populous cities, where land is very valuable, and it is the constant practice to place buildings side by side," but he then *applied* the doctrine to a house in the town of Belvidere, Warren County. In *Cherry v Stein*, 11 Md. 1 (1858) at 21, Maryland's Justice John Eccleston, rejecting the doctrine, explained that "to adopt it would, greatly interfere with, and impede, the rapid changes and improvements which are here constantly going on," but he *applied* the implied-grant rule in the case at hand, *and* he indicated that the tolerating of the eaves of plaintiff's house overhanging defendant's property and depositing rain runoff on that property for over twenty years *would* constitute a lawful easement through adverse possession. See also *Gerber v Grabel*, 16 Ill. 217 at 223–24 (1854) (Scates, J.); and *Powell v Sims*, 5 W.Va. 1 (1871).

19. As in *Pierre v Fernald*, 26 Me. 438 at 441 (1847).

20. See, for example, *Napier v Bulwinkle* at 321.

21. In *Parker v Foote*.

22. In *Guest v Reynolds* (Breese, C. J.).

23. In *Parker v Foote*; and *Pierre v Fernald*. Cf. Justice John Pierpont's remarks in *Hubbard v Town*, 33 Vt. 283 (1860).

Needless to say, those opinions in which the doctrine was *adopted* were doctrinal as well. Thus Justice J. B. O'Neall of South Carolina allowed that the doctrine might be "an unwise one and inapplicable to this country," but felt that such an argument "may very properly be addressed to legislators; with judges, it can have no weight." *McCready* v *Thomson*, 1 Dud. L. (23 S. C.) 131 at 133 (1838). Just so, Illinois' Justice John Caton: "That the public good would be promoted by [the doctrine's] repeal, I may admit, but the constitution has not made me a judge of that." *Gerber* v *Grabel*, 16 Ill. 217 at 225 (1854).

24. George, and John Stuart Mill before him, aptly called this increase the "unearned increment." He recommended a "single tax" on such undeveloped property to induce its owners to action. Henry George, *Progress and Poverty* (New York, 1879), bk. 8, chap. 3.

25. Dicta in *Hoy* v *Sterrett*, 2 Watts (Pa.) 327 at 331 (1834), italics mine; Dicta in *Haverstick* v *Sipe*, 33 Pa. St. 368 at 371 (1860). See also *Mullen* v *Stricker*, 19 Ohio St. 135 (1869) at 144: The ancient-lights doctrine was "not in accordance with the common understanding of the community." Here land changed hands so often "as almost to become a matter of merchandise." And see *Myers* v *Gemmel*, 10 Barb. (N.Y. Sup. Ct.) 538 (1851) at 542–43: Americans were "confident that the future will add to the value of their lands, and create the expediency and necessity of improving them by more extensive buildings."

26. *Stein* v *Hauck*, 56 Ind. 65 at 69 (1877).

27. Horwitz, *Transformation 1*, 46.

28. *Mahan* v *Brown*, 3 Wend. 261 (1835).

29. *Parker* v *Foote*, 19 Wend. 309 at 318 (1838). The "overthrow" of ancient lights in New York was a tenuous one. After the supreme court split two to one in *Parker*, the still separate vice chancellor, Lewis Sandford, carefully avoided declaring whether or not his court would observe the doctrine fully nine years later in *Banks* v *American Tract Society*, 4 Sandf. Ch. 438 at 464 (1847). In any event he enjoined the completion of another offending defendant's wall. Similarly, in *Myers* v *Gemmel*, 10 Barb. (N.Y.) 538 (1851) the recently created New York Court of Appeals also split two to one on the question of whether the doctrine of ancient lights had truly been extinguished in that state. Justice Samuel Selden mentions the "ancient" right again in *Lampman* v *Milks*, 21 N.Y. 505 at 511 (1860). And see the survival of the right to light, be it ancient or no, in *Doyle* v *Lord*, 64 N.Y. 432 (1876) (one cannot build in back yard and stop light to lessees in building, under implied grant theory); *Patten* v *N.Y. El. RR*, 3 Abb. N. C. (N.Y.) 306 at 321 (1878) (hotel owner entitled to special damages for obstruction of long-enjoyed light and air from street); *Story* v *N.Y. El. RR*, 90 N.Y. 122 at 142, 146 (1882) (abutting landowner, whose light now of "a flickering character" may recover damages from elevated railway); *Peyser* v *Met. Ry.*, 13 Daly (N.Y. Com. Pl.) 123 (1885); and *Pond* v *Metrop. Elev. Ry*, 42 Hun (N.Y. Sup. Ct.) 567 at 568 (1886) (abutting landowner can recover twenty-five hundred dollars from elevated railway for loss of easement of light).

30. *Hubbard* v *Town*, 33 Vt. 283 at 302 (1860). Contrast Bronson's and Pierpont's emphasis on "neighborly" behavior with Oliver Wendell Holmes's toleration of more malicious "spite fences," even where the Massachusetts legislature had addressed the subject and the defendant had acted "malevolently," if the plaintiff could offer another credible reason for the tall offensive fence. *Rideout* v *Knox*, 148 Mass. 368 at 373 (1889).

31. Horwitz, *Transformation 1*, 281; Noyes, "Legal Rules," 46.

32. In *Pierre* v *Fernald*.

33. Noyes, "Legal Rules," 51–52, 56, 58.

34. Ibid., 50, 51–53, 59.

35. Melville, "Bartleby the Scrivener: A Story of Wall Street," *Putnam's Monthly Magazine*, November–December 1853.

36. Noted in William Deverell, *Railroad Crossing: Californians and the Railroad, 1850–1910* (Berkeley and Los Angeles: University of California Press, 1994), 44.

37. Mass. Stats. 1852, ch. 144. Earlier in Rev. St. Ch. 60, secs. 27 & 28, the Massachusetts legislature had provided "a very simple mode of preventing the mere use of light and air from ripening into a right, by filing a notice in the office of the register of deeds, and serving a copy of the same upon the party enjoying the use of such light and air." Dewey J. in *Atkins v Chilson*, 7 Met. (48 Mass) 398 (1844). Here was a positive way around the "odious" wall.

38. And in any event, the doctrine of "ancient lights" may not have been terribly problematical. It is unmentioned, for example, in Stanley Schultz, *Constructing Urban Culture: American Cities and City Planning, 1800–1910* (Philadelphia: Temple University Press, 1989).

FIVE

1. Morton Horwitz, *The Transformation of American Law, 1780–1860* (Cambridge, Mass.: Harvard University Press, 1977), 186.

2. Ibid., 187.

3. 6 N. H. 481 (1834).

4. Horwitz, *Transformation* 1, 170, 172, 184, 187–88, 332.

5. Ibid., 188, 333. Sanford Jacoby and Jay Feinman both take this view with regard to nineteenth century judicial disinctions between contractors and personal service workers and both cite Horwitz. (Jacoby, "The Duration of Indefinite Employment Contracts in the U.S. and England: An Historical Analysis," *Comparative Labor Law* 5 (1982): 85, at 94; Jay M. Feinman, "Critical Approaches to Contract Law," *UCLA Law Review* 30 (1983): 741, at 850. Horwitz correctly cites *Hayward v Leonard*, 24 Mass. (7 Pick.) 181 (1828), the leading case in this genre; he observes that New York's court did not make the distinction he describes.

Wythe Holt has greatly elaborated on one aspect of Horwitz's analysis, that of the legal plight of workers who quit. Holt agrees with Horwitz that jurists in early nineeenth century America displayed "class bias" when they fashioned a "new system" of law with regard to breaches of labor contracts that was decidedly less fair to workers than the earlier standard, and which favored building contractors or service workers. "Simply put," Holt put it (a little too simply), "the entrepreneur wins, the laborer loses."

Holt, like Horwitz, notes that *Britton v Turner* was an exception to these "new tools of thralldom," and he allows that a few other states adopted the *Britton* standards "in the last half of the century," though "only Indiana" actually reversed its previous adherence to the new and unfair standard. When workers won, courts acted "grudgingly." Occasional victories like *Britton* "operated to lull workers into a false sense of eqality and security." In fact, "all" of the state decisions regarding workers who quit "actually promote[d] the interests of employers" by facilitating "worker subservience." The freedom of workers in labor contracts was only "apparent." They were held to the terms of contracts "whether they understood what they had agreed to or not."

Holt faults the jurists for failing to promote "socioeconomic equality," but, unlike Horwitz, he sees no conspiracy at work. "Every judge attempted to answer the problems before him in a principled fashion." The problem was that the judges "found the values of entrepreneurial, individualistic, competitive capitalism to be good obvious and true. The arguments made by the employers resonated with that world view." Hence the arguments of those representing the workers could be "disregarded." Holt, "Recovery by the Worker Who Quits: A Comparison of the Mainstream, Legal Realist, and Critical Legal Studies Approaches to a Problem of 19th Century Contract Law," *Wisconsin Law Review* (1986): 677 at 679, 682–84, 688, 691, 710, 727–28; Holt, "Labor Conspiracy Cases in the U.S., 1805–1842: Bias and Legitimation in Comon Law Adjudication," *Osgoode Hall Law Journal* 22 (1984): 591 at 656.

6. See examples given in S. F. C. Milsom, "Reason in the Development of the Common Law," *Law Quarterly Review* 81 (1965): 507–10; A. W. B. Simpson, *A History of the Common Law of Contract* (Oxford: Clarendon Press, 1975), 47–51, 260–62, 268–80; and Potter's *Historical Introduction to English Law* by A. K. R. Kiralfy (London: Sweet and Maxwell, 1958), 464.

7. 23 Edw III, ch. 1 (1349); 5 Eliz. I, ch. 4 (1562); 6 Geo. III, ch. 25 (1765); 5 Geo. IV, ch. 34 (1823); Patrick S. Atiyah, *The Rise and Fall of Freedom of Contract* (Oxford: Clarendon Press, 1979), 444; Jay M. Feinman, "The Development of the Employment at Will Rule," *American Journal of Legal History* 20 (1976): 118, 120.

The Statute of Artificers and Apprentices (1562) did require three months' notice by one or the other of the parties before the termination of their contract, and Edmund Morgan, "The Labor Problem at Jamestown, 1607–1618," *American Historical Review* 76 (1971): 604, offers evidence that some masters in seventeenth-century Somerset, Sussex, and Herford were forced by courts to maintain servants for the full contract period.

8. David H. Morgan, *Harvesters and Harvesting, 1840–1900: A Study of the Rural Proletariat* (London: Croom Helm, 1982), 124–26, 131–33.

See *Whittle v Frankland*, 2 B. & S. 49, 121 ER 992 (Q. B. 1862), for an example of a collier whose imprisonment for one month's hard labor for quitting in breach of an entire contract was upheld by Queen's Bench, even though he was not being paid by his employer at the time.

9. Otto Kahn-Freund, "Blackstone's Neglected Child: The Contract of Employment," *Law Quarterly Review* (1977): 509, 519.

10. Sidney Pollard, *The Genius of Modern Management: A Study of the Industrial Revolution in Great Britain* (Cambridge, Mass.: Harvard University Press, 1965), 188, 191; Jacoby, "Duration of Indefinite Employment Contracts," 85, at 98.

11. Morgan, *Harvesters*, 47, 101; E. L. Jones, "The Agricultural Labor Market in England, 1793–1872," *Economic History Review*, 2nd ser., 17 (1965–66): 329; T. M. Devine, ed., *Farm Servants and Labour in Lowland Scotland, 1770–1914* (Edinburgh: John Donald, 1984), 1–5, 80. Some farmers paid their hired hands more regularly than this. Folio eleven in Thomas Tusser's *Five Hundred Pointes of Good*

Husbandrie (London, 1580) reads: "Paie weekle thy workman, his household to feed / Paie quarterle servants, to buie as they need."

12. William Blackstone, *Commentaries on the Laws of England*, 4 vols. (London, 1765–69), 1:425.

13. See, for example, Ann Kussmaul, *Servants in Husbandry in Early Modern England* (Cambridge: Cambridge University Press, 1981), 32; *Newby v Wiltshire*, 4 Doug. 284, 99 ER 883 (K. B. 1785) (Lord Mansfield, C. J.), *Wennall v Adney*, 3 Bosq. and Pull. 247, 127 ER 137 (C. P. 1802); and James Kent's *Commentaries on the American Law*, 11th ed., by George Comstock, 4 vols. (Boston, 1867), 2:301–2 n. 2. And see text at notes 162 and 163 in chapter 3.

14. Richard Burn, *The Justice of The Peace*, 12th ed. (London, 1772), 4:111, 116, 120. Moreover, they might be dismissed with only partial pay before the end of a yearly hire in order for the parish to avoid becoming responsible for the laborer in the event he was without work in the future, since a year's residence constituted the legal requirement for "settlement" (residency). See, *Rex v Inhabs. of Pucklechurch*, 102 ER 1116 (K. B. 1804); and K. D. M. Snell, *Annals of the Labouring Poor: Social Change and Agrarian England, 1660–1900* (Cambridge: Cambridge University Press, 1985), 70, 77 94, 98–99.

15. *Turner v Mason*, 14 Mees. & W. 112, 153 ER 411 (Ex., 1845). Seaman, however, fared better than domestic servants and hired hands, and their treatment by the courts appear to have improved slightly as well throughout the eighteenth century, getting "liberation" as well as wages when their contract was broken by their employer. See Marcus Rediker, *Between the Devil and the Deep Blue Sea: Merchant Seamen, Pirates, and the Anglo-American Maritime World, 1700–1750* (New York: Cambridge University Press, 1987), 116–52.

16. *Spain v Arnott*, 2 Stark. 256, 171 ER 638 (N. P. 1817).

17. Cited in Alastair Orr, "Farm Servants and Farm Labour in the Forth Valley and South-East Lowlands," in Devine, *Farm Servants*, 46. Cf. Pollard, *Genius of Modern Management*, 191; Kahn-Freund, "Blackstone's Neglected Child," 521.

18. W. R. Cornish and G. de N. Clark, *Law and Society in England, 1750–1950* (London: Sweet and Maxwell, 1989), 286; *Veer v York and Others*, in N. Nielson, ed., *Year Books of . . . 1490* (London: Selden Society, 1931), 164, cited in Robert Steinfeld, *The Invention of Free Labor: The Employment Relation in English and American Law and Culture, 1350–1870* (Chapel Hill: University of North Carolina Press, 1991), 150; Glanville Williams, "Partial Performance of Entire Contracts," *Law Quarterly Review* 57 (1941): 373–99 (for reference to two fifteenth-century Yearbook cases); Michael Dalton, *Country Justice* (London, 1622), chap. 58, p. 129, citing 10 Ed 4, 2, and 49 H19; *Countess of Plymouth v Throgmorton*, 1 Salk. 65, 91 ER 60 (K. B. 1687); Charles Viner, *Abridgement of the Laws of England*, 2nd. ed., 24 vols. (London, 1791), 3:5–9; *Pordage v Cole*, 1 Wms. Saund. 319, at 320, 85 Eng. R. 449, at 451 (K. B. 1669); *Cutter v Powell*, 6 T. R. 320, 101 ER 573, 575 (K. B. 1795); *Hulle v Heightman*, 2 East. 145, 102 ER 324, (K. B. 1802); *Appleby v Dods*, 8 East. 300, 103 ER 356 (K. B. 1807); *Jesse v Roy*, 1 C. M. & R. 316, 149 ER 1101 (Ex. 1834); *Lilley v Elwin*, 11 Q. B. 742, 116 ER 652 (Q. B. 1848); *Saunders v Whittle*, 24 Weekly Rptr. 406 (Mar. 11, 1876); Charles Bradlaugh, *Labor and Law* (London, 1891), 11. Cf. Alan W. B. Simpson, "The Horwitz Thesis and the History of Contracts," *Uni-*

versity of Chicago Law Review 46 (1979): 533, 588, who notes *Cutter v Powell* and observes that "there is no evidence" that there had "ever generally been" any apportioning on a quantum meruit count of "entire" contracts in England. See also J. L. Barton, "Contract and *Quantum Meruit*: The Antecedents of *Cutter v Powell*," *Journal of Legal History* 8 (1987): 46 for a similar view. And see Sarah C. Maza, *Servants and Masters in 18th Century France* (Princeton: Princeton University Press, 1983), 98, 164, for evidence of an equally harsh rule for servants who quit "entire" contracts in eighteenth-century France.

19. Laurence Friedman, *A History of American Law*, 2nd ed. (New York: Simon and Schuster, 1985), 85. Cf. Abbott E. Smith, *Colonists in Bondage: White Servitude and Convict Labor in America, 1607–1776* (Chapel Hill: University of North Carolina Press, 1947); Laurence Towner, "A Fondness for Freedom: Servant Protest in Puritan Society," *William and Mary Quarterly*, 3rd ser., 19 (1962): 201–19 (for evidence of some 200 apprentice/indentured servant complaints in colonial Massachusetts, some 650 cases of complaints by masters of servant impropriety, and some 800 cases of servant contract breaches by flight ["runaways"]); and Howard Lamar, "From Bondage to Contract: Ethnic Labor in the American West, 1600–1890," in Stephen Hahn and Jonathan Prude, eds., *The Countryside in the Age of Capitalist Transformation* (Chapel Hill: University of North Carolina Press, 1985), 293–324 (on peonage, indenture servitude, and harsh labor contracts among native Americans, Hawaiians, and Chinese in the West).

20. Richard B. Morris, *Government and Labor in Early America* (New York: Columbia University Press, 1946) 399–400; *Archives of Maryland*, 70 vols., continuing (Baltimore: Maryland Historical Soc., 1915–), 70:455 (hereafter cited as *Archives of Md.*); Edmund Morgan, "Masters and Servants in Early New England," *More Books* (September 1942), 311–27.

21. See, for example, *Records of the Colony and Plantation of New Haven, 1638–49*, ed. Charles Hoadly (Hartford, 1857), 35–38, 51–56 (for the "rates of wares and work" for 1640 and 1641 and the example of one John Reader, fined forty shillings on February 7, 1641, by the New Haven Town Court for "exacting" greater wages than the court allowed).

22. Percy W. Bidwell and John I. Falconer, *History of Agriculture in the Northern U.S., 1620–1860* (Washington, D.C.: GPO, 1925), 118, 163, 274; Morris, *Government and Labor in Early America*, 213–14.

23. *Dowlan v Blomfield*, Md. (1679), *Archives of Md.* 68:201–2; *Gilbert v Worgan*, Md., (1678), ibid., 67:259; Maryland Statutes, 1671, 1676, ibid., 2:288, 529.

24. *Price v Wheeler*, *Archives of Md.* 53:385–86; Morris, *Government and Labor in Early America*, 240–42, 250, 262n; *Archives of Md.* 70:128–34, (1682); Dorothy S. Towle, ed., *Records of the Rhode Island Vice-Admiralty Court, 1716–1752* (Washington, D.C.: American Legal Records, AHA, 1936), 3:408 (*Brown, et al., v The Dolphin* [1747]), 450 (*Boswell v The Noble James* [1747]), and 500 (*Conway v The Prince Fredrick* [1749]). Cf. Nelson, *Americanization of the Common Law*, 50–51.

Similarly, as David Galenson notes, there was "a standard provision" in the contracts of indentured servants in the colonies, "the servant's freedom dues," which "constituted a nonvested pension and therefore also acted to discourage servants from running away." Galenson, *White Servitude in Colonial America* (Cambridge: Cambridge University Press, 1981), 101.

25. *Fern* v *Edward*, New Haven Colony Historical Society, *Ancient Town Records: Vol. 1*, ed. Franklin B. Dexter (New Haven, Conn.: New Haven Historical Society, 1917), 84–85 (1651); *Archives of Md.* 23:130 (1697). See also the Dutch, Civil Law cases in New Amsterdam of "The 3 workmen at the Graght" (1658), "Reintje the Mason" (1658), *Hendrick Hutson* v *Gysbert* (1663), *Tomas Quick* v *Symon Claasen* (1662), and *Lourenz Holst* v *Abel Hardenbroeck* (1668), in *Records of the Courts of Burghers and Schoepers of New Amsterdam* 4:164, 211; 6:142; and 7:173, 202. (Employers won all but the last of these actions. The court ordered the employees who "quit" [*Gysbert*] or "ran away and let the work stand" ["The 3 workmen at the Graght"; "Reintje the Mason"; *Quick*] to "begin" or go to prison. But it ordered Abel Hardenbroeck to pay Lourenz Holst twelve florins of wampum for an assault.) Dalton's *Country Justice* (69) taught seventeenth-century Englishmen and English colonists that courts could commit "without baile" a servant who quit without one quarter's warning until the servant agreed to return to his work.

26. J. Davis, *The Office and Authority of a Justice of the Peace* (New Bern, N. C., 1774), 312–13; George Webb, *The Office and Authority of a Justice of the Peace* (Williamsburg, Va., 1736), 292.

27. Damages ("liquidated," not entire penal bonds) were also awarded by juries to plaintiffs complaining in covenant or action on the case for the "nonperformance of the articles of agreement" regarding the building of houses, mills, chimneys, barns, for joinery work on house frames, and for charcoal-making in seventeenth century Plymouth, Essex County, Massachusetts, and New Haven. See *Records of the Colony of New Plymouth in New England: Judicial Acts of the General Court, 1636–1692*, vol. 7, ed. Nathaniel B. Shurtleff (Boston, 1857), *Clarke* v *Bowker*, 1665 (122), *Ellis* v *Ewen*, 1669 (156), *Denham* v *Mylam*, 1673 (175), and *Doten* v *Southworth*, 1681 (239, 245); *Leonard* v *Makefashion* and *Ramdell*, 1673, in *Records and Files of the Quarterly Courts of Essex County, Massachusetts*, 8 vols. (Salem, Mass.: Essex Institute, 1911–18), 5:196 ("for not coaling wood, for brands left in the woods which would have made a load of coals, wood at ye stump at 4d per cord . . . , for a month's rent that [Leonard, owner of an ironworks] was forced to lie still for want of the coles . . . for 3 hands lieing still 4 weeks, etc."); *Wakefield* v *Beach*, 1642, *Records of the Colony of New Haven*, ed. Hoadly, 75 ("for not performing covenant in the worke which he undertook to doe att the mill, which he was to doe strongly and substantially, butt did itt weaklly and sleightly as was proved by . . . testimony . . . also nott denying itt").

28. Stephen Innes, *Labor in a New Land: Economy and Society in Seventeenth Century Springfield* (Princeton: Princeton University Press, 1983), 79, 110n.

29. Morris, *Government and Labor in Early America*, 214; Ross Beales, "The Rev. Ebenezer Parkman's Farm Workers, 1726–1782," *Proceedings of the American Antiquarian Society* 99 (1989): pt. 1, 121 at 133. See also Steinfeld, *Invention of Free Labor*, 48–50, 114; Christopher Tomlins, *Law, Labor and Ideology in the Early American Republic* (Cambridge: Cambridge University Press, 1993), 242 nn. 43 and 49, 243, 272.

30. Steinfeld, *Invention of Free Labor,* chap. 5; *Wheateley v James.* Md (1649), *Archives of Md.* 9:472, 70:1360.

31. Morris, *Government and Labor in Early America,* 252; see *Archives of Md.* 70:169 (1682), for a court order to Wm. Harper to find a surgeon to treat his servant, the petitioner, Wm. Douglas, for a "Miserable sore legg" at the master's "owne proper cost and charge."

32. Morris, *Government and Labor in Early America,* 215n, 216; *White* and *Holmes v Russell* (1673), *Plymouth Judicial Records,* 7, *Hoxsea v Polock & Levy,* D. Towle, ed., *Records of The Rhode Island Vice-Admiralty Court,* 542; *Records of Quarterly Courts of Essex County,* 421–22 (but see 443); *Flower v Scott,* 1730; *Dodge v Berrian,* 1750, *Select Cases of the Mayor's Court of New York City,* vol. 2, ed. Richard B. Morris (Washington, D.C.: American Legal Records, AHA, 1935), 472, 505–10.

33. Jeremy Atack and Fred Bateman, *To Their Own Soil: Agriculture in the Antebellum North* (Ames: Iowa State University Press, 1987), tables 11.3 and 13.7; James T. Lemon, *The Best Poor Man's Country: A Geographical Study of Early Southeastern Pennsylvania* (Baltimore: Johns Hopkins University Press, 1972), 179; David E. Schob, *Hired Hands and Plowboys: Farm Labor in the Midwest, 1815–1860* (Urbana: University of Illinois Press, 1975), 162, 252–53, 257, 262; Paul Gates, *The Farmer's Age: Agriculture, 1815–1860* (N.Y., Holt, Rinehart, 1960), 198, 271, 275–76. See also the opinion of a Scottish farmer, Patrick Shirreff: "The abundance of land induced labourers to turn landowners, and reward others with high wages, who likewise became landowners." Shirreff, *A Tour Through North America* (Edinburgh, 1835), 400. Ann Kussmaul has calculated that it took a hired hand and his wife ten years of work and saving in late-eighteenth-century England to afford to rent a twelve-acre farm. Kussmaul, *Servants in Husbandry,* 82. Mary Schweitzer's data indicates that wages in Chester County, Pennsylvania, were three times higher than English wages in the mid-eighteenth century. *Custom and Contract* (New York: Columbia University Press, 1987), 54. Cf. Robert L. Jones, *History of Agriculture in Ohio to 1880* (Kent, Ohio: Kent State University Press, 1983), 35; Howard Russell, *A Long, Deep Furrow: Three Centuries of Farming in New England* (Hanover, N. H.: University Press of New England, 1976), 314. But see Carville Earle and Ronald Hoffman, "The Foundation of the Modern Economy: Agriculture and the Costs of Labor in the U.S. and England, 1800–1860," *American Historical Review* 85 (1980): 1055–94, for evidence of relatively lower U.S. wages in the grain belt.

34. This was so for urban artisans as well as farm workers, of course. See Susan Salinger, "The Transformation of Labor in Late 18th Century Philadelphia," *William and Mary Quarterly,* 2nd ser., 40 (January 1983): 62–84, for a good account of the drift from indenture to apprenticeship to free contracting by 1800 in that northern city.

35. Jacoby, "Duration of Indefinite Employment Contracts," 85 at 93, offers a good account of the steady elimination of the corporal punishment of servants in the United States in the early and mid-nineteenth century. See also Christopher Tomlins, "The Ties that Bind: Master and Servant in Massachusetts, 1800–1850," *Labor History* 30 (1989): 193, at 208–9.

36. Snell, *Annals of the Poor,* 13; Shirreff, *Tour Through North America,* 341. See

also the views of Kentucky's Humphrey Marshall in the 1780s: "It is peculiarly difficult for a man of property to hire a laborer; he must humor him a good deal and
make him sit at the same table with him." Patricia Watlington, *The Partisan Spirit:
Kentucky Politics, 1779–1792* (New York: 1978), 189. Cf. James S. Buckingham,
America, Historical Statistics Descriptive, (London, 1841), 2:412–16; Schob, *Hired
Hands*, 184n. Farm journals in the mid-nineteenth-century United States recorded
the relatively good state of housing and treatment of farm laborers and urged all employers to meet such standards in order to retain good hired hands (Gates, *Farmer's
Age*, 275). As Shirreff put it: "In no other part of the world is industry, sobriety, and
worth so richly rewarded" (*Tour Through North America*, 347). See Worthington
C. Ford, *George Washington as an Employer and Importer of Labor* (Brooklyn,
1889), for examples of wages and contracts for artisans, overseers and ploughmen
in late eighteenth century Virginia and Pennsylvania. Cf. Merle Curti, *The Making
of an American Community: A Case Study of Democracy in a Frontier County*
(Stanford: Stanford University Press, 1959), 147–49.

37. Jack Larken, "The Farm Laborers of the Ward Family of Shrewsbury, Mass.,
1787–1860," *Proceedings of the American Antiquarian Society* (1989): 189–226,
esp. 212, 214; Commonwealth of Mass., Bureau of Statistics of Labor, *3rd Annual
Report, Bureau of Statistics of Labor* (Boston, 1872), 31.

38. See Paul McGouldrich, *New England Textiles in the Nineteenth Century:
Profit and Investment* (Cambridge, Mass.: Harvard University Press, 1968), 273.

39. Jonathan Prude, *The Coming of Industrial Order: Town and Factory Life in
Rural Massachusetts, 1810–1860* (Cambridge, Mass.: Harvard University Press,
1983), 150, 230; Ray Ginger, "Labor in a Massachusetts Cotton Mill: 1853–60,"
Business History Review 28 (1954): 67, at 88–89.

For evidence that some New England manufacturers in the 1820s actively recruited the workers of other manufacturers see *Boston Glass Manufactory* v *Binney*, 4 Pick. (Mass.) 425 (1827).

Contract laborers in labor-scarce late-nineteenth-century Hawaii were occasionally able to exert similar pressure for wage increases, as when the manager of the
Ewa Plantation "claimed that he had been forced to raise the contract workers' pay
to keep them from leaving or disputing their contracts." Edward D. Beechert, *Working in Hawaii: A Labor History* (Honolulu: University of Hawaii Press, 1985), 108.

40. Ibid., 150–52.

41. Ibid., 152; William A. Sullivan, *The Industrial Worker in Pennsylvania, 1800–
1840* (Harrisburg, Pa.: Pennsylvania Historical and Museum Commission, 1955),
35–36; *Potter* v *Cain*, 117 Mass. 238 (1875) (for a description of the Hamilton
Woolen Company's contract in 1872, which required thirty days' notice of employees, but also promised thirty days' severance pay in the event of layoffs.) Anthony
F. C. Wallace, *Rockdale: The Growth of an American Village in the Early Industrial
Revolution* (New York: Knopf, 1978), 163, 172, 179. In 1869 Massachusetts mills
were holding back pay for anywhere from three to twenty-eight days, with the typical duration being fifteen days. Mass., *Statistics of Labor*, 3:90–91, 206.

42. Wallace, *Rockdale*, 179.

43. Mass., *Statistics of Labor*, 1:353–55.

44. *Craig* v *Darrett*, 24 Ky. 365 at 366 (1829). See also *Garahan* v *Weeks*, 10 Mar-

tin's R. (La.) 96 (1829); *Smith* v *Smith*, 5 Martin's R. (La.) 197 (1821); *Dirs. of House of Employment of Western County* v *Murry*, 32 Pa. St. 178 (1858); *Riggs* v *Horde*, 25 Texas Sup. 456 (1860); *Blood* v *Enor*, 12 Vt. 625 (1839).

45. Zephaniah Swift, *Digest of the Laws of the State of Connecticut* (New Haven, Conn., 1822), 682–83; 13 Johns. (N.Y.) 94 (1816).

46. J. S. Sanders, *The Law of Pleading and Evidence in Civil Actions*, 3rd American ed., 2 vols. (Philadelphia, 1837), 2:959. See also William Wetmore Story, *A Treatise on The Law of Contracts*, 4th ed., 2 vols. (Boston, 1856), 1:516. Neither this edition nor Melville Bigelow's 1874 (5th) edition made any mention of *Britton* v *Turner*.

47. *Reports of Cases in Viceadmiralty-New York, 1715–1788*, ed. Charles M. Hough, (New Haven, Conn.: Yale University Press, 1925), 245. The records of these cases, however, are incomplete.

Seamen, in any event, were treated as special "wards of the court," and in *Hart* v *the Littlejohn* (1 Pets. Adm. 115, 11 Fed Case 687, #6,153 [1800], a seaman recovered *full* wages on an entire contract to go from North Carolina to Liverpool and back after the cargo was delivered in Liverpool and the ship was then captured by the French. This was, of course, consistent with *Cutter* v *Powell*, because Joseph Hart had fulfilled his part of the contract and the freight ["the mother of wages" for seamen] had been delivered).

48. 12 Johns. (N.Y.) 165 (1815).

49. Ibid., at 167.

50. 13 Johnson 94 (1816).

51. See, for example, *Webb* v *Duckingfield*, 13 Johns. (N.Y.) 390 (1816); *Reab* v *Moor*, 19 Johns. (N.Y.) 337 (1822); and *Marsh* v *Rulesson*, 1 Wend. (N.Y.) 514 (1828).

52. 2 Cranch CC 423, 15 Fed. Cases 482, £8, 322 (1823).

53. *Stark* v *Parker*, 19 Mass. (2 Pick.) 267 (1824).

54. Christopher Tomlins reads *Stark* v *Parker* as a departure from an earlier Massachusetts *pro rata* rule favoring the hired hand who quit an entire contract before the fulfillment of the contract, and he quotes from a *Boston Courier* story of 23 July 1824 about the case: Pro rata recovery was "generally understood to be the common law of the state, although no decision of the Supreme Court had ever sanctioned it." But Tomlins, who has ably combed the records of the trial courts of early nineteenth century Massachusetts, offers no such trial court cases himself, and without a careful analysis of the *fact* situation of such a pre-*Stark* decision at the trial court level, it would be unwarranted to conclude, on the basis of this newspaper account alone, that hired hands were being released from entire contracts by trial courts and awarded quantum meruit or pro rata recovery without there having been given some evidence of a mutual agreement of this kind with their employers or without evidence of language in the contract giving it a clear pro rata character. Tomlins relies on the dicta of Lawrence, J., who had offered one of the four King's Bench seriatim opinions in *Cutter* v *Powell*. Lawrence had distinguished between a written "entire" contract and "the common case" of a servant hired "in a general way." Such a servant, by "the general understanding upon the subject," was "entitled to his wages for the time he serves though he do not continue in the service during the whole year." Lawrence may have been referring to domestic servants, who were, by

custom, considered to be hired by the month. Or he may have been referring to an "at mutual will" practice that had developed in Georgian London, something that one finds evidence of in antebellum America. In any event, Lawrence's dicta did find its way into two treatises and one early-nineteenth-century reporter's footnote as sanctioning quantum meruit or pro rata apportionment when a worker quit an "entire" oral contract. And this leads Tomlins to describe the New York Supreme Court's opinion in *McMillan* v *Vanderlip* as an "innovation". But when a custom, recognized only in dicta, flourishes for all of three decades, it can be argued that its rejection by a high court in favor of a rule deemed to be much older does not merit the appellation "innovation." And, in any event, as Robert Steinfeld says, "what was new" about *Stark* v *Parker* "was not that laborers were being denied recovery of any part of their wages for departing during the term. What was new was that no one ever imagined that they might be compelled to serve out their time." Employers were not testing the limits of an old, proworker rule; "workers were doing the testing." Tomlins, "The Ties that Bind," *Labor History* 30, at 219, 273–74; Lawrence, J., in *Cutter* v *Powell*, 101 ER 573 at 576–77 (K. B. 1795); Steinfeld, *Invention of Free Labor*, 150.

55. 19 Mass. at 271 and 274.

Justice Lincoln maintained that "the employer and employee alike universally" understood the principles of "entire" contracts. However, neither he nor his colleagues believed that "minors" or "infants" (in law, those under twenty-one years of age) understood such principles. A worker who was "under-age" was "not presumed to be capable" of contracting or of judging of the value of his services," and was free to abandon an "entire" contract at any time and collect on a quantum meruit count. This was an "elementary principle." The jury was free to determine such wages; "no injustice will be done, because the jury will give no more than under all circumstances the services were worth." Chief Justice Isaac Parker in *Moses* v *Stevens*, 2 Pick. (19 Mass.) 332, at 335 (1824). Cf. *Vent* v *Osgood*, 19 Pick. (36 Mass.) 572 (1837), and *Moulton* v *Trask*, 9 Met. (50 Mass.) 577 (1845).

56. 36 Mass 528 (1837).

57. Ibid., at 528–29. Cf. *Davis* v *Maxwell*, 53 Mass. 286 (1847), and *Tatterson* v *Suffolk Mnfrg. Co.*, 106 Mass. 56 (1870).

58. Cf. *DeCamp* v *Stevens*, 4 Blackford's Report (Ind.) 24 (1829).

59. *Wright* v *Turner*, 1 Stew. (Ala.) 29 (1827); *Norris* v *Moore*, 3 Ala. 676 (1842); *Pettigrew* v *Bishop*, 3 Ala. 440 (1842). See also *Mitchell* v *Scott* & *Brown*, 41 Mich. 108, 1 NW Rpt 968 (1879), for an elaborate discussion of *Cutter* v *Powell*.

60. *Crump* v *Mead*, 3 Mo. 233 (Houck 129)(1833). Cf. *Schneer* v *Lemp*, 19 Mo. 40 (1853), and *Aaron* v *Moore*, 34 Mo. 79 (1863). But see *Downey* v *Burke*, 23 Mo. 228 (1856).

61. 24 Mass. (7 Pick.) 180 (1828).

62. 6 N. H. 481, at 483–84 (1834).

63. Ibid., at 489, 494; Hugh Clokie, "Parker, Joel," *Dictionary of American Biography*, 14:230; Phillip Paludan, *A Covenant With Death: The Constitution, Law, and Equality in the Civil War Era* (Urbana: University of Illinois Press, 1975), 166–67.

Horwitz, *Transformation 1*, 333, faults Parker in *Britton* v *Turner* for allowing defendants to prove damage offsets to such quantum meruit recoveries, but the charge is unfair; Parker was merely stating established rules of contract law. See, for example, the rule regarding damage awards in contract cases as it was expressed by John B. Colvin, *The Magistrates' Guide and Citizen's Counsellor* (Fredricktown, Md., 1805), 186: "If I fail in my part of the agreement, I shall pay the other party such damages as he has sustained by such my neglect or refusal."

64. Floyd R. Mechem, *A Treaise on The Law of Agency* (Chicago, 1889), sec. 636; Theophilus Parsons, *The Law of Contracts* (Boston, 1855), 1:525–26; George W. Field, *A Treatise on the Law of Damages* (Des Moines, Iowa, 1876), 327, 332–35. James Kent, *Commentaries on American Law*, 3rd ed. (New York, 1840), 2:258: "The old rule is now held to be relaxed, and wages it is understood may be apportioned, upon the principle that such is the reasonable construction of the contract of hiring." Cf. John D. Lawson, *Leading Cases Simplified* (St. Louis, 1882), 124 n. 1.

Parsons noted that "the principles of this case are better adopted to do adequate justice to both parties and wrong to neither, than those of the numerous cases which rest upon the somewhat technical rule of the entirety of the contract," but he maintained (in 1855) that *Britton v Turner* had not been adopted in other states. Indeed, it was not until the 1893 edition of *Parsons on Contract* (2:41 n. l) that mention was made in that treatise of the acceptance of *Britton v Turner* by any other states. I suspect that Morton Horwitz, who cites the 1855 edition of Parsons on this issue, may have relied on that source for his judgment that *Britton v Turner* was "the solitary challenge" to "the doctrine against quantum meruit recovery in labor cases" (*Transformation 1*, 332).

65. Robert Campbell's *English Ruling Cases*, ed. Irving Browne, 26 vols. (Boston, 1894–1902), 6:639. See also J. C. Perkins, ed., Joseph Chitty's *A Practical Treatise on the Law of Contracts*, 6th American ed. (Springfield, Mass., 1844), 580.

66. 6 Vt. 383 at 387 (1834), affirming *Hair v Bull*, 6 Vt. 35 (1834), a case in which a jury had denied recovery to a ship-joiner who left after he objected to be assigned other work.

67. *Hair v Bull*, 6 Vt. 35 (1834); *St. Albans Steamboat Co. v Wilkins*, 8 Vt. 54 (1836); *Brown v Kimball*, 12 Vt. 617 (1839); *Ripley v Chipman*, 13 Vt. 268 (1841); *Winn v Southgate*, 17 Vt. 355 (1845).

In *Winn v Southgate* the plaintiff Thales Winn, a journeyman tailor, quit shortly after learning that another journeyman tailor "in the same village" had secured a contract "to reckon 24 work days as a month." When Winn's employer refused to revise the terms of his contract accordingly, Winn consulted an attorney to see if he could quit after five and a half months of a six-month contract and claim for all six months, reckoning twenty-four days to the month. The attorney "advised him to return to his labor." He did so, but became offended at being shifted to a different task after again arguing with his employer, and, ignoring his attorney's advice, he quit and sued.

68. Redfield, dissenting in *Fenton v Clark*, 11 Vt. 557, at 568 (1839).

69. 8 Vt. 204 (1836). This case can be contrasted with *Stephens v Baird*, 4 Wend. (N.Y.) 604 (1830): Another woodcutter quit before clearing all the land agreed on, but the New York Supreme Court refused to allow him any quantum meruit.

70. In *Booth v Tyson*, 15 Vt. 515 (1843). It was said of Redfield that he "did much towards tempering the rules of the common law by an infusion of equity principles." R. S. Taft, "The Supreme Court of Vermont," *Green Bag*, March 1894, 128.

71. Taft, "Supreme Court of Vermont," at 204. Cf. *Gilman, Gilman & Cole v Hall*, 11 Vt. 510 (1839), involving an imperfectly built stone fence, *Booth v Tyson*, 15 Vt. 515 (1843), involving the making of furnace moldings; and *Patnote v Sanders*, 41 Vt. 66 (1866).

President Judge Henry St. George Tucker of the Virginia Supreme Court took a similar position in *Bream v Marsh*, 4 Leigh (Va.) 21 (1832), and Justice James Worden (quoting from *Britton v Turner*) in *Wolcott v Yeager*, 11 Ind. 84 (1858). See also *Dayton v Dean*, 23 Conn. 99 (1954).

72. *Hays v Marsh*, 11 La. 369 (1837); *Eldridge v Rowe*, 7 Ill. (2 Gil.) 91 (1845); *Badgley v Heald*, 9 Ill. (4 Gil.) 64 (1847); *Angle v Hannah*, 22 Ill. 429 (1859); *Swanzey v Moore*. 22 Ill. 63 (1859); *Hansell v Erickson*, 28 Ill. 257 (1862); *Miller v Goddard*, 34 Me. 102 (1852); *Hutchinson v Wetmore*, 2 Cal. 310 (1852); *Hughes v Cannon*, 33 Tenn. 623 (1853); *Erving v Ingram*, 24 N.J. 520 (1854); *Larkin v Buck*, 11 Ohio St. 566 (1860). Cf. Justice Hugh Henry Brackenridge in *Woods v Ingersoll* and *Dallas*, 1 Binney (Pa.) 145, at 151 (1806), who "could form no idea of a *quantum meruit* for half services."

Louisiana's high court denied an overseer remuneration who quit an annual contract after eight months, "in the busiest season of the year . . . without taking off" the sugar cane crop, but the court relied on article 2721 of the state legislature's statutory code, a mix of Continental civil and English common law. Neither the counsel for the planter nor the court referred to any English or American judicial decisions. This statute-based decision can be contrasted with those of provincial courts in Quebec and Montreal, both of which rendered *Britton v Turner*–like decisions where workers quit entire contracts. (See *Bilodeau v Sylvain*, 4 Lower Can. R.26 (1853), and *Madon v Ollivon*, 15 Lower Can. Jurist 280 [1871].) Nevertheless, since Louisiana is one of the states, for all its civil law background, and since its high court reaffirmed *Hays v Marsh* in the era of Reconstruction, I count Louisiana as a "*Cutter v Powell*" state. (*Bartell v Lallande*, 23 La. Ann. 317 (1871), concerned a sharecropper on an entire contract.)

73. *Eldridge v Rowe*, 7 Ill. (2 Gil.) 91 at 92–96 (1845). Koerner was a "close friend" of Abraham Lincoln; he took over some of his cases in 1860–61 and served as his minister to Spain in 1862. Julius Goebel, "Korner, Gustav P.," *Dictionary of American Biography*, 10:496.

Georgia's high court announced in obiter dicta for the all-or-nothing standard in an ambiguous case in which the facts found at the trial level were inconclusive as to whether plaintiff, an overseer, quit or was fired. (*Henderson v Stiles*, 14 Ga. 135 [1853].)

74. *Badgley v Heald*, 9 Ill. (4 Gil.) 64, at 66 (1847).

75. *Hansell v Erickson*, 28 Ill. 257, at 259 (1862), citing *Spain v Arnott*, 2 Starkie 256, 171 ER 638 (N. P. 1817), and other English and American cases.

76. Hitchcock in *Witherow v Witherow*, 16 Ohio 238, at 242, 244 (1847); Peck in *Larkin v Buck*, 11 Ohio St 561, at 568 (1860).

77. Read in *Witherow v Witherow* at 245.

78. Chitty's *Practical Treatise on the Law of Contracts*, 6th American ed., by J. C. Perkins (Springfield, Mass., 1844), 580.

79. *Miller v Goddard*, 34 Me. 102 at 105 (1852). However, the Maine high court held in *Dargin v Baker*, 32 Me. 273 (1850), that where a plaintiff agreed to "labor for

the defendant" for six months at thirteen dollars per month, "if they could agree," the plaintiff was entitled to his pay if he quit after two months. And in the case of a minor who quit on "entire" contract for labor, quantum meruit recovery was allowed. (*Judkins* v *Watker*, 17 Me. 38 [1840].)

80. *Hughes* v *Cannon*, 33 Tenn. 623, 627 (1853). Cf. *Hutchinson* v *Wetmore*, 2 Cal. 310 (1852), *Erving* v *Ingram*, 24 N.J. 520 (1854), and Justice Stacy Potts in *Has-lack* v *Mayers*, 26 N.J. 290, at 292 (1857): The "leading case is *Cutter* v *Powell*," and *Britton* v *Turner* "has not been followed, and is clearly not law."

81. *Coe* v *Smith, Adm.*, 4 Ind. 79 (1853), overruling *Cranmer* v *Graham* and *De-Camp* v *Stephens*. Cf. *Manville* v *McCoy*, 3 Ind. 148 (1851). And see *Downey* v *Burke*, 23 Mo. 228 (1856) (quantum recovery for work done on a stone wall not accepted by defendant. Justice Abiel Leonard offered an early "unjust enrichment" rationale: It was "generally true in morals that one who is made rich by the act of another . . . ought to recompense the party, at least so far as he himself is a gainer; and the legal doctrine laid down in *Britton* v *Turner* . . . is, we think, a just application of the principles of morality to transactions of this character.")

82. *Dayton* v *Dean*, 23 Conn. 99 (1854); *Ryan* v *Dayton*, 25 Conn. 188 (1856) (both are farm "hired hands" cases); *Allen* v *McKibbin*, 5 Mich. (1 Cooley) 450 (1858); *Pixler* v *Nicholas*, 8 Iowa 106 (1859); *McClay* v *Hedge*, 18 Iowa 66 (1864); *Byerlee* v *Mendel*, 39 Iowa 382 (1874). See also *Dibol* and *Plank* v *Minott*, 9 Iowa 403 (1859), for an example of the adoption of Redfield's "severable" rule in *Dyer* v *Jones*, 8 Vt. 204 (1836). In *Dibol* two painters had agreed to paint and glaze ten houses; they completed only four. Iowa's high court viewed the contract as a severable one.

83. *Ryan* v *Dayton*, 25 Ct. 188 at 193–94 (1856).

84. *Allen* v *McKibbin* at 454.

85. See *Pixler* v *Nicholas*.

86. *McClay* v *Hedge* at 68.

This, of course, is the John Dillon who later, upon resigning from the U.S. Circuit Court, served as counsel to the Union Pacific Railroad, Western Union, and Jay Gould. His practice "was lucrative, he was a shrewd businessman, and he left a substantial estate." Yet he favored *Britton* v *Turner* over *Cutter* v *Powell*. Robert Cushman, "Dillon, John," *D. A. B.* Dillon may have borrowed the term "bottomed upon . . . justice" from Justice Spencer Roane in *Jones* v *Commonwealth*, 5 Va. 555 (1799), or from a more "venerable" English jurist.

87. I am not counting the high courts of Vermont, Massachusetts, Connecticut, California, or Oregon, each of which adopted Redfield's rule that, where work was by the task and a price per task was mentioned in the contract, workers who quit could collect pro rata. (See *Thayer* v *Wadsworth*, 36 Mass. 349 [1837]; *Dayton* v *Dean*, 23 Conn. 99 [1854]; *Hogan* v *Titlow* & *Price*, 14 Cal. 255 [1859]; *Steeples* v *Newton*, 70 Ore. 110 [1879].) As C. Harding, a hired hand's attorney in *Scherr* v *Lemp*, 19 Mo. 40 (1853) put it: "The hardship and injustice occasioned by the old rule's enforcement have led courts to evade its operation as far as possible."

88. Horwitz, *Transformation* 1, 186.

89. *Hays* v *Marsh*, 11 La. 369, at 373 (1837). Cf. Justice R. K. Howell in *Bartell* v *Lallande*, 23 La. Ann. 317, at 318 (1871): "The great importance of the agricultural interests of this country demand that these rules of law and justice [requiring share-

croppers who abandoned work without permission to forfeit everything and repay all wages paid on an entire contract] be maintained in all their vigor and integrity."

Later, after emancipation, southern legislatures sought to bind the former slaves to labor with statutes making an employee's breach of a contract a crime and permitting the farming out to private contractors of such misdemeanants (most of whom were black). See William Cohen, "Negro Involuntary Servitude in the South, 1865–1940: A Preliminary Analysis," *Journal of Southern History*, 42 (February 1976): 31–60.

90. *Isaacs v McAndrew, et al.*, 1 Mont. 437 (1872). (The "servant" was a mine superintendent offered a five-year contract at four thousand dollars per year.)

91. *Lee v Davis*, 5 Ky. Op. 617 (1871); *Asher v Tomlinson*, 22 Ky. 1494, 60 S. W. 714 (1901); *Duncan v Baker*, 21 Kansas 99 (1878); *Ryan v Cranston*, 27 Kansas 672 (1882); *Parcell v McComber*, 11 Neb. 209, 7 N. W. 529, at 530 (1880); and *McMillan v Malloy*, 4 N. W. (Neb.) 1004 (1880).

92. *Neliehka v Esterley*, 12 N. W. Rep. 457 (Minn.) (1882); *Diefenback v Stark*, 56 Wis. 462 14 N. W. 621 (1883); *Timberlake v Thayer*, 71 Miss. 279, 14 So. 446 (1894); *Bedow v Tonkin*, 5 S. D. 432, 59 N. W. R. 222 (1893); *Lynn v Selby*, 29 N. D. 420, 151 N. W. 31 (1915); *Matthews v Jenkins*, 80 Va. 463 (1885); *Chamblee v Baker*, 95 N. C. 98 (1886); *Oliver v McArthur*, 158 N.Y. App. Div. 241, 143 N.Y. Sup. 126 (1913); *Lawyer's Reports Annotated*, 1916E, 792; "Note," *Harvard Law Review* 8 (1895): 364; Carl McGowan, "The Divisibility of Employment Contracts," *Iowa Law Review* 21 (1935): 50, at 65–66 (on CA & IL).

93. *Harmon v Salmon Falls Manufacturing Co.*, 35 Me. 447, at 450, 452–53 (1853). See also Horace Gay Wood, *A Treatise on The Law of Master and Servant* (San Francisco, 1877), who defends (281, 293) the harsh "entirety" rule vis-à-vis labor contracts as one "predicated upon a sound public policy, and in the interest of the industrial interests of the country." No other treatise writer offers such a statement.

94. *Bradley v Salmon Falls Manufacturing Co.*, 30 N. H. 487 (1855). Cf. Chief Justice Isaac Parker's similar ruling in *Stevens v Reeves*, 9 Pick. (Mass.) 197 (1829), involving a weaver working piecerate for an Andover factory who quit and claimed unfamiliarity with the severance rule.

95. Justice Dillon in *McClay v Hedge*, 18 Iowa 66 (1864); Kellogg in *Oliver v McArthur*, 143 N.Y. Supp. 126 at 127 (1913).

96. *Hansell v Erickson*, 28 Ill. 257 (1862); *McMillan v Vanderlip*, 12 Johns. (N.Y.) 165 (1817); Holt, "Recovery by the Worker who Quits," *Wisconsin Law Review* (1986): 679, 681, 687n, 698, 729–30.

97. Oliver Wendell Holmes Jr., *The Common Law*, ed. Mark DeWolfe Howe (Boston, 1881; reprint, Boston: Little, Brown, 1963), 263–64.

98. Ray Ginger, "Labor in a Massachusetts Mill," *Bus. Hist. Rev.* 28, nn. 15–20.

99. Richard Posner, *Economic Analysis of Law*, 3rd ed. (Boston: Little Brown, 1986), 236–37.

100. *Eldridge v Rowe*; *Badgley v Heald*.

101. Atack and Bateman, *To Their Own Soil*, 242; *Hunt's Merchants Magazine*, 41 no. 69 (December 1859): 759.

102. See Earle and Hoffman, "Foundation of the Modern Economy."

103. Holt, "Recovery by Worker who Quits," 716–20. Specific performance

rather than monetary damage was often ordered by the courts of some socialist states in cases of breach of contract. See Bernard Grossfeld, "Money Sanctions for Breach of Contract in a Communist Economy," *Yale Law Journal* 72 (1963): 1326; and E. L. Johnson, *An Introduction to the Soviet Legal System* (London: Methuen, 1972), 163–64, 192–215. In the People's Republic of China workers in both state-owned and foreign-investment enterprises must "show cause" before quitting before their employment contracts end, and one in a training program may be ordered to reimburse the enterprise for the cost of the training if one quits before the year-long program ends. One must give one month's notice before quitting, and workers with frequent unexplained absences or workers who violate the work rules of the shop may be fired (*chuming*). Henry R. Zheng, *China's Civil and Commercial Law* (London: Butterworths, 1988), 399–403.

104. *Hughes* v *Cannon*, 33 Tenn. 623 (1853); Karl Llewellyn, *The Common Law Tradition: Deciding Appeals* (Boston: 1960).

105. Schob, *Hired Hands*, 162; Atack and Bateman, *To Their Own Soil*, 242. See also Kussmaul, *Servants in Husbandry*, 179–80. For an example of a contract that appeared to reflect this newer permissive relationship, see the one signed by plantation owner Ruth Hairston and overseer Jackson Carrol in North Carolina, December 11, 1862, wherein Hairston was free "to dismiss" Carrol "at any time" and Carrol was "to be at liberty to quit . . . at any time" and "to recve in proportion to the . . . Sum of one hundred & Twenty dollars as may be in proportion to the time during which . . . Carrol remained upon the . . . plantation." William K. Scarborough, *The Overseer: Plantation Management in the Old South* (Athens: University of Georgia Press, 1984), 23.

Steinfeld, in *Invention of Free Labor*, clearly demonstrates that jurists in the late eighteenth century were becoming more generous toward indentured servants, as were their judicial ancestors in the early nineteenth century with regards to apprentices and slaves in states that abolished slavery. See also Charles Quill [James Alexander], *The Working-Man* (Philadelphia, 1839), 115–18: "It is less common than it used to be for [apprentices] to serve out their whole time. . . . And when they abscond from their proper service, it is not every employer who now thinks it worth his while to take the legal measures for recovering their time. . . . The old-fashioned system is found to be ineffectual."

106. Horwitz, *Transformation* 1, 187; Karen Orren recently made the same claim in an otherwise excellent book. Orren, *Belated Feudalism: Labor, the Law, and Liberal Development in the United States* (Cambridge: Cambridge University Press, 1991), 84–85.

107. *Thorne* v *White*, 1 Pet. Adm. 168, 23 Fed Cases 1133 (1806)). See *Limland* v *Stephens*, 3 Esp. 269, 170 ER 611 (N. P., 1801), for a similar English case with a similar verdict.

108. *Ward* v *Ames*, 9 Johns. (N.Y.) 138 (1812).

109. *DeCamp* v *Stevens*, Blackf. (Ind.) 24 (1835). See *Lilley* v *Elwin*, 11 Q. B. 742, 116 E. R. 652 (Q. B. 1848), for a similar English "hired hand" case with a similar verdict.

110. *Patterson* v *Gage*, 23 Vt. 558 (1851).

111. *Cody* v *Raynaud*, 1 Colo. 272 (1871).

112. *Forsythe* v *Hastings*, 27 Vt. 646 (1855).

113. *Abernathy* v *Black*, 2 Cold. (42 Tenn.) 314 (1865).

114. *Hannu* v *Williams, et al.* 2 Haw. 233, at 237 (1860). This court was fully attentive to developments in the United States, and referred in passing to *Britton* v *Turner*. Its defense of the contract rights of workers is evident at times, not as evident at other times. See Beechert, *Working in Hawaii*, esp. 54 and 110. In *Erving* v *Ingram*, 24 N.J. 520 (1854), the New Jersey Supreme Court remanded the case for a rehearing to permit the jury to hear evidence regarding the extent of "ill usage" involved.

115. Some workers may have been conscious of this judicial propensity. In *Ford* v *Danks*, 16 La. Ann. 119 (1861), an overseer left the plantation for a day after working three and one half months of a one year contract for $800, vowing that he would not work any longer and would demand the full $800, inasmuch as the planter he had contracted with had sold the plantation. However, "being advised by others that it would be better to return and be discharged, he went back." (He was then fired, but was offered a pro rata sum of $198. by the previous owner, and the court ordered that his recovery be allowed, but limited to that amount.)

116. *Adams* v *Hill*, 16 Me (4 Shep.) 215 (1839); *Chamberlain* v *McCallister & Sanders*, 6 Dana. (36 Ky.) 352 (1838); *Stewart* v *Walker*, 14 Pa. 293 (1850); *King and Graham* v *Steiren*, 44 Pa. St. 99 (1862); *Webster* v *Wade*, 19 Cal. 291 (1861); *Green* v *Hulett*, 22 Vt. 188 (1850); *Williams* v *Anderson*, 9 Minn. R. 50 (1864); *Madden* v *Porterfield*, 53 N. C. 166 (1860); *Whitney* v *Brooklyn*, 5 Ct. 405 (1824); *Williams* v *Chicago Coal Co.*, 60 Ill. 149 (1871); *Hoyt* v the *Wildfire*, 3 Johns. (N.Y.) 518 (1808); *Costigan* v *Mohawk & Hudson RR Co.*, 2 Denio (N.Y.) 609 (1846); *Colburn* v *Woodsworth*, 31 Barbour (N.Y.) 381 (1860); *Mackabin* v *Clarkson*, 5 Minn. R. 247 (1860); *Newman* v *McGregor*, 5 Hammond (Ohio) 349 (1832); *Alexander* v *Hoffman*, 5 Watts & S. (Pa.) 382 (1843); *Laurence* v *Gullifer*, 38 Me. 582 (1854); *Walworth* v *Pool*, 9 Ark. 394 (1849); *Wright* v *Morris*, 15 Ark. 444 (1855); *Meade* v *Rutledge*, 4 Tex. 44 (1853); *Hassell* v *Nutt*, 14 Tex. 260 (1855); *Nations* v *Cudd*, 22 Tex. 550 (1858); *Gordon* v *Brewster*, 7 Wis. 355 (1858); *Rogers* v *Parham*, 8 Ga. 190 (1850); *Cox* v *Adams*, 1 Nott & McCord (S. C.) 284 (1818); *Nears* v *Harbert*, 25 Mo. 352 (1857); *Rankin* v *Darnell*, 11 B. Monroe (50 Ky.) 30 (1850); *Swift* v *Harriman*, 30 Vt. 607 (1858); *Hoy* v *Gronoble*, 34 Pa. St. 9 (1859); *Williams* v *Bemis*, 108 Mass. 91 (1871); *Given* v *Charron*, 15 Md. 502 (1860); *Jenkins* v *Long & Byrne*, 8 Md. 132 (1855); and *Rick* v *Yates, Adm.*, 5 Ind. 115 (1854). Cf. *Howard* v *Day*, 61 N.Y. 362 (1875); and *Bull* v *Schuberth*, 2 Md. 38 (1852).

I have reported the occupations of these workers to indicate that American courts did not favor white-collar over blue-collar employees; at least one English court did: In *Beeston* v *Collyer*, 4 Bing. 309, 130 ER 786 (C. P. 1827), an army agent who had fired without cause his clerk of fifteen years was ordered to pay the man eighty-three pounds in damages, one-quarter year's severance, for violating the contract. Chief Justice Best observed (at 311) that "it would be, indeed, extraordinary if a party in his station in life could be turned off at a month's notice, like a cook or scullion." American courts sometimes made distinctions regarding implied periods of "notice," but not as consistently and never with such overtones of class and status. (See Jacoby, "Duration of Indefinite Employment," 101, for further evidence of the class consciousness of English courts regarding contract durations.)

As in England, New York's high court did not allow the employer any set-off for the value of wages the unjustly fired worker had earned after the firing but before the end of the contract term, but those of Minnesota and Arkansas did. *Costigan* v *Mohawk & Hudson RR Co.*; *Williams* v *Anderson*, and *Walworth* v *Pool, loc. cit.* See *Beckham* v *Drake*, 2 HLL 579, 9 ER 1213, esp. 1223 (H. L. 1849), and Atiyah, *Rise and Fall*, 425, on the English standard. For the complete story of this facet of the law regarding breaches of labor contracts see Louis Wolcher, "The Privilege of Idleness: A Case Study of Capitalism and the Common Law in Nineteenth Century America," *American Journal of Legal History* 36 (1992): 237, who concludes that the end result of the judicial application of the set-off rule was that white-collar workers benefited more than unskilled and semiskilled laborers, who were expected to find any available work.

117. These cases, all cited in note 116, are *Nears* v *Harbert* (Mo.), *King and Graham* v *Steiren*, (Pa.), *Webster* v *Wade* (Cal.), *Laurence* v *Gullifer* (Me.), *Hoyt* v *The Wildfire* (N.Y.), and *Costigan* v *Mohawk & Hudson RR Co.*, (N.Y.). See also *Ward* v *Ames*, 9 Johns. (N.Y.) 138 (1812); *Clark* v *Marsiglia*, 1 Denio (N.Y.) 317 (1845), *Whitney* v *Brooklyn*, *Hoy* v *Gronoble*, and *Walworth* v *Pool*, in note 116 above. A boot maker in Vermont, denied leather by his employer in the midst of his contract term was entitled to all of a penalty bond posted at the outset. *Boardman, Adm.* v *Keeler*, 21 Vt. 78 (1848).

118. This was the case in *Brinkley* v *Swicegood*, 65 N. C. 626 (1871), and in *Newman* v *McGregor*, 5 Hammond (Ohio) 349 (1832), both won by the plaintiff-respondents without representation on appeal.

In "Development of the Employment at Will Rule," 118–35, Jay M. Feinman has argued that courts were, by the end of the nineteenth century, sanctioning the firing of midlevel managerial personnel on the grounds (laid out in Wood's *Master and Servant*) that, unless clearly specified to the contrary, contracts were understood to be quarterly or monthly, rather than yearly, and continuation of employment was at the will of the employer. But his focus is on the benefits such a development had for employers who chose to *fire* workers; it ignores the benefit of "employment at will" for employees who *quit*. They now had a stronger claim for pro rata payment. (See for example, *Boogher* v *Maryland Life Insurance Co.*, 8 Mo. App. 533 (1880) (where the court observed that by allowing quantum meruit recovery to one who quit before the end of the year, the worker was "thus relieved from the injustice of the English rule."); *Oliver* v *McArthur*, 158 N.Y. App. Div. 241, 143 N.Y. Sup. 126 (1913); *Chamblee* v *Baker*, 95 N. C. 98 (1886); *Matthews* v *Jenkins*, 80 Va. 463 (1885); the note in *Lawyer's Reports Annotated*, XXIV (1894), 231, at 234; and Andrew D. Hill, *"Wrongful Discharge" and the Derogation of the At Will Employment Doctrine* (Philadelphia: Wharton School, 1987), esp. chap. 8, for a good analysis of the potential consequences of a legislated return to the earlier standard.) Moreover, employees no longer had to rely on common law court acceptance of *Britton* v *Turner*. Beginning with Massachusetts, in 1875, some thirty-odd states had by 1920 passed wage payment statutes. Twenty-four of these provided that, upon discharge, the worker's wages "became due and payable" "in full," and half of these extended that mandate to cases where workers quit and sought wages. Moreover, employers who withheld wages from workers who quit without notice were liable to similar forfeitures if they fired workers without notice. Note, "Legislation," *Harvard Law Review* 43 (1929): 641; McGowan, "Divisibility of Employment Contracts," 50, 69–

75; C. B. Labatt, *Commentaries on the Law of Master and Servant*, 2 vols. (Rochester, N.Y.: Lawyer's Cooperative, 1913), 2:2320–21.

119. *Clark v City of Manchester*, 51 N. H. 594, 595 (1872).

120. *Helm v Wilson*, 4 Mo. 43 (1838); *Fenton v Clark*, 11 Vt. 557 (1839); *Fuller v Brown*, 52 Mass. (11 Metc.) 440 (1846); *Seaver v Morse*, 20 Vt. 620 (1848); *Hubbard v Belden*, 27 Vt. 645 (1854); *Fahy v North*, 19 Barbour (N.Y.) 341 (1855); *Patrick v Putnam*, 27 Vt. 759 (1855); *Ryan v Dayton*, 25 Conn. 188 (1856); *Wolfe, Ex. v Howes*, 20 N.Y. (6 Smith) 197 (1859); *Green v Gilbert*, 21 Wis. 395 (1867); *Harrington v Fall River Iron Works*, 119 Mass. 82 (1876); *Lakeman v Pollard*, 43 Me. 463 (1857). Cf. *Parker v Macomber*, 17 R. I. 674 (1892).

Once again, I take issue with Wythe Holt's treatment of these cases: He regards the Vermont high court's opinion in *Fenton v Clark* as "unusual," and writes that they "proceeded to enact an 'illness' exception." ("Recovery by the Worker who Quits," 685–86.) They simply applied the existing English rule, as in *Bailey v Rimmell*, 1 M. & W. 505, 150 ER 534 (Ex. 1836).

121. *Givhan v Dailey's Adm.*, 4 Ala. 336 (1842).

122. *Beach v Mullen*, 34 NJLR 343 (1870).

123. *Byrd v Boyd*, 4 McCord (S. C.) 246 (1827); *McClure v Pyatt*, 4 McCord (S. C.) 26 (1826); *Eaken v Harrison*, 4 McCord (S. C.) 249 (1827); *Pritchard v Martin*, 27 Miss. 305 (1854). The Virginia case was actually a Richmond county court judgement in 1744. An overseer fired for killing slaves successfully sued for his share of the year's crop. See Gwenda Morgan, *The Hegemony of the Law: Richmond County, VA., 1692–1776* (New York: Garland, 1989), 83.

124. *Byrd v Boyd* at 247–48.

Actually, the English standard was itself becoming less severe as well. In *Callo v Brouncher*, 4 Car. & P. 518, 172 ER 807 (N. P. 1831), Justice Parke set forth the conditions (moral misconduct, willful disobedience, or habitual neglect) that would warrant a servant's dismissal, in a case in which he found that the employer had wrongfully fired her servant. (See *Archard v Horner*, 3 Car. & P. 349, 172 ER 451 [N. P. 1828], for the recovery terms for a domestic servant wrongfully discharged, and *Gandell v Pontigny*, 4 Camb. 374, 171 ER 119 [N. P. 1816] for those of one paid by the quarter.) Nonetheless, English justice could still be harsh. In *Turner v Robinson*, 5 B. & Ad. 789, 110 ER 982 (K. B. 1833), a foreman in a silk factory, fired for helping some apprentices "to go to America," first lost a damage suit for forty shillings brought by his employer (for the apprentices' breach of contract), and then lost his own suit to recover his wages pro rata.

125. *Posey v Garth*, 7 Mo. 96, 97 (1841). Posey had served for three months on a one-year contract before being fired for the killing. He sued for the full year's wages. His attorney cited *Cutter v Powell*. The jury awarded him wages for the three months, *and the man appealed*, claiming "all or nothing." He got nothing.

126. In *Partington v Wamsutta Mills*, 110 Mass. 467 (1872), two mill operatives, husband and wife, had left the mill at 4:00 P.M. one day, without notifying the foreman, after one of ten looms they tended had broken down. They returned at 5:30 P.M., explained their reason for leaving to the foreman, and were told to return home and await orders. Upon reporting for work the next day they were fired and were told that they had forfeited their two-week bond. The trial jury awarded them recovery, but the high court ordered a rehearing with clearer judicial instructions to

the jury regarding the question of whether they had violated shop rules and whether these rules were reasonable.

127. Another involved several members of the crew of an American ship, who went ashore in Havana to complain to the U.S. consul of mistreatment. When the consul refused to hear their complaint (contrary to the terms of the Merchant Seaman's Act of 1802), they returned to the ship, were imprisoned and their wages ordered forfeit by the master. A U.S. district court ordered that their wages be paid. *Hart, et al.* v *The Otis,* 11 Fed. Cases 689, #6, 154 (1836). See also *Foster* v *Watson,* 16 B. Monroe (55 Ky.) 377 (1855).

128. *Sloan* v *Hayden,* 110 Mass. 141 at 143 (1872). Recall that this is the same Marcus Morton who, in *Olmstead* v *Beale,* 30 Mass. 528 (1837), had held to the *Cutter* v *Powell* standard in a very clear case.

129. *Heber* v *U.S. Flax Manufacturing Co.,* 13 R. I. 303 at 305 (1881). Cf. *Collins* v *New England Iron Co.,* 115 Mass. 23 (1874), and *Commonwealth* v *Baird,* 1 Ashmead (1st Jud. Dist. of Pa.-Phila.) 267 (1826), where the claim of factory owners of a right to have a young apprentice who worked for him beaten with a leather strap for negligence or disobedience was challenged by Philadelphia Quarter Sessions president Judge Edward King: "It may be convenient, in large manufactories, that such a power should exist in proprietors in order [for] the preservation of order among so numerous a body of young persons as are sometimes employed in these establishments. Our answer to this argument must on all occasions be, that such is not the law of the land, nor have we the power or the inclination to mould it to accommodate individual convenience or peculiar emergencies." See also *Matthews* v *Terry,* 10 CT 455 (1835). (But see *Naylor* v *Fall River Iron Works,* 118 Mass. 317 [1875], where a roller in an iron foundry who took a three day "excursion" in defiance of instructions to the contrary was fired and denied recovery of his ten day's "trustee money" by the court for his breach of contract. See *Preston* v *American Linen Co.,* 119 Mass. 400 [1876], for a similar case.)

130. *Hunt* v *The Otis Co.,* 4 Metc. (45 Mass.) 464, at 466–67 (1842); Mechem, *Treatise on Agency,* sec. 641.

131. My sorties into the nineteenth-century trial court records of Nevada, Colorado, Allegheny County, Pennsylvania, and various New Zealand cities seem to me to indicate that J. P. and common-law trial courts confronted with wrongful discharge claims were applying the high court rules fairly. See, for example, *Pierson* v *Fast Freight Express Co.,* Ormsby County Court, Nevada, no. 1358, 1865; and *Bolles* v *Mountain Queen M. & M. Co.,* Ormsby County Court, Nevada, no. 2146, 1893.

132. Kent's *Comentaries,* 2:289n. Comstock was commenting on the case of *Turner* v *Mason,* 14 Mees. & W 112, 153 ER 411 (EX. 1845), discussed in note 15. Cf. J. C. Perkins, the American editor of the sixteenth edition of Joseph Chitty's *Treatise on Pleadings and Parties to Actions,* 2 vols. (Springfield, Mass., 1879), 2:208 n. f.: "If a servant leaves 'improperly,' in England he has no recovery," but a different rule has been adopted in "several" of "the American states, and the servant has been allowed to recover even after dismissal for good cause, at least so far as his services have been beneficial to his employer."

133. Horwitz., *Transformation 1,* 187–88.

134. Even more striking was the fate of sellers of goods on "entire" contracts who delivered only a part of the order and sought to apportion the contract. In the course of my study of labor contracts, I read a total of eight such cases, from five different states. In no instance did the appellate court allow any pro rata apportioning, or any quantum meruit or quantum valebant recovery. The English "entire" rule was strictly applied—indeed, more strictly than in England itself. (See *Shipton v Casson*, 5 B. & C. 378, 108 ER 141 [K. B. 1826] and Justice Parke in *Read v Rann*, 10 B. & C. 438, at 441 109 ER 513, at 514 [K. B. 1830]: "In some cases, a special contract, not executed, may give rise to a . . . *quantum meruit* [as] when a special contract has been made for goods, and goods sent, not according to the contract, are retained by the party, there a claim for the value on a *quantum valebant* may be supported, but then, from the circumstances, a new contract may be implied." These cases involving the partial deliveries of hay, wood, corn, malt, lumber, grocery stock, ice, and coal, can be [and, in *Lynn v Selby*, 151 N. W. 31, *were*] distinguished from suits where workers and contractors quit before completing *their* "entire" contracts. The difference is that these goods could always be returned to the seller, placing the parties back "*in statu quo*," whereas, in most cases, the partially completed labor of hired hands, operatives, mechanics and artisans had already benefited their employers and could *not* be "returned" to the worker or contractor, a point Justice Parker made in *Britton v Turner*.) *Champlin v Rowley*, 18 Wend. (N.Y.) 187 (1837); *Harris v Liggett*, 1 Watts & S. (Pa.) 301 (1841); *Witherow v Witherow*, 16 Ohio 238 (1847); *McKnight v Dunlop*, 4 Barb. (N.Y.) 36 (1848); *Paige v Ott*, 5 Denio (N.Y.) 406 (1848); *Haslack v Mayers*, 2 Deutch. (26 N.J.) 291 (1857); *Bersch v Sander*, 37 Mo. 105 (1865); *Shinn v Bodine*, 60 Pa. R. 182 (1869).

135. *Hayden v Inhabs. of Madison*, 7 Greenl. (Me.) 76 (1830); *McKinney v Springer*, 3 Ind. 59 (1851); *Dyer v Seals*, 7 La. 131 (1834); *Lee & Dolen v Ashbrook*, 14 Mo. 379 (1851); *Hillyard v Crabtree*, 11 Texas 264 (1854) (a case in which the failure to complete was due to the illness and death of the contractor); *Eyser v Weissgerber*, 2 Cole's Ed. (Iowa) 463 (1856); *Grimes v Howard*, 2 Mich. N. P. 167 (1871); *Hollis v Chapman*, 36 Tex. 1 (1871). The court relied on *Britton v Turner* in four of the five of these cases decided after Parker's opinion appeared.

To get a sense of how small some of these "contractors" were one has only to note that many of the awards were for well under one hundred dollars, or that, as the court noted in one Texas decision, the plaintiff, a carpenter, was "only one of four or five contractors on the same building." (*Hollis v Chapman*, 36 Tex. 1.) Hence it is not surprising that most courts saw little reason to distinguish "contractors" from "servants" in any truly significant fashion. Cf. Sean Wilentz, "Subcontracting and the Building Trades," in *Chants Democratic: New York City and the Rise of the American Working Class, 1788–1850* (New York: Oxford University Press, 1984), 132–34.

136. *Faxon v Mansfield*, 2 Mass. 147 (1806); *Pedan v Hopkins*, 13 S. & R. (Pa.) 47 (1825); *Brumby v Smith*, 3 Ala. 123 (1841); *Easton v Pa. & Ohio Canal Co.*, 13 Ohio 79 (1844); *Wooten v Read*, 2 S. & M. (Miss.) 585 (1844); *Swift v Williams*, 2 Ind. 365 (1850); *Hawkins v Gilbert*, 19 Ala. 54 (1851); *Coates v Sangston*, 5 Md. 121 (1853); *Slater v Emerson*, 20 Howard (60 U.S.) 224 (1856); *Cunningham v Jones*, 3

E. D. Smith (N.Y. C. P. R.) 650 (1857); *Allen v Curles*, 6 Ohio St. 505 (1856); *Finegan v L'Engle*, 8 Fla. 413 (1859); *Malbon v Birney*, 11 Wis. 107 (1860); *Central Military Tract RR Co v Spurk, et al.*, 24 Ill. 588 (1860); *Carpenter v Gay*, 12 R. I. 306 (1879).

137. *Allen v Curles* at 507–8.

138. *Peeters v Opie*, 85 ER 1144 (K. B. 1671).

139. *Farnham & Pollar v Ross, et al.*, 2 Hall's N.Y. Sup. Ct R. 187 (1829); *Carroll v Welch*, 26 Tex. 147 at 149–50 (1861).

140. *McVoy v Wheeler*, 6 Porter (Ala.) 201 (1837); *Jewell v Blanford*, 37 Ky. (7 Dana) 472 (1838).

141. *Preble v Bottom*, 27 Vt. 249 (1855); *Dobbins v Higgins*, 78 Ill. 440 (1875). But only if adequate proof of the work completed was introduced as evidence. See *Cunningham v Morrell*, 10 Johns. (N.Y.) 203 (1813).

142. Similarly, Louis Wolcher has found that builders and unpropertied laborers were treated in the same fashion by high courts in the second half of the nineteenth century in cases involving the new, and oft-ignored, rule that wrongfully fired employees were expected to seek other work rather than continually offering their services to their former employer until the end of the agreed-upon term of service. Wolcher, "Privilege of Idleness," 237 at 248 n. 33.

143. *Farnsworth v Garrard*, 1 Camp. 40, 170 ER 867 (N. P. 1807); *Ellis v Hamlen*, 3 Taunt. 52, 128 ER 21 (C. P. 1810); *Munro v Butt*, 8 El. & Bl. 739, 120 ER 275 (Q. B. 1858). In the latter two cases the courts rejected the arguments of the contractor's attorneys to the effect that since the imperfectly built houses were on the employer's own land, this fact automatically constituted use and benefit of the value of the labor and materials. As Chief Justice Sir James Mansfield put it in *Ellis v Hamlen*: "Is he to have his ground covered with buildings of no use . . . ?"

144. *Burn v Miller*, 4 Taunt. 744, 128 ER 523 (C. P. 1813). The employer-defendant was, however, allowed damage setoffs equal to his costs in bringing the road, wall, or building up to the contractually stipulated standard.

But see George J. Bell, *Commentaries on the Laws of Scotland*, 4th ed. (Edinburgh, 1821), 456, for evidence that Scottish courts allowed builders quantum meruit and quantum valebant recovery for imperfect work to the extent that it benefited the other party.

145. *Willey v Fredericks*, 10 Gray (76 Mass.) 357 (1858); *Haven and White v Wakefield*, 39 Ill. 509 (1866); Kussmaul, *Servants in Husbandry*, 32.

146. The Minnesota high court, however, was noteworthy for its strict adherence to the all-or-nothing rule in entire contracts and its complete rejection of *Britton v Turner* and *Hayward v Leonard*. See especially Justice Issac Atwater in *Mason v Heyward*, 3 Minn. R. 182 (1859).

147. *Cooke v Rhine*, 1 Bay (South Car.) 16 (1784); *Jewell v Schroeppel*, 4 Cowen (N.Y.) 564 (1825); *Hayward v Leonard*, 7 Pick. (24 Mass.) 180 (1828); *Smith v Proprietors of 1st Cong. Meetinghouse in Lowell*, 8 Pick. (25 Mass.) 178 (1829); *Loreau v DeClouet*, 3 La. 1 (1831); *Wadleigh v Town of Sutton*, 6 N. H. 15 (1832); *Brewer v Inhabitants of Tyringham*, 12 Pick. (29 Mass.) 547 (1832); *Liggett v Smith*, 3 Watts (Pa.) 331 (1834); *Jewett v Weston*, 11 Me. 346 (1834); *Norris v School Dist. £1*, 12 Me. (3 Fairf.) 293 (1835); *Elliot v Wilkinson*, 8 Yerg. (16 Tenn.) 411 (1835); *Gazzam v Kirby*, 8 Porter (Ala.) 253 (1838); *Gilman v Hall*, 11 Vt. 510 (1839); *Danville Bridge Co. v Pomeroy*, 3 Harris (15 Pa. St.) 151 (1850); *Bassett v Sanborn*, 63 Mass. (9

Cush.) 58 (1851); *Downey v Burke*, 23 Mo. 228 (1856); *Smith v Gugerty*, 4 Barb. (N.Y.) 614 (1848); *Mitchell v Wescotta Land Co.*, 3 Cole's Ed. (Iowa) 209 (1856); *Demoss v Noble*, 6 Iowa 530 (1858); *Taylor v Williams*, 6 Wis. 363 (1858); *Dermott v Walter*, 31 Mo. 516 (1862); and *McClay v Hedge*, 18 Iowa 66 (1864).

148. *Pullman v Corning*, 9 N.Y. 93 (1853); *Haven & White v Wakefield*, 39 Ill. 509 (1866), and *Willey v Fredericks*, 76 Mass. 357 (1858); *Bryant v Stillwell*, 24 Pa. St. 314 (1855); *Taft v Inhabitants of Montague*, 14 Mass. 282 (1817); *Morford v Mastin*, 22 Ky. 609 (1828); *Lewis v Blanchard*, 10 Martin's R. (La.) 151 (1829); *Shaw v Lewiston & K. Turnpike Co.*, 2 P. & W. (Pa.) 454 (1831); *Stagg v Munro*, 8 Wend. (N.Y.) 399 (1832); *Mason v Heyward*, *supra* note 154; *Trustees of Monroe Female University v Broadfield*, 30 Ga. 1 (1859). In this last case Justice Richard Lyons, setting aside two consecutive jury findings that absolved the contractors of fault, offered an early example of the modern rejection of the "accepted work" doctrine. When the roof of a repaired assembly hall leaked and the ceiling fell, the contractors were held liable, despite the fact that the trustees had accepted the work, because, as Lyons wrote, the trustees "were not presumed to know how many [pillars] were necessary" to hold the ceiling and "could not see and examine the [inadequate but hidden] girder themselves." See also *Feagan v Meredith*, 4 Mo. 514 (1837).

149. *Sinclair v Tallmadge*, 35 Barb. (N.Y.) 602, at 604 (1861).

150. Perhaps that should read "Republicanism." For what it is worth, every one of the staunch defenders of *Britton v Turner* as "good policy" (Parker, Dillon, Cobb, G. W. Field, and James Campbell) were Republicans, while none of the five most vigorous defenders of *Cutter v Powell* as "good policy" were ever Republicans. (Three—Holman, Caruthers, and Breese—were Democrats, one [Spencer] was a Whig; the other [Isaac Parker of Massachusetts] may have been a Federalist.) And there is evidence that Republican leaders in Indiana and Illinois in 1856 and 1860 appealed deliberately and with some effect to farm laborers, which would be consistent with the "free labor" ideology of the party. See Schob, *Hired Hands*, 239–40.

151. See *Bradley v Mnfg. Co.*, 30 N.H. 487 (1855); *Stevens v Reeves*, 9 Pick. (Mass.) 197 (1829).

SIX

1. Karen Orren, *Belated Feudalism: Labor, the Law, and Liberal Developments in the United States* (Cambridge: Cambridge University Press, 1991), 63, feels (incorrectly) that the champerty rule was still present in New York in 1835. Kenneth DeVille, *Medical Malpractice in Nineteenth Century America* (New York: New York University Press, 1990), 195, feels that the phenomenon first significantly affected the field of medical malpractice in the 1880s. Randolph Bergstrom, *Courting Danger: Injury and Law in New York City, 1870–1910* (Ithaca, N.Y.: Cornell University Press, 1993), 88–91, 113, notes the antebellum origin of the change in New York, but argues that it was not being used in 1870 in New York City, but was in use by 1890. Lawrence Friedman, *A History of American Law*, 2nd ed. (New York: Simon and Schuster, 1985), 482; Edward Purcell, *Litigation and Inequality* (New York: Oxford University Press, 1992), 150, 340; and Kermit Hall, *The Magic Mirror: Law in American History* (New York: Oxford University Press, 1989), 215, associate it simply with the late nineteenth century. Tony Freyer, as usual, is closest to the truth in this regard, noting the use of contingency-fee contracts "at least by the

1850s." *Producers versus Capitalists: Constitutional Conflict in Antebellum America* (Charlottsville: University of Virginia Press, 1994), 172.

Edward Purcell indicates that the typical percentage fee for personal injury suits in 1900 was 20 percent (*Litigation and Inequality*, 312.)

2. *Slywright* v *Page*, 1 Leon. 167, 74 ER 153 (Q. B. 1589).

3. Sir William Hawkins, *A Treatise of the Pleas of the Crown*, 2 vols. (London, 1724), vol. 1, chap. 83–84, sec. 38; Charles Viner, *A General Abridgement of Law and Equity*, 2nd ed. (London, 1793), 15:148–51. Cf. 32 Henry VIII (barring assignment of a chose in action).

4. *Box* v *Barnaby*, Hobart 118, 80 ER 266 (K. B. 1617).

5. In *Priestley* v *Fowler*, 150 ER 1030 (Ex. 1837).

6. In *Findon* v *Parker*, 11 M. & W. 675, 152 ER 976, at 979 (Ex. 1843). Despite Abinger's dicta, English courts continued to bar the contingency fee. See *Kennedy* v *Brown*, 2 F. & F. 801, 175 ER 1292 (N. P. 1862); 3 Ridg. P. C. 501, 143 ER 268 (C. P. 1863) (Champerty is "the worst kind of maintenance"); and *Hilton* v Woods, LR, 4 Eq. 432 (1867).

7. John Leubsdorf, "Toward a History of the American Rule of Attorney Fee Recovery," *Law and Contemporary Problems* 47 (1984): 9.

8. Peter Bartrip and Sandra Burman, *Wounded Soldiers of Industry* (Oxford: Oxford University Press, 1983), 116–17, 111.

9. H. H. Brackenridge, *Law Miscellanies* (Philadelphia, 1814), xx. See also the defense of "contingent fees" in David Hoffman, *A Course of Legal Study* (Baltimore, 1836), 761.

10. *Arden* v *Patterson*, 5 Johns. Ch. (N.Y.) 44 (1821); *Thurston* v *Percival*, 1 Pick. (18 Mass.) 415 (1823); *Rust* v *Larue*, 4 Lit. (14 Ky.) 411 (1823); *Kay* v *Vattier*, 1 Ohio 132 (1823); *State* v *Chitty*, 1 Bailey (So. Car.) 401 (1830); *Holloway* v *Lowe*, 7 Port. (Ala.) 488 (1838); *Backus* v *Byron*, 4 Mich. 536 (1857); *Scobey* v *Ross*, 13 Ind. 117 (1859). Cf. *Martin* v *Clarke*, 8 R. I. 389 (1866); and *Livingston* v *Cornell*, 2 Martin's (O. S.) (La.) 280 (1812), where the court noted that Roman law barred such fees.

11. *State* v *Chitty*, 1 Bailey's Law (17 S. C.) 375 at 401 (1830); *Arden* v *Patterson*, 5 Johns. Ch. (NY) 44 at 49 (1821). Cf. *In re Bleakley*, 5 Paige Ch. (N.Y. Ch.) 311 (1835); *Merritt* v *Lambert*, 10 Paige (N.Y. Ch.) 352 (1843).

See also the voiding of "champertous" contracts for "secret" lobbying before legislative committees for contingent fees: *Clippinger* v *Hepbaugh*, 5 W.&S. (Pa.) 315 (1843); *Harris* v *Roof*, 10 Barb. (N.Y. Sup. Ct.) 489 (1851); *Marshall* v *B.& O. RR*, 57 U.S. 324 (1853); *Frost* v *Belmont*, 6 Allen (Mass.) 152 (1863), noted in Herbert Hovenkamp, *Enterprise and American Law, 1836–1937* (Cambridge, Mass.: Harvard University Press, 1991), 123. See also *Trist* v *Child*, 63 U.S. 441 (1874).

12. See *Clay* v *Ballard*, 9 Rob. (La.) 308 (1844); *Central Law Journal* 59 (1904): 401; *Kendall* v *U.S.*, 74 U.S. 113 (1868); *Wylie* v *Coxe*, 56 U.S. 415 (1853); *Trist* v *Child*, 63 U.S. 441 (1874).

13. See Paul Gates, "Tenants of the Log Cabin," in Gates, *Landlords and Tenants on the Prairie Frontier* (Ithaca: Cornell University Press, 1973); Alan Taylor, *Liberty Men and Great Proprietors: The Revolutionary Settlement on the Maine Frontier, 1760–1820* (Chapel Hill: University of North Carolina Press, 1990); and Patricia Watlington, *The Partisan Spirit: Kentucky Politics, 1779–1792* (New York, 1978).

14. For examples of contingency-fee contracts involving land title disputes, inheritance of property, or suits to protect the value of squatter improvements, where the litigant entering into the contract with an attorney was "very poor," or "too poor" to pay up-front fees, see *Campbell's Rep. v Kinkaid*, 19 Ky 68 (1825); *Wilhite v Roberts*, 34 Ky 172 (1836); *State v Chitty*, 1 Bailey (S. C.) 401 (1830); *Moore, et al. v Trs. of Campbell Academy*, 17 Tenn. 115 (1836); *Ramsey's Dev. v Trent*, 10 B. Monroe (Ky) 336 (1850); *Johnson v Bright*, 4 Cal. 392 (1854); *Wright v Meek*, 3 Greene (Iowa) 472 (1852); *Lytle v State*, 17 Ark. 608 (1857); *Newkirk v Cone*, 18 Ill. 449 (1857); and *Backus v Byron*, 4 Mich. 536 (1857).

15. *Kay v Vattier*, 1 Ohio 132 at 135, 141, 146, and 147 (1823). Cf. *Weakly v Hall*, 13 Ohio 167 at 175 (1844).

16. *Rust v Larue*, 4 Lit. (14 Ky.) 411 at 412, 421, 424 (1823); Leubsdorf, "Toward a History." Hardin was at it again, with a similar contingency-fee agreement in 1822 for a third of a fifteen-hundred-dollar debt. See *Caldwell's Adm. v Shepherd's Heirs*, 6 T. B. Mon. (22 Ky.) 389 (1827). Cf. *Campbells's Heirs v Kinkaid*, 3 T. B. Mon. (19 Ky.) 68 (1825); *Thurston v Percival*, 1 Pick. (18 Mass.) 415 (1823); *Holloway v Lowe*, 7 Port. (Ala.) 488 at 491 (1838); and *Robbins v Harvey*, 5 Ct. 335 (1824). (At issue in *Robbins* was an implied contract for services (quantum meruit), not, strictly speaking, a contingency-fee arrangement, but the attorney-plaintiff made clear that his client had been "wholly destitute of property to enable her to prosecute her claim," and he noted that he had agreed to work "with no other prospect of remuneration" for his services, "owing to the entire poverty" of his client, "than what he might receive from the estate expected to be recovered." Thus this arrangement has several of the elements of a contingency fee. The Connecticut Supreme Court found the admission in the trial of his evidence of the poverty of his client to be error and ordered a new trial.)

17. *Patten v Wilson*, 34 Pa. St. 299 at 300 (1859). Similarly, in England August 1851, *Herpath's Journal* bemoaned the fact that "law sharks," "hunting" for "cases to try," were winning "ruinous" awards against railway companies, and the chief solicitor of the London and North Western Railway told the Select Committee on Railway Accidents in 1870 that he was "sorry to say that there is never any difficulty in [lower-income accident victims] getting lawyers." *Parliamentary Papers, 1870* 10:232–33. (Cited in Rande Kostal, *Law and English Railways* [Oxford: Oxford University Press, 1994], 294, 378–79).

18. See especially *Scobey v Ross*, 13 Ind. 117 (1859); *Martin v Clarke*, 8 R. I. 389 (1866); *Butler v Legro*, 62 N. H. 350 (1882); and the language of Justice S. M. Green in *Backus v Byron*, 4 Mich. 536 at 539 (1857) ("venerable code of rules"). But the reporter of this case noted that the Michigan legislature sanctioned contingency fees in 1 Session Laws 1867, p. 83, and 2 Comp. Laws, 1871, sec. 7427.

19. *Thallhimer v Brinckerhoff*, 3 Cow. (N.Y.) 622 at 648 (1824); *Flower v O'Conner*, 7 La. 199 at 207 (1834); *[Henry] Clay v Ballard*, 9 Rob. (La.) 308 (1844); *Wilhite v Roberts*, 4 Dana (34 Ky.) 172 (1836); *Evans v Bell*, 6 Dana (36 Ky.) 479 (1838); *Ramsey's Dev's v Trent*, 10 B. Mon. (49 Ky.) 336 (1850); *Moore, et al. v Trustees of Campbell Academy*, 17 Tenn. 115 (1836); *Bayard v McLane*, 3 Harr. R. (Del.) 139 at 219–20 (1840); *Stoecker v Hoffman*, 19 Pa. St. 223 (1852); *Ogden v Des Arts*, 4 Duer (N.Y. Sup. Ct.) 275 (1855); *Sedgwich v Stanton*, 14 N.Y. 289 (1856); *Benedict v Stu-*

art, 23 Barb. (N.Y.) 420 (1856); *Rooney v 2nd Ave. Ry,* 18 N.Y. 371 (1858); *Rasquin v Knickerbocker Stage Co.,* 12 Abb. Prac. (N.Y.) 324 (1861); *Porter v Parmly,* 7 Jones & Sp. (N.Y. Sup.) 219 (1875); *Martinez v Vines,* 32 La. Ann. 305 (1880).

For evidence of the use of contingency fees in the practice of law in antebellum North Carolina and Texas see Fannie M. Farmer, "Legal Practice and Ethics in North Carolina, 1820–1860," *North Carolina Historical Review* 30 (1953): 329 at 352; and Maxwell Bloomfield, *American Lawyers in a Changing Society, 1776–1876* (Cambridge, Mass.: Harvard University Press, 1976), 278.

20. *Sherley v Riggs,* 11 Hump. (30 Tenn.) 53 at 56–57 (1850); *Wright v Meek,* 3 Greene (Iowa) 472 (1852); *Wyllie v Coxe,* 56 U.S. 415 at 420 (1853); *Baldwin v Bennett,* 4 Cal. 392 (1854); *Newkirk v Cone,* 18 Ill. 449 (1857); *Johnson v Bright,* 15 Ill. 464 (1854); *Major's Exr. v Gibson,* 1 Pat. & H. (Va. Ch.) 48 (1855); *Lytle v State,* 17 Ark. 608 (1857); *Nesbit v Cantrell,* 29 Ga. 255 (1859); *Hill v Cunningham,* 25 Tex. 25 (1860); *Christie v Sawyer,* 44 N. H. 298 at 303 (1862); *Ryan v Martin,* 16 Wis. 59 at 64 (1862) (sanctioned by a statute, Public Law of 1856, ch. 120, sec. 214. Here the contingency fee-making plaintiff was Edward G. Ryan, who was to be the railroad-regulating chief justice of the Wisconsin Supreme Court in 1874); *McDonald v Chicago & N. W. RR,* 29 Iowa 170 (1870); *Richardson v Rowland,* 40 Ct. 565 (1873); *Duke v Harper,* 2 Mo. App. 1 (1876); *Schomp v Schenck,* 40 N.J.L. (11 Vro.) 195 (1878); *Weeks v Circuit Judges,* 73 Mich. 256, 41 N. W. 269 (1889); *Potter v Ajax Mining Co.,* 22 Utah 273, 61 Pac. 999 (1900). Cf. *Smith v Young,* 62 Ill. 210 (1871); *Howard v Throckmorton,* 48 Cal. 482 (1874); *Allison v Chicago & N. W. RR,* 42 Iowa 274 (1875); *Wildey v Crane,* 63 Mich. 720, 30 N. W. 327 (1886); *Blaisdell v Ahern,* 144 Mass. 393, 11 N. E. 681 (1887); *Aultman v Waddle,* 40 Kan. 195, 19 Pac. 730 (1888); and *Omaha & R. V. RR v Brady,* 39 Neb. 27, 57 N. W. 767 (1894). The English bar on fees for barristers working for the indigent is in *Dody v Great N.Ry.,* 4 El & Bl. 341 at 345, 119 ER 131 (Q. B. 1854). But see *Butler v Legro,* 62 N. H. 350 (1882), and *Atchison, Topeka & Santa Fe v Johnson,* 29 Kan. 218 (1883), and criticism of contingent fees and "ambulance chasing" by editor Irving Browne and some prominent jurists in *Albany Law Journal* 23 (1881): 485 and ibid. 24 (1881): 26. But then see Judge Edwin Countryman's vigorous response to those criticisms in *The Ethics of Compensation for Professional Services* (Albany, N.Y., 1882), esp. 20, 69, 87, and 111.

21. Chancellor Kent in *Arden v Patterson,* 5 Johns. Ch. (N.Y.) 44 (1821); Justice S. M. Green in *Backus v Byron,* 4 Mich. 536 (1857); Justice Henry Goldthwaite in *Holloway v Lowe,* 7 Port. (Ala.) 488 (1838).

22. *Thurston v Percival,* 1 Pick. (18 Mass.) 415 at 417 (1823).

23. *Major's Exr. v Gibson,* 1 Pat. & H. (Va. Ch.) 48 at 57 and 84 (1855); T. Sedgwick, *How Shall the Lawyers be Paid?* (N.Y. 1840), 3–7; *Backus v Byron,* 4 Mich. 536 (1857) (reporter's note on 1 Session Laws 1867, p. 83); *Ryan v Martin,* 16 Wis. 59 at 64 (1862); *Porter v Parmly,* 7 Jones & Sp. (N.Y. Sup.) 219 (1875); Leubsdorf, "Toward a History," 9, at 18, 20 (on Field and Sedgwick). See also the dicta of Justice Adair Wilson in *Casserleigh v. Wood,* 14 Colo. App. 265, 59 PAC 1024 at 1028 (1900), sanctioning a contingency fee in a mining claim: "Freedom of contract is essential to that unrestricted trade which the spirit and enterprise of the age demand, and especially in countries like this, boasting a republican form of government."

412

24. Thompson in *Major's Exr. v Gibson,* 1 Pat. & H. (Va. Ch.) 48 at 82 (1855);

Skinner in *Newkirk v Cone*, 18 Ill. 449 at 453 (1857). Countryman, *Ethics of Compensation*, 69, 87.

25. *Moore v Trustees of Campbell Academy*, 17 Tenn. 115 (1836).

26. *Bayard v McLane*, 3 Harr. R. (Del.) 139 at 207, 219–20 (1840). The two men were not speaking hypothetically: The client of this contingency-fee arrangement was suing the Philadelphia millionaire merchant Stephen Girard!

27. *Lytle v State*, 17 Ark. 608 at 670 and 677 (1857).

28. Justice A. W. D. Totten in *Sherley v Riggs*, 11 Hump. (30 Ten.) 53 at 56–57 (1850); Justice Moses Walker in *Bentnick v Franklin & Galveston City Co*, 38 Tex. 458 at 473 (1873); Justice Lucas Thompson in *Major's Exr. v Gibson*, 1 Pat. & H. (Va. Ch.) 48 at 83 (1855); Justice John Kinney in *Wright v Meek*, 3 Greene (Iowa) 472 at 484 (1852); Chief Justice Samuel Bell in *Christie v Sawyer*, 44 N. H. 298 at 303 (1862) (Bell was both quoting and paraphrasing the dicta of Chief Justice William Richardson in *Shapley v Bellows*, 4 N. H. 347 at 355 [1828]); Judge Robert Bakewell in *Duke v Harper*, 2 Mo. App. 1 at 10 (1876) ("Many a poor man with a just claim would find himself unable to prosecute his rights, could he make no arrangement to pay his advocate out of the proceeds of the suit"); *Schomp v Schenck*, 40 NJL 195 at 206 (1878) (the champerty rule was "unsymetrical"); *Dunne v Herrick*, 37 Ill. App. 180 (1890); Chancellor Theodore Runyon in *Hassell v Van Houten*, 39 N.J. Eq. 105 at 110 (1884); and Justice James Miner in *Potter v Ajax Mining Co.*, 22 Utah 273, 61 PAC 999 (1900). Judge Bakewell also commented on the popularity of contingency-fee contracts in Missouri and noted that "if they are immoral or illegal, there are perhaps few attorneys in active practice amongst us who have not been habitual violators of the law." Cf. the remarks of Judge Kane in *Ex Parte Plitt*, 2 Wall, Jr., 453, 19 Fed. Cas. 875 at 883 (1853).

29. Note, "Contingency Fees in Divorce Cases," *Virginia Law Review* 21 (1935): 446; *Jordan v Westerman*, 62 Mich. 170, 28 N. W. 826 (1886); *Price v Caperton*, 62 Ky. 207 (1864); *Houlton v. Dunn*, 60 Minn. 26, 61 N. W. 898 (1895); *Spaulding v. Ewing*, 149 Pa. St. 375 (1892); *Richardson v Scotts Bluff County*, 59 Neb. 400, 81 N. W. 309 (1899).

30. Robert Silverman, *Law and Urban Growth: Civil Litigation in the Boston Trial Courts, 1880–1900* (Princeton: Princeton University Press, 1981), 191; and information available for eighty-seven plaintiffs in my appellate personal injury case population, described in chapter 9.

31. "The Solicitation of Cases," *American Law Review* 63 (1929): 135; Paul Holmes, "The Ambulance-Chasing Panacea," *Marquette Law Review* 12 (1928): 193.

32. "Contingency Fees," *Central Law Journal* 59 (1904): 401 at 402.

33. See Jeffrey O'Connell et al., *Rethinking Contingency Fees* (New York: Manhattan Institute, 1994).

SEVEN

1. These are the words used by Justice Daniel Valentine, summarizing the record of the first trial court, in *Kansas Central RR v Fitzsimmons*, 18 Kan. 34 at 35 (1875).

2. *Kansas Central RR v Fitzsimmons*, 22 Kan. 686 (1879).

3. *Nagel v Missouri Pacific RR*, 75 Mo. 653, at 658 (1882). This report of the case also notes that the Missouri Pacific Railway relinquished its rights to the property

on which this turntable stood, by deeding the land back to the City of Jefferson by quit-claim some four months after the accident that took young Albert Nagel's life. Whether this is mere coincidence or whether the company sought to avoid a similar damage suit in the future is unclear.

4. *York* v *Pacific & I. N. RR*, 8 Idaho 574, 69 PAC 1042 (1902).

5. *Harriman* v *Pittsburgh, Cincinnati, and St. Louis RR*, 45 Ohio St. 11, 12 N. E. 451 (1887).

6. Justice Augustus Summers in *Wheeling and Lake Erie RR* v *Harvey*, 77 Ohio St. 235, 83 N. E. 66 (1907), citing *Ryan* v *Towar*, 128 Mich 463, 87 N. W. 644 (1901). Both Summers and Hooker cited the opinion of Michigan's Chief Justice Thomas Cooley in *Powers* v *Harlow*, 53 Mich. 507, 19 N. W. 257 (1884), whose obiter views appeared to reject the attractive-nuisance doctrine.

7. Thus Michigan's Justice Frank Hooker would refer to "the generic term . . . attractive nuisance" in that state's "leading case," *Ryan* v *Towar* (1901).

8. Grant Gilmore, *The Age of American Law* (New Haven, Conn.: Yale University Press, 1977), 41–67, calls it the "Age of Faith." Morton Horwitz, "The Rise of Legal Formalism," 19 *Amer. Journal of Legal History*, 251 (1975), Lawrence Friedman, *A History of American Law*, 2nd ed. (New York: Simon and Schuster, 1985), 383–84, Kermit Hall, *The Magic Mirror: Law in American History* (N.Y.: Oxford University Press, 1989), 211ff., and Morton G. White, *Social Thought in America: The Revolt against Formalism* (New York: Viking, 1949), prefer the term "Age of Formalism."

9. *Henderson* v *Cont. Refining Co*, 219 Pa. 384 (1908); *Millum* v *Lehigh & Wilkes-Barre Coal Co.*, 225 Pa. 214 (1909); *Ziehm* v *Vale*, 98 Ohio St. 306, 120 N. E. 702 (1918). The post-1925 history of the doctrine is beyond the scope of this study, but suffice it to say that by 1980 some thirty-five states had adopted section 339 (which does not require that the danger actually be "alluring"), and only five state courts still rejected it. For more on that story see Eugene Thatch, "Note: Demise of the 'Attractive Nuisance' Concept [in Mississippi]," *Mississippi College Law Review* 2 (1980): 41, and R. A. K., "Note: Attractive Nuisance: A Logical Extension or Expansion of an Already Expanded Liability?" *Albany Law Review* 36 (1972): 439. Cf. Clark, C. J., in *Kermarec* v *C. G. T.*, 245 F 2nd 175, at 180 (1957): "[The distinctions between invitees, licensees, and trespasser] have become more and more obscured during the last century as courts have moved towards imposing on owners a single duty of reasonable care." The leading case that formally abolished the distinction in tort between trespassers and invitees seems to be *Rowland* v *Christian*, 69 Cal. 2nd 108, 443 PAC 2nd 561, 70 Cal. Rpt. 97 (1968).

10. Thus the high courts of Connecticut, Rhode Island, Michigan, Massachusetts, New Jersey, and New York, in addition to Ohio and Pennsylvania, have now reversed themselves and are in the ranks of those accepting section 339 of the *Second Restatement* while the legislatures of Virginia and West Virginia had, between 1929 and 1939, *directed* their high courts to hold property owners of dangerous artificial conditions liable for injuries to "expected trespassers." (Thatch, "Note," 57, 58 n. 78.) See also R. Neal Batson, "Trespassing Children: A Study in Expanding Liability," *Vanderbilt Law Review* 20 (1966): 139.

11. Lon Fuller uses the attractive-nuisance doctrine as an example of "a doctrine

that is plainly fictitious" in his *Legal Fictions* (Stanford, Calif.: Stanford University Press, 1967), 66–71.

12. *Kansas Central RR v Fitzsimmons*, 22 Kan. 686 (1879); *Union Pacific RR v Dunden*, 37 Kan. 1, 14 PAC 501 (1887); *Powers v Harlow*, 53 Mich. 507, 19 N. W. 257 (1884); *Kopplekom v Colorado Cement Co.*, 16 Col. App. 278, 64 PAC 1047 (1901); *Temple v McComb City Elec. Light & Power Co.*, 89 Miss. 1, 42 50 874 (1907); *Day v Consol. Light, Power, & Ice Co.*, 136 Mo. App. 274, 117 S. W. 81 (1909); *Thompson v Baltimore & Ohio RR*, 218 Pa. 444, 67 ATL 768, at 774 (1907).

13. See for example, Friedman, *History of American Law*, 300, 469; Horwitz, *Transformation* 1, xvi, 102, and chap. 8 ("The Rise of Legal Formalism"); Karl Llewellyn, *The Common Law Tradition: Deciding Appeals* (Boston: Little, Brown, 1960), 37.

14. Wilkes, J., offers the distinction just summarized in *Gautret v Egerton*, *Law Reports* II C. P. 371 (1872).

15. *Townsend v Walthen*, 9 East 277, 103 ER 579 (K. B. 1808); *Bird v Holbrook*, 4 Bing. 628, 130 ER 911 (C. P. 1828); *Blyth v Topham*, Cro. Jac. 158, 79 ER 139 (K. B. 1608), known to later jurists via Sir John Comyns's *Digest* (numerous English and American editions) under "Action on the Case for Nuisance: C"; *Sarch v Blackburn*, 4 Car & P 299, 172 ER 712 (N. P. 1830).

16. *Hounsel v Smyth*, 7 CB (NS) 743, 141 ER 1003 (C. P. 1860); *Bolch v Smith*, 31 L. J. 201 (Ex. 1862); *Sharrod v London & WW RR*, 4 Exch. 580, 154 ER 1345 (1849); *Mangan v Atterton*, Times Law Rpts, 1 Exch. Cases 239 (1866). Cf. *Singleton v Eastern Counties Ry*, 7 CB (NS) 287, 141 ER 827 (C. P. 1859) (where the legs of a three-year-old girl, trespassing on the parapet of a bridge, were lost to a passing train whose engineer saw her peril, blew his whistle, but did not brake).

17. *Lynch v Nurdin*, 1 Ad & El (NS) 29, 10 L. J. (NS) 73, 113 ER 1041 (Q. B., 1841).

18. Anderson, B., and Pollock, C. B., in *Lygo v Newbold*, 9 Ex. 302, 156 ER 129 (Ex. 1854). Cf. *Hughes v McAffie*, 2 Hurl. & Col. 744, 159 ER 308 (Ex. 1863); *Ross v Keith*, 16 Scot. Session Cases, 4th series, 86 (1888); *Patterson v Borough of Woollahra*, 16 New South Wales—Cases at Law 229 (1895); and *Slade v Victorian Ry*, 15 Victorian Law Rpts 190 (1889).

19. See, for example, Justice Esek Cowen's obiter dicta in *Loomis v Terry*, 17 Wendell (N.Y.) 494, at 500 (1837): "The business of life must go forward, and the fruits of industry must be protected." Unintended injuries could occur to trespassers without liability, he noted, offering several examples from English cases. Cf. *Brown v European & North American RR*, 58 Me. 384 (1870) (C. J. Appelton); *Severy v Nickerson*, 120 Mass. 306 (1876); and *Maenner v Carroll*, 46 Md. 193 (1877).

20. *Loomis v Terry*; *Johnson v Patterson*, 14 Ct. 1 at 5 (1840). Justice Sherman (son of the "Founding Father") did note that English law allowed spring guns *if* neighbors had been *warned* of that fact, something he condemned as "aristocratic and feudal, and the offspring of the peculiar state of society which existed three centuries ago" (5).

21. *Daley v Norwich and W. RR*, 26 Ct. 591, at 598 (1858). Chief Justice Samuel Church had similarly sidestepped the trespass problem nine years before in *Birge v Gardner*, 19 Ct. 507 (1849), where a property owner's poorly secured heavy gate had

broken off from his fence and injured a six-year-old child who had been tugging at it. The court affirmed a jury verdict of $160, citing *Johnson* v *Patterson*.

22. *Whirley* v *Whiteman*, 1 Head (38 Tenn.) 610, at 622 (1858).

23. McKinney, an Irish-born Presbyterian, was a foe of slavery and a Unionist in 1861. He was also clearly comfortable with Lord Denman's argument, since he used his language (622).

24. See for example, *Prosser on Torts*, 364, and literally every article on the doctrine.

Justice James Campbell's forerunning opinion in *Hargreaves* v *Deacon*, 25 Mich. 1 (1872), skirts the question of whether attractive and dangerous artificially-created objects injurious to trespassing children might lead to landowner liability. The case was one in which a boy fell into an uncovered cistern on another's property. The court would not hold the owner liable but Justice Campbell would "express no opinion concerning cases where the nature of the business is such as to present peculiar attraction to children." (5)

25. *Stout* v *Sioux City & Pacific RR*, 2 Dillon 294, 23 Fed. Cases 183 (1872).

26. 84 U.S. (17 Wall.) 657 (1873) (Justice Ward Hunt, former chief justice of the New York Supreme Court and a Republican, wrote the opinion).

27. *Central Law Journal* 2 (reported March 12, 1875): 176. This instruction was reproduced by the editors of the *Central Law Journal*, quite deliberately, in order to provide the reader with a view alternative to that of the one they had just drawn favorable attention to, the Minnesota high court's *reversal* of Judge Hall's directed verdict for the company. Here was professionalism at work. The editor of the spanking new *Central Law Journal* was none other than John Forrest Dillon, whose instructions in *Stout* the Minnesota high court had just praised in reversing Judge Hall. The associate editor of the *Journal* was Seymour Thompson, whom Dillon had just appointed his Master in Chancery, and who was to praise Dillon's *Stout* instructions extravagantly within a few years in his *Law of Negligence* (1886).

28. Dean Prosser, describing the emergence of the attractive-nuisance doctrine, refers to *Keffe* and its author, "an obscure Minnesota judge named Young" (William Prosser, "Trespassing Children," *California Law Review* 47 [1959]: 430n). The historian can give Justice Young more in the way of flesh and bones. He was a minister's son, born in Boston in 1840, a graduate of Harvard Law in 1863 where he studied torts with the Royall Professor of Law, Joel Parker, the author of *Britton* v *Turner* (6 N. H. 481 [1834]). He migrated to Minnesota shortly after graduation and was named to the court to fill an unexpired term in April 1874. He left the court in January 1875, the same day that the *Keffe* decision was handed down. He set up an office in a building one floor above that of James J. Hill, the entrepreneur who was reorganizing bankrupt railroad companies into the Northern Pacific, and by 1877 was serving as Hill's chief counsel. Federal Circuit Court Judge John Dillon, behaving with circumspection and equanimity, was the man overseeing the receivership of the bankrupt lines (possibly with the assistance of his master in chancery, Seymour Thompson). Young travelled to Judge Dillon's court and chambers in 1878 and 1879 on Hill's behalf; he was paid eight thousand dollars for his handling of one of Hill's suits in the 1880s, and he presented Hill's brief to the U.S. Supreme Court in *Northern Securities* v *U.S.*, 193 U.S. 197, at 241 (1903). (*Who Was Who in America*, vol. 1, 1897–1940) (Chicago: Marquis—Who's Who, 1942) 1:1391; Albro Martin, *James*

J. Hill and the Opening of the Northwest (New York: Oxford Univerrsity Press, 1976), 133, 159, 162, 164, 171, 178–79, 359.)

29. *Keffe* v *Milwaukee & St. Paul RR*, 21 Minn 207, at 210–13 (1875).

30. *Mullaney* v *Spence*, 15 Abbott's Practice Rpts (NS) 319 at 322 (1874). (Judge Reynolds also cited *Lynch, Birge*, and *Whirley*.)

31. *Govt. St RR* v *Hanlon*, 53 Ala. 70 (1875); *Kansas Central RR* v *Fitzsimmons*, 18 Kan. 34 (1875); *Nagel* v *Missouri Pacific RR*, 75 Mo. 653 (1882); *Koons* v *St. Louis & Iron Mt RR*, 65 Mo. 592 (1877); *Phila. Hydraulic Works* v *Orr*, 83 Pa. 332, at 336 (1877).

32. L. R., 3 Q. B.Div 327 (1878); S. D. Thompson, *The Law of Negligence in Relations Not Resting in Contract*, 2nd ed. (San Francisco, 1886), 1:305.

33. See for example, *Bransom's Adm.* v *Labrot* 81 Ky. 638 (1884); *Harriman* v *Pitts., C. & St. L. RR*, 45 Ohio St. 11, 12 N. E. 451 (1887); *Westerfield* v *Levis*, 43 La. Ann. 63, 9 SO 52 (1891); *Brinkley Car-Works* v *Cooper*, 60 Ark. 545, 31 S. W. 154 (1895); *City of Pekin* v *McMahon*, 154 Ill. 141, 39 N. E. 484 (1895); *Price* v *Atchison Water Co*, 58 Kan. 551, 50 PAC 450 (1897); *Franks* v *Southern Cotton Oil Co.*, 78 S. C. 10, 58 S. E. 960 (1907); *Bjork* v *City of Tacoma*, 135 PAC (Wash.) 1005 (1913); *Coeur d'Alene Lumber* v *Thompson*, 215 Fed (9th Cir.) 8 (1914). See also *Ft Wayne & N. Ind. Traction* v *Stark*, 74 Ind. App. 669, 127 N. E. 460 (1920).

34. Thompson, *Law of Negligence*.

35. *A & N RR* v *Bailey's Admin.*, 11 Neb. 332, 9 N. W. 50 (1881); *Evansich* v *The G. C. & S. F. RR*, 57 Tex. 123 (1882); *Nagel* v *Missouri Pacific RR*, 22 Kan. 686 (1879); *Bransom's Adm.* v *Labrot*, 81 Ky. 638 (1884); *Ferguson* v *Columbus & Rome RR*, 75 Ga. 637, 77 Ga. 102 (1885); *Bridger* v *Asheville & Spartenburg RR*, 25 S. C. 24 (1885); *City of Indianapolis* v *Emmelman*, 108 Ind. 530, 9 N. E. 155 (1886); *Harriman* v *Pitts., C. & St. L. RR*, 12 N. E. 451 (1887); *Mackey* v *Mayor of City of Vicksburg*, 64 Miss. 777, 2 SO 178 (1887).

36. *Ilwaco RR & Navigation Co.* v *Hedrick*, 1 Wash. 446, 25 PAC 335 (1890). (Chief Justice T. J. Anders staked out the strictest liability rule of any high court toward turntable owners when he ruled that the company's evidence that it was the custom of other railroads to leave turntables unfastened (evidence relevant to the "reasonable man" standard in negligence) was not admissible, because such a custom would be "manifestly unreasonable and negligent." For the opposite view, that evidence of unlocked turntables being characteristic of railroad company policy was admissible and relevant see Chief Justice James Gilfillan's observations in *Kolsti* v *RR*, 32 Minn. 134, 19 N. W. 655 (1884).) *Westerfield* v *Levis*, 9 SO 52 (1891); *Barrett* v *Southern Pacific RR*, 91 Cal. 296, 27 PAC 666 (1891); *City of Pekin* v *McMahon*, 154 Ill. 141, 39 N. E. 484 (1895); *Brinkley Car-Works* v *Cooper*, 31 S. W. 154 (1895); *East Tennessee & Western North Carolina RR* v *Cargille*, 105 Tenn. 628, 59 S. W. 141 (1900); *Edginton* v *Burlington RR*, 116 Iowa 410, 90 N. W. 95 (1902); *Denver City Tranway* v *Nicholas*, 35 Col. 462, 84 PAC 813 (1906). Cf. *Kopplekom* v *Colo. Cement Co.*, 16 Col. App. 278, 64 PAC 1047 (1901); *Brown* v *Salt Lake City*, 33 Utah 222, 93 PAC 570 (1908); *Taylor* v *Manila Elec. RR & Light Co.*, 16 Phil. 8 (1910); *Meyer* v *Menominee Light & Traction Co.*, 138 N. W. (Wis.) 1008 (1912); *Riggle* v *Lens*, 71 Ore. 125, 142 PAC 346 (1914); *Baxter* v *Park*, 184 N. W. (S. D.) 198 (1921); *Stark* v *Holtzclaw*, 90 Fla. 207, 105 SO 330 (1925); *Cooke* v *Midland G. W. RR of Ireland*, Law Rpt. App. Cases 229 (1909). Cf. *Harrold* v *Watney*, 2 Law Rpt.

2B 320 (1898); and *Jewson v Gatti*, 2 Times Law Rpt 381, at 441 (1886) (A girl lean-ing against a railing [which gave way] to see scenes being painted in a basement. "It must have been known that painting would attract children; and then a bar was put up ostensibly as a protection, against which children would naturally lean while looking down into the cellar. This was almost an invitation—certainly an induce-ment—to the child to lean against the bar.").

37. *Union Pacific RR v Dunden*, 37 Kan. 1, 14 PAC 501 (1887); *O'Malley v St. Paul, M. & M. RR*, 43 Minn. 289, 45 N. W. 440 (1890); *Gulf, Colorado & Santa Fe RR v McWhirter*, 77 Tex. 356, 14 S. W. 26 (1890); *Ft Worth and Denver City RR v Measles*, 81 Tex. 474, 17 S. W. 124 (1891); *Callahan v Eel River & E. R. Co.*, 92 Cal. 89, 28 PAC 104 (1891); *Alabama Gr. Southern RR v Crocker*, 131 Ala. 584, 31 S. W. 561 (1901); *Chicago, Burlington & Quincy RR v Krayenbuhl*, 91 N. W. (NEB) 880 (1902); *Chicago & E. R. Co. v Fox*; Ind. App., 70 N. E. 81 (1904); *Berry v St. Louis, M. & SE RR*, 214 Mo. 593, 114 S. W. 27 (1908); *Taylor v Minn. & St. Louis RR*, 163 N. W. (Iowa) 405 (1917).

38. *Siddall v Jansen*, 168 Ill. 43, 48 N. E. 191 (1897) (an elevator shaft and a five-year-old boy); *Dublin Cotton Oil Co. v Jarrard*, Texas Ct Civ App. 40 S. W. 531 (1897) (a seven-year-old girl "enjoying the whir and buzz of the machinery," "charmed with the novel and alluring scenes," but unaware of the "swift but lurking dangers"); *Jensen v Wetherell*, 79 Ill. App. 33 (1898) (a planing mill's cogwheels); *Force v Standard Silk Co.*, 160 Fed. 992 (1908) (child caught in silk mill machine belt); *Nashville Lumber v Busbee*, 100 Ark. 76, 139 S. W. 301 (1911) (wheelcogs in box factory); *Biggs v Consol. Barbed Wire Co.*, 60 Kan. 217, 56 PAC 4 (1899) (a pro-jecting bolt and coupling that caught and killed a boy); *Henderson v Cont. Refining Co.*, 219 Pa. 384 (1908) (unenclosed cogwheels for a pumping machine killing a seven-year-old boy); *Millum v Lehigh & Wilkes-Barre Coal Co.*, 225 Pa. 214 (1909) (pulley and wheel in unfenced mine company lot injuring a four-year-old boy); *Brown v Rockwell City Canning Co.*, 110 N. W. (Iowa) 112 (1906) (a corn husking machine was not inherently attractive or dangerous); *Stamford Old Mill Co.*, v *Barnes*, 103 Tex. 409, 128 S. W. 375 (1907) (a cotton gin's conveyor belt not inher-ently attractive to children); *Rodgers v Lees*, 140 Pa. 475, 21 ATL 399 (1891) (a mov-ing ball chain used to haul materials at a mill).

39. *Mattson v Minn. & N. W. RR*, 104 N. W. (Minn.) 443 (1905); *Hayko v Colo. & Utah Coal Co.*, 77 Col. 143, 235 PAC 373 (1925).

40. *Conol. Elec. Light & Power v Healy, et ux.*, 65 Kan. 798, 70 PAC 884 (1902); *Daltry v Media Elec. Light & Power*, 208 Pa. 403, 57 ATL 833 (1904); *Day v Consol. Light, Power & Ice Co.*, 136 Mo. App. 274, 117 S. W. 81 (1909); *Meyer v Menomi-nee & Marinette Light & Traction Co.*, 138 N. W. (Wis.) 1008 (1912); *Hayes v Southern Power Co.*, 78 S. E. (S. C.) 956 (1913); *Ft. Wayne & N. Ind. Traction v Stark*, 74 Ind. App. 669, 127 N. E. 460 (1920); *McCoy v Texas Power & Light*, Tex. unrpt, 239 S. W. 1105 (1922); *Stark v Holtzclaw*, 90 Fla. 207, 105 SO 330 (1925). Cf. *Guinn v Del. & A. Tel. Co.*, 72 N.J.L. 276, 62 ATL 412 (1905); *Sheffield Co. v Mor-ton*, 161 Ala. 153, 49 SO 772 (1909).

41. *Govt. St. RR v Hanlon*, 53 Ala. 70 (1875); *Biddle, et ux. v Hestonville, M. & F. P. RR*, 112 Pa. 551, 4 ATL 485 (1886); *Texas & Pacific RR v Brown*, Tex. Ct Civ App., 33 S. W. 146 (1895); *Denver City Tramway v Nicholas*, 35 Col. 462, 84 PAC 813 (1906); *Cahill v E. B. & A. L. Stone & Co.*, 153 Cal. 571, 96 PAC 84 (1908);

Ziehm v *Vale*, 98 Ohio St. 306, 120 N. E. 702 (1918); *Central Branch U. P. RR* v *Henigh*, 23 Kan. 244 (1880); *Robinson* v *Oregon Short Line & Utah RR*, 7 Utah 493, 27 PAC 689 (1891); *Barnhill's Adm.* v *Mt. Morgan Coal Co.*, 215 Fed. 608 (1910); *Emerson Adm.* v *Peteler*, 35 Minn. 481, 29 N. W. 311 (1886); *Catlett* v *St. Louis, Iron MT., & Southern RR*, 57 Ark. 461, 21 3 W 1062 (1893); *Underwood* v *Western & Atlantic RR*, 105 Ga. 48, 31 S. E. 123 (1898); *Swartwood* v *Louisville & Nashville RR*, 111 S. W. (Ky.) 305 (1908); *Zigman* v *Beebe & Runyan Furniture Co.*, 97 Neb. 689, 151 N. W. 166 (1915).

42. *Brinkley Car-Works* v *Cooper*, 31 S. W. 154 (1895); *Duffy* v *Sable Ironworks*, 210 Pa. 326, 59 ATL 1110 (1904); *Kinchlow* v *Midland Elev. Co.*, 57 Kan. 374, 46 PAC 703 (1896); *Schmidt* v *Kansas City Distilling*, 90 Mo. 284, 1 S. W. 865 (1886); *Briscoe* v *Henderson Lighting & Power Co.*, 148 N. C. 396, 62 S. E. 600 (1908).

43. *Kopplekom* v *Colo. Cement Co.*, 16 Col. App. 278, 64 PAC 1047 (1901); *Snare & Triest Co.*, v *Friedman*, 169 Fed. 1 (1909); *Foster* v *Lusk*, 129 Ark. 1, 194 S. W. 855 (1917). But see *Missouri, Kansas & Texas RR* v *Edwards*, 90 Tex. 65, 36 S. W. 430 (1896).

44. *Penso* v *McCormick*, 125 Ind. 716, 25 N. E. 156 (1890); *Union Pacific RR* v *McDonald*, 152 U.S. 262 (1894); *Roman* v *City of Leaverworth*, 90 Kan. 379, 133 PAC 551 (1913); *Carr* v *So. Pa Traction Co.*, 253 Pa. 274 (1916); *Erickson* v *Great Northern RR*, 82 Minn. 60, 84 N. W. 462 (1900).

45. *Peirce* v *Lyden*, 157 Fed. 552 (1907); *Brown* v *City of Minneapolis*, 136 Minn. 177, 161 N. W. 503 (1917).

46. *Machey* v *Mayor of City of Vicksburg*, 64 Miss. 777, 250 178 (1887); *Baxter* v *Park*, 184 N. W. (So. Dak.) 198 (1921). (But see *Zagar* v *Union Pacific RR*, 214 PAC (Kan.) 107 (1923), where the Kansas court cited *United Zinc & Chemical* v *Britt*, 258 U.S. 268 (1922), in ruling that an excavation not visible off the company's property did not constitute an attractive nuisance.) *Cincinnati & Hammond Spring Co.* v *Brown*, 32 Ind. App. 58, 69 N. E. 197 (1903); *Harris* v *Cowles*, 38 Wash. 331, 80 PAC 537 (1905).

47. *Brown* v *Salt Lake City*, 33 Utah 222, 93 PAC 570 (1908); *City of Indianapolis* v *Williams*, 58 Ind. App 447, 108 N. E. 382 (1915); *Salladay* v *Old Dominon Copper Mining & Smelting Co.*, 12 Ariz. 124, 100 PAC 441 (1909) (an open irrigation flume in which a three-year-old girl drowned); *Riggle* v *Lens*, 71 Ore. 125, 142 PAC 346 (1914).

48. *Tucker* v *Draper*, 62 Neb. 66, 86 N. W. 917 (1901) (a disused open well); (S. C. Commissioner Roscoe Pound concurring); *Franks* v *Southern Cotton Oil Co.*, 78 S. C. 10, 58 S. E. 960 (1907); *Bjork* v *City of Tacoma*, 135 PAC 1005 (1913); *Coeur d'Alene Lumber* v *Thompson*, 215 Fed. (9th Circ.) 8 (1914). But see *Dobbins* v *Missouri, Kansas, & Texas RR*, 91 Tex. 60, 41 S. W. 62 (1897) (an artificially created trench with water in which a two-year-old girl drowned); *Gillespie* v *McGowan*, 100 Pa. 144 (1882); *Klix, Adm.* v *Nieman*, 68 Wis. 271, 32 N. W. 223 (1887); *Peters* v *Bowman*, 115 Cal. 345, 47 PAC 113 (1896).

49. See, for example, *Garza* v *Texas Mexican RR*, Tex. Civ App., 41 S. W. 172 (1897) (a standing railroad car not intrinsically attractive); *N.Y., N. H. & Hartford RR* v *Fruchter*, 260 U.S. 141 (1922) (no implied invitation to climb the girder of a bridge which had live wires close to it); *San Antonio & Arkansas Pass RR* v *Morgan*, 92 Tex. 98, 46 S. W. 28 (1898) (a turntable not alleged to be attractive); *Curtis* v *Ten-*

nino Stone Quarries, 37 Wash. 355, 79 PAC 955 (1904) (machinery not attractive to children).

In 1920 the Illinois Appellate Court anticipated the Second Restatement's abandonment of the "attractiveness" requirement when it argued that dangerous electric lines in a tree that children might be expected to climb would suffice to hold a company liable for injury to a trespassing child despite their finding that the wires were not themselves alluring. *Ft Wayne & N. I. Traction Co.* v *Stark*, 74 Ind. App. 669, 127 N. E. 460 (1920).

50. *St. Louis, Iron Mt & So. RR* v *Waggoner*, 166 S. W. (Ark.) 948 (1914) (an empty alcohol barrel not known to be dangerous); *Kressine* v *Janesville Traction Co*, 175 Wis. 192, 184 N. W. 777 (1921) (a stationary trolley car sufficiently disconnected and disabled).

51. *St. Louis, Vandalia, & Terre Haute RR* v *Bell*, 81 Ill. 76 (1876) (a turntable too isolated from public or noncompany property to be visible or attractive); *Meyer* v *Menominee & Marinette Light & Traction Co*, 151 Wis. 279, 138 N. W. 1008 (1912) (an electrical wire not noticeable off the premises); *Ramsay* v *Tuthill Bldg. Material Co.*, 295 Ill. 395, 129 N. E. 127 (1920) (a ten-year-old boy killed by a sandslide in the company's bins, where the court said "there is no implied invitation from the mere existence of a dangerous attraction which is not discoverable off the premises."); *United Zinc & Chemical Co.* v *Britt*, 258 U.S. 268 (1922) (two boys killed swimming in a pool of water and sulfuric acid left in the basement of a building). Oliver Wendell Holmes Jr. wrote the majority opinion, denying recovery because the danger was not discoverable off the premises, and Holmes has been treated as the author of this exception to the rule. As the cases cited before *Britt* in this note make clear, he was not its author, but after *Britt*, his opinion would be the one critics of the exception would deal with. See *Hayko* v *Colo. & Utah Coal Co.*, 77 Colo. 143, 235 PAC 373 (1925), and Leon Green, "The Basis of Responsibility in Tort," *Michigan Law Review* 21 (1925): 495, at 521, where Green rejected "the idea of 'attractiveness'" and anticipated its abandonment as an element of liability in section 339 of the *Second Restatement of Torts*.

52. *Ky. Central RR* v *Gastineau's Adm*, 83 Ky. 119 (1885) (a fourteen-year-old boy too old to be unaware of dangers); *Bates* v *Nashville, C. & St. L. RR*, 90 Tenn. 36, 15 S. W. 1069 (1891) (a boy who said he was "going to get on" a moving turntable "or die" was aware of the dangers, and the effort required to unblock and rotate the turntable too substantial (three or four older boys needed to remove bolts and crossties and to turn the turntable)); *Stamford Oil Mill Co* v *Barnes*, 103 Tex. 409, 128 S. W. 375 (1907) (a boy thoroughly familiar with machinery); *Taylor* v *Manila Elect RR & Light Co.*, 16 Phil. 8 (1910) (a fifteen-year-old boy too familiar with dangers); *Central of Ga. RR* v *Robins*, 95 SO (Ala.) 367 (1923) (a fifteen-year-old boy too aware of dangers); *Branan* v *Wimsatt*, 54 U.S. App. (D. C.), 394, 298 Fed. 833 (1924) (a twelve-year-old girl too aware of dangers).

53. Lawrence Friedman, *Total Justice* (New York: Russell Sage Foundation, 1985), 63. In two of these forty-two cases (from 1873 to 1917) the jury had found for the company and the high court set a figure itself. Fifteen of the cases were turntable cases; for these the average award was higher—$3,538. These figures were consistent with those Friedman reports for Alemeda County, California, tort awards by

juries, 1880–1900. See Lawrence Friedman, "Civil Wrongs: Personal Injury Law in the Late 19th Century," *Amer. Bar Assoc. Res. Journal* (1987): 351, at 358.

54. Illinois, Indiana, Maine, Massachusetts, Minnesota, Colorado, Nebraska, New Hampshire, New York, Oregon, Wisconsin, West Virginia, Connecticut, and Missouri had five-thousand-dollar wrongful death limits (*Wilmot v McPadden*, 65 Atl 157 [1906]; *Nagel v Mo. Pac. RR*, 75 Mo. 653 [1882]; C. Patterson, *Railway Accident Law* [Phila. 1886], sec. 414, p. 494.) Most states limited these damages further to income the child might have earned until age twenty-one. See *Clark v Manchester*, 62 N. H. 577 (1883); and *Caldwell v Brown*, 53 Pa. 453 (1866). Only Louisiana appeared to sanction damages for the pain and suffering the child endured before death. (*Westerfield v Levis*, 43 La. An. 63, 9 So. 52 [1891].) Other states limited suits by the guardian (where the child had survived the accident) to the doctor's bills, the parent's lost labor in caring for the child, and the diminished value of the child's services to the parent to age twenty-one. (See, for example, *Ft. Worth & Denver City RR v Measles*, 81 Tex. 474, 17 S. W. 124 [1891]). And, as Edward Purcell has recently pointed out, when railroads managed to remove the case on diversity to a more distant and unfamiliar federal court for trial, plaintiffs sometimes decided to reduce their claim to $1,999, a sum just below the jurisdictional limit (after 1887) for the federal courts to avoid this removal. (Purcell, *Litigation and Inequality: Federal Diversity Jurisdiction in Industrial America, 1870–1958* [New York: Oxford University Press, 1992], 92–94).

55. Friedman, "Civil Wrongs," 351 at 366 n. 41; U.S. Dept. of Commerce, Bureau of the Census, *1980: Census of Population*, vol. 1, chap. C (Washington, D.C.: GPO, 1983), table 92.

56. *Kansas Central RR v Fitzsimmons*, 22 Kan. 686 (1879); *Nagel v Missouri Pacific RR*, 75 Mo. 653 (1882) at 663a; *City of Indianapolis v Emmelman*, 9 N. E. 155 (1886) (an excavated creek bed at a street crossing, leading to the drowning of a five-year-old boy); *Westerfield v Levis*, 9 So 52 (1891) (an untended gravel roller pulled by a mule) (In this Louisiana case the jury had found the five-year old boy contributorily negligent and gave the victory to the defendant. The court, guided by the Louisiana Code's comparative-negligence rule, reversed the verdict and directed an award of one thousand dollars); *City of Pekin v McMahon*, 39 N. E. 484 (1895) (a city-owned lot with deep water pits and poor fences); *Price v Atchison Water Co.*, 58 Kan. 551, 50 PAC 450 (1897) (an eleven-year-old boy drowned in a reservoir); *Harriman v Pittsburgh, Chicago & St. Louis RR*, 45 Ohio St. 11, 12 N. E. 451, at 458 (1887). Justice Marshall Williams was referring to signal torpedoes negligently left by the railroad tracks (which tracks were themselves also "inviting to children and likely to tempt them to wander and play"). But he was also remarkably frank in dicta (perhaps at the request of formalist colleagues)—regarding the rationale for the doctrine in the original turntable cases. Of these, he wrote, "It is said children had an implied invitation to go upon them because their being attracted to them might have been reasonably expected. . . . There is in reality no invitation; it is implied from slight circumstances" (458).

57. Thomas Cooley, *A Treatise on the Law of Torts or the Wrongs which Arise Independent of Contracts* (Chicago, 1880), 606, 606n; Christopher Patterson, *Railway Accident Law* (Philadelphia, 1886), sec. 196; Thomas Sherman and Amasa

Redfield, *A Treatise on the Law of Negligence*, 5th ed. (1898), vol. 1; sec 31; Cf. Thomas Atkins Street, *The Foundations of Legal Liability: A Presentation of the Theory and Development of The Common Law* (Northport, N.Y., Edw. Thompson, 1906), 1:160.

58. *Clark* v *Manchester*, 62 N. H. 577, at 580 (1883); *Frost* v *Eastern RR*, 62 N. H. 220, 9 Atl 790, at 791 (1887).

59. *Daniels* v *N. E. RR*, 154 Mass. 349, 28 N. E. 283 (1891). See also *Gay Admin.* v *Essex Elec. St. Ry Co.*, 159 Mass. 238, 34 N. E. 186 (1893); and *Cherney* v *Fitchburg RR*, 160 Mass. 211, at 214 (Holmes, J.) (1893); *Walsh* v *Fitchburg RR*, 145 N.Y. 30, 39 N. E. 1068 (1895), where Justice Rufus Peckham distinguished the English precedent, *Lynch* v *Nurdin*, by emphasizing that the attractive object there (an egg merchant's cart) had been left in a public street, incorrectly representing Lord Dennman's opinion to apply only to children playing in a nontresapatory manner with dangerous and negligently maintained property.

60. *Holbrook* v *Aldrich*, 168 Mass. 16, 46 N. E. 115 (1897). Note that the facts of this case had clearly allowed Holmes, had he been so inclined, to find the plaintiff to have been an invitee, or at the very least, a licencee. It will come as no surprise that Holmes cited *Mangan*. Holmes's *Holbrook* opinion is quoted in Jeremiah Smith, "Liability of Landowners to Children Entering without Permission," *Harvard Law Review* 11 (1898): 349; *Delaware, L. & W. RR* v *Reich*, 61 N.J.L. 635, 40 Atl 682 (1898); *Paolino* v *McKendall*, 24 R. I. 432, 53 Atl 268 (1902); and numerous other early-twentieth-century eastern decisions.

61. J. Smith, "Liability of Landowners," 349, 435, 352, 355, 352 n. 1, 353 n. 243, 354, 353, 436 (1898).

62. He is cited at length in *Delaware, L. & W. RR* v *Reich*, 40 Atl 682 (1898); *Ryan* v *Towar*, 128 Mich. 463, 87 N. W. 644 (1901); *Paolino* v *McKendall*, 24 R. I. 432, 53 Atl 268 (1902); and numerous other early-twentieth-century opinions involving injury to trespassing children.

63. Chief Justice William Magie in *Turness* v *N.Y., S., & W. RR*, 61 N.J.L. 314, 40 Atl 614, at 615 (1898) (a turntable case). The rule's logic, to Magie, was also "absurd." "A solid foundation"—Justice William Gumere (albeit with three dissenters) in *Delaware, L. & W. RR* v *Reich*, 61 N.J.L. 635, 40 Atl 682 (1898) (another turntable case in which a thirteen-year-old girl's foot was crushed as she tried to rescue her six-year-old brother from a similar fate); "what a constant menace."—President Judge Henry Brannon in *Uthermohlen* v *Bogg's Run Machinery and Manufacturing Co.*, 50 W.Va. 457, 40 S. E. 410, at 412 & 414 (1901) (involving a coal car cable's pulleys that caught a boy's leg). Cf. *Ritz* v *City of Wheeling*, 31 S. E. 993 (W.Va. S. C.) (1898) (a reservoir drowning). (Admirers of West Virginia Judge Marmaduke Dent may be surprised to learn that he did not dissent from either of these opinions. The politics of opinions is an understudied [and difficult to document] subject; conceivably Dent was engaged in trading votes.)

64. *Ryan* v *Towar*, 87 N. W. 644 (1901); *Paolino* v *McKendall*, 53 Atl 268 (1902); *Walker's Adm.* v *Potomac F. & P. RR*, 105 Va. 226, 53 S. E. 113 (1906) (a turntable case); *Wilmot* v *McPadden*, 79 Ct. 367, 65 Atl 157 (1906) (a house demolition case); *Wheeling & Lake Erie RR* v *Harvey*, 77 Ohio 235, 83 N. E. 66 (1907) (a turntable case); *Thompson* v *Baltimore & Ohio RR*, 218 Pa. 444, 67 Atl 768 (1907) (another turntable case); *Briscoe* v *Henderson Lighting & Power Co.*, 148 N. C. 396, 62 S. E.

600 (1908) (a hot water well in an alley); *Bottum's Adm.* v *Hawks*, 84 Vt. 370, 79 Atl 858 (1911) (a mill conduit drowning); *Nelson* v *Burnham & Morrill Co.*, 114 Me. 213, 95 Atl 1029 (1915) (an elevator shaft in a canning factory).

65. Justice Frank Hooker in *Ryan* v *Towar* (Michigan) at 648; Justice D. Newlin Fell in *Thompson* v *Baltimore & Ohio RR*, 67 Atl 768 (1907) at 770; Justice George Powers in *Bottum's Adm.* v *Hawks*, 79 Atl 858 (1911) at 860; Justice Augustus Summers in *Wheeling & Lake Erie RR* v *Harvey*, 83 N. E. 66 (1907) at 72.

66. I prefer this term to one I regard as less precise ("formalism"). Lon Fuller's description of the "doctrinal" jurist is useful; he is one who "does not consider that it is the primary function of judges or legal scholars to weigh the practical consequences of deciding a particular case one way or the other. Rather [he] regards them as having a purely deductive function. The starting point for the deciding of any case is to be found in certain premises dictated by the nature of law and legal relationships. Each relationship or transaction has its 'essential nature.' " Lon Fuller, *Basic Contract Law* (St Paul: West, 1947), 520.

67. Justice Samuel Hunter in *Dublin Cotton Oil Co.* v *Jarrard*, Texas Ct. Civ. App., 40 S. W. 531, at 534 (1897).

68. Some 114 of 136 accidents suits (83.8 percent) resolved at a level reported in published reports involved boys; some 81.4 percent of those in which the child's age could be ascertained (105 of 129) were ten years of age or younger.

69. Chief Justice Albert Whitfield in *Temple* v *McComb City Electric Light & Power Co.*, 89 Miss. 1, 42 SO 874, at 875 (1907); Justice Daniel Valentine in *Kansas Central RR* v *Fitzsimmons*, 22 Kan. 686 at 691 (1879); Needham Collier in *Central Law Journal* 72 (1914): 122; Browne, *American Law Review* 31 (1897): 904.

This masculine appreciation for the vigorous activities of small boys could cut two ways in these cases: Justice William Ellis flavored his dissent in a Florida high court case in 1925, allowing recovery by an eight-year-old boy who lost two fingers to an uninsulated wire passing through a magnolia tree near his school, with gender-specific language. The boy had been picking magnolia blossoms on a spring day. Ellis dismissed this behavior: "Boys rather effect a contempt and disdain for such girlish trophies" as flowers (*Stark* v *Holtzclaw*, 90 Fla. 207, 105 SO 330, at 335 [1925]).

70. Justice Daniel Hydrick in *McLendon* v *Hampton Cotton Mills*, 95 S. E. (S. C.) 781 at 782 (1917), (a six-year-old boy drowned in a reservoir); *Ryan* v *Towar*, 87 N. W. 644 (1901) at 645; *Heva* v *Seattle School District #1*, 110 Wash. 622, 188 PAC 776 (1920); *Twist* v *Winona*, 39 Minn. 165, 39 N. W. 402 (1888); *Iamurri* v *Saginaw City Gas Co.*, 148 Mich. 27, 111 N. W. 884 (1907); *Missouri, Kansas & Texas RR* v *Edwards*, 90 Tex. 65, 36 S. W. 430 (1896); *Ritz* v *Wheeling*, 45 W.Va. 267, 31 SE 993, at 996 (1898); *Nicolosi* v *Clark*, 169 Cal. 746, 147 PAC 971 (1915) (a ten-year-old boy took dynamite caps from a road construction box); *Catlett* v *St. Louis, Iron MT. & Southern RR*, 57 Ark. 461, 21 S. W. 1062 (1893) (a boy swinging on the ladder of a moving freight train); Justice S. M. Weaver in *Edginton* v *Burlington RR*, 90 N. W. 95 (1902) at 104 (a turntable case).

71. Lyman Wilson (a Cornell Law School professor), "Limitations on the Attractive Nuisance Doctrine," *North Carolina Law Review* 1 (1923): 162, at 164 n. 7–10.

72. See the cases cited in notes 69–70.

73. See cases in note 70.

74. Thompson, *Law of Negligence*, sec. 1040; Friedman, *Total Justice*, 56, 63.

75. U.S. Bureau of Census, *Twelvth Census: Manufacturing: 1900* 8:983–89.

76. Bureau of Census, *12th C.: Abstract: 1900*, at 3233; Bur. of Cen., *12th C: 1900: Mnfg.*, at pt. 1, lxv.

77. U.S. Bureau of Census, *Abstract of the 12th Census of the U.S. (1900)* (Washington, D.C.: GPO, 1902), table 51, p. 66; *Census of the U.S. (1900), III, Vital Statistics*, pt. 1, table 26.

78. U.S. Bureau of Census, *Twelveth Census: 1900: Manufacturing* 8:983–89.

79. Bruce Trimble, *Chief Justice Waite: Defender of the Public Interest* (Princeton: Princeton University Press, 1938), 18–19. *Frost v Eastern RR*, 62 N. H. 220, 9 Atl 790, at 791 (1887), and *Ritz v City of Wheeling*, 31 S. E. (W.Va.) 993 at 996, (1898), offer such examples, and these were then quoted by several eastern courts following the *Frost* precedent.

80. See, for example, Richard Posner, "A Theory of Negligence," *Journal of Legal Studies* 1 (1972): 29; Richard Posner, *Economic Analysis of Law*, 3rd ed. (Boston: Little, Brown, 1986), 46–47; Richard Posner and William M. Landes, *The Economic Structure of Tort Law* (Cambridge, Mass.: Harvard University Press, 1987), 86–87, 95–97.

81. *Tucker v Draper*, 62 Neb. 66, 86 N. W. 917, at 920 (1901). (Commissioner Roscoe Pound concurred in this opinion.); *Chicago & E. R. Co v Fox*, Ind. App., 70 N. E. 81, at 84 (1904); *Nashville Lumber v Busbee*, 100 Ark. 76, 139 S. W. 301 (1911); *Briggs v Consol. Barbed Wire Co.*, 60 Kan. 217, 56 PAC 4 (1899); Justice S. L. Mestrezat, dissenting, in *Thompson v Baltimore & Ohio RR*, 218 Pa. 444, 67 ATL 768, at 775 (1907). Cf. *Whirley v Whiteman*, 38 Tenn. (1 Head) 610 (1858), and *Schmidt v Kansas City Distilling*, 90 Mo. 284, 1 S. W. 865, at 868 (1886), where the summary of trial court testimony reports that the "defendant could have put up a fence enclosing the [scalding water] pipes without difficulty."

A later opinion by the Nebraska Supreme Court may serve as an even better example of this cost-benefit analysis in action: In *B. & O. RR v Krayenbuhl*, 65 Neb. 889, 903–4, 91 N. W. 880, 882–83 (1902), Supreme Court Commissioner I. L. Albert observed, in a case involving an unlocked, unfenced turntable and a trespassing child: "The danger . . . may be lessened by the use of a lock . . . ; the interference with the proper use of the turntable occasioned by the use of such lock is so slight that it is outweighed by the danger to be anticipated from an omission to use it." Commissioner Albert allowed that turntables were to be distinguished in this regard from ponds on vacant lots: "The public good would not require the owner of a vacant lot on which there is a pond to fill up the pond or enclose the lot with an impassable wall to insure the safety of children resorting to it, because the burden of doing so is out of proportion to the danger to be anticipated from leaving it undone." (Noted in Posner and Landes, *Economic Structure of Tort Law*, 86).

82. J. Smith, "Liability of Landowners," 360–61, 369, 439, 443.

83. Justice Andrew Cobb in *Underwood v Western & Atlanta RR*, 105 Ga. 48, 31 S. E. 123, at 124 (1898); President Judge Henry Brannon in *Uthermohlen v Bogg's Run Mining & Mnfg. Co.*, 50 W.Va. 457, 40 S. E. 410, at 414 (1901). Cf. *Harris v Cowles*, 38 Wash. 331, 80 PAC 537 (1905); Justice Frank Hooker in *Ryan v Towar*, 128 Mich. 463, 87 N. W. 644, at 645 (1901); Justice William Gumere in *Delaware, L. & W. RR v Reich*, 61 N.J.L. 635, 40 Atl 682, at 683 (1898); Justice George Powers in *Bottum's Adm. v Hawks*, 84 Vt. 370, 79 Atl 858, at 865 (1911).

84. Chief Justice Edward Kent in *Salladay v Old Dominion Copper Mining & Smelting Co.*, 12 Ariz. 124, 100 PAC 441, at 442 (1909). (Cf. the language of Lord Justice Clerk in *Ross v Keith*, 16 Scot. Session Cases, 4th series, 86 at 90 [1888].) Kent, a Harvard graduate, regarded open flume irrigation ditches to be necessary for the "prosperity" of miners and farmers. (The Arizona court *did* accept the rule in more explicitly "attractive" invitation cases such as turntables.)

85. Justice James Whitfield in *Stark v Holtzclaw*, 90 Fla. 207, 105 SO 330, at 334 (1924) (an electrocution case); Street, *Foundations of Legal Liability*, 1:160. And see notes 58–67.

86. Justice William Allen in *Clark v Manchester*, 62 N. H. 577, at 580 (1883) (a drowning); Chief Justice James Mitchell (dissenting) in *Duffy v Sable Ironworks*, 210 Pa. 326, 59 Atl 1110, at 1102 (1904) (a hot grease vat accident); Justice John Buchanan in *Walker's Adm. v Potomac, F. & P. RR*, 105 Va. 226, 53 S. E. 113 (1906) (a turntable case); Justice D. Newlin Fell in *Thompson v Baltimore & Ohio RR*, 218 Pa. 444, 67 Atl 768, at 770 (1907) (a turntable case); Justice William Gumere in *Delaware, L. & W. RR v Reich*, 40 Atl 682 (1898) (a turntable case). Chief Justice Henry Brannon in *Uthermohlen v Bogg's Run Mach. & Mnfg. Co.*, 40 S. E. 410 (1901) (pulleys of a coal car cable catching a boy's leg).

Some of our "formalist" critics of the rule also seem to have identified with the ideology of "possessive individualism," laissez-faire, or social Darwinism. (See text at notes 85–87.) I do not regard this ideological perspective as being the determinative element in their judicial philosophy; this I believe to be doctrinal formalism. But I recognize that the two perspectives were sometimes present in the same opinion and that they were often complimentary.

87. Justice George Powers in *Bottum's Adm. v Hawks*, 84 Vt. 370, 79 Atl 858, at 864 & 865 (1911) (a drowning); Chief Justice Albert Savage in *Nelson v Burnham & Morrill Co.*, 114 Me. 213, 95 Atl 1029, at 1032 (1915) (an elevator accident). Cf. Justice James Campbell in *Hargeaves v Deacon*, 25 Mich. 1 (1872).

88. Justice Oliver Wendell Holmes Jr., describing Justice Clarke's dissent from *Britt* to Sir Fredrick Pollock, March 29, 1922, *Holmes-Pollock Letters*, ed. M. DeW. Howe (Cambridge, Mass.: Harvard University Press, 1941), 2:92.

89. Justice Whitefield in *Stark v Holtzclaw*, 105 So 330 (1925).

90. Justice Frank Hooker in *Ryan v Towar*, 87 N. W. 644 (1901) at 650 (a waterwheel accident); Justice Augustus Summers in *Wheeling & Lake Erie RR v Harvey*, 83 N. E. 66 (1907) at 72 (a turntable case).

The *Keffe* case's trial judge, it will be recalled, also preferred "resort . . . to . . . the legislature" for "protection" against "accidents of this nature" and refused to depart from "established principles of law" himself (*Central Law Journal* 2 [Mar. 12, 1875]: 176). See also Justice Leroy Denman in *Dobbins v Mo, K. & T. RR*, 91 Tex. 60, 41 S. W. 62 (1897) (a drowning): Courts "yielding to the hardships of individual instances where owners have been guilty of moral, though not legal, wrongs . . . have passed beyond the safe and ancient landmarks of the common law, and assumed legislative function's imposing a duty where none existed. [Legislatures] may, and doubtless should, . . . compel the enclosure of pools, etc. . . . . attractive and dangerous, and impose criminal and civil liability."

91. Justice J. J. DeHaven in *Barrett v Southern Pacific RR*, 91 Cal. 296, 27 PAC 666, at 667 (1891) (a turntable case) (rejecting *Frost* as "a departure from well-settled principles"). Justice Frank Doster in *Consol. Elec. Light & Power v Healy*,

425

65 Kan. 798, 70 PAC 884 (1902) (an electrocution case), also implied that precedent was on the side of the attractive nuisance rule when he described it as "the sounder exposition of the law." A few years later Doster while identifying himself with the socialism of Eugene Debs, would speak of the law as a "science." (Michael Brodhead, *Persevering Populist: The Life of Frank Doster* [Reno: University of Nevada Press, 1969], 144–45).

92. Comment [Jerrilyn Marston], "The Creation of a Common Law Rule: The Fellow Servant Rule, 1837–1860," *Univ. of Pennsylvania Law Review* 132 (1984): 579.

93. *Barrett v Southern Pacific RR*, 91 Cal. 296, 27 Pac 666 (1891) at 667.

It is likely that the "leading case" *Stout* decision, coming as it did from the portals of the U.S. Supreme Court, carried the weight of "authority." Tennessee's *Whirley* decision was certainly comparable to Stout in its "principled" character, but not in its import.

Moreover, a few "frontier" western jurisdictions were still (federal) territorial courts, or had benches whose member, at the time of their "first impression" attractive-nuisance ruling, had recently served as territorial judges. By virtue of the fact that as territorial judges they had accepted the U.S. Supreme Court's opinion as stare decisis, these jurists may have been predisposed to accept *Stout* as guiding precedent. This may explain why Chief Justice Edward Kent of the Arizona Territorial Court announced the adoption of the rule for the Arizona Territory in 1909, for *turntable* accidents, but not for a three-year-old girl drowned in the open flume of an irrigation ditch that was necessary for the "prosperity" of miners and farmers; property with an artificially made, dangerous character did not have to be "child-proof" (Kent's quotation marks). (*Salladay v Old Dominion Copper Mining & Smelting Co.*, 12 Ariz. 124, 100 PAC 441 [1909].)

I was surprised to see that only 5 percent of the attractive nuisance cases reported between 1873 and 1925 were in the federal courts; I had thought that the diversity suit would have generated more business. I detected only one case where a party appealed the judgement of a state high court (*Friedman v Snare & Triest Co*, 71 N.J.L. 605, 61 Atl 401 [1905]) (reversing a lower court award of seven thousand dollars in an accident involving children playing on unstably piled I-beams that then fell) to a federal court: *Snare & Triest Co v Friedman*, 169 Fed. (3rd circuit) 1, at 9 (1909) (in diversity, where the court denied the company's claim that the state court decision was binding, absent a state statute on the subject, citing *Swift v Tyson* [16 Pet. (US) 1, 1842]; it then cited *Stout* as "the rule of law.") Perhaps those corporations doing business in more than one state had been prompted by the *Stout* decision to take adequate remedial action to reduce the likelihood of injuries to trespassing children (for evidence of this see text at note 123). Perhaps the consistency of the U.S. Supreme Court's position on the attractive nuisance rule (as in *Union Pacific RR v McDonald*, 152 U.S. 262 [1894]) led companies to settle out of court or to capitulate after trial at the federal district level. Perhaps 5 percent is not an unsubstantial percentage of the reported cases. After all, many of the corporations were small, intrastate entities. Edward Purcell has made clear that railroad corporations often did seek to remove tort cases to the federal courts in these years where a majority were settled, dismissed, or voluntarily discontinued. Plaintiffs often faced greater distances for witnesses to travel and greater delays between commencement of their action and the trial date. But plaintiffs could forestall this removal by limiting their claims to $1,999. Surely this led to a higher than usual percentage of cases in state courts. (*Litigation and Inequality,* 50, 85–90.)

94. Chief Justice David Agnew in *Hydraulic Works v Orr,* 83 Pa. St 332 (1877) at 336; Justice Eugene Gary in *Franks v Southern Cotton Oil Co.,* 78 S. C. 10, 58 S. E. 960 (1907) (a drowning); Justice J. J. DeHaven in *Barrett v Southern Pacific RR,* 27 Pac 666 (1891); Justice S. L. Mestrezat (dissenting) in *Thompson v Baltimore & Ohio RR,* 67 Atl 768 (1907) at 774.

95. Chief Justice Agnew in *Hydraulic Works v Orr,* 83 Pa. St. 332 (1877) at 336; Justice S. M. Weaver in *Edgington v Burlington RR,* 116 Iowa 410, 90 N. W. 95, at 97 (1902) (a turntable case); Justice W. H. Holt in *Kentucky Central RR v Gastineau's Adm.,* 82 Ky. 119, at 125 (1885). Cf. Justice William Morrow in *Coeur d'Alene Lumber v Thompson,* 215 Fed (9th Ctr.) 8, at 13 (1914) (a drowning).

96. Justice Isaac Gordon in *Biddle & Wife v Hestonville, M. & F. P. RR,* 112 Pa. St. 551, 4 Atl 485 (1886) (a street car accident); Justice Henry Lamm in *Berry v St. Louis, M. & S. E. RR,* 214 Mo. 593, 114 S. W. 27, at 31 (1908) (a turntable case).

97. *Berry v St. Louis, M. & S. E. RR,* 114 S. W. 27 (1908) at 33; Justice R. M. Wanamaker in *Ziehm v Vale,* 98 Ohio St. 306, 120 N. E. 702 at 704 (1918) (an automobile case). (This is the Ohio case that reversed the rejection of the rule in the turntable case described in the opening paragraphs of this essay.)

98. *Hydraulic Works v Orr,* 83 Pa. St. 332 (1877) at 336; *Berry v St. Louis, M. & S. E. RR,* 114 S. W. 27 (1908) at 33.

99. In *Price v Atchison Water Co.,* 50 PAC (KAN.) 450 (1897).

100. John Andrew Hamilton, "Denman, Lord Thomas," *Dictionary of National Biography,* ed. Sir Leslie Stephen and Sir Sidney Lee (London: Oxford University Press, 1917–), 5:808–10; Sir William Holdsworth, *A History of English Law* (London: Methuen, 1965), 15:395ff.

101. James G. Rogers, *American Bar Leaders* (Chicago: ABA, 1932); *Union Pacific RR v McDonald,* 152 U.S. 262 (1894).

102. Dillon, "Property—Its Rights and Duties in Our Legal and Social Systems," *American Law Review* 29 (1895): 161.

103. Arnold M. Paul, *Conservative Crisis and the Rule of Law: Attitudes of Bench and Bar, 1887–1895* (Gloucester, Mass.: P. Smith, 1976), 29, 79, 80; Edwin Gre, "Dillon's Rule and the Cooley Doctrine: Reflections of the Political Culture," *Journal of Urban History* 8 (1982): 271 at 288.

104. Tyrrell Williams, "Thompson, Seymour" *Dictionary of American Biography,* ed. Allen Johnson and Dumas Malone, 20 vols. (New York: C. Scribner's Sons, 1937), 18:471; Thompson, *Law of Negligence,* 168; Paul, *Conservative Crisis,* 43, 48–49, 57, 183.

105. *National Cyclopedia of American Biography* 12:125; Michael Brodhead, *Persevering Populist: The Life of Frank Doster* (Reno: University of Nevada Press, 1969), 8–12, 47, 59–60, 88, 102, 137, 144–45.

106. Could he have met with and discussed the issues of the *Keffe* case with his Harvard Law School peer, Justice George Young of the Minnesota bench during this time?

107. Zechariah Chafee Jr., "Smith, Jeremiah," *Dictionary of American Biography* 12:292–93; Jeremiah Smith, "Sequel to Workmen's Compensation Acts," *Harvard Law Review* 27 (1913): 235.

108. Grandfather Jackson was quite comfortable with the way that the late medi-

eval English courts had generated solutions to the legal problems of property law: "I was well convinced that the system of real [property] actions established by the common law needed only to be known, to be universally approved." His *Treatise on the Pleadings and Practice in Real Actions* (Boston, 1828) won the praise of New York's Chancellor James Kent. Sheldon Novick, *Honorable Justice: The Life of Oliver Wendell Holmes, Jr.* (Boston: Little, Brown, 1989), 6.

109. Novick, *Honorable Justice*, passim; Felix Frankfurter, "Holmes, Oliver Wendell Jr.," *Dictionary of American Biography*, supplement 1, 417–27.

110. Novick, *Honorable Justice*, 202; Gary Aichecle, *Oliver Wendell Holmes, Jr.: Soldier, Scholar, Jurist* (Boston: Twayne, 1989), 143 (Holmes had written to Dean John Wigmore of Harvard Law in 1915 that this "squashy sentimentalism" made him "puke."); *Holmes-Einstein Letters*, ed. James Peabody (New York: St. Martin's Press, 1964), 48, 58, 106; Holmes, "The Path of the Law" in *Collected Legal Papers* (New York: Harcourt, Brace, 1920), 171; Mark DeWolfe Howe, *Justice Holmes: Vol. II: The Proving Years, 1870–1882* (Cambridge: Belknap, 1963), 256.

111. I find Patrick J. Kelley, "A Critical Analysis of Holmes' Theory of Torts," *Washington Univ. Law Quarterly* 61 (1983): 681 (on Mill), and H. L. Pohlman, *Justice Oliver Wendell Holmes, Jr., and Utilitarian Jurisprudence* (Cambridge, Mass.: Harvard University Press, 1984) (on Bentham and Austin), convincing on this score regarding Holmes's legal *philosophy*, but see text at note 114 regarding Holmes judicial *practice*. Holmes's "legal theologian" reference was, of course, to Dean C. C. Langdell of Harvard Law in Holmes's review of Langdell's *Selection of Cases on the Law of Contracts*, 2nd ed., in *American Law Review* 14 (March 1880): 234.

112. Oliver Wendell Holmes, *The Common Law*, ed. Mark DeWolfe Howe (Boston: Little, Brown, 1963), 5.

113. See Patrick Kelley, "Holmes on the Supreme Judicial Court: The Theorist as Judge," in *The History of the Law in Massachusetts: The Supreme Judicial Court, 1692–1992*, ed. Russell Osgood (Boston: Supreme Judicial Court, 1992), 275–352.

114. *Heard v Sturgis*, 146 Mass. 545, at 548–49 (1888) (citing Hobbes, Bentham, and Austin); Novick, *Honorable Justice*, 184; *Dempsey v Chambers*, 154 Mass. 330, at 331, 28 N.E. 279, at 280 (1891). Cf. Holmes in *Hicks v Guinness*, 269 U.S. 71 (1925); *Stack v NY, NH & Hartford RR*, 177 Mass. 155, at 157, 58 N.E. 686, at 688 (1900). See also his infamous doctrinal dissent in the debt peonage case, *Bailey v Alabama*, 219 U.S. 219, at 245 (1911).

115. Since both Morton Horwitz's and H. L. Pohlman's otherwise insightful analyses of Holmes rests almost exclusively on Holmes's book and articles, since Horowitz cites only four of Holmes's Massachusetts decisions and Pohlman cites only a tiny handful of (constitutional) cases, they have both missed this dichotomy between the scholar and the practitioner. (Horwitz, *The Transformation of American Law, 1870–1960* [New York: Oxford University Press, 1992], chap. 4.) Pohlman (*Holmes and Utilitarian Jurisprudence*, 149) writes that Holmes's "theory of liability reduced the conditions of legal liability to one—unreasonably dangerous action. If the agent acted dangerously, caused damage, but violated no one's rights" (precisely the case with trespassing children), the courts "could still hold him liable according to Holmes's theory, but not according to the orthodox approach." Had Pohlman read *Holbrook* and *Britt* he would not have offered such an opinion.

116. Hoyt L. Warner, *The Life of Mr. Justice Clarke* (Cleveland: Western Reserve

University Press, 1959), 12, 17, 68, 74, 88, 205; "John Clarke," in *The Supreme Court Justices*, ed. Clare Cushman (Washington, D.C., GPO, 1993), 337, 339.

117. On the other hand, the fact that several jurists *had* offered cost-benefit analyses must have been of some significance to the decision of the authors of the *Second Restatement of Torts* in 1934 to include in their "Artificial Conditions Highly Dangerous to Trespassing Children" this element: "d) the utility to the possessor of maintaining the condition and the burden of eliminating the danger [must be] slight as compared with the risk to the children involved."

118. Alexis de Tocqueville, *Democracy in America*, ed. J. P. Mayer and Max Lerner, trans. George Lawrence (New York: Harper and Row, 1966), 246. Tocqueville was referring to both English and American jurisprudence in the first cited sentence; he referred more particularly to English jurists in the rest of the passage, but I find his remarks applicable to Americans as well.

119. Deaths of trespassers on railroad property alone averaged about three thousand per year from 1891 to 1920, a rate higher than that of workers and passengers combined, and in 1900 approximately 24 percent of all persons living in the United States were under the age of ten. U.S. Bureau of the Census, *Historical Statistics of the United States* (Washington, D.C.:. GPO, 1957), 8, 10, 367, 437.

120. Anon., *The Seasons* (New York, 1814), 21; Anon., *School of Good Manners* (New London, Conn., 1796), cited in Monica Kieffer, *American Children Through their Books, 1700–1835* (Philadelphia: University of Pennsylvania Press, 1948), 191; "The Religion of Childhood," *Sunday-School Journal* 28 (November 18, 1857): 169; "Social Entertainments for Sunday-Schools," *Sunday-School World* 1 (November 1861): 130, cited in Anne Boylan, *Sunday School: The Formation of an American Institution, 1790–1880* (New Haven, Conn.: Yale University Press, 1988), 148–49; Bernard Wishy, *The Child and the Republic: The Dawn of Modern American Child Nurture* (Philadelphia: University of Pennsylvania Press, 1968), 20–24; E. Douglas Branch, *The Sentimental Years* (New York: Hill and Wang, 1934); Carol Z. and Peter N. Stearns, *Anger: The Struggle for Emotional Control in American History* (Chicago: University of Chicago Press, 1986), 51; Peter Coveney, *The Image of Childhood: The Individual and Society* (London: Penguin, 1967); Priscilla F. Clement, "The City and the Child, 1860–1885," in *American Childhood*, ed. Joseph Hawes and N. Ray Hiner (Westport, Conn.: Greenwood, 1985); Kate D. Wiggin, *Children's Rights* (Boston, 1892); Horace Bushnell, *Views of Christian Nurture* (Hartford, 1847), 291–99; Jacob Abbott, *Gentle Measures in the Managment and Training of the Young* (New York, 1871), 167–73. Cf. Louisa May Alcott, *Little Men* (Boston, 1871); Mark Twain, *The Adventures of Tom Sawyer* (Boston, 1885); and Thomas Baily Aldrich, *The Story of a Bad Boy* (New York, 1870), 138.

121. *Dublin Cotton Oil Co.*, v *Jarrard*, Texas Ct. Civ. App., 40 S. W. 531, at 534 (1897).

122. Chief Justice Albert Whitfield in *Temple* v *McComb City Electric Light & Power Co.*, 89 Miss. 1, 42 SO 874, at 875 (1907); H. C. S., "Subject Note: Attractive Nuisances," *Lawyers Reports Annotated (NS)* 19 (1909): 1094, at 1114.

123. *Barrett* v *Southern Pacific RR*, 91 Cal. 296, 27 PAC 666 (1891). (Bicknell was commenting on the trial court award of $12,500, not the appellate court's later upholding of the award.)

124. Cited in Gordon Bakken, *The Development of Law in Frontier California:*   **429**

Civil Law and Society, 1850–1890 (Westport, Conn.: Greenwood Press, 1885), 81–82; Bakken, *Practicing Law in Frontier California* (Lincoln: University of Nebraska Press, 1991), 163.

125. I refer to the "Dillon's rule" known to students of American urban and constitutional history: If there exists "any fair, reasonable, substantial doubt concerning the existence of a power" claimed by a municipal corporation, the courts will deny the municipality the power. This "rule," attributed (incorrectly) to Dillon, is derived from a U.S. Supreme Court decision that a municipality defaulting on its properly issued bonds cannot escape its liability because of a state statute enacted after the issuance of the bonds or because of a state court judgment releasing it from liability, and the federal courts will uphold the claims of the bondholders "with a firm hand." Dillon was simply summarizing the law as mandated by the U.S. Supreme Court; he was *not* fond of that rule. See *Hanson* v *Vernon,* 27 Iowa 28 (1869); Dillon, *Commentaries on the Law of Municipal Corporations,* 5th ed. (Boston: Little, Brown, 1911), vol. 2, sec. 897, p. 515.

EIGHT

1. See David Nasaw, *Children of the City* (New York: Oxford University Press, 1985), 20–23; Peter Opie and Iona Opie, *Children's Games in Street and Playground* (Oxford: Clarendon, 1969), 10–11; Mark Twain, *The Adventures of Tom Sawyer* (Boston, 1885); Thomas Bailey Aldrich, *The Story of a Bad Boy* (New York, 1870); Mary Antin, *The Promised Land* (Boston: 1912); Michael Gold, *Jews without Money* (New York: Avon, 1930).

2. Nasaw, *Children of the City,* 38.

3. As in *Lynch* v *Nurdin,* 1 Ad. & El. (n.s.) 29, 113 ER 1041 (Q. B. 1841).

4. As was the plight of Mike Gold's friend, Joey Cohen, in New York, c. 1899. Gold, *Jews without Money* (New York: Avon, 1930), 31.

5. Ida Tarbell, "Who Is to Blame for Child Killing?" *Colliers* 70 (October 7, 1922): 12, cited in Viviana A. Zelizer, *Pricing the Priceless Child: The Changing Social Value of Children* (New York: Basic Books, 1985), 40; Jane Addams, *The Spirit of Youth and the City Streets* (New York: Macmillan, 1909), 55–57; Nasaw, *Children of the City,* 1, 22–23.

The words of Jane Addams, Marcus Dow, and Ida Tarbell on the "reckless spirit" of children in the streets is not the fabrication of insensitive middle-class moralists or sadistic police. The recollection's of children growing up in Boston and New York in the 1890s confirm them. See Mary Antin's words cited in the prologue to this section and Samuel Chotzinoff, *A Lost Paradise* (New York: Knopf, 1955), 88: "There were ambulances to be run after and horsecars to hang on to, unobserved by the conductor."

The appearance of automobiles in early-twentieth-century American towns and cities provided children with new "games" (running "into streets on the approach of autos and throw[ing] their hats beneath the wheels or hit[ting] the car with sticks as it passes, or standing in front and waiv[ing] their arms until the car is almost upon them" *New York Times,* April 25, 1909, p. 4]). But as late as 1908 *wagons* were still the greatest reported national killers (469) of children under sixteen years of age in streets, followed by streetcars (346) and autos (110); "Trolley Accidents," *Outlook* 68 (May 25, 1901): 202. Marcus Dow, "Accident Prevention in Relation to Child

Welfare," *4th International Congress on School Hygiene*, vol. 4 (New York: 1913), 612; Philip Davis, *Street-Land: Its Little People and Big Problems* (Boston: Small, Maynard, 1915), 33–34; Zelizer, *Pricing the Priceless Child*, 46.

6. *Flanders* v *Meath*, 27 Ga. 358 at 362 (1859).

7. *Baltimore City Passenger Co.* v *McDonnell*, 43 Md. 534 at 553 (1876). Cf. *Mangam* v *Brooklyn RR*, 38 N.Y. 455 (1868), where the driver had "caught a pigeon which he had in his hands, and was sitting down looking at it, having wound his lines around the brake, and was paying no attention" to the road.

8. Wex Malone, "The Formative Era of Contributory Negligence," *Illinois Law Review* 41 (1946): 151 at 181; *Hartfield* v *Roper*, 21 Wend. (N.Y.) 615 (1839). Malone's essay is cited as authority in Lawrence Friedman, *A History of American Law*, 2nd ed. (New York: Simon and Schuster, 1985), 471.

The masculine gender is used in describing injured children because in approximately five of every six such cases the injured plaintiff was male. Boys were given more freedom and took greater risks.

9. *McAllister* v *Hammond*, 6 Cow. (N.Y.) 342 (1826); *Hartfield* v *Roper*, 21 Wend. (N.Y.) 615 at 620 (1839).

10. *Hartfield* v *Roper*, 21 Wend. (N.Y.) 615 at 618, 620 (1839); Karl Llewelyn, *The Common Law: Deciding Appeals* (Boston: Little, Brown, 1960), 426.

11. It did survive for a few decades, but only in a tiny handful of cases. See *infra* notes 18–20, and 24, and *Brown* v *European and North American RR*, 58 Me. 384 at 389 (1870).

12. 11 East 60, 103 ER (1809).

13. *Boss* v *Litton*, 5 Car. & P. 409, 172 ER 1030 (N. P. 1832).

14. 113 ER 1041 (Q. B. 1841).

15. *Lygo* v *Newbold*, 9 Ex. 302, 156 ER 129 at 130 (Ex. 1854); *Waite* v *Northeastern RR*, 28 LJ (Q. B.) 258 (Ex. 1859); *Singleton* v *Eastern Counties RR*, 7 LB (N. S.) 287, 141 ER 827 (C. P. 1859); *Hughes* v *Macfie & Others*, 2 Hurl. & Cot. 744, 159 ER 308 (Ex. 1863); *Mangan* v *Atterton*, Times L. R., 1 Ex. Cas. 239 (1866).

16. *Birge* v *Gardiner*, 19 Ct. 507 at 512 (1849); *Daley* v *Norwich & Worcester RR*, 26 Ct. 591 at 598 (1858). Justice William Ellsworth, the author of the latter opinion, cited *Birge* v *Gardiner*, *Lynch* v *Nurdin*, and *Robinson* v *Cone*, on this subject.

17. *Robinson* v *Cone*, 22 Vt. 213 at 215, 220, 224–26 (1850). Hamilton, L. J., offered a similar critique of attempts to apply a general theory of contributory negligence to children in *Lathan* v *Johnson*, 1 K. B. 398 at 416 (1913): "Children's cases are always troublesome. . . . Each decision seems clear enough, but to fit them all into their places in the theory of negligence is not so easy."

18. Oliver Wendell Holmes Jr., *The Common Law* (Boston, 1881), 99, 101–2; *Callahan* v *Bean*, 9 Allen (91 Mass.) 401 (1864); *Carter* v *Towne*, 98 Mass. 567 (1868); *Wright* v *Malden & Melrose Ry*, 4 Allen (86 Mass.) 283 (1862); *Lovett* v *Salem & South Danvers RR*, 9 Allen (91 Mass.) 557 (1865); *Casey* v *Smith*, 152 Mass. 294 (1890). But see *Munn* v *Reed*, 86 Mass. 431 (1862) (a four year old bitten by a dog); *Mulligan* v *Curtis*, 100 Mass. 512 (1868) (nonsuit in death of three year old reversed and case remanded since parental contributory negligence was "a question for the jury."); *Lynch* v *Smith*, 104 Mass. 52 at 57 (1870); *Gibbons* v *Williams*, 236 Mass. 366 (1883) (a nineteen-month-old child run over by an ice cart; case remanded because judge had directed a verdict for defendant on grounds of parental

contributory negligence); *McGeary* v *Eastern RR*, 136 Mass. 363 (1883); *O'Connor* v *Boston & Lowell RR*, 136 Mass. 352 (1883) (award of ten thousand dollars to a four-year-old boy who lost both feet; the question of parental contributory negligence had been "correctly" left to the jury; hence the judgment was affirmed); and *McGuiness* v *Butler*, 159 Mass. 233 at 236 (1893), for examples of cases involving two, three, and four year olds, where the question of parental contributory negligence was to be left to the jury.

19. *Stinson* v *City of Gardiner*, 42 Me. 248 (1856); *Brown* v *European & N. A. RR*, 58 Me. 384 (1870). Cf. *O'Brien* v *McGlinchy*, 68 Me. 552 (1878) (contributory negligence of a three-and-a-half-year-old boy left to jury).

20. *Honesberger* v *2nd Ave. Ry*, 33 How. Prac. (N.Y.) 193 at 197, 201 (1864). Cf. *Kreig* v *Wells*, 1 E. D. Smith (N.Y.C. P.) 74 (1850).

21. *Costello* v *Syracuse, Bing. & N.Y. RR*, 65 Barb. (N.Y. Sup. Ct.) 92 at 104 (1873).

22. On this point see also *Byrne* v *N.Y. Central & Hudson River RR*, 83 N.Y. 620 at 621 (1881) and *Washington & Georgetown Ry* v *Gladmon*, 82 U.S. 401 (1872) (Justice Hunt of New York).

23. *Mangam* v *Brooklyn Ry*, 38 N.Y. 455 at 461 (1868). Cf. *Mowrey* v *Central City Ry*, 66 Barb. (N.Y. Sup. Ct.) 43 (1867), affirmed in 51 N.Y. 666 (1873); *Ihl* v *42nd St. Ry*, 47 N.Y. 317 (1872); *Thurber* v *Harlem Bridge, Morrisania & Fordham Ry*, 60 N.Y. 327 (1875); *Dowling* v *N.Y. Central & Hudson River Ry*, 90 N.Y. 670 (1882); and *Kunz* v *City of Troy*, 104 N.Y. 344 (1887).

As in Massachusetts, New York's jurists did not permit attempts to impute parental contributory negligence to older children (eight or nine years of age) who were presumed to be capable or walking to school or the store by themselves. See *McMahon* v *City of New York*, 33 N.Y. 642 at 647 (1865); *Drew* v *6th Ave. Ry*, 26 N.Y. 49 (1862) ("It was not, as a matter of law, negligent or in any way improper for the plaintiff to send her [eight-year-old] son to school without an attendant."); and *Thurber* v *Harlem, etc., Ry.*, at 333: Parents of a nine-year-old boy were justified in letting him "go abroad and to his school without the protection of some elder person to look after and care for him."

24. *Bannon* v *Baltimore & Ohio RR*, 24 Md. 108 at 125 (1865).

25. *Baltimore City Passenger Co.* v *McDonnell*, 43 Md. 534 at 551, 553 (1876); *Baltimore & Ohio RR* v *Freyer*, 30 Md. 47 (1869); and *McMahon* v *Northern Central RR*, 39 Md. 438 at 456, 460 (1874). Cf. *Baltimore Traction Co.* v *Wallace*, 77 Md. 435, 26 Atl. 518 (1893).

26. *Pittsburgh, Ft. Wayne & Chicago RR* v *Vining's Adm.* 27 Ind. 513 (1867); *Hathaway* v *Toledo, Wabash, & Western RR*, 46 Ind. 25 (1874); *Citizen's St. Ry* v *Stoddard*, 37 N. E. (Ind. App.) 723 at 724 (1894); *Louisville, New Albany & Chicago RR* v *Sears*, 38 N. E. (Ind. App.) 837 (1894); *Cleveland, Cincinnati, Chicago, & St. Louis RR.* v *Keely*, 138 Ind. 600, 37 N. E. 406 (1894); *Karr* v *Parks*, 40 Cal. 188 (1870); *Meeks* v *Southern Pacific RR*, 52 Cal. 602 (1878); *St. L., I., M., & S. RR* v *Freeman*, 36 Ark. 41 (1880); *Boland* v *Missouri RR*, 36 Mo. 484 (1865); *Louisville & Portland Canal Co.* v *Murphy, Adm.*, 9 Bush (72 Ky.) 522 (1872); *Johnson* v *Chicago & N. W. RR*, 14 N. W. (Wis.) 181 (1882); *Fitzgerald* v *St. Paul, Minneapolis & Manitoba RR*, 29 Minn. 336, 13 N. W. 168 at 169 (1882); *Walters* v *C. R. I. & P. RR*, 41 Iowa 71 (1875); *Westbrook* v *Mobile & Ohio RR*, 66 Miss. 560, 6 So 321 (1889); *Barksdull* v *New Or-*

leans & Carrollton Ry, 23 La. Ann. 180 (1871); *Payne* v *H. & S. RR*, 31 N. W. (Iowa) 886 (1887); and *Kyne* v *Wilmington RR*, 8 Houst. (Del.) 185, 14 Atl. 922 (1888).

27. Were the parents to sue on their own behalf, for lost income from a child *killed* by a careless driver or engineer, they might well have to answer to a defense that their own lack of care for the child had figured significantly into the accident's causality (as in *Glassey* v *Hestonville, Mantua & Fairmont Pass. RR*, 57 Pa. 172 (1868)). This they did *not* have to do in at least nineteen of thirty-one jurisdictions if they were suing as *guardians* for their still-living child.

28. *City of Chicago* v *Major*, 18 Ill. 349 at 352 and 361 (1857). Cf. *Chicago & Alton RR* v *Gregory*, 58 Ill. 226 (1871) (mother had "gone out to milk," leaving four-year-old boy temporarily unattended); *Chicago City Ry* v *Robinson*, 27 Ill. App. 26 (1888) (Melville Fuller represented the mother of a five-year-old boy killed crossing a track on the way to a funeral); *Chicago West Div Ry* v *Ryan*, 31 Ill. App. 621 (1889) (a one-year-old boy in the care of his older brother, the brother's carelessness not to be imputed via the parents to the boy).

29. *O'Flaherty* v *Union Ry*, 45 Mo. 70 (1869) (five-thousand-dollar award affirmed, the statutory limit.) Other examples: *Isabel* v *Hannibal Ry*, 60 Mo. 475 (1875); *Frick* v *St. Louis, Kansas City & Northern RR*, 75 Mo. 542 (1882); *Rosenkranz* v *Lindell Ry*, 108 Mo. 9, 18 S. W. 890 (1891). Cf. *Boland* v *Mo. RR*, 36 Mo. 484 (1865).

30. M. A. Low, "Note," *Central Law Journal* 2, ed. John Forrest Dillon and Seymour Thompson (September 1875): 594.

31. *Rauch* v *Lloyd & Hill*, 7 Casey (31 Pa.) 358 at 370 (1858); *Pennsylvania RR* v *Kelly*, 7 Casey (31 Pa.) 372 at 378 (1858). Cf. *Oakland RR* v *Fielding*, 48 Pa. 320 (1864); and *Smith* v *O'Connor*, 48 Pa. 218 at 222 (1864), where Justice William Strong noted that *Lynch* v *Nurdin* is "founded in better reason" than *Hartfield* v *Roper* and is "intrinsically just," and praised *Robinson* v *Cone* and *Birge* v *Gardiner* as well.

32. *Kay* v *Pa. RR*, 65 Pa. 269 at 272 (1870). Cf. *N. Pa. RR* v *Mahoney*, 57 Pa. 187 (1868); and *Warner* v *RR*, 25 Phila. Rpts. 52 (1868).

33. *Phila. & Reading RR* v *Long*, 75 Pa. St. 257 at 265–66 (1874).

34. *Karr, pro ami* v *Parks*, 40 Cal. 188 (1870) (a ten-year-old girl horned by a cow while walking in the main street of Marysville "to pick flowers"); *Walters* v *C. R. I. & P. RR*, 41 Iowa 71 (1875); *Hedin* v *City & Suburban Ry*, 26 Ore. 155, 37 Pac. 540 (1894); *[John Pierpont] Morgan, Receiver* v *Illinois & St. Louis Bridge*, 17 Fed. Cas. 749 (1878) (Report by Seymour Thompson, master in chancery; opinion by Judge John Forest Dillon); *Butler* v *N.Y., N. H. & Hartford RR*, 177 Mass. 191, 58 N. E. 59 (1900) (O. W. Holmes Jr, J.); *East Saginaw City Ry* v *Bohn*, 27 Mich. 503 at 509 (1873) (Justice Thomas Cooley, in the case of a four-year-old boy, accompanied by a twelve-year-old brother, whose leg was crushed leaving a streetcar: "[This mode of conveyance) is supposed to be especially adapted to the needs of those classes of the community whose . . . limited means put the more expensive modes of conveyance beyond their reach . . . , to the poor laborer employed at a distance from his home . . . [and] the families of laboring men who by means thereof are enabled to enjoy occasional holidays in the public parks, or in forest and open fields, which otherwise would only be accessible to them at an expense beyond their means. . . . The State would never grant the corporation privileges on any other supposition

[than that the "mode of conveyance they provide" is "reasonably safe"]." Cf. *San Antonio & A. P. RR v Vaughn*, 5 Tex. Civ. App. 195, 23 S. W. 745 (1893).

35. *Walters v C. R.I & P. RR*, 41 Iowa 71 at 78 (1875).

36. Christopher Patterson, *Railway Accident Law* (Philadelphia, 1886), sec. 81. *Contra* see Charles F. Beach, *A Treatise on the Law of Contributory Negligence* (New York, 1885), 143: A "sense of justice and instincts of humanity" was leading of number of jurisdictions to reject *Hartfield v Roper*, since "the children of the poor can have no place of resort but the streets."

37. In a few cases some courts decided that the evidence of contributory negligence by child or parent was so great that the trial judge should have nonsuited the plaintiff himself, but California's high court defended the harsh result of such a rule with the doctrinal remark that it was "constrained by the settled rules of law" to act thusly. That opinion bore no jurist's name. *Meeks v Southern Pacific RR*, 52 Cal. 602 at 604 ("By the Court") (1878).

38. *Whirley v Whiteman*, 1 Head (38 Tenn.) 610 at 620, 622 (1858). Cf. *East Tennessee & Georgia RR v St. John*, 5 Sneed (37 Tenn.) 524 at 530 (1858). ($962 for an eight-year-old slave child killed while sleeping on the tracks; Justice Caruthers noted that the company enjoyed "a monopoly" and should have kept a "constant and vigilant lookout," while "certainly the master was not required to watch his negro children and keep them from the road.")

39. *Honegsberger v 2nd Ave. Ry*, 33 How. Prac. (N.Y.S. C.) 193 (1864); *Lannen v Albany Gas Light Co.*, 46 Barb. (N.Y.S. C.) 264 at 270 (1865), affirmed in 44 N.Y. 459 (1870); cited by Chief Justice James Arnold in *Westbrook v Mobile & Ohio RR*, 66 Miss. 560, 650, 6 So. 321 at 322 (1889), and elsewhere.

40. *Bellefontaine & Indiana RR v Snyder*, 18 Ohio St. 399 at 409 and 415 (1868); *RR v Mahoney*, 57 Pa. St. 187 (1868). Welch also cited *Lynch v Nurdin* and held that railroads should be required to exercise "a high degree of caution" because of "the common dictate of humanity," but his challenge to the interval logic of the negligence imputation rule is clearly his opinion's most noteworthy contribution. Cf. *St. Clair Street Railway v Eadie*, 43 Ohio St. 91, 1 N. E. 519 (1885). See also the opinion of Justice William Strong in *Smith v O'Connor*, 48 Pa. 218 at 222 (1864), which came close to enunciating this rule.

41. *Government St Ry v Hanlon, pro ami*, 53 Ala. 70 at 82 (1875). Brickell cited *Keefe v RR*, "reported in the 11th number of the *Central Law Journal* for the present years," as "an illustration of the doctrine" to be found in the "very just" case of *Lynch v Nurdin*, in affirming an award of $6,830.43 to a three-year-old boy whose leg was crushed by a horse-drawn sweeper car following a passenger streetcar too closely on "one of the main thoroughfares" of Mobile some seventy-five feet from his home.

42. *Norfolk & Petersburg RR v Ormsby*, 27 Gratt. (Va.) 475 (1876); *G. H. & H. RR v Moore*, 59 Tex. 64 (1883); *Huff v Ames*, 16 Neb. 139, 19 N. W. 623 (1884); *Ferguson v Columbus & Rome Ry*, 77 Ga. 102 (1886); *Battishill v Humphrey*, 64 Mich. 494, 31 N. W. 894 (1887); *Bisaillon v Blood*, 64 N. H. 565, 15 Atl 147 (1888); *RR v Whipple*, (Kan.) 18 Pac. 730 (1888). See also *St. Clair Street Railway v Eadie*, 43 Ohio St. 91, 1 N. E. 519 at 522 (1885), where Justice Johnson declined to follow *Thorogood v Bryan*, 8 C. B. 115, 137 ER 452 (C. P. 1849): "If her father's misconduct or negligence contributed to the injury, why should that fact exonerate a joint

wrong-doer?" Cf. *Union Pacific RR* v *Young*, 57 Kan. 168, 45 PAC 580 (1896); and *Shippy* v *Village of Au Sable*, 85 Mich. 280, 48 N. W. 584 (1891).

43. Francis Warton, *A Treatise on the Law of Negligence* (Philadelphia, 1874), sec. 310, p. 283.

44. See text at note 36.

45. Thomas M. Cooley, *Treatise on the Law of Torts*, 2nd ed. (Chicago, 1888), 821 n. 1.

46. *Cauley* v *Pitts., Civic., & St. L. RR*, 95 Pa. St. 398 at 401–2 (1880).

47. Joel Bishop, *Commentaries on the Non-Contract Law . . . or the Every-day Rights and Torts* (Chicago, 1889), secs. 581–87, esp. 582. Bishop (b. 1814) had been editor of the New York Anti-Slavery Society's journal, the *Friend of Man*, in the 1830s and 1840s. In 1844 he entered the practice of law in Massachusetts. In the 1850s he began a remarkable career of treatise writing with a treatise on marriage and divorce. His introduction to his treatise on torts, as well as those of his other treatises, make it clear that he sought to portray the law as a set of logically interconnected principles. Cf. Michael Grossberg, *Governing the Hearth: Law and the Family in Nineteenth-Century America* (Chapel Hill: University of North Carolina Press, 1985), 22.

48. *C. B. & Q. RR* v *Dewey, Adm.*, 26 Ill. 255 (1861); *City of Chicago* v *Starr, Adm.*, 42 Ill. 174 (1866); *Chicago & Alton RR* v *Murray*, 71 Ill. 601 (1874); *Toledo, Wabash & Western RR* v *Grable*, 88 Ill. 441 (1878).

49. *Chicago City Ry* v *Wilcox*, 33 Ill. App. 450 (1889), 24 N. E. 419 (1890); and 138 Ill. 370, 27 N. E. 899 (1891).

50. Chief Justice Beasley in *Newman* v *Phillipsburg Horse-Car Ry*, 52 N.J.L. 446 at 450, 19 Atl. 1102 at 1104 (1890). Cf. *Westbrook* v *Mobile & Ohio Ry*, 66 Miss. 560, 6 So 321 (1889); *Wymore* v *Mahaska County*, 78 Iowa 396, 43 N. W. 246 (1889); *Hyde* v *Union Pacific RR*, 7 Utah 356, 26 PAC 979 (1891); *Bottoms* v *Seaboard & Roanoke RR*, 114 N. C. 699, 19 S. E. 730 (1894); *Atlanta & C. Air-Line RR* v *Gravitt*, 93 Ga. 369, 20 S. E. 550 (1894); *Dicken* v *Liverpool Salt & Coal Co.*, 41 W.Va. 511, 23 S. E. 582 (1895); *Roth* v *Union Depot Co.*, 13 Wash. 525, 43 PAC 641 (1896); *Union Pacific RR* v *Young*, 57 Kans. 168, 45 PAC 580 (1896).

See also Seymour Thompson, *Commentaries on the Law of Negligence in all Relations*, 6 vols. (St. Louis: W. H. Stevenson, 1901–5), vol. 1, chap. 11, pp. 277–78, sec 289: (*Hartfield* v *Roper* was "harsh" law and the imputation of parental negligence to the child was "cruel, heartless and wicked. It can only hold in jurisdictions where *property* is placed above humanity." Courts "have taken a more humane view of cases of this kind." A child "does not select his custodian."); Thomas Shearman and Amasa Redfield, *Treatise on the Law of Negligence*, 4th ed., 3 vols. (New York, 1888), 1:sec. 73; Beach, *Contributory Negligence*, sec. 42.

51. A. L. I., *Restatement of Torts*, reporter, Francis Bohlen (St. Paul: West, 1934), vol. 2, sec. 488, p. 545.

52. Malone, "Formative Era"; Justice Cowen in *Hartfield* v *Roper*, 21 Wend. (N.Y.) 615 (1839).

53. *Waite* v *N. Eastern Ry*, El., Bl., & El. 719, 120 ER 679 (1858).

54. 17 Ind. 102.

55. It was, however, cited with approval in Ontario. See *Anderson* v *Northern Ry.*, 25 Up. Can. C. P. 301 (1875).

56. *Eckert, Adm.*, v *L. I. Ry.*, 43 N.Y. 502 at 506 (1871).

57. *Corbin* v *Phila.*, 195 Pa. St. 461 at 474 (1900). (The dissenters were James Mitchell, Newlin Fell, and Henry Green).

58. *Linnehan* v *Sampson*, 126 Mass. 506 (1879); *Donahoe* v *Wabash, St. L. & Pac. Ry.*, 83 Mo. 560 (1884); *Spooner* v *Del., Lack., & West. RR*, 115 N.Y. 22 (1889); *Peyton* v *Texas & P.RR*, 41 La. Ann. 861, 6 So. 690 at 691 (1889); *Louisville N.RR* v *Orr*, 121 Ala. 489, 26 So. 35 (1899); *Liderman* v *West. Chic. St. Ry*, 187 Ill. 463, 58 N. E. 367 (1900). See also *Mullikin* v *C. C. C. & St. L. Ry*, 164 Ill Ap. 37 (1911).

59. *Pa. Co.* v *Langendorff*, 48 Ohio St. 316, 28 N. E. 172 at 174 (1891).

60. *Walters* v *Denver Consol. Elec. Light Co.*, 12 Colo. C. of A. 145, 54 Pac 960 at 962 (1898).

61. *Cottrill, Adm.* v *Chic., Milw. & St. P.RR*, 47 Wis. 634, 3 N. W. 376 at 378 (1879); *Pa. Co.* v *Roney Adm.*, 89 Ind. 453 at 456 (1883); *Central R. R.* v *Crosby*, 74 Ga. 737 at 750 (1885). And see *Condiff* v. *R. R.*, 45 Kans. 256, 25 PAC 562 (1891).

62. *Md. Steel* v *Marney*, 88 Md. 482, 42 Atl. 60 at 66 (1898). I couldn't determine who it was that Justice Pierce was quoting despite the efforts of colleagues in our English Department, but he must have felt the phrase would be familiar to his audience a century ago.

NINE

1. On the modern "liability crisis" and its exaggerated nature, see Robert Hayden, *The Cultural Logic of a Political Crisis: Common Sense, Hegemony, and the Great American Liability Insurance Famines of 1986* (Madison, Wisc.: Institute for Legal Studies, 1989).

2. See, for example, *Scott* v *Sheperd*, 95 ER 1124 (K. B. 1773); J. Wentworth, *A Complete System of Pleading* (London, 1798), 437; Joseph Chitty, *A Treatise on Pleading*, 2 vols. (London, 1809), 1:238–41.

One *can* find one or two earlier affirmed awards for personal injury due to a defendant's negligence, as in *Angell* v *Shatterton*, 1 Sid. 232, 82 ER 1000 (K. B. 1663), where ten pounds had been awarded to one who lost both an eye and a leg due to the negligent firing of a ship's gun, but here there was no reference to compensation for the plaintiff's pain and suffering. In *Weaver* v *Ward*, Hob. 136, 80 ER 284 (K. B. 1617) (negligent discharge of firearm) there was made reference to "hurt" in the plea regarding damages.

3. *Pippin & wife* v *Sheppard*, 11 Price 400, at 405, 147 ER 512 (Ex. 1822).

4. *Mitchell* v *Allestry*, 3 Keb. 650, 84 ER 932 (K. B. 1676); damages noted in J. H. Baker and S. F. C. Milson, eds., *Sources of English Legal History: Private Law to 1750* (London: Butterworths, 1986), 573.

5. *Pippin & wife* v *Sheppard*.

6. *White* v *Boulton & Others*, Peake 113, 170 ER 98 (N. P. 1795); *Bush* v *Steinman*, 1. Bos. & Pul. 404, 126 ER 978 (C. P. 1799); *Leslie* v *Pounds*, 4 Taunt. 649, 128 ER 485 (C. P. 1812); *Matthews* v *West London Water Works Co.*, 3 Camp. 401, 170 ER 1425 (N. P. 1813) (£525 jury award to man who broke leg in fall from stagecoach due to hole in street where water pipes being laid); *Bretherton* v *Wood*, 3 Brod. & B. 54, 129 ER 1203 (Ex. 1821); *Bremner* v *Williams*, 1 Car. & P. 414, 171 ER 1254 (N. P. 1824); *Hall* v *Smith*, 2 Bing. 156, 130 ER 265 (C. P. 1824); *Daniels* v *Potter*, 4 Car. & P. 262, 172 ER 697 (N. P. 1830); *Woolf* v *Beard*, 8 Car. & P. 374, 173 ER 538

(N. P. 1838); *Sleath* v *Wilson* 9 Car. & P. 605, 173 ER 976 (N. P. 1839); *Kramer* v *Waymark*, 35 LJ, Ex. 148 (1866) (£150 for kick by horse); *Cotterill & Wife* v *Starhey*, 8 Car. & P. 691, 173 ER 676 (N. P. 1839); *Armytage* v *Haley*, 4 Q. B. 917, 114 ER 1143 (Q. B. 1843) (settled out of court). Note that in this last case, where the jury had given 1 farthing to a pedestrian whose thigh had been broken when struck by a negligently driven omnibus, the jurist ordering a new trial on the grounds that the first jury's verdict was inconsistent with the evidence and unfair was our English maverick, Lord Denman.

7. *Times* (London), December 29, 1845, 4; *Burgess* v *Gray*, 1 C. B. 578, 135 ER 667 (C. P. 1845) (£45 to a paper-stainer who "under-went great pain" in a highway accident); Willes, J., in *Limpus* v *London General Omnibus Co.*, 1 H.&C. 526, 158 ER 983 at 998 (Ex. 1862). Cf. *Dudley* v *Smith*, 1 Camp. 167, 170 ER 915 (N. P. 1808) (£100 to a woman injured on a stagecoach); *Jones* v *Boyce*, 1 Stark. 493, 36 Dig. Rep. 23 (N. P. 1816) (£300 to a passenger of a stage-coach); *Boss* v *Litton*, 5 Car. & P. 409, 172 ER 1030 (N. P. 1832) (£20 for a paralytic hit by a horse and cart); *Moreton* v *Hardern*, 4 B.& C. 223, 107 ER 1042 (K. B. 1825) (£200 for a leg broken by a careless stagecoach company); *Sharp* v *Grey*, 9 Bing. 457, 131 ER 684 (C. P. 1833) (£500 for fractures when the stagecoach axle broke); *Withers* v *Great Northern Ry*, 1 F.&F. 165, 175 ER 674 (N. P. 1858) (£1,500 to a manager injured in a derailment); *Wyborn* v *Great Northern Ry*, 1 F.&F. 162, 175 ER 673 (N. P. 1858) (£250); *Britton* v *South Wales Ry*, 1 F.& F., 171, 175 ER 677 (N. P. 1858) (£2000); *Roberts* v *Eastern Counties Ry*, 1 F.& F. 459; 175 ER 808 (N. P. 1859) (£250); *Ford* v *London & S. W. Ry*, 2 F.& F. 730, 175 ER 1260 (N. P. 1862) (£1,500); *Mose & Wife* v *Hastings & St. Leonards Gas Co.*, 4 F.& F. 324, 176 ER 584 (N. P. 1864) (£160 for injuries from a gas explosion); *Bilbee* v *Brighton Ry.*, 18 CBNS 584, 144 ER 571 (C. P. 1865) (£60 in crossing injury); *Rowley* v *London & North Western Railway Co.*, LR, 8 EX 221, at 230 (1873); and *Cowley* v *Mayor of Sunderland*, 6 H. & N. 565, 158 ER 233 (EX. 1861) (£50, by defective steam-powered wringer).

I did find two nineteenth-century English personal injury awards affirmed on appeal for princely sums (one for £7,000; the other for £5,250), but these awards were, essentially, for lost past and future *income*, not for pain and suffering, and the issues on appeal concerned the proper calculation of the value of these two plaintiff's future earning power. One was a prominent physician, the other a "gentleman of good prospects." *Phillips* v *London & Southwestern Ry*, L. R., 5 Q. B. 78 (1879); and *Fair* v *London & Northwestern Ry*, 21 L. T. (N. S.) 326 (1869). These awards, consequently, accord with the status-conscious nature of an older era of delicts, when men were "worth" so many marks or shillings or hides depending upon their status (or, in Saxon days, on their *wergeld*). Loss of past and future income is an important element in American awards too (as in *Ballou* v *Farnum*, 11 Allen [93 Mass.] 73 [1865], where the plaintiff, a textile print manufacturer, was awarded $9687.50, much of it clearly for his loss of income). But in America the element of pain and suffering counted for much more than it did in England. See note 102.

8. *Armsworth* v *South Eastern Ry.*, 11 Jurist 758 at 760 (1847); *Theobald* v *Railway Passenger Assurance Co.*, 18 Jurist 583, at 585–86 (Ex. 1854).

9. In *Carpue* v *London & Brighton Ry* (5 Q. B. 747, 114 ER 1431 [1844]).

10. W. Cornish and G. de N. Clark, *Law and Society in England, 1750–1950* (London: Sweet and Maxwell, 1989), 493–94.

11. See notes 21, 22 and 23.

12. Thesinger in *Blake* v *Midland Ry*, 18 Q. B. 98, at 104, 118 ER 35, at 39 (1852). Shannon Stimson, *The American Revolution in the Law: Anglo-American Jurisprudence Before John Marshall* (Princeton: Princeton University Press, 1990), 31.

Actually, the phrase "stiff upper lip" and its stoical meaning originated in *New England* in these years, first appearing in John Neal's *The Down Easters* (New York, 1833). But the term never caught on in America as it did in Britain, which is further evidence of this particular cultural difference between mid-nineteenth-century Britain and America. If "stiff upper lip" stoicism was essentially an upper- and middle-class phenomenon, this would have affected the awards that English juries and jurists offered to working-class plaintiffs, given the property qualification for jurors and the absence of elections for judges and justices in Britain.

13. £100 was the median British jury award, 1773–1873 (n=38) for personal injury/pain and suffering caused by negligence. In this regard it is worth noting that the butcher's assistant who sued his employer for his fractured thigh in the landmark fellow-servant doctrine case of *Priestley* v *Fowler*, 3 M. & W. 1, 150 ER 1030 (EX. 1837) was awarded £100 by the trial jury. Cf. *Lamphier* v *Philpos*, 8 Car. & P. 475, 173 ER 581 (N. P. 1838) (£100 in a medical malpractice suit.) £100 was worth about $600 in 1870. (B. R. Mitchell, *British Historical Statistics* (Cambridge: Cambridge University Press, 1988), 702. As in America, English juries awarded those injured by railway companies much more than those injured by individuals or small partnerships. (See note 73.) In 1890 the average damage award under the terms of the Employer's Liability Act of 1880 (facilitating personal injury suits for workers in railway and industrial firms) was £41 4s. (David G. Hanes, *The First British Workman's Compensation Act, 1897* (New Haven, Conn.: Yale University Press, 1968), 24–25). The number of cases involving personal injury negligence cases involving pain and suffering that I have detected in early- and mid-nineteenth-century English courts, however, is too small (n=38) to conclude any more than what I have said— that their legal system was not nearly as generous as ours. They still aren't; the median British award in an auto accident in 1974 was £1,819; in San Francisco in that same year it was $26,000, constituting about a one-to-seven ratio. John G. Fleming, *The American Tort Process* (Oxford: Clarendon, 1988), 2n. Cf. W. R. Cornish, *The Jury* (London: Allen Lane, 1968), 236 (English awards for pain and suffering "are much lower than in . . . the United States.")

14. Damages for *intentionally* inflicted suffering, as in slander, libel, assault, and battery, had been lawful as early as the thirteenth century in England. O'Connell and Bailey, appendix 5 to O'Connell and Rita J. Simon, "Payment for Pain and Suffering," *Univ. of Illinois Law Forum* (1972), 88–89; Sir Fredrick Pollock and F. W. Maitland, *The History of English Law*, 2nd ed., 2 vols., (Cambridge: Cambridge University Press, 1898), 2:527–538. O'Connell and Bailey also offer a summary of the early Roman, civil, and Saxon law of delicts and conclude that compensation for pain and suffering in those systems was allowed only "when wrongs were inflicted intentionally" (86).

According to the West German Great Civil Senate (1955), "[German] legal history shows that damages for pain and suffering have their origin in criminal law." The Prussian Code of 1792 allowed for compensation for pain and suffering, but not to "peasants or common citizens"; this passage of the code may have been intended to provide for the mental suffering of a nobleman or gentleman whose honor had been assailed. In any event, section 847 of the German Imperial Code of 1896 is the first clear authority for "non-pecuniary losses" in cases of negligently caused personal injury. B. S. Markesinis, *A Comparative Introduction to the German Law of Tort* (Oxford: Clarendon, 1986), 562; Rudolph Huebner, *A History of Germanic Private Law* (Boston: Little, Brown, 1918), 578–79.

In 1740 Lord Bathurst referred to language calling for compensation for pain in "the Jewish constitution" (the Talmudic tracts on Jurisprudence) whenever one "hurt his neighbor," but this appeared, both in the Talmud and the Bathurst's treatise, in a discussion of assault and battery, not negligence. Sir Francis Buller (originally written by Lord Bathurst), *An Introduction to the Law Relating to Trials at Nisi Prius*, 7th ed., ed. R. W. Bridgman (London, 1817), 21–22; *The Babylonian Talmud*, ed. Michael L. Rodkinson, 20 vols. (Boston: Talmud Society, 1916–18), 10:182–83.

15. One might argue that the median figure to use in this analysis should be that of *all* awards heard on appeal, those affirmed *and* those remanded or remittured. I have separately calculated the medians of awards remanded or remittured as "excessive." They do not differ in size from those affirmed. The problem with calculating a median for those awards remanded for other reasons (n=30) is that no award figure generally appears in these cases. (Exceptions: *Crofts v Waterhouse*, 3 Bing. 319, 130 ER 536 (C. P. 1825) (£150 in a stagecoach accident case, reversed for improper instructions regarding liability rules); *Taylor v Rainbow*, 12 Va. (2 Hen. & M.) 423 (1808) (£900 for "the pain he suffered" and loss of limb due to the negligent discharge of a musket, reversed because case was pleaded rather than trespass); *Gonzales v N.Y. & Harlem RR*, 39 How. Pr. (N.Y. Sup. Ct.) 407 (1870) ($5,000 awarded; new trial ordered). More common: *Dalton v Favour*, 3 N.H. 465 (1826) ("great carelessness" in discharging of a musket, putting the plaintiff to "great pain, etc." but no award amount noted.) Moreover, inasmuch as this study's primary focus is on jurists, I felt that restricting our attention to *affirmed* awards was appropriate.

Richard Posner analyzed all American appellate court negligence cases reported in the first quarter of 1875 (as well as those for 1885, 1895, and 1905), a year very close to my median year. He found the mean bodily injury awards for that quarter (n=9) to be $4,794. Posner, "A Theory of Negligence," *Journal of Legal Studies* 1 (1972): 29, at 79.

Note that these cases all involved *living* plaintiffs. In most states no heirs/administrators were allowed to claim damages for the pain and suffering of those wrongfully killed, even after the passage of Lord Campbell's Act, allowing wrongful death suits by such parties. See *Sherman v Western Stage Co.*, 24 Iowa 55 (1868); and *Quin v Moore*, 15 N.Y. 432 (1857). Other states did permit such damage awards to the estate so long as the victim had been conscious for some time, in pain, before dying. Marcus Plant, "Damages for Pain and Suffering," *Ohio State Law Journal* 19 (1958): 200.

16. Using the cases cited in O'Connell and Bailey, in Comment, "Instructions: Damages for Pain and Suffering," *Annotated Law Reports* 85 (1933): 1010; and in the Century Edition of the *American Digest* (under "Damages"), 50 vols. (St. Paul, 1898–1904), vol. 15, and then by "reverse shepardizing" these cases, I was able to

identify some 207 appealed personal injury negligence cases in thirty-five high court jurisdictions from 1808 to 1897 wherein questions had been raised by one party as to damage awards for pain and suffering. Of these, 73 percent of the plaintiff awards were affirmed on appeal (149). Six awards were disallowed and the cases remanded because the trial judge had incorrectly instructed the jury that punitive ("exemplary") damages (or "smart money") might be awarded for the defendants, intentional or grossly negligent act where the evidence showed only negligent behavior by the defendant, or where the defendant was a municipal corporation, against which no jury had a right to award punitive damages. ("Against such a body they should only be compensatory." (J. Pinkney Walker in *City of Chicago* v *Langlass*, 52 Ill. 256, at 259 (1869). See also *Woodman* v *Nottingham*, 49 N. H. 387 (1870); and the remarks of C. J. Sidney Breese in *City of Chicago* v *Martin*, 49 Ill. 242 (1868): "The city is not a spoliator, and should not be visited by vindictive damages." (He had just offered the example of several outrageous railroad accidents where punitive damages *had* been sanctioned against these profit-oriented common carrier "spoliators.") Cf. *Goodno* v *City of Oshkosh*, 28 Wis. 300 (1871).) Thirteen other awards, all but five of them from either Illinois or Wisconsin appellate courts, were remanded either because the trial judge's instructions regarding future pain and suffering were too generous or because the award revealed jury "prejudice" and was "excessive" (median: five thousand dollars; lowest three thousand dollars; highest twenty-five thousand dollars). Nineteen awards averaging eighty-seven hundred dollars apiece, were reduced by remitter by an average of 36 percent but then affirmed, and three other awards were remanded at the plaintiff's behest, because the trial judge had failed to allow the plaintiff instructions to the jury on the right to damages for mental suffering, or for past and "reasonably certain" future pain and suffering. (*Smith* v *Overby*, 30 Ga. 241 (1859); *McLaughlin* v *City of Corry*, 77 Pa. St. 109 (1874); *Townsend* v *City of Paola* (Kan.), 21 PAC 596 (1889)). At least four awards were reversed because of the *inadequacy* of the award. *Richards* v *Sandford*, 2 E. D. Smith (N.Y.C. P.) 349 (1854) (court recommended increasing a ten-dollar jury award to one hundred dollars); *Peatz* v *City of Cohoes*, 8 Abb. Pr. (N.Y. Supreme Ct.) 392 (1880); *Smith* v *Dittman*, 16 Daly (21 N.Y. Com. Pl.) 427 (1890); Louisiana's high court went so far as to reverse a jury verdict for a defendant and to direct an award of one thousand dollars for a child, crushed by a street roller, who had suffered "intense agony" for nine days before his death. (*Westerfield* v *Levis*, 43 La. Ann. 63, 9 So. 52 (1891)). About 9 percent of our cases were remanded for reasons having nothing to do with the question of damages. It might appear, then, that the plaintiffs "won" well over eighty percent of our 207 cases, in the sense that even with the 13 plaintiffs whose cases were remanded as excessive, one can be fairly certain that every plaintiff ultimately would be awarded and receive *some* damages for pain and suffering (either from a courtroom judgement or a settlement). See, for example, *Meeks* v *Southern Pacific RR*, 52 Cal. 602 (1878), a ten-thousand-dollar award remanded, and *Meeks* v *S. P. R.R*, 56 Cal. 513 (1880), an unspecified award at a second trial affirmed, and *Beisiegel* v *N.Y. Central*, 34 N.Y. 622 (1866), a nonsuit reversed and remanded for trial on appeal, *Beisiegel* v *RR*, 40 N.Y. 9 (1869), reversed for retrial, and *Beisiegel* v *RR*, 14 Abb. Pr. (N. S.) 29 (1873), third jury's award affirmed on appeal.

17. Randolph Bergstrom, *Courting Danger: Injury and Law in New York City*,

1870–1910 (Ithaca, N.Y.: Cornell University Press, 1992), 163. Lawrence Friedman, "Civil Wrongs: Personal Injury Law in the Late 19th Century." 1987 *American Bar Foundation Research Journal* 351, at 358. (Friedman reports the averages of the two jurisdictions separately; the figures are similar, and, for purposes of simplification, I have computed a single average for both, weighting each by the number of cases in each.) A congressional committee report on Employer Liability and Workman's Compensation in 1912 calculated the average award between 1900 and 1910 for the loss of a foot to be $3,492, for permanent partial disability to be $3,515, and for permanent total disability to be $11,272. Cited in Edward Purcell, *Litigation and Inequality* (New York: Oxford University Press, 1992), 43, 312. Posner, "Theory of Negligence," 94 reports an average award for personal injury in trial courts of Cook (Chicago) and DuPage Counties, Illinois, in the late nineteenth century of $2,731, but he is unclear as to the number of his cases (I estimate about thirty to forty), and does not specify the years of these trials (though his study would suggest that they must have been drawn from the years 1875, 1885, 1895, and 1905).

18. Stephen Daniels and Joanne Martin, "Jury Verdicts and the 'Crisis' in Civil Justice," *Justice System Journal* 11 (1986): 321. Cf. George L. Priest and Mark Peterson, *The Civil Jury: Trends in Trials and Verdicts, Cook County, Illinois, 1960–79* (Santa Monica, Calif.: Rand Corp., Institute for Civil Justice, 1982), 25; Jury Verdict Research, *Personal Injury Verdict Survey, Pennsylvania Edition* (Solon, Ohio: Jury Verdict Research, 1987).

19. *Newsweek*, August 26, 1991, 58 ("increasingly generous juries"); Brian Ostrom, David Rottman and Roger Hanson, "What are Tort Awards Really Like? The Untold Story from the State Courts," *Law and Policy* 14 (1992): 77; James W. Geary, *We Need Men: The Union Draft in the Civil War* (DeKalb: Northern Illinois University Press, 1991), 144–45, 186; Clarence D. Long, *Wages and Earnings in the United States, 1860–1890* (Princeton, N.J.: National Bureau of Economic Research, 1960), 14–15, 59; John McClymer, "Late 19th Century American Working Class Living Standards," *Journal of Interdisciplinary History* 17 (1986): 379 at 397 (*average* male income in Massachusetts [a highly industrialized state] in 1875 may have been as high as $568 [but this was an *average*, and in a state that was not typical]; U.S. Department of Commerce, Bureau of Economic Analysis, cited in *New York Times*, September 29, 1992, p. A11.

Median personal injury awards in the early 1980s ranged from about $10,000 in communities in Georgia, Kansas, and Cook County (Chicago), Illinois, to $60,020 in Alameda County (Oakland), California, to a high of about $100,000 for the New York City boroughs. About one in seven were for product liability or medical malpractice, and were much higher than for street and vehicular accidents, the sorts of personal injuries most like the ones compensated in our cases from nineteenth-century courts, but the median product liability and medical malpractice awards in 1988 (Ostrom: Rottman and Hanson) were still only about ten times the median income in that year, almost exactly the ratio for all median personal injury awards and median income in the late nineteenth century. Street defect and vehicular accidents produced much smaller awards in the 1980s than they had a century ago. The median jury award, 1981–84, for a vehicular accident in Cook County was $5,698, San Francisco, $36,517, Alameda County, California, $28,190, and New York (Manhattan), $118,300. The median jury award for a "street hazard" accident (such as our defective sidewalk awards) was $25,900 in Alemeda County, $72,015, in San Francisco, $29,733, in Cook County, and $164,550 in New York City. Stephen Daniels and Joanne Martin, "Jury Verdicts and the 'Crisis' in Civil Justice," *Justice System Journal* 11 (1986): 321.

20. Friedman, "Civil Wrongs," 351–52, 355, 377. (His phrase was "damage awards have exploded.")

21. Ibid., 373, 369, 374. Lawrence Friedman and Thomas Russell, "More Civil Wrongs: Personal Injury Litigation, 1901–1910," *American Journal of Legal History* 34 (1990): 295 at 303. See also Thomas Russell, "Historical Studies of Personal Injuries Litigation: A Comment on Method," *Georgia Journal of Southern Legal History* 1 (1991): 109 at 112; Lawrence Friedman, *Total Justice* (New York: Russell Sage Foundation, 1985), chap. 4; and Lawrence Friedman, *A History of American Law*, 2nd ed. (1987), 481, 485. Herbert Hovenkamp relies on Friedman and Jack Ladinsky ("Social Change and the Law of Industrial Accidents," *Columbia Law Review* 67 [1967]: 50 [probably at 66]) in maintaining that nineteenth-century judges and juries were stingy in their treatment of those suing for personal injuries: "The compensation was barely enough to cover legal fees or burial costs." ("Pragmatic Realism and Proximate Cause in America," *Journal of Legal History* 3 [1982]: 3 at 24). While it was true that many awards *were* well below a median of over three thousand dollars, the facts remain that (1) many of these injuries were not disabling; (2) many legal fees were provided for by the contingency fee; and (3) burial costs, in death cases, were often provided for either by worker mutual aid society insurance policies or company grants. On this subject see chapter 3, section on assumption of risk.

22. Friedman, *Total Justice*, 60–63. Richard Posner believed that 1875 was the appropriate year to begin a study of negligence awards in America because "before 1875 the [negligence] standard was rather new . . . and the reported decisions few." ("Theory of Negligence," 29 at 34). Kermit Hall, *The Magic Mirror* (New York: Oxford University Press, 1989), 297, 299, adopts Friedman's position. G. Edward White, *Tort Law in America: An Intellectual History*, 2nd ed. (New York: Oxford University Press, 1985), 62, holds a similar view: "The primary function of tort liability has been seen (in nineteenth century America) as one of punishing or deterring blameworthy civil conduct. A conception of tort law as a 'compensation system' is a distinctly twentieth century phenomenon, brought about by an altered view of the social consequences of injuries." See also Morton Horwitz, *The Transformation of American Law, 1780–1860* (Cambridge, Mass.: Harvard University Press, 1977), 81–84: Tort damage awards were larger before 1800 than they were to be in the nineteenth century and judges could now control the "measure of damages" that juries awarded and "set aside jury verdicts that were excessive."

Of considerable value in my reconstruction of the development of pain and suffering damages was Jeffrey O'Connell and Theodore Bailey, "The History of Payment for Pain and Suffering," appendix 5 to O'Connell and Rita J. Simon, "Payment for Pain and Suffering: Who wants What, When and Why?" *University of Illinois Law Forum* (1972): 83. However, as with Friedman, they suppose the size of these awards to be steadily increasing throughout the past century, with the most significant increase coming since World War II (101–4, 109). Thus they see the nineteenth-century record as mere backdrop to the "bloated and dysfunctional" awards of the post–World War II era. Useful as their survey is, it is flawed; they cite figures only impressionistically.

23. Leon Green, *Traffic Victims: Tort Law and Insurance* (Evanston: Northwestern University Press, 1958), 33–34. See (for the *single* example of Green's claim that I detected) the indication in *Stockton v Frey*, 4 Gill (Md.) 406 at 412 (1846), that a passenger injured when a bolt popped out of a stagecoach axle during a race between two coaches told a witness that he "knew such accidents would unavoidably occur."

Randolph Bergstrom's fine new book, *Courting Danger: Injury and Law in New York City, 1870–1910* (Ithaca, N.Y.: Cornell University Press, 1992), argues that injured victims in New York City were largely unwilling to sue until very late in the nineteenth century. Utilizing the trial court records of the New York City division of the New York Supreme Court for 1870, 1890, and 1910, he finds a twenty-three-fold increase in the number of litigated suits for personal injury. After factoring in the role of population growth, accident frequency, new technologies and dangers, and such common-law and statutory rule changes as occurred in these decades, he concludes that these account for only a fraction of the large increase. The rest he attributes in part to the rise after 1870 of the contingency-fee arrangement (89) and more significantly to a broader cultural change that led greater numbers of injured persons to expect and thus to seek compensation from those entities that had injured them. (His work, while in dissertation form, attracted the attention and approval of Thomas Russell, "Historical Study of Personal Injury Litigation: A Comment on Method," *Georgia Journal of Southern Legal History* 1 [1991]: 109.)

Bergstrom's method is sophisticated and compelling, but I am not completely convinced. As I indicated in chapter 6, contingency-fee contracts were sanctioned in New York as early as 1824 by the courts, and, more explicitly still, in 1848 by the legislature. Moreover, Bergstrom's data set of trial court cases for 1870 and 1890 do not include trials of personal injury suits in the City Court of New York City, the Superior Court for New York City, the New York City Common Pleas Court, the New York City Marine Court, or the District Courts of the City of New York. Several of these (Superior, Common Pleas, and Marine) were discontinued in 1894 and their dockets taken over by the Supreme Court (Ellen Gibson, *New York Legal Research Guide* (Buffalo, N.Y.: W. S. Hern, 1988), 123). And we know that juries of these courts *had* awarded damages to plaintiffs suing for personal injury in 1870 and 1890. See, for example, *Gonzales v N.Y. & Harlem RR*, 39 How. Pr. 407 (1870), reporting an appeal from a New York Superior Court jury award of five thousand dollars in June 1870; *Bateman v Ruth*, 3 Daly (New York Common Pleas) 378, reporting an appeal of a suit for injuries suffered in a fall into a sewer being built on Seventh Avenue before a jury of the marine court, April 5, 1870; *Belton v Baxter*, 32 N.Y. Superior Ct. (2 Sweeney) 339 (1870), reporting an appeal from a New York Superior Court jury award to a man hit by a cart on Second Avenue and Fourth Street; *Seitz v Dry Dock, E. B., & B. RR*, 16 Daly (21 N.Y.C. P.) 264 (1890), affirming an appeal from the City Court of New York; *Buddin v Fortunato*, 16 Daly 195 (1890), affirming a district court verdict for plaintiff in a blasting accident on Ninety-first Street; *Morsemann v Manhattan Ry*, 16 Daly 249 (1890), affirming a jury verdict and award for one injured by a falling crowbar while driving under an elevated railway; *Treanor v Manhattan Ry*, 28 Abbotts' N. C. (N.Y.C. P.) 47 (1891), an appeal from a city court judgment; *Rosevelt* v *Manhattan Ry,* 27 Jones & Sp. (N.Y. Superior Ct.) 197 (1891) an appeal decided Mar. 9, 1891, from a jury verdict for loss of an arm; *Smith* v *Dittman,* 16 Daly 427 (Dec. 1890), appeal from a jury award in the Court of Common Pleas for a woman hit by a falling bale of cloth; *Lynch* v *3rd Ave. Ry,* 27 Jones & Sp. 371 (Apr. 1891), appeal from a jury verdict in the superior court; *O'Neil* v *Dry Dock, E. B. & B. RR,* 27 Jones & Sp. 123 (Mar. 1891), appeal from a Superior Court jury verdict; *Duncan* v *Preferred Mutual Accident Assoc. of N.Y.,* 27 Jones & Sp. 145 (Mar. 1891), appeal from jury verdict in Superior Court; *Mele* v *Del. & Hudson Canal Co.,* 27 Jones & Sp. 367 (May 1891), appeal reversing twenty-five-thousand-dollar Superior court jury award to worker; *Shanley* v *Stanley,* 27 Jones & Sp. 495 (July 2, 1891), appeal from five-hundred-dollar superior court jury award to worker; and *Schneider* v *2nd Ave. Ry,* 27 Jones & Sp. 536 (July 2, 1891), appeal affirming Superior court jury award of fifteen thousand dollars to worker in streetcar collision.

In short, Bergstrom has understated by an unknown number the personal injury cases tried in New York in 1870 and 1890. Were *these* to be added to his figures, his large increase per capita between 1890 and 1910 of persons willing to sue would decline, and we can only estimate how much that decline would affect his findings. On the speculative *assumption* that the addition of the trial records of these five additional courts would triple or quadruple the numbers of his figure for 1870, and perhaps for 1890 as well, we would still have to account for the growth between 1870 and 1890. Population increase, the advent of new dangers (elevators, more street railway trackage, taller buildings), greater travel-to-work distance, more illuminating gas and electricity, larger horse-drawn trucks, and, after 1890, the advent of automobiles, subways, electric streetcars, and both safety legislation and statutes weakening employer defenses when workers were injured, can account for the differences between the new estimated figures for 1890 and the actual figures for 1910, but they may well fail to account for a substantial fraction of the difference between the number of suits in 1870 and those in 1890, as Bergstrom argues, persuasively. Nonetheless, it is worth noting that there was an eighty-eight-fold increase in the number of the faster, quieter electric streetcars in the nation between 1885 and 1890. (J. W. Hurst, *Law and the Conditions of Freedom in Nineteenth-Century United States* (Madison: University of Wisconsin Press, 1956, 88.) Moreover, fatal accidents involving streetcars and railways in Philadelphia increased by over sevenfold between 1875 and 1895. (Roger Lane, *Violent Death in the City* [Cambridge, Mass.: Harvard University Press, 1979], 40.) And it is worth noting that the numbers of tort cases in the circuit courts of two rural Illinois counties merely doubled over the years 1870–85 and 1890–1910. See Steven Daniels, "Continuity and Change in Patterns of Case Handling: A Case Study of 2 Rural Counties," *Law and Society Review* 19 (1985): 381 at 408. There may well have been a significant rise in willingness-to-sue in the 1870s and 1880s, and *possibly* thereafter as well, in New York. I offer one theoretical explanation that Bergstrom did not consider: These are the decades that large numbers of eastern Europeans, many of a socialist ideology and perspective, began to arrive in New York City, and who, by 1912, constituted the main voting bloc of support for the socialist presidential candidate, Eugene V. Debs, in New York. Conceivably this community, with its anticapitalist, pro-union window on the world, was more likely to sue than were its native-born neighbors.

In any event, Bergstrom's thesis does not greatly affect the claims I am advancing in this chapter, because, as his figures show, jury awards in 1870 averaged $3,637, about 65 percent *more* than the comparable figures for either 1890 or 1910. And juries were far *more* willing to find for the plaintiff in Bergstrom's personal injury suit trials in 1870 (92 percent of the cases) than they were in 1890 (57 percent) or 1910 (45.5 percent).

24. Friedman, "Civil Wrongs," 376–77; Rabin, "The Historical Development of the Fault Principle: A Reinterpretation," *Georgia Law Review* 15 (1981): 925.

25. In *Armsworth* v *S. E. Ry.*, 11 *Jurist* 758 (1847). One New York judge may have shared some of Pollock's stoicism. Judge Albert Cardozo's instructions to the jury in *Doran* v *East River Ferry* allowed that, while some personal injuries were compensable, others were among "those misfortunes to which all human beings are liable, and for which there is no legal responsibility." Randolph Bergstrom draws our attention to these instructions and claims that "most" of the New York Supreme Court adhered to this stoic view of injuries. (Bergstrom, *Courting Danger*, 172.) What he does not tell us is that, after hearing these instructions, the jury found for the plaintiff and, on appeal, the New York Supreme Court affirmed the judgement. (*Doran* v *East River Ferry*, 3 Lans. 105 [1870].) (Nor does he remind us that Judge Cardozo resigned in disgrace two years later after charges of impeachment for corrupt behavior were drawn up.) One more important American jurist (and treatise writer) clearly did see things Sir Frederick's way, but his words indicate that his view was not shared by his countrymen. Justice Isaac Redfield of Vermont praised these words of Sir Frederick (in his *Practical Treatise on the Law of Railways*, 2nd ed. [Boston, 1858], 347) for their "philosophic and Christian temper," and observed that it was "sometimes refreshing to find minds soaring above the dead level of pecuniary equivalents," but, as such, he was acknowledging that "pecuniary equivalents" were being sought in mid-nineteenth-century American courts.

26. See chapters 3, 7, and 8.

27. See Silverman, *Law and Urban Growth: Civil Litigation in the Boston Trial Courts, 1880–1900* (Princeton: Princeton University Press, 1981), 103, for examples of this phenomenon in Boston.

28. *Fales* v *Dearborn*, 1 Pick. (18 Mass.) 344 (1823); *Bigelow* v *Inhabs. of Weston*, 3 Pick. (20 Mass.) 267 (1825); *Springer* v *Inhabs. of Bowdoinham*, 7 Greenl. (Me.) 442 (1831); *Howard* v *North Bridgewater*, 16 Pick. (33 Mass.) 189 (1834); *Ware* v *Gay*, 28 Mass. 106 (1831); *Worster* v *Props. of Canal Bridge*, 16 Pick. (33 Mass.) 544 (1835); *Jacobs* v *Town of Bangor*, 16, Me. 187 (1839); *Whipple* v *Walpole*, 10 N. H. 130 (1839); *Wheeler* v *Troy*, 20 N.Y. 77 (1849); *Frost* v *Inhabs. of Portland*, 11 Me. 271 (1834); *Hunt* v *Pownall*, 9 Vt. 418 (1837); *Stokes* v *Saltonstall*, 13 Pet. (38 U.S.) 181 (1839); *Canning* v *Inhabs. of Williamstown*, 1 Cush. (55 Mass.) 451 (1848); *Powell* v *Deveney*, 3 Cush. (57 Mass.) 300 (1849); *McKinney* v *Neil*, 1 McLean (U.S. Circ.) 540, 16 Fed. Cas. 219 (1840); *Maury* v *Talmage*, 2 McLean 157 (U.S. Circ.), 16 Fed. Cas. 1182 (1840) (This $2,325 award went to Lieutenant Matthew Fountaine Maury, the naval scientist, injured in a stagecoach accident, for $250 of medical treatment for a fractured thigh and fractured kneecap accompanied by a "good deal of pain"); *Wheeler* v *Troy*, 20 N. H. 77 (1844); *Churchill* v *Rosebeck*, 15 Ct. 359 (1843); *Diblin* v *Murphy*, 3 Sanf. (5 NY. Super.) 19 (1849). Cf. *Verrill* v *Inhabitants of Minot*, 31 Me. 299 (1850); *Derwort* v *Loomer*, 21 Ct. 245 (1851); *Erie City* v

Schwingle, 22 Pa. St. 384 (1853); *Mason* v *Ellsworth*, 32 Me. 271 (1850); *Seger* v *Town of Barkhampsted*, 22 Ct. 289 (1853); *Wilson* v *Cunningham*, 3 Cal. 241 (1853); *Farrish* v *Reigle*, 11 Gratt. (Va.) 697 (1854); *Fairchild* v *California Stage Co.*, 13 Cal. 599 (1859); and *Masters* v *Town of Warren*, 27 Ct. 293 (1858).

29. William James, *Varieties in Religious Experience*, ed. Joseph Ratner (New York: Modern Library, 1936), 297–98.

30. Martin Pernick, *A Calculus of Suffering: Pain, Professionalism, and Anesthesia in Nineteenth Century America* (New York: Columbia University Press, 1985), 43–45, 78, 209–10; Kenneth Lockridge and Jan Lewis, " 'Sally has been sick': Pregnancy and Family Limitation among Virginia Gentry Women, 1780–1830," *Journal of Social History* 22 (1988): 5; Daniel de Moulin, "A Historical-Phenomenological Study of Bodily Pain in Western Man," *Bulletin of History of Medicine* 48 (1974): 540–70.

31. On these topics see, generally, Frank Klingberg, *The Anti-Slavery Movement in England* (New Haven, Conn.: Yale University Press, 1926), chaps. 2 and 3; and Crane Brinton, "Humanitarianism," in *Encyclopedia of the Social Sciences* (New York: Macmillan, 1937). More specifically, see Sir William Blackstone, *Commentaries on the Laws of England*, 4 vols. (London, 1765–69), 1:245; James Thomson, *The Seasons*, "Winter," lines 322 and following in *Complete Poetical Works*, ed. J. L. Robertson (Oxford: W. Frowde, 1908); Marcello Maestro, *Voltaire and Beccaria as Reformers of Criminal Law* (New York: Columbia University Press, 1942); Harold Langley, *Social Reform in the U.S. Navy, 1798–1862* (Urbana: University of Illinois Press, 1967); Seymour Drescher, *Econocide: British Slavery in the Era of Abolition* (Pittsburgh: University of Pittsburgh Press, 1984); James Turner, *Reckoning of the Beast: Animals, Pain, and Humanity in the Victorian Mind* (Baltimore: Johns Hopkins University Press, 1980), 79–83; William L. Brown, *An Essay on Sensibility: A Poem in Six Parts* (2nd ed., London, 1791); John H. Langbein, *Torture and the Law of Proof: Europe and England in the Ancient Regime* (Chicago: University of Chicago Press, 1977); Peter Karsten, *Law, Soldiers, and Combat* (Westport, Conn.: Greenwood, 1978), 21–22; Geoffrey Best, *Humanity in Warfare* (New York: Columbia University Press, 1980); Myra Glenn, *Campaigns against Corporal Punishment . . . in Antebellum America* (Albany: State University of New York Press, 1984); Louis Masur, *Rites of Execution: Capital Punishment and the Transformation of American Culture, 1776–1865* (New York: Oxford University Press, 1989).

32. See Thomas Haskell, "Capitalism and the Origins of the Humanitarian Sensibility," pts. 1 and 2, *American Historical Review* 90 (1985): 339–361, 547–66.

33. See Patrick Atiyah, *The Rise and Fall of Freedom of Contract* (Oxford: Clarendon, 1979) 368–72; David M. Gold, *The Shaping of Nineteenth Century Law: John Appleton of Maine and Responsible Individualism* (Westport, Conn.: Greenwood, 1990), 9, 41–42, 123–24; and Christopher Tomlins, *Law, Labor, and Ideology in the Early American Republic* (New York: Cambridge University Press, 1993), chaps. 5, 6, 8, and 10.

34. See, for example, Chief Justice John Appleton's opinion in *Brown* v *European & North American RR*, 58 Me. 384 (1870).

35. Sir William Blackstone's term, in book 1, "The Laws of England," in *Commentaries on the Laws of England* (London, 1765).

36. *McNamara* v *King*, 7 Ill. 432, at 436 (1845). Cf. *Grey* v *Grant*, 2 Wils. K. B.

251, 95 E. R. 794 (K. B. 1764); and Linda Schlueter and Kenneth Redden, *Punitive Damages*, 2nd ed., 2 vols. (Charlottesville, Va.: Michie Co., 1989), vol. 1, chap. 1: "The History of Punitive Damages."

The exceptions were Massachusetts, New Hampshire (after 1870), and Nebraska, whose courts did not permit punitive damages in civil trespass suits where criminal fines might also be imposed. (See *Boyer v Barr*, 8 Neb. 68 [1878]; and *Fay v Parker*, 53 N. H. 342 [1872] for a good summary of the cases and reasoning by Justice William Foster.)

37. These were: *Chamberlain v Chandler*, 3 Mason 242 (C. C. U.S.), 5 Fed. Cas. 413 (1823) (Daniel Webster for the plaintiff; Justice Joseph Story the trial judge); *Reed v Davis*, 21 Mass. (4 Pick.) 215 (1826); *Lindsley v Bushnell*, 15 Ct. 225 (1842); *Cook v Ellis*, 6 Hill (N.Y.) 466 (1844); *McKenzie v Allen*, 3 Strob. (S. C.) 546 (1849); *Pendleton v Davis*, 46 N. C. (1 Jones) 98 (1853); *Bell v Morrison*, 27 Miss. 68 (1854); *McWilliams v Bragg*, 3 Wis. 424 (1854); *Taber v Hutson*, 5 Ind. 322 (1854); *Brichard v Booth*, 4 Wis. 67 (1855); *Hagins v DeHart*, 12 How. Prac. (N.Y.) 322 (1856); *Donnell v Sandford*, 11 La. Ann. 645 (1856); *Slater v Rink*, 18 Ill. 527 (1857); *Weed v Panama Ry*, 17 NY 362 (1858); *Roberts v Mason*, 10 Ohio St. 277 (1859); *Nay v Byers*, 13 Ind. 413 (1859); *New Orleans, Jackson, & Great Northern RR v Hurst*, 36 Miss. 660 (1859); *Chiles v Drake*, 2 Met. (Ky.) 146 (1859); *Hendrickson v Kingsbury*, 21 Iowa 379 (1866); *Little v Tingle*, 26 Ind. 168 (1866); *Towle v Blake*, 48 N. H. 91 (1868); *Taylor v Grand Trunk RR*, 48 N. H. 304 (1869); *Green v Craig*, 47 Mo. 90 (1870); *Goddard v Grand Trunk RR*, 57 Me. 202 (1869); *Bryant v Rich*, 106 Mass. 180 (1870); *Sherley v Billings*, 71 Ky. 147 (1871); *Hanson v European & N. A. RR*, 62 Me. 84 (1873); *Dailey v Houston*, 58 Mo. 361 (1874); *McKinley v C. & N. W. RR*, 44 Iowa 314 (1876); *Lake Erie & Western RR v Fix*, 88 Ind. 388 (1882); *Smith v Bagwell*, 19 Fla. 117 (1882); *Borland v Barrett*, 76 Va. 128 (1882); *Ward v White*, 86 Va. 212, 9 S. E. 1021 (1889); and *Nichols v Brabazon* (Wis.), 69 N. W. 342 (1896). In *Jones v Commonwealth*, 5 Va. 555 (1799), three assailants were jointly assessed £106.

38. Bergstrom, *Courting Danger*, 161, and Bergstrom, "Courting Danger" (Ph.D. diss., Columbia University, 1991), 39, 45; found that assault and battery damage awards in New York City's trial courts, 1870, 1890, and 1910 (n=9), averaged $1,220.

39. Justice Carrington in *Jones v Comm.*, 5 Va. 555 at 559 (1799).

40. One has only to recall the award of fifteen hundred pounds in the famous case of *Forcey v Cunningham* to the merchant assaulted by another on The Battery in New York City in 1764 to appreciate that juries *were* willing to levy hefty awards when the assailant's means allowed. See the excellent essay on *Forcey v Cunningham* by Herbert Johnson in his *Essays on New York Colonial Legal History* (Westport, Conn.: Greenwood, 1981), 171–192.

This is not to say that the sentiments of jurists towards the victims of intentionally-inflicted injuries and their assailants were less "sympathetic" than they would be towards those injured by negligent corporations. Justice Samuel Putnam, for example, observed of a couple injured by their mortgagor (who had broken into the house in an attempt to evict them): "[The jury] have discovered a determination to vindicate the rights of the poor against the aggressions of power and violence. These motives are sound, and should be cherished. . . . There is nothing more abhorrent to the feelings of the subjects of a free government, than oppressing the poor and distressed under the forms and color, but really in violation of the law." (The jury had awarded the couple five hundred dollars.) *Reed v Davis*, 4 Pick. (21 Mass.) 215, at 217–18 (1826).

41. *Fair v London & Northwestern Ry*, 21 L. T. (N. S.) 326 (1869). Mr. Harcourt was also to argue, to no avail, that "the companies are really made insurers, without having any premiums."

The jury bias allegedly extended to the original question of the corporate defendant's liability as well. In 1880, a contributor to *Solicitor's Journal* complained that "things no one would dream of treating as negligence in the case of ordinary individuals are treated as negligence in the case of companies," and "it is no use ordering new trials when the jury is sure to find the same way, and so the whole standard of what constitutes negligence gradually becomes warped." *Solicitors Journal* 24 (1880): 305, cited in J. H. Baker, *An Introduction to English Legal History*, 3rd ed. (London: Butterworths, 1990), 475.

It is worth noting that recent research into the actual *payments* to judgement creditors in the 1980s established that corporate defendants paid 77 percent of the value of the award, while individual defendants paid only 58 percent of it (this despite the fact that the larger awards, which tended to be levied against "deep pocket" defendants, were often contested at the appellate level). Michael G. Shanley and Mark A. Peterson, *Postrial Adjustments to Jury Awards* (Santa Monica, Calif.: Rand Institute for Civil Justice, 1987), x. Wouldn't this have been the case in the nineteenth century as well?

42. Calculated from the lists of "representative awards" in appendices to Kenneth A. De Ville, *Medical Malpractice in Nineteenth Century America: Origins and Legacy* (New York: New York University Press, 1990); and from *Bellinger v Craigue*, 31 Barb. (N.Y.) 534 (1860); *Wood v Clapp*, 4 Sneed (Tenn.) 65 (1856); *Tefft v Wilcox*, 6 Kans. 46 (1870); *Musser's Ex. v Chase*, 29 Ohio St. 577 (1876); *Ballou v Prescott*, 64 Me. 305 (1874); *Bowman v Woods*, 1 Greene (Iowa) 441 (1848); *Carpenter v Blake*, 60 Barb. (N.Y.) 488 (1871); *Smothers v Hawks*, 34 Iowa 286 (1872); *Long v Morison*, 14 Ind. 595 (1860); and *Almond v Nugent*, 34 Iowa 300 (1872). Cf. Chester R. Burns, "Malpractice Suits in American Medicine before the Civil War," *Bulletin of the History of Medicine* 43 (January–February 1969): 41–56.

43. Moreover, as was the case with my personal injury judgments against corporations in the mid-nineteenth century, mid-nineteenth-century medical malpractice awards were *larger*, as a function of the typical doctor's ability to *pay*, than they would be in 1950. (De Ville, *Medical Malpractice*, 3, 16, 190.)

44. *Ibid.*, 32, 57, 67. In the South, DeVille argues (91, 133–35), practitioners were less attuned to these measures, and expectations were lower. Moreover, religious conservatism-fatalism was greater, and consequently malpractice suits were less common. But see Lockridge and Lewis, "Sally Has Been Sick," *Journal of Social History* 22 (1988).

45. 22 Pa. St. 261.

46. *Ibid.*, at 264, 269; *Smothers v Hanks*, 34 Iowa 286 at 297 (1872).

Justice Woodward's high "standard of ordinary skill" was, as DeVille points out, and *Smothers* indicates, not shared by all high courts. King's Bench found no fault in the trial judge's remarks to a jury in 1807 that "he was at a loss to state to the jury what degree of skill ought to be required of a village surgeon." *Seare* v *Prentice*, 8 East 348, 103 ER 376. Massachusetts offered a "locality rule" in 1880 in *Small* v *Howard*, 128, Mass. 131 (1880), which set a lower standard for "country doctors." For a regional borrowing of this standard see *Zirkler* v *Robertson*, 30 Nova Scotia R. 61 (1897) at 70.

47. De Ville, *Medical Malpractice*, 89, 192, 195.

48. Ibid., 22.

49. Dr. Asabel Humphrey in *Landon* v *Humphrey*, 9 Ct. 209, at 214 (1832). (Dr. Humphrey might have been better off with legal counsel; by accepting the plaintiff's counsel's language ["ordinary skill," ordinary diligence"] rather than insisting that it was extraordinary skill that was being expected of him, he yielded too much: Blackstone's definition of malpractice was less than ordinary skill).

50. 28 Me. 97, at 101 (1848). Cf. Justice Samuel Dana Bell's remarks in *Leighton* v *Sargent*, 27 N. H. 460 at 468 (1853): "At the present moment, it is to be feared, there is a tendency to impose some perilous obligations, beyond the requirements of the law, upon some classes of professional men."

51. *Ibid.*, 59, 203. See also *Craig* v *Chambers*, 17 Ohio St. 253 (1867); *Bellinger* v *Craigue*, 31 Barb.(N.Y.) 534 (1860); *Tefft* v *Wilcox*, 6 Kans. 46 (1870); *Hawthorn* v *Richmond*, 64 Me. 305 (1874); *Bowman* v *Woods*, 1 Gr. (Iowa) 441 (1848); *Smothers* v *Hanks*, 34 Iowa 286 (1872); and *Almond* v *Nugent*, 34 Iowa 300 (1872).

52. Posner, "Theory of Negligence," 51, 89, 95; Friedman, "More Civil Wrongs," table 10, p. 309; Gary Schwartz, "Tort Law in America," 1764; Francis Laurent, *The Business of a Trial Court* (Madison: University of Wisconsin Press, 1959), 249–50; Silverman, *Law and Urban Growth*, 45; Wayne McIntosh, "150 Years of Litigation and Dispute Settlement: A Court Tale," 15 *Law and Society Review* 823, at 839 (1981); Bergstrom, *Courting Danger*, 138 (corporation and government defendants); Frank Munger, "Social Change and Tort Litigation: Industrialization, Accidents, and Trial Courts in Southern West Virginia, 1872–1940," *Buffalo Law Review* 36 (1987): 75. These ratios are consistent with the more recent findings of Daniels and Martin, "Jury Verdicts," 321, at 329; and Priest and Peterson, *Civil Jury*, 8. Edson Sunderland, "Trial by Jury," *University of Cincinnati Law Review* 11 (1937): 120 at 123–28; Harry Kalven and Hans Zeisel, *The American Jury* (Boston: Little, Brown, 1966), 64 *n*; Kalven, "The Dignity of the Civil Jury," *Virginia Law Review* 50 (1964): 1055 at 1071–72; Harry Kalven, Hans Zeisel, and Bernard Buchholz, *Delay in the Court* (Boston: Little, Brown, 1959). In early-twentieth-century Wayne County (Detroit), Michigan, the difference between the percentage of jury and bench verdicts for tort plaintiffs was more modest (61 to 51 percent), while in early-twentieth-century Kent County, Michigan, and mid-twentieth-century New York City, jury and bench verdicts in tort cases were of equal frequency (64 percent in Michigan; 55 percent in New York); but jury *awards* in Kent County and New York were 15 to 20 percent higher than bench awards to these accident victims.

53. (See DeVille, *Medical Malpractice*, 209–10, on patient contributory negligence defenses.)

54. Rabin, "Historical Development of the Fault Principle," 953. But see Hendrik Hartog, *Public Property and Private Power: The Corporation of the City of New York in American Law, 1730–1870* (Chapel Hill: University of North Carolina Press, 1983), 233: Municipal corporations like New York were, by midcentury,

"largely shorn of the immunities to which other public institutions and offices were entitled."

55. *Lindley* v *City of Salem*, 137 Mass. 171 (1884) (fireworks); *Wixon* v *City of Newport*, 13 R. I. 451 (1881) (school); *Bigelow* v *Inhabs. of Randolph*, 80 Mass. 541 (1860) (school); *Hill* v *Boston*, 122 Mass. 344 (1877) (school); *Burrill* v *City of Augusta*, 78 Me. 118 (1886) (fire engine); *Wild* v *Mayor of Paterson*, 47 N.J.L. 406, 1 Atl. 490 (1885) (fire engine). But see *City of Lafayette* v *Allen*, 81 Ind. 166 (1881) (fire engine boiler bursts: city liable); and *Kies* v *City of Erie*, 135 Pa. 144 (1890) (fire house door springs poorly designed: city liable). I have omitted consideration of the question of immunity of charitable institutions, but see *Maximillian* v *Mayor of New York*, 62 N.Y. 160 (1870), where no recovery was allowed the heirs of one killed by a recklessly driven *city* ambulance under the sovereign immunity principle.

56. 2 Term R. 667 at 672, 100 ER 359 at 362 (K. B. 1788) (Lord Kenyon, C. J.: "recourse must be had to the Legislature.")

57. *Drake* v *City of Lowell*, 54 Mass. 292 (1847) (awning fell onto road); *Rowell* v *City of Lowell*, 7 Gray (73 Mass.) 100 (1856) (ice on post office steps); *Hixon* v *City of Lowell*, 79 Mass. 59 (1859) (snow falling from building onto highway); *Shepherd* v *Inhabs. of Chelsea*, 4 Allen (86 Mass.) 113 (1862) (sledding on icy road); *Clark* v *Inhabs. of Waltham*, 128 Mass. 567 (1880) (iron nail in commons); *Bartlett* v *Crozier*, 17 Johns. (N.Y.) 439 (1820) (county bridge); *Altwater* v *Mayor of Baltimore*, 31 Md. 425 (1869) (sled hit woman); *Chidsey* v *Town of Canton*, 17 Ct. 475 (1846) (sidewalk); *Hedges* v *County of Madison*, 1 Gil. (6 Ill.) 567 (1844) (county road); *Freeholders of Sussex County* v *Strader*, 3 Harr. N.J.R. 108 (1840) (county road); *Comms. of Hamilton County* v *Mighels*, 7 Ohio St. 106 (1857) (county courthouse); *Eastman* v *Merrdith*, 36 N. H. 284 (1858) (town hall floor collapses); *Wood* v *Tipton County* 7 Bax. (66 Tenn.) 112 (1874) (county road); *Young* v *City Council of Charleston*, 20 S. C. 116 (1883) (hidden drain hole); *Barber* v *City of Roxbury*, 94 Mass. 318 (1865) (rope across highway); *City of Arkadelphia* v *Windham*, 49 Ark. 139, 4 S. W. 450 (1887) (city RR crossing). In *Young* v *Commissioners of the Roads*, 11 S. C. (2 Nott & Mc.) 537 (1820) (defective bridge) the court denied recovery, citing *Russell* v *Men of Devon*, but two justices dissented, claiming the road commissioners *were* "liable."

58. The Massachusetts and New Hampshire statutes (of 1693 and 1719, respectively) also imposed a fine of one hundred pounds, payable to next of kin, in the event that the "defective waye" or bridge led to loss of life.

One of the first appellate cases affirming such statutory-imposed standards, *Worster* v *Props. of Canal Bridge*, 16 Pick. (33 Mass.) 544 (1835), involved a defective railing on the Charles River Bridge. The Bridge's Proprietors (essentially Harvard College) were represented by Charles G. Loring, who was to go on seven years later to represent Nicholas Farwell, with equal lack of success, in the famous fellow-servant case. See also *Bigelow* v *Inhabs. of Weston*, 3 Pick, (20 Mass.) 267 (1825); *Howard* v *North Bridgewater*, 16 Pick. (33 Mass.) 189 (1834); *Currier* v *Lowell*, 16 Pick. (33 Mass.) 170 (1834); *Springer* v *Inhabs. of Bowdoinham*, 7 Greenl. (Me.) 442 (1831); *Hunt* v *Pownall*, 9 Vt. 418 (1837); *Frost* v *Inhabs of Portland*, 11 Me. 271 (1834); *Whipple* v *Walpole*, 10 N. H. 130 (1839); *Wheeler* v *Troy*, 20 N. H. 77 (1844); *Jacobs* v *Town of Bangor*, 16 Me. 187 (1839); *Snow* v *Inhabs. of Adams*, 1 Cush. (55 Mass.) 443 (1848); *Canning* v *Inhabs. of Williamstown*, 1 Cush. (55 Mass.) 451

(1848); *Palmer v Inhabs. of Andover*, 2 Cush. (56 Mass.) 600 (1849); *Cogswell v Inhabs. of Lexington*, 4 Cush. (58 Mass.) 307 (1849); *Fitz v City of Boston*, 4 Cush. (58 Mass.) 365 (1849); *Bacon v City of Boston*, 3 Cush. (57 Mass.) 174 (1849); *Kimball v City of Bath*, 38 Me. 219 (1854); *City of St. Paul v Seitz*, 3 Minn. 297 (1859); *Verrill v Inhabs. of Minot*, 31 Me. 299 (1850); *Seger v Town of Barkhampsted*, 22 Ct. 289 (1853); *Smoot v Mayor of Wetumpka*, 24 Ala. 112 (1854); *Masters v Town of Warren*, 27 Ct. 293 (1858); *Lund v Inhabs. of Tyngsboro*, 11 Cush. (65 Mass.) 563 (1853); *Stickney v Town of Maidstone*, 30 Vt. 738 (1858); *Savage v Town of Bangor*, 40 Me. 176 (1855); *Hayden v Inhabs. of Attleborough*, 7 Gray (73 Mass.) 338 (1856); *Willey v Portsmouth*, 35 N. H. 303 (1857); *Merrill v Inhabs. of Wilbraham*, 11 Gray (77 Mass.) 154 (1858); *Runsch v City of Davenport*, 6 Iowa 443 (1858); *Davis v Town of Hill*, 41 N. H. 329 (1860); *Davis v Inhabs. of Leominster*, 1 Allen (83 Mass.) 182 (1861); *Wilson v Jefferson County*, 13 Iowa 181 (1862); *Brown v Jefferson County*, 16 Iowa 339 (1864) (despite the county's posting and obstructing a defective bridge); *Soper v Henry County*, 26 Iowa 264 (1868); *Oliver v City of Worcester*, 102 Mass. 489 (1869); *McCalla v Multnomak Cty.*, 3 Ore, 424 91869); *Woodman v Nottingham*, 49 N. H. 387 (1870); *Collins v City of Council Bluffs*, 32 Iowa 324 (1871); *Ward v Town of Jefferson*, 24 Wis. 342 (1869); *Butler v City of Bangor*, 67 Me. 385 (1877); *Sheff v City of Huntington*, 16 W.Va. 307 (1880); *Wilson v City of Wheeling*, 19 W. Va. 323 (1882); *Yeager v City of Bluefield*, 40 W. Va. 484 (1895); and *Taylor v Mayor of Cumberland*, 64 Md. 68, 20 Atl. 1027 (1885) (hit by boy on coasting sled while crossing street; statute held city responsible if notice had been given).

59. This was *Mayor of Lyme Regis v Henley*, 1 Bing N. C. 222, 131 ER 1102 (C. P. 1834). Cf. *Mayor of Lynn v Turner*, 1 Cowp. R. 86, 98 ER 980 (K. B. 1774); and *Cowley v Mayor of Sunderland*, 6 H. & N. 565, 185 ER 233 (Ex. 1861). But see also *Newton v Ellis*, 5 El. & Bl. 115, 119 ER 424 (Q. B. 1855), and cases cited in note 63.

60. *Browning v City of Springfield*, 17 Ill. 143 (1855) (Lincoln and Herndon for the plaintiff; C. J. Walter Scates cited *Mayor of Lyme Regis v Henley* and the *sic ut ere tuo* maxim to establish municipal liability for defective roads and bridges in the absence of a statute establishing such liability); *City of Chicago v Langlass*, 52 Ill. 256 (1869); *City of Peru v French*, 55 Ill. 317 (1870); *City of Chicago v Dermody*, 61 Ill. 431 (1871); *City of Chicago v O'Brennan*, 65 Ill. 160 (1872); *City of Freeport v Isbell*, 83 Ill. 440 (1876); *City of Chicago v Hoy*, 75 Ill. 530 (1874); *Blake v City of St. Louis*, 40 Mo. 569 (1867); *Higert v City of Greencastle*, 43 Ind. 574 (1873); *Grove v City of Ft. Wayne*, 45 Ind. 429 (1874); *Bd. of Commissioners of Howard County v Legg, Adm.*, 93 Ind. 523 (1883); *Milcairns, Adm. v City of Janesville*, 67 Wis. 24, 29 N. W. 565 (1885).

Michigan's high court originally took the same position on this question as had Illinois' (*City of Detroit v Corey*, 9 Mich. 165 [1861]), but nine years later C. J. Campbell's dissenting voice in *Corey* had become the voice of the court, holding that a statute imposing liability was necessary (*City of Detroit v Blackby*, 21 Mich. 84 [1870]). Now it was Justice Thomas Cooley's turn to dissent: When the legislature grants a municipal charter, that act itself "imposes concurrent duties" (121). He cited *Weet v Brockport*, 16 N.Y. 161 (1853).

61. *Dean v New Milford Township*, 5 W. & M. (Pa.) 545 (1843) (The mere existence of a county fund was sufficient to warrant liability). Cf. *Erie City v Schwingle*, 22 Pa. 384 (1853); *Scott Township v Montgomery*, 95 Pa. 444 (1880); *Pa. & Ohio Ca-*

nal Co. v *Graham*, 63 Pa. 290 (1869); *Norristown* v *Moyer*, 67 Pa. 355 (1871); *McLaughlin* v *City of Corry*, 77 Pa. 109 (1874); *Kibele* v *Philadelphia*, 105 Pa. 41 (1884); *Barthold* v *Philadelphia*, 154 Pa. 109 (1893); *Weet* v *Brockport*, 16 N.Y. 161 n. (1853); *Galvin, Admx.* v *Mayor of New York*, 112 N.Y. 223 (1889); *Mayor of Baltimore* v *Marriott*, 9 Md. 160 (1856) (citing *Erie City* v *Schwingle*); *County Comns. of Anne Arundel Cty.* v *Duckett*, 20 Md. 468 (1864); *Mayor of Savannah* v *Cullens*, 38 Ga. 334 (1868); *Parker* v *Mayor of Macon*, 39 Ga. 725 (1869); *Jones* v *City of New Haven*, 34 Ct. 1 (1867).

62. *Harris* v *Baker*, 4 M. & S. 26, 105 ER 745 (K. B. 1815) (road company not liable to one who fell over excavation earth negligently left with a warning light overnight even though governing statute required lights); *Hall* v *Smith*, 2 Bing. 156, 130 ER 265 (C. P. 1824); *Duncan* v *Findlater*, 6 Cl. & F. 894, 2 (Scot.) Session Cas. 139 (1839); *Holliday* v *Vestry & Parish of St. Leonard*, 11 C. B. (N. S.) 192, 142 ER 769 (C. P. 1861); *Newton* v *Ellis*, 5 El. & Bl. 115, 119 ER 424 (Q. B. 1855). But see *Scott* v *Mayor, etc. of Manchester*, 1 H.&N. 58, 156 ER 1117 (Ex. 1856) (Where municipality's own workers caused the injury, the authorities were liable).

63. Rev. J. O'Hanlon, *The Irish Emigrants' Guide for the United States* (Boston, 1851), 74.

64. *Bartlett* v *Crozier*, 17 Johns. (N.Y.) 434 at 456 (1820).

65. William E. Nelson, *The Americanization of the Common Law: The Impact of Legal Change on Massachusetts Society, 1760–1830* (Cambridge, Mass.: Harvard University Press, 1975), 147. W. T. Jackman, *Transportation in Modern England* (Cambridge: Cambridge University Press, 1916), 312–18; Robin Einhorn, *Property Rules: Political Economy in Chicago, 1833–1872* (Chicago: University of Chicago Press, 1991), 110. I do not mean to imply that America's roadbeds were immediately macadamized. (See Jean Labatut and Wheaton Lame, eds., *Highways in our National Life* [Princeton, N.J.: Princeton University Press, 1950], 74–82, to the contrary.) But the technique *was* available, it was used in many cities, and its reputation was spreading.

66. *Fitz* v *City of Boston*, 4 Cush. (58 Mass.) 365 at 368 (1849). Shaw may have been aware of (but he did not cite) *Rex* v *Henley Inhabitants*, 2 Cox C. C. 334 (1847), where Queen's Bench approved of Patteson, J.'s, instructions to a Suffolk assizes jury: "It was not enough to say [a road] was as good as ever it was, or as it usually has been; [since] it was a public road, and the necessity of the public required it, the inhabitants might be bound to convert it from a green road into a hard road." This, however, was an action by the English public prosecutor. English jurists had a much lower standard for municipalities in *private* actions against them for nonfeasance.

67. This is the language of a Maryland Act of 1853; see *County Comns. of Anne Arundel Cty.* v *Duckett*, 20 Md. 468 (1864).

In some instances counties and municipalities did *not* request their new roads; when New England's turnpike and bridge corporations failed in the mid-nineteenth century with the advent of state-supported railways and bridges, the state legislature sometimes compelled towns and county commissioners to assume their "maintenance." Oscar Handlin and Mary Handlin, *Commonwealth: A Study of the Role of Government in the American Economy: Massachusetts, 1774–1861*, rev. ed. (Cambridge, Mass.: Belknap, 1969), 237–38.

68. As in *Dean* v *New Milford Township*, 5 W.& M. (Pa.) 545 (1843); *Weet* v *Brockport*, 16 N.Y. 161 n. (1853); *Browning* v *City of Springfield*, 17 Ill. 143 (1855); and *City of Detroit* v *Corey*, 9 Mich. 165 (1861). Even those "new state" jurists who were reluctant to abandon the older sovereign immunity rule where municipal road contractors had been negligent acknowledged by mid-century "the great struggle in the courts" to place municipal corporations "on the same footing in liability as natural persons." Justice John Ryland in *Barry* v *City of St. Louis*, 17 Mo. 121 at 125 (1852).

69. In *Browning* v *City of Springfield*, 17 Ill. 143 at 148 (1855).

70. *Lloyd* v *City of New York*, 5 N.Y. 369 at 373 (1851).

71. Awards to the victims of road, bridge, and sidewalk accidents tended to cluster at the round numbers one thousand dollars, two thousand dollars, and three thousand dollars. Those of railroad and streetcar accidents tended to cluster at five thousand dollars and ten thousand dollars.

72. Bergstrom, *Courting Danger*, 164; *Bretherton* v *Wood*, 3 Brod. & B. 54, 129 ER 1203 (Ex. 1821); *McLane* v *Sharpe, et al.*, 2 Del. (2 Harr.) 481 (1838); *M'Call* v *Forsyth*, 4 W. & S. (Pa.) 179 (1842); *Diblin* v *Murphy*, 3 Sandf. (N.Y. Sup. Ct.) 19 (1849); Martin, B., cited in Rande Kostal, *Law and English Railway Capitalism, 1825–75* (Oxford: Oxford University Press, 1994). The victims of English railway accidents received at least 50 percent more from the hands of juries than did those injured by less affluent defendants. Successful personal injury suits against English railways in the years 1864–70 averaged £219. (The median award was lower; about £150, but still over 50 percent higher than the median of the remaining, nonrailway accident cases. Rande Kostal derived these figures from London and North Western Ry. payments in 1864–69, London and Brighton Ry. payments in 1869, and North London Ry. payments in 1870 (Kostal, *Law and English Railway Capitalism*, 375–76 n. 14). See also Select Committee of House of Commons on Railway Accidents, *Parliamentary Papers*, 1870, vol. 10 [207], 255.) Note also that coroner's juries required deodand forfitures (surrender by the defendant of the object causing the death) of low value as late as the 1820s, whereas the value of these rose with the advent of railway accidents. (Harry Smith, "From Deodand to Dependency," *American Journal of Legal History* 11 [1967]: 389.) Locomotives were simply more expensive than bulls, cartwheels, or horses. Moreover, when in 1842 one railroad appealed a coroner's jury verdict of forfiture of a £500 locomotive, the two Exchequer Barons known, one as the planter, the other as the nurturer of the infamous fellow-servant rule, Lord Abinger and Sir Edward Alderson, ordered the full sum to be paid. "It is in the power of the defendants to redeem the whole sum of £500 by giving up the engine," wrote Sir Edward, "and if they ask us for equity, they must begin by doing equity themselves." (*Queen* v *Eastern Cities Ry Co.*, 10 M.& W. 56, 152 ER 380 at 382 (Ex. 1842).)

It is worth noting in this regard that *today* the median award in a vehicular accident, where the defendant is generally an individual, is *lower* than the median award in street accidents, where the defendant is more frequently a municipality. See note 19.

73. Swift to A. Phelps, October 7, 1853, cited in Thomas Cochran, *Railroad Leaders, 1845–1890: The Business Mind in Action* (Cambridge, Mass.: Harvard University Press, 1953), 470; Tony Freyer, *Producers and Capitalists: Constitutional*

Conflict in Antebellum America (Charlottesville: University of Virginia Press, 1994), 184; O. W. Holmes, "The Path of the Law," *Harvard Law Review* 10 (1897): 457 at 466; Charles Francis Adams, *Notes on Railroad Accidents:* (New York, 1879), 267. Adams then pointed out that three accidents he had described previously cost the companies an average of $500,000 apiece.

Coroner's juries appear to have been equally hard on railroads. Philadelphia's issued only thirty-five censures in the years 1854–57 and 1878–80 (years that records of coroner jury actions have survived). Roger Lane found that twenty-three of these thirty-five censures were directed at railroads. (Lane, *Violent Death in the City* [Cambridge, Mass.: Harvard University Press, 1979], 38–39.) Streetcar companies, by my reckoning, were in the same boat as railroads with regard to liability. And, confirming Charles Francis Adams's point, streetcar corporations spent 10 percent of their expenses in 1900 on damages and legal expenses. Responding to these liability costs, to public opinion, and to conscience, the Brooklyn Transit Company pioneered a "Children's Safety Crusade" in 1913, offering leaflets, lecturers in schools, badges, and so on. Viviana Zeliger, *Pricing the Priceless Child*, 39, 44; Dept. of Commerce and Labor, Bureau of Census, *Street & Electric Railways*, 1902, p. 79, cited in Silverman, *Law and Urban Growth*, 192.

74. Leo Marx, *The Machine in the Garden: Technology and the Pastoral Ideal in America* (New York: Oxford University Press, 1964), is the classic treatment of this theme.

75. Adams, *Notes on Railroad Accidents*, 231, 236, 268, and 2: "Both by public opinion and the courts of law the companies are held to a most rigid responsibility. The causes which led [to each serious accident] are anxiously investigated by ingenious men, new appliances are invented, new precautions are imposed, a greater and more watchful care is indicated." See also Adams, "Our Railroad Death-Rate," *Atlantic Monthly*, February 1876; and the British Board of Trade's Report on the subject in 1874, noted in R. Vashon Rogers, *Law of the Road*, American ed. (San Francisco, 1884), 185–86.

76. James A. Ward, *Railroads and the Character of America, 1820–1887* (Knoxville: University of Tennessee Press, 1986), 124, 127; *American Railway Journal*, May 13, 1848.

77. *Chicago and Alton RR v Adler*, 56 Ill. 344 (1870); *Chicago and Western Indiana RR v Bingenheimer*, 116 Ill. 226, 4 N. E. 840 (1886); *Atchison, Topeka & Santa Fe v Chance*, 57 Kan. 40, 45 Pac. 60, at 61 (1896). See also *Hudson v St. Louis, Kansas City & N. RR*, 53 Mo. 536 (18); *Montgomery v Wabash, St. Louis & P. RR*, 90 Mo. 446, 2 S. W. 409 (1886); *Kumli v Southern Pacific RR*, 21 Ore. 505, 28 Pac. 637 (1892); and *McLaughlin v Louisville Elec. Light Co.*, 100 Ky. 173, 37 S. W. 851 (1896) (a stockholder of the light company not qualified to be a juror).

There is also evidence of a *pro*-railroad bias in a few jurors who "did business" with or received "favors" from railroads. See *Denver, S. P. & P. RR v Driscoll*, (Col.) 21 Pac. 708 (1889); *Omaha & Republican Valley RR v Cook*, 37 Neb. 435, 55 N. W. 943 (1893); (the remaining jurors then awarded the plaintiff, a thirteen-year-old girl whose foot had been amputated $11,500, affirmed on appeal); and *Omaha Street Ry. v Craig*, 39 Neb. 601, 58 N. W. 209 (1894). All these jurors were successfully challenged for cause, as was a railroad employee (*Central RR v Mitchell*, 63 Ga. 173

[1879]). But a juror who had worked for the plaintiff for the past year was allowed to sit in a personal injury suit against a railroad (*East Line and Red River RR* v *Brinker*, 68 Tex. 500, 35 S. W. 99 [1886]).

78. In remitting from six thousand to four thousand dollars (still a princely sum in 1854) a jury award for a passenger whose leg had been broken in a collision, in *Clapp* v *Hudson River RR Co.*, 19 Barb. (N.Y. Supr. Ct.) 461 at 464 (1854).

79. In *American Law Review* 22 (1888): 347 at 364.

80. Robert MacCoun, "Differential Treatment of Corporate Defendants by Juries," *Law and Society Review* 30 (1996): 121–35; Valerie Hans and M. D. Erman, "Responses to Corporate versus Individual Wrongdoing," *Law and Human Behavior* 13 (1989): 151–63.

81. Silverman, *Law and Urban Growth*, 42, 45, 191; David Bodenhamer, "The Democratic Impulse and Legal Change in the Age of Jackson: The Example of Criminal Juries in Antebellum Indiana," *Historian* 45 (1982): 206, at 218; Tony Freyer, *Producers versus Capitalists*, 22, 144, 173.

82. *The History of the Law in Massachusetts: The Supreme Judicial Court, 1692–1992*, ed. Russell Osgood (Boston: Supreme Judicial Court Historical Society, 1993), 132; The Duke's Law, 1664, New York, noted in John Aiken, *Utopianism and the Emergence of the Colonial Legal Profession: New York, 1664–1710, a Test Case* (New York, 1989), 106; Daniel Klein and John Majewski, "Economy, Community and Law: The Turnpike Movement in New York, 1797–1845," *Law and Society Review* 26 (1992): 469 at 484.

It is also worth noting that later antitrust legislation called for threefold damage awards, and that the laws of the Salian Franks called for the tripling of fines where injury was willful, brutal, or where the victim was of a protected status (a boy under twelve years or a woman of child-bearing age). Shari Diamond and Jonathan Casper, "Blindfolding the Jury to Jury Consequences: Damages, Experts, and the Civil Jury," *Law and Society Review* 26 (1992): 513; *The Law of the Salian Franks*, ed. Katherine F. Drew (Philadelphia: University of Pennsylvania Press, 1991), 86, 162, 178, 180, 200.

83. Friedman, *History of American Law*, 300–302; 469–72; Horwitz, *Transformation 1*, 99, 166–67; 208–10.

84. 44 Wis. 282.

85. See Robert S. Hunt, *Law and Locomotives: The Impact of the Railroad on Wisconsin Law in the Nineteenth Century* (Madison: University of Wisconsin Press, 1958), 98–131; and *Attorney General* v *Railway Companies*, 35 Wis. 425 (1874).

86. *Brown* v *Swineford*, 44 Wis 282, at 294 (1878).

87. *Verrill* v *Inhabitants of Minot*, 31 Me. 299 (1850); *Matteson* v *NY Central RR*, 62 Barb. (N.Y. Sup. Ct.) 364, at 368 (1862); *Curtiss* v *Rochester & Syracuse RR*, 20 Barb. (N.Y. Supreme Ct.) 282 at 288, (1855); *Ransom* v *NY & Erie RR*, 15 N.Y. 415, at 417 (1857); *Masters* v *Town of Warren*, 27 Ct. 293 (1858) *Shaw* v *Boston & Worcester RR*, 74 Mass. (8 Gray) 45, at 63 and 81 (1857) (but see the concession by attorneys for the railroad, E. R. Hoar and Benjamin F. Butler, on appeal after retrial (82) that "a reasonable *solatium*, or satisfaction, for . . . pain of body and mind" was lawful for the jury to award, though this jury had exceeded that "reasonable"

standard); *Pennsylvania RR v Allen,* 53 Pa. 276, at 277 (1866); *City of Chicago v Jones,* 66 Ill. 349 (1872); *Solen v Virginia & Truckee RR,* 3 Nev. 106 at 113 (1878); *Georgia Pacific RR v Freeman,* 83 Ga. 583, 10 S. E. 277 (1889).

88. Attorney Ebenezer R. Hoar in *Shaw v Boston & Worcester RR.* Cf. the entry in the English *Herapath's Journal* for August of 1851, regarding the "ruinous" awards levied against railroads: "The whole of their profit will be swept away." (Cited in Kostal, *Law and English Railway Capitalism,* 88.)

89. This, I confess, was actually the rationale of an *English* Queen's Counsel, one Harcourt, in *Fair v London and Northwestern Railway,* 21 L. T. (N. S.) 326 (1869), but the principle was expressed as well in American courts. (See also the observation in *Railway Record,* 5 August 1854: "The payment of a few shillings under the designation of *fare* can hardly be construed to a legal *consideration* for a contingent risk of 4000!" In fact, by 1850 the English Great Western Railway was insuring itself against lawsuits flowing from a major accident.

Just as *American* jurists rejected this Horwitzian/Posnerian reasoning, the English Court of Common Pleas rejected Harcourt's argument as well and affirmed an award of £5,250 to this "gentleman of good prospects."

90. William Yerger and James Yerger, counsel for the New Orleans, Jackson, & Great Northern Railroad in *N. O., J. & G. N. RR v Bailey,* 40 Miss. 395 at 407–8 (1866).

91. Attorney Herbert in *Mason v Ellsworth,* 32 Me. 271 (1850). (Herbert's opposing counsel was John Appleton.)

92. Hoar and Benjamin F. Butler in *Shaw v Boston & Worcester RR,* 74 Mass. 45 (1857). Cf. the brief of B. C. Whitman (a former Nevada Supreme Court Justice, later Chief Justice of the California Supreme Court) for the railroad in *Solen v Va. & Truckee RR,* Nevada State Archives, Carson City, Supreme Court Records, file no. 852; and the argument of defendant's counsel in *Porter v Hannibal & St. Joseph Railway,* 71 Mo. 60, at 69 (1879).

93. *Morse v Auburn & Syracuse RR,* 10 Barb. (N.Y. Sup. Ct.) 621, at 624 (1851). I recognize that the N.Y. Court of Appeals was superior to the New York Supreme Court by 1851, and that, as such, this decision did not bind New York jurists to any rule of precedent, but the fact is that Chief Justice Hiram Denio and Justice Henry Cowen of the Court of Appeals, referring to "numerous authorities", took the same position in *Ransom v N.Y. & Erie RR,* 15 N.Y. 415, at 417 (1857). Denio also observed of the railroad counsel's "no standard to compute" objection to pain and suffering awards: "No authorities are referred to to sustain this position." Compare the remarks of Justice Joseph G. Baldwin (author of *Flush Times in Alabama*) in *Fairchild v California Stage Co.,* 13 Cal. 599, at 601 (1859); Justice Samuel Wells in *Verrill v Inhabitants of Minot,* 31 Me. 299 (1850); Justice Joseph Howard in *Mason v Ellsworth,* 32 Me. 271 (1850); Justice T. R. Strong in *Curtiss v Rochester & Syracuse RR,* 20 Barb. (NY Sup. Ct.) 282 (1855); Chief Justice Ira Perley in *Hopkins v Atlantic & St. Lawrence RR,* 36 N. H. 9 (1857) ("a subject in which all the travelling public are deeply interested, for railroads have now a practical monopoly for transporting passengers on all the principal lives of travel"); Justice H. K. McCay in *Atlanta & Richmond Air Line RR v Wood,* 48 Ga. 565, at 570 (1873) ("a gross wrong, and the company ought to pay for it").

94. *Morse v Auburn & Syracuse RR,* 10 Barb. (N.Y. Sup. Ct.) 621 (1851).

95. *Farwell* v *Boston & Worcester RR*, 45 Mass. 49 (1842).

96. *Shaw* v *Boston & Worcester RR*, 74 Mass. (8 Gray) 45, at 66 (1857). Cf. *Worster* v *Props. of Canal Bridge*, 16 Pick. (33 Mass.) 544, at 547 (1835); *Linsley* v *Bushnell*, 15 Ct. 225, at 236 (1842); *Canning* v *Inhabs. of Williamstown*, 1 Cush. (55 Mass.) 451 (1848); *Seger* v *Town of Barkhampsted*, 22 Ct. 289, at 298 (1853).

97. *Frink & Co.* v *Coe*, 4 Greene (Iowa) 555, at 559 (1854).

98. *New Jersey Railroad* v *Kennard*, 21 Pa. St. 203 (1853). Cf. *Pa. RR* v *McCloskey's Admin.*, 23 Pa. St. 526 at 532 (1854), where Lowrie, J., speaks of the jury's "loving mercy." And see *Flinn* v *P.,W., & B. RR*, 1 Houst. (Del.) 467 (1857) (jury award of thirteen thousand dollars to a sheep drover injured in a collision.)

99. *Joliet, Aurora & Northern RR*, 36 Ill. App. 450, at 458 (1889). See also the weight given to each side of the cost-benefit equation by Chief Justice Charles Lawrence eighteen years earlier in *RR* v *Gregory*, 58 Ill. 226 at 228 (1871): "We cannot regard the saving of a few minutes of time . . . a matter of such importance as to justify a railroad in permitting its fastest trains to dash with unabated speed through villages, where men, women and children are liable at all times to be on the open and unguarded track. . . . Accidents may be less common than one would suppose; but that [this] must be dangerous is self-evident, and the law requires of these companies the greatest precautions for the safety of human life."

100. *Smith* v *Dittman*, 16 Daly (22 N.Y.C. P.) 427 at 431 (1890). See also *Richards* v *Sandford*, 2 E. D. Smith (N.Y.C. P.) 349 (1854); *Peatz* v *City of Cohoes*, 8 Abb. Pr. (N.Y. Sup. Ct.) 392 (1880); *Westerfield* v *Levis*, 43 La. Ann. 63, 9 So. 52 (1891).

101. *Donnell* v *Sandford*, 11 La. Am. 645, at 646 (1856). (This, however, had been a *battery* action against an individual for biting a carpenter's thigh, which led to infection and amputation.) *Merrill* v *City of St. Louis*, 12 Mo. App. 466, at 469 (1882); *Pa. RR* v *Allen*, 53 Pa. St. 276, at 277–78 (1866); *Dimitt* v *Hanibal & St. Joseph RR*, 40 Mo. App. 654, at 658 (1890). Cf. the instructions of federal district judge Benedict in *Reiss* v *North-German Lloyd*, 11 Fed. R. 844 (1881); and *Holyoke* v *Grand Trunk Ry*, 48 N. H. 541, at 545 (1869). (But see *Malone* v *Hawley*, 46 Cal. 409 (1873), where a new trial was granted because the jury had been instructed to take the plaintiff's "condition in life" into account.)

However, in 1891 the Pennsylvania Supreme Court refused to tolerate a trial judge's remark in his jury instructions that "no person would voluntarily endure such pain." There was to be "no market" assumed by the jury with regard to pain, and they were not to be invited to imagine how much *they* would want to be paid for such pain as the plaintiff was suffering. *Baker* v *Pa. Co.*, 142 Pa. 503, at 510, 21 Atl. 979 (1891). Cf. *Dunn* v *Pa RR*, 20 Phil. 258, at 261 (Ct. C. P. 1890).

102. See *Donnell* v *Sanford*, 11 La. Ann. 645 (1856); *Caldwell* v *N.J. Steamboat Co.*, 56 Barb. (N.Y. Sup. Ct.) 425 (1870); *Miller* v *The W. G. Hewes*, Cir. Ct. E. D. Tex., 16 Fed. Cas. 363 (1870); *City of Chicago* v *Elzeman*, 71 Ill. 131 (1873); *Pittsburgh, Cincinnati & St. Louis RR* v *Spoiner*, 85 Ind. 165, at 173 (1882); *Merrill* v *St Louis*, 12 Mo. App. 466, at 468–69 (1882); *City of Salina* v *Trosper*, 27 Kan. 544 (1882); and *Atchison, Topeka, and Santa Fe RR* v *Chance*, 57 Kan. 40, 45 PAC 60 (1896). See also *I. & G. N.RR* v *Underwood*, 64 Tex. 463 (1885), where the plaintiff specifically asked for $500. for medical bills, $2500. for lost income, five thousand dollars for pain and suffering, and twenty thousand dollars for loss of limbs (future income and mental suffering); and *Atlanta & West Point RR* v *Johnson*, 66 Ga. 259

(1881), where the plaintiff asked for ten thousand dollars for loss of past and future income (his left hand had to be amputated. He was a "trainhand"), ten thousand dollars for pain and suffering, and five thousand dollars for medical expenses. Cf. William Zelermyer, "Damages for Pain and Suffering," *Syracuse Law Review* 6 (1954): 27, at 27f; and Comment, "A Quantum Study of Pain and Suffering awards in the Louisiana Appellate Courts . . . 1976–78," *Loyola Law Review* 25 (1979): 117.

103. President Judge John Phillips in *Fell v Rich Hill Coal Mining Co*, 23 Mo. App. 216 (1886).

104. Briefs for *Solen, Resp., v Virginia & Truckee RR, Appl.*, 13 Nev. 106 (1878), no. 852, pp. 43, 45, Supreme Court Records, Nevada State Library and Archives, Division of Archives and Records, Carson City.

105. Comment, "Loss of Enjoyment," *ALR* 120 (1939): 535.

106. *Taber v Huston*, 5 Ind. 322 (1854); *Toledo, Wabash, & Western RR v Baddeley*, 54 Ill. 19, at 25 (1870); *Walker v Erie RR*, 63 Barb. (N.Y.) 260 (1872); *Louisville & Nashville RR v Mitchell*, 87 Ky. 327, 8 S. W. 706 (1888); *Heddles v Chicago & N. W. RR*, 77 Wis. 228, 46 N. W. 115, at 118 (1890). Cf. *Cox v Vanderkleed*, 21 Ind. 164 (1863); *Chicago City Ry v Wilcox*, 33 Ill. App. 453 (1889); and *American Strawboard Co. v Foust*, 12 Ind. App. 421, 39 N. E. 891 (1895). Cf. *Phillips v London & SW RR*, L. R., 50 B 78 at 80 (1879).

107. I have added the racial qualifier to this statement both because, as a generalization, blacks shared few of the benefits of economic growth in nineteenth century America and, more specifically, because each time I could clearly identify a tort plaintiff as being a free black, I found little or no humanity displayed by the appellate court. (*Turner v North Beach & Mission RR*, 34 Cal. 594 (1868); *Pleasants v North Beach & Mission RR*, 34 Cal. 586 (1868); and *Sibley v Smith*, 46 Ark. 275 (1885)).

108. Justice Theron Metcalf in *Canning v Inhabitants of Williamstown*. 1 Cush. (55 Mass.) 451, at 452 (1848).

109. Simon Greenleaf, *A Treatise on the Law of Evidence*, 3 vols. (Cambridge, Mass., 1850), vol. 2, sec. 267, italics mine (first vol. published in 1842).

110. Theodore Sedgwick, *A Treatise on the Measure of Damages* (New York, 1847), 45, app., 652–72 (sec. 484). Cf. *American Law Reporter*, June 1847.

111. By Justice Greene in *Frink & Co v Coe*, 4 Greene (Iowa) 555, at 556 (1854); by Justice Ellsworth in *Masters v Town of Warren*, 27 Ct. 293 (1858); and by Justice Henry in *Porter v Hannibal & St. Joseph RR*, 71 MO. 66, at 81–83. (Justice Henry, in proper juridical fashion, preferred to imagine Greenleaf's seeming misunderstanding of the meaning of Justice Theron Metcalf's opinion in *Canning v Inhabitants of Williamstown*, as "a typographical error" (83), but the fact is that Metcalf was the sole mid-nineteenth century jurist to show any sympathy with Greenleaf's position. (*American Jurist* 3 [1830]: 287.) Cf. Justice Walton in *Goddard v Grand Trunk RR of Canada*, 57 Me. 202, at 220 (1869).

112. See, for example, Justice Storrs in *Seger v Town of Barkhampsted*, 22 Ct. 289, at 298 (1853) ("His mind is no less a part of his person than his body.") and Chief Justice Gilfillan in *Pureell v St. Paul City Ry*, 48 Minn. 34, 50 N. W. 1034, at 1035 (1892) ("The mind and the body operate reciprocally on each other.")

113. *Schmitz v St. Louis, Iron Mt., & Southern RR* (Mo.), 24 5W 472, at 477

(1893) (denying that a nine-year-old boy "could be capable of suffering mental anguish.") (The court disagreed and affirmed a $5,708 award.)

114. *Victorian Ry Commissioners v Coultas*, L. R., 13 App. Cas. 222, at 226 (H. of L., 1888).

115. See *Wyman v Leavitt*, 71 Me. 227 (1880); and *Trigg v St. Louis, Kansas City, and Northern RR*, 74 Mo. 147 (1881). It *remained* the case in Massachusetts (*Spade v Lynn & Boston Ry*, 172 Mass. 488 (1899); and Pennsylvania (*Ewing v P., C., & St. L. RR*, 147 Pa. St. 40 (1892).

116. Edward Brown, "Regulating Damage Claims for Emotional Injuries before the First World War," *Behavioral Sciences and the Law* 8 (1990): 421; *Purcell v St. Paul City Ry*, 48 Minn. 34, 50 NW 1034, at 1035 (1892); *Illinois Central RR v Latimer*, 128 Ill. 163, 21 NE 7 (1889); *Hill v Kimball*, 76 Tex. 210, 13 SW 59 (1890); *Missouri Pacific v Kaiser*, 82 Tex. 144, 18 SW 305 (1891); *Sloane v Southern California RR*, 111 Cal. 688, 44 Pac. 320 (1896); *Yoakum v Kroeger*, (Tex. Civ. App.), 27 5 W 952, at 954 (1894); *Mack v South Bound RR*, 52 S. C. 323, 29 S. E. 905 (1898); and *Mitchell v Rochester Ry*, 4 Misc. Rpts. 575, 25 NY Sup. 744, at 749 (1893), where Justice William Rumsey observed that while British decisions still did not allow such recovery, "the weight to be given to any decided case as an authority depends not alone upon the rank of the court, but upon the solidity of the reasons upon which the decision is founded, and the perspicuity and precision with which those reasons are expressed." Here was a New York (lower) appellate court of the Age of Formalism that did not blindly follow precedent. Cf. *Homans v Boston Elevated RR*, 180 Mass. 456 at 457, 62 N. E. 737 (1902), where Chief Justice Holmes called the physical touching rule "arbitrary," but then observed it. But see *Simone v The R. I. Co.*, 28 R. I. 186, 66 Atl. 202 (1907) where *Coultas* was rejected despite *Homans*.

Robert Rabin, in an otherwise excellent essay, "Historical Development of the Fault Principle," 925 at 949, notes the reluctance of earlier nineteenth century courts to allow damages for "non-touching" emotional distress and misses this late-nineteenth-century development. Cf. Francis Bohlen, "The Right to Recover for Injury Resulting from Negligence without Impact," in Bohlen, *Studies in the Law of Torts* (Indianapolis: Bobbs-Merrill, 1926), 252–90.

117. *Schroeder v Chicago, Rock Island & Pacific RR*, 47 Iowa 375, at 379 (1877). A New York Superior Court judge drew these analogies more explicitly nine years before *Schroeder*. He added that he could find "no recorded case" on the subject of courts requiring medical examinations of plaintiffs in personal injury cases and he suspected that "no such application was ever made." He ordered the examination of a seven year-old girl in a malpractice suit. *Walsh v Sayre*, 52 How. Prac. 334, at 344, (1868). Either court (or both) may have been aware of the passage of a Parliamentary statute in 1868 granting to railroads the right to have their own physicians examine plaintiffs suing for personal injuries (Reg. of Railways Act, 31 & 32 Vic. c 119, s 26).

118. *Atchison, Topeka & Santa Fe RR v Thiel*, 29 Kan. 466 (1883) (in a new trial, after the railroad's expert medical examination *was* admitted into evidence, the second jury returned a verdict five times as large as the first one had! *Atchison, T. & S. F. RR v Thiel*, 32 Kan. 160, 4 Pac. 352 (1886)); *Fitzgerald v Dobson*, 78 Me. 559, 7 Atl.

704 (1887) (a dog bite case in which the Supreme Court, despite some prejudicial error to the defendant, refused to grant a new trial because it was appalled by the defendant physicians' examination of the nine year-old female plaintiff and did not want to "subject this little girl to similar treatment" again); *RR v Underwood*, 64 Tex. 463 (1884); *Missouri Pacific RR v Johnson*, 72 Tex. 95, 10 S. W. 325 (1888) (the court may refuse the defendant's request for a medical examination of the plaintiff where the defendant insists on a particular physician who is objectionable to the plaintiff).

119. *Miami & Montgomery Turnpike Co. v Baily*, 37 Ohio St. 104, at 107 (1881). Cf. *McGovern v Hope*, 63 N.J.L. 76, 42 Atl. 830 (1899); *Terre Haute & I. R. Co. v Brunker*, (Ind.) 26 N. E. 178 (1890); and *Hess v Lowery*, 122 Ind. 225, 23 N. E. 156 (1890) (the court may refuse to allow a physical examination of the plaintiff during the defendant's presentation of the case but after the plaintiff had rested its case).

120. *Roberts v Ogdensburgh & Lake Champlain RR*, 29 Hun (N.Y. Sup. Ct.) 154, at 156 (1883); *McSweeny v Broadway & 7th Ave RR*, 7 N.Y. Sup. 456 (1889) (a streetcar passenger who "suffered great pain" when she fell, fracturing her hip entering the car when it started prematurely, did not have to submit to a physical examination); and *McQuigan v RR*, 129 N.Y. 50, 29 N. E. 235 (1891). Barbara Welke has, similarly, found that jurists treated female plaintiffs in alighting accidents to a different, less rigorous standard of care. Welke, "Unreasonable Women: Gender and the Law of Accidental Injury, 1870–1920," *Law and Social Inquiry* 19 (1994): 369.

121. *Parker v Enslow*, 102 Ill. 272 (1882); *Chicago & Eastern Ill. RR v Holland*, 18 Ill. App. 418, at 421 (1886) (a thirty-year-old train conductor who suffered "destruction of his genital powers and the gradual failure of his mind and memory" in a train wreck did not have to submit to a medical examination, and a twenty-five-thousand-dollar judgment in his favor was affirmed). Cf. *Shephard v RR*, 85 Mo. 629 (1885); *Owens v Kansas City, St. Joseph & Council Bluffs RR*, 95 Mo. 169, 8 S. W. 350 (1888); *Union Pacific RR v Botsford*, 141 U.S. 250 (1891) (John Forrest Dillon unsuccessfully argued on behalf of the Union Pacific for the court to require an injured passenger to submit to an examination. The court declined to do so, and affirmed a ten-thousand-dollar award to her).

122. *Johnson v Wells Fargo & Co.*, 6 Nev. 224, at 239–40 (1870). Justice Whitman also excoriated the Pennsylvania legislature for having recently set a three-thousand-dollar maximum on personal injury caused by negligent railroads. Such legislation was just as "absurd and unjust" as were those judges and juries who offered unreasonably large awards to those injured by corporate defendants. This is the same B. C. Whitman who as a *former* Nevada Supreme Court justice, was to argue cases before that court on behalf of the Virginia City and Truckee Railroad.

Baron Bramwell, one of the more conservative English jurists of the nineteenth century, also offered a *taschen* metaphor (albeit disparagingly) in testimony before Parliament in 1877: "The only reason for going against the [corporate] employer [whose servant's negligence led to another's injuries] is the great convenience of his always having his pockets full." *Parl. P. 1877* (285) X. Q. 1179.

123. *Goddard v Grand Trunk RR*, 57 Me. 202 at 224 (1869); *N. O., J. & G. N. RR v Bailey*, 40 Miss. 395 at 456–57 (1866).

124. *McKinney v Neil*, 1 McLean (U.S. Circuit) 540, 16 Fed. Cas. 291, at 221, 223.

(1840). Cf. Justice William Daniel in *Farrish & Co.* V *Reigle*, 11 Gratt. (Va.) 697, at 722 (1854) ("his agonies, physical and mental, must have been intense.")

125. In *Cooper* v *Mullins*, 30 Ga. 146, at 152 (1860).

126. *Memphis and Charleston RR* v *Whitfield*, 44 Miss. 466 at 500–501 (1871).

127. *Deppe* v *Ch., R. I., & P. Ry*, 38 Iowa 592, at 598 (1874). Cf. the remarks of Justice George Wright, affirming an $8000 award to one falling into an opening in a sidewalk in *Rowell* v *Williams*, 29 Iowa 210 (1870) ("suffering intense pain for many months"); Chief Justice William Hyman, affirming an award of $25,000 to a passenger who lost his legs in a train collision in *Chappin* v *New Orleans & Carrollton R. R.*, 17 La. Ann. 19 (1865) ("a miserable cripple . . . long months of physical suffering"); and Chief Justice Silas Sanderson, affirming an award of $2,250 to an iron foundry worker who lost two toes due to company carelessness in *Aldrich* v *Palmer*, 24 Cal. 513, at 518 (1864).

But see Justice Charles Lawrence on the man "not much hurt" when the train he was riding in hit a cow on the track in 1868: "We can not . . . resist the conviction that his recovery [from "merely a muscular injury"] would have been much more rapid if he had no claim for damages, and that a verdict of $5000, which the state fixes as the maximum limit of damages for death itself . . . is wholly disproportionate to the injuries received." *Chicago, Rock Island & Pacific RR* v *McAra*, 52 Ill. 296, at 298 (1869). See also Chief Justice Sidney Breese on the award to a twenty-year-old girl who fell on a defective sidewalk suffering pain which "was not shown to be very severe": "Juries seem to entertain the idea that when a corporation is defending, the amount of damages they shall pay . . . shall be, not in proportion to the injury actually done, but according to the ability of the defendants to pay." *City of Decatur* v *Fisher*, 53 Ill. 40, at 409–10 (1870). And see Justice Austin Adams remitting $1500 of a $4000 award to a railroad worker whose broken leg was healing well: "We cannot avoid the conviction that if the defendant had been other than a corporation, the verdict would have been less. . . . The jury was influenced by prejudice." *Lombard* v *Chicago, Rock Island & Pacific RR*, 47 Iowa 494, at 498 (1877). Cf. Justice Anthony Thornton in *Chicago & Northwest RR* v *Fillmore*, 57 Ill. 265, at 267 (1870); and the views of former Judge Samuel Hand before the New York State Bar Association in 1879: "The communistic tendencies of the present time produce enormous verdicts [in personal injury suits]—fortunes in themselves . . . ." Quoted in "The Ethics of Professional Compensation," *Albany Law Journal*, June 18, 1881.

128. Evidence of judicial empathy can sometimes be detected in judicial dicta as well. Maine's Justice Charles Walton noted in *Goddard* v *Grand Trunk RR*, 57 Me. 202 at 224 (1869), that railroad corporations were capable of hiring "careful baggagemen . . . who will not handle and smash trunks and band-boxes as is now the universal custom." And Justice John O'Neall of South Carolina's high court spoke of how he knew "from a somewhat intimate acquaintance with this mode of [railway] transporation, how important it is to make no unnecessary relaxation of . . . railway . . . vigilance and care." *Zemp* v *W. & M. RR*, 43 S. C. (9 Rich.) 84 at 91 (1855). Thus Justice Joseph Story suffered an "unlucky accident" (Story and Baron Pollock were of the same mold on this score) when runaway horses on his Washington to New York stagecoach trip led to his being flung from the coach and his being left with a "lame arm" for the rest of his life. William Wetmore Story, *Life and Letters of Joseph Story*, 2 vols. (Boston, 1851), 1:418–19. Judge James Burnside of Penn-

sylvania was killed when he was thrown out of a buggy in 1859, and Justice Isaac Preston of Louisiana was killed in 1851 when the boiler of the SS *St. James* exploded. Thomas Roberts, *Memoirs of J. B. Gibson* (Pittsburgh, 1890), 88n.

129. *Baker v Bolton*, 1 Camp. 493, 170 ER 1033 (N. P. 1808); *Cross v Guthery*, 2 Root (Ct.) 90 (1794); *Ct. Mutual Life Ins. Co. v N.Y. & N. H. RR*, 25 Ct. 265 (1856); *Ford v Monroe*, 20 Wend. (N.Y.) 210 (1838); *Green v Hudson River RR*, 28 Barb. (N.Y. Sup. Ct.) 9, at 22 (1858); Wex Malone, "The Genesis of Wrongful Death," *Stanford Law Review* 17 (1965): 1043 at 1063–65.

130. *Carey v Berkshire RR*, 1 Cush. (Mass.) 475 (1848); *Eden v Lexington RR*, 14 B. Mon. (Ky) 165 (1853); *Lyons v Woodward*, 49 Me. 29 (1860); *Wyatt v Williams*, 43 N. H. 102 (1861); Wex Malone, "The Formative Era of Contributory Negligence," *Illinois Law Review* 41 (1946): 151 at 170–72.

131. *Plummer v Webb*, 15 Fed. Cas. 895 (Cir. Ct. D. Mass. 1825); *James v Christy*, 18 Mo. 162 (1853); *Shields v Young*, 15 Ga. 349 (1854); *Cutting v Seabury*, 6 Fed. Cas. 1083 (Dist. Ct. D. Mass. 1860). Cf. *Tilley, Adm. v Hudson River RR*, 24 N.Y. 471 (1862).

132. *Sullivan v Union Pacific RR*, 23 Fed. Cas. 368 (1874). (The case was not reviewed by the U.S. Supreme Court, either because it was not appealed or because the Supreme Court refused to review it.) The term "scot-free" describes the corporate tortfeasor under the regimen of *Baker v Bolton*, but in fact early-nineteenth-century Scottish jurists did *not* allow negligent defendants to evade liability simply because the victim had died. See *Brown v McGregor*, 17 Fac. Coll. 232 (26 Feb. 1813).

133. *Guy v Livesey*, 3 Cro. Jac. 501, 79 ER 428 (K. B. 1619).

134. Blackstone, *Commentaries* 3:143; *Blake v RR*, 16 Jur. 562, 18 Q.B. 93 (1852).

135. *McIntyre v N.Y. Central RR*, 37 N.Y. 287 at 296 (1867). Cf. *Tilley, Adm. v Hudson River RR*, 24 N.Y. 471 (1862) (wife had made shirts in her home piecework; children owed by railroad damages for loss of "nurture and of intellectual, moral and physical training"). In *Ford v Monroe*, 20 Wend. (N.Y.) 210 (1838), the New York Supreme Court, even before that state's wrongful death statute, had affirmed a two-hundred-dollar damage award to the parents of a boy run over and killed by a carriage for the medical treatment the wife had experienced due to the shock to her maternal feelings.

136. *Pennsylvania RR v Goodman*, 62 Pa. St. 339 (1869). See also *RR v Freeman*, 97 Ala. 289, 11 So. 800 (1892); *Petrine v RR*, 29 S. C. 303, 7 SE 515 (1888); *Balt. & Ohio RR v State*, 24 Md. 271 (1866); *Webb v RR*, 7 Utah 17, 24 Pac. 616 (1890). But see *Caldwell v Brown*, 53 Pa. St. 453 (1866); *Hyatt v Adams*, 16 Mich. 180 (1867); *Little Rock & Ft. Smith RR v Barker*, 33 Ark. 350 (1878); *Cincinnati Stret Ry v Altemeier*, 60 Oh. St. 10, 53 N. E. 300 (1899); *Birkett v Kickerbocker Ice Co.*, 110 N.Y. 504, 18 N. E. 108 (1888); *Ag. & Mech. Assoc. v State*, 71 Md. 86, 18 A 37 (1889) for more conservative constructions of those state's wrongful death statutes regarding loss of companionship.

137. *Beeson v Mining Co.*, 57 Cal. 20 at 33 (1880); *Munro v Pacific Coast Dredging & Reclamation Co.*, 84 Cal. 515, 24 PAC 303 (1890); *Goodsell v Hartford & New Haven RR*, 33 Ct. 51 (1865).

138. *Florida Central RR v Foxworth*, 41 Fla. 1, 25 So. 338 (1899); *Strother v S. C. RR*, 47 S. C. 375, 25 S. E. 272 (1896).

139. *Oldfield* v *N.Y. & Harlem River RR*, 14 N.Y. 310 (1856) ($1300 for a six year old); *Ihl* v *42nd St. Ry*, 47 N.Y. 317 (1872) ($1800 for a three year old); *Potter* v *Chicago & N. W. RR*, 21 Wis. 377 (1867), cited in Zelizer's excellent study, *Pricing the Priceless Child*, 143–51.

140. Zelizer, *Pricing the Priceless Child*, 11, 24–26; Phillip Aries, *The Hour of our Death* (N.Y., 1982), 536; Ann Douglas, *The Femimization of American Culture* (New York: Knopf, 1977), 243–56.

141. *B.& O. RR* v *Wightman's Adm.*, 29 Gratt. (70 Va.) 431 (1877); *B.& O. RR* v *Noell's Adm.*, 32 Gratt. (73 Va.) 394 (1879); *Turner* v *Norfolk RR*, 40 W. Va. 688, 22 S. E. 83 (1895); *Kelley* v *Ohio RR*, 58 W. Va. 216 (1905); *Brickman* v *Southern RR*, 74 S. C. 306, 54 S. E. 553 (1906); *Anderson* v *Great Northern RR*, 15 Id. 513, 99 PAC 91 (1908); *Beaman* v *Martha Washington Mining Co.*, 23 Utah 39, 63 PAC 631 (1901); *Seaboard Air Line* v *Moseley*, 60 Fla. 186, 53 So. 718 (1910); *Fla. East Coast RR* v *Hayes*, 65 Fla. 1, 60 So. 792 (1913).

A classic "deep-pockets" statute was Florida's (ch. 3147 of 1906, amending ch. 4722 of 1899) in that it applied *only* to corporate defendants.

142. *Hicks* v *Newport, A, & H. Ry*, (1857), ref. to in *Pym, Adm.*, v *Great Northern Ry.*, 4 B.&S. 396, 122 ER 508 at 510 (Ex. 1863).

143. *Harding* v *Town of Townsend*, 43 Vt. 536 (1870); *B & O RR* v *Wightman's Adm.*, 70 Va (29 Gratt.) 431 (1877). Cf. *The Propeller Monticello* v *Gilbert Mollison*, 17 How. (U.S.) 152 (1854); *Althorpe* v *Wolfe*, 22 N.Y. 355 (1860); *Pitts. & Cinc. RR* v *Thompson*, 56 Ill. 138 (1870).

144. James Hunt, "Private Law and Public Policy: Negligence Law and Political Change in Nineteenth Century North Carolina," *North Carolina Law Review* 66 (1988): 421.

145. Marston, "Creation of a Common Law Rule," *Univ. of Pa. Law Review* 132 (1984), 609 n. 177; Seymour Thompson, *A Treatise on the Law of Negligence*, 2 vols. (San Francisco, 1886), 2:1005, discussing *Schultz* v *Pacific RR*, 36 Mo. 13 (1865), and *Proctor* v *Hannibal, etc. RR*, 64 Mo. 112 (1876); Robert Hunt, *Law and Locomotives*, 58.

146. Kermit Hall, "Progressive Reform and the Decline of Democratic Accountability: The Popular Election of State Supreme Court Judges, 1850–1920," *American Bar Foundation Research Journal* (1984): 345, esp. 365; Hall, "Dissent on the California Supreme Court, 1850–1920," *Social Science History* 11 (1987). (Hall focused on the judiciary of California, Ohio, Tennessee, and Texas. Only those on the federal bench and the state courts of South Carolina and Massachusetts, appointed to their positions, were free of any popular election recall.)

147. 118 Cal. 55, 50 PAC 25.

148. Hall, "Progressive Reform," 364.

149. *Fox* v *Oakland Consolidated RR*, 118 Cal. 55, 50 PAC 25 (1897) 27. This was the rule as well in Illinois (*City of Chicago* v *Major*, 18 Ill. 349 at 361 [1857]); California (*Karr* v *Parks*, 40 Cal. 188 [1870]); Missouri (*O'Flaherty* v *Union RR*, 45 Mo. 70 [1869]); Iowa (*Walters* v *C. R. & P. RR*, 41 Iowa 71 [1875]); Oregon (*Hedin* v *City and Suburban RR*, 26 Ore. 155, 37 PAC 540 [1894]); and Pennsylvania (*Kay* v *Pa. RR*, 65 Pa. St. 269 [1870]). It had been rejected in Wisconsin (*Potter* v *Chicago & N. W. RR*, 22 Wis. 586 [1868]); and Indiana (*City of Delphi* v *Lowery*, 74 Ind. 520 [1881]).

150. Christopher Patterson, *Railway Accident Law* (Phila., 1886), sec. 81 (ellipses mine; not in opinion). Patterson, a director of the Pennsylvania Railroad and member of the Philadelphia Bar, also called *RR* v *Stout* (the leading "attractive nuisance" case) "a miscarriage of justice" (sec. 196).

151. *Fox* v *Oakland Consol. St RR*, 118 Cal. 55, 50 PAC 25 (1897).

152. *San Francisco Examiner*, October 25, 1898, p. 2; cited in Hall, "Progressive Reform," 364.

153. Michael P. Rogin and John L. Shover, *Political Change in California Elections and Social Movements, 1890–1966* (Westport, Conn.: Greenwood, 1970), 25–28; I am indebted to Melody Andersen of the California State Archives, Sacramento, for providing me with copies of the 1898 San Francisco County returns.

154. This pattern persists, of course. Hammitt, Carroll and Relles have found that in 1979 tort defendants in personal injury cases in Cook County, Illinois, were assessed rather differently by juries, depending upon whether they were individuals, physicians, government entities, or for-profit corporations. Government defendants paid twice as much as individual defendants'; doctors paid almost two and a half times as much as individuals; for-profit corporations paid 1/3rd more than individuals unless the injuries were "serious;" then they paid almost four and a half times as much as individuals. James Hammitt, Stephen Carroll and Daniel Relles, "Tort Standards and Jury Decisions," *Journal of Legal Studies* 14 (1985): 751 at 754.

CONCLUSION

1. I found no specific evidence that jurists were consciously and willfully aiding corporations or other entrepreneurs, and several biographies of important state chief justices have found no such evidence. See, for example, Leonard Levy, *The Law of the Commonwealth and Chief Justice Shaw* (Cambridge, Mass.: Harvard University Press, 1957); John Phillip Reid, *Chief Justice: The Judicial World of Charles Doe* (Cambridge, Mass.: Harvard University Press, 1967); Reid, *An American Judge: Marmaduke Dent of West Virginia* (New York: New York University Press, 1968); David Gold, *The Shaping of Nineteenth Century Law: John Appleton and Responsible Individualism* (Westport, Conn.: Greenwood, 1990); Alan Jones, "Thomas M. Cooley and the Michigan Supreme Court, 1865–1885," *American Journal of Legal History* 10 (1968): 17; M. Brodhead, *Persevering Populist: The Life of Frank Doster* (Reno: University of Nevada Press, 1969). However, in the published state reports that served as my primary source of information, I did uncover some further evidence of judicial behavior that seems antithetical to a "corporate bias" story. Inadvertently, I noticed that some fifteen individual jurists "recused" themselves (withdrew from sitting on a case) because one or another was "a stockholder in the Canal Company" or "the Railroad Company" being sued; *Easton* v *Pa. & Ohio Canal Co.*, 13 Ohio 79 (1844); *Tonawanda RR* v *Munger*, 5 Denio (N.Y.) 266 (1848); *N. O., Jackson & Gr. N. RR* v *Harris*, 27 Miss. 517 at 541 (1854); *Flinn* v *Phil., W. & B RR*, 6 Del. (1 Houst.) 469 at 472 (1857); *Ponton* v *Wilmington & Weldon RR*, 51 N. C. (6 Jones) 245 (1858); *N. O., Jackson & Gr. N. RR* v *Allbritton*, 38 Miss. 242 at 280 (1859); *Langhoff* v *Milw. & P. du Ch. RR*, 19 Wis. 489 (1865); *Hartford Bridge Co.* v *East Hartford*, 16 Ct. 149 at 179 (1844); "related to some of the stockholders in the . . . Steamboat Company" being sued; a citizen of

the municipality being sued; *Hubbard* v *Concord*, 35 N.H. 52 at 58 (1857); or former counsel to a railroad or municipality being sued; 1 N.H. 44 (1817); 36 Mo. 352 (1865); 37 Ct. 199 (1870); 24 N.E. (N.Y.) 834 (1890). This is not to say that *every* jurist who should thereby have recused himself actually did so; it is simply to say that clear evidence exists that jurists were *expected* to recuse themselves whenever a potential conflict of interest arose, and that a number of them did so.

2. See, for example, G. Edward White, *Tort Law in America: An Intellectual History* (New York: Oxford University Press, 1985), chaps. 3–7; Kermit Hall, *The Magic Mirror: Law in American History* (New York: Oxford University Press, 1989), 294–99.

3. For an example of a treatise writer using such language see Theophilus Parsons's views on marine insurance in his *Treatise on the Law of Marine Insurance* (Boston: Little, Brown, 1868) at 6–10, brought to light in Morton Horwitz, *The Transformation of American Law, 1780–1860* (Cambridge, Mass.: Harvard University Press, 1977), 236.

4. I borrow this label from Jonathan Prude's edition of essays, *The Countryside in the Age of Capitalist Transformation* (Chapel Hill: University of North Carolina Press, 1985).

5. I have in mind Lawrence Friedman, Christopher Tomlins, Wythe Holt, and James Willard Hurst. For example, I find Wythe Holt's "Labor Conspiracy Cases in the U.S., 1805–1842: Bias and Legitimation in Common Law Adjudication," *Osgoode Hall Law Journal* 22 (1984): 591, to be persuasive, even though its message is inconsistent with my own. I have not examined labor conspiracy cases in this work. Karen Orren's study, *Belated Federalism: Labor, the Law and Liberal Development in the United States* (Cambridge, 1991), explains judicial behavior with regard to these sorts of issues in a way consistent with my own thesis, but I don't claim that she is right and Holt wrong on *that* score. Both studies are thoughtful and well argued. Hence one who is to judge their merits must get into the trenches and dig as they have, and I simply haven't done that with labor conspiracy cases.

6. See chapters 1 through 6.

7. Richard Posner, "A Theory of Negligence," *Journal of Legal Studies* 1 (1872): 72; Richard Posner, *Economic Analysis of Law*, 3rd ed. (Boston: Little, Brown, 1986), 21. But see Richard Posner, *The Economics of Justice* (Cambridge, Mass.: Harvard University Press, 1981), 115; "Wealth Maximizing is not . . . the only conception of the good or the just that has influenced law."

8. See chapters 3 and 7 and the "Entr'acte."

9. See Posner, *Economic Analysis of Law*, 47, 81, 85, 97, 106, 114, 230; Posner, "Theory of Negligence," at 44. See chapters 2, 3, 7, 8, and "Entr'Acte."

10. Adam Smith had long been concerned with "moral sentiments," but these were not of the "ideal" or Christian, but the ordinary human sort. Jeremy Bentham's "benevolence" always coincided with utility and self-love. The American Jurisprudence of the Heart was inspired more by theology than by economics. See A. Smith, *The Theory of Moral Sentiments*, ed. D. Raphael and A. MacFie (1759; reprint, Oxford: Clarendon, 1976); A. Smith, *Lectures on Jurisprudence*, ed. R.L. Meek et al. (1762–66; reprint, Oxford: Clarendon); Kenneth MacKinnon, "The 'Reasonable Man' as an Impartial Spectator" and Stephen Hicks, "The Revolution in Social Theory in the Early Nineteenth Century: From Sympathy to Disinterest-

edness with an Afterword on the Origin of the Tort of Negligence," both in *Law and Enlightenment in Britain,* ed. Tom O. Campbell (Aberdeen: Aberdeen University Press, 1990); and N. MacCormack, "Adam Smith on Law," *Valpariso Univ. Law Review* 15 (1981): 243.

11. These questions have been raised by R. B. Ferguson, "The Horwitz Thesis and Common Law Discourse in England," *Oxford Journal of Legal Studies* 3 (1983): 34; David Flaherty, *Michigan Law Review* 76 (1978): 556; and especially Robert W. Gordon, *Harvard Law Review* 94 (1981): 907 (in a review of G. Edward White's *Tort Law in America: An Intellectual History* [New York: Oxford University Press, 1980]): Gordon observes that it would be extremely difficult to insist that the fault principle in tort liability emerged in American law in response to the needs of industrialization, "for one would then have to explain, for instance, why England and the United States seem to have undertaken the systematic generalization of the fault principle to include all tort liability at the same time (1870s and 1880s) despite England's much earlier industrialization, as well as why Germany responded to industrialization by *imposing* strict liability on railroads and industrial concerns for accidents by way of exception to a pre-existing fault standard."

12. For an example, see *Reygasse v Plazon,* Fr. Cour de Cassation, Recueil Periodique et Critique (D. P.), I, 273 (1841). Others appear in chapters 3, 5, 7, and 9.

13. A. W. B. Simpson, "The Horwitz Thesis and the History of Contracts," *University of Chicago Law Review* 46 (1979): 533 at 591, citing Richard Danzig, "*Hadley v Baxendale* [breach of contract of timely delivery of new machine part; question of damages]: A Study in the Industrialization of the Law," *Journal of Legal Studies* 4 (1975): 249 at 250.

14. Cross, *The Burnt-Over District: The Social and Intellectual History of Enthusiastic Religion in Western New York, 1800–1850* (Ithaca, N.Y.: Cornell University Press, 1950); Tyler, *Freedom's Ferment* (New York: Harper and Bros., 1962); Perry Miller, "The Evangelical Basis," in *The Life of the Mind in America from the Revolution to the Civil War* (Boston, 1965).

15. I remind you again that Oliver Wendell Holmes Jr. was the central figure in this dismal crowd.

16. Atiyah, *The Rise and Fall of Freedom of Contract* (Oxford: Clarendon, 1979), 130. I am indebted to Walter Pratt, "American Contract Law at the Turn of the Century," *South Carolina Law Review* 39 (1988): 415, for many of these references and for the basic content of my argument here.

17. Posner, *Economic Analysis of Law,* 97, 106.

18. *Ex parte Young,* 30 Fed. Cas. 828 (N. D. Ill. 1874); *Beveridge v Hewitt,* 8 Ill. App. 467 (1881) (speculator was a twenty-five-year-old clerk); *Heard v Russell and Potter,* 59 Ga. 25 at 39 (1877).

19. *Brua's Appeal,* 55 Pa. St. at 299 (1867); *Waterman v Buckland,* 1 Mo. App., 45 at 48 (1876) (options on the price of "mess pork" leading to "the demoralization of society"; English cases sanctioning these contracts of "wager" had "never been regarded as good precedents in Missouri"); *Nave v Wilson,* 12 Ind. App. 38 at 45, 38 N. E. 876 at 878 (1894); *Webster v Sturges,* 7 Ill. App. 560 at 564 (1880); *Justh v Holliday,* 13 D. C. (2 Mackey) 346 (1883)(a case involving the reckless speculations of Colonel George Custer on the eve of his further recklessness at Little Big Horn).

Jurists were not alone, of course, in condemning stock speculation for its effect on "the humble." When John W. Reynolds migrated to San Francisco from the Midwest in 1875 he wrote home of the "speculative mania" that "gripped" that city. It was "all the go here-even the mechanics & servant girls who get $100 ahead put into Mining Stocks & either double it or lose it in a short time." Quoted in William Deverell, *Railroad Crossing: Californians and the Railroad, 1850–1910* (Berkeley and Los Angeles: University of California Press, 1994), 35.

20. *Sawyer, Wallace & Co. v Taggart*, 77 Ky. (14 Bush) 727 (1879); *Melchert v American Union Teleg. Co.*, 11 Fed. R. 193 at 195 (C. C. D. Iowa 1882); *Heard v Russell & Potter*, 59 Ga. 25 at 38 (1877).

21. *Heard v American Union Telegraph Co.*; *Melchert v Russell & Potter.*

22. *J. B. Lyon & Co. v Culbertson, Blair & Co.*, 83 Ill. 33 at 53 (1876).

23. Compare Lord Kenyon's dicta in *Rex v Rusby*, Peake Ad. Cas. 189, 170 ER 241 (1800), affirming a judgment against one who bought and sold oats in the same market: "The Legislature is never so well employed as when they look to the interests of those who are at a distance from them in the ranks of society. It is their duty to do so; religion calls for it; humanity calls for it . . . The law has not been disputed, for though in an evil hour all the statutes which had been existing above a century were at one blow repealed, yet thank God, the common laws were not destroyed."

After I completed this draft, I found William Novak's essay, "Public Economy and the Well-ordered Market: Law and Economic Regulation in 19th-Century America," *Law and Social Inquiry* 18 (1993): 1. Novak offers many additional examples from antebellum high courts of judicial antipathy to "free trade" arguments, and he also notes that Georgia's Judge Lumpkin appeared to be unresponsive to them.

24. Kevin Teeven, *A History of the Anglo-American Common Law of Contract* (New York: Greenwood, 1990), 184–85, 248–51. But see also Paula Dalley, "The Law of Deceit, 1790–1860: Continuity Amidst Change," *American Journal of Legal History* 30 (1995): 407, who demonstrates that there was essentially no change in these years of "instrumentalism" in the rules of contract regarding deceit.

25. In *King v Greenhill*, 4 Ad. & El. 624, 111 ER 922 (K. B. & H. of L. 1836).

26. See *Foster v Alston*, 6 How. (Miss.) 406 at 433–34 (1842); *Miner v Miner*, 11 Ill. 43 at 49 (1849); *Mercein v People*, 25 Wend. (N.Y.) 64 at 106 (1840); M. Grossberg, *Governing the Hearth: Law and the Family in Nineteenth Century America* (Chapel Hill: University of North Carolina Press, 1985), 240–41. To be sure, reactionary jurists could and did at times quote the Bible as authority too. And Heart judgments by the New York Senate's Court of Errors could be evaded on rehearing by reactionary jurists (as in *People v Mercein*, 3 Hill 399 [1842], where Justice Esek Cowen held that *Patria potestas* was "in accordance with the law of God."

27. M. Salmon, *Women and the Law of Property in Early America* (Chapel Hill: University of North Carolina Press, 1986), 185; C. Klafter, *Reason over Precedents: Origins of American Legal Thought*, (New York: Greenwood, 1993), 105, 121; B. Welke, "Unreasonable Women: Gender and the Law of Accidental Injury, 1870–1920," *Law and Social Inquiry* 19 (1994): 369–401, for evidence of the paternalism of many nineteenth-century jurists.

28. Kenneth Winkle, *The Politics of Community: Migration and Politics in Antebellum Ohio* (New York: Cambridge University Press, 1988), 58–60; Amy Dru Stanley, "Beggars Can't be Choosers: Compulsion and Contract in Postbellum

America," *Journal of American History* 78 (1992): 1265 at 1280; *People v Phillips*, 1 Edm. Sel. Cas. (N.Y.) 386 (1847); *In re Forbes*, 19 How. Pr. (N.Y.) 457 (1860); *State v Custer*, 65 N. C. 339 (1871); *Bouls v State*, 49 Ala. 22 (1873); *Walters v State*, 52 Ga. 574 (1874); *Taylor v State*, 59 Ala. 19 (1877); *Hicks v State*, 76 Ga. 326 (1886); *In re Conroy*, 54 How. Pr. (N.Y.) 432 (1878); *In re Jordan*, 90 Mich. 3, 50 N. W. 1087 (1892); *Comm. v Kehoe*, 11 Pa. Comm. Ct. 516 (1892); *People v Denby*, 108 Cal. 54, 40 PAC 1051 (1895). Freedmen and freedwomen in the post-Reconstruction South were often held in virtual peonage by anti-enticement, contract-enforcement, emigrant-agent, criminal-surety, and vagrancy statutes, and that while some of these were declared unconstitutional, most were not. See William Cohen, "Negro Involuntary Servitude in the South, 1865–1940," *Journal of Southern History* 42 (1976): 31.

29. A. Steinberg, *The Transformation of Criminal Justice: Philadelphia, 1800–1880* (Chapel Hill: University of North Carolina Press, 1989), 90, 214; A. J. Kier Nash, "A More Equitable Past? Southern Supreme Courts and the Protection of the Antebellum Negro," *North Carolina Law Review* 48 (1970): 197. But see Thomas Russell, "South Carolina's Largest Slave Auctioneering Firm," *Chicago-Kent Law Review* 68 (1993): 1241, for evidence that southern jurists were, ultimately, indifferent to the fate of slave families, broken at court-ordered auctions ("sales by operation of law").

30. Hall, *Magic Mirror*, 372. But see Stephen Schlossman, *Love and the American Delinquent* (Chicago: University of Chicago Press, 1977), 42–44; and William F. Kuntz, *Criminal Sentencing in Three Nineteenth Century Cities: Social History of Punishment in New York, Boston and Philadelphia; 1830–1880* (New York: Garland, 1988).

31. I owe the term to Peter Hoffer, who suggested it after reading a first draft of this book.

32. See the continued resistance to *Britton v Turner* in chapter 6, table 1, and see Peter Karsten, "The 'Discovery' of Law by English and American Jurists of the 17th, 18th, and 19th Centuries: Third-Party Beneficiary Contracts as a Test Case," *Law and History Review* 9 (1991): 327.

33. These were: the invocation of "fundamental" law on behalf of manumitted, fugitive, and sojourner slaves, the rejection of "ancient lights," the prudent investor rule, quantum meruit recovery in breaches of labor contracts, the "superior servant," different department, and safe tool and place exceptions to the fellow-servant rule, the "balancing of equities" in pollution nuisance cases, the attractive nuisance rule, ceasing to impute parental contributory negligence to children, freeing those injured in the act of saving others from contributory negligence, the favoring of third-party gift- over third-party creditor-beneficiaries, allowing the creation of charitable trusts by bequest, leaving the question of plaintiffs' contributory negligence as a fact question for the jury, the competent servant, subcontractor, complaint-of-hazard, and no-warning-of-hazard exceptions to the assumption-of-risk rule, the allowing of contingency-fee contracts, resistance to the adoption of the fellow-servant rule, allowing plaintiffs to "come to the nuisance," rejecting the "industrial zone" defense in pollution nuisance cases, allowing most "private" nuisance bills and suits, refusing to allow common carriers to contract out of liability, rejecting sovereign immunity for injuries caused by negligent road and bridge authorities, refusing to order examinations of plaintiffs by defendants' physicians in

personal injury cases, and the allowing of damage awards for mental shock where no "touching" of the injured plaintiff had occurred.

34. It also mixes the two "pro-entrepreneurial" innovations ("balancing the equities" in pollution-nuisance cases, and the prudent-investor rule) in with the other, almost entirely proplaintiff innovations, but this doesn't trouble me, because the scale measures propensity to *innovate*, not "humaneness" or the "developmentalist" thesis that I have rejected in the qualitative analysis throughout the book.

35. Some possible explanations: New Hampshire's court was led in the antebellum years by the innovative Joel Parker, in the later nineteenth century by the innovative Charles Doe. It seemed at times to enjoy sparring with its doctrinal neighbors, Massachusetts and Maine. Louisiana, with its mix of codified civil law and adopted common law, may be an anomaly. Minnesota's score does resemble those of Wisconsin's and Michigan's, and all three of these Old Northwest high courts attracted large numbers of New England–trained jurists.

36. Strong in *Annals of Iowa*, 3rd ser., 1:255 (1894), cited in Charles Fairman, *Mr. Justice Miller and the Supreme Court, 1862–1890* (Cambridge, Mass.: Harvard University Press, 1949), 22–23; Fairman, "Miller, Samuel," *Dictionary of American Biography*, 639; Miller, *Albany Law Journal*, July 5, 1879, 5. Compare the distinction made in William R. Johnson, *Schooled Lawyers: A Study in the Clash of Professional Cultures* (New York: New York University Press, 1978), 177; and Friedman, *History of American Law*, 394.

37. Posner, "Theory of Negligence," 29 at 89, 95.

38. See text at note 190 in chapter 3.

39. *RR v Ross*, 112 U.S. 377 (1884); *RR v Baugh*, 149 U.S. 368 (1893); *RR v Dixon*, 194 U.S. 338 (1904). Edward Purcell, *Litigation and Inequality*, 78–81, draws attention to these cases, and notes elsewhere (62), the tendency of opposition to the drift of the federal courts away from plaintiff-oriented positions to have come from the south, midwest and west.

40. See *Cooper v Sunderland*, 3 Clarke (Iowa) 114 at 140 (1856); *Lehow v Simonton*, 3 Colo. 346 (1877); George Dargo, *Jefferson's Louisiana: Politics and the Clash of Legal Traditions* (1975), 237; Gordon Bakken, *Practicing Law in Frontier California* (Lincoln: University of Nebraska Press, 1991), 28–31, 149; Bakken, *The Development of Law in Frontier California, 1850–1890* (Westport, Conn.: Greenwood, 1985), 7, 38.

41. This East-West propensity can even be detected within a state: The Massachusetts constitutional convention of 1853 included a provision for the election of judges, but while this was approved by western counties, it was rejected when the eastern counties voted against it. Jean Matthews, *Rufus Choate: The Law and Civic Virtue* (Philadelphia: Temple University Press, 1980), 190.

For a good overview of "the legal culture of the Great Plains," with much more attention to statutory innovations than this book offers, see Kermit F. Hall, "The Legal Culture of the Great Plains," *Great Plains Quarterly* 12 (1992): 86. See also Evan Haynes, *The Selection and Tenure of Judges* (1944), 90–135.

42. Robert Hunt, *Law and Locomotives*, 109 (Taylor chose Edward G. Ryan. He was not disappointed.)

43. See Freyer, *Producers and Capitalists*.

44. U.S. Bureau of the Census, *Historical Statistics of the United States: Colonial Times to 1957* (Washington, D.C.: GPO, 1961), 7, 284, 366.

45. Jon Butler, *Awash in a Sea of Faith: Christianizing the American People* (Cambridge, Mass.: Harvard University Press, 1990), 270; Richard Carwardine, *Evangelicals and Politics in Antebellum America* (New Haven, Conn.: Yale University Press, 1993), 44.

46. William Miller, quoted by Nathan Hatch, "*Sola Scriptura* and *Novus Ordo Seclorum*," in *The Bible in America*, ed. Nathan Hatch and Mark Noll (New York: Oxford University Press, 1982), 75; John Nevin, quoted in Hatch, ibid., 60.

47. See, for example, David Gold, *The Shaping of Nineteenth Century Law: John Appleton and Responsible Individualism* (New York: Greenwood, 1990); and Christopher Tomlins, *Law, Labor and Ideology in the Early American Republic* (New York: Cambridge University Press, 1993).

48. Hatch, "*Sola Scriptura*", 61.

49. See Butler, *Awash in a Sea of Faith*; Hatch, "The Democratization of Christianity," in *Religion and American Politics*, ed. Mark Noll (New York, 1990); Anne M. Boylan, *Sunday School: The Formation of an American Institution, 1790–1880* (New Haven, Conn.: Yale University Press, 1988); Lori Ginzberg, *Women and the Work of Benevolence: Morality, Politics and Class in the Nineteenth Century United States* (New Haven, Conn.: Yale University Press, 1990); Carroll Smith-Rosenberg, *Religion and the Rise of the American City: The New York City Mission Movement, 1812–1870* (Ithaca: Cornell University Press, 1971); Martha T. Blauvelt, "Society, Religion and Revivalism: The Second Great Awakening in New Jersey, 1780–1830" (Ph.D. diss., Princeton University, 1975). An older but still valuable analysis of this sort is Cross, *Burned-Over District*.

50. Magoon, *Republican Christianity* (Boston, 1849), 312–23, cited in Merle Curti, *The Growth of American Thought*, 2nd ed. (New York: Harper and Bros., 1951), 308.

51. Francis Asbury, quoted by Richard Carwardine, "Methodist Ministers and the 2nd Political System," in R. Richey and K. Rowe, eds., *Rethinking Methodist History* (Nashville: Methodist Church of U.S. Society, 1988), 134–47. Benevolent societies did *not* simply "labor to make men behave," as Clifford Griffin would have it in *The Brothers' Keepers: Moral Stewardship in the United States, 1800–1865* (New Brunswick: Rutgers University Press, 1965), xii. Much "benevolence" was inspired by concern for the victims of slavery, drink, and cruelty, not simply the minds (or souls) of their tormentors. See also Lois Banner, "Religious Benevolence as Social Control: A critique of the Interpretation," *Journal of American History* 60 (1973): 34; and Lori Ginzberg, *Women and the Work of Benevolence*.

52. Lori Ginzberg, *Women and the Work of Benevolence*, 70 n. 5.

53. Cited in ibid., 27 n. 39.

54. Isaac Cornelison, quoted in Robert T. Handy, *Undermined Establishment: Church-State Relations in America, 1880–1920* (Princeton: Princeton University Press, 1991), 11. See also Handy, *Undermined Establishment*, 26.

55. Geoffrey Blodgett, "A New Look at the Gilded Age," in Daniel W. Howe, ed., *Victorian America* (Philadelphia: University of Pennsylvania Press, 1976), 99. See also the studies cited in the Introduction, notes 19–21, and Blodgett's further observations on this subject (101): "While considerable attention has been focussed on

the changing nature of markets, on the decline of independent artisans and farmers and the rise of the American working class, surprisingly little energy has gone into exploring the dynamics of insurgent religious movements. This neglect stems both from the neo-Marxist preoccupation with the formation of social class and the assumption that religion is generally a conservative force and a pernicious one. What these studies fail to take into account is that for better or worse, the most dynamic popular movements in the early republic were expressly religious."

56. E. A. Penniman to Bigler, quoted in William Gienapp, *The Origins of the Republican Party, 1852–56* (New York: Oxford University Press, 1987), 144; Fillmore supporter, cited in Carwardine, *Evangelicals and Politics*, 261. See also Edw. Pierce to Salmon P. Chase, November 5, 1855: "The people will not confront the issues we present. They want a Paddy hunt & on a Paddy hunt they will go." Gienapp, *Origins*, 223.

57. We know more about the elections of state legislators than we do state supreme court jurists. See Phillip Vandermeer, *The Hoosier Politician: Officeholding and Political Culture in Indiana, 1896–1920* (Urbana: University of Illinois Press, 1985); and Dennis Downey and Francis Bremer, eds., *A Guide to the History of Pennsylvania* (New York: Greenwood, 1993). Perhaps jurists have always seemed less interesting than "politicians" and "lawmakers" to political historians. And that may explain why these historians sometimes fail to recognize, or at least to mention, that candidate A or B had been an important supreme court justice before the election at hand. Thus Gienapp identifies our Justice Greene Bronson, the "Hard" Democrat's gubernatorial candidate in 1856, simply as a former Collector of the Port of New York (*Origins*, 156), and Ronald Formisano quotes Isaac Christiancy several times without mentioning that he was elected to the Michigan Supreme Court in 1857 and served until 1875, and as chief justice for two of those years. Formisano, *The Birth of Mass Political Parties: Michigan, 1827–1861* (Princeton: Princeton University Press, 1971), 253, passim.

58. Kermit Hall, *The Politics of Justice: Lower Federal Judicial Selection and the 2nd Party System, 1829–1861* (Lincoln: University of Nebraska Press, 1979), 10–12, 24–26, 143; *New York Tribune*, April 26, 1858, p. 4.

59. Quoted in Kermit Hall, "The Judiciary on Trial: State Constitutional Reform and the Rise of an Elected Judiciary, 1846–1860," *Historian* 45 (1983): 337 at 347.

60. Gienapp, *Origins*, 94–95, 99, 227; John Coleman, "The Public Career of James Campbell," *Pennsylvania History* 5 (1962): 24; Samuel T. McSeveney, *The Politics of Depression: Political Behavior in the Northeast, 1893–1896* (New York: 1972), 42–43, 50, 245. Campbell and Maynard lost, both running well behind other candidates for office in their party. In Campbell's case, some non-Catholic Democrats in Pennsylvania (chiefly Episcopalians and German Lutherans) were not prepared to vote for a Catholic in 1851. In Maynard's case, some Democrats in Grover Cleveland's wing of the party in New York were critical of the steps he had taken to produce Democratic control of the state senate.

61. Gienapp, *Origins*, 501, 508, 523. See also Victor Howard, "The 1856 Election in Ohio: Moral Issues in Politics," *Ohio History* 80 (1971): 24.

62. Thus Samuel McSeveney (*The Politics of Depression*, 150), notes that when New Jersey's equity court chancellor, Alexander McGill, was nominated for governor in 1895, none of his decisions as a chancellor were at issue. The only bone of con-

tention was his vote on a Catholic Protectory bill before the New Jersey legislature some twenty years before, while he was a legislator.

63. Methodist minister Orange Scott at New England Anti-Slavery Society meeting in 1837, noted in William Wiecek, "Slavery and Abolition before the U.S. Supreme Court, 1820–1860," *Journal of American History* 65 (1978): 34 at 40; Boston abolitionist W. I. Bowditch to Senator Charles Summer, April 23, 1852, noted in Hans Trefousse, *The Radical Republicans* (Baton Rouge: Louisiana State University Press, 1968), 19.

64. Vroman Mason, "The Fugitive Slave Law in Wisconson," *Proceedings of the State Historical Society of Wisconsin* 117 (1895): 140–41; E. Peshine Smith to Henry Carey, March 17, 1856, quoted in Gienapp, *Origins*, 313.

65. 8 Wallace 603 (1870).

66. 9 Ohio State 198 (1859).

67. Robert Cover, *Justice Accused: Antislavery and the Judicial Process* (New Haven, Conn.: Yale University Press, 1975), 256.

68. 19 Howard 393 (1857); 21 Howard 506 (1859).

69. *Ex Parte Bushnell*, 9 Ohio St 198 at 229 (1859). Brinkerhoff had been an antislavery Congressman, a supporter of the Wilmot Proviso.

70. Cover, *Justice Accused*, 178.

71. John Phillip Reid, *An American Judge: Marmaduke Dent of West Virginia* (N.Y., 1968).

72. And, in any event, we don't know enough about the jurists of most state courts in the nineteenth century. Three exceptions: Carol Chomsky, "Progressive Judges in a Progressive Age: Regulatory Legislation in the Minnesota Supreme Court, 1880–1925," *Law and History Review* 11 (1993): 383; R. Heiberg, "Social Backgrounds of Minnesota Supreme Court Jurists, 1858–1968," *Minnesota Law Review* 53 (1969): 901; and Leonard Levy's appendix (on Shaw's colleagues) to *The Law of the Commonwealth and Chief Justice Lemuel Shaw*.

73. Stephen S. Gregory, "Sidney Breese," in *Great American Lawyers*, ed. W. D. Lewis, 7 vols. (Philadelphia: John C. Winston, 1907–8), 4:462–76; Finkelman, *Imperfect Union*, 99n.; *Hansell v Erickson*, 28 Ill. 257 (1862); *Peoria Bridge Assoc. v Loomis*, 20 Ill. 236 at 251 (1858). Cf. *G. & Ch. RR v Jacobs*, 20 Ill. 478 (1858).

74. *Munn v People*, 69 Ill. 80 (1873); *Hunt v Hoyt*, 20 Ill. 544 (1858); *Lalor v C. B. & B.RR*, 52 Ill. 401 at 404 (1869); *Bass v C. B. & Q.RR*, 28 Ill. 9 at 19 (1862); *Ill. Central RR v Jewell*, 46 Ill. 99 at 101 (1867).

75. Cooley, *Treatise on Constitutional Limitations*, 335; Alan Jones, "The Constitutional Conservatism of Thomas McIntyre Cooley: A Study in the History of Ideas" (Ph.D. diss., University of Michigan, 1960), 24, 27, 23n, 59, 86; *Marquette & O. RR v Taft*, 28 Mich. 289 at 298 (1873); chapter 8, note 34.

76. Zachariah Chaffee's words in his entry on Smith in the *Dictionary of American Biography*.

77. Reid, *Chief Justice: The Judicial World of Charles Doe* (Cambridge, Mass.: Harvard University Press, 1967), 256, 313, 319, 327, 393–400; Reid, "The Reformer and the Precian: A Study in Judicial Attitudes," *Journal of Legal Education* 12 (1959): 157.

78. Carpenter's brother-in-law, Jonathan Ross, became the chief justice of the Vermont Supreme Court. His son-in-law, Frank Streeter, served as chief counsel to

the Concord Railroad. "Carpenter, Alonzo," *National Cyclopedia of American Biography*, vol. 12 (New York: J. T. White, 1933), 326; J. P. Reid, "The Reformer and the Precian: A Study in Judicial Attitudes," *Journal of Legal Education* 12 (1859): 157 at 160–61, 164, 168, 177.

79. Reid, *Chief Justice Doe*, 398.

80. *Buch* v *Amory Mnfg. Co.*, 69 N. H. 257, 44 Atl. 809 at 810–11 (1898).

81. Carpenter could be just as adamantly determined that plaintiffs would recover against railroads when he was satisfied that "the law" was on their side, and from these verdicts Doe could end up dissenting, as in *Mitchell* v *Boston & Main RR*, 68 N. H. 96, 34 Atl. 674 (1894).

82. Hugh H. Brackenridge, *Law Miscellanies* (Philadelphia, 1814), 67; Nathaniel Chipman, *Principles of Government: A Treatise on Free Institutions* (Burlington, Vt., 1833), 165; *Kaufman* v *Oliver*, 10 Pa. St. 514 (1849); Albert Bell, *Memoirs of Bench and Bar of Westmoreland County* (n.p., n.d., 1933), 37; "William Strong," in *The Supreme Court Justices*, ed. Clare Cushman (Washington, D.C., GPO, 1993); Robert Kaczorowski, *The Politics of Judicial Interpretation: The Federal Courts, the Department of Justice and Civil Rights, 1860–1876* (Dobbs Ferry, Oceana, 1985), 201; Harlan, quoted in G. Edward White, *The American Judicial Tradition*, rev. ed. (New York: Oxford University Press, 1988), 132–33.

Note that three of the leading voices of the Jurisprudence of the Head, Oliver Wendell Holmes Jr., Lemuel Shaw, and Maine's admirer of Adam Smith, John Appleton, were Unitarians. But then so were Heart jurists Samuel Miller of Iowa and Frank Doster of Kansas.

Index of Characters

This index lists significant references to the nineteenth-century "characters" in this Tale of Two Voices: jurists, with their jurisdictions; treatise writers; counsel; commentators; and key contemporaries. Page numbers in bold designate significant discussions of a subject.

Abinger, Lord (Ex.), 119, 192, 453 (n. 72)
Adams, Charles Francis, Jr. (Chair, Mass. Board RR Commisioners), 271
Agnew, Daniel (Pa.), 6, 246–47, 286, 318, 319
Albert, I. L. (Nebr.), 424 (n. 81)
Alderson, Justice Edward (C.P.), 90, 241, 453 (n. 72)
Allen, Elisha (Hawaii Terr.), 183
Allen, William (N.H.), 215
Allen, William F. (N.Y.), 188, 253
Alvanley, Lord (C.J., C.P.), 118
Anders, T. J. (Wash.), 417 (n. 36)
Appleton, John (Maine), 242, 329 (n. 9), 446 (n. 34)
Ardmillan, Lord Ordinary (Scot.), 120

Bakewell, Robert (Mo.), 413 (n. 28)
Baldwin, Henry (U.S.—Pa.), 130
Barculo, Seward (N.Y.S.C.), 96, 97
Bartley, Thomas (Ohio), 18, 19, 105, 187, 317
Bay, J. Elihu (S.C.), 31
Beach, Charles, 123, 434 (n. 36)
Beck, Joseph (Iowa), 107, 265, 281, 284
Bell, Samuel Dana (N.H.), 198, 449 (n. 50)
Bemis, George, Esq., 276
Bentham, Jeremy, 223, 229, 262, 300, 329 (n. 9), 465 (n. 9)
Best, Chief Justice (C.P.), 89, 207, 403 (n. 116)
Bicknell, John D., Esq., 232–33

Bigelow, George (Mass.), 136
Biggs, William (Mo.), 279
Binney, Horace, Esq., 25
Bishop, Joel (treatise writer), 70, 250–51, 319, 435 (n. 47)
Bissell, Clark (Conn.), 18, 19
Black, Jeremiah (Pa.), vii, 32
Blackstone, William, Sir (*Commentaries on the Laws of England*; 1765–69), 29, 31, 83, 138, 160, 337 (n. 29), 449 (n. 49)
Blake, Sarah, 314
Bledsoe, Jesse (Prof., Judge, Disc. of Christ Minister), 7
Bliss, Philemon (Mo.), 107
Bowen, Ozias (Ohio), 18
Bowie, Richard (Md.), 244
Brackenridge, Hugh Henry (Pa.), vii, 29, 35, 193, 323
Bracton (*DeLegibus*), 83
Bradbury, Joseph (Ohio), 253–54
Bradley, Joseph (U.S.—N.J.), 330 (n. 26)
Bramwell, Baron (Ex.), 111, 141, 461 (n. 122)
Bredin, Presiding Judge (Pa.), 264–65
Breese, Sidney (Ill.), 112, 173, 188, 280, 319, 461 (n. 127)
Brewer, David (U.S.—Ky.), 318
Brickell, Robert (Ala.), 249
Brinkerhoff, Jacob (Ohio), 18, 19, 317, 319
Bronson, Greene (N.Y.), 152–53, 341 (n. 57)
Browne, Irving (ed., *Albany Law Jour-*

nal, American Reports, and *Campbell's English Ruling Cases*), 94, 172, 218, 412 (n. 20)

Burnet, Jacob (Ohio), 195

Butler, Benjamin F., Esq., 276

Byles, Justice (C.P.), 122

Cadwalader, John (U.S. Dist. Ct., E. Pa.), 315

Campbell, James (Mich.), 175, 189, 416 (n. 23)

Campbell, James, Esq., 315

Cardozo, Albert (N.Y.S.C.), 445 (n. 25)

Cardozo, Benjamin (N.Y.), vii, 102

Careton, Henry (La.), 176

Carpenter, Alonzo (N. H.), 321–22, 473 (n. 81)

Caruthers, Robert (Tenn.), 174, 188

Catline, Richard (Sgt.), 52

Caton, John (Ill.), 245

Cavendish, Chief Justice (K.B.), 83

Chambre, Justice (C.P.), 118

Chapman, Reuben (Mass.), 104

Chase, Salmon P. (U.S.—Ohio), 316

Child, Linus, Esq., 194

Chipman, Nathaniel (Vt.), 323

Chitty, Joseph (*Treatise on Contracts*; 1842 ed.), 66, 174

Choate, Rufus, Esq., 277, 336 (n. 19)

Church, Samuel (Conn.), 241

Church, Sandford (N.Y.), 253

Clarke, John (U.S.—Ohio), 230, 319

Clay, Henry, Esq., 194

Clemens, Samuel Langhorne. *See* Twain, Mark

Clerke, Thomas (N.Y.), 18

Cobb, Amasa (Nebr.), 176, 189

Cockburn, Lord (C.J., Q.B.), 93, 263

Coke, Edward, Sir (K.B.), 29, 54

Cole, Erasmus (Wis.), 289

Coley, William (Calif.), 290

Colvin, John (*The Magistrate's Guide*; 1805), 398 (n. 63)

Comstock, George (N.Y.; ed., Kent's *Commentaries*, 11th ed.), 70, 186

Comyns, Lord Chief Baron (*Digest* of), 68

Cooley, Thomas McIntyre (Mich.; chair, I.C.C.), 214, 250, 272–73, 320, 329 (n. 9), 433 (n. 34), 451 (n. 60)

Coulter, J. Richard (Pa.), 323, 334 (n. 52)

Countryman, Edwin (N.Y.S.C.), 197

Cowen, Esek (N.Y.), 152, 208, 240, 415 (n. 19), 467 (n. 26)

Cranworth, Lord Chancellor, 149

Crawford, Samuel (Wis.), 18

Crocker, Charles (Pres., So. Pac. RR), 154

Crompton, Charles, Sir (Justice, Q.B.), 111

Dalton, Michael (*County Justice*; 1622), 161–62, 393 (n. 25)

Daniel, William (Va.), 90

Davis, David (U.S.—Md.), 73

Davison, Andrew (Ind.), 111

Day, James (Iowa), 112, 247

Deady, Matthew (Fed. Dist., Wash.), 123

Denman, Leroy (Tex.), 425 (n. 90)

Denman, Thomas, Lord (C.J., Q.B.), 93, 208, 210, **226**, 241, 242, 304, 319, 384 (n. 59), 416 (n. 23), 439 (n. 6)

Dent, Marmaduke (W.Va.), 318, 422 (n. 63)

Dickey, T. Lyle (Ill.), 303

Dillon, John Forrest (Iowa, later Fed. Circ.), 123, 175, 189, 210, 212, **226–27**, 285, 312, 319, 324, 329 (n. 10), 400 (n. 86), 416 (n. 27), 430 (n. 125)

Dixon, Luther (Wis.), 105–6, 120, 289

Doe, Charles (N.H.), 120, 321

Doster, Frank (Kans.), 225, 228, 312, 319

Dudley, John (N.H.), 28

DuPonceau, Peter, Esq., 37

Durfee, Thomas (R.I.), 185, 312, 319

Earl, Robert (N.Y.), 88

Eastman, Crystal, 366 (n. 72), 378 (n. 196)

Eldon, Lord Chancellor, 26, 34

Ellenborough, Edward Law, Lord (K.B.), 40, 94, 284
Elliot, Byron (Ind.), 254
Ellis, William (Fla.), 423 (n. 69)
Ellsworth, W. W. (Conn.), 209, 319
Ely, Richard, 139
Eustis, George (La.), 333 (n. 45)
Eyre, Lord Chief Baron (Ex.), 49, 344 (n. 9)

Field, David Dudley, Esq., 26, 196
Field, George W. (treatise writer), 172
Field, Stephen J. (U.S.—Calif.), 31
Field, Walbridge (Mass.), 230
Fitzherbert (*Natura Brevium*; 1534), 54
Folger, Charles (N.Y.), 253
Foot, Samuel (N.Y.), 269
Foster, Dwight (Mass.), 107

Gamble, Hamilton (Mo.), 17
Gardiner, Addison (N.Y.), 13
George, Henry, 151, 388 (n. 24)
Gibson, John Bannister (Pa.), vii, 14, 18, 25, 28, 32, 37, 55–56, 92, 277, 329 (n. 9)
Gilfillan, Chief Justice (Minn.), 281
Gordon, Isaac (Pa.), 140
Gould, George (N.Y.), 93
Gould, James (Conn.), 38
Gray, Hiram (N.Y.), 69, 73
Gray, Horace (Mass.), 40, 384 (n. 58)
Gray, John Chipman, 133–34
Green, George (Iowa), 277
Green, Nicholas St. John, Esq., 102, 108, 123
Greene, Richard (R.I.), 34
Greenleaf, Simon (treatise writer), 103, 280
Grover, Martin (N.Y.), 70, 253
Guffy, B. L. D. (Ky.), 94

Hall, William Sprigg (Cnty. Ct., Minn.), 211, 425 (n. 90)
Hammond, Charles, Esq., 194
Hammond, Creed, Esq., 232–33

Hand, Learned (U.S. 2nd Circ.), 106
Harcourt, Q. C., 263, 448 (n. 41)
Hardin, Benjamin, Esq., 195
Hare, Clark (Phila.), 101
Harlan, John Marshall (U.S.—Ky.), 323–24
Harrington, Samuel (Del.), 197
Harris, Ira (N.Y.S.C.), 272
Harris, William (Miss.), 283
Haywood, John (Tenn.), 7
Hitchcock, Peter (Ohio), 174
Hoar, Ebenezer, Esq., 276
Hobart, Henry, Sir (C.P.), 192
Hobson, J. P. (Ky.), 218
Hoffman, David, vii, 35
Hogeboom, Henry (N.Y.), 243, 248–49
Holman, Jesse (Ind.; Baptist minister), 171, 188, 315
Holmes, Oliver Wendell, Jr. (Mass.), 85, 102, 136, 137, 179, 215, 228–30, 271, 319, 329 (n. 9), 388 (n. 30), 420 (n. 51)
Holt, Lord (C.J., K.B.), 52, 84, 117, 337–38 (n. 29)
Hooker, Frank (Mich.), 203–4
Hosmer, Titus (Conn.), 37
Hubbard, Samuel (Mass.), 185
Hunt, Ward (N.Y.), 101, 104
Hutchinson, Thomas (Mass.), 28, 344 (n. 11)

Jackson, Andrew, 315
Jackson, Charles (Mass.), 228, 427–28 (n. 108)
Jackson, James (Ga.), 254
James, William, 261
Johnson, David (S.C.), 185
Johnson, Thomas (N.Y.S.C.), 276
Johnson, William (reporter), 31
Jones, Casey (engineer), 254
Jones, William, Sir, 28, 85; *Treatise on Bailments* (1781), 360 (n. 22)

Kearney, Dennis, 154
Kellogg, John (N.Y.), 178
Kendall, Amos, Esq., 194

Kennedy, John (Pa.), 25

Kent, Edward (Ariz. Terr.), 426 (n. 93)

Kent, James (N.Y.), vii, 31, 32, 33, 34–35, 54, 73, 131, 172, 193, 268, 338 (n. 32), 339 (n. 41), 398 (n. 63)

Kenyon, Lord (K.B.), 36, 50, 162

King, Edward (J., Phila. Quart. Sess.), 406 (n. 129)

Koerner, Gustav (Ill.), 174, 399 (n. 73)

Langdell, Christopher Columbus (Dean, Harv. Law Sch.), 225

Lawrence, Charles (Ill.), 105, 319, 457 (n. 99), 461 (n. 127)

Learned, William (N.Y.S.C.), 282

Leonard, Abiel (Mo.), 400 (n. 81)

Lincoln, Levi (Mass.), 170, 188

Lincoln and Herndon (law firm), 269, 451 (n. 60)

Livermore, Samuel (N.H.), 28

Loring, Charles, Esq., 124, 276, 450 (n. 58)

Low, M. A., Esq., 246

Lumpkin, Joseph (Ga.), 236, 365 (n. 71)

Lyon, William Penn (Wis.), 293

Lyons, Richard (Ga.), 409 (n. 148)

McAdam, John, 268

McCurdy, Charles (Conn.), 286

McFarland, T. B. (Calif.), 290

McKinney, Robert (Tenn.), 92, 123, 209, 248, 319, 416 (n. 23)

McLean, John (U.S.—Ohio), 17, 87, 283, 316

Madison, James, 26

Magoon, Elias, Rev., 313

Mansfield, William Murray, Lord (K.B.), 26, 65, 73, 118

Marshall, Humphrey, 394 (n. 36)

Marshall, John (U.S.—Va.), 335 (n. 2)

Martin, Baron (Ex.), 271

Martin, F. X. (La.), 318

Mason, Charles (N.Y.), 244

Maynard, Isaac, Esq., 316

Mechem, Floyd (treatise writer), 172, 186

Melville, Herman ("Bartleby the Scrivener"), 154

Merrick, E. T. (La.), 278

Metcalf, Theron (Mass.), 70

Miller, Samuel (U.S.—Iowa), 106, 133, 308–9

Moncure, Richard (Va.), 333 (n. 46)

Morton, Marcus (Mass.), 170, 185

Mullin, Joseph (N.Y.S.C.), 243

Nelson, Samuel (N.Y.), 58, 153

North, Francis (Lord Keeper), 51

Nottingham, Lord Chancellor, 54

Noyes, William C., Esq., 153, 154

Oliver, Benjamin (*Forms of Practice*; 1828), 359 (n. 20)

O'Neall, John B. (S.C.), 31, 387 (n. 23)

Orton, Harlow (Wis.), 254

Page, Herbert, 281

Paine, Byron (Wis.), 316

Parke, Baron (Ex.), 257

Parker, Isaac (Mass.), 39, 44, 178, 196

Parker, Joel (N.H.), 171, 172, 189, 319

Parsons, Theophilus, Sr. (Mass.), 29

Parsons, Theophilus, Jr., 30, 398 (n. 64)

Patterson, Christopher (*Railway Law*), 214, 247–48, 289–90, 464 (n. 150)

Paxon, Edward (Pa.), 250

Peck, William (Ohio), 174

Peckham, Rufus (N.Y.), 113, 253, 422 (n. 59)

Perkins, J. C. (ed., *Chitty on Contracts*), 172, 406 (n. 132)

Perkins, Samuel (Ind.), 116

Perley, Ira (N.H.), 32, 456 (n. 93)

Phelps, Samuel (Vt.), 172

Pierce, James (Md.), 254

Pierpont, John (Vt.), 153

Pollock, Fredrick, Sir, Sr. (Chief Baron, Ex.), 111, 116, 119, 241, 257, 260

Porter, John (N.Y.), 97

Powell, Justice (K.B.), 52

Preston, Isaac (La.), 87

Pryor, Roger (N.Y. Ct., C.P.), 278
Putnam, Samuel (Mass.), 131, 447–48
  (n. 40)
Pyncheon, John (J.P., Springfield, Mass.),
  164

Rapallo, Charles (N.Y.), 253
Read, John (Pa.), 133
Read, Nathaniel C. (Ohio), 174
Reade, Edwin (N.C.), 331 (n. 29)
Redfield, Isaac (Vt.), 26, 38, 72, 108, 112,
  122, 173, 189, 242, 319, 398 (n. 70),
  445 (n. 25)
Reece, William (Tenn.), 197
Reeve, Tapping (Conn.), 38
Richardson, John (S.C.), 360 (n. 29)
Richardson, Robert (Va.), 112–13
Richardson, William (N.H.), 32, 413
  (n. 28)
Riddle, Samuel (manufacturer), 167
Roane, Spencer (Va.), 329 (n. 10), 339
  (n. 39)
Robbins, Alexander (ed., *Central Law
  Journal*), 199
Robertson, George (Ky.), 121, 126, 141,
  319
Robinson, Jonathan (Vt.), 12
Rogers, Molton (Pa.), 151
Rolle, Chief Justice (K.B.), 65, 117
Rooke, Justice (C.P.), 118
Roosevelt, James (N.Y.S.C.), 37
Root, Jesse (Conn.), 25
Ryan, Edward (Wis.), 275, 412 (n. 20),
  469 (n. 42)

St. George Tucker, Henry (Va.), 339
  (n. 39), 399 (n. 71)
Sander (*Law of Pleading and Evidence*;
  1837 ed.), 109, 168
Savage, John (N.Y.), 152
Scates, Walter (Ill.), 269
Scott, Christopher (Ark.), 197
Scott, William (Mo.), 17
Sedgwick, John (N.Y.), 87
Sedgwick, S. H. (Nebr.), 222

Sedgwick, Theodore (treatise writer),
  103, 196, 280–81, 346 (n. 24)
Sergeant, Thomas (Pa.), 72
Shackelford, James (Tenn.), 123
Sharswood, George (Pa.), 249
Shaw, Lemuel (Mass.), 28, 34, 41, 43–44,
  45, 68, 85, 91, 92, 108, 119, 121, 137,
  138, 154, 268, 276, 308
Shearman, Thomas, and Amasa Redfield
  (*Law of Negligence*, 1869 ed.), 103,
  112, 214
Shepley, Ether (Maine), 32, 153, 176–77
Sherman, Roger M. (Conn.), 209, 319,
  415 (n. 20)
Shirreff, Patrick, 166, 394 (n. 33), 395
  (n. 36)
Skinner, Onias (Ill.), 197
Slidell, Thomas (La.), 361 (n. 29)
Smith, Abram (Wis.), 18, 312, 319
Smith, Adam, 52, 262, 300, 329 (n. 9),
  337 (n. 20), 465 (n. 10)
Smith, Jeremiah, 215, 223, 319, 321
Spencer, Ambrose (N.Y.), 30, 131, 169,
  188
Spencer, John (N.Y. Sen., Ct. of Errs.),
  338 (n. 31)
Stephens, Linton (Ga.), 283
Story, Joseph (U.S.—Mass.), 17, 32, 35,
  36, 38, 49, 124, 131, 334 (n. 52)
Story, William Wetmore, 49
Strong, William (U.S.—Pa.), 73, 279, 323
Sutliff, J. Milton (Ohio), 317
Swan, Joseph (Ohio), 18, 317
Swift, William (Pres., Phila., Wilm. &
  Balt. RR), 271
Swift, Zephaniah (Conn.), 30, 38, 168,
  337 (n. 29)

Tappan, Benjamin, Esq., 315
Tarbell, Jonathan (Miss.), 284
Taylor, David (Wis.), 280
Taylor, George (Huntingdon Cnty., Pa.),
  120
Taylor, William R. (Wis. Gov.), 312
Tenderden, Lord (C.J., K.B.), 90

Thesiger, Fredrick, Sir (Q.C.), 257

Thompson, Charles (Colo.), 254

Thompson, Lucas (Va.), 197

Thompson, Samuel G. (Pa.), 382 (n. 43)

Thompson, Seymour (St. Louis Ct. of Appeals; *Law of Negligence*; ed., *Central Law Journal*), 113, 212, 219, 220, 227–28, 278–79, 312, 319, 416 (n. 27), 435 (n. 50)

Thorton, James (Calif.), 95

Tilghman, William (Pa.), 18, 25

Tindal, Chief Justice (C.P.), 85, 207

Tocqueville, Alexis de, 171, 231–32

Trippe, R. P. (Ga.), 41

Twain, Mark, 86, 360 (n. 27), 362 (n. 33)

Tyler, John (Pres.), 37

Underwood, Joseph (Ky.), 168

Van Fleet, William (Calif.), 289–90, 312

Vaughan, Chief Justice (K.B.), 338 (n. 34)

Verplanck, Gulian (treatise writer), 347 (n. 36)

Viner, Charles (*Abridgement*), 29, 65, 162

Wade, Benjamin (Ohio 3rd Circ., U.S. Senate), 316

Wagner, David (Mo.), 112, 121, 123, 246, 312, 319

Waite, Morrison (U.S.—Ohio), 221

Walmsley, Thomas, Sir (Justice, C.P.), 84

Walton, Charles (Maine), 283

Weaver, S. M. (Iowa), 7

Webster, Daniel, Esq., 10, 194

Welch, John (Ohio), 249

Wells, Samuel (Maine), 174, 265

Wharton, Francis (treatise writer; Episcopal minister), 32, 74, 101, 102, 104, 249–50, 319, 368 (n. 93)

Whitman, B. C. (Nev.), 279, 282, 460 (n. 122)

Whiton, Edward (Wis.), 18

Willes, Justice, 257

Williams, John (*Reports of Sir Edmund Saunders*), 149, 153, 162

Williams, Marshall (Ohio), 421 (n. 56)

Williams, Thomas (Conn.), 18, 19

Wilmot, John, Sir (K.B.), 149, 153

Wilson, James (U.S.—Pa.), 130

Wood, Bradford, Esq., 315

Wood, Horace Gay (*Law of Master and Servant*; 1877), 123, 401 (n. 93); *Law of Nuisance* (1875), 140

Woodbury, Levi (U.S.—N.H.), 17

Woodruff, Lewis (N.Y. Ct. of C.P.), 242–43

Woods, Andrew (N.H.), 178

Woodward, George (Pa.), 95, 195, 246, 264–65

Worden, James (Ind.), 399 (n. 71)

Wright, William (N.Y.), 18

Young, George Brooke (Minn.), 211, 212, 216, 416 (n. 28)

Zabriskie, Abraham (N.J.), 138

Index of Cases ("Texts") Discussed

Abelman v. Booth (U.S., 1859), 316, 317

Alden v. New York Central RR (N.Y., 1862), 92, 93

Anderson v. Poindexter (Ohio, 1856), 19, 317

Arden v. Patterson (Ch., N.Y., 1821), 193–94

Armsworth v. South Eastern Railway (Ex., 1847), 257

Baker v. Bolton (N.P., 1808), 284, 285

Baltimore & Ohio RR v. Baugh (U.S., 1893), 311

Bayly v. Merrel (K.B., 1606), 98

Beeston v. Collyer (C.P., 1827), 403 (n. 116)

Bemis v. Upham (Mass., 1825), 44–45

Birge v. Gardiner (Conn., 1849), 241, 242

Blymire v. Boistle (Pa., 1837), 72, 73

Bourne v. Mason (K.B., 1669), 65, 69

Bradshaw v. Nicholson (1601), 84

Brainton v. Pinn (K.B., 1290), 82

Britton v. Turner (N.Y., 1834), 158, 171–72, 173–78, 180, 181, 184, 189, 319, 389 (n. 5), 398 (n. 64)

Brown v. Swineford (Wis., 1878), 274

Buch v. Amory Manufacturing Co. (N.H., 1898), 322–23

Bush v. McRath (V. Adm., N.Y., 1786), 169

Butterfield v. Forester (K.B., 1809), 241, 242

Butterfield v. Hartshorn (N.H., 1834), 70

Byrd v. Boyd (S.C., 1827), 185

Carey v. Berkshire (Mass., 1848), 285

Carnegie v. Morrison (Mass., 1841), 69

Carroway v. Cox (N.C., 1852), 71

Cary v. Daniels (Mass., 1844), 41–44

Chicago & Milwaukee RR v. Ross (U.S., 1884), 311

Clark v. Chambers (Q.B., 1878), 212

Clark v. City of Manchester (N.H., 1872), 184

Clark v. Foot (N.Y., 1811), 83

"Clifford v. Overland Mail Co." (Nev., 1862), 109–10

Cook v. Jennings (K.B., 1797), 49

Cook v. Western & Atlantic RR (Ga., 1883), 110

Cooke & Lathame v. Barker (Plymouth, 1645), 83–84

Cooper v. Hall (Ohio, 1832), 342 (n. 68)

Coultas v. Victorian Railway Commissioners (H.L., 1888), 281

Crow v. Rogers (K.B., 1727), 65, 69, 353 (n. 93)

Cuddee v. Rutter (Ch., 1720), 60

Cutter v. Powell (K.B., 1795), 162, 168, 169, 171, 172, 173, 174, 176, 180, 184, 188, 189

Davies v. Mann (Ex., 1842), 81

Downey v. Burke (Mo., 1856), 400 (n. 81)

Dred Scott v. Sanford (U.S., 1857), 317

Dutch v. Warren (K.B., 1720), 60

Dutton v. Poole (K.B., 1677), 65, 70, 73, 76

Eckert v. Long Island Railway (N.Y., 1871), 252–53

Ernst v. Hudson River RR (N.Y., 1866), 97

Escola v. Coca-Cola Bottling (Calif., 1944), 85, 91, 95

Evansville & Crawfordsville RR v. Hiatt (Ind., 1859), 252

Ex Parte Bushnell (Ohio, 1859), 317

Farrish & Co. v. Reigle (Va., 1854), 90

Farwell v. Boston & Worcester RR (Mass., 1842), 108, 114, 119, 120, 121, 126

Fent v. Toledo, Peoria & Warsaw RR (Ill., 1871), 105

Fields v. State (Tenn., 1829), 333 (n. 42)

Forcey v. Cunningham (N.Y., 1764), 447 (n. 40)

Ford v. Danks (La., 1861), 403 (n. 115)

Ford v. Monroe (N.Y., 1838), 285

Fox v. Oakland Consolidated Street Railway (Calif., 1897), 289–90

Gardiner v. Pullen & Phillips (Ch., 1700), 60

Gibbons v. Pepper (K.B., 1696), 82

Goodson v. Walkin (K.B., 1376), 98

Griffith v. Spratley (Ex., 1787), 49

Hadley v. Baxendale (Ex., 1854), 300

Hargreaves v. Deacon (Mich., 1872), 416 (n. 24)

Haring v. New York & Erie RR (N.Y.S.C., 1852), 96

Harmon v. Salmon Falls Manufacturing Co. (Maine, 1853), 176–77

Hart v. The Littlejohn (Fed. Adm., 1800), 396 (n. 47)

Hartfield v. Roper (N.Y., 1839), 240, 242, 243, 244, 248

Harvard College v. Amory (Mass., 1830), 132

Hatch v. Dwight & Burnell (Mass., 1821), 44

Hay v. Marsh (La., 1837), 173, 399 (n. 72)

Hayward v. Leonard (Mass., 1828), 171

Heathcock v. Walker (Vt., 1802), 12

Heber v. U.S. Flax Manufacturing Co. (R.I., 1881), 185 l

Hepburn v. Griswold (U.S., 1870), 316

Honegsberger v. Second Avenue Railway (N.Y.S.C., 1864), 243

Hoopes v. Dundas (Pa., 1848), 37

Howard v. Grover (Maine, 1848), 266

Hoyt v. Jeffers (Mich., 1874), 104

Hubbard v. Town (Vt., 1860), 153

Hughes v. Cannon (Tenn., 1853), 174–75

Hunt v. The Otis Co. (Mass., 1842), 185

In re Booth (Wis., 1854), 18

Jackson v. Bulloch (Conn., 1837), 19

Jennings v. Camp (N.Y., 1816), 168, 169, 170

Kansas Central RR v. Fitzsimmons (Kan., 1875 and 1879), 201

Kay v. Pennsylvania RR (Pa., 1870), 246–47

Kay v. Vattier (Ohio, 1823), 194–95

Keffe v. Milwaukee & St. Paul RR (Minn., 1875), 211, 212, 213

Kellogg v. Chicago & Northwest RR (Wis., 1870), 105–6

Kerwacker v. Cleveland, Columbus & Cincinnati RR (Ohio, 1854), 105

Lalor v. Chicago, Burlington & Quincy RR (Ill., 1871), 112

Lannen v. Albany Gas Light Co. (N.Y.S.C., 1865), 248–49

Lawrence v. Fox (N.Y., 1859), 62, 69–70, 73, 74

Lewis v. Esther (D. C., 1823), 169

Lexington & Ohio RR v. Applegate (Ky., 1839), 121, 141

Losee v. Buchanan & Bullard (N.Y., 1873), 88–89

Louisville & Nashville RR v. Collins (Ky., 1865), 121–22

Lynch v. Nurdin (Q.B., 1841), 208, 209, 210, 211, 225, 226, 241, 242, 243, 244, 246, 248

McCandless v. McWha (Pa., 1853), 264–65

McCord & Hunt v. Iker (Ohio, 1843), 135

McFarland v. Newman (Pa., 1839), 55–56

McMahon v. Davidson (Minn., 1867), 87–88

McMillan v. Vanderlip (N.Y., 1815), 169, 170

MacPherson v. Buick Motor Co. (N.Y., 1916), 85, 102

Mahan v. Brown (N.Y., 1835), 152, 154

Mangan v. Atterton (Ex., 1866), 212, 215

Mann v. Oriental Print Works (R.I., 1875), 26

Manning v. Manning (N.Y., 1815), 35

Mellen v. Whipple (Mass., 1854), 70

Merritt v. Parker (N.J., 1795), 42

Miller v. Goddard (Maine, 1852), 174

Moseley v. Chamberlain (Wis., 1861), 120

Murray v. South Carolina RR (S.C., 1841), 119, 126

Nagel v. Missouri Pacific RR (Mo., 1882), 202–3

Nasworthy v. The Glaudina (V. Adm., N.Y., 1786), 168–69

Newby v. Wiltshire (K.B., 1785), 98, 118

New Jersey RR v. Kennard (Pa., 1853), 277–78

Northern Pacific RR v. Dixon (U.S., 1904), 311

North Pennsylvania RR v. Mahoney (Pa., 1867), 249

O'Flaherty v. Union Railway (Mo., 1869), 246

Ogle v. Barnes (K.B., 1799), 82

Olmstead v. Beale (Mass., 1837), 170

Parker v. Foote (N.Y., 1839), 152–53

Partington v. Wamsutta Mills (Mass., 1872), 405 (n. 126)

Pennsylvania Coal Co. v. Sanderson, (Pa., 1886), 140–42

Perley v. Eastern RR (Mass., 1868), 104

Philbrook v. Belknap (Vt., 1834), 172

Pickering v. Thoroughgood (1533), 159

Pike v. Butler (N.Y., 1850), 13–14

Posey v. Garth (Mo., 1841), 405 (n. 125)

"*Price v. Wheeler*" (Charles Cnty., Md., 1662), 163

Priestley v. Fowler (Ex., 1837), 91, 109, 114, 118, 119, 121, 126

Railroad v. Stout (U.S., 1873), 210, 211, 212, 213, 215, 225

Rex v. Ward (K.B., 1836), 384 (n. 59)

Robinson v. Campbell (U.S., 1818), 35

Robinson v. Cone (Vt., 1850), 241–42, 244

Russell v. Men of Devon (K.B., 1788), 267

Rust v. LaRue (Ky., 1823), 195

Ryan v. New York Central RR (N.Y., 1866), 101, 102, 103, 104, 106

Rylands v. Fletcher (H.L., 1868), 88

Sands v. Taylor (N.Y., 1810), 30

Scott v. Emerson (Mo., 1852), 17

Scott v. Sheperd (K.B., 1773), 256

Sergeant Maynard's Case (Ch., 1676), 54

Sexias v. Woods (N.Y., 1804), 54

The Slave Grace (Adm., 1827), 16

Slingsby v. Barnard & Hall (K.B., 1617), 341 (n. 54)

Sloan v. Hayden (Mass., 1872), 185

Smith v. Dittman (N.Y.C.P., 1890), 278

"*Smyth v. Beach*" (New Haven, 1643), 83

Stark v. Parker (Mass., 1824), 170, 174, 181

Stokes v. Eastern Counties Railway (N.P., 1860), 93

Sullivan v. Union Pacific RR (Fed. Circ., 1874), 285

Tenant v. *Goldwin* (K.B., 1705), 84

Theobald v. *Railway Passenger Assurance Co.* (Ex., 1854), 257, 279

Thompson v. *Harcourt* (H.L., 1722), 60

Thorp v. *Freed* (Mont., 1872), 343 (n. 73)

Thurston v. *Hancock* (Mass., 1815), 39

Trustee of Monroe Female University v. *Broadfield* (Ga., 1859), 409 (n. 148)

Tweddle v. *Atkinson* (Q.B., 1861), 67, 74

United Zinc & Chemical Co v. *Britt* (U.S., 1922), 420 (n. 51)

Vaughan v. *Menlove* (C.P., 1837), 85

Wesson v. *Washburn Iron Co.* (Mass., 1866), 136

Wheeling & Lake Erie RR v. *Harvey* (Ohio, 1907), 203

Whirley v. *Whiteman* (Tenn., 1858), 209, 210, 211, 212, 225, 248

Winn v. *Southgate* (Vt., 1845), 398 (n. 67)

Winterbottom v. *Wright* (Ex., 1842), 86, 91

Wordworth v. *Willan & Others* (N.P., 1805), 82

York v. *Pacific & Idaho Northern RR* (Idaho, 1902), 203

General Index

Page numbers in bold designate significant discussions of a subject.

Accepted work doctrine: abrogation of, 409 (n. 148)

"Age of Formalism": doubts about, 3–4, 204, 205, 214, 251, 423 (n. 66), 459 (n. 116)

American Digest (Century edition, 1897), 111, 351 (n. 71)

American Law Institute's *Second Restatement of Torts* (1934), 206, 251

American Party, 314

"Ancient lights," 41, 147–56; and elevated railway, 150; and skyscrapers, 150; and implied grants, 150, 155; and developmental consequences, 151; and "unneighborly" walls, 152–53

Appellate reports, 14, 29–32

Assault and battery, 263–64

Assumption-of-risk doctrine, 80, 88, 108–14; *Henry V* and, 109; question of, left to jury, 111; exceptions to, 111–13

Attractive-nuisance rule, 201–33

Bailment leases, 56–59

Baker, John H., 82, 83, 357 (n. 1)

Bakken, Gordon, 21, 232, 311

Barton, Michael, 9

Beard, Charles, 8, 301, 331 (n. 28)

Bergstrom, Randolph, 21, 80, 99, 258, 260, 443–45 (n. 23)

"Best interest of the child" doctrine, 304

Bible: references to, 6, 10, 19, 152, 174, 225, 231, 243, 248, 249, 275, 293, 313–14, 321–24, 330 (n. 26), 467 (n. 26). *See also* Christian/Christianity

Boiler explosions: liability in cases of, 86–89, 360 (n. 28)

Bona fide purchasers, 12

Bridwell, Randall, 337 (n. 29)

Burkman, Jack, 344 (n. 6)

Caveat emptor, 12, 52–56, 343 (n. 4)

Champerty, 191–95. *See also* Contingency-fee contracts

Chattel mortgages, 56–59, 349 (n. 53)

Chomsky, Carol, 472 (n. 72)

Christian/Christianity, 4, 6, 10, 11, 12, 207, 225, 227, 229, 254, 262, 293, 305, 313–24, 445 (n. 25). *See also* Bible

Coase, Ronald, 300

Comity, 17–19, 316–17, 332 (n. 38)

Common-carrier liability, 86–95, 103–4, 105–8, 360 (n. 29)

Conditional sales, 56–59, 349–50 (nn. 55–57)

Consideration: adequacy of, 49–50, 344 (n. 9); moving of, 65, 352 (n. 76)

Contingency-fee contracts, 191–99, 317; and "loser pays" rule, 192, 195; and squatters, 194; and rights of poor, 195–98; and "ambulance chasing," 198, 271

Contract ("agreements"): law of, 47–78, 157–99, 296–98. *See also* Conditional sales; Contingency-fee contracts; "Fairness" doctrine; Labor contracts, breaches of; Third-party-beneficiary contracts; "Will-of-the-parties" theory of contract

Contributory-negligence rule, 80, 95–

101; imputing of parent's to child, 97, 215, 236–55, 289–90; question of, for jury, 98–99, 244–45; exceptions to, 100, 249, 252; and "means test" for parents' contributory negligence, 245–48

Cook, Charles, 336 (n. 14)

Corbin, Arthur, 351 (n. 69)

Corporations: suits against sanctioned, 92; high standard of liability for, 92–95, 310; lack of jury sympathy for, 96, 99, 102, 271–73, 275–76; stock of sanctioned for trust funds, 131; "pocket nerve" of, 282–83, 454 (n. 73), 463 (n. 141), 464 (n. 154). *See also* Common-carrier liability; Railroads

Cost-benefit analysis. *See* Law and Economics reasoning

Cover, Robert, 15, 17, 317, 332 (n. 38)

Cross, Whitney, 301

Culture, American nineteenth-century, 6, 301; child-centered interpretation of, 217–18, 232, 236, 286–88; and "pursuit of happiness," 280; ethnocultural interpretation of, 313–18

Dalley, Paula, 467 (n. 24)

Damages. *See* Jury awards

Damnum absque injuria, 207

Democracy and mass-movement politics, 262–63, 306–12

Democratic Party, 9, 132, 139, 230, 288, 290, 317, 321

Deville, Kenneth, 264

Diamond, Stephen, 330 (n. 27)

Dicta, 13, 192, 341 (n. 57), 344 (n. 9), 415 (n. 19)

Dillon's rule, 233, 430 (n. 125)

"Doctrinal" method, 3, 4, 20–22, 26–127 passim, **63–76**, 423 (n. 66). *See also* Precedent

Dorsey, Stuart, 371 (n. 126)

Ducker, James, 107

Economic efficiency. *See* Law and Economics reasoning

Economic-oriented paradigm, 2–3, 9, 11, 38–39, 41, 47–49, 53, 54–55, 56–57, 60, 62, 79–80, 81, 86, 95–96, 101–2, 108, 114, 134, 141, 148, 157–58, 175, 237–38, 251, **298–303**, 325–28

Election of jurists. 288–90, 312, 315–18

Electric shocks: liability for, 94–95, 420 (n. 49)

Elevators: liability for defects in, 95

Epstein, Richard, 332 (n. 37)

Equity, 34, 50, 72, 130–31, 138–43, 160–61, 175, 189, 293, 301, 305–6, 338 (n. 34), 344 (nn. 9, 12), 345 (n. 14), 356 (n. 136), 385 (n. 63), 453 (n. 72)

Expectation damages, 30, 59–61, 350 (nn. 61, 63)

Fairman, Charles, 310

"Fairness" doctrine: nonexistence of, 48–51

Fede, Andrew, 332 (n. 38)

Federal court "diversity"/"removal" issues, 21, 426 (n. 93)

Feiman, Jay, 404 (n. 118)

Fellow-servant rule, 80, 88, 114–28; and "labor aristocracy," 116; and watchful-worker rationale, 116; historic roots of, 117–20; exceptions to, 121–24

"Field Code" of Civil Procedure (N.Y., 1848), 69, 71, 72, 73, 306

Finkelman, Paul, 15, 17, 334 (n. 50)

Fire: liability for spread of, 83, 101–7

"Foreseeability," 83, 101–2, 107–8

Free-Soil Party, 314

Freyer, Tony, 409 (n. 1)

Friedman, Lawrence, 8, 28, 48, 62, 79, 95, 127, 214, 219, 258, 259, 260, 298, 300, **327–28**, 337 (n. 25), 343–44 (n. 45), 347 (n. 31), 348 (n. 39), 357 (n. 145), 360 (n. 22), 370 (n. 105), 375 (n. 165), 465 (n. 5)

Fugitive Slave Act of 1850, 316, 317

Fuller, Lon, 414–15 (n. 11), 423 (n. 66)

Galeson, David, 392–93 (n. 23)
"Gate-keeper" rules, 8, 15, 77, 303, 308
Gienapp, William, 316, 471 (n. 57)
Gilles, Stephen, 81
"Golden Age of American Law," 2, 28
Gordon, Robert, 466 (n. 11)
Grady, Mark, 368 (n. 94), 369 (n. 97)
Granger movement, 312
Green, Leon, 257, 260, 310, 420 (n. 51)
Grossberg, Michael, 304

Hall, Kermit, 48, 54, 288–89, 298, 305,
    328, 334 (n. 48), 343 (n. 4), 348 (n. 39),
    357 (n. 2), 469 (n. 41)
Hans, Valerie, 273
Haskell, Thomas, 262
Hatch, Nathan, 313
Heckman, Charles, 349 (n. 46)
Helmholz, R. H., 358 (n. 9)
Hening, Crawford, 67
Hill, Andrew, 404 (n. 118)
Hoffer, Peter, 328 (n. 5), 338 (n. 35), 468
    (n. 31)
Holt, Wythe, 178–80, 300, 389 (n. 5), 465
    (n. 5)
Horwitz, Morton, 8, 30, 44, 48, 83, 140,
    152, 153, 182, **298–99**, 300, 326, 340
    (n. 50), 341 (n. 57), 343 (n. 1), 348
    (nn. 42, 45), 358 (n. 9), 359 (n. 20),
    367 (n. 89), 397–98 (n. 63), 428 (n.
    115), 465 (n. 3)
Hovencamp, Herbert, 442 (n. 210)
Howe, Daniel Walker, 10
Hoyt, Jeff, 37
Humanity/humaneness, 6, 7, 10, 16, 73,
    76, 112, 113, 118, 123, 133, 225, 244,
    245, 250, 251–54, 262, 283–84, 286,
    301, 304, 313–14, 331 (n. 29), 333
    (n. 46), 361 (n. 30), 434 (nn. 36, 40),
    470 (n. 51)
Hunt, James, 288, 330 (n. 20)
Hurst, James Willard, 8, 10, 300, 325,
    330–31 (n. 28)

*In jure non remota causa, sed proxima
    causa*, 101; criticized, 108

"Instrumentalism," 5, 33, 36, 52, 71, 137,
    206, 225

Jacoby, Sanford, 394 (n. 35)
Josephson, Matthew, 301
Jurisprudence of the Hand, 131–43, 243,
    296, 298–99, 387 (n. 18)
Jurisprudence of the Head: noted, vii, 7,
    10, 15, 16, 17, 18, 27–45, 104, 113, 115,
    121, 126, 168–89, 206, 224, 252, 294,
    296, 303, 314, 321–22, 333 (n. 45);
    defined, 3, 4
Jurisprudence of the Heart: noted, vii, 5,
    7, 10, 15–20, 104, 113, 121–22, 133–
    34, 171–72, 174–89, 206, 225, 250,
    253, 261, 262, 296, 304, 314, 317, 333
    (n. 46); defined, 3, 4; explained, 305–
    18
Jurors: views of, expressed during voir
    dire, 272, 454 (n. 77)
Jury awards: personal injury ("compen-
    sation"), 214, 255, 256–80, 360 (n. 25);
    assault-and-battery ("compensation"
    and "punitive"), 263–64; for medical
    malpractice, 264–67; for defective
    roads and bridges, 267–70; where pri-
    vate corporation is defendant, 271–79;
    in England, 438 (n. 13)

Kaczorowski, Robert, 328 (n. 5), 332
    (n. 38), 357 (n. 1), 360 (n. 26), 366
    (n. 76)
"Keep a stiff upper lip": origins of, 438
    (n. 12)
Klafter, Craig, 37, 304, 337 (n. 29)
Krauss, E. P., 342 (n. 68)
Kurtz, Paul, 136, 142
Kussmaul, Ann, 394 (n. 33)

Labor contracts, breaches of, 157–89; in
    England, 159–62; in colonies, 162–64;
    "Damage of Disappointment" in, 164;
    in nineteenth-century U.S., 166–89; by
    quitting, 168–82; by firing, 182–88;
    involving minors, 397 (n. 55)

LaPiana, William P., 36
Lateral support of buildings, 38–41, 340 (n. 50)
Law and Economics reasoning, 12, 41, 55–56, 63, 71–72, 90, 94, 106, 113, 131, 134, 139, 151, 197, 250, 275, 277, 299, 300–332, 325–26; and "watchful-worker" rationale, 116–17, 121; and "balancing-the-equities," 139, 457 (n. 99); and "harsh" rule in breaches of labor contracts, 179–80, 188–89, 404 (n. 118); and laborers versus contractors, 186–88; and attractive-nuisance rule, 221–24
Law as "science," vii, 36, 37–38, 426 (n. 91)
"Legal fictions," 206, 210–12, 214–17, 224, 269, 286, 414–15 (n. 11)
Legal Tender Act, 316
Legislation: deference of jurists toward, 17–18, 37, 77, 243, 267, 285, 387 (n. 23), 406 (n. 127), 425 (n. 90); "strict" reading of by jurists, 384 (n. 58)—use of: to alter common law of property, 129, 137, 141, 149, 387 (n. 15), 389 (n. 37); affecting third party beneficiary contracts, 77, 356 (n. 143); to abrogate fellow-servant rule, 115, 124; affecting contingency-fee contracts, 196; to make streets safer, 261, 452 (n. 67); to make steamboats safer, 360 (n. 28); and wrongful death damage limits, 421 (n. 54)
Liberty Party, 314
Life insurance policies, 77, 110, 287–88, 356 (n. 143)
Llewylln, Karl, 181, 335 (n. 37)
Lord Campbell's Act (9 & 10 Vic., 1846), 284, 285, 286
Loss of companionship (consortium), 285–86
Loss of enjoyment, 280
Louisiana's Civil Code, 348 (n. 40), 399 (n. 72), 421 (n. 56)

McBride, Michael, 136
MacCoun, Robert, 273
McLaren, John, 143, 386 (n. 7)
Malone, Wex, 96–98, 251
Mann, Bruce, 51
Marston, Jerrilyn, 121, 124, 224, 328 (n. 5)
Master and Servant Act (1747), 159
Medical malpractice, 264–67; "locality" rule in, 448–49 (n. 46)
"Mental suffering," 280–81
Merchant Seaman's Act (1802), 406 (n. 127)
Methodology: author's, 11–14, 258–60, 306, 331 (nn. 34–36), 351 (n. 71), 439–43 (nn. 15–22)
Miller, Perry, 7, 301
Milsom, S. F. C., 81
Morris, Richard, 83
Morris, Thomas, 332 (n. 38)
Moulin, Daniel de, 261

Nash, A. E. Keir, 15, 305
Nedelsky, Jennifer, 382 (n. 42)
Neighborly behavior, 6, 12, 40, 41, 153–54, 171–72, 208, 209, 212, 220, 230
Nelson, William E., 15, 45, 327, 332 (n. 38), 341 (n. 54), 382 (n. 36)
Non sui juris, 244
Nourse, David, 339 (n. 38)
Novak, William, 130, 328 (n. 5), 467 (n. 23)
Nuisances: pollution, 134–43; "balancing of the equities" in, 135, 138–42; and "aggregation" of private actions, 136; and "industrialization" defense, 137–38; "coming-to-the-nuisance" defense, 138–39; and damages at common law, 142–43

Oral tradition, 30
Orren, Karen, 465 (n. 5)

"Pain and suffering," 255–80, 445 (n. 28), 457–58 (nn. 101, 102), 461

(n. 127)

Painkillers, 261–62

Palmer, Vernon, 66

"Pocket nerve" of corporations, 282–83, 454 (n. 73), 460 (n. 122), 463 (n. 141), 464 (n. 154)

Pohlman, H. L., 428 (n. 115)

Polanyi, Karl, 301

Populist (People's) Party, 228, 288, 290, 330 (n. 20)

Posner, Richard, 8, 106, 221, 299–300, 302–3, 325–26, 327, 385 (n. 1)

"Possessive individualism," 425 (n. 86), 465 (n. 10)

Pound, Roscoe, 27, 119, 310

Precedent, 30–37, 40, 49–50, 57, 120–21, 148, 189, 195, 204, 226, 228, 285, 293, 297, 304, 317, 321–22, 434 (n. 37); and "principle," 37–38, 153, 170–71, 225, 230, 242, 336 (n. 19), 337 (n. 29), 338 (nn. 31, 32, 34), 339 (n. 38), 459 (n. 116); counsel's quest for "principled exceptions" to, 126

"Principle." *See* Precedent

Product liability: early proxy for, 85–95

Property: law of, 13, 15, 19, 38–46, 129–42, 296. *See also* "Ancient lights"; Lateral support of buildings; Nuisances; Prudent investor rule; Riparian rights; *Sic utere tuo, ut alienum non laedas*; Slavery; "Spendthrift" trusts; Tenant's agricultural improvements

Prosser, William, 85

Proximate cause, 80, 101–7, 250

Prude, Jonathan, 167

Prudent-investor rule, 131–32

Purcell, Edward, 21, 80, 421 (n. 54), 469 (n. 39)

Rabin, Robert, 260, 267

Railroads: defective equipment of, 91–94; turntables of, 201–33; trackage of, 219–20; safety devices of, 271, 454 (n. 75). *See also* Common-carrier liability; Fellow-servant rule

"Reason." *See* Precedent

"Reasonable man" standard of care, 85, 417 (n. 36), 465 (n. 10)

Recusal of jurists: evidence of in cases involving corporations, 464 (n. 1)

Reid, John Phillip, 321–22

Republicanism, 56, 189

Republican Party, 9, 139, 175, 226, 227, 228, 288, 290, 314, 317, 330 (n. 20), 332 (n. 30), 409 (n. 150)

Res ipsa loquitur, 100, 367 (nn. 86, 87)

Respondeat superior, 117–18

"Responsible individualism," 56

Right to examine tort plaintiff, 281–82

Riparian rights, 41–45

Rose, Carol, 342 (n. 69)

Rosen, Christine, 139, 140

Rostow, Walt Whitman, 301

Rothenberg, Winifred, 51

"Rules of the road," 84, 98

Russell, Thomas, 80, 259, 334 (n. 57)

Sale of goods, 48–63; breaches of contract in, 407 (n. 154)

Salinger, Susan, 394 (n. 34)

Salmon, Marlynn, 304

Schafer, Judith, 332 (n. 38)

Scheiber, Harry, 130

Scheppele, Kim Lane, 55, 96, 348 (n. 39)

Schlesinger, Arthur, Jr., 301

Schwartz, Gary, 328 (n. 5)

Second Great Awakening, 262, 264

Sic utere tuo, ut alienum non laedas, 84, 140, 212, 225, 231, 248, 277, 323, 451 (n. 60)

Silverman, Robert, 259, 273

Simpson, A. W. Brian, 51, 61, 300, 343 (n. 3), 347 (n. 30), 392 (n. 18)

Slavery, 15–19, 315, 316, 317, 332 (n. 38), 434 (n. 38), 468 (n. 29); and assumption-of-risk rule, 112

"Spendthrift" trusts, 132–34

"Spite" fences, 154, 388 (n. 30)

Stagecoach defects, 89–91

"Standing," 8, 15, 77, 303, 308

Stanley, Amy Dru, 304

Stare decisis, 32, 174, 308

Statute of Artificers and Apprentices
(1562), 390 (n. 7)

Statute of Frauds (1677), 66

Statute of Labourers (1350–51), 159

Steinberg, Allen, 304–5

Steinfeld, Robert, 402 (n. 105)

Strict liability: nonexistence of, 81–85

Super antiquas vias, 35, 36, 37, 339
(n. 41)

Symmetry, vii, 7, 38, 301, 319, 340
(nn. 48, 49)

Teeven, Kevin, 61, 303, 350 (n. 61)

Tenant's agricultural improvements rule,
131

Third-party beneficiary contracts, 62–
77; creditor-beneficiaries to, 63–66,
68–74, 76–77; gift-beneficiaries to, 64,
67, 73, 76–77

Tomlins, Christopher, 121, 126, 300, 327,
357 (nn. 1, 5), 375 (nn. 162, 165), 396–
97 (n. 54), 465 (n. 5)

Tort: law of, 79–127, 201–92, 295–96.
See also Assumption-of-risk doctrine;
Attractive-nuisance rule; Common
carrier liability; Fellow-servant rule;
Loss of companionship; Loss of enjoyment; Product liability; Proximate
cause; Railroads; Right to examine
tort plaintiff; *Sic utere tuo, ut alienum
non laedas*; Traffic on roadways;
Wrongful death

Traffic on roadways, 84, 98, 99, 101, 241,
242, 243, 244, 246, 247, 250, 251, 268–
69, 430 (n. 5), 432 (n. 23), 444 (n. 23)

Traynor, Roger (Calif.), 85, 91, 95, 310

Trespass: and case, 81–83, 359 (n. 20);
and children, 201–33

Trial court judges, 21–22, 87, 97, 99–
100, 120, 170, 173, 211, 242, 249, 264,
331 (n. 35), 448–49 (n. 46)

Tushnet, Mark, 15

Tyler, Alice Felt, 301

Warren, Earl (U.S.—Calif.), 316

Webb, Walter Prescott, 311

Weinberg, Harold, 331 (n. 32)

Welke, Barbara, 304, 460 (n. 120)

Whig Party, 9, 288, 314, 317

White, G. Edward, 442 (n. 22)

Whiteside, James, 365

Whitten, Ralph, 337 (n. 29)

"Will-of-the-parties" theory of contract,
48, 52–53, 346 (n. 24)

Winkle, Kenneth, 304

Wolcher, Louis, 404 (n. 116), 408 (n. 42)

Wrongful death, 284–87; and mother's
"tender solicitude," 286; and insurance payment offsets, 287–88